THE GUIDE TO
CAREER EDUCATION

Second printing, March 1975

Copyright © 1974 by Muriel Lederer

All rights reserved, including the right to reproduce this book
or portions thereof in any form. For information, address:
Quadrangle/The New York Times Book Co., 10 East 53 Street,
New York, N.Y. 10022. Manufactured in the United States of
America. Published simultaneously in Canada by Fitzhenry &
Whiteside, Ltd., Toronto.

Library of Congress Catalog Card Number: 73-90169

International Standard Book Number: hardcover: 0-8129-0409-5
paperback: 0-8129-6260-5

THE GUIDE TO
CAREER
EDUCATION

Muriel Lederer

QUADRANGLE/THE NEW YORK TIMES BOOK CO.

To my husband,
    my children,
       and my mother
           who have always backed me
           in everything I wanted to do.

Acknowledgments

I am deeply grateful for the help which came from many people in every aspect of compiling this book. Special thanks to Gladys Walker and Barbara Plunkett for invaluable research and editorial assistance, and to Terry Macri for the endless typing job so well done.

Appreciation is extended to all the professional and trade associations, unions, corporations, schools, and other groups who so generously supplied background information and advice necessary for research. Among those to whom I am particularly indebted for help are the following: American Association of Community and Junior Colleges, American National Cattlemen's Association, American Association of Nurserymen, American Meat Institute, Association of Independent Schools and Colleges, American Bar Association, American Forest Institute, American Hospital Association, American Personnel and Guidance Association, American Vocational Association, Carl Byoir & Associates, Inc., Battelle Columbus Laboratories, Bell & Howell Schools, B'nai B'rith Vocational Service, Council on Hotel, Restaurant and Institutional Education, Communications Workers of America, Center for Urban Education, City University of New York, City Colleges of Chicago, Connecticut State Department of Education (Bureau of Vocational Education), State of California (Department of Human Resources Development), Daniel J. Edelman, Inc., Engineers' Council for Professional Development, Gas Appliance Manufacturers Association, Guidance and Testing Center (University of North Carolina), Goodwill Industries of Western Connecticut and Sheltered Workshops, Inc., Harshe-Rotman & Druck, Inc., Dr. Kenneth B. Hoyt, Instrument Society of America, International Association of Machinists and Aerospace Workers, Congressman Stewart B. McKinney (Barbara C. Norris and William Sangiovanni), National Association of Trade and Technical Schools, National Home Study Council, State of New Jersey (Department of Education), Public Relations Board, Inc., Dr. Edwin L. Rumpf, Director, Field Coordination (Center for Adult, Vocational Technical and Manpower Education), U.S. Office of Education, Staples High School, Westport, Connecticut (Guidance Department), Scholarship Search, Technical Education Research Centers, U.S. Bureau of Labor Statistics (Don Dillon), U.S. Department of Agriculture, U.S. Department of Health, Education and Welfare (Office of Education and Division of Manpower Development and Training), U.S. Bureau of Apprenticeship and Training, United Auto Workers, Westport (Connecticut) Public Library Reference Staff.

Photo Credits

Aeronautics. United Air Lines Photos: pages 91, 93, 97, 99, 101; Federal Aviation Administration: 94; American Airlines Photo: 95.

Agriculture. California Almond Growers: page 103; USDA Photo: 106; St. Regis Paper Co.: 108; Horticulture Dept., Michigan State University: 109; Geo. A. Hormel & Co.: 110.

Art. Newspaper Comic Council, Inc.: page 114; Rochester Institute of Technology: 115; Eleanor Lambert, Inc.,: 117; Walter Dorwin Teague Assoc., Inc.: 118; Environmental Consultants Interiors: 120; National Broadcasting Co.: 122.

Automotive Industry. American Association: page 126; Ford Motor Company, Educational Affairs Dept.: 129, 130.

Business. American Institute of CPA: page 133; National Association of Bank-Women, Inc.: 135; Holiday Inns, Inc.: 137; Allstate Insurance Co.: 139; U.S. Department of Justice: 141; International Association of Personnel Women: 143. St. Francis Hospital, Evanston, Illinois: 144.

Clerical Occupations. National Association of Bank-Women, Inc.: Page 147; Pitney Bowes-Alpex Inc.: 149; Bridgeport Hospital, Bridgeport, Conn.: 150, 153; Holiday Inns, Inc.: 152; St. Regis Paper Co.: 155, 156; National Cash Register Co.: 158; Southern New England Telephone Co.: 159; American Association of Medical Assistants, 161.

Communications. Carl Byoir, Inc.: pages 164, 167; Miami-Dade Community College: 165; National Broadcasting Co.: 169, 171, 174; Rochester Institute of Technology: 172.

Conservation. Environmental Protection Agency: pages 176, 184; U.S. Department of Commerce, National Marine Fisheries Service: 180; USDA Photo: 181.

Construction Industry: International Masonry Institute: pages 189, 198, 207; National Association of Home Builders: 190; Lincoln Technical Institute, 192; Armstrong Cork Co., 194; International Brotherhood of Painters and Allied Trades: 196, 200; Wood, Wire and Metal Lathers International Union: 197; International Masonry Institute: 198, 207; Ryder Technical Institute: 199; National Roofing Contractors Association: 205; St. Regis Paper Co.: 206; U.S. Department of Interior: 210.

Data Processing. International Business Machines Corp.: page 213; Honeywell, Inc.: 214.

Electric and Telephone. St. Regis Paper Co.: page 216; Kansas Power & Light Co.: 217; U.S. Atomic Commission: 219; National Cash Register Co.: 220; A.T.&T.: 222, 224, 226; Southern New England Telephone Co.: 225.

Engineering. National Cash Register Co.: pages 228, 235, 239, 243; Sikorsky Aircraft: 232; Miami-Dade Community College: 233, 234, 238, 247; RCA: 236; U.S. Atomic Energy Commission: 237, 245, 252; Eastman Kodak Co.: 240, 248; Smith Kline & French Laboratories: 241; Ingersoll-Rand Co.: 244; American Society for Metals: 249; Lawrence Radiation Laboratory, Livermore: 250; Union Camp: 253.

Graphic Communications. U.S. Government Printing Office: pages 257, 258, 260, 261, 263, 264.

Health Service. Career Academy: pages 268; National Association of Dental Laboratories, Inc.: 270; University of Missouri at Kansas City: 271; American Optometric Association: 272; Optical Wholesalers Association: 273; American Association of Certified Orthoptists: 274; St. Francis Hospital, Evanston, Illinois: 275, 290; American Association of Medical Assistants: 277; Bridgeport Hospital, Bridgeport, Conn.: 278, 285, 289, 291; Park City Hospital, Bridgeport, Conn.: 279, 287, 290; Duke University Medical Center: 281; American College of Radiology: 282; Easter Seal Rehabilitation Center of Eastern Fairfield County, Conn.: 284; Irene B. Bayer, New York City: 286.

Machining Occupations. National Tool, Die and Precision Machining Association: pages 296,

299, 300, 301; Instrument Society of America: 297.

Mechanics and Repairmen. Cape Fear Technical Institute: pages 305, 311; Association of Home Appliance Manufacturers: 307; National Cash Register Co.: 309; John Deere: 313; Giddings & Lewis, Inc.: 314; Instrument Society of America: 316; St. Regis Paper Co.: 318; Ingersoll-Rand Co.: 319; General Electric Color Television Dept.: 321; Joseph Bulova School of Watchmaking: 322.

Performing Arts. Long Wharf Theatre: page 325; Bambi Linn, Westport, Conn.: 326; Ro-Jon, Westport, Conn.: 328; American Music Conference: 330; National Broadcasting Co.: 332.

Sales. Equitable Life Assurance Society of the U.S.: pages 337, 345; ITT Educational Services, Inc.: 339; H. F. Philipsborn & Co.: 341; National Cash Register Co.: 343; Merrill Lynch, Pierce, Fenner & Smith: 344.

Service Industries. Vaughn Barber Schools, Inc.: page 349; Servicemaster Industries, Inc.: 350, 355; National Hairdressers & Cosmetologists, Inc.: 352; New York City Fire Dept.: 353; Chicago Police Dept.: 357; American Library Association: 360; National Recreation and Park Association: 361; Miami-Dade Community College: 363; State University Agricultural and Technical College, Delhi, New York; 365, 369; Pepperidge Farm, Inc.: 367.

Transportation. Miami-Dade Community College: page 371.

Manual Occupations. Better Heating-Cooling Council: page 375; National Association of Metal Finishers: 376; St. Regis Paper Co.: 378; American Foundrymen's Society: 379, 380, 381; Geological Institute of America: 382; Rochester Institute of Technology: 385; Con Edison: 387; Ingersoll-Rand Co.: 389; American Gas Association: 390.

Contents

Preface

If you're asking yourself, "Where do I go from here?" perhaps you'll find your answer in this book.

Exciting new career opportunities are opening up everywhere. High school graduates are asking the question, "Is college really necessary?" The answer for many is, "No, you don't need four years of college to get a good job. What you do need is further education in the form of job training or career education." Career education today is your admission ticket to the world of work.

I feel there is a strong need, previously unsatisfied, to provide a basic reference book pulling together materials from many sources into one easy-to-read volume for quick reference or for easy browsing. This book does not represent an attempt to list or judge career education schools. Such lists can be found in other books, already in print, which you'll find in the bibliography at the end of this volume. This is an attempt to acquaint counselors, parents, and students with the numerous opportunities open for post-high school career education. There is unquestionably a very wide range of jobs open to those who get the proper career training.

As used in this book the words "career education" refer to post-high school training you receive to prepare you specifically for your chosen occupation, e.g., legal assistant or airline pilot. This training can be obtained in many ways, as described later on. Career education is a much misunderstood subject! In the past it has been the most controversial subject in American education. But now its time has finally come!

This book is an effort to give information that will increase the number of options open to students who are looking for paths to higher education, outside a standard four-year baccalaureate program.

Although you may not want to undertake a full four-year program, don't stop with just your high school diploma! You should definitely consider an occupation which calls for a limited amount of additional schooling—anywhere from three weeks to three years. America is full of jobs just looking for the right person. If you are prepared, these well-paying jobs are waiting for you! Don't be hampered all your life by lack of a salable skill.

College is not the only answer! We must stop thinking the plumber, who learned his skills in an apprenticeship program, does not deserve the same respect we pay a physician who learned his skills in a college.

Until just recently, our society has believed a four-year college was the only path to a successful career. In the case where students, who are seriously *not interested*, are forced into four-year college programs by well-meaning teachers and parents, the result is restlessness, dissatisfaction, and disillusionment all around.

In many respects the American pressure for collegiate education for everyone is the result of unrealistic thinking, misinformation, and misguided intentions. We have a distorted view of education which ignores the many ways a person can develop competence. We all must have training for our technological society, but we don't necessarily need strict academic education. *What you do need is career education leading to job opportunities.*

As a result of the advances in our technology, we are faced with manpower shortages in skilled and technical occupations. But remember, in spite of the shortages, it is increasingly difficult for young people to break into the world of work . . . unless they have well-trained skills. Today no one need settle for a mediocre job. The opportunities for well-paying, rewarding careers exist for the high school graduate through career education and training.

A wise man once pointed out not everyone can become a successful nuclear physicist, surgeon, or businessman. But, the individual who can work with his hands is just as important to our society as the individual who works with his mind. A pair of skilled hands is more valuable to our increasingly service-oriented society than the output of a second-rate mind!

The possession of a college degree doesn't guarantee you competence or happiness. A college degree isn't even a sure guarantee of financial success, as recent studies have shown.

Not all people are alike in their aptitudes, interests, and abilities. Your own abilities may suit you for training of a different kind from that offered in college. Just because your abilities are different does not imply they are inferior.

You *can* achieve job status, financial rewards, and family security; you *can* have an attractive future—through professional preparation and training.

In the modern world, to be without skills is a serious handicap. We are lucky there are so many alternatives for career education open to us. The question of what type of training is best can only be answered by you. Success has many definitions, and excellence is the result of effort rather than the automatic by-product of a college degree.

Muriel Lederer

Note: The information in this book is as accurate as it is possible to make it. Because this field is changing so rapidly, it is advisable for you to double-check what truly interests you to be sure the facts are still the same at the time you intend to pursue your career education.

If Not College, What?

What Is Career Education?

Are you career shopping? Looking for ideas on what to do with your life? Did you wake up Monday determined to become a scientist, switch to an accountant on Wednesday, and on Friday throw up your hands in despair?

Whether you are undecided or already know what you want to be, one thing you ought to consider is a good, practical course which will lead you directly to the job you want.

You and your parents probably always believed college was the best place for you to go after high school. But, now you're not so sure! There are alternatives you ought to consider.

This is a book about alternatives—those things you can do other than go to a four-year college or university.

The accent in career education today is on "do," "perform," "create," "make it," in the world of work. You emerge from your education with a marketable skill.

Career education is training for the world of work that does not require a bachelor's degree. It includes training in public high schools; in junior and community colleges and technical schools; in private vocational schools; in business, industry, and government; and in union apprenticeship programs.

It is vocational or technical training or retraining to prepare individuals for gainful employment as semiskilled or skilled workers or technicians or subprofessionals in recognized occupations. It does not include any program to prepare individuals for employment in occupations generally considered to be professional or which require a baccalaureate or higher degree.

Why not take a good look now at what is happening in career or vocational education? There is a whole new "glow" to this growing phenomenon. Vocational schools aren't what they used to be! Neither are their students. No longer are they merely trade schools teaching just mechanics and drafting to students of limited ability. In the past several years U.S. vocational enrollment in all types of programs jumped to over three million post-high school students coming from every type of family, everywhere. American students are enrolled in institutions of all kinds from tiny barber colleges to huge, 3,000-student technical institutes.

Our changing world of work is largely responsible for this great boom. The number of jobs requiring untrained minds and physical strength have greatly declined, while jobs requiring advanced education and perfected skills have sizably increased. Today nearly 80 percent of all jobs available require some vocational or technical skill. We need two technicians for every engineer or professional physical scientist, six to ten technicians for every medical doctor or professional researcher in the health field, and four to five technicians for every professional biological scientist. The fact we are far short of these standards explains why graduates of vocational schools are in great and increasing demand.

Many new kinds of occupations have appeared which require high levels of specialized technical knowledge. Technical training no longer refers to just jobs in engineering, industry, or manufacturing. For example, you can combine an interest in agriculture and distribution for a technical type job which relates to both fields, such as agribusiness technician. There are new combinations being developed every day which in turn lead to new classifications of technical occupations. Before an awestruck world could watch and listen to moonwalking Americans describing their step-by-step actions, thousands of earthbound men and women worked behind the scenes to make the feat possible. When you think of the skills needed to send men to the moon, you think in terms of Ph.D.'s: aerodynamicists, astrophysicists, chemical engineers whose depth of scientific and technical knowledge lies at the base of the space program. But, many big jobs in the NASA space program—satisfying and high salaried—did not require college degrees. They were filled by graduates of vocational and technical schools. One vocational school graduate was the technical supervisor of the voice control room at Goddard Space Flight Center at Greenbelt, Maryland. He was responsible for repair and maintenance of the maze of equipment which brought together the voices of the astronauts with those of the men operating NASA's tracking stations over the world.

1

Why career education is good insurance for your future

What about the students who don't plan to go to college? Are they doomed to unemployment? To unhappy, unfulfilled and unsuccessful lives?

After putting two years of hard study toward a degree in education, Heidi Peterson, 20, became a college dropout. "The employment situation for teachers was so bad I was just wasting my time and money in college," she said.

So, Miss Peterson quit her teachers' college. Then she promptly enrolled in a career education program at her district community college to learn how to be a therapist for patients who have difficulty breathing. "I'll be able to get a job at any hospital in the country and earn $12,000 to $15,000 a year. Why do I need a college degree?" she asked.

Miss Peterson's case is far from unusual. It's clear that vocational training gives people an edge in the job market compared with those who lack formal training. National unemployment among teenagers stands at nearly 16 percent, but the rate for teens with vocational training is only 5 percent, according to the United States Office of Education.

Career education programs offer you the chance to prepare yourself for the rest of hour life. Today, there is a bewildering proliferation of jobs, many of which didn't exist ten or even five years ago. Yet, virtually all of them require training—specific job-oriented training—not necessarily the education you receive at a four-year college with its basic core of liberal arts and general education.

One big reason you may be clinging to the belief you need a four-year college education is that you aren't aware of the alternatives. The possession of a college diploma does not guarantee competence, happiness, success, or personal adjustment. It may be a colossal waste of time and money. It's not even a sure guarantee of financial success. Some students would be horrified to learn just how many diploma-holders earn considerably less than the skilled workmen who built their dormitories. As a pair of researchers at Columbia University put it, " ... there is some indication college education already is not paying off as well as it may have done in the past." They estimate in 1966 salaried college graduates averaged about $8,400 a year—only a little ahead of unionized construction workers, with $8,000!

By 1976, who will be ahead? If your main reason for going to college is to boost your earnings, why go if blue-collar workers make more than college graduates? The time is coming, if not already here, when millions of shrewd parents will be advising Junior to go for a union card rather than a college diploma.

Consider these good jobs: an x-ray technician who is a paramedical worker with enough training to relieve doctors of many duties earns $7,000 to $8,000; medical technologists average over $10,000; an old-fashioned trade, carpentry, will provide 40,000 new openings each year, many of them leading to wages of $12 an hour, including union fringe benefits; plumbers earn over $13 an hour, certainly a better financial return than earned by many professional people.

Specialized training, rather than college, is all you need for these occupations: computer programmer and data processor, cook and chef, airline pilot, automobile salesman, electronic engineering technologist, bank teller, legal assistant, dental hygienist, office electronic computer operator, hotel and restaurant manager, architectural technician, and television and radio repairman.

What we all really desire is to find a place in adult life for which we are best suited. This will occur only if we try seriously to match our aptitudes, abilities, and interests with job requirements, regardless of the social status of the job in question. This can be done, and it does pay off.

A few years ago a study of several hundred graduates of Wilmington, Delaware, high schools was conducted. They were given a complete battery of tests and a personal aptitude profile was drawn up for each. The students were shown descriptions of a widespread variety of jobs in which they could succeed based on their aptitude profiles.

A year after they had been graduated, a follow-up study of the students located two groups: those who were in occupations for which their aptitude profiles were suitable; and those who were in jobs which called for a different aptitude profile. The results were clear and definite. Those who were in occupations for which their aptitudes suited them were more contented with their work and were rated by their employers as better employees than were the students whose aptitude profiles were not compatible with the job requirements. This suggests that if we aim for a successful future, we must look beyond the pressures of social status—being in the swim just because everyone else seems to be. The person who is unhappy on his job and who feels defeated in his work is very likely to feel unhappy and defeated in other aspects of his life. His problems won't be left in the office!

A study of job prospects for the 1970s has found eight out of ten jobs will be open to young workers with less than a college degree. But, the report stresses the fact that *young people who have acquired a skill or good basic education will have a better chance at steadier jobs.* With all the competition for good jobs, the boy or girl who doesn't have good preparation will find the going more difficult. Young people who have continued their education beyond high school will be in the best position to get jobs in the 1970s.

Some of the saddest cases personnel directors see—and they see them every day—are the young women who went through school, took academic courses which didn't prepare them to get a job. They didn't expect to work because they only wanted to get married; they did, and had a child or two. But then they were divorced or widowed and now have children to support and no way to do it. These women come into employment offices every day in desperate need of jobs. But they can't find jobs because they haven't any skills to offer employers.

By enrolling in one of the many public or private postsecondary programs, you can be prepared to earn respectable income with honor and dignity. An individual's ready employability as he leaves school, and throughout his working life, is one of the major goals of vocational and technical education.

What career education will do for you

There are many avenues to successful and happy living outside the domain of a full college education.

Today's vocational schools may lack the ivy-covered trappings of the academic world, but they do offer a storehouse of no-nonsense schooling for career-minded students. Most of the students at these institutions are fresh out of high school. Others have tried college or spent a few years in the armed forces. Some are mature married people. All have a desire to improve themselves through training. They are spurred on by the knowledge that plumbers, carpenters, and electricians earn more than many school superintendents and college presidents! Graduates of the Bergen (New Jersey) Technical Institute courses in commercial baking step into jobs which, within a period of time, pay up to $19,000 a year!

Not everyone is alike in his aptitudes, interests, and ability. Your particular pattern of ability may suit you for training of a different kind from that offered in a four-year college. And college is only one kind of education. *It is not the only key to your future! The main ingredient for a good job is the ability to do something and to do it reasonably well.*

The key word for your future is training

Vocational schools exist in order to give students occupational skills they can use in obtaining and holding a job. The schools and programs we are talking about concentrate on specialized skills and technical training. For teacher and student as well as for employer, the question no longer is: "What grade did you get?" The question is, "What can you do?" The performance is what counts! It is all that counts.

Many employers also feel vocational school graduates perform certain jobs better than their college-trained counterparts. Argonne National Laboratory, an Atomic Energy Commission laboratory near Chicago, used to hire all its computer programmers from among the ranks of college graduates. Now, more than half are graduates of junior colleges that provide vocational training programs. "College graduates are more interested in broad theory than in practical application, so they tend to make more programming mistakes," an official claims. "That can get pretty costly in terms of lost computer time."

There are all kinds of ways to make a living. Practicing medicine or law is just as much a vocation as being a mechanic. Be realistic: the fact that you have to work most of your life requires that you prepare for a job in which you can be productive, successful, and happy!

Career education should lead to fulfillment. Money can, without question, fulfill a lot of desires, but it can never be a substitute for the deep-down satisfaction obtained from accomplishment in work you enjoy. The figures which suggest people earn more money in their lifetime if they have a college degree are quite true, but do the figures also testify these people are happier in their jobs than those who did not go to college?

Why career education hasn't been more popular before

Suddenly career education, too long the stepchild of American education, is emerging from its second class citizenship to become the "Cinderella" of the school scene.

Career education has always had an "image problem." The National Advisory Council on Vocational Education said in 1968, "At the very heart of our problem is a national attitude that says vocational education is for somebody else's children . . . . We [Americans] have promoted the idea the only good education is an education capped by four years of college. This idea . . . is snobbish, undemocratic, and a revelation of why schools fail so many students."

The stigma of vocational education is steadily fading now, though slowly, as students' disillusionment with college education increases. The scarcity of jobs for graduates, especially those in the liberal arts, is encouraging many young people to switch to vocational training after high school. The rate of U.S. college enrollment is slowing down.

We are in the midst of a healthy re-evaluation of educational priorities. "Our higher education programs are turning out more graduates than the economy can absorb," says Dr. Edwin L. Rumpf, formerly acting director of vocational and technical education for the U.S. Office of Education. "In many cases people are spending four years in college and aren't prepared to do any specific job when they finish ... we are just beginning to recognize college isn't the only way to get to heaven."

There has been a lot of reassessment in recent years. People are asking, "Does everyone need a college degree?" Very recently society has begun to realize that it is "overengineered" and "over-teachered." The lead story in the Springfield, New Jersey, *Leader* of July 8, 1971, reports more than 900 teachers applied for about fourteen openings in the town's public school system! Meanwhile, "body and fender" jobs go begging, even though they may offer better pay than teaching positions.

For too long high school counselors have emphasized the need for a college degree in order to make a decent living. Too many students waste time (and money) taking classes which leave them bored, disillusioned, and bitter simply because they feel family pressure not to change a course of study once a decision is announced. Forcing high school graduates on to college indiscriminately is like taking horses to water and then emptying the trough over their heads. Many of them will drink very little and some cannot drink at all. The results clearly can be harsh. Dropouts reject themselves, feel worthless and humiliated. Their failure is a stigma they could have been spared. And the presence of aimless students on college campuses dilutes the efforts of the colleges to provide first-rate education to those students who do have genuine academic interest.

There seems little doubt a good many students in college today have no bona fide purpose for being there. They are not really intent on jobs requiring higher learning. They are there because they see nothing more promising off the campus and because a college degree has unfortunately become a status symbol. We are suffering from a pay and status myth. Americans have the mistaken idea vocational-technical education leads to lower pay and career status than liberal arts and the pure humanities.

In industrial plants, design draftsmen, tool and instrument makers, and engineering technicians can earn at least $15,000 per year, which is a respectable salary for any engineer with a number of years experience. And anyone who has built a house, an office building, or a plant, knows the incomes of craftsmen and journeymen in the construction trades have increased faster than any of the other occupational groups in the country.

Job status is a more elusive thing to communicate but there is no question successful competion of the most demanding technical production depends heavily on skilled methods of tooling set-ups, efficient automated-circuit design, appropriate maintenance of terribly complicated test equipment, etc. In other words, the technical skills involved are just as vital to the process as the administrative and managerial skills.

Are there any drawbacks to vocational education? "The biggest handicap vocational schools face today," says Dr. Kenneth Hoyt, an authority in this field, "is the low status they enjoy in our society. Too many parents and students still think of these schools as 'second-best' choices for 'second-class' people when, in fact, this simply is not true. The vocational school represents the really *best* choice for hundreds of thousands of people—including thousands of those who make the mistake of entering four-year colleges each fall and simply don't belong there."

In many respects, the pressure of the last twenty years for collegiate education for all is the result of unrealistic thinking, misinformation, and misguided intentions. Too often there has been a demand that secondary schools concentrate on the training of college-bound students to the exclusion of providing worthwhile kinds of training for youths with other interests. Too often pressure has been put on colleges and universities to be something other than what they should be. Far too often pressures have been put on all children to orient themselves toward a college education. Americans have developed a myopic view of education which results in ignoring many ways in which a person may develop competence without going to college.

There is also a mistaken notion that occupational or vocational education is obsolete; that the best occupational preparation is a solid background in the liberal arts. For some people and for many vocations, this is true. The notion that liberal arts training is essential for all job applicants comes most often from corporation executives, rarely from the recruiters in the field. Although you often see ads asking for secretaries trained in shorthand, accountants trained in business data processing, and electronic technicians with a knowledge of transistor circuits, you never see notices asking for individuals with a good general education. The point is that the requirement for an entry job is the ability to *do* something, and to do it reasonably well.

Fortunately, we are in the midst of a general drift away from value-oriented education (the humanities and liberal arts), and toward a vocational-oriented education (the health sciences, professional schools and applied social sciences). For both boys and girls today the horizon is wide, with the opportunities for a great variety of careers there for the taking.

Why we need career education now

Before we became a technological society, the youth who did not graduate from high school could become contributing citizens in our society; the only prerequisites were a willingness to work, good health, and brawn.

What then is the future for the almost one million youngsters who now drop out of high school each year? We know, and the dropout learns, the lack of a high school diploma spells disaster. Today's work world has no place for him. High school dropouts have an unemployment ratio nearly double that of graduates.

About 70 percent of today's 23-year-olds have had no job training in schools and have not completed a college education. Yet, nearly 80 percent of all jobs available in the United States require some vocational or technical skill.

Dr. Sidney P. Marland, Jr., former Assistant U.S. Secretary of Education, says, "America, richest of all nations, has the additional distinction of the highest youth unemployment rate in the world. Why? Our high schools have not been able to make sure every young man and woman who receives a diploma is qualified for either immediate employment or further education."

We hear most parents want their children to receive a college education, yet fewer than one in three high school graduates enters college. Of these only about half graduate from college. It is up to schools and the parents to do a better job of counseling students on vocational options open to them and educational opportunities for them beyond high school and other than four-year colleges. We must help students understand the varied choices open to them in their post-high school years.

Each year, unfortunately, thousands of high school graduates who should be attending such schools enter the labor market with no real job skills. The sky-high unemployment rates among such youth, their use in unskilled and semiskilled jobs, far below their potential job competence, their bitter frustrations and disappointments are a national disgrace.

In looking to the future, we are sure the world will become more crowded. Jobs will become increasingly specialized and competition very keen. The standards for vocational education and training will rise considerably. Those who are unqualified or who are poorly trained will have a tough time getting jobs.

A long-range projection shows that by 1975, 14 million people should be receiving some sort of vocational technical education. In 1968, only 3.8 million were getting such training in secondary schools.

Why vocational education? Young people seeking a toehold in the labor force often have trouble simply because they lack *relevant* work experience. Also, they face competition for jobs from other persons who are better educated.

Career opportunities, not dead-end job opportunities are the answer.

A Nobel prize winner has pointed out technology has advanced sufficiently to free people from many menial tasks. He recommends men gear themselves to giving personal service to one another. People consider service jobs as a form of slavery, but we have to change this attitude if there is to be happiness.

The notion someone who goes to college is better than someone who does not must be changed so a first-rate artisan who works with his hands is held in as high esteem as the graduate of a liberal arts college. Our country no longer has a place for a person who is not going on to college and doesn't possess a salable skill.

Badly needed new support for vocational education is now putting in an appearance on many fronts. For reasons no one exactly understands, the American school system has been designed and maintained as though each of its pupils was destined for Harvard or Oxford. We need to develop a new attitude that education should lead to a job.

The National Advisory Council on Vocational Education in 1970 advised, "In America, every child must be educated to his highest potential, and the height of the potential is not measured by the color of the collar. Plumbers, carpenters and electricians make more than many school superintendents and college presidents; only the arrogant will allow themselves to feel that one is more worthy than another."

It's absurd to suggest general knowledge for its own sake is somehow superior to useful knowledge.

John W. Gardner, former Secretary of Health, Education and Welfare, has written: "We live in a society which honors poor philosophy because philosophy is an honorable calling, and ignores good plumbing because plumbing is a humble occupation. Under such practices, we will have neither good philosophy nor good plumbing. Neither our pipes nor our theories will hold water."

Don't settle for a mediocre job. The opportunities for well-paying, rewarding careers exist for the high school graduate who isn't college bound.

Employment growth will be fastest among those occupations requiring the most education and training to enter. A high school education has become standard for American workers. Employers are looking for people with higher levels of education because jobs are more complex and require higher levels of skill. Good quality vocational education is what you need.

You can achieve job status, financial rewards, and family security. You can have an attractive future through the kind of professional preparation and training described starting on page 28.

Is Career Education For You?

Who goes to vocational schools and training programs

Peggy North, a twenty-year-old medical technology student at a Dayton, Ohio technical school, finds there's no comparison between her studies and her unhappy first year at a large state university. She thought college was a "dog-eat-dog world" with so much competition she didn't get the feeling anybody cared about her at all.

She was in the same program she is now, but wasn't getting what she wanted because there were so many unrelated requirements to get out of the way before she could begin studying what she came to college for. She finds the 126-student technical school much more to her liking. "Here you get right into the "meat" of your field and you're a person, not a number. You come here not to socialize but to learn. You're here to learn a trade. If you take care of that, though, the fun falls into place."

Vocational schools are for the student who wants to learn something that will make him more employable. They are no longer places for students who are not qualified for four-year colleges.

Many young people want to attend vocational schools and technical institutes, but are discouraged from doing so by their parents, guidance counselors, and others. What these well-meaning people don't realize is how much the schools have changed from the 1940s and 1950s. The truth is, students looking for personal attention and the immediate study of career-related courses are likely to feel more at home in a small career school than at a large university.

Bill James, 18, a recent Milwaukee, Wisconsin high school graduate, is a good example: "I wanted to do something to help mankind, to help save human lives. I chose this community college because of the personal attention students get. The sense of dedication among the students is impressive, too. There is no playing around here. We are preparing for professional work. You have a different attitude toward school when you're studying exactly what you want, when you're not being forced to take a lot of extra things you aren't interested in."

Joe Beames, a 24-year-old California student, though qualified to attend a four-year college, is taking an industrial technology course at a Los Angeles community college. It is one of the 58 programs his school offers. He gets greater satisfaction from finishing a woodwork project than from paperwork. His course offers a little more action, and that's what he and his classmates want.

Steve Simpson, 20, of Buffalo, New York, gave up the promise of a well-paying future as a tool-and-die worker to study dental technology. After completing a two-year trade school course to equip him to follow in his father's footsteps, he refused several job offers, fearing he would become "just another punchcard in a factory." Talks with the family dentist sparked an interest in dental technology. "It's very precise work with your hands," Steve explained. "I like to do small things, to work with a micrometer. And it's not routine work. Every job is a new challenge. You have the chance to be something of an artist, to do a piece of real individual craftsmanship."

Another thing students today want is fast money! A Michigan electronics school student found he could start earning after just a year of his two-year course. If he'd gone to a four-year college, he wouldn't be useful to any company till he'd been handed his degree.

Some high school gradates who in other years might have gone to college are now bypassing it in favor of trade schools. Midwesterner Alan Wood, 18, graduated at the top of his high school class, but he enrolled in a union sponsored work-study program to become an apprentice electrician. "A lot of my friends agree with me. College just isn't worth the hassle anymore," he says. "You can earn just as much in the trades as you can as a professional, and you don't have the expense of four years of college either."

Another group swelling the ranks of vocational students are veterans returning from Vietnam. "They're really no-nonsense students," says an official of Los Angeles Trade Technical Institute. "There are always some classes, like fashion design and photography, that continually attract more students than we can place in jobs. But these veterans come in and ask, 'Where are the job openings?' If we tell them, 'Auto Repair,' they sign right up. They really have their feet on the ground."

So students may be high school graduates who either don't wish to go to college, or those who transfer from college in search of practical career training. There are also homemakers headed back to work who enroll in home study courses to prepare themselves for a career. Another group of students are mature people looking for retraining who enroll in such courses as those directed toward a retirement-type career in hotel-motel operation.

Are there any differences between freshmen and sophomore students attending four-year colleges and those going to two-year institutions? Plenty, according to the U.S. Census Bureau. An October 1970 survey found there were 6.3 million undergraduate college students at all types of schools. Of these, 1.7 million (27 percent) were enrolled at two-year colleges and 2.2 million (36 percent) as freshmen or sophomores at four-year colleges.

The report by the Census Bureau declares students at two-year colleges are twice as likely to be at least twenty years old, twice as likely to be married, almost three times as likely to be attending classes on a part-time basis, and more than twice as likely to be living on the West Coast.

A student of a vocational program is more interested in being trained than in being educated. There are more boys than girls at post-secondary level vocational and technical schools. About half of all secondary and post-secondary students work full or part-time and one half of these have jobs related to their program of study.

In the past the bulk of students have been drawn from the lowest socio-economic level of society. They have generally been the children of workers rather than of professional men.

With the new acceptance of technical education, this has begun to change. Also by broadening the concept of technical education to include preparation for highly skilled technicians for other fields, e.g., health and science, more children of middle- and upper-class families can be expected to enroll in career education courses.

Career education for girls

Girls are finding that if college isn't possible financially, or not a wise choice, they still have a good chance to prepare for careers in expanding fields ... perhaps as technicians or apprentices in some craft. Today the entire world of work is open to qualified women. Why not a lady plumber? Or a dispensing optician? Or a TV repairwoman?

"They still get funny looks on their faces when I show up carrying a case of tubes and my tools," says Diana Ildefonso. "When I walk in that door, I have to prove myself, or I might as well quit." Diana is a young television repairwoman who showed such aptitude for electronics she attended a service training school and did

better than most of her boy classmates. She now has a job with a television dealer in Linden, New Jersey, makes house calls with a fellow worker, and does an exceptionally competent job.

Though girls have been slow to enter the skilled trades, there is now a marked movement of women into some crafts. In fact, in the last ten years more girls than boys have become auto mechanics, bakers, compositors and typesetters, decorators and window dressers, opticians, lens grinders and polishers, tailors and upholsterers. Girls have worked in some crafts and service fields since colonial days, but present-day technology has created job openings unheard of before. Girls who are looking for more than "just a job" are registering in courses that will qualify them for the more interesting and satisfying careers which fully use their abilities and talents.

A revolution has taken place in the life patterns of girls and women. A girl today can anticipate a very different way of life from her grandmother and even her mother. Most girls today work for several years after completing their schooling, then devote themselves to marriage and motherhood before returning to the labor force. About half of today's girls marry by the time they are 21 and have their last child at about 30. After her youngest child has entered school, a mother may have thirty or thirty-five more years of active life before her. Thus, a woman is almost as likely to be working at age 45 as she is at age 20 to 24.

This means that as a girl, your career may be interrupted by marriage and childbearing. But you'll be a happier person and have a more satisfying life before marriage, and later as a wife and mother, if you consider family life and career as related, rather than conflicting ideas.

Because the chances of marriage for a girl today are almost 100 percent, it's unrealistic for a girl to concentrate on the big man hunt or to look on marriage as the sole preoccupation of her future. You'll be better off preparing yourself for a satisfying and interesting career that runs along with a hoped-for marriage to the man of your dreams.

With the time for domestic chores shortened by work-saving appliances, married women are freer to choose how they will make their contribution to the family and the community. Opportunities for paid employment and challenging volunteer service are increasing. As a result, 31.5 million women are now in the labor force (by 1980 there probably will be about 37 million), while other millions are devoting their talents and energy to much needed volunteer work.

Because you can look forward to spending more years working at a paid job, it is essential you give serious thought now to the type of work you will be able to do. Education and training are just as important to a girl's future as they are to a boy's.

In the past one of the groups least served vocationally has been women. The old and weak argument that training for girls was wasted is no longer valid. Girls have traditionally had fewer career options than boys. This is all changed now. Until the last few years girls who didn't plan to go to college were mostly limited in the vocational courses they could take to beauty trades, retail sales, needleworking, or office work. This didn't bother girls apparently because they saw themselves as only capable of entering these relatively few occupations.

Since 1964 and the Equal Opportunities Act, men and women are equal under the law insofar as employment opportunities are concerned. Despite this legislation, men are still somewhat "more equal" than women when it comes to pay scales and entry into many trades and professions in other than token numbers.

There is no legitimate reason for this discrimination except prejudice in almost every instance. We need skilled women in all career areas. But, according to the U.S. Department of Labor Statistics, only 14 percent of all employed women are professional or technical workers.

Although more than 250 distinct occupations are listed in the Bureau of the Census tabulations, half of all women workers were employed in only twenty-one occupations in 1969. About a fourth of all employed women were in five occupations: secretary-stenographer, household worker, bookkeeper, elementary school teacher, and waitress. Secretary and stenographer jobs alone accounted for one of every ten women workers. Only 1 percent of the total female work force is employed in the four top professional career groups: law, medicine, engineering, and scientific research.

Women are concentrated in certain occupations because they have always been discouraged from trying to enter others. Some jobs in the construction trades, for instance, require lifting or carrying weights that are beyond the capability of most women. And some occupations require much longer periods of preparation than many women are able or willing to undertake. Work requiring a professional degree, for example, is open to fewer women than men, since the number of women workers who have four years of college is so much smaller than the number of men.

But discrimination and, perhaps even more important, widely held prejudices that some jobs are feminine and others are masculine have artificially restricted women's jobs far beyond what is reasonable.

In a sense the concentration of women in certain jobs is the result of the lack of men in them. Attitudes of what is masculine or feminine have played a part here, too. But low wages in many of the "women's occupations" have been

an important reason. Because men failed to choose the occupation, women found it easier to land the job; for example, nursing.

Many factors today seem to encourage women workers to spread out. Physical requirements, for example, aren't as important as technological innovations lessen the strength requirements in many jobs. Widespread use of aptitude and interest tests is slowly effecting changes in attitudes regarding "appropriate" or "inappropriate" jobs for women or men. Rising salaries in teaching and social work have attracted more men to these occupations, further lessening the concentration of women.

The average earnings of women who work all year at full-time jobs are still far below those of their male counterparts. They amounted to $5,323 in 1970—only 59 percent of the $8,966 earned by men. Although this does not necessarily mean that women are receiving unequal pay for equal work, it is true they are more likely to be employed in the lower skilled, lower paying jobs. Women and girls consistently have been channeled into these jobs by the preparation they have received in the schools and by the expectations of the community. They desperately need a chance to improve their position and to move into new careers and nontraditional job opportunities.

Vocational education is the best chance you have for opening doors now and in the future and for increasing your earning ability and your status. It would seem to make best sense to enroll in programs offering preparation for the new and emerging job areas. More women workers in the 1970s must prepare to enter work outside the traditional "women's occupations" if they expect to find a job in keeping with their ability.

Women can provide the labor America requires. But the requirements are becoming more and more specific. Needs are in the individual occupations, not in the broad unskilled labor market. And those needs change, for at any one time some occupations are growing very rapidly, others are growing slowly, and some are declining numerically.

A girl who wants both a career and a family must choose her career—and her husband—with care. *It's not a matter of deciding between a career and a family.* Improved day care services due to recently established federal standards will enable many future mothers to go to work part-time, once their children are out of diapers. And in most states, compulsory kindergarten within the next few years will probably take preschoolers out of their homes for a good part of the day.

You can plan for a realistic career that enhances, rather than conflicts with, your expectations as a woman. The same opportunities are available to girls as to boys. There need be no limitations to your ambitions because you are a girl. But because some prejudices still linger you must plan to make the system work for you rather than against you.

Don't allow parents, teachers, counselors or cultural prejudices to decide your future as a woman. If you hunger to be competent, useful, productive and interested, you can now enter any field, save those that make physical demands that are best fulfilled by men.

Who should consider career education

Dr. Kenneth B. Hoyt, a leading voice in the fight for better recognition of vocational education, says, "The prime reason for choosing a vocational school rather than some other type lies in the educational motivations of the student. In the 11,000 cases I have studied, the students most frequently expressed their reasons in these terms: 'Here we study only what we need to know—not things like poetry and history.'"

When asked what kind of students he recommends considering vocational schools, Dr. Hoyt said, "The increasingly technological nature of our occupational society leads me to believe roughly two out of every five high school graduates should give serious consideration to attending vocational schools." Students who should go include those whose main reason for attending school is to acquire an occupational skill; those who have an aversion to liberal arts kinds of courses; those who have a real and sincere interest in the occupation, or occupations for which the school offers training; and those who are willing to work long, hard hours to gain their vocational skills.

Another vocational education authority has said his school has found many prep school students are late bloomers, capable youths who treated high school as a lark and spent their school years passing courses without really trying to learn anything. After graduation they discovered, much to their chagrin, they were qualified only for unskilled, low-paying jobs. *Vocational schools represent a second chance to those young people.*

Vocational education is for the person who believes he or she will do the very best a person can do in every job he works on. He regards himself as a professional at his particular job. There is no better way for a person to find fulfillment, no matter what he does.

There is no shortcut, no magic carpet sweeping you swiftly from desire to achievement. If you are to be a respected man or woman, your biggest asset will be to have self-discipline which allows you to master your job or craft. This means a dedication and a work schedule that sometimes can be rather dismaying. Still, there is no other way to acquire that standard of excellence which is the mark of the professional and the major ingredient for achievement.

Who should not consider career education

"I think," says Dr. Hoyt, "all students should consider vocational education along with all other kinds of alternatives available to them. Those who should reject vocational education include: people who like to learn just for the sake of learning but who do not want to get ready to go to work; those students who are content with or unable to do more than hold a job at the unskilled or semiskilled level; and students who have not accepted for themselves the values of a work-oriented society. The vocational school is no place for the 'hippie,' the pseudo-intellectual, or the 'playboy.' It is a serious place for students who consider their training as a means of getting and holding a good, rewarding job."

Facts You'll Need to Know About Career Education Programs

Accreditation and What It Means

If you're planning to enroll in a school, you want to know the quality of the school before you commit yourself. Some schools do just what their advertising promotion says they can do. Others make wildly exaggerated claims to attract applicants.

How can you tell which is which? Your choice of a school to attend should be made in the light of all the available information about both the institution and its students. Although the accredited status of a college is the best guide to its general standing or quality, it's true some departments of study in an unaccredited institution may be better than the corresponding departments in an accredited school.

It is also possible a particular course of study you are looking for may happen to be given more satisfactorily, conveniently, or economically in a school without the highest quality. This is an area you must look into very carefully.

A few states have practically no control over the establishment of institutions with respect to their educational legitimacy. In such states almost any person or group can set up and operate an educational enterprise, granting diplomas and degrees of all kinds, whether or not they meet any standards for a sound program of instruction. This absence of control in certain states has encouraged the establishment of a number of so-called "diploma mills," which sell degrees, diplomas, and credentials to anyone for a price, without requiring the usual academic achievement by students. Some of these fraudulent organizations eventually are discovered and stopped by the Federal Trade Commission through "cease and desist" orders, after it has been established that they are guilty of practices that violate the Federal Trade Commission Act.

Even after a cease and desist order has been issued, it is relatively easy for the operator to open up again under a slight variation in name, or in a different location, and to continue to sell academic credentials until he is caught again. Most institutions of this type give only correspondence instruction and so their "students" may never discover they don't even have the usual facilities for a college program. Many people are not aware of the fact that degrees granted for work done entirely by correspondence are not recognized by accredited colleges and universities or by examining boards of the different professions.

Until the states provide closer supervision over educational enterprises, the only protection a prospective student may have is a warning to be on your guard against a prospectus that offers educational credentials without the usual academic effort.

See also pages 77-79 for more information on how to choose a school.

What accreditation means

Accreditation is the process whereby an association or agency grants public recognition to a school as having met certain established qualifications or standards. Such approval is granted by one or more of the regional or professional "accrediting" associations and agencies that exist in the United States.

If a school is accredited, it means the school has a competent faculty; it offers educationally sound and up-to-date courses; it screens students carefully for admission; it provides satisfactory educational services; it has demonstrated ample student success and satisfaction; its tuition charges are reasonable; it advertises its courses truthfully; and it is financially able to deliver what it promises.

It is in general not the policy of the voluntary accrediting agencies to rate their member institutions or to make distinctions among those they have accredited. The organizations publish only a single list—those institutions they have accredited—without any indication that one college may rate higher than another. In some cases the accredited list may give information concerning the type of institutions, e.g., junior college, or college for teachers. A few of the accrediting agencies indicate probationary or provisional membership.

No recognized authority in this country in recent years has made a rate of institutions to determine "the best" or "the ten best" in any field. From time to time publications appear reporting ranks according to limited criteria.

Such reports as a rule are restricted in scope and frequently out of date as soon as they are published.

Accreditation is a process of recognizing those educational institutions whose performance and integrity entitle them to the confidence of the educational community and the public. In the United States this recognition is extended largely through nongovernmental or voluntary agencies which have assumed responsibility for establishing criteria, visiting and evaluating institutions at the institution's request, and approving those institutions that meet their criteria.

In American higher education accreditation performs a number of important functions. For example, it helps intensify the effort each institution makes toward being educationally effective. The accrediting process of most agencies requires each institution to examine its own concepts, goals, and operations, supported by the expert criticism of a visiting team which later reports back to the institution through the accrediting agency. And, since the accredited status of an institution is reviewed periodically (normally, at least once every ten years or after a major change of purpose or program), the institution is encouraged continually to study itself and improve itself.

One of the most important factors involved is that any institution eligible to be considered for accreditation must voluntarily ask to be considered. It must analyze itself and submit to an on-site evaluation by a team of visitors assigned by the appropriate accrediting commission.

How schools get accreditation

The United States is the only country in the world whose system of higher education is evaluated by individuals outside the government. Most members of the accrediting associations and agencies evaluation committees are drawn from the educational community itself. Thus accreditation is controlled by people in the field of education and in the professions, not by civil servants or politicians.

Neither the American Council on Education nor the Federation of Regional Accrediting Commissions of Higher Education accredits institutions. The Federation develops national standards in accrediting for regional application by the six-member associations.

The Office of Education does not rate or accredit institutions. It has no procedure of its own for determining whether one institution is better than another. The Office of Education does furnish information about the accreditation of institutions by other recognized agencies.

Accrediting agencies are actually voluntary nongovernmental associations of institutions already judged as meeting the established standards. If an institution is admitted to membership in the association, it means it is accredited by that group. The accrediting agencies announce new accreditations each year. It is wise to check the latest list at your library or school if your preferred school is a fairly new one and hasn't been previously listed as accredited. It might be accredited now.

The Regional Accrediting Associations, of which there are six, are concerned with both secondary schools and institutions of higher education within a particular geographic region. The professional agencies, of which thirty-three were recognized by the Office of Education in April 1970, are national organizations concerned only with programs leading to a particular profession (e.g., legal assistant). Until quite recently professional training programs have existed primarily at universities. With the growth and development of new programs for paraprofessional workers (practical nurses, for example) many of which are given jointly in community colleges and hospitals, clinics, or other institutions, the professional agencies have enlarged the scope of their accrediting activities.

Among the regional associations there is great diversity in the degree of influence each has had on institutions it has tried to stimulate to improve and develop. The activity of a regional agency is voluntary and selective; no institution is required to belong. In fact the initiative for accreditation must be taken by the institution. After written application for accreditation has been made to the regional association, an appointed committee of representatives visits the school or college and subsequently submits written evaluations to the association based on its findings.

The criteria on which judgments are made are fairly uniform and usually include: previous preparation of students and effectiveness of admissions procedure; training and performance of faculty and administrative offices and the quality of the relationships between these two; extent and suitability of curriculum in relation to the institution's stated goals; size and appropriateness of library facilities; adequacy and condition of physical plant; and the institution's finances.

There is normally a period of a year or two or even longer between application and approval. During this period, if an institution is judged to be in a sufficiently advanced stage of development, it is said to be "in correspondence with" or "an associate of" the association. When the association is satisfied an institution meets its standards adequately, approval is given and the institution's name is included in the association's printed list. In order to insure future maintenance of standards, periodic revisits and reevaluations are made. Lists are revised and updated frequently.

Professional agencies, the only accrediting groups that operate nationally, function in much the same way as do the regional associations. But each agency is concerned only with the part of an institution's curriculum that is intended to prepare students to enter a particular profession. For example, the American Association of Architects accrediting committee visits, examines, and evaluates only schools of architecture; the American Chemical Society examines and evaluates undergraduate and graduate curricula in chemistry and sets its own requirements for admission to the American Chemical Society.

A high percentage of the professional accrediting agencies require an educational institution first be evaluated and approved by the appropriate regional accrediting association before application is made to the professional agency for evaluation. There are instances in which graduate schools in particular professional categories are approved by the professional agencies but have not received regional approval, but these are exceptions rather than the rule. Many institutions are accredited by more than one association or agency.

Accrediting of special schools

Less than half of all states license and regulate private vocational schools. Very few of these states carefully supervise the instructional programs offered by the licensed schools. Therefore, the findings of a visiting team from a group like the National Association of Trade and Technical Schools (NATTS) are the main way of evaluating a trade or technical school. Such a team would be made up of industry experts who examine the course content and instruction in their relevant fields. The schools' business practices are examined, including job placement records and student recruitment procedures, especially when a school's representatives are paid on a commission basis. Impressions of students are sought through random interviews. Accrediting teams evaluate a school on the basis of its success in meeting its self-stated objectives.

Business schools are evaluated by the Association of Independent Colleges and Schools, a recognized accrediting body.

Home study schools are accredited by the National Home Study Council (NHSC) or the National Association of Trade and Technical Schools (NATTS), both recognized by the U.S. Office of Education as official accrediting agencies.

Like other educational institutions, private vocational school must apply for accreditation on a voluntary basis. In general, they are evaluated by private accrediting groups.

So, though we have no single institutional accreditation system in the United States, all reputable voluntary agencies share the same basic philosophy. All are concerned with the quality of the total effort of an institution to achieve what it says its purpose is. The courses offered in two institutions may be quite different, not at all comparable, even though both institutions have been adjudged to be of high quality and are, therefore, accredited. See pages 13-14 for list of accrediting agencies recognized by the U.S. Office of Education.

How to find out if the school you are interested in is accredited

You can avoid "fly-by-night" schools if you find out whether the school has been approved and accredited. Check its reputation with guidance counselors, state employment services, state office of education, Veterans Administration, and such groups as the National Association of Trade and Technical Schools or the National Home Study Council. Some states require private schools be approved by the Office of Superintendent of Public Instruction. It is wise to check if your chosen school has been so approved. Ask the local Better Business Bureau or Chamber of Commerce whether any complaints have been received against the school. Ask employers in the field you're going to be trained for what they think of the school.

If a school is properly accredited, its ads or catalog might have statements like, "Accredited member of the NATTS," "Eligible institute under the Federally insured Student Loan Program," "Approved U.S. Department of Justice for nonimmigrant Alien Students," "Approved for Veterans' Training Benefits," or "Approved N.Y. State Education Department for the training of veterans eligible under the Federally insured Student Loan Programs."

Because of the wide variations in practices among the states, the United States Office of Education doesn't try to maintain complete, up-to-date lists of state approved institutions in all the fields in which each state happens to do accrediting. You can get information concerning the approved status of an institution within any state by writing directly to the Department of Education in that state.

You can also get information about the accredited status of a school which interests you by asking the school registrar for its annual catalog. The catalog will usually tell about the agencies which have accredited it and its programs of study.

There are a number of respectable educational organizations that do not accredit institutions of higher education, but whose names are similar to those of recognized accrediting agencies. Frequently institutions are somewhat careless in their catalogs in listing memberships in educational and professional organizations in a way that does not distinguish clearly between those by which they are accredited and those they have joined merely by making application and paying the annual dues. Among well-known educational organizations that do not carry on accrediting activities, but which are frequently listed by colleges as having "accredited" them, are the American Council on Education, the Association of American Colleges, the National Education Association, and American Association of Junior Colleges.

The Veterans Administration has on file the names of institutions that have been approved for the attendance of students obtaining veterans' benefits. In general, the information in the file was supplied by state authorities and includes all kinds of instruction, such as secondary schools, trade schools, and schools for adults, as well as institutions of higher education. You can get information concerning a specific institution or a particular course from the Veterans Administration regional office servicing the territory in which the school is located.

The Immigration and Naturalization Service of the U.S. Department of Justice also maintains a list of institutions that have been approved by the Attorney General for the enrollment of non-immigrant alien students. The fact that an institution has been included as being an "established institution of learning or other recognized place of study" does not mean the Attorney General is listing the Institution as being accredited in the way we have used that word in talking about educational institutions in this chapter.

Reasons for these precautions

Unfortunately all these precautions are necessary because of the number of fraudulent schools in the country. In Miami, Florida, a private computer school recruited two Mississippi black girls for nonexistent courses. When the girls arrived in Miami, they found the balance of their educational contracts had been sold to a finance company, which threatened them with lawsuits if they didn't pay.

Until recently most educators held private vocational schools in low esteem because of too frequent abuses, such as ads which promised high-salary jobs to graduates but the training provided was often inadequate. While the situation is better and improving many states still have no laws regulating the schools. The proprietary schools' industry has set up voluntary accrediting boards, but many schools have ignored them because they can fill their classes without accreditation.

The Federal Trade Commission has been steadily cracking down. It has issued guidelines to keep the school advertising honest. It has taken specific action against offenders repeatedly in recent years.

Transfer of credit from one institution to another usually must be between accredited institutions, and most professional licenses, certificates, and academic degrees are awarded on the basis of work done in institutions or programs that have been either regionally or professionally accredited.

If you are trying to plan a study program for yourself, you would do well to understand what accreditation is and how it works so you can choose wisely the institution in which you register. For example, the content of a course might be precisely the same when given under the auspices of a voluntary organization or in a nearby college. But credits toward an academic degree would be earned most easily by taking the course in the college. This fact may or may not be important to you.

Although the regional associations exert no legal control over academic standards, they are very influential indeed. Students can consult the regional lists for help in choosing a college or university in which to register; admissions officers often want to know if a student's previous work has been done in an accredited institution; and most government agencies and professional organizations recognize credits only from the educational institutions that have been listed by the regional associations.

Because standards vary somewhat among the associations and agencies, it should not be assumed that any course taken in an institution whose name appears on one list is automatically transferable to another, similarly listed institution. You must always ask specifically at the institution where you wish the credit to be accepted if it will be accepted.

For more information, write:

Accrediting Commission
Association of Independent Colleges and Schools
1730 M Street, N.W.
Suite 401
Washington, D.C. 20036
Ask for: *Directory of Accredited Institutions 1973*, $.50 (accredited business schools).

National Commission on Accrediting
1 Dupont Circle, N.W.
Washington, D. C. 20036
Ask for: Accrediting information on junior colleges, technical institutions and other types of schools.

U.S. Government Printing Office
Public Documents Distribution Center
5801 Tabor Avenue
Philadelphia, Pennsylvania 19120
Ask for: *Accredited Postsecondary Institutions and Programs* (ask for most recent revised edition), HE 5.250:50066–S/N 1780–1065, $1.25.

Accrediting Agencies and Associations recognized by the U.S. Office of Education which evaluate and accredit postsecondary institutions.

Regional Accrediting Associations

Middle States Association of Colleges and Secondary Schools
225 Broadway
New York, New York 10007

New England Association of Colleges and Secondary Schools, Incorporated
50 Beacon Street
Boston, Massachusetts 02108

North Central Association of Colleges and Secondary Schools
5454 South Shore Drive
Chicago, Illinois 60615

Northwest Association of Secondary and Higher Schools
Commission on Higher Schools
University of Washington
Seattle, Washington 98105

Southern Association of Colleges and Schools
795 Peachtree Street, N.E.
Atlanta, Georgia 30308

Western Association of Schools and Colleges
c/o Modesto Junior College
Modesto, California 95350

Professional Associations:

Accrediting Bureau of Medical Laboratory Schools
166 East Superior Street
Chicago, Illinois 60611

Accrediting Commission for Business Schools
Suite 724, New Center Building
7430 Second Boulevard
Detroit, Michigan 48202

American Board of Funeral Service Education
9 Jackson Avenue
Naperville, Illinois 60540

American Dental Association Council on Dental Education
211 East Chicago Avenue
Chicago, Illinois 60611

Cosmetology Accrediting Commission
1601 Eighteenth Street, N.W.
Washington, D.C. 20009

Council on Medical Education of the American Medical Association (in collaboration with other professional associations)
535 North Dearborn Street
Chicago, Illinois 60610

Department of Transportation
Federal Aviation Administration
Washington, D.C. 20590

Engineers Council for Professional Development
345 East 47th Street
New York City, New York 10017

National Association of Schools of Art
1225 Connecticut Avenue, N.W.
Washington, D.C. 20036

National Association of Trade and Technical Schools
2021 L Street, N.W.
Washington, D.C. 20036

National Council of Technical Schools (Engineering Technician)
1835 K Street, N.W.
Washington, D.C.

National Home Study Council
1601 Eighteenth Street, N.W.
Washington, D.C. 20009

National League for Nursing
10 Columbus Circle
New York City, New York 10019

Financial Help and How to Get It

How much your career education will cost

City or community colleges are usually tuition-free to legal residents of the area, but are open to nearby residents for tuition fees often less than the same courses would cost in a private college. All students provide their own books and supplies and are charged small laboratory fees and general service fees.

At a private vocational school you can expect to pay tuition ranging from $800 to $2,500 a year. An electronics course may run $1,400 to $2,000 per year; $1,300 per academic year for a good computer studies course; something over $300 for a ten-week secretarial course; and advanced flight training could exceed $5,000.

Private vocational school courses normally range from three-month highly specialized programs to three-year engineering technology courses. Most are one to two years in length. Most private vocational schools operate on a half-day schedule so their students can work part-time to meet their expenses. The emphasis is on helping students to achieve the best possible jobs in the shortest possible time.

Financial help and how to get it

"But I don't have the money for education beyond high school," you may say.

It isn't always necessary. Though money is often a stumbling block, there are many ways you can get help for more schooling—if you are an interested and capable student, and if you really want to get more training.

Today many families can't afford to pay the full cost from their income or from savings. But you can put together the amount you'll need by combining money from family income (remember home expenses may be cut if you are living away at a school), money from part-time and summer jobs while you are at school, and money from scholarships, loans, grants and other sources.

There are literally thousands of scholarships, loan funds, gratuities and other educational aids offered by schools, foundations, private organizations and by federal and state legislation. A scholarship almost never provides the entire amount of money you need; but almost every school will help you obtain a part-time job or a loan to cover part of your expenses.

There's no point in your trying for aid until you know how much you'll need for the schools you'd like most to attend. Also, since aid is most often adjusted according to financial need, you should know roughly how much you might expect to be offered in the light of your own need. How much scholarship help to look for—how much you may need—depends on just two things: your own and your family's resources and the costs at the school you choose.

The search for financial aid may be very difficult because accurate and timely information about an appropriate program may not be easy to find. It is estimated $3 billion is available in loans, scholarships, and part-time jobs for college students. Approximately two-thirds come from colleges, individuals, foundations, organizations, and state or local governments.

A wide variety of organizations and agencies provide financial aid for students. Civic and cultural groups, local and state organizations, educational foundations, scholastic organizations such as the National Merit Scholarships, business and industry, religious denominations, and various clubs award approximately $50 million annually in student aid. The rest of the funds come through the federal government and the schools themselves. There are also a large number of contests awarding scholarships to the winners. A list of approved contests is published each year by the National Association of Secondary School Principals, 1201 Sixteen Street, N.W., Washington, D.C. 20036.

If you really want more education, don't let a lack of money stand in your way. Here is a plan to get you started in your search for financial help.

1. Start early; your junior year in high school is best, the beginning of your senior year at the latest.

2. Pick your schools. Before applying for financial help, be sure you are eligible to enter those schools.

3. If you need financial help or advice of any kind, speak to your high school counselor, principal, the admissions office or financial aid officer of the institution you hope to attend. They'll tell you of some of the possibilities for aid and help you apply. *Don't expect them to do the whole job for you.* They just don't have enough time to cover all the possibilities.

4. You and your parents will have to consider the combination of savings, scholarships, loans and your part-time employment to meet your school expenses.

5. Ask your parents to check with their employers and/or unions to see if there are any scholarship aids or loans for which you might qualify. If you've worked after school or summers your employers, too, might have scholarship funds available (some food chains, for example, will help boys and girls who have worked as checkers or stock boys during their high school years).

6. Check with each organization to which you and your parents belong for information about possible scholarships or loans. This includes lodges, PTA, clubs, church, fraternal orders, veterans' groups, professional and industry associations, Junior Achievement, and many other types of groups.

7. Check Federal and state veterans' benefits carefully to see if you are entitled to any special benefit. Being the child of a veteran in some states entitles you to scholarships at state schools.

8. *Finally, do as much researching as possible.* There are a number of places to go for more information listed at the end of this chapter.

There is something else you can do. A New York City company called Scholarship Search has programmed thousands of scholarships into a computer. These include aid from government, industry, foundations, private donors, social and political organizations and religious groups. You complete a questionnaire-application form which includes such information as residence, ethnic origin, vocational preference, social or religious affiliations, and scholastic achievement.

For a $29 fee paid in advance, Scholarship Search feeds this information into a computer and gives you a personalized listing of as many as fifteen to twenty financial aid sources for which you may be eligible. You are told the names, type and value of each award and when and where to apply for each. You get a full refund of your $29 if the computer can't give you five or more sources of aid!

One thing to remember is there is much financial aid available that has nothing to do with your scholastic ability—it might be available because of your interest in a particular vocation, or perhaps because of your name, your ethnic origin, or even the town you were born. For further information, write to:

Scholarship Search
7 West 51st Street
New York, New York 10019

The financial aid programs

What is financial aid? Financial aid is the difference between what it costs to attend school and the financial resources of the student to meet this expense. The general policy in making application for financial aid is *the student must be accepted by the school before considerations are given for financial aid.* This does not mean you cannot send your application for financial aid to the school before you are accepted. A good plan of action would be to send your application for financial aid to the school when you apply for admission. Forms for financial aid can be obtained from the school you are applying to, your high school counselor, or your financial aid officer if you are considering a transfer.

A variety of financial aid programs to help needy students achieve their educational goals are available. To determine how much aid you actually need some schools participate in the College Scholarship Service (CSS) Need Analysis Program. This is a nonprofit organization which assists schools in determining the student's need for financial aid. CSS forms and instructions for processing them are usually available from the financial aid office of the schools you hope to attend.

Another service comparable to CSS is also provided by the American College Testing Service, P.O. Box 168, Iowa City, Iowa 52240.

If you are offered aid, you'll most probably find you are awarded a "package." This may mean a combination of grant, job, and loan. Though you may prefer an outright grant or scholarship, the package idea does allow the school to help more students; today many schools have 30 to 50 percent of their student bodies on financial aid of some type.

Because of proposed changes by the Federal government, some of the assistance programs are subject to change. Be sure to ask if a program which interests you is still in effect or how it has been changed.

The financial aid package, designed to supplement the family's or student's resources, may include a combination of one or more of the following:

Scholarships from private sources won in open competition based on merit and need.

Grants (nonrepayable sums to students on the basis of merit and need or creative promise) may be from a private source, or if the student is from a low income family, he may be eligible for a Federal Education Opportunity Grant.

Low-interest loans from the university or college loan program, state or federal loans or from private sources. All or most of these loans provide for long term repayment.

Regular loans from commercial banks, loan associations and private organizations. Repayment usually begins immediately and interest is at commercial rates.

Part-time and/or summer employment offered by the school job placement service or through a federally guaranteed College Student Work Program if the institution is a participant and if the student needs a job to stay in school.

Cooperative education programs which offer periods of full-time employment in fields related to courses alternating with periods of full-time study.

Installment payments arranged by the school itself or a recommended private time payment organization. Such arrangements are frequently made to students whose family income and assets are above the "low" or "moderate" income level.

As a rule, the greater the student's need, the better are his chances of obtaining a packaged form of assistance. The packages come in all combinations, depending on the need and the circumstances.

The major sources of student aid

As a starter it may be helpful to identify the kinds of organizations and institutions which, in general, represent the main sources of student aid. These include—

Educational institutions; the junior college, technical institutes, vocational schools and other places that offer postsecondary education and occupational training.

Organizations interested in a particular discipline in the occupation of your choice.

Organizations interested in providing educational opportunities for particular groups of young people.

The state government in many, but not all states.

The federal government, under a wide range of provisions each focused on a particular need.

Here are some of the basic programs you'll find at most accredited schools.

Scholarships

A scholarship is a sum of money or other financial aid which goes to an undergraduate student to further his education for which no return of service or repayment is required.

Though no two scholarship programs are exactly alike, there are many similarities among them. Many have requirements as to financial need, personal qualification, school standing; and a considerable number require written examinations. But academic requirements vary. It is by no means always necessary to have a "straight A" high school record. Even so, it stands to reason the better your academic record, the better your scholarship prospects.

Some scholarships are for one year; others are renewable for a year at a time; still others cover the total program in which you are enrolled. A few are large enough to meet all or nearly all of your expenses; most represent only a fraction of the cost. Small as some of them are, a scholarship may be just enough to make up the difference that family resources and student earnings just can't cover.

When you apply to a school, ask about student aid. Don't overlook the possibility a school some distance from your home might offer more student aid than one nearby—and thus more than offset your travel expenses.

Find out if there are special scholarship programs for training in the career of your choice—nursing or medical technology, for example. Such "earmarked" scholarships are widely available. Some of them are offered by health organizations, others by civic organizations interested in a particular career area.

But just because you are going into a particular field does not necessarily mean you would be limited to these "earmarked" sources. You may also be eligible for a general scholarship depending on whether you can meet its particular requirements.

Though these scholarships are general in the sense they aren't tied to a particular course of study, each has a particular focus of interest—a particular group of students to whom its assistance is directed. In scholarship size as well as in eligibility requirements, these programs are as varied as their sponsoring organizations. Such well-known national competitive awards as those under the National Honor Society Program and the National Merit Scholarship Program also are not the only ones. There are many scholarship programs representing a special interest on the part of the sponsor. For example, there are scholarships offered to children of a particular national origin or church affiliation; children of a particular college's alumni; children of veterans or children of members of a fraternal organization or a labor union; children of employees in a particular sponsoring industry; or a stipulation that the student must enroll at a specified school, or in a highly specialized field. Contrary to general belief, scholarships are not always easy to obtain, for competition is exceedingly keen.

Nevertheless, it has been said, and it's probably true, thousands of scholarships go begging each year, due in part to lack of knowledge or their existence. However, the most important reason so many scholarships go unclaimed is a great number of these awards have special restrictions. Some awards may be conditional; to receive them the student may need to reject all others or limit the amount of other scholarships. Several organizations offer scholarships to special groups such as Afro-Americans, Puerto Ricans, Mexican Americans, Indians, or new Americans such as Cuban refugees.

Scholarships are granted either on the basis of overall superior scholastic achievement or won in open competition against other outstanding or gifted students. While excellence is an eligibility requirement for scholarships, increasingly the trend is to scale the amounts granted upward or downward, according to need.

With more able students entering postsecondary schools, the search for scholarships grows more intense. Existing scholarship funds must be stretched to accommodate a larger number of students; hence smaller scholarships.

Scholarships cover but a small part of the cost of education, and are no longer the major way needy students get through college. The financial aid package, a combination of aids arranged by the educational institution replaces the large scholarship grant. However, the brighter and needier the student, the larger the monetary worth of the scholarship portion of the aid package.

It is impossible to list all the sources of scholarships since so many groups grant them. Private foundations, fraternal orders, medical society and hospital auxiliaries, service clubs, religious and nationality groups, etc., offer scholarships and/or low-interest loans. In 35 states 350 *Dollars for Scholars* chapters (Citizens Scholarship Foundation of America) award scholarships for postsecondary study. Labor-financed scholarships are available. Get the *Higher Educational Kit* from the AFL-CIO, 815 16th Street, N.W., Washington, D.C. 20006.

Minority students may qualify for aid provided by various organizations. For information, write National Medical Fellowship, 3935 Elm Street, Downers Grove, Illinois, 60515. Black students should apply through their high school for the National Achievement Scholarship Program. Minority group students in junior college may be eligible for Ford Foundation scholarships to go on for baccalaureate degrees.

Qualified physically disabled students can obtain free education through state Vocational Rehabilitation offices to study for careers such as medical laboratory work. State scholarships are offered to so many students that it's a good place to start your search. More suggestions are made in the references at the end of this chapter.

State scholarships

The student aid programs administered by many state governments represent an important source of scholarships. These government sponsored scholarships are usually open only to the state's own young people. For example, Illinois students who are full-time students and Illinois residents may qualify for an Illinois State Scholarship, which covers payment of tuition and mandatory fees in schools in the state. In addition to covering study at in-state schools, some of these programs have certain provisions covering study at out-of-state schools as well.

Most states, including the District of Columbia, have statutes which authorize educational assistance and loan funds for students. Forty-five states and the District of Columbia have laws authorizing educational assistance for sons or daughters of veterans, particularly the children of deceased and disabled veterans.

Most states require applicants with reasonably good grades in high school. They must also meet the academic standards acceptable to the school in which they are enrolled. If you apply for state educational aid, you should do it well in advance of when you plan to enroll in school. Your own high school can probably give you information about the scholarship program in your state. If not, your questions will be answered and the required application form will be sent from your state department of education. (See page 22 for where to write for information on state operated programs.)

Grants

A grant is a gift of financial aid which does not take into account academic excellence. It is an outright, nonrepayable sum of money not requiring competitive examinations. Both grants and scholarships are based on need. Sometimes they are also called "scholarship aid to needy students."

Grants are offered by federal agencies, state governments, or the federal government to children of deceased or disabled veterans or to veterans themselves. Some schools also offer grants-in-aid in return for services of the student. Such a grant might be in recognition of some outstanding activity such as drama, or music, or athletics, where the student must participate in one of the school athletic programs, for example, in return for his tuition grant.

Here are some of the special grant programs that might apply to you.

Basic educational opportunity grant program

Students from low-income families may qualify for grants of $200 to $1,000 in an academic year under the Education Opportunity Grant Program. The awards, however, can cover no more than one-half the total assistance received by the student, and are available for a maximum of eight semesters or an equivalent number of terms or quarters. Cumulative award is limited to $4,000 for four years.

Eligibility and application procedures: a student must be enrolled or accepted for enrollment at an eligible institution, must need such assistance in order to pursue his education, and must be enrolled for at least half-time study. Students apply directly to the participating institution which is responsible for selecting the recipients and determining the amount of their grants. For further information, write to Division of Student Financial Aid, Bureau of Higher Education, U.S. Office of Education, Washington, D.C. 20202.

Special services for disadvantaged students

Tutoring and other academic services in summer residential and academic year follow-up programs are available for potential college students from low-income families. During the summer programs students also receive room and board and may receive stipends during both summer and academic year programs. Programs are operated by institutions of higher learning and, in some instances, by high schools or combinations thereof.

Eligibility and application procedures: Projects may include such activities as identifying educationally disadvantaged youths who might be capable of pursuing college or vocational postsecondary education and encouraging them to do so. Talent Search programs are also intended to encourage high school dropouts to reenter school; they also publicize forms of student aid for continuing education beyond high school. Grants are not made to individuals but to institutions, agencies and in some cases to nonprofit private organizations. For further information, contact your local Talent Search or Upward Bound representative, or write to:

Student Special Services,
Bureau of Higher Education
U.S. Office of Education
Washington, D.C. 20202

Social Security or Railroad Retirement Student Benefits

Students aged 18 to 22 can continue their education if their major breadwinning parent is retired, disabled, or deceased. A monthly stipend of up to $110 is available to students up to age 22 who are enrolled or entering an accredited college, technical or business school. However, *they must be full-time students.* Marriage disqualifies students from receiving continued payments.

The student or his family must notify the nearest Social Security office that the student will be continuing his education. Otherwise, Social Security payments for dependents cease at the age of 18. Many students may be eligible for retroactive payments. They should get in touch with their nearest Social Security office in person, at once, to find out if they qualify. Your high school guidance counselor or your college financial aid officer can advise on procedure for eligibility to payments while you are in full-time study.

Similar benefits are also available to college, business, or technical school students of deceased or disabled parents who worked under the Railroad Retirement System. Eligible students should contact the nearest Railroad Retirement System Office.

Junior GI Bill (War Orphans Education Program—Title 38 U.S. Code Chapter 38)

More than 200,000 children of deceased or totally disabled war veterans are eligible for federal financial aid for a maximum of 36 months training or education at a business, trade, or technical school or college. Payments under this program start at age 18 and continue to the recently extended age of 26. If an eligible student is a veteran of the Cold War, he is eligible for an additional 12 months education or training.

Unlike the Social Security education payments to children of retired, disabled, or deceased parents, under the Junior GI Bill marriage does not disqualify an eligible student. The eligible student need not be in full-time attendance at school.

Students eligible under this program receive $130 per month upon completion of each month of full-time training or study; $95 per month upon completion of three-fourths time training or study; $60 per month upon completion of one-half time training or study.

To be eligible a student's parent must have been:

1. Deceased or totally or permanently disabled from disease or injury incurred or aggravated in the Spanish-American War, World Wars I or II or the Korean War; or,

2. Deceased or permanently disabled while in the armed services between peace-time periods of September 11, 1940 to December 1941; January 1, 1947 to June 26, 1950; or

3. Deceased or disabled during service in the armed forces while selective service was in operation from the end of the Korean War, January 31, 1955.

Tragically, studies have shown less than half of the eligible students have ever applied for or received benefits from this law!

Students whose parents were deceased, or totally or permanently disabled during the periods listed above should contact the Veterans Administration office in their locality. If you are eligible, an educational plan will be worked out with the VA counselor and you (if you are over 21) or your remaining parent (if you are under 21).

State war orphan grants

Most states offer educational grants to children of deceased or disabled veterans. Some offer education grants to unmarried widows of deceased veterans. Eligibility requirements differ from state to state. A few state programs pay the entire amount of tuition and a few for four years, others pay for three years. Students who may be eligible should consult their high school guidance counselor or college financial aid officer, State Education Department or State Veterans Department.

Loans

If for some reason you don't get a scholarship or grant, don't give up the idea of school. Nearly every college and vocational school has loan funds at its disposal. Many organizations also offer loans. Most loans provide for repayment

plans following graduation. You are betting on yourself when you borrow to further your education.

If you plan to attend an accredited school, loans are usually available to students from four sources: school funds; U.S. Office of Education financial aid programs (federally supported); loans from banks insured under the terms of the Education Amendments of 1972; and private sources. These loans primarily are long-term, low-interest and are meant to help needy students borrow money for their postsecondary education.

You can look for low-interest loans from private, nonprofit groups such as those connected with health professions, Cuban Refugee programs, state associations of the Congress of Parents and Teachers, Inc. (PTA); Independent Order of Odd Fellows Revolving Loan Fund (IOOF), some private foundations, and many large corporations.

The *Guaranteed Student Loan Program* of the U.S. Office of Education enables you to borrow money directly from a bank, credit union, savings and loan association, or other participating lender. The loan is guaranteed by a state or private nonprofit guarantee agency or insured by the federal government.

You may borrow up to a maximum of $1,500 per academic year. (In some states the maximum is $1,000 per academic year and lenders must adhere to state regulations.) You may borrow up to a total of $7,500.

If your adjusted family income is less than $15,000 per year, the federal government will pay the interest on the loan while you are attending school and until the beginning of the repayment period. The repayment period begins between nine and twelve months after you leave school or complete your course of study.

You may normally take five to ten years to repay the loan. However, the minimum monthly payment of $30 may reduce the repayment period, depending upon the size of your loan. Repayment may be deferred for up to three years while you serve in the military, Peace Corps, or VISTA; or for any period that you return to full-time study.

You may borrow under this program if:

1. You are enrolled or have been accepted for enrollment as an undergraduate or graduate student—on at least a half-time basis—at an eligible college or university or hospital school of nursing; or

2. You are enrolled or have been accepted for enrollment on at least a half-time basis in an approved vocational, technical, trade, business, or home study school.

Your regional office of the U.S. Office of Education, state guarantee agency, lender, or school student financial aid officer will be able to provide you with

1. Specific information regarding the operation of the program in your state

2. The necessary application forms

3. Information on the eligibility of your school

4. An affidavit (OE Form 1260) which you must sign, declaring that your loan will be used only for education purposes. This must be notarized.

You may obtain loans from banks, savings and loan associations, pension funds, credit unions and insurance companies. Some schools also qualify as lenders. Loans are approved or denied at the discretion of the lender. An insurance premium of one-fourth of one percent is charged on each loan. If the borrower dies or becomes permanently disabled, his loan is cancelled.

It's wise to apply for your loan early as banks have limited funds available for student loans, and you don't want to be turned away because all the available educational funds are already committed for the period.

Under a federally insured loan program, you can learn, thus earn, then repay your loan. The negotiation of each loan is between the student and the lending institution. See page 22 for sources of information on the Guaranteed Student Loan Program.

Other loan programs may be available to you. The *National Vocational Student Loan Insurance Act* provides loan programs for college students. Students accepted for enrollment in an eligible public or nonprofit vocational school may apply for such loans through the schools. The bonus opportunity here is you don't have to be a high school or even a grade school graduate, as long as you're accepted by the vocational school.

Another good loan program is the *Nursing Student Loan Program*, which gives loans up to $1,500 or the amount of financial need (whichever is the lesser). Interest of 3 percent a year is paid by the federal government while the borrower is in school. Repayment of the loan must begin no later than nine months after the borrower ceases to be a full-time student and must be completed within ten years. If the student becomes employed as a professional nurse in the field of Nurse Training and serves in any public or nonprofit private institution or agency, up to 50 percent of the loan may be canceled at the rate of 10 percent for each year of employment. If the student meets the same requirements and also serves in an area with a substantial shortage of nurses, up to 100 percent of the loan plus interest at the rate of 15 percent for each year of full-time service may be canceled.

Veterans' benefits

The GI Bill, formerly available only to veterans who had served during or just after World War II or during the Korean War, was made permanent in 1966. Veterans honorably discharged from the U.S. Armed Forces after January 31, 1955 (except for six-month enlistees, who are ineligible) now qualify for benefits from the G.I. Bill, which provides for a program of education assistance. Veterans with at least 18 months of service can get up to 36 months of educational assistance from the Veterans Administration. Those with less than 18 months of service can get one and a half months of assistance for each month of service. This program, therefore, can be of great benefit to those who decide to enter military service before entering or completing college.

Widows of veterans who died of service-connected injury or disease also now are eligible for VA college or other educational benefits on either a full or part-time basis.

Many schools have a Veterans Counselor to help students. If the school is properly accredited, veterans may use their educational benefits under the GI Bill to meet expenses. Ask your school's Veterans Counselor to help you apply.

College Work-Study Programs (Self-Help Programs)

Both Cooperative Education and the College Work-Study Programs are formal self-help procedures that permit students to be gainfully employed during the academic year. These programs give qualified students the opportunity to earn enough money while they are attending school to pay for most or all of their education.

The Cooperative Plan of Education, or the Co-op Program as it is commonly called, differs from the Work-Study Program in several ways. The Co-op Program consists of alternate periods of full-time residence in school and full-time employment in industry or in governmental service. Employment under this program ordinarily does not begin until after the student has completed one or more semesters in school. One big feature of Cooperative Education is practical, on-the-job training. In the series of work periods, the employment assignments are varied and upgraded to complement as nearly as possible the advancing progress of the students' education.

This background of experience becomes a tremendous asset to you when you graduate and go to look for your first permanent position. During the training-employment period, you ordinarily receive the base rate of pay for the type of work to which you are assigned. The compensation usually is enough to meet all living and college expenses for an unmarried student from the time of entry into the program until the time he graduates.

The general qualifications for admission to a Co-Op Program are at least average grades, good health, and a willingness to work.

The College Work-Study Program (CWSP) is authorized by the federal government and is administered by the U.S. Department of Health, Education and Welfare. Under this program, jobs for students are provided on campus. Funds for wages are supported by both federal and state funds. Qualified students may work up to fifteen hours each week during the academic year. If not attending classes during the summer, students may work forty hours a week, but earnings must be used for expenses of attending school during the next school year.

To qualify for admittance to the Work-Study Program you must be from a family with financial need and you must be a regular full-time student making satisfactory progress toward a degree.

An ever-growing number of formal self-help programs is expected for the future (the number of schools offering these programs grows every year) because of the mounting costs of education and the increasing demands for more education for all people.

CWSP may assist you by providing a job opportunity at the college itself or with a public or private nonprofit agency (such as a school, a social agency, or a hospital) working in cooperation with your school. In general, the salary paid is at least equal to the current minimum wage, although it is frequently higher. The school financial aid officer is responsible for determining the students to be employed, selecting suitable jobs for them, handling the payroll, and the general administration of the program.

The work must be for a nonprofit organization; the government pays 80 percent of the student's wages, and the institution providing the work pays the rest. Federal studies show that the average amount earned by students under this program is $600 per year. Preference is given to students from families receiving or eligible to receive public or private welfare assistance or from families with combined incomes below $7,500.

The jobs are guaranteed and might be on campus or as playground supervisors at a school, or maintenance work, or in community action poverty programs such as tutors to disadvantaged children, or in day-care centers, for example.

The amount earned this way plus the financial aid package will make up the amount needed to cover your school expenses.

To be eligible a student must

1. Be enrolled or accepted for enrollment as a full-time student in an educational institution participating in the College Work-Study Program;

2. Be in need of earnings from this program to pursue a course of study at this institution;

3. Be capable of maintaining good standing in the course of study under this program;

4. Be a citizen of the U.S. or owe pertinent allegiance to the U.S. or meet other criteria regarding residence or immigration status.

Because the list of participating institutions changes from time to time, students are advised to inquire about the availability of this program when writing to the school of their choice about admission and financial aid.

Manpower Development Training Act

The U.S. Government also helps with tuition in private schools under the Manpower Development and Training Act (MDTA), which is designed for unemployed and underemployed or disadvantaged people who are looking for a skill-oriented education. Your state employment office, school counselor, or the National Association of Trade and Technical Schools can help you find out more about this type of help which is open to ambitious young people who want to make their way into the right slot. See also page 68 for more details.

For more information, write:

If you know what career field you plan to train for, financial aid may be available from the professional society, trade association or unions in that field. You can find out about possible help by writing to the appropriate group which may be listed at the end of the section describing the particular occupation, starting p.83 and following.

Director
Air Force Aid Society
National Headquarters
1117 North 19th Street, Suite 700
Arlington, Virginia 22209
Ask for: Vocational Training and Undergraduate College Loans: Air Force Aid Society. The General H. Arnold Educational Fund, 1972 (financial aid to children of USAF personnel).

The American Legion
National Headquarters
P.O.Box 1055
Indianapolis, Indiana 46206
Ask for: *American Legion Education and Scholarship Program, the Viet-Nam GI Bill* (revised) 1972 *Need a Lift? To Educational Opportunities, Careers, Loans, Scholarships, Employment!* (22nd edition). Free to schools and libraries, $.50 to individuals.

B'nai B'rith Vocational Service
1640 Rhode Island Avenue, N.W.
Washington, D.C. 20036
Ask for: *Student Aid Planning in the Space Age: A Selected Bibliography,* $.50.

College Entrance Examination Board
P.O. Box 592
Princeton, New Jersey 08540

Ask for: *Do-It-Yourself College Financial Planner for Parents*. 1972, free.

College Opportunities, Inc.
492 Pedretti Street
Cincinnati, Ohio 45238
Ask for: *Vocational-Occupational Training and Financial Aids*, Lewis D. Hall, editor, $1.95 prepaid. (State by state paperback books describing schools and training programs and financial aspects. Ask for specific state.)

Communications Workers of America (AFL-CIO)
1925 K Street, N.W.
Washington, D.C. 20006
Ask for: *Membership Guide to College Financing*.

Publications Service
Haskell Indian Junior College
Lawrence, Kansas 66044
Ask for: *Scholarships for American Indians*, U.S. Department of the Interior, Bureau of Indian Affairs, free.

International Brotherhood of Teamsters, Chauffeurs, Warehousemen and Helpers of America
25 Louisiana Avenue, N.W.
Washington, D.C. 20001
Ask for: *Financing your Higher Education*, 1972, free; and, *Scholarship Guidebook 1972–73* (available from James R. Hoffa Scholarship Fund).

Research Division
National Education Association
1201 16th Street, N.W.
Washington, D.C. 20036
Ask for: *Sources of Information on Student Aid*, a comprehensive reference $.25.

Bureau of Naval Personnel (Pers-P511)
Navy Department
Washington, D.C. 20370
Ask for: *Scholarship Pamphlet for USN, USMC, USCG Dependents* (Navpers 15003-C), 1972, free.

Division of Student Assistance
U.S. Office of Education
Washington, D.C. 20202
Ask for: general information on all U.S. aid programs and *Information for Students*.

Superintendent of Documents
U.S. Government Printing Office
Washington, D.C. 20402
Ask for: *Federal and State Student Aid Programs*, 1972 No. 5271–00324, $.45 (lists all programs available in each state). *Trio, Talent Search, Upward Bound Special Services*, 1972. No. HE 5.237:37101 S/N 1780–01022, $.20.

Veterans Administration
Washington, D.C. 20420
or
Your state Veterans Administration headquarters

Ask for: *Benefits for Veterans and Servicemen with Service since January 31, 1955, and their Dependents, VA* Pamphlet 20–67–1, revised February, 1972.

Additional Reading:

Barron's Handbook of Junior and Community College Financial Aid, Woodbury, New York: Barron's Educational Series, Inc. 1970, $6.95.

Sources of information on the guaranteed student loan programs and other state operated loan programs

ALABAMA
Director of Higher Education
Office of Education, Region IV
50 Seventh Street, N.E.
Atlanta, Georgia 30323

ALASKA
United Student Aid Funds, Inc.
845 Third Avenue
New York, New York 10022

ARIZONA
Director of Higher Education
Office of Education, Region IX
50 Fulton Street
San Francisco, California 94102

ARKANSAS
Student Loan Guarantee Foundation of Arkansas
Suite 515, 1515 West 7th Street
Little Rock Arkansas 72202

CALIFORNIA (see Arizona)

COLORADO
Director of Higher Education
Office of Education, Region VIII
9017 Federal Office Building
19th & Stout Streets
Denver, Colorado 80202

CONNECTICUT
Connecticut Student Loan Foundation
251 Asylum Street
Hartford, Connecticut 06103

DELAWARE
Delaware Higher Education Loan Program
University of Delaware
207 Hollihen Hall
Newark, Delaware 19711

DISTRICT OF COLUMBIA
D.C. Student Loan Insurance Program
1329 E Street, NW
Washington, D.C. 20004

FLORIDA (see Alabama)

GEORGIA
Georgia Higher Education Assistance Corporation
Post Office Box 38005
Capitol Hill Station
Atlanta, Georgia 30339

HAWAII (see Arizona)

IDAHO
Director of Higher Education
Office of Education, Region X
1321 Second Avenue
Seattle, Washington 98101

ILLINOIS
Illinois Guaranteed Loan Program
102 Wilmot Road, P.O. Box 33
Deerfield, Illinois 60015

INDIANA
Director of Higher Education
Office of Education, Region V
226 West Jackson Boulevard
Chicago, Illinois 60606

IOWA
Director of Higher Education
Office of Education, Region VII
601 East 12th Street
Kansas City, Missouri 64106

KANSAS (see Iowa)

KENTUCKY (see Alabama)

LOUISIANA
Louisiana Higher Education Assistance Commission
Post Office Box 44095
Capitol Station
Baton Rouge, Louisiana 70804

MAINE
Maine State Department of Education
Augusta, Maine 04330

MARYLAND
Maryland Higher Education Loan Corporation
2100 Guilford Avenue
Baltimore, Maryland 21218

MASSACHUSETTS
Massachusetts Higher Education Assistance Corporation
511 Statler Building
Boston, Massachusetts 02116

MICHIGAN
Michigan Higher Education Assistance Authority
309 North Washington Avenue
Lansing Michigan 48902

MINNESOTA (see Indiana)

MISSISSIPPI (see Alabama)

MISSOURI (see Iowa)

MONTANA (see Colorado)

NEBRASKA (see Iowa)

NEVADA
State Department of Education
Carson City, Nevada 89701

NEW HAMPSHIRE
New Hampshire Higher Education Assistance Foundation

3 Capitol Street
Concord, New Hampshire 03301

NEW JERSEY
New Jersey Higher Education Assistance Authority
65 Prospect Street
Post Office 1293
Trenton, New Jersey 08625

NEW MEXICO
Director of Higher Education
Office of Education, Region VI
1114 Commerce Street
Dallas, Texas 75202

NEW YORK
New York Higher Education Assistance Corporation
50 Wolf Road
Albany, New York 12205

NORTH CAROLINA
State Education Assistance Authority
1307 Glenwood Avenue
Post Office Box 10887
Raleigh, North Carolina 27605

NORTH DAKOTA (see Colorado)

OHIO
Ohio Student Loan Commission
Wyandotte Building
21 West Broad Street
Columbus, Ohio 43215

OKLAHOMA
Oklahoma State Regents for Higher Education
State Capitol Station, P.O. Box 53383
Oklahoma City, Oklahoma 73105

OREGON
Oregon State Scholarship Commission
1445 Willamette Street
Eugene, Oregon 97401

PENNSYLVANIA
Pennsylvania Higher Education Assistance Agency
Towne House, 660 Boas Street
Harrisburg, Pennsylvania 17102

PUERTO RICO
Director of Higher Education
Office of Education, Region II
26 Federal Plaza
New York, New York 10022

RHODE ISLAND
Rhode Island Higher Education Assistance Corporation
Room 414, 187 Westminster Mall
P. O. Box 579
Providence, Rhode Island 02901

SOUTH CAROLINA (see Alaska)

SOUTH DAKOTA (see Colorado)

TENNESSEE
Tennessee Education Loan Corporation

State Department of Education
313 Capitol Towers
Nashville, Tennessee 37219

TEXAS (see New Mexico)

UTAH (see Colorado)

VERMONT
Vermont Student Assistance Corporation
191 College Street
Burlington, Vermont 05401

VIRGINIA
Virginia State Education Assistance Authority
1116 United Virginia Bank Building
Richmond, Virginia 23219

WASHINGTON (see Idaho)

WEST VIRGINIA
Director of Higher Education
Office of Education, Region III
Post Office Box 12900
Philadelphia, Pennsylvania 19108

WISCONSIN
Wisconsin Higher Education Corporation
State Office Building
115 West Wilson Street
Madison, Wisconsin 53702

WYOMING (see Colorado)

AMERICAN SAMOA (see Arizona)

GUAM (see Arizona)

TRUST TERRITORY (see Arizona)

VIRGIN ISLANDS (see Alaska)

A.E.T.   Associate in Engineering Technology
A.F.A.   Associate in Fine Arts
A.G.Ed.   Associate in General Education
A.G.S.   Associate in General Studies
A.L.A.S.   Associate in Letters, Arts and Sciences
A.L.A.   Associate in Liberal Arts
A.Mus.   Associate in Music
A.N.   Associate in Nursing
A.P.A.   Associate in Practical Arts
A.P.S.T.   Associate in Public Service Technology
A.R.L.   Associate in Recreation Leadership
A.R.A.   Associate in Religious Arts
A.S.   Associate in Science
A.S.B.E.   Associate in Science in Basic Engineering
A.S.B.   Associate in Science in Business or Associate in Science in Business or Associate in Specialized Business
A.S.Ed.   Associate in Science in Education
A.S.E.E.T.   Associate in Science in Electronic Engineering Technology
A.S.E.   Associate in Science in Engineering
A.S.N.   Associate in Science in Nursing
A.S.R.L.   Associate in Science in Recreation Leadership
A.S.A.   Associate in Secretarial Administration
A.S.S.   Associate in Secretarial Science
A.T.A.   Associate in Technical Arts
A.T.E.   Associate in Technical Education
A.T.   Associate in Technology
A.Th.   Associate in Therapy
A.W.T.   Associate in Wildlife Technology

Degrees Granted

In many major fields of study at community and junior colleges and technical institutes associate degrees are awarded after completion of the course, usually two years. There are many different associate degrees. Not all are offered at every school. The following are among those you'll find most frequently.

Associate Degrees
A.A.A.   Associate in Applied Arts
A.A.S.   Associate in Applied Science
A.A.   Associate in Arts
A.A.B.   Associate in Arts in Business
A.A.F.A.   Associate in Arts in Fine Arts
A.A.L.E.   Associate in Arts in Law Enforcement
A.A.Mus.   Associate in Arts in Music
A.A.N.   Associate in Arts in Nursing
A.Bus.   Associate in Business Administration
A.B.S.   Associate in Business Science
A.B.T.   Associate in Business Technology
A.C.   Associate in Commerce
A.C.J.   Associate in Criminal Justice
A.Ed.   Associate in Education
A.E.   Associate in Engineering

Glossary

Acceptance: Approval of an application for admission.

Accreditation: A school is certified as meeting the standards for excellence as set up by a particular academic association. Schools are accredited by either regional or professional bodies; not by government agencies.

Allied health: A new general term used to refer to all areas of occupational learning which deal with the mental and physical well-being of people. Included are such fields as nursing, inhalation therapy, medical assistant and dozens of other categories.

Application fee: A sum of money charged for making application for entrance to a particular school. It is often nonrefundable.

Apprentice: A person who works for someone else in order to learn a trade. This arrangement is formalized with an apprenticeship agreement.

Apprenticeship agreement: A written agreement between the apprentice (or his parent or guardian if he is a minor) and his employer. The agreement is approved by the local area or state joint apprenticeship committee of the trade involved and lays out the terms and conditions of the apprenticeship.

Associate degree: A degree awarded by junior and community colleges, some trade and technical schools, and some universities in the United States to a person who has completed a required course of study, usually requiring two years of work. The degree may be in either arts or sciences.

Baccalaureate degree: A degree awarded by a college or university to a person who has completed a required course of study, usually requiring four years of work. It is also called a bachelor's degree.

Career: A whole lifetime series of jobs and occupations. This includes jobs a worker may have while he is still a student and then all the jobs all the way through his life. Through his working life, the worker moves up a career ladder—his personal pathway of advancement from one level to another.

Certificate: A document serving as evidence that a person has completed a vocational or technical course. Generally certificate programs are shorter than two years.

Certified: A document given to a person who has satisfied educational and professional requirements for a particular occupation. Such certification is granted after examination by an association to which members of the particular profession belong.

Committee (Union Apprenticeship Committee): The joint apprenticeship committee represents the union and the employer which has the job of developing and administering the apprenticeship programs as provided for in the local apprenticeship standards.

Community college: A two-year postsecondary institution that is publicly supported and meets the needs of the people in the area which sponsors it. Not all junior colleges are community colleges.

Cooperative program: An arrangement offered by some schools for combining gainful employment with study. Sometimes one or more semesters in school are alternated with semesters of work in fields related to the student's career interests.

Correspondence school: All educational institutions that provide study courses by mail. Also called home study schools.

Dead end job: A job with no hope of progress or being able to move upward into a better position.

Degree: An academic award given by an educational institution to show the student has successfully completed the prescribed course. The associate degree is most often granted by two-year schools.

Degree-granting and non-degree granting: Some institutions award degrees to students who successfully complete the course of study (degree-granting). Other institutions offer programs which lead to awarding of a diploma or certificate when the course is successfully completed (non-degree granting).

Entry-level job: The first level of job in which a beginner may start to work in a particular field. Such a job requires the least amount of training of any job in the field and can lead to jobs up the career ladder as the worker gains experience.

Evening school: Courses offered by an educational institution at night (also called night school). The evening school may or may not be accredited, and the student may or may not receive credit for courses he takes.

Full-time student: A student who takes the normal number of courses allowed at a time by the school. He may also have a part-time job, but this is in addition to the full-time schedule he follows.

Guidance counselor: A trained person who through personal interviews helps a student make his own choices about a suitable career or place to get the proper training. Counselors are found in high schools, colleges, employment service offices, community organizations, private agencies, and many other places where students can go for assistance.

Home study school: An educational institution that provides study courses by mail. Also called correspondence school.

Journeyman: A person who has served his apprenticeship at a trade or handicraft and is certified to work in that trade.

Junior college: A two-year college of higher education.

Liberal arts college: A college which emphasizes a program of general undergraduate courses, including the arts, humanities, social sciences and natural sciences.

Low-income family: A family where income is below the level necessary to maintain a decent standard of living. The family cannot reasonably be expected to contribute very much toward a child's educational expenses.

Matriculated: To be enrolled in a program at an educational institution leading to a certificate or a degree.

Nonmatriculated: To be enrolled as a student at an educational institution taking courses not for credit and not leading to a certificate or degree.

Occupation: A collection of tasks a worker performs for pay. It is a particular set of jobs for which he is trained and at which he may spend the largest middle section of his life. He may be promoted through a series of increasingly responsible jobs in his occupational field.

Open-door admission policy: A postsecondary institution which accepts all students who apply for admission, regardless of their previous academic record. Some schools do require a high school diploma or a high school equivalency (GED) certificate.

Paraprofessional: A trained person who performs the simpler tasks previously performed by a professional. The paraprofessional or subprofessional does not have the extensive education or professional competence of the professional. There are paraprofessionals in many occupational fields including health, education, law, architecture, recreation, and others.

Part-time employment off-campus: Jobs with employers near the educational institution open to all students regardless of financial need. Work might be available for sales clerks, factory laborers, office personnel, baby sitters, or waiters.

Part-time employment on-campus: Students are offered jobs working in laboratories, libraries, offices, food service areas, and other locations on campus.

Part-time student: A student who takes less than the normal full load of courses allowed by the institution at one time.

Private college: An institution that is not supported by public taxes. It can be independent or church-related.

Proprietary school: An educational institution that is privately owned usually with no public control or supervision. It is operated as a profit-making business.

Public college: Any college that is supported by public taxes and run on a nonprofit basis.

Registry agency: This is the Bureau of Apprenticeship and Training, U.S. Department of Labor, or a state apprenticeship agency recognized by and conforming to the students established by the Federal Committee on Apprenticeship.

School dropout: A pupil who leaves school, either during high school or earlier, before he graduates or completes a program and does not transfer to another school.

Semiskilled worker: A person who has more training or skill than an unskilled worker, but less than a skilled worker.

Simulated work situation: A copy of an actual work situation set up in a classroom for training purposes. It would include machines, tools, or anything else the worker uses in performing his job.

Skilled worker: A worker who has competence and experience in any craft, trade or job that requires manual dexterity or special training.

Subprofessional: Same as paraprofessional.

Technical program: A postsecondary course leading to a job as a technician or technologist or any other job requiring scientific training.

Technician: A person who has been trained specifically to carry out particular procedures necessary to perform scientific or artistic jobs. The work must be done precisely and skillfully.

Technologist: A person who deals with the techniques and skills involved in applied sciences, industrial arts, engineering, etc. Similar to technician.

Terminal institution or program: A course of study designed to prepare a student for immediate employment in a related field. The programs are usually vocational or technical, highly specialized and concentrated and will usually not be accepted as transfer credit at four-year colleges.

Transcript: A student's official high school academic record used as a basis for admission to a postsecondary institution. Or it can be the college record used as basis for admission to another school if the student wishes to transfer.

Transfer: A student who has been registered in one school and changes to another.

Transfer program: A course of study at a two-year college designed to prepare students to transfer to a four-year college. The credit accumulated by a student in a transfer program will usually be accepted by a four-year college and applied toward a baccalaureate degree.

Tuition: The charge made by the educational institution for instruction. Sometimes the tuition is stated in an amount per credit hours. For example, if tuition is $50 per credit hour, the cost of a three-credit hour course is $150.00.

Underemployed: A person who is working below his skill ability, is receiving or has received notice he will be working less than full-time in his industry or occupation, or has received notice he will be unemployed because his skills are becoming obsolete.

Undergraduate: A person who has not yet received his bachelor's degree.

Union: The recognized or certified bargaining agency for a group of workers.

Upgrade: To improve the rank or position or job of a worker. This most often occurs when a worker has accumulated additional skill and training and is ready to move up the career ladder.

Veteran: A person who served at least one day in the active service of the armed forces of the United States during any of the war periods and who has been discharged or released under other than dishonorable conditions. See the Veterans Administration for exact war periods and benefits provided.

Vocational program: A school course which emphasizes occupational training rather than academic subjects. It leads directly to a job upon completion of the course. See also terminal programs.

Vocational rehabilitation: Programs designed to develop and restore the working usefulness of handicapped people to the point where they may become self-supporting.

Waiting list: A list of accepted students for

which the school does not have room. As openings occur, these students are notified and admitted.

Work-study programs (or College work-study program): Either a cooperative program combining employment and study; or a program subsidized by the federal government whereby students from low-income families who need earnings from part-time jobs are paid an hourly rate for up to 15 hours a week of work in their school libraries or administrative offices. The earnings help pay the students' college expenses.

What Are the Alternatives?

If you think the only way to get ahead and be somebody is by getting a four-year college education, you're wrong. A college education is not always the essential ingredient for a successful career. You may not need a bachelor's degree to enter the labor market with a good job. The choice is strictly yours. All it really takes to get ahead is the desire to do something that needs doing—*and the ability to do it well.* That means getting the education you need for the career you want.

What do you really want out of life? If you're not sure your future depends on a college degree, or if you just can't see yourself in college, you do have other choices that will lead to good jobs with a good future. There are different ways to get your education.

Americans have created the myth that to be a success you must have a college degree and be a white collar worker.

Because career education has been thought of as inferior, parents often insist their children go to college even though the student may not want to go. The sad part of this situation is that the vast majority of the jobs of the future won't require a college degree, but rather some form of vocational or technical education.

Emerging from its long tradition of second-class citizenship, career education has some exciting new choices to offer anyone wanting to continue his education. There has been a sharp increase in vocational enrollments not only at the secondary level, but also at the postsecondary level. In just five years, 1965 to 1970, postsecondary enrollments increased from about 200,000 to over a million in public programs alone.

We are finally experiencing a fundamental change in attitude toward college. More and more people feel they can live satisfactorily without a college degree. There is a burgeoning desire for the "no nonsense" practical job training to be found in vocational programs.

Of the students who complete their program requirements, 90 percent of those who are available for job placement (some go into the armed forces, others continue their education, others get married) find jobs in their field or a closely related one.

New programs emerge every year to meet present day manpower needs. Some of the newest courses are for jobs as mental health technicians, surgical technicians, urban planning assistants, water and wastewater technicians, pesticide technicians, air pollution technicians, laboratory animal care technicians, biomedical equipment technicians, and police science and crime lab specialists.

Career education comes in packages of all shapes and sizes. Technical education, for example, varies greatly depending on the needs of a particular job area. Instruction is given on many different levels to meet many different needs.

Graduates of two-year junior or community colleges or technical institute programs earn an associate degree. About 25 percent of these students eventually go on to a four-year institute and complete work for a bachelor's degree.

Here are some of the best ways of acquiring organized, planned training for employment in occupations not requiring a college degree.

Junior and community colleges (public and private)

Most junior colleges and nearly all public community colleges offer vocational courses as well as courses in academic subjects. At Chicago City College, for example, there are courses for medical paraprofessionals in operating room technology, pharmacy, psychiatric nursing, medical secretarial skills, and child care.

The Cape Fear Technical Institute (Wilmington, North Carolina) has a two-year marine technology program which is preparing technicians in oceanography, marine biology, and fishing industries as well as ship engineers and deck personnel. Male and female students from sixteen states attend the Institute which has a fleet of fifteen vessels, three of which are more than 100 feet in length.

Private trade, technical, and business schools

There are some 7,000 privately owned trade and technical schools. These schools specialize in the highly desirable occupations wide open to the noncollege graduate—job areas like computer programmer and data processor, cook and chef, medical and dental assisting, radio and television broadcasting, airline pilot, electronic engineering technologist, bank teller, advanced police and detective service, and health service worker.

Home study

Home study courses are another way of acquiring a vocational skill. With home study, you can learn practically anything, including subjects you can't find in a local school. Many courses provide complete vocational training. Others prepare you for upgrading your present job without losing experience and seniority.

Where the skill being taught requires equipment, such as electronics, often a kit is furnished giving the student practice in assembling a radio or television set as part of the course. There are over five million Americans studying in all types of institutions offering courses by correspondence.

Apprenticeships

Unions do a lot of true job training in the form of apprenticeships. An apprenticeship involves on-the-job practice plus related classroom instruction. There are about 400,000 registered apprentices in training in the U.S. and there are probably half again as many working in small shops who aren't actually registered as apprentices.

Cooperative programs (work-study)

At most vocational adult education schools, both daytime and evening courses are held. Under the cooperative work-study program offered by many schools, you actually receive school credit for on-the-job training and related in-school instruction.

You might find a program like hotel training provided by the Lindsey Hopkins Vocational School in Miami, Florida, which prepares students for such jobs as front office clerk, hotel maid, linen room attendant, office machine operators, or switchboard operators.

The Air Transportation Occupation program of the Rochester, New York Board of Education was begun in 1969. It uses a nontraditional approach for training students of all ability levels to enter the air transportation field. A student can spin off after a short period of training or continue through a four-year sequence, ultimately becoming licensed as a commercial pilot or air frame-power plant mechanic. The flight program has been fully approved by the Federal Aviation Authority, which administers tests for various licenses. The program utilizes the Monroe County Airport as well as the Vocational Center on Whitney Street. Its advisory committee has representatives from three major airlines, the FAA, the state coordinator of air transporta-

tion, and an airport manager. The program also provides guidance, psychological, clinical, and placement services for students.

The Wicomico County (Maryland) Board of Education has a manpower training program at the Peninsula General Hospital which has proven most effective in developing certified laboratory assistants. The one-year program, approved by the American Socity of Clinical Pathologists and the American Society of Medical Technologists, also was cited recently not only for the large number of students who stayed with it over the period of four and a half years it has been in operation, but also for the fact that every trainee who has completed the program has found a job in this field.

Industry training programs

Private employers are heavily into job training, especially the big corporations. General Motors, for instance, operates the GM Institute in Flint, Michigan. High school graduates apply and, if admitted, spend alternate periods of six weeks in work and study for four years. The Institute includes an engineering college and runs numerous technical and management training programs. Virtually every GM plant has a director of training; and in the United States alone, more than 30,000 GM employees attend training programs each year.

Many other companies conduct a variety of employee training programs including orientation; instruction in additional skills for job advancement or job transfer; supervisory training and management development. Sometimes there are programs for new and potential employees. One Pennsylvania manufacturer recruits fifteen high school graduates each year and gives them two and a half months training as laboratory technicians.

Programs for handicapped

Rehabilitation is a public service designed to develop and restore the working usefulness of handicapped individuals to the point where they may become self-supporting. We have both public and private vocational rehabilitation programs to train or retrain handicapped persons for jobs suited to their needs. Every state has a Vocational Rehabilitation Service and in many communities you'll also find private, nonprofit organizations like Goodwill Industries which offer excellent programs.

Manpower development and training programs

These are special programs sponsored by state and federal government to give training in job skills to the unemployed and underemployed. The purpose is to open up new career opportunities particularly for the disadvantaged.

No matter which alternative you choose,

keep your career goals clearly in mind. The first and most important thing is the starting point. You can't climb the career ladder of your choice until you get yourself in shape. Once you've picked your course, patience and a willingness to learn are all you'll need.

Junior And Community Colleges

Two-year colleges are not ordinary places.

From 7 A.M. to 10 P.M. some 38,000 students swarm through facilities at Miami-Dade (Florida) Junior College costing $45 million—a downtown center and two sprawling suburban campuses studded with filigreed concrete buildings, palm trees, contoured plaza, and landscaped parking lots.

Students range in age from 17 to 70, their intelligence from subnormal to genius, their diligence from full-time preparation for senior colleges to a single one-hour course before Christmas in fancy giftwrapping.

And their interests span the seven stages of man, from "Maternal and Child Health Nursing," to "Marriage and the Family," to "Advanced Embalming."

A junior or community college is an institution of higher education which offers usually the first two years of college instruction, which grants an associate rather than a bachelor's degree. It can be either private or public. Course offerings include academic college transfer courses and programs; vocational, technical, and semiprofessional occupational programs; and general education programs for post-high school students. It is a place where after two years, you can be ready for immediate employment or transfer to a four-year college.

The distinguishing characteristic of these schools is that they offer something to everyone—whether you are interested in satisfying the two-year basic course requirements before transferring to a four-year institution or are interested in a terminal program which will give you all you need to know to get an entry-level job in a particular field.

The schools differ widely in nature, facilities and objectives, ranging from new public institutions open to virtually everyone to venerable private liberal arts institutions of high academic quality that still are much like "finishing schools."

Two-year colleges may be residential or nonresidential (primarily local). Residential colleges provide dormitory facilities for most of the student body which come from all over. Nonresidential colleges serve just local students. Local, nonresidential junior and community colleges or technical institutes which are public and controlled by local, county, or state agencies are intended to serve the educational needs of local

students only. They are forbidden or actively discouraged from enrolling students from other parts of the country.

The big break in the career education boom has been the phenomenal growth of the tax-supported community colleges. Ten years ago there were 656 of these publicly supported colleges. There are now about 1200 and more being opened each year.

In the fall of 1971 more students enrolled as freshmen in the junior and community colleges of the U.S. than in the nation's four-year institutions. In fact, enrollment in two-year colleges has grown from 600,000 students in 1960 to three million in just ten years. While total university enrollment doubled in the 1960s, enrollment in the public two-year colleges quadrupled. Experts figure the number will swell to 3.3 million by September, 1975. Of the schools in operation, about 950 are public and about 250 are private.

These schools have grown so rapidly for five good reasons: they are economical to attend because tuition fees are minimal; they are close to the homes of their students; they are responsive to local demands because the courses offered are usually geared to the needs and opportunities of the area the school serves; their programs are flexible, yet thorough; through their adult education programs they provide opportunities for continuing education.

Because half the students will eventually transfer to four-year institutions and half will enter the world of work, equal attention is given to academic and career programs.

These colleges come in incredibly varied sizes, locations, and aims. Miami-Dade (Florida) Junior College, serving the city and county it is named for, is now the largest of the approximately 950 public two-year colleges in the country. They are tax supported, open at little or no cost (Miami-Dade's fees total $125 a term) to virtually any resident ·who wants to enter. In the southern suburbs of Washington, "Novacoco" (Northern Virginia Community College) now has overflowed into a second campus. In Cleveland, acres of inner city slum have been replaced by the handsome Cuyahoga Community College. In Los Angeles, some 100,000 students attend eight public junior colleges.

Some schools proudly proclaim, "*Yes*, we have *NO* tradition or ivied philosophies," and offer instead new approaches to vocational training based on individual needs. The City Colleges of Chicago have nine campuses throughout the city serving 39,000 students. Courses are tuition-free to residents of Chicago, but also are open to suburban residents for tuition fees often less than the same courses would cost in a private school. Programs vary in length and students may take one course, a short sequence, or a full two-year program. Courses provide college credits as well as job skills. Students can even take the course right at home through the TV College which leads to an Associate in Arts degree.

In Wisconsin, the nonresidential Milwaukee Area Technical College offers programs on five levels of difficulty, ranging from basic courses for functional illiterates to a two-year associate arts degree program in the most sophisticated technologies. Two-thirds of the school's 11,000 full-time enrollment is at the postsecondary level.

Why should there be two-year colleges? Originally the reason was largely that it was hard for girls to get into four-year colleges and universities. The first junior colleges were private and enrolled mainly privileged young ladies. The first public two-year college was not founded until 1901 in Joliet, Illinois, and the schools moved slowly till after World War II.

Then by strongly relating schooling to the realities of the world, and by placing continuing stress upon the uses of knowledge, it was discovered that career education in schools such as junior colleges answers both academic and vocational needs.

Community colleges have been creating programs as quickly as possible to fill local manpower needs and at the same time fulfilling individual job requirements of young people and adults of the community being served. Providing "relevant" education has been a basic commitment of the community college and perhaps that may account for the boom in popularity. In addition to opening doors to those going on to four-year institutions, they give high priority to training people at semiprofessional and technical levels.

Community colleges have close ties with local business and industry and thus are able to direct their programs to employment conditions not as they are thought to exist by someone a thousand miles away, but as they actually are. One Eastern community college dropped its courses for Library Assistants because the job demand in its area was all filled with no promise of substantial openings in the near future. No point in training people for jobs which just aren't available within a reasonable distance from home.

Community colleges hold a special promise for the disadvantaged because they are close to home and double the chances for bright students from lower socioeconomic levels to receive higher education. The open-door admissions policy and nominal tuition charges help, too.

Many community colleges have also discovered that they have more students coming to their evening divisions than to daytime sessions. One such school is Los Angeles Trade-Technical College where most of the extended-day students are attending college to maintain or improve their job skills, prepare for occupational advancement, or prepare for a new occupation—all while holding down daytime jobs.

While the public colleges are growing so greatly, the number of private junior colleges declines. You'll find private schools doing much the same thing as the public ones do. There are schools which teach the technical and mechanical trades leading to an associate degree and feature what amounts to a one-to-one tutorial schedule. Tuition costs are more than for public schools, but generally less than at private four-year colleges. You'll find men's, women's, and coed schools, residential and nonresidential and many fully as flexible as public schools as far as work-study, financial aid, starting times, and administrative policy are concerned. Most are geared to both academic and career education and definitely prepare you with specific job skills.

Subjects taught

According to a recent survey, junior and community colleges offer 10,624 occupational education programs leading to a two-year associate degree. In addition they offer a total of 3,708 occupational education programs leading to a certificate or job entry requirement below the associate degree. And still another 3,970 occupational education programs are now in various stages of planning and development. Shortly there will be over 20,000 occupational programs in community colleges in the fifty states.

When you think about enrolling in a community college, it means you'll have to ask yourself some hard questions about your goals and about the program you want. In a liberal arts program you choose from a variety of academic subjects that will help you select an area of academic concentration or eventual career. If you are planning to transfer to a four-year college, courses are chosen from this general academic field. On the other hand, a two-year program leading to an associate in arts degree in a job-oriented field is the basis of career education.

Two-year colleges offer certificates of achievement and associate degrees in fields where the training and education had normally come on the job in the past. Today students have the opportunity to get their education while they are learning an occupation.

These schools have an obligation to prepare students for a job when he leaves a school, not to prepare him for what appears to be an exciting field that may or may not offer jobs.

All kinds of creative and innovative programs exist in two-year colleges. On one campus, education students work as teacher aides in preschool centers located in poverty areas of the city. Another two-year college has a special preparatory program for biology students who perform laboratory work in the community's facilities.

There are also mini-semesters in which students have a break of several weeks between semesters to involve themselves in a variety of off-campus programs of study apart from regular course work for which they can receive academic credit.

There are accelerated admissions programs for high school juniors. With permission of their school, applicants can be admitted to college after three years of high school. Upon completion of one year of college, students admitted through this process are eligible for their high school diplomas.

There are weekend colleges in which classes are offered only on Saturday. These courses lead to a degree program for students who have full-time jobs.

Many schools have an extension of the college day so that classes are held from 7:30 a.m. to 10:00 p.m. Class scheduling is more flexible and students can hold down jobs while they go to school. Some colleges hold classes outside the physical setting of the classroom in community buildings, facilities, and stores in order to be close to students' working and living environment. This also means the college becomes a real part of the community.

Junior college career-oriented programs fall into three broad categories. The first includes training that has been traditionally offered at junior colleges but which has been recently expanded to meet changing needs. For example, many junior colleges that have long offered courses in mechanical drafting have expanded their curriculums to provide training in advanced technical aspects of engineering technology. Junior colleges have also developed courses to meet demand in occupations for which post-secondary training has not been historically necessary but in which it is becoming increasingly desirable, though not required. For example, many junior colleges now offer courses in law enforcement designed to train policemen. The third category of training leads to employment in the newly developing paraprofessional and aide occupations in public service fields—often through the New Careers program.

New Careers aims to recruit disadvantaged persons—many without high school diplomas—and to offer them training in both classroom and on-the-job situations to prepare them for teacher aide, welfare aide, and other paraprofessional jobs in various public service areas and to make possible further advancement in these jobs.

Community colleges may give special courses needed by these trainees. The course may be basically the same as the one taught to entering freshmen, although it might be less concentrated; or it may be a special course set up specifically for the trainee class. The credit earned often can be applied as credit toward an associate degree if the trainee should later decide

to continue his education. In some junior colleges if the trainee has not yet completed high school, the credits are held and granted when he completes his high school equivalency education. New Careers emphasizes further education for trainees. A trainee who wishes to advance his education after his initial training is complete may work toward an associate degree and perhaps go on to earn a bachelor's degree.

Many junior colleges offer a variety of courses pertaining to aide occupations—welfare, recreation, teacher—outside the New Careers program as well as within it. Such courses have been developed as a response to the increasing demand for personnel in aide occupations to help ease the shortage of professional manpower in certain "helping occupations."

Two-year colleges are in a unique position to respond to the career needs of their communities. One Michigan community college recently designed and offered a program for structural steel draftsmen to train students to fill a gap in the local steel industry. In North Carolina, officials realized a need for technicians in the fields of air and water pollution control. A local community college began to offer such a program and now graduates are working on the problem in their own communities.

At a college in a big city, where local industry is much more diversified, the range of occupational programs will be greater. Miami-Dade (Florida) Junior College offers more than fifty technical and business careers on its three campuses. Some are courses you'd expect to find like accounting or secretarial science. But there is also heavy demand for courses in air conditioning and refrigeration technology, data processing, and aeronautical technology. Colby Community Junior College in Kansas has courses in feed year technology, meat inspection, and animal hospital technology.

At Malcolm X, one of the City Colleges of Chicago, the practical curriculum enables its 4,100 full- and part-time students to enroll either in strictly academic or career-oriented subjects ranging from plant engineering and civil technology to urban studies. Individualized remedial instruction in reading and composition is given to more than 2,000 students by English teachers and tutors.

There is nothing unimaginative about these new skills taught at two-year colleges. Many schools combine occupational courses interdepartmentally to come up with some unique programs such as one for an executive secretary pilot. It's a two-year curriculum, part flight training and part secretarial science, to prepare a student as a secretary who can fly his or her boss to a meeting, take notes, and then fly back again. Far out? Maybe, but the community college tries to meet real needs.

Many career education programs come into

being in response to changing times, needs, and popular concerns. As the cry for pollution control has gone up throughout the land, many community colleges have mounted programs to train technicians to take part in the fight to preserve the land, the water, the air—to improve the quality of living. More than seventy two-year colleges have associate degree programs in environmental education. There are sixty different programs in environmental-ecological education that are being offered currently by community and junior colleges. They are listed under the four main headings: pollution prevention and control, disease prevention, environmental planning, and resources conservation.

Another relevant field that community colleges are preparing students for is health. Today, most community and junior colleges have paramedical programs, filling an enormous need. Colleges that have such programs work closely with hospitals and clinics in planning programs and in providing on-the-job training.

Community colleges are making a similarly important contribution in training people for public service jobs, and as the need for qualified personnel has expanded, so has the range of programs being offered. Some prepare employees of local, state, and federal agencies to assume greater responsibilities, others to train persons for entrance into mid-level or intermediate careers in government. Thus, the colleges are producing teacher aides, day care center assistants, and social service technicians. Students are offered courses in law enforcement, in urban planning, and in the corrections field. Surely you can find a program to suit your interests and abilities. Consider what some of these schools are offering:

The Williamsport (Pennsylvania) Area Community College operates a program in Service and Operating of Heavy Equipment at the college's Earth-Science facilities near Allenwood, Pennsylvania. The heavy-equipment students share a 160-acre site with the forestry and ornamental horticulture students. Thirty-five students were graduated from the two-year certificate program in 1971, and the salary range of those graduates ran from $4,160 to $13,645.

Flathead Valley Community College in Montana recently offered a training and education course called "Timber Fallers." Students in the program received on-the-job training in felling trees, scaling timber, and practicing safety on the job. They also received instruction in business operations and management. The twenty students who completed the latest Timber Fallers course, five weeks in duration, were immediately employed in jobs paying an average daily wage of $55.

Because Chicago is a major transfer center for the nation's land, sea and air traffic, many jobs are available to people trained in various phases of transportation. One of the City Colleges of Chicago, located in the heart of the city's trucking industry, offers four programs in its Motor Transportation Program. Students who enroll in the two-year course are trained for supervision and management jobs in the industry and receive an Associate in Applied Science degree. They receive on-the-job training in local transportation companies for which they are paid the firm's standard wages.

A policeman's job was never easy, but the complexity of urban society has made it even more demanding. A police officer today needs to be a social worker, a psychologist, and a doctor all at once. Recruits to the Chicago Police Department are learning more than standard police procedure in a joint effort of the Public Service Institute and Loop College, another one of the City Colleges of Chicago. Under the expanded program, recruits take the extra courses at Loop College. The subjects which can be applied toward an Associate in Arts Degree in law enforcement include two classes in behavioral sciences, two in history and theory of law enforcement, and one in applied psychology. Recruits also learn the history and culture of Chicago's ethnic groups and study youth development theories.

The new $13-million Southwestern Indian Polytechnic Institute in Albuquerque, New Mexico's west mesa, opened in 1971 to about 700 young Indians from 64 tribes throughout the United States. The school operates year round with 500 students living on campus and 200 in off-campus housing in the community. The curriculum involves a ladder concept so that a student can start at whatever level is best suited for him. His instruction will be individualized and geared so that he may get off the ladder at any level he chooses.

When the school first opened it offered training in business management, clerical work, drafting, electronics, radio, television, engineering, offset lithography, commercial food preparation, telecommunications, and optical technology. Programs are to be added in automotive mechanics, aircraft maintenance, building trades, and machine shop.

A supermarket management program is attracting many Chicago area students at College of DuPage, Glen Ellyn, Illinois. Backed by all major retail food chains, cooperatives, independents and retail food associations of Greater Chicago, the program is recognized as a model in training students for positions in the food industry and for advanced degrees in supermarketing at four-year colleges. The program offers early morning hours which permit the student, usually a retail food store employee, to attend class and still have enough time to return to work or to other schedules.

San Francisco's allure for tourists is indicated

by courses at the City College of San Francisco designed to help meet the manpower needs of the hotel and restaurant industry through a variety of programs operated in cooperation with and sometimes taught by, prominent restaurateurs and hotel executives. Florida Keys Junior College, surrounded by ocean waters, is big on marine diesel technology, marine propulsion and environmental marine science.

Career training programs offer some fine opportunities; training that leads to employment in two years; a chance through on-the-job training programs to experience working in a community; and familiarity with a variety of subjects. While not all schools offer all programs, most offer a wide range of choices to meet the growing need for trained workers.

Length of time programs last

Career education programs offered in junior colleges vary in length and in the nature of the diploma granted. Most programs last two years and lead to an associate degree. If fewer "general education" courses are taken, the award may be a certificate or a diploma. For example, a program in business data processing would lead to an Associate in Arts in Business Administration degree after a two-year course.

Some courses offered are of short duration, ranging from less than six months to a year in length. In these programs, diplomas, or certificates rather than formal degrees are awarded. Other courses, especially those in the health occupations, may extend to three years if actual hospital experience is included. But the schools are flexible and often a student can finish sooner or take longer.

Degrees granted

The number of recipients of associate degrees from all junior college programs, including occupational programs, has increased from nearly 95,000 in 1966 to well over 200,000 in 1970. Among graduates of occupational programs at the technical or semiprofessional level, most students completed programs in business and commerce-related studies. The next largest group graduated from mechanical and engineering technology courses and the next largest group was health science programs. Women receive about 43 percent of all the associate degrees. Three-fourths of the graduates were from public colleges and the rest from private schools. See page 24 for more information on the degrees granted.

Students at junior and community colleges

One college president calls his students a "grass roots—to hell with tradition" group, who are generally more conscientious, and no longer going to school because of parental pressure or prestige. The community college's flexibility allows a student to go to school on his own terms, holding a job at the same time if he or she chooses, and easily enrolling or pulling out of classes when it becomes necessary. Perhaps this is why 60 percent of freshmen today enter two-year colleges and 40 percent enter four-year colleges.

Some schools look for a diverse student body, while others are designed to serve a specific clientele: members of a particular church, residents of a given area, or students interested in some specialized field of study. All kinds of people go to these schools, which is why they are often called "people's colleges." There are:

Students who want to prepare themselves as rapidly as possible to compete on the job market;

Students who haven't taken full advantage of previous schooling and are still trying to find themselves;

Students whose family obligations make going away to college difficult, if not impossible;

Students who are disadvantaged and need help in overcoming the limitations of their earlier schooling;

Students who are ambitious but can't afford to go to school away from home;

Academically capable students who prefer the relatively sheltered environment of a small college during their transition from adolescence to young adulthood.

Students go to two-year colleges because the education offered is relevant to their needs. The courses are a quick answer to economic self-sufficiency. The two-year college can do so much for a student so quickly. Not only do the transfer students go on to further study; many of the career students who only intended to go for two years (those in terminal programs) keep studying and eventually earn bachelor's degrees. These students have been "turned on" educationally and are being given more than just a prescribed program when they attend a junior college.

These schools are not dumping groups for students who do not have the ability to qualify for university or four-year college level work. The range of ability represented in occupation-centered courses is almost as great as that of college students in general. But these students differ from other junior college students in interests and personality. They are interested in the applied fields because they are seeking a lifestyle they cannot get if they were to study the humanities or more theoretical sciences.

Dr. Kenneth B. Hoyt, who has studied the growth of two-year schools, finds that the students are likely to be around 20 years old; to work part-time and attend classes part-time; about a third are married (especially the men); most come from families without any college education; most come from families with lower incomes than students in four-year colleges; half the students come from suburbs of metropolitan areas and 92 percent attended public schools; half are from the top half of their high school classes and 7 percent said they were high school dropouts; most had taken a general course in high school with about a quarter taking vocational education in high school; about 28 percent had been encouraged to attend a two-year college. They appear to be more willing to follow their own instincts as to how to lead their lives rather than bow to strong bias of teachers, parents, or guidance counselors in favor of four-year college education. Some students enroll in vocational or technical courses after actually attending a four-year college and finding out it wasn't really what they wanted to do. Pride of workmanship is the rising tide among such students.

Students come directly from high school or from the armed services, they are transfers from other schools, they are unemployed to be trained, and adults are there for retraining to change their occupation.

The advantages and disadvantages of junior college education

There is a great advantage to students who attend a comprehensive college which includes both academic and occupational students. A student gets an awareness of the range of opportunities and obligations which face him. He has a chance to rub elbows with students of all ability levels and interests and to decide for himself which way he'll go. He can choose between technical training for highly skilled occupations and occupational training for clusters of jobs as well as the newer career programs. One advantage usually found at community colleges is that the instructors have usually had actual experience working at the skill being taught. A woman teaching secretarial skills will have held a job as a secretary; a man teaching mechanical arts will have worked as a mechanic.

There are some disadvantages to a junior college education. Most two-year graduates will not enter work with full professional status. You frequently begin as an assistant or trainee. When you enter the field of accounting, for example, you may begin as a junior accountant, perhaps in some specialized area such as accounts receivable. Much the same thing can be said for the beginning worker in personnel, purchasing, or buying. If you were to enter management, you'd usually begin as a trainee or assistant.

Your salary generally will be somewhat below that for graduates of four-year colleges in the same position; but you would be paid the same as other people with similar educational preparation. How fast you advance in position and earnings will depend on your own initiative, motivation, and ability. In some occupations you can compete successfully with graduates of four-year colleges.

You should weigh the advantages of lower training expense and income after only two years of education compared with the normally higher expense of training in a four-year institution followed by probably higher initial earnings and potentially greater advancement. See page 9 for more information on who should and who shouldn't consider going to these schools.

How good the schools are at job training

Richard Blumenthal enrolled first in one of the senior colleges at City University of New York. Later he transferred to CUNY's New York Community College in Brooklyn because he wanted the practical course of study offered by the college in its hotel and restaurant management program. One of the major factors in his decision was that faculty members in the department are all practitioners with many years of experience in this field.

After graduating from the Community College, he took a job as food management trainee with Treadway Inns in New England. Later he became a management trainee with Restaurant Associates in New York. This company operates 187 restaurants in 35 cities, including the Four Seasons Restaurant in New York. Blumenthal is now president of the company's restaurant division and corporation senior vice-president.

Community college administrators and teachers are concerned about the quality of learning. They emphasize good teaching, and they are constantly expanding and experimenting in curriculum and instructional development. The community college may be different in some important ways from other colleges and universities, but it is not different in its commitment to creating the best possible conditions for learning.

Delphi Agricultural and Technological Institute, Delphi, New York, is one of the state's six new agricultural and technical institutes. It is a two-year school, open to high school graduates. The Institute awards associate degrees in such subjects as biological technology, hospital management technology, dental hygiene, food processing technology, X-ray technology, industrial instrumentation technology, measurement science, and construction technology. The campus at Delphi is beautiful. It's new and the quality and volume of its equipment is outstanding. The "shop," if you can call it that, is a vast room, almost as big as a football field, five stories high with a glass-enclosed balcony where visitors can watch the students and their instructors. But the thing that catches the eye is a simple little sign in one of the medical laboratories. It reads: "There is nothing second class about a first rate technician."

There are experimental new programs at Central Nebraska Technical College unlike any others you have ever seen. A student may enter the college at any time of the year and on any working day (though preferably on a Monday), proceed at whatever pace he sees fit, and receive his associate of science degree whenever he has demonstrated mastery over whatever course of study he selected. Anyone "of good moral character" not currently enrolled in a high school and at least 16 years old is welcome.

There are no classrooms and no lectures as such. Life at Central Nebraska is a lively mixture of media centers, demonstration films, cassette-type tapes, study centers, laboratories, and individual study stations or carrels, plus individual attention from an instructor whenever it is needed.

The individualized approach covers 33 areas of occupational training scattered among six divisions covering automotive technology, business and office work, electronics, construction and allied fabrication skills, agriculture, and dental technology.

The approach works. The dropout rate is something less than 5 percent.

And on the other side of the coin, the school has regularly been placing nearly every one of its graduates in skilled jobs, even while the economy nationally has been in the doldrums and many a graduate from four-year academic institutions has been pounding the streets seeking employment. "In some instances," says the President, "we've had ten jobs waiting for a student. There's no difficulty whatsoever in placing all our graduates who want to work."

Of the 1970–71 graduates, 81 percent found employment immediately, 5 percent continued their education and 8 percent entered the armed forces. The greatest majority of the graduates who went to work found jobs in the immediate area served by the college.

A recent study of the educational and occupational experience of 1966 graduates of the Community Colleges of CUNY asked whether the career training received at the community college provided the respondent with the means to fulfill his goals. Could he earn enough to support himself and implement his educational plans? Would a liberal arts degree have provided a viable job opportunity and salary? Of those who answered these questions over 70 percent believed that their community college training helped them locate a job sufficiently remunerative to permit furthering their education. Only 25 percent felt that a liberal arts degree would have served the same function.

More than 85 percent of the respondents viewed their first job as directly related to their college training and over 75 percent of them view their present job similarly. More than half started with jobs in the $5,000 to $7,500 range. At present, over half are earning between $7,500 and $10,000. The remainder are divided almost evenly between over $10,000 and under $7,500.

How much it costs

Students who attend a two-year college are likely to save in two ways. First, tuition fees are low at the church-supported colleges, ranging from $300 a year to $900, and are nonexistent at most of the municipal and state institutions. Even at the private junior colleges, annual tuition is not likely to be more than $900. Many junior colleges offer scholarships. Second, community colleges are just that: institutions so close to the students' homes that they are able to commute by car or city transit. In this way they and their families eliminate the expense of dormitory room and board, and all the many costs of out-of-town living (long distance calls, air or train transportation during holidays and vacations, etc.). However, many of the junior colleges do attract students from all parts of the nation, and even from all parts of the world.

Community and junior colleges aim to make education accessible financially. Many two-year colleges offer a variety of loans and scholarships. These are often made possible by local civic and business groups and are usually awarded on a need basis.

Federal aid to community colleges is also important. Over 100,000 students in community colleges received loans, grants, and work/study assistance from the Federal Government.

While it is difficult to generalize about the total number and amount of loans, grants and scholarships available in two-year colleges, one trend is universal. Because most two-year college students work, these schools rely heavily on self-help and concentrate on work/study programs. Work/study means that the college will help the student find a job either within the school itself or in the community as training in the particular area he or she is studying. The student is paid for working.

Malcolm X College, one of the City Colleges of Chicago, has 75 percent of its students coming from families with incomes under $6,000 a year. This school has steadily expanded its financial aid program. In 1967, the college had 50 students on work/study, its only student-aid program at the time. Today about 1,000 of its nearly 10,000 students are receiving financial aid under four major programs.

Many students who begin to work after school while still in high school continue to hold those jobs through college, paying their way and training themselves for more responsible work at the same time.

A significant point to keep in mind when evaluating the price of education at a two-year college is that costs to students are kept to a minimum at a time when everything else is costing more. Tuitions average about $250 per year, and many students live at home, saving considerably on room and board.

If you're a veteran, it's even easier. Educational benefits are the legal right of every veteran (except reservists) who has completed 181 days of consecutive service since January 31, 1955. A veteran has eight years from his day of discharge to use his benefits. War widows, war orphans, and wives and children of men with 100 percent disability also have educational benefits. Under new laws, veterans are also allowed an allotment for tutoring assistance while attending regular college programs. See page 20 for more details.

Financial aid

There are a number of federal financial aid programs available to junior college students.

Approximately $72 million was earmarked in fiscal 1971 for 183,000 community junior college students in Educational Opportunity Grants and College Work Study (both under title IV HEA) and National Defense Student Loans (title 11 NDEA). Educational Opportunity Grants enable academically qualified high school graduates of exceptional financial need to attend college. College Work Study grants make part-time employment possible for postsecondary students— particularly those from low income families— who need extra money to pursue their studies. The NDEA loan program places funds with postsecondary institutions for making low interest loans to students.

Community junior college students also participate in the Guaranteed Student Loan Program (title IV as amended). Through this program the Government insures low interest loans made to students by banks and other lending institutions. These loans need not be repaid until after a student completes his studies. Last year more than a million postsecondary students borrowed $1 billion through this program.

The Upward Bound Program (title IV HEA) provides funds for precollege preparation of high school students from low-income backgrounds and for students with poor records of academic achievement and motivation. An allotment of $618,000 was provided for the assistance of 800 students in 11 community colleges. Likewise, Talent Search, which seeks under the same title students of financial or cultural need who have exceptional potential for postsecondary education, supplied $342,000 to six community junior colleges and thereby were able to approach some 12,000 students.

Title IV HEA also establishes Special Services for Disadvantaged Students, a program meant to provide physically, culturally or economically handicapped students with remedial or other kinds of help in order that they may start or continue their postsecondary studies. Approximately $3 million was allotted to assist 10,000 community junior college students. In addition, the Cooperative Education Program under the same title set aside an estimated $324,000 for 20 communities' junior colleges to plan, establish, expand, or carry out programs that enable students to alternate periods of full-time study and periods of full-time employment.

Title III of the Higher Education Act— Strengthening Developing Institutions—provides funds for colleges that are struggling to survive and need to bolster their academic, administrative, and students services programs. Fifty-nine community junior colleges in this category were awarded $7.8 million. See also pages 14-24 for full details on getting financial help.

Entrance requirements

Public community or junior college admission is based on your high school record (transcript), or information from your previous college if you are a transfer student. In applying have your records mailed directly from your high school to the Director of Admission of the school you wish to enter. You may be asked to take tests, such as the American College Testing Program (ACT) before registration. If you are a legal resident of the college district, admission is fairly easy.

Most community colleges operate with an open door admission policy. This is usually translated as meaning the college will admit all persons, whether they are high school graduates or not, who could benefit by the instruction offered.

General admission is less competitive than in most four-year schools. But the schools vary in their admissions requirements. Some require an interview with an applicant on campus or with a representative of the school.

One college administrator puts it this way, "Our original admissions requirement was the ability to turn left off 27th Avenue to reach the college. We're still pretty close to that."

You'll find both day and evening courses, and you can enroll on a part-time basis. You may usually enroll as a matriculated student, a nonmatriculated student, or as a special student in the extension program. You are considered matriculated when you are officially accepted as a degree candidate on a full-time or evening basis. A nonmatriculated student takes degree-credit courses, but hasn't yet been accepted as a degree candidate. You can also take any courses you wish for no credit.

Many students at community colleges could have registered at universities had they not preferred to enroll in two-year institutions. Others could not have met entry requirements for four-year programs. There are many reasons: insufficient high school grades and constantly rising competition for slots in a university program, among them. And increasingly in many states, the two-year college is marked as the starting point for growing numbers of young people.

Two-year colleges are of particular help to

those who could not, for some reason, enter universities. They offer upgrading work to bring the student with a below average scholastic background up to college level. Extensive counseling programs are available.

Open admission is one of the most exciting innovations in higher education in recent years. Because of this policy, community college students are more representative of the general population of the United States than are students in any other major segment of higher education. The above-average as well as average and below-average students, in terms of scholastic records, make up the diverse population of the community college. They come from all economic strata, though families of students fall most frequently into average and below-average income brackets.

If you are planning to transfer to a four-year program, you are able to do so after completing the program at an accredited two-year college. In fact, many four-year colleges are encouraging junior college transfers to enroll. At one top university the number of transfer students has quadrupled in the past four years, and statistics show that 80 percent of these students graduate. That is a higher percentage of transfer students graduating than the percentage of freshmen who enter the same university and graduate.

Many two-year colleges offer special recruitment programs for veterans, members of minority groups, and adults who want to return to school. Reports show that 38 percent of all black students who enter college begin in two-year colleges. Two-year colleges recognize their responsibility to such groups of potential students and have planned programs oriented to them. In several colleges, black and Spanish-speaking students are involved in developing their own ethnic-oriented curriculums.

Campus life

The community and junior colleges offer more variety and opportunity in campus life than most of the other postsecondary schools. You may find lounges where students gather informally between classes. Cafeterias are open for all meals and generally serve hot food as well as sandwiches. There are sometimes school sponsored social and athletic activities such as picnics, bowling leagues, film series, and dances. The usual range of activities including student government, extracurricular clubs, and honor societies are also available.

Some two-year colleges orient extracurricular activities to off-campus interests while others place emphasis on such traditional activities as athletics, newspapers, and yearbooks. Many two-year colleges sponsor cultural and entertainment events which the public is invited to participate in and attend. But, whatever the activity, one thing is sure: extracurricular activities are created and organized almost always by the students. Prison inmates, housewives, businessmen, high school dropouts, students bound for four-year colleges—all these people make up the two-year college. It is not usual to find a college that opens its doors to everyone from early morning until late evening, and meets in a city hospital, factory cafeteria, county courtroom, or a brand new campus.

Every student lives two lives at college—one academic and one social. And you learn much from each. The total environment your school provides is important to your development. You will be affected by the other students; by their abilities, their variety of interests, and the nature and scope of their ambitions.

If your school is primarily a commuter college where large numbers of students attend class and then leave for home, it'll be very different from a school where substantial numbers of students live on campus. The latter will provide a more active satisfactory campus environment. The percentage of students leaving campus on weekends may be important for the student from another part of the country. Though many students may live on campus, if their homes are close by, they make a habit of going home on weekends. If you live far away, you may find yourself on a deserted campus come Friday afternoon.

The rules governing student conduct that are enforced by the college may have an important influence on your happiness and success. Institutions' policy varies from the very strict to the very permissive, where minimum rules limit students' behavior and individual responsibility is encouraged.

Everyone is a joiner—the clique, the gang, or the club. This is a strong psychological need. Many of the extracurricular activities at a two-year college are geared to providing students with opportunities to participate in community improvement and to develop a sense of civic responsibility, as well as to further their knowledge of particular vocational fields.

Job placement

Follow-up information on job placement of junior college graduates is hard to find. However, since junior colleges are usually local institutions drawing both students and financial support from a fairly small area, their programs are often designed to fit community manpower needs. As a result, students from occupational programs generally have little difficulty in finding jobs in the areas of their training.

Community colleges are strategically located close to where people live. The curriculum is usually geared to the needs and opportunities of the area the school serves. The demand for graduates of these schools is so great in some fields that industry hires the students before they complete their two years, then supports them the rest of the way through school. The employment services run by the colleges are able to place most students in jobs before they graduate.

Choosing a school

Here are some things to look for when you choose a school. What educational setting the school offers; range of academic opportunity; intensity of the pressures you will meet; your chance for scholastic success. You can judge all this by examining the kind of programs the school offers and determining the degree of success its students enjoy.

Degrees granted by a school show the type of academic program it offers. Look at the majors for a recent graduating class which are often listed in order of popularity. This will give you an idea of where the school's strengths lie— where its major resources are channeled. A look at the number of students who complete terminal programs in comparison with the number taking transfer programs in preparation for further study at four-year institutions also gives you clues as to the quality of the school. How you can be sure it's the right school for you. See pages 77-79 for what to check.

School accreditation

What does accreditation mean? Junior colleges, like other institutions of higher education, seek accreditation through regional accreditation commissions. They are accredited on the basis of standards the colleges already accredited have set for themselves as a group. The accrediting commissions obviously influence school programs and policies by their standards, published points of views and recommendations of evaluation teams.

Institutions are required to do a self-study to begin the accreditation or renewal process. This gives them a health stimulus for institutional self-improvement.

Most community colleges are also evaluated by state agencies and some seek professional accreditation for specific programs, such as accreditation of associate degree nursing program by the National League for Nursing. It's a good idea to be sure the school you plan to attend is accredited and that the vocational or technical program you plan to take is also accredited. See pages 10-14 for a full explanation of accreditation.

The future of junior and community colleges

Community colleges have all the essential requisites for a bright future: they are a logical first step in postsecondary education. They are comprehensive in their offerings. They are less costly and more convenient for the student. They are closely linked to their own communities. And they have a steadily increasing possibility of transfer upward for the student.

But the big strength of the junior college is that it offers all the people of the region it serves the services of its vocational guidance and counseling services as well as the educational opportunity to carry out a plan laid out by the counselors. The colleges are designed to serve those who are unemployed, underemployed, who want to change jobs, who are not as yet in the labor force, and those who need help in making major vocational decisions.

The better schools are equipped to provide individual and group counseling, administer vocational aptitude interest tests, provide materials for vocational exploration and arrange on-site visits so that people will have a better understanding of the occupations in which they are interested.

Another big advantage is the emphasis on individual attention. This service is particularly helpful to the high school graduate uncertain of his occupational goals. The schools offer wide open options, depending upon what you want to study.

For more information, write:

American Association of Community and Junior
    Colleges
One Dupont Circle, N.W.
Suite 410
Washington, D.C. 20036
Ask for: *Junior College Directory*, revised annually, $5.00 (gives current data on costs, accreditation, and other necessary information).

National Council of Independent Junior Colleges
One Dupont Circle, N.W.
Washington, D.C. 20036
Ask for: Information on private junior colleges.

If you want to know where the closest community college is to your home, write to your Director of Community Colleges at your State Department of Education.

Private Trade, Technical, and Business Schools

America's 7,000 private trade and technical schools may lack the ivy-covered trappings of the collegiate world, but they offer a needed storehouse of no-nonsense job-oriented training for you—if you're career-minded.

These schools don't usually have football teams, beautiful campuses, or stately buildings; yet their graduates are among the most sought-after by business firms. These schools offer over 550 different courses. Somewhere between

1,500,000 and 2,000,000 students attend each year, including adult and evening school students. In 1960, there were only about 750,000 students. In 1973 these private schools registered about ten percent of the U.S. population enrolled in higher education.

Girls as well as boys are included in most schools. The courses last from a few weeks to three years and tuition fees range from $200 to $1,800 a course. These schools specialize in the highly desirable occupations open to the noncollege graduate. Emphasis is on teaching what you need to know to get a job as quickly as possible.

Most students at these schools are fresh out of high school. Others have tried college or spent a few years in the armed forces. All, however, have decided not to settle for the mediocre jobs open to the unskilled when today there are so many opportunities for well-paying, rewarding careers for anyone with good training.

The schools are usually small, only a few number over 2,000 students, and the average enrollment is much less than 350. The schools generally can have limited objectives, which explains why there are so many schools.

Private schools are called "proprietary" because they make profits for their owners. A private trade school is a profit-making institution owned by an individual or corporation which offers training leading to employment in a specialized trade or vocation.

The quality of training may vary greatly from school to school. The cost or tuition of private trade school training not only must cover the full cost of educating the students, but it must also provide a profit to the owners of the school. This is the thing which makes private trade schools different from the many vocational schools that are public, tax-supported, and may be either free or inexpensive. Some private trade schools offer day or evening courses, some offer resident courses, some offer correspondence courses, and some offer combinations to suit the student's needs.

Many people think of these schools as "third floor walk-up schools" that have but one interest—getting the student's money. Nothing could be further from the truth.

Subjects taught

A trade or technical school will teach you only a specific skill, what you need to know to get a job. The practical requirements of the prospective employer affect the contents of every course. The emphasis is on helping students to qualify for the best possible job in the shortest possible time. You won't find subjects like poetry or history listed in their catalogs. They offer only selected practical courses which lead directly to a job.

Modern vocational schools offer an ever changing list of courses in areas where job opportunities are especially good. They add or drop courses to meet the fluctuating manpower needs of industry as well as to provide people to fill the new jobs being created almost daily by industry and government.

Whatever fields have a shortage of trained people, you'll find those fields recognized in the curriculum of local vocational schools. The payoff is three or four jobs offered to each student who graduates with those skills.

There is a course offered somewhere for almost every type of job. Just recently, the National Association of Trade and Technical Schools helped two high school seniors find schools for monument engraving and Western saddlery. The monument engraving schools were located in New York and Georgia; the saddlery school was in Wyoming.

Proprietary schools train students for a wide range of careers from drafting to radio-TV broadcasting. A school outside Philadelphia teaches students how to tell male from female chickens, a skill needed by commercial poultry producers; four others in Las Vegas train card dealers.

Preparation for more than 200 different occupations is offered—some courses for occupations like baseball umpiring and fire and explosion investigation are offered in few, if any, other institutions. Many areas of instruction are in the fields of growing job opportunities. Each course has a precise employment objective. You'll find a far broader variety of short-term courses offered than in most public schools.

The atmosphere in which you study for your future career will be different from high school classes. Your curriculum will be completely oriented toward your chosen field.

If you are attending a private business school for a secretarial course, some schools may include a charm course to give you ideas on cosmetics, clothes and appearance, but even that will be oriented toward your appearance on the job. The curriculum will focus on shorthand, typewriting, filing, English, and secretarial office training. The course will run from six months to two years, depending on whether you choose to specialize in a certain area. There are longer programs available for those who want to become executive secretaries or administrative assistants. In these programs more emphasis is placed on accounting and other business courses such as mathematics, law, economics, and psychology.

Some schools offer specialization in legal or medical secretarial and technical training. The legal area might include extra courses in legal terminology, legal documents, and business, besides shorthand, typewriting, and filing. Some schools include field trips to court so students can observe the procedures. The medical training would focus on subjects needed to work in a doctor's office, hospital, or research lab.

Here are some of the programs offered by schools in different parts of the country.

There are private schools which offer courses dealing with law enforcement on several levels. One features home study courses and regional seminars in such subjects as Explosives and Home Made Bombs; Arson Investigation; The Law of Arrest, Search & Seizure; and Drug Addiction. The courses cost from $20 to $60 each and give policemen a chance to earn an Associate in Police Science Degree.

Gem City College, a 102-year-old private school in Quincy, Illinois, gives individual instruction for careers in watchmaking, engraving, jewelry-diamond setting, and jewelry store management. Even though it's one of the largest schools in this field, the program accommodates only 150 students at a time. Enrollment begins on any Monday.

There are schools to learn floral art, bartending, photography, printing and lithography, truck driving, welding, dog grooming, electronic equipment servicing (radio, TV, stereo, transistor), hotel management, trained draftsman, air conditioning and refrigeration. You can train for an entry-level job in medical or dental fields in just four months with day or evening classes or study at home in your spare time.

One school offering Fashion Merchandising features visits to mills, manufacturers, and advertising media as part of its courses. It also offers paid on-the-job training in local stores to its students.

You can obtain an associate degree in the Culinary Arts at a school with a two-year course preparing you for a career as a cook, chef, pastryman, buffet caterer, food supervisor or food manager.

Length of time programs last

Courses run from half a week for an entry-level job to three years for an engineering technology degree course. Most courses are one to two years long. A New York City school which offers a course in air conditioning and refrigeration advertises that it takes five months of daytime classes or ten months of evening classes to complete the course. It also conducts classes in Spanish as well as English.

The schools usually operate throughout the year (no summer vacations) to allow students to complete an already compact course quickly. Some have fall, winter, and summer semesters. Others start a course each month or each Monday or whenever there is enough demand.

Once you enroll in a private vocational school, you can attend classes year-round with a week off at Christmas and a week off in July. Students in most courses graduate at different time intervals, depending on their individual achievement. If you are a hard-working, serious student you can finish sooner. If you are a slow learner or are out because of illness or other problems, many schools allow you to repeat part of or even an entire course, usually at no extra tuition.

Degrees granted

In contrast to many community colleges that are concerned with students' transferability to four-year colleges, most private vocational schools are content to remain nondegree granting (or terminal) institutions. However most do award certificates or diplomas when you successfully complete a course. At some schools there is an actual graduation ceremony. Others hold none at all. Those schools which do grant degrees usually award associate degrees. See page 24 for a list of such degrees.

The students

At 18, Anne Meyer was a discouraged liberal arts student at Nassau Community College on Long Island. "I really felt that I was accomplishing nothing," she recalls. "I was learning things but nothing that I could use in the future." She dropped out of college to enroll in the Katharine Gibbs Schools, which promised her secretarial skills that would enable her to get a job immediately after graduation.

Since it has been proven that most students in the proprietary schools meet the admission requirements of the junior or community colleges or the evening adult education programs, why do they choose to invest a substantial sum for a study program that is also being offered at no charge in a public institution? Students most frequently mention time, convenience, and course content in explaining their decision to enroll in a proprietary school program. They say they usually can start class within a week after enrolling, and they can complete the course within a relatively short period of time—less than a year and often under six months. They point out that the curriculum is entirely skill-oriented and free of what they consider to be nonessential subjects. Finally, many students mention job placement service. A private school's continuation as a successful business depends on how successful its students are in securing employment after training. Individual attention and relaxed classroom atmosphere are other major reasons mentioned.

Positive encouragement and practical guidance are given by either the instructors or guidance counselors in many schools. Students are briefed on how to get a job and how to hold onto it.

Many students are over-educated, that is, they have more years of school than are actually required for courses. This often happens because the students are college dropouts. Most students are from 17 to 26 years old and if they work, it is part-time only. Students who work full-time are more likely to be older and attending night classes. There are some students as old as 60, however. Though most students live near their schools, many schools do have foreign students who are in the United States for their schooling.

"Here, I don't have to bother with English composition, physical education, history or science," says a California girl enrolled in secretarial training. "I spend all my time on business courses, and, after all, that's what I need for a job."

Students begin classes when they want to and get to work much sooner than in public schools where they see courses added "to drag out the time." They feel the early paychecks compensate for high study costs.

Though instructional programs are similar to those in many public schools, students feel that proprietary school teachers are closer to the job market, more aware of conditions, better able to help them find jobs.

For both the schools and their students, an impressive degree is less important than job placement. New York's highly rated RCA Institutes, owned by RCA Corporation, operates three shifts a day training TV and electronics technicians in a former warehouse and places 79 percent of the graduates. Half of RCA's nontenured faculty lack college degrees, but nearly all have job experience. Such a practical approach attracts students like Angelo Gomez, 23, who briefly considered going to college, then decided, "What I'm really after is money." His benchmate, Bob Kane, 19, a dropout from the City University of New York, agrees. "As a technician you can still get rich."

Who should and who should not go to these schools

Private vocational schools are for the student who wants to learn something that will make him more employable and is only interested in training for a specific occupation.

You will find high school dropouts with no previous occupational training; high school graduates of general education programs; high school graduates preparing for licensable occupations; college dropouts; college students and graduates taking an otherwise unavailable course, such as computer programing; and older people who have come back to school for particular training for one reason or another.

Despite financial pressures, the student dropout rate is lower than the rates for either high school or college students, partly because of the self-selection of courses. Financial problems and the need to go to work full-time are the main reasons given when students do drop out. Only about 15 percent of those who do drop out do so because of lack of ability.

It is one educator's belief that many high school students now take one of the first jobs offered them. The job may look pretty good at first but after a year or two they begin to look around for something better. What a loss of valuable time and talent! Why spend your valuable time job experimenting? With business college training, for example, you get added poise, increased self-confidence and the resources of the business college through its proximity to business. You can be placed in a top position from the start—or at least in a position with a future. The best time to develop marketable skills is at an age when you don't yet have the responsibilities of job and marriage.

To take one example, every June thousands of high school graduates armed with typing and stenography skills choose to spend more time in class, paying tuition to one of the 1,500 private independent business schools located throughout America, instead of immediately taking a job with a regular paycheck.

Why? Mostly because the investment of additional time and money leads to a better, more rewarding position.

The secretarial field is a competitive one; the keener your skills and the more and self-confident you are, the more likely you are to get the job you want.

There is Sandy, for example, a Washington, D.C. secretary, working in a plush office environment. She chose to go on to business school because, "My parents wanted me to go to college, but I didn't want to spend another four years in school; yet my business skills weren't that good."

What did Sandy gain through the added education? "For one thing, the classes were smaller so that in a business machines course I didn't have to wait my turn to practice. There was a lot of work involved, especially in the area of shorthand, where we concentrated all the shorthand into nine months. When I graduated I really felt confident enough to handle the job offered to me."

A vocational school education can be valuable to almost any high school graduate. Such a school can take the student with no training and equip him with marketable skills in a much shorter time than junior college or college because of the concentrated course it offers. Here is where the potential college dropout could be aided if he had good advice and counseling before going through the bitter taste of failure in an academic college.

Vocational school education is not better than an academic college education. But some students are more suited to one area of schooling than another, and it is a shame to waste valuable time and money studying in an area not suited to your own needs and talents.

How good the schools are at job training

There appear to be some very good and some very bad schools. The better vocational schools feel it is their responsibility to see that students get successfully through their course, once accepted. The attitude is that a student is there to be trained for a job, and it's up to the school to deliver relevant training on up-to-date equipment.

The emphasis is definitely on the practical side. A student pays money to be trained for a job. He naturally expects the school to deliver. Vocational schools must change the courses to meet the challenging job picture. The specialized nature of courses and the primary objective of preparing students for employment prompts most schools to maintain close but informal contacts with employers. Course content is easily modified as a result of frequent exchanges of information. Innovations made in employers' plants, offices and laboratories are reflected in changes in the courses to be sure students are realistically prepared for jobs.

Because students select occupational courses which they prefer, they are much more likely to be motivated than if they had no free choice. The students tend to do very well and the instruction is especially attractive to students who want short, intensive courses containing only a minimum of academic content.

Commenting on his school's philosophy, the president of RCA Institute, Inc., says, "It is our principal purpose to provide programs in electronic technology which will both qualify graduates for responsible positions in industry, and also provide the more able and ambitious students with the foundation and incentive for more advanced education." He said many of his graduates go on to college to obtain their degrees afterwards. "In contrast to many college graduates," he pointed out, "our graduates are prepared to assume an immediately productive role in industry because they have received a practical blend of theory and industry-oriented laboratory work with modern equipment."

Graduates of the RCA Institute have no trouble getting jobs. They are employed around the globe installing, operating, and maintaining electronic equipment ranging from computers and missile instrumentation to radio and TV broadcasting and receiving units. "We train young men not for specific jobs in industry, but rather in the broad concept of fundamental electronics and its application in modern industry." The curriculum in good vocational schools emphasizes changes to keep pace with the technical skills taught by industry.

Some private firms contract with private schools to meet their training needs. And many private schools have been bought by large corporations, which brings about an even closer tie of the schools' training courses with specific industry needs.

How the schools accomplish the training is important. In one radio and television broadcasting course, for example, you can get training as a newscaster, disc jockey, sportscaster, or announcer. The radio and television training laboratories include a model radio broadcasting studio and a model television studio. In the television laboratory, a student's work is videotaped, permitting him to instantly view himself on a television monitor.

At a technical school, laboratories are a vital part of education. If the lab doesn't have the latest devices and isn't well-equipped, you will not be adequately trained.

Because only those theoretical or academic concepts related to the performance of a job are dealt with, only a small amount of home work is required for many of the courses. And the concepts are integrated with the practical instruction. For example, if you were studying auto mechanics, you'd be taught only the physics of combustion and of electrical hydraulics that pertains directly to automobiles.

Another significant feature is that training is usually at various levels of accomplishment within a group of related occupations. For example, at one school you can shift your study from a radio-television repair course to a more sophisticated course in electronics technology, or vise versa, depending on your aptitudes or interests or abilities. If you cannot pass the courses at the highest level, there are a number of lower levels available to you, each of which makes you immediately employable after graduation. It is important to train for a meaningful job and train in such a way that will let you move from one job level to another.

It is the instructor's job in this type of school more so than in a public school to see that a student is successful. Most schools consider that if there are many student failures in one course, it's the instructor's fault and something needs to be done.

Classes are small and most instruction is individualized. The instructors have to be very adept at working with each student and tailoring the course to fit his needs, meet his deficiencies and not keep him waiting unnecessarily. The better schools use team teaching and many hire specialists as teachers. They are constantly encouraging their students and urging them to better themselves. Students are put into job-like training settings. The schools attempt to stimulate and relax new students who might not have been entirely successful in schools they attended before.

Much motivation is provided by instructors who frequently emphasize the employment opportunities open to successful graduates. Students are often instructed in grooming and personal behavior because employers are interested in their employees' appearance. Neatness counts, not necessarily new or fancy clothing, as long as you are neatly dressed. Punctuality and regular attendance are checked because the schools feel it is important to develop habits of regular attendance and being on time. Lateness and absence records are more often the cause of student failure to succeed in school than lack of ability. Schools insist on promptness.

Many schools have a preparatory educational program which is designed to tutor you in any areas in which you are deficient and need the background to understand the material in your chosen course. For example, if you need to understand a certain amount of math to be a draftsman, you may need some preparatory course in math to make up for something you did not do well in high school.

Instructional methods are geared to making sure a student succeeds. A course is broken down into short units or topics which encourage and motivate the student to take one small step forward at a time rather than becoming discouraged by tedious or too difficult material. One student said, "You're here to learn things. It's not like high school where you can get away with goofing off."

Private schools attempt to simulate shops, labs, and other actual settings. In one school student desks have been completely removed and replaced by stools and benches. At a school in New York City automobiles are accepted from private persons and engine and body repairs are made by the students at no charge. At the Culinary Institute of America top grade foods are used for classes so students learn how such food tastes and learn to distinguish between quality of foods.

Most schools give letter or number grades to show the student his progress; but many schools also use a review of the work in the classroom or the shop or the individualized instructor with student conferences as the principal way of grading.

Because securing employment, as related to training, is the objective of programs in private vocational schools, the students, instructors, and school administrators are most concerned with successful completion of the course. This means the school gives a verbal guarantee for a comparatively meaningful education for most students who are accepted by a school. Graduation requirements in some occupations like medical technician include a service of "internship." Before students get their diplomas they must finish six months employment and receive the employer's recommendation.

School owners realize that graduates can affect the school's reputation. Some schools will not give a certificate to graduates whose performance is only barely satisfactory. Student transcripts and recommendations are sent to prospective employers which detail how well you did in the program.

What is a vocational school diploma worth? Over 90 percent of the graduates from the schools studied in a broad survey obtained jobs. Over 80 percent obtained jobs directly related to the training they received, often through the job placement departments of their schools. Many graduates are content with their training and the jobs they are able to get. They consider themselves better prepared for their jobs than employees who come from other programs.

But if you have chosen your field of study and are considering a vocational school, you must always check to see if you will have any advantages over the trainees in the industry's own programs. An airline personnel director says he has hired airline school graduates, but they still have to go through the airline's program. The airline has no special arrangement with any school to insure hiring.

How much it costs

"Tuition usually runs from $800 to $2,000 a year. The average is about $1,200. There are extremes both ways; advanced flight training could exceed $5,000," says W. A. Goddard, Executive Director of the National Association of Trade and Technical Schools.

The tuition varies from school to school, depending on the type of school and its location. Most schools allow monthly or quarterly payments or even deferred payment plans. The schools have a businesslike outlook. Not only are the courses short, but the tuition is cheap per classroom hour compared with college charges ($1.50 per classroom hour vs. $4 or more).

Only a small number of students have their tuition paid by parents—more than 60 percent work part time. Most schools help students find part-time jobs that not only help with expenses, but add to on-the-job training and will not interfere with studies or the school's activities.

There are many possibilities for financial aid. The Office of Educational Opportunity's Talent Search program is one way. The Talent Search looks for young people who ought to be in vocational schools and guides them in suitable choices of study programs, application procedures, and sources of financial aid. Send a postcard to Student Aid, U.S. Office of Education, Washington, D.C. 20202. Ask for the name of a Talent Searcher in your area.

Help is also available from the Veterans' Assistance Benefits, "G.I. Bill"; various government grants, loans, and scholarships; and broader provisions under the Vocational Educational Amendment of 1968. Ask the school that interests you for help in applying for aid.

Under the Government Guaranteed Loan Program, students attending an accredited private vocational school can borrow up to $1,500 for the tuition. The student or his parents borrow the money through a bank or savings and loan association. See also pages 14-24 for more information on financial aid.

Entrance requirements

Generally you apply for admission by filling out an application for admission and forwarding it to the Registrar's Office. You must also ask your high school to send a transcript of your grades. If you are transferring from another college or other school, you'll need a transcript from that school as well as your high school record. You may be asked for a registration fee with your application—usually $10 and not refundable.

Always file a formal application for admission prior to the semester you wish to enroll. Generally you are eligible for entrance to a private school only if you are a high school graduate or the equivalent (e.g. the High School Equivalency Diploma). Once you have applied, a representative of the school will interview you. Before you are admitted, the school will consider your background, high school transcripts, interests, and recommendations of the high school principal and guidance counselor. Certain technical schools may require some high school mathematics and science courses, and others may require entrance tests such as the Scholastic Aptitude Test. Pre-admission counseling and advisement is always available to anyone applying to a vocational school.

You may find specific entrance requirements for the field you plan to enter. For example, the Academy of Aeronautics in New York feels it is important that each of its graduates meet industry standards for education, physical health, and personal integrity. The rigid physical requirements of the flight crew members do not apply to engineering technicians. However, even they must be in good health, with no physical defects that would hinder their employment. Therefore a statement of general physical health is required on the application for admission.

It may be surprising to you to learn that the typical vocational school of today does not accept just anyone willing to pay tuition. A student may be unacceptable if he has poor personality traits, low high school scholarship record, physical handicaps (some schools, however, pride themselves on being able to help the physically handicapped), low intelligence, lack of interest, truant record in high school, or a poor study or work attitude.

The feeling in regard to accepting students seems to be summed up in the statement of one business school director: "Each graduate represents us. He makes or breaks our reputation with some employer. We enroll only those we believe we can honestly train—and place."

Another school, which requires applicants to take an aptitude test for specialized data-processing training, reports that 30 to 40 percent of the applicants fail to pass and are refused admission. Any business that will turn away profit in the best interests of its applicants should certainly gain the respect of the public.

Once accepted, you'll find the schools' course schedules are adjusted to fit your needs. Students may attend day or evening sessions; full or part-time programs can be arranged.

Campus life

While few schools sponsor social schedules, there is campus life at some of the schools. You may find student lounges where students gather informally between classes. There are sometimes school-sponsored social and athletic activities such as dances, picnics, bowling leagues and get-togethers. Cafeterias are open for all meals. They generally serve hot food as well as sandwiches.

As for the lifestyle while attending a private vocational school, that depends on what type of environment you want. For those who want the aura of college life, there are schools that have developed campuses complete with dormitories and social activities centers. If it's a residential school, there will probably also be a housing director on hand to arrange and supervise housing for out-of-town students. You may live in school-approved dormitories, or with approved private families in nearby homes. Many schools are adding dormitory facilities, thus drawing students from farther away. Many female students who stay with private families can earn their room, board, carfare, and some spending money in return for baby-sitting and mother's helper duties. Other schools cater to commuters or "day hops." Most of these schools are easy to reach by public transportation.

Remember, for the most part these are cost-conscious schools in rented buildings in urban areas using leased equipment instead of handsome campuses in country settings. There are no summer vacations or frills. As one proprietary school administrator puts it, "If you want a gym, go to the Y."

Job placement

All accredited private schools are required to operate free job placement departments. Part-time placement assistance while in training is usually also offered. Naturally, a school cannot guarantee you employment because individual willingness and ability vary, but most school placement departments report 85 to 95 percent of their graduates go to work in the fields for which they were trained.

The close contacts with employers create mutual trust and give the schools a significant course for their placement of graduates. Often employers will send their representatives to the schools to recruit graduating students.

Many schools have a lifetime placement bureau. This means you can always go through their placement office when looking for another job. Some schools (particularly business schools) charge a fee to the employer while others perform the service free.

You should always ask about the placement service when interviewing the school personnel. If it's a good school usually there is little difficulty in finding a job at graduation time. Schools are often on the personnel lists of businesses and receive calls to send students for interviews. Most schools have more employment inquiries than students to fill the requests. Two business schools said they receive twenty-five calls per graduate! The graduates usually receive higher starting salaries and increased opportunities for promotion once on the job.

A New York electronics school maintains a job placement service supervised by a full-time Placement Administrator. This service is available without charge to all prospective graduates, attending students, and alumni. Prospective graduates are introduced to firms looking for full-time employees. Attending students are given information on part-time employment. Many companies visit the school to interview prospective graduates and may invite students to visit them at their places of business.

At some schools near the end of your course the placement office will send information on your scholastic record and interests to companies throughout the country. This will give you more job openings to consider before making your final choice.

Choosing a school

How can you make the best decision? Take your time! A decision which will affect the entire future course of your life should not be reached overnight. Go over your plans with your high school counselor or principal. They are in the best position to help you obtain the information that you need to reach a decision.

Next, ask several employers in the line of work which you hope to enter to give you the names of schools which offer good training for their trade. Write letters to these institutions asking for information concerning their offerings, requirements, length of course, and tuition. Try to find out from the institution how it is rated by examining or accrediting bodies. Distrust any school that fails to answer your ques-

tions concerning standing or is vague in its answers to other specific questions.

Ask about tuition costs, how much will be needed for books and supplies, and whether the school offers a reimbursement policy if you find that you must drop the course. Read carefully and be sure that you understand all enrollment blanks and applications before signing them. Such blanks sometimes turn out to be promissory notes which bind the signer to pay exorbitant tuition fees even though he may later decide not to attend the school. Consider contract agreements. All states have certain regulations regarding the execution of written contracts or application forms. In some instances, a person under 21 must also have all papers signed by a parent or legal guardian before they become binding. A check with a lawyer regarding the legal aspects of these documents is always advisable. Make sure you understand any contract provisions for cancellation and refunds of fees and tuition. This is particularly important because, if your school sells your contract to a finance company, you will probably have no recourse against the finance company even if the school is no good, or fails to fulfill its part of the contract.

Visit the school. See for yourself what it has to offer. Get someone to visit the school with you who is qualified to judge the type of equipment and facilities and the quality of instruction offered. If you plan to attend school away from home, now is the time to ask about living accommodations. Should the school have dormitories, ask for a tour. If there are none, then inquire about finding a room. Most schools will help you locate one.

Ask the Better Business Bureau whether any complaints have been made against a particular school. Inquire also at the local Chamber of Commerce or the state consumer fraud bureau. Your high school teachers and guidance counselor may also have opinions.

If you are seeking a career in a particular field, do not fail to check on the openings available to you without training. A trade school can be an expensive employment agency if all it really does is to help you gain employment. Many times, if you are interested and have the ability, employers will hire you and give you the training on the job. Contact the personnel director of a firm in the industry you wish to enter and ask for the minimum requirements of job applicants.

To further protect yourself, ask the school to send you the names of former students and employers who have hired them in your area: see what they think of the school. Talk with graduates. Find out if they feel that their training was worthwhile.

Even if you attend a reputable school and finish the course there's no guarantee you will be able to find a job where you live, or that the course will be acceptable to potential employers. It's best to spot check a few employers in advance to see if training such as you are planning would qualify you as a beginner in their companies. Continue to investigate. Even after you are out of high school you may wish to return to your school counselor for help in selecting a school.

And in the event you decide to go on to college after completing a vocational school course, some colleges will accept a certificate from a recognized school for credit toward a bachelor's degree. So, you're a winner, no matter what you decide.

See also pages 77-79 for more information on choosing a school.

School accreditation

How reliable are these schools? Some are; some are not. How can you tell?

Is the school accredited? Accreditation is the process whereby an association or agency grants public recognition to a school as having met certain established qualifications of standards.

If a school is accredited, it means the school has a competent faculty; it offers educationally sound and up-to-date courses; it screens students carefully for admission; it provides satisfactory educational services; it has demonstrated ample student success and satisfaction; its tuition charges are reasonable; it advertises its courses truthfully; and it is financially able to deliver a high quality of education.

Almost all trade schools, public and private, claim some type of accreditation or approval. Some accrediting agencies are responsible, independent agencies which thoroughly evaluate schools seeking approval. Other agencies may be little more than mutual admiration societies which assume little or no control over the quality of the school. Your high school counselor is in a position to help you obtain reliable information about schools you are considering.

Many private trade or correspondence schools are required by law to register with some department of government. It should not be taken for granted that such registration means approval. Again, your counselor may be your best guide.

Thus, when a private trade or correspondence school claims approval or accreditation, this actually holds little meaning for you, the prospective student. The agency granting the accreditation may be reputable, but you should never take that for granted. In fact, the poorer the school, the more likely that it will rely upon impressive-sounding claims of approval or accreditation.

The best private vocational schools are accredited by the National Home Study Council (NHSC) or the National Association of Trade and Technical Schools (NATTS), both recognized by the U.S. Office of Education as official accrediting agencies. See pages 13-14 for a complete list of the accrediting agencies.

Less than half of all states license and regulate private vocational schools and very few of those states carefully supervise the instructional programs offered by the schools. Therefore, a visiting team from a group like the NATTS is the main way of evaluating a school. Such a team would be made up of industry experts who examine the courses' content and instruction in their relevant fields. The school's business practices are examined, including job placement records and student recruitment procedures, especially when a school's representatives are paid on a commission basis. Impressions of students are sought through random interviews. See also pages 10-13 for a full explanation of accreditation and what it means.

Other things you should check

There are many very good private vocational schools. Several universities (including the University of Minnesota and Southern Illinois University) have begun accepting transfer students from approved private vocational schools. In nine states private vocational schools are allowed to confer "associate" degrees. And Congress has authorized grants for financing poor students who enroll in accredited proprietary schools under the Higher Education Act passed in June, 1972.

Most private trade schools are reliable institutions, but some of them are frauds. You should beware, therefore, of magazine advertisments, catalogs and bulletins of schools that make extravagant claims concerning their buildings, equipment, and instruction, and exaggerated statements about the number of persons who, with the proper training, could be placed immediately in lucrative positions.

Do not rely too much upon any unusual promises made by the representatives of these schools. Salesmen sometimes try to rush young people into signing contracts or paying tuition in advance by offering what they call "special bargain rates" or "scholarships" or by flattering their prospects into feeling that they have been recommended to the schools as outstanding students.

Some disreputable institutions guarantee jobs to all who finish the course. They then make the last lessons so difficult that very few students ever succeed in completing them. Others promise to get jobs for their students only so long as they are still enrolled in the school. Those who finish the course are often kept on indefinitely and charged additional tuition by the week or the month with the hope that the school will eventually place them in in good positions. There have been cases in which students who had been guaranteed jobs were "hired" by fake employers and discharged when the school was ready to give the "jobs" to other graduates.

The Federal Trade Commission has now put a stop to the false advertising of certain vocational schools which had been conveying the impression that they prepared students for civil service examinations and they had the inside connections for securing government positions for them.

Although these schools are no longer allowed to use pictures of Uncle Sam, the National Capitol, and other symbols which, by implication, link the school with the United States Government, some of them still imply that they are approved by the government and that those who take the courses will be given special consideration when trying to get civil service jobs. Salesmen who make such promises should be asked to put the promises in writing and to sign the paper.

How to guard against "gyp" schools

To be sure, there are many good private trade schools which are well equipped and prepared to give adequate instruction. But, before you enroll in any school, you should investigate it. Be sure that it will give you enough hours of training to enable you to master the subject. It should have teachers who not only know the subject but also know how to teach it and who give their students individual instruction and explanations. The school should provide modern machinery and equipment in sufficient quantity to serve all the students.

The books used should be neither too difficult nor too simple. Some inferior schools will give a new student a book he cannot understand, assign him to a machine, and expect him to work out his own problems.

If, after carefully considering whether you have the time, the money, the aptitude, and the desire to study a particular trade, you decide that it will be to your advantage to attend a vocational school, you will certainly want to select the school that will give you the best possible training.

Your choice of a trade or correspondence school may be one of the most important decisions you will ever make. Your whole way of life, the kinds of jobs you will hold, the opportunities for advancement, the kinds of people you meet, will be affected by this decision. If you are like many other students who have faced this decision, you will want to avoid the following pitfalls:

1. The salesman who offers you a "substantial" discount on the registration fee or tuition in exchange for an immediate cash payment.

2. The salesman who insists that you make up your mind at once because he is leaving the area and will not return for several months or because he has just one or two openings left.

3. The school which seems reluctant to refer you to its graduates for recommendations.

4. The schools which promise a fabulous career in a glamorous industry after only a few weeks of training.

5. The private correspondence school which promises degrees or diplomas usually granted only by colleges and universities.

6. The sometimes meaningless words: "Registered," "Approved," "Accredited."

7. The school which seems reluctant to allow you visit before making up your mind.

8. The school which makes extravagant claims for placement and employment.

9. The school which does not have a fair refund policy clearly stated in the bulletin.

Finally, once again you can avoid "fly-by-night" schools if you find out whether the school has been approved and accredited by checking its reputation with guidance counselors, state employment services, state office of education, Veterans Administration, and the National Association of Trade and Technical Schools or National Home Study Council, and the lists of accredited private schools. Some states require that private schools be approved by the Office of the Superintendent of Public Instruction. It is wise to check if your chosen school has been approved before enrolling. Ask the local Better Business Bureau or Chamber of Commerce whether any complaints have been received against the school. Ask employers in the field you're going to be trained for what they think of the school.

Private vocational schools will continue to grow in acceptance in the 1970s. They will remain more experimental than public schools in initiating new courses and revising old courses. A private school is flexible enough to expand or revise its services in direct response to students' needs or advice from its instructors.

For more information, write:

Association of Independent Colleges and Schools
1730 M Street, N.W.
Washington, D.C. 20036
Ask for: list of accredited business schools.

National Association of Trade and Technical Schools
2021 L Street, N.W.
Washington, D.C. 20009
Ask for: *Directory of Accredited Private Trade and Technical Schools* (rev.), free.

National Home Study Council
1601 18th Street, N.W.
Washington, D.C. 20009
Ask for: *Directory of Accredited Private Home Study Schools*, free.

Also contact:

For a list of approved schools in your state, write to the State Department of Education in your state or whatever state the school you are considering attending is in.

Home Study

Home study courses are another route to career education. With study by mail you can learn practically anything, including subjects you can't find offered by schools in your area. Many courses provide complete vocational training, others prepare you for upgrading your present job without losing experience and seniority.

There are now over 5,000,000 Americans studying with all types of institutions that offer courses by correspondence.

The enrollment figures are impressive. The largest single operator of correspondence schools, the federal government, has two million students participating: the four branches of the armed forces provide military and technical courses for more than a million officers and enlisted personnel, and the U.S. Armed Forces Institute conducts academic courses from grade school to university level for another 350,000 service men and women. The U.S. Departments of State and Agriculture and several other federal agencies also operate sizable programs.

The 188 accredited private correspondence schools who belong to the National Home Study Council account for a total enrollment of 1,600,000; other private home study schools enroll about 250,000; college and university extension courses enroll about 250,000 students, and thousands more are taking courses conducted by business and industrial firms for their employees. All this makes a goodly number of Americans who choose to study at home at their own pace.

There are two basic types of institutions which offer instruction by correspondence. One type is the college or university which has a correspondence department where students are enrolled to study by mail some of the same courses taught on campus. The same textbook and study outlines are used; the same faculty members read and correct the papers; and often the same exams are given. There are definite entrance requirements.

The other type of institution is the private correspondence school. Altogether there are 700 of these schools which are businesses-operated for profit. Some are old, well-established reliable institutions, while others are diploma-mills or fly-by-night operations. Some offer a great variety of courses, while others specialize in one field, such as photography. Some have definite entrance requirements as to age, aptitude and previous training; while others enroll anyone regardless of his ability to do the work. The

better private schools give entrance exams supervised by respectable officials; the inferior ones give no exams at all.

Subjects taught

There are courses in just about everything: art and cartooning, architectural drawing and design, office management, accounting, highway engineering technology, quality control, warping and weaving, locksmithing, ecology, refrigeration and air conditioning, hotel-motel management, diesel mechanics, real estate brokerage. You name it—there must be a home study course somewhere that teaches it. Through such courses you can learn to repair anything from a transistor radio to a bulldozer.

You can study practically anything: business; skilled trades; preparation for professional licenses; profitable hobbies; and academic subjects. Emphasis is on learning what you need to know to get a job in your chosen field.

For example, you can prepare for a career in the travel industry with either a course from the American Society of Travel Agents (ASTA) or a course from one of several private correspondence schools. The ASTA course features programmed instruction in which you learn by doing. You actually perform such tasks as filling facsimile airline tickets, selecting a cabin from an ocean liner deck plan, and planning a special European Tour for a client from start to finish. The 14-lesson course costs $200 and covers all the responsibilities and duties of a travel agent.

The students

A glance at the enrollment blanks shows that typical home study student is married, has a family, and can't leave his job to go back to school. Correspondence is the only practical way for such students to continue their education. They are men and women who didn't finish school when they were younger; or students who are ambitious but who can't stop working to go to school; or those who need technical or specific training to enter a different trade or profession; or those who want to study subjects not taught in their local schools; or people who live in isolated, rural districts, mountainous regions, or on ranches where there are no regular schools close by.

Also some corporations have contracts with correspondence schools for the training of their employees. Some employers pay all or part of the tuition for those employees who enroll in courses to improve their specific abilities.

Who should and who should not take home study courses

Students who find home study courses rewarding usually have a strong desire to learn, well-defined goals and plans, and a sympathetic and understanding family. They are personally orderly, curious, independent, and realistic about their educational background and aptitudes and expectations.

The fact that not all students are successful at home study courses is indicated by the large number of dropouts before the courses are completed. If you need to be prodded or are in the habit of putting things off, this type of program may not be for you.

What you can expect to learn

With correspondence school courses, the school comes to you. Correspondence school instruction follows the learn-by-doing method that frequently includes materials and equipment at least equivalent to those found in classrooms and labs. New combinations of study-by-mail are continually being developed using mail, TV, radio, and teaching machines. Other innovations are designed to bridge the distance between the school and the student with a personal approach: booklets introducing the faculty members to the students, handwritten corrections on papers, and immediate response to queries are some of the typical methods.

When you enroll in a correspondence school, you receive textbooks, assignments, and lists of questions from the school. Sometimes supplementary books and mimeographed materials are sent to take the place of a library. The assignments usually consist of directions for study and suggestions for reading, preparing reports or solving problems. You follow the instructions and mail your completed lessons to the school. The instructor then looks over your lessons, corrects them, and returns them with his comments.

When the skill being taught requires equipment, such as in electronics, a kit is often furnished giving you practice in assembling a radio or television set as part of the course. Emphasis is on learning what you need to know to do the particular job. Instructional materials in accredited schools are up-to-date, clearly written, and easy to understand. See pages 10-13 and 77-79 for more information.

Studying at home means you won't have to give up your job while you prepare yourself for a better one. You can study at your own pace, reviewing and rereading until you've satisfied yourself. There's usually a quiz after each lesson, and if you have a special problem or question not answered in the test, your instructor will send a complete reply. Quizzes and questions are graded and answered by qualified faculty members.

How much it costs

Home study courses cost anywhere from $100 to $1,000, with the average running about $500 to $700.

Financial aid

Financial aid is available through the G.I. Bill, federally insured student loans and, through time payment plans offered by some schools. See pages 14-24 for more information.

Entrance requirements

The entrance requirements vary, but usually you'll find the average student is at least a high school graduate.

Job placement

Some schools do offer job placement, but you must ask specifically if the school which interests you does so. Sometimes they arrange job interviews, but often the "job placement" just consists of advice on how to go about finding your own job.

The advantages of home study courses

There are several advantages to be found in study by mail. It's usually less expensive than going to a regular school. You can hold down a full-time job and study at your own convenience. You aren't rushed forward or held back by other members of a class, but can progress at your own rate of speed. Each student must prepare every lesson, and so you cover the work more thoroughly than if you were reciting in a class. Subjects that aren't taught in local schools can be taken by correspondence. If you are housebound or miles away from an educational center, a home study course may be your best choice.

All the ingredients of any learning situation are present: the student, the instruction materials, and the instructor. The difference is that communication between teacher and student takes place through the written rather than the spoken word. And each student receives individual attention from the instructor. Studies have shown home study students tend to retain more of what they learn than regular classroom students.

Home study is flexible. It permits you to adjust to the time and place of study. You can complete your course quickly or over an extended period. You can study whenever your time permits and whenever it's convenient—in bed, in the bathtub, or at the kitchen table. You go through the same learning process as students in a classroom, but you set your own pace.

The disadvantages of home study courses

Along with the advantages, there may be drawbacks for you personally. You may have trouble learning without a teacher standing over you, and you'll probably feel the lack of classroom stimulation you personally may need to learn. The periodic deadlines will force you to produce a certain amount of work. You must have the ability to do it without the discussions between teachers and other students. You'll have no chance to participate in classroom discussion—often more helpful to a student than lectures or individual study. You have no bells to mark study periods, libraries to help with reference questions, or contact with other students.

Some correspondence courses are hard for those who don't read well. If you can't express yourself clearly in writing, you'll be at a serious disadvantage in some courses. If you have no aptitude or insufficient background for the particular subject, you'll find it difficult to succeed in home study.

The hardest part of all may be for you to know enough about yourself to be sure you will have the stick-to-it-iveness to finish something you begin. Once you pay money for your course, you'd suffer not only financial loss (usually tuition is not returnable), but a sense of inadequacy in yourself because you started something you didn't finish.

Choosing a correspondence school

If you decide on correspondence study with a private home study school, how do you select a school? You are more likely to be on safe ground if you choose an accredited correspondence school. The National Home Study Council (NHSC) has been designated by the U.S. Office of Education as the recognized accreditation agency for private home study schools. While many nonaccredited schools may be reliable, only 188 of about 700 private correspondence schools in operation at present are accredited. To check on schools that are not accredited, contact your state department of education, local chamber of commerce, Better Business Bureau, or the Veterans Administration.

The NHSC will give you information concerning the particular subjects taught in their member schools, and will also investigate and see that fitting action is taken against any of its member schools reported to be guilty of fraudulent or unethical practices.

It is always wise for you to investigate the school you are considering. Some of the best-known correspondence schools don't deliver what they claim in their advertising copy. In order for you to judge whether a correspondence school will give you what you are looking for, find out how a good one works, what to look for in its description of courses, and what a school should not promise. Then decide if you're apt to get your money's worth. Your guidance counselor can help you with this information and a Better Business Bureau in the area where the school is located will tell you if the school has a record of fraudulent practice.

After you have decided what you want to study, write to three or four schools offering the subject and ask for descriptive information about the courses. Ask for a sample lesson or a part of one. This could help you decide how valuable the courses would be. You can also ask for the names of recent graduates in your area and either call or write them asking their opinions of the courses.

Make comparisons between the schools which give the particular course you want to take. It is well to look for a school that has been in operation for several years, has adequate equipment, uses up-to-date textbooks, and can supply satisfactory references concerning its character. Be suspicious of private correspondence schools that accept anyone for admission without questions or restrictions; those that make impossible promises, extravagant guarantees, and offers of free scholarships and reduced tuition rates; and those that do not provide for refunds of tuition if the course is only partially completed.

Before seriously considering enrolling with a correspondence school, obtain in writing a statement concerning the percentage of students who have actually completed the courses for which they enrolled and also a statement as to the proportion of graduates who have obtained jobs, the kind of jobs, the average salaries, and the length of time they have held the jobs. Do not sign any contract or agreement without reading it through carefully. If you do not thoroughly understand every point in the agreement, ask some competent person to explain it to you.

If you are hoping to qualify for a particular type of job by completing a home study course, check with local employers concerning the merits of the course you are considering.

Be sure you understand clearly the total cost of the course, when payment is due, and exactly what is included before you sign any contract or pay any registration fee. When you sign a contract for a home study course, it is a legally binding contract. Refund policies vary. But all schools belonging to the NHSC must refund money for incompleted lessons. If teaching aids in the form of kits are part of the course, their cost should be included in the overall price for the course. While some schools have arrangements for deferred payment plans, watch out for interest charges—which are likely to be quite high.

Many schools obligate their students to pay the tuition in full whether or not the course is completed, and then furnish lessons so difficult that only a few can master them. Others offer good instruction, but accept students whose backgrounds are such that they cannot hope to understand the work. Some correspondence schools are much more interested in collecting tuition than in helping students to complete their courses. For this reason, you should check carefully on all claims made by school representatives, and have all specific promises in writing. As a further check, consult the Better Business Bureau of the city in which the correspondence school is located. Also write to the NHSC, which was organized to promote fair practices among correspondence schools.

A word of warning about fraudulent correspondence school operations. The Post Office Department finds prosecution of correspondence schools for mail frauds has increased four-fold in the last few years. Con men have set up quickie, learn-by-mail "schools" in states that have no regulations in this field or only minimum license requirements. Don't be taken in by glaring advertising that makes extravagant claims about placement services and refunding money if the student doesn't get a job after finishing the course. No school can guarantee you that!

And after you have chosen your school, enrolled and started your studying, there's something else to keep in mind. Many correspondence students don't really know how much their instructor's comments on their work is supposed to help them. If a school doesn't give enough real guidance to a student in the form of written commentary, telephone conversation, or notes on exams, it can lose its accreditation. But many schools operate on a thin borderline. Be alert to the fact that your school may not be helping you as much as it is supposed to do. If the written comments you receive do not seem to apply to your work or that seem over a period of time to be just lifted from a list of generalized comments, report what is happening to the school's administration, the accrediting association, or the Better Business Bureau.

For more information, write:

Accrediting Commission of the National Home Study School Council
1601 Eighteenth Street, N.W.
Washington, D.C. 20009
Ask for: *Directory of Accredited Private Home Study Schools,* free.

Council of Better Business Bureaus, Inc.
1150 17th Street, N.W.
Washington, D.C. 20036
Ask for: *Tips on Home Study Schools,* publication No. 229, free.

National University Extension Association
Suite 360
1 Dupont Circle, N.W.
Washington, D.C. 20036
Ask for: list of accredited colleges and universities offering extension courses, $.50.

Additional reading:

Jensen, Jo. *College by Mail.* New York: Arco Publishing Co., Inc. 219 Park Avenue South, New York 10003. 1972. 78 pgs. $4.00

Apprenticeships

People can be trained for jobs in many ways. But the oldest and one of the most effective ways of handing down skills from one generation to another is to apprentice young people to a skilled craftsman or mechanic.

Perhaps the most famous apprentice to learn the printing trade was Ben Franklin. In his day, young men who signed on as apprentices had to agree that they would remain single, would not gamble, and would stay away from alehouses. Today, most apprenticeship agreements simply require that you "perform diligently and faithfully the work of said trade or craft."

Apprenticeship is not only a system of learning-by-doing, but of learning-while-earning. It combines day-to-day, on-the-job training with basic technical instruction in the classroom. You start to earn, learn, and work at the same time.

This differs from other on-the-job programs because apprenticeship is based on a formal written agreement with your employer stating the conditions of your training period; length of time, amount of pay, and rate of periodic increases, with certification as a journeyman on completion of the term. You will be qualified as a skilled craftsman and so recognized throughout the industry, wherever you may go, for you will have learned your craft according to that industry's standards.

Apprenticeship is a method of acquiring a skill. It can be a golden opportunity to learn. The U.S. Office of Education says there are about 400,000 persons enrolled in full-time apprenticeship programs; 140,000 of whom also attend school and study related subjects. These students might be apprentice draftsmen who also study blueprint reading; apprentice compositors who take special English courses; or electricians studying math and basic science.

There are more than 350 approved occupations in this country, ranging from bookbinding, printing, and engraving to upholstery and plumbing that accept apprentices. The advantage of such an apprenticeship is that, in the words of Abraham Lincoln, "He who has a craft has a fortune." It means an income that is assured.

The potential is limited only by the mental ability and the ambition of the graduate apprentice. Apprenticeship provides not only many supervisors in our production lines, but also many managers in American business. Surveys have shown many top officials of corporations began their careers as apprentices. Many project managers, superintendents, and foremen also began as apprentices.

On completing your training, you will be a recognized craftsman. If the program in which you have participated is registered with the U.S. Department of Labor's Bureau of Apprenticeship and Training or a recognized state approved agency, you will, on recommendation of the industry, be issued a Certificate of Apprenticeship, attesting to your all-round training.

How apprenticeship operates

Basically an apprentice is taken into a place of business as a beginner; is paid wages; and is taught the basic skills of the trade under the constant supervision of a master craftsman. The fact that the apprentice is paid while learning and that he has an opportunity to learn all phases of the trade is a definite advantage of this type of training.

In 1937, Congress decided that it would be good for the entire country if employers and labor, working as a team, were to establish programs of apprenticeship. Accordingly, a law was passed which, among other things, authorized the Secretary of Labor to set up labor standards that would safeguard the welfare of apprentices, bring management and labor together to formulate apprenticeship programs, cooperate with state agencies interested in starting their own apprenticeship programs, and to publish information relating to apprenticeship standards. The Bureau of Apprenticeship was subsequently established to carry out the objectives of the act and a Federal Committee on Apprenticeship was appointed to develop standards and policies. Today, apprenticeship programs are conducted through the voluntary cooperation of labor, management, schools, and government throughout the country.

The Bureau of Apprenticeship and Training in the Manpower Administration of the Department of Labor and the cooperating state apprenticeship agencies operate through a network of field offices throughout the United States.

Programs registered by the Bureau of Apprenticeship and Training must provide that:

- the starting age of an apprentice is not less than 16
- there is full and fair opportunity to apply for apprenticeship
- selection of apprentices is based on qualifications alone
- there is a schedule of work processes in which an apprentice is to receive training and experience on the job
- the program includes organized instruction designed to provide the apprentice with knowledge in technical subjects related to his trade (a minimum of 144 hours per year is normally considered necessary)
- there is a progressively increasing schedule of wages
- proper supervision of on-the-job training with adequate facilities to train apprentices is insured
- the apprentice's progress, both in job performance and related instruction, is evaluated periodically and appropriate records are maintained
- there is employee-employer cooperation
- successful completions are recognized
- there is no discrimination in any phase of apprenticeship employment and training

The trainer is usually an employer who needs highly skilled workers in his plant or business. The trainer could be a labor organization with an agreement with management to conduct the training under joint auspices. The employer may be in any industry: manufacturing, building and construction, transportation, communications, wholesale and retail, or services, as long as there is a need for highly skilled workers. For many years the Federal Government has been training apprentices in its own shops and plants such as arsenals, printing and engraving establishments, and its several Navy Yards. And the employer must be willing to invest capital and time to obtain this type of worker as part of his regular cost of doing business.

The apprentice is an employee subject to the same rules and policies governing other employees in the firm or organization. He is called an apprentice because he is learning his skill on the job, in a wide range of skills, over a period of at least two years, under a written agreement with his employer, and going to job-related classes at a vocational school. He is usually selected as an apprentice on the basis of what will be required of him to be a skilled worker in a particular occupation. This may mean that he should have a high school education, or a knowledge of math, or ability to use his hands, or special sense of eye or art, or good physical health, or superior intellect. Whichever of these prerequisites he will need depends on the demands of the skill he chooses to learn. A program may be set up for one apprentice or a thousand, depending on the need of the employer.

Joint apprenticeship committees

These are national trade committees representing national organizations. The national committees formulate, with the Bureau of Apprenticeship and Training Assistance, national policies on apprenticeship in the various trades and issue basic standards to be used by affiliated organizations. In many local areas the principal crafts have joint apprenticeship committees of six members, three from management and three from labor. These committee members are responsible for conducting and supervising their crafts' local apprentice programs.

They test, select, and sign up (indenture) the apprentice and register him with the U.S. Department of Labor's Bureau of Apprenticeship and Training, or with the state apprentice agency, if there is one.

They supervise and evaluate the variety and the quality of the apprentice's work experience.

They certify the apprentice as a journeyman after he has satisfactorily completed the apprentice program.

Apprentice programs are closely related to the manpower needs of employers, who train for existing or prospective job vacancies. For a list of careers that accept apprentices, see page 62.

How to choose an apprenticeship

If you are thinking about becoming a craftsman in one of the skilled trades, here are some of the points you should consider. Choosing a trade means taking the measure of a big field. There are more than 350 different trades from which to choose. A wise choice will pay rich dividends in later years.

If you have been accustomed to thinking of apprentices as doing heavy work in industry, and you can't or don't want to do work like that, remember there are many, many choices open to you that involve varying amounts of physical strength. Particularly if you are a girl, remember there are skilled jobs in electronic assembly plants, but also there are service-type apprenticeships as bakers; chefs; dental, optical, or pharmaceutical workers. All require skills learned through apprenticeship.

In choosing a trade, you have access to a variety of occupational material to assist you in making an intelligent choice. Take advantage of the guidance counseling available to you. Aptitude tests are also available in school offices and local employment offices to help you determine your greatest potentialities.

Discuss the selection of a trade with your parents and those of your friends already working in the various trades and occupations. Determine the advantages and problems in the various trades and weigh them against your own abilities and shortcomings. Try to get advice from someone who knows both you and something about the various trades in which you are interested. Generally, the best training is found in any apprenticeship program when the apprentice has curiosity and ambition and the desire to learn.

How to be sure apprenticeship is right for you

How do you know if you would make a good apprentice? A variety of abilities, aptitudes, and personal qualities are looked for when choosing apprentices. No one person is expected to have all of them. They are just clues to placing the right person in the right job.

If you like to tinker with the family car or fix things around the house; if you like to make things or are interested in how they are made; if you enjoy reading about new inventions, you probably have some mechanical ability and should consider entering the skilled trades.

Do you have a high school or vocational school education? Perhaps you studied math, chemistry, physics. Or took industrial or manual arts courses. Or liked drawing or other creative activities. Maybe all of these. Is your health good? Do you have good coordination of hands and eyes? Ability to recognize and match various forms? Finger dexterity? A good memory? A talent for solving problems? Are you ambitious? Will you stay on the job until it is done and learn all you can? Apprenticeship training is not a temporary, short term job. It is the basis of a fine career for life. It is hard work, exacting work, rewarding work.

If you are not sure you are qualified, should you rule out the skilled trades as a career? No. You may have talents of which you are unaware. You should take stock of your particular abilities and aptitudes and seek the help of a qualified counselor to determine your interests and qualifications.

To attract more able young men and women to apprenticeship in the years when they are making career decisions, apprenticeship preparatory courses are given in some high schools, vocational, and technical schools. These acquaint youth with the great opportunities in crafts and trades and give them some theoretical and technical instruction in specific fields.

On-the-job training for six to eight weeks is provided in apprenticeship pre-job programs. The purpose is to introduce potential apprentices to specific skilled trades and to determine their suitability for the particular work involved. When students successfully complete the introductory period, they may continue with placement in regular apprenticeship training programs.

The advantages of apprenticeship

For young persons just starting out in the world of work, apprenticeship has important advantages. It offers an efficient way to learn skills, for the training is planned and organized and is not hit-or-miss.

Training in the skilled trades is good insurance. In addition to opportunities for promotion and steady employment, it gives you something that no one can take away from you: a life-long insured earning capacity which will enable you to hold down a well-paying job in your home town or anywhere else in the country. Skilled hands give the owner a greater feeling of security, in some ways, than money in the bank.

The apprentice earns as he learns, for he is already a worker. And when apprenticeship is completed, he is assured of a secure future and a good standard of living because training is in the crafts where skills are much in demand. Opportunities for employment and advancement open up with the recognition that he is now a skilled craftsman.

Apprenticeship also offers:

- A lasting lifetime skill leading to security and knowing you can always get a good job.

- More exciting creative work will be given to you as a skilled craftsman than to a semiskilled worker.
- Faster upgrading because the apprentice trained skilled worker is always first in line for promotion to higher paying or supervisory jobs.
- Job availability trends in the industrial field are never ending. So long as industry exists, there will be need for skilled workers.
- You may want to go into business yourself someday and you'll be better qualified to do so.

Industry, too, benefits greatly. Out of apprenticeship programs come all-round craftsmen, competent in all phases of their trades and able to work without close supervision because their training has enabled them to use imagination, ability, and knowledge in their work. When changes are made in production, these workers provide the versatility needed for quick adaptation of work components to suit the changing needs. An adequate supply of skilled workers with these qualities is vital to the industrial progress.

Apprenticeship has become a dependable resource to meet industrial needs for both shop supervision and top level staff.

Is it possible to learn a trade without going through so many years of required training? You can learn some aspects of a trade without being enrolled in an apprentice program but you become a registered and recognized skilled craftsman (journeyman) only through apprentice training. There is a big difference in pay and career outlook when you go through this training and learn by progressive steps the right way to work. You'll have a thorough knowledge of your entire craft, not just a part of it—as most semiskilled workers do. There is a trend now toward many apprentices completing their technical instruction in postsecondary institutions and moving toward an associate degree.

Who should and who should not apply

If you're looking for a soft touch, forget an apprenticeship. This isn't an easy job. Apprenticeship is no snap. It demands hard work and the competition is tough. You've got to have the will to see it through. This takes ambition, drive, and courage. Many an apprentice has fallen by the wayside because he sees his buddies making more money right out of high school in jobs with little future.

You can't let this happen to you. The temptation will be to drop out of an apprentice program and get some kind of job that pays more money now. If you want a real career, not just "some kind of job," apprenticeship is for you, but realize in advance you are signing a formal agreement, and it won't always be easy to stick with your part all the way through to the end.

Women as apprentices

In a book on apprentices written as recently as 1958 women were excluded because apprenticeships for women were so rare the author felt there was no point in discussing them. He added that perhaps the nation was beginning to reconsider its longstanding prejudice against women as skilled workers.

Apprenticeship opportunities today are open to boys, girls, and minorities. However, it is only fair to say there have always been more applicants than apprenticeship openings. Therefore, no employer may be out actively advertising for applicants.

Although women are highly competent in many industrial skills in a wide range of occupations, only a minimal proportion (about one percent) of the estimated 400,000 registered apprentices in training are women.

Women today are in more than 60 occupations out of 370 offering apprenticeship training. These include among others: pharmaceutical laboratory technician, gyro repairer, aircraft instrument mechanic, compositor, barber, upholsterer, and dry cleaner. The Women's Bureau of the U. S. Department of Labor is working to interest employers, labor organizations, and prospective trainees in opportunities for women in apprenticeship trades which traditionally have been reserved for men and where the opportunities are new or growing. As a result of this activity, there has been a significant increase in the number of women registered as apprentices in recent years.

What you can expect to learn

On-the-job training is the heart of apprenticeship. Working side by side with skilled craftsmen, under the direct supervision of a foreman or a training director, the apprentice learns all the tricks of the trade under conditions of actual production. He also learns how to get along with the men in his craft.

Training in theory is equally important. Usually this training is called related technical instruction, supplemental instruction, or just related training. Actually, related instruction involves more than theory. It often includes training in reading blueprints and other mechanical drawings, and in actually making them. Many apprenticeships also include instruction in safe working habits and in human relations.

Registered apprenticeships require a minimum of 144 hours per year of related instruction, which amounts to a little more than two hours a week. There are many apprenticeships, however, in which six or eight hours a week of related instruction are considered essential.

Responsibility for providing the necessary instruction rests with the sponsors of the apprenticeship program, usually a joint committee of labor and management. In most cases, related instruction is given at local trade or vocational school either after working hours or during working hours. Otherwise, the apprenticeship sponsors may develop course material and conduct their own related instruction programs, or use the services of private educational consultants.

An increasing number of employers and joint committees are turning to correspondence courses, not only to provide apprentices with related instruction, but also to keep qualified journeymen up-to-date. In all cases, related instruction for the apprentice is part of the apprenticeship agreement, and the apprentice does not pay for it. Sometimes, however, the apprentice will be required to buy a few tools or miscellaneous items for his education and training.

Home study programs are also used to help apprentices who have not graduated from high school to make up their requirements. A number of large corporations are using home study programs to qualify apprentices and other on-the-job trainees for higher education at technical schools, junior colleges, community colleges, and universities. In many cases the cost of the program is borne by the employer.

To show you what related instruction will be offered to you, here's what a catalog for the Bullard-Havens Regional Vocational-Technical School in Bridgeport, Connecticut, lists. There are "Trade Related Subjects Classes for Employed Apprentices." The courses are free and conducted by the State Department of Education. There are opportunities for technical instruction related to the apprentice trade which

the average shop is not equipped to give. The catalog lists evening classes in subjects including Light and Power, Electrical Math, Motor Control, Electrical Code, Barbering, Masonry, Carpentry, Woodworking, Plumbing, Cook and Chef, and Welding.

Apprenticeship is a no-nonsense system. Detailed work and study records are kept, and the training program of the apprentice is evaluated frequently. The length of the training period varies with the occupation, but ranges generally from two to four years.

How much it costs

One of the best things about apprenticeship is that you are paid while you learn. Starting pay is usually 40 to 50 percent of the journeyman's going rate. In most areas it will vary from $2.50 to $5.00 an hour.

More than that, if you make satisfactory progress, you get a raise in pay every six momths, until you are earning about 90 percent of the journeyman's current rate during the last six-month period. And then there are fringe benefits; paid vacations, paid holidays, insurance, hospitalization, and retirement pension plans.

Here's an example of how it works:

Suppose you are a construction trades apprentice in the Washington, D.C. area. The lowest starting wage for apprentices in these trades is $3.50 an hour.

Let's say you have selected a trade which pays $7 an hour to the finished craftsman. The apprenticeship requires four years. The following tables show what you could be earning during each six-month period as you move ahead:

Training Period	Weekly Pay	6-Month Total
First 6 months	$140	$3,640
Second 6 months	155	4,030
Third 6 months	170	4,420
Fourth 6 months	185	4,810
Fifth 6 months	220	5,200
Sixth 6 months	215	5,590
Seventh 6 months	230	5,980
Eighth 6 months	250	6,500
		$40,170

Now, $40,170 is not a small sum to earn while you learn in a four year apprenticeship program. This figures out to $10,000 a year.

For eligible veterans there is an additional pleasant financial twist. The Vietnam ERA Veterans Readjustment Assistance Act of 1970 provides the following:

Regardless of the wages paid by the employer, VA's monthly training assistance allowance to a veteran pursuing a full-time approved apprenticeship is as follows:

Periods of Training	No dependents	One dependent	Two or more dependents
First 6 months	$160	$179	$196
Second 6 months	120	139	156
Third 6 months	80	99	116
Fourth & any succeeding 6-month period	40	59	76

After completing a four year construction trades apprenticeship, you could be making an average of $280 a week as a journeyman at present rates of pay, not including overtime and not counting other fringe benefits.

The national average journeyman rate for 30 trades (building and construction, metal, foundry, printing and automotive) comes to $15,454 a year, while an apprentice starts at about $8,500 a year.

Also, an apprentice starting out now with one of America's largest automobile manufacturers in any one of eight major occupational categories (mostly metal trades) would earn an average of $12,480 as a journeyman.

It has been found that the graduate apprentices (journeymen) will not only maintain full employment, but are the ones picked for many overtime hours and faster promotions. A survey in the Painting and Decorating industry showed that at the end of ten years, a graduate apprentice was earning 25 percent more than an average journeyman and 75 percent more than an untrained journeyman. The apprentice started out earning far less than the other two men, but once he graduated and had his certificate, he quickly passed them and stayed well ahead.

How to apply for an apprenticeship

The first step in search of an apprenticeship should be a visit to the local state employment office, which is well-equipped to help you. It has information on any apprenticeship employment opportunities in the local area, elsewhere in the state, and in other states; current requirements for various apprenticeships; current pay; working conditions; and advancement opportunities in particular skills.

Through its testing and counseling services the office can help you estimate your own capabilities for a particular apprenticeship; and, it can help you obtain an apprenticeship that will meet the requirements of the U.S. Bureau of Apprenticeship and Training. If you can't get all the information you need from your state employment service office, then get in touch with the nearest field office of the U.S. Bureau of Apprenticeship and Training.

If you're interested in an apprenticeship, then try these sources:

Is your mother or father employed by a company that has an apprenticeship program? If so, it's possible that you can apply for apprenticeship training in the same plant.

The U.S. Bureau of Apprenticeship and Training regional office (listed on pages 59-60). For the local office near you, consult your telephone book.

The Apprenticeship Information Centers (listed on pages 60-62). In many labor market areas, these centers have been set up. Used by thousands of young people, the centers are operated by the state employment services and provide a wide range of information on apprenticeship and also counsel applicants. The centers can tell you which programs have openings and when the entrance tests will be given. In addition the centers prescreen applicants for referral to employers, unions, and the local joint apprenticeship and training committees for final selection of the youth to receive training.

The Director of Vocational Education in your town school office, your high school, or community college.

The nearest state employment service office (consult your telephone book). No charge for counseling help.

The Urban League in your city.

A business firm that has workers in the trade in which you are interested. See potential employers personally.

The local union that represents the trade in which you are interested.

Any friends you may have in the skilled trades.

How you are chosen to become an apprentice

Apprentices are chosen in accordance with the provisions of the written apprenticeship program for each local plan or trade. Usually there are more applicants seeking jobs than there are openings to be filled. Apprenticeship openings are limited to the number of apprentices who can be assured employment after completing their training. Sons and daughters of workers in a trade or industry are chosen first if they are qualified. Other apprentices are usually selected from those applicants registered at the local office of the state employment service. Applicants for some trades are given aptitude tests to better determine their fitness as well as predict how well they will do in the particular trade.

The requirements for apprentices vary somewhat from place to place and from industry to industry. Here are the general requirements you must present to the Joint Apprenticeship Committee.

1. You must be between the ages of 17 and 26 (veterans may add their years of service to the 26-year limit).

2. You must be in good physical condition, capable of performing the work of the trade. You must have more than average ability to work with your hands and your head, and be good at both.

3. Some trades require a high school diploma or its equivalent. Other trades prefer it, but don't insist on it. Sometimes an industry will recognize that some specific knowledge you have is sufficient for entry to their apprentice program.

4. You may be required to have better than average mechanical aptitude to suit your chosen trade.

5. You must have good moral character as proven by your letter of recommendation. You must have perseverance, ambition, and initiative.

6. You must agree to remain with the employer until you have finished your apprenticeship.

7. You must agree to do the outside studying necessary to learn whatever related subjects are needed in your trade.

8. You must pass an entrance test.

Assistance to help pass entrance tests is being offered to those who may not have all the necessary background. This help is being offered in most of the big cities through such organizations as the local AFL-CIO building and construction trades council, the Urban League, Worker's Defense League, and other community action agencies.

If you want to be an electrician, for instance, and you don't think your high school studies are good enough to let you pass the math and physics questions, check with the building trades council or the Urban League or the Apprenticeship Information Center or your local employment service office. They will have information about attending one of the special four week courses conducted to prepare applicants for apprenticeships tests as openings for electrician apprentices become available.

The country has become increasingly aware that many Americans are being left out of the main areas of employment because they are disadvantaged or members of minority groups or are women. To help you make your way into the skilled crafts and trades, federal regulations on nondiscrimination in apprenticeship and training have been put into effect by the U.S. Secretary of Labor. There are set policies and procedures for equality of opportunity—without regard to race, color, national origin, sex, or occupationally irrelevant physical requirements—in apprentice programs registered with the U.S. Bureau of Apprenticeship and Training. State apprenticeship agencies have adopted similar policies.

More than regulations are needed. Youth in disadvantaged groups often know little about apprenticeships and have to find openings or how to pass entrance exams. To meet these needs, "Outreach" programs have been formed to inform and prepare interested youth. The programs operate under the Manpower Development and Training Agency and are carried forth by private, interested groups, such as the building and construction trades councils of the AFL-CIO, the Worker's Defense League, the Urban League, the United Automobile Aerospace and Agricultural Implement Workers of America (UAW), the Negro Trade Union Leadership Council and others. A very successful program now established in twenty cities is called the Recruitment and Training Program. It recruits apprentices and offers tutoring and counseling services, and assistance to minority contractors. In the past five years it has recruited 5,000 apprentices in highly skilled trades. There are more minority group members in the construction trade than any other.

Another program has been backed by the Women's Bureau and the Bureau of Apprenticeship and Training, both of the U.S. Department of Labor, to stimulate and encourage women to serve in apprenticeship programs. Though apprenticeships are open to men and women, some unions are hesitant about hiring women for a number of reasons; they may not stay on the job after marriage; they may not complete the apprenticeship program; they may not be able physically to do the work.

The future of this type of program

The apprenticeship system has grown up with America. Like America, it is still growing and changing. Today it serves a far different nation from the one of pioneer days. To meet the needs for changes in production methods and products, apprenticeships have been set up in new trades, and those in older trades have been updated. Increasing numbers of women in apprenticeship reflect some of our changing attitudes about whose hands may do our skilled work.

Because of rapid changes in our industrial systems, we need a large body of skilled workers who are able to carry out technical specifications and who can supervise less skilled members of the work force.

National projections of the number of skilled workers we will need prepared by the Bureau of Labor Statistics, U.S. Department of Labor, shows a rise in the number of skilled workers from 9.2 million in 1965 to 11.4 million by 1975.

Apprenticeship has proven over the years to be one of the best ways of training skilled craftsmen that has ever been devised.

In time of economic depression, all workers suffer. But a smaller proportion of skilled workers lose their jobs than is the case with unskilled or semiskilled workers. This has been true in the past and the outlook for the future is entirely in favor of skilled workers.

Apprenticeship lays a foundation on which you can build according to your own ability and your determination to get ahead. Don't forget that many of the key men in today's industry started as apprentices.

For more information, write:

Bureau of Apprenticeship and Training
Manpower Administration
U.S. Department of Labor
Washington, D.C. 20210
Ask for: *The National Apprenticeship Program,* 1972 (rev.) free. *Apprenticeship, Past and Present,* 1971, free.

Manpower Administration
U.S. Department of Labor
Washington, D.C. 20210
Ask for: *Jobs for Which Apprenticeships Are Available,* and *Veterans! Train for a Skilled Trade Through Apprenticeship,* both free.

U.S. Superintendent of Documents
U.S. Government Printing Office
Washington, D.C. 20402

Ask for: *Apprentice Training: Sure Way to a Skilled Craft,* U.S. Department of Labor. Manpower Administration. 1973 (rev.) Stock Number 2906–00006, $.20. *Skilled Trades for Girls,* Women's Bureau, Wage and Labor Standards Administration, U.S. Department of Labor.

Also contact:

When looking for a regional office of a federal agency in your local phone book, look up listings under U.S. Government—U.S. Department of Labor.

When contacting a regional office of the U.S. Bureau of Apprenticeship and Training, mention the trade in which you are interested and ask about the opportunities for training in your vicinity. Ask for names of firms in your area that have apprenticeships training programs. Then, write to those firms and ask for detailed information.

U. S. Bureau of Apprenticeship and Training

Bureau of Apprenticeship and Training
Manpower Administration
U.S. Department of Labor
Washington, D.C. 20210

Regional Offices:

Location	States Served	
Region I		
John F. Kennedy Federal Bldg., Room 1703-A Government Center Boston, Massachusetts 02203	Connecticut Maine Massachusetts	New Hampshire Rhode Island Vermont
Region II		
1515 Broadway, 37th Floor New Yori, N.Y. 10036	New Jersey New York	Puerto Rico Virgin Islands
Region III		
P. O. Box 8796 Philadelphia, Pa. 19101	Delaware Maryland Pennsylvania	Virginia West Virginia
Region IV		
1371 Peachtree Street, N.E. Room 700 Atlanta, Ga. 30309	Alabama Florida Georgia Kentucky	Mississippi North Carolina South Carolina Tennessee
Region V		
300 South Wacker Drive, 13th Floor Chicago, Illinois 60606	Illinois Indiana Michigan	Minnesota Ohio Wisconsin
Region VI		
1512 Commerce Street, Room 704 Dallas, Texas 75201	Arkansas Louisiana New Mexico	Oklahoma Texas
Region VII		
Federal Office Bldg. Room 2107 911 Walnut Street Kansas City, Mo. 64106	Iowa Kansas	Missouri Nebraska

Location	*States Served*	
Region VIII		
Republic Bldg., Room 232A	Colorado	South Dakota
1612 Tremont Place	Montana	Utah
Denver Colo. 80202	North Dakota	Wyoming
Region IX		
450 Golden Gate Avenue, Room 9001	Arizona	Hawaii
P. O. Box 36017	California	Nevada
San Francisco, Calif. 94102		
Region X		
Arcade Plaza Building, Room 2055	Alaska	Oregon
1321 Second Avenue	Idaho	Washington
Seattle, Wash. 98101		

Apprenticeship Information Centers

1816 Eighth Avenue, North
Birmingham, Alabama

438 West Adam Street
Phoenix, Arizona

555 Pennsylvania Avenue, N.W.
District of Columbia

321 South State Street
Chicago, Illinois

737 Washington Street
Gary, Indiana

141 West Georgia Street
Indianapolis, Indiana

150 Des Moines Street
Des Moines, Iowa

1309 Topeka Avenue
Topeka, Kansas

402 E. Second Street
Wichita, Kansas

1100 North Eutaw Street
Baltimore, Maryland

408 South Huntington Avenue
Boston, Massachusetts

8600 Woodward Avenue
Detroit Michigan

917 Plymouth Avenue, North
Minneapolis, Minnesota

390 North Robert Street
St. Paul, Minnesota

1411 Main Street
Kansas City, Missouri

505 Washington Avenue
St. Louis, Missouri

558 Federal Street
Camden, New Jersey

1004 Broad Street
Newark, New Jersey

301 Graham Avenue
Paterson, New Jersey

119 West Chippewa Street
Buffalo, New York

255 West 54th Street
New York, New York

108 E. Seventh Street
Cincinnati, Ohio

779 Rockwell Avenue
Cleveland, Ohio

239 South Fourth Street
Columbus, Ohio

1030 N.E. Couch Street
Portland, Oregon

1221 North Broad Street
Philadelphia, Pennsylvania

915 Penn Avenue
Pittsburgh, Pennsylvania

72 Pine Street
Providence, Rhode Island

1295 Poplar Avenue
Memphis, Tennessee

301 James Robertson Parkway
Nashville, Tennessee

2613 Austin Street
Houston, Texas

904 Granby Street
Norfolk, Virginia

609 East Main Street
Richmond, Virginia

515 Thomas Street
Seattle, Washington

State Apprenticeship Agencies
(including the District of Columbia,
Puerto Rico, and the Virgin Islands)

Arizona
Arizona Apprenticeship Council
1623-B West Adams
Phoenix 85007

California
Division of Apprenticeship Standards

Department of Industrial Relations
455 Golden Gate Avenue
P.O. Box 603
San Francisco 94102

Colorado
Apprenticeship Council
Industrial Commission Offices
200 East Ninth Avenue, Room 216
Denver 80203

Connecticut
Apprentice Training Division
Labor Department
200 Folly Brook Boulevard
Wethersfield 06109

Delaware
State Apprenticeship and Training Council
Department of Labor and Industry
618 North Union Street
Wilmington 19805

District of Columbia
D.C. Apprenticeship Council
555 Pennsylvania Avenue, N.W.
Room 307
Washington 20212

Florida
Bureau of Apprenticeship
Division of Labor
State of Florida Department of Commerce
Caldwell Building
Tallahassee 32304

Hawaii
Apprenticeship Division
Department of Labor and Industrial Relations
825 Mililani Street
Honolulu 96813

Kansas
Apprentice Training Division
Department of Labor
401 Topeka Boulevard
Topeka 66603

Kentucky
Kentucky State Apprenticeship Council
Department of Labor
Frankfort 40601

Louisiana
Division of Apprenticeship
Department of Labor
State Capitol Annex
P.O. Box 44063
Baton Rouge 70804

Maine
Maine Apprenticeship Council
Department of Labor and Industry
State Office Building
Augusta 04330

Maryland
Maryland Apprenticeship and Training Council
Department of Labor and Industry

203 East Baltimore Street
Baltimore 21202

Massachusetts
Division of Apprentice Training
Department of Labor and Industries
State Office Building
Government Center
100 Cambridge Street
Boston 02202

Minnesota
Division of Voluntary Apprenticeship
Department of Labor and Industry
110 State Office Building
St. Paul 55110

Montana
Montana State Apprenticeship Council
1331 Helena Avenue
Helena 59601

Nevada
Nevada Apprenticeship Council
Department of Labor
Capitol Building
Carson City 89701

New Hampshire
New Hampshire Apprenticeship Council
Department of Labor
State House Annex
Concord 03301

New Mexico
New Mexico Apprenticeship Council
Labor and Industrial Commission
1010 National Building
505 Marquette, NW
Albuquerque 87101

New York
Bureau of Apprentice Training
Department of Labor
The Campus, Building No. 12
Albany 12226

North Carolina
Division of Apprenticeship Training
Department of Labor
Raleigh 27602

Ohio
Ohio State Apprenticeship Council
Department of Industrial Relations
220 Parsons Avenue, Room 314
Columbus 43215

Oregon
Apprenticeship and Training Division
Oregon Bureau of Labor
Room 115, Labor and Industries Building
Salem 97310

Pennsylvania
Pennsylvania Apprenticeship and Training Council
Department of Labor and Industry
Room 1547

Labor and Industry Building
Harrisburg 17120

Puerto Rico
Apprenticeship Division
Department of Labor
414 Barbosa Avenue
Hato Rey 00917

Rhode Island
Rhode Island Apprenticeship Council
Department of Labor
235 Promenade Street
Providence 02908

Utah
Utah State Apprenticeship Council
Industrial Commission
431 South 6th East
Room 225
Salt Lake City 84102

Vermont
Vermont Apprenticeship Council
Department of Industrial Relations
State Office Building
Montpelier 05602

Virginia
Division of Apprenticeship Training
Department of Labor and Industry
P.O. Box 1814
9th Street Office Building
Richmond 23214

Virgin Islands
Division of Apprenticeship and Training
Department of Labor
Christiansted, St. Croix 00820

Washington
Apprenticeship Division
Department of Labor and Industries
314 East 4th Avenue
Olympia 98504

Wisconsin
Division of Apprenticeship and Training
Department of Labor, Industry and Human Relations
Box 2209
Madison 53701

Career Apprenticeships

These are some of the occupations listed with the U.S. Bureau of Apprenticeship and Training and the state agencies. The number of years listed for each applies to the usual term of apprenticeship, with variations depending upon the particular industry and its requirements.

The trades listed here are only the basic classifications. You'll find many additional jobs within each classification. This list is by no means final or complete. It changes constantly, and you must check with your Apprenticeship Information Center for the most up-to-date information.

Trade	Years
Aircraft Fabricator	3
Airplace Mechanic	3–4
Arborist	3
Asbestos Worker	4
Automotive Body Builder-Repairman-automobile manufacturing	3–4
Automotive Mechanic	3–4
Baker	3
Barber	2
Blacksmith	4
Boilermaker	4
Bookbinder	2–4
Brewer	2–3
Bricklayer	3
Butcher-Meatcutter	3
Cabinetmaker-Millman	3–4
Candy Maker	4
Canvas Worker	3
Carman	4
Carpenter	4
Cement Mason	3
Cook	3
Cooper	4
Cosmetician	2
Dairy Products Maker	2–3
Draftsman-Designer	3–5
Dry Cleaner	3–4
Electrical Worker	4–5
Electroplater	3–4
Electrotyper	5–6
Engraver	4–5
Fabric Cutter	3–4
Farm Equipment Mechanic	3–4
Floor Coverer	3–4
Foundryman	2–4
Furrier	3–4
Glazier-Glass Worker	2–4
Heat Treater	4
Iron Worker	2–4
Jeweler	2–4
Lather	2–3
Lead Burner	5
Leather Worker	3–4
Lithographer	4–5
Machinist	4
Mailer	4–5
Maintenance Mechanic Repairman	3–4
Marking-Device Maker	2–3
Mattress Maker	2–3
Metal Polisher-and-Buffer	3–4
Miller	4
Millwright	4
Model Maker	4
Musical Instrument Mechanic	3–4
Operating Engineer	3–4
Optical Technician	4
Orthopedic-Prosthetic Technician	3–4
Paint Maker	3–4
Painter and Decorator	2–4
Patternmaker	5

Trade	Years
Photoengraver	5–6
Photographer	3
Plasterer	3–4
Plate Printer	4
Plumber-Pipefitter	4–5
Pottery Worker	3
Printing Pressman	3–5
Rigger	2
River Pilot	3
Roofer	2–3
Rotogravure Engraver	5–6
Sheet Metal Worker	3–4
Sign, Scene and Pictorial Artist	3–4
Silversmith	3–4
Stationary Engineer	3–4
Stereotyper	5–6
Stone Worker	2–3
Stonemason	3
Stone Mounter	3
Tailor	4
Telephone Worker	4
Terrazzo Worker	3
Textile Technician Mechanic	3–4
Tile Setter	3
Tool and Die Maker	4–5
Upholsterer	3–4
Wallpaper Craftsman	4–5
Wire Weaver	3–4
Wood Carver	3–5

Cooperative Programs (Work-Study)

A cooperative program is a work-study arrangement between your school and your employer- giving you both instruction in required academic courses and related vocational instruction and experience. You alternate study in school with on-the-job training in your occupational field. These two experiences must be planned and supervised by your school and employer so each contributes to your education and employability. Work periods and school attendance may be on alternate half-days, full-days, weeks, or other periods of time agreed upon which fulfill the cooperative vocational education work-study program. On-the-job training may be provided by government agencies, trade unions, or reliable private enterprises.

Cooperative programs are most effective in teaching completely relevant skills. Co-op education contains elements of apprenticeship training and on-the-job experience along with classroom work in related subject matter. You can immediately apply what you learn in the classroom to actual job conditions.

LaGuardia College, a new community college of the City University of New York, is the first community college in the country to offer work-study programs to all of its 524 students. The cooperative program holds a great attraction for the students. A business administration major says, "This is such a good break for us. We can get a chance to see what a job is like so we won't make mistakes later on."

LaGuardia's academic year is set up on the basis of four semesters, each lasting thirteen weeks. All freshmen are in the classroom for the first two semesters, then alternate a semester of work and a semester of classes for the rest of their stay. A cooperative education department locates jobs for students connected with their field of interest. In this way students can earn money and at the same time see what life in the practical working world is like.

A cooperative work-study program will help you support yourself or pay your school expenses. At the same time it enriches your experiences and may help in making your career choice. Your salary is paid by your off-campus employer. See pages 20-21 for more information on the financial side of work-study programs.

Some of the cooperative education projects are designed specially to serve minority groups. For example, Hostos Community College in New York City serves mostly Puerto Rican and black students. In its cooperative education program this school fills jobs in the health sciences that lead to paraprofessional status.

At Seminole Junior College in Oklahoma, the school's many Indian students assists the community in its transition from an agriculturally supported to a semi-industrial economy.

Two hundred employees of Mount Sinai Hospital in Manhattan are enrolled in a college credit program planned by the hospital and City University of New York to help students advance to specialized, better paying jobs in the health field. Courses are given by CUNY's Borough of Manhattan Community College.

Classes meet at the hospital at the end of the work day so that enrollees can avoid extra travel time. Freshmen courses in liberal arts and science—English, speech and mathematics—are scheduled for the first semester. As the program continues, students have a choice of more technical subjects. They are preparing for jobs now available at Mount Sinai as medical secretaries, registered nurses, medical record technologists, and accountants.

There is a new two-year educational program, providing retail employees with an associate degree in business at Purdue University, Lafayette, Indiana. The program, which could lead to a bachelor's degree, is designed to fulfill the needs of Indiana retailers. The curriculum has been set up according to the advice of educators and retailing consultants. The purpose of the courses is to give students skills they can use in the retailing field. Retailers are cooperating by giving jobs to students to work part-time as they study.

In all cooperative programs the key is the vital combination of school and work.

How good is it? The National Advisory Council on Vocational Education reports that cooperative education had the best record of all vocational education programs in terms of the preparation of students placed in occupations for which they were trained.

For more information, write:

Cooperative Education Association
Drexel University
Philadelphia, Pennsylvania 19104
Ask for: *Directory of Cooperative Education: Its Philosophy and Operation in Participating Colleges in the United States and Canada,* January, 1973. $6.00.

Industry Training Programs

Job training within industry ranges from the most casual form of pick-up training to highly structured apprentice programs. This section covers industrial training other than apprenticeships.

Today most large corporations like Sperry Rand, IBM, Portland Cement, Caterpillar Tractor, and Eastman Kodak have training and development programs of their own. One survey shows that $30 billion are spent yearly by industry in education and training of employees. This has come about because management in most cases has realized they could not expect efficiency and good productivity from untrained personnel assigned to operate expensive and sophisticated equipment. In other words, a company which has complicated automated equipment needs trained workers to make it go. American industry can be profitable only with systematically operated job training that turns out skilled workers. These workers are more flexible and adaptable to changes and have fewer accidents, higher productivity records, and are less apt to change jobs.

Job training given by industry has changed. It used to be that as an employee taking job training you were taught only how to do a particular job. Today you are more apt to learn not only how to do it but why. You are no longer locked into a particular dead-end type of job, but rather your training will give you the chance to move either up the ladder or the chance to do different types of work at the same level of ability.

Unlike apprenticeships, there is no formal written agreement between employer and employee and no certificate is awarded.

Job training in industry covers those training techniques which are worker oriented, not management or supervisor oriented, and are done during the regular working hours of occupation, and for which a minimum or beginning wage is paid. This definition includes an array of job training techniques used within private industry, one of which is on-the-job training.

The training can range in time anywhere from 80 hours or two working weeks or more. It may be in informal sessions with a foreman or formal sessions with a company trainer, for a semiskilled worker, or to train a skilled worker requires more than 80 hours to complete. This can also be done informally or formally.

Industry uses job training to train a newly employed worker, to change an existing employee to another position, to promote a worker, to produce and service a new product, to initiate a new manufacturing procedure, or to increase safety. One place where job training is essential is in teaching employees to cope with the manufacturing and maintenance of new equipment. "For UAW craft members," one report states, "the skills required by new and changing technologies have started to take shape ... For example, computer programmed operation, numerically controlled machines, and technologically affected maintenance systems are becoming fact rather than conversation in a growing number of plants and shops ... industrial robots present immediate challenges to, for example, maintenance skills."

Because workers today are just as interested in nonfinancial rewards from work as financial rewards, industry has found increased productivity is based on more than just job knowledge and pay.

The new look to industrial job training means you are quite likely to be taught: human relations (causes of human behavior, individual differences, performance and abilities, development through training, motivation, individual company goals, solving the problems of frustration, attitudes and understanding them, seeking help through counseling, importance of group attitude, communicating, responding to leadership); health related information (personal hygiene, proper diet, adequate sleep, drugs, diagnosis and care of specific diseases, recreation, family planning and housing); financial-legal (family budgeting, consumer buying, borrowing, living and working within the law, and legal service); job related factor orientation (transportation, safety and security measures, identification badge, company history and philosophy, description of company regulations and policies, union contract, absenteeism, chain of command, orientation to work environment, and worker benefits); labor information (seniority provision, job classification, licensing in specifics, occupations, collective bargaining and grievance procedures); specific job content (use of manuals, safety, job environment orientation and specific skill needed for job.)

Upgrading your job through retraining is also possible through industry training. Once you are employed, many companies have regular programs to help their employees climb the job ladder. AT&T has 139 standardized training courses with instructional material, text material, instructors' guides and exercises geared to specific job requirements.

Many companies give you an opportunity for self-development by supplying tuition aid to all employees who take correspondence courses or attend night school.

Another type of job training you may find in your area is a program whereby industry and local schools combine to give job training courses to those either newly hired or already employed. The City Colleges of Chicago, which are free public community colleges, offer a series of job training courses developed by 260 local industries and educators and planned for the urban student. They run from four to eight weeks and cover the fields of health occupations, civil technology, public service, and commercial training. Under this type of program you can work and at the same time study operating room technology, medical secretarial skills, child care, airline baggage handling, air-conditioning and refrigeration, highway engineering, motor fleet supervision, law enforcement, air pollution control and many other occupations.

Private hospitals in their trend toward modernization have become good places to look for job training. Dozens of new categories of jobs are being created (see pp. 266-293) and in order to provide people to fill these new jobs and to provide better qualified people for already existing jobs, hospitals have become involved in teaching. Up till a few years ago the only training a hospital offered was internships for doctors and schools for nurses. The new training tends to be formalized either at the hospital or a nearby public school. One hospital gives a four-week course for nurses' aides and a five-week course for ward clerks. Some hospitals will take people without high school diplomas. The training is all free. The best programs are those which include practical training and academic instruction that will equip a person who has the ability to advance as far as possible in hospital work. The purpose is to eliminate dead-end jobs.

One of the most exciting ventures in training hospital personnel involves about fifteen metropolitan hospitals and the City Colleges of Chicago. The program, called Allied Health, has as its basic course a noncredit, 28-week program for aides. Students take fourteen weeks of courses in basic medical concepts, nursing arts, communications, and basic science at the college.

They then spend fourteen weeks at local hospitals, receiving clinical training in one of ten specialized fields ranging from community health to psychiatric and transfusion therapy.

Upon graduation from the program, trainees are ready to be hired by hospitals as aides and are quickly employed.

The program is geared toward movement. Administrators hope that those who have been graduated from the 28-week course will become more specialized by going back to take longer courses while earning money as aides. The longer courses also offer transferable credit so that a person who wants to change his specialty can do so.

Suppose you want to become an insurance agent. Most insurance companies offer job training. For example, Nationwide Insurance requires two and a half years of free formal classes and on-the-job training for its agents. Intensive and exhaustive, it equips an agent to pass required state and federal licensing tests. The training is professional and once the man or woman qualifies as an agent, he or she has numerous continuing educational opportunities open to him through the company.

Where will you get your training? Some industries use the actual production line as the only training facility. Other industries use a classroom plus a simulation of the production line to give on-the-job training. Some companies use the facilities at nearby schools. Many of the larger industrial corporations have set up sophisticated lectures and laboratory facilities for job training. They might also use audio-visual and electronic equipment and programmed instruction.

How much does it cost the company to train you? No one knows for sure, but it probably ranges from $300 per trainee for a semiskilled worker to well over $1,000 for a skilled worker. The wages paid while you are learning do not cover the cost of teaching you the job.

There are some advantages to job training. You have the feeling of realism—the atmosphere and discipline of the world where you will actually be working is right there. That's often hard or impossible to duplicate in a classroom. Training can take as long as it takes you to catch on. You can repeat the steps as often as you need without being held to a set class period schedule of weeks or semesters or years.

On the other hand a distinct disadvantage is that you will not receive as broad an education as you would in a regular vocational school situation. Your training will be for a specific job in line with the company's needs.

To find out what programs might be available in your area, go to your state employment office. They will have listings of companies who offer industry training and can help you apply. You might also inquire at hospitals, banks, telephone company or any place else you'd like to work. Guidance counselors or your local trade or technical institute, community college, or your high school may also have programs to suggest.

Programs for the Handicapped

According to the U.S. government definition, "handicapped persons" means mentally retarded, hard of hearing, deaf, speech impaired, visually handicapped, seriously emotionally disturbed, crippled, or other health impaired persons who because of their handicapped condition cannot succeed in a vocational or consumer and homemaking education program designed for persons without handicaps, and who for that reason require special educational assistance or a modified vocational or consumer and homemaking education program.

Rehabilitation is a public service designed to develop and restore the working usefulness of handicapped individuals to the point where they may become self-supporting. Our public vocational rehabilitation program is a state-federal partnership with state vocational rehabilitation agencies in each state providing vocational rehabilitation services directly to their handicapped clients. Each state vocational rehabilitation agency maintains local offices throughout the state, usually in larger cities and at institutions and facilities at which they operate special vocational rehabilitation programs.

You are eligible for help if you have a physical or mental disability; if you have a substantial handicap to employment; and if there is reasonable expectation that giving you vocational rehabilitation services will make you employable. Just being disabled doesn't in itself make you eligible for vocational rehabilitation.

When you apply for vocational rehabilitation, you will be given a thorough diagnostic study which includes a comprehensive evaluation of the medical, psychological, vocational, educational, cultural, social, and environmental factors in your particular case. The counselor who is assigned to you arranges for the study as well as an evaluation of your personality, intelligence level, educational achievement, work experience, vocational aptitudes and interests, personal and social adjustment, employment opportunities, and anything else which might be helpful in determining both your eligibility for vocational school and the kind of vocational rehabilitation in which you should participate.

Once the agency determines you are elibible, you will receive services such as the following:

1. Counseling and guidance in laying out a plan for you to achieve good vocational adjustment.

2. Physical restoration to correct, reduce or remove a physical or mental condition which is stable or slowly progressive. This includes such things as dental treatment or surgical services, speech therapy, hearing aids, and many other needs.

3. Training:

Personal adjustment training to help you acquire personal habits, attitudes and skills needed so that you can function effectively in a vocation in spite of your disability; *Prevocational training* to get you ready for specific training or work opportunities by using actual or simulated work tasks in a special sheltered workshop, or in a school or community work situation, for periods of training or work experience. This includes remedial education in such areas as reading or mathematics; *Vocational training* arranged for you at the school or in specialized rehabilitation centers including sheltered workshops and adjustment centers in the community, full-time or part-time, in either formal vocational classes or on-the-job training.

4. Maintenance might include lunches, community work assignments, or other help should you be unable to get it from home or at school.

5. Placement includes job placement activities and counseling with both you and your employer to be sure a job will be satisfactory to you both.

6. Followup to help you get along in your job.

7. Transporation when you need it or other services listed by your counselor under your personal plan.

8. Reader services for the blind and interpreter services for the deaf.

9. Services to members of your family if it could help your rehabilitation.

10. Other goods and services necessary to make you employable, e.g., tools, equipment, and licenses for work on a job or in establishing a small business of your own.

How you benefit

These services are provided at public expense to meet your individual needs so that you may work at a safe and suitable occupation.

Many physical and mental handicaps can be removed through vocational rehabilitation services. Others may be corrected to the point where they do not interfere with work demands of properly selected jobs.

The success of the rehabilitation program

If you can attain paid employment, the program has been judged successful for you. More than 300,000 people are rehabilitated into employment each year.

It is no longer enough for any person entering the labor force to be able and willing to work. The premium today is on education and training. This is even more so for the handicapped. There is a need to stay in school longer and obtain the highest training and education possible. Even if the work does not require a high school diploma, the employer often does.

Handicapped people seeking work, including those now on the job, will need much more technical and vocational training than ever before. They need to keep up with changing occupational trends and new developments in their own fields. So many jobs have been phased out or are simply not growing and so many new ones have come into existence that it takes study just to keep up with vocational trends.

Who is eligible for state vocational rehabilitation

Any handicapped person living in the state who can reasonably expect to profit by rehabilitation services should apply for consideration. Disabled veterans are eligible to the extent that they are not entitled to or are receiving similar benefits through the Veterans Administration.

People with disabilities from birth, disease, accident, from emotional or behavioral causes are served. These include arm and leg deformities, amputations, heart ailment, tuberculosis, hearing, speech and eye defects, mental illness, environmental and many other handicapping conditions.

How to apply

If you need assistance you can either get in touch with a counselor at the Vocational Rehabilitation Service or be referred to a counselor by someone else, such as a teacher or school guidance counselor.

To find your nearest office, look in the phone book under your state Board of Education. It'll probably list "Vocational Rehabilitation Services." For example, in Connecticut you would look under "Connecticut, State of, Board of Education, Vocational Rehabilitation Service."

In most states there are two agencies—one for people who are blind, the other for people with any other disability. In the rest of the states, a single rehabilitation agency accepts people with any disability, including blindness.

By phone, letter, or personal visit arrange an interview with a rehabilitation counselor at your nearest state rehabilitation agency office. Many services are free. Those services which are necessary to evaluate your case, such as medical exams are free. Counseling is also free. You may be asked to share in the cost of other services if you are able.

Some of the rehabilitation programs

Your state may have a variety of rehabilitation facilities to help you. For example, under federal law arrangements can be made for you to attend an approved private postsecondary vocational training school if comparable training is not available in local public agencies or institutions. You can get a list of such institutions by writing to the Division of Vocational and Technical Education, Office of Education, Washington, D.C. 20202. Private vocational schools have been leaders in training handicapped people because of their ability to develop highly individualized courses and techniques.

Junior and community colleges also offer some specialized educational facilities.

It is possible for some handicapped people to attend schools like Missoula Technical Center, Missoula, Montana, which is a public postsecondary vocational education institution with a large adult evening program. It takes courage and determination to function as equals among equals at a school which accepts both normal and handicapped students, but this may be your best path to rehabilitation.

This school has no classes set aside for the handicapped. They study side by side with normal students. Informal remedial help or counseling is always available to anyone who asks for it. Many of the handicapped students have a hard time. The staff has found that people who have been in special classes most of their lives or people who have been injured after being out of school for several years are often far more troubled by their educational handicaps than their physical handicaps. The school has eliminated hazards like steps, doors, and thresholds to make it easier for those in wheelchairs. Courses are offered in heavy equipment mechanics, forestry, bookkeeping, mid-management, welding, data processing, and many other vocational fields as well as adult basic education classes for those who haven't finished their high school work.

Missoula Tech's counselors and the graduate assistants got a sort of backhanded compliment for their work from the younger brother of a 22-year-old student during his second year in the program. Handicapped all his life, he had been submissive and easy to manipulate, but his experience at Missoula Tech evidently gave a large boost to his confidence and independence. The brother complained to one of the staff members that the young man had become somewhat argumentive and "now he thinks he's somebody."

Another place you can turn for vocational rehabilitation is Goodwill Industries, a nonprofit community service organization with branches in 150 cities. This is a program of self-help for handicapped and now includes ex-drug addicts in some cities.

Goodwill provides a new way of life through the rehabilitation of the total person. Beginning with psychological testing and medical examinations, counseling and vocational testing, Goodwill's staff provides the client with evaluation, work adjustment, training, and interim employment. Goodwill offers vocational rehabilitation, training, and employment to the handicapped. The purpose is to lead a person through the rehabilitation process to a job in private industry. For those who can't qualify for jobs in private industry, Goodwill offers extended employment at a salary in keeping with the person's individual productivity.

The public supports Goodwill mainly by contributing materials no longer needed, yet still useful. They are used as training tools in the workshop, and then when properly repaired or reconditioned, are sold in the Goodwill store to provide income for the program and salaries for the handicapped workers. A broken radio, for example, is repaired by a trainee taking radio repair and then sold in a Goodwill store by a clerk learning to work in a retail establishment. Goodwill workshops also perform sub-assembly work, perhaps mailing and simple machine work and other functions for industry on contract. Wages are paid to each individual, depending on his ability, with the average being $1.25 an hour.

People are referred to Goodwill by the state department of Vocational Rehabilitation, Veterans Administration, Public Welfare Department, hospitals, physicians, and private social agencies. You must be at least 15 years old to work the machines. No other training or education is necessary. The training is free to the client; it is paid for by your state department of Vocational Rehabilitation.

If you are referred to Goodwill, you go through an evaluation program for the first twenty days. This determines vocational aptitudes, interests and work tolerances before you are given comprehensive training. You are directed to areas where you are likely to succeed and much of your frustration is therefore eliminated.

After the twenty-day evaluation program you are put through a three-month training period in a specific area. During this time you'll be paid between $.80 and $2.00 an hour depending on the job. After completing your training, hopefully you'll be hired by someone in the community.

If you don't adjust in three months, you are put back into training for another three months. If the Evaluation Committee doesn't think you will be able to compete in a community atmosphere, you are placed in the "sheltered workshop." The people in this workshop never work on a competitive level. For this work they are paid less than the legal minimum wage (truck drivers and retail clerks get minimum wage if work is on a competitive level).

Goodwill offers training in about forty-five different fields, e.g., switchboard, radio dispatch, truck driving, clerical, retail sales, chambermaid, day care, kitchen work, printing, cashiering, machine operating, clothing repair, automotive repair, dry cleaning, furniture repair and finishing, appliance repair, grounds keeping, and others.

One new center in Bridgeport, Connecticut, for example is a handsome functional building geared to serve 350 handicapped clients a day. It offers programs in sub-contracting, training in service areas, crafts, auto mechanics, building maintenance and ground care. The new building features a residence to house handicapped clients coming from rural areas, the blind, and those returning from general and mental hospitals.

The new residence made possible the development of a training program for hotel or motel housekeepers, maids, custodians, all areas of food services such as cooks, dishwashers and counter workers, and programs to train for the care and maintenance of buildings and grounds. These trained people can then be placed in the community in jobs in their fields.

In addition to Goodwill there are probably other private, nonsectarian and nonprofit agencies in your area which will give you guidance and information and may offer actual training usually in sheltered workshops. You can inquire about them through your local community fund.

For more information, write:

B'nai B'rith Career and Counseling Services
1640 Rhode Island Avenue, N.W.
Washington, D.C. 20036
Ask for: Feingold, S. Norman and Rose, Jaren
    Student Aids in the Space Age–Educational
    Resources for the Handicapped. 1971. $.50.

Division of Vocational and Technical Education
U.S. Department of Health, Education and Welfare
7th and D Streets, S.W.
Washington, D.C. 20202

President's Committee on Employment of the Handicapped
Washington, D.C. 20210
Ask for: *Accessibility of Junior Colleges for Handicapped. A Survey by the Education Committee of the President's Committee on Employment of the Handicapped,* 1973. (Gives information on ramped or ground floor entrances, doors wide enough for wheelchairs, etc.)

Manpower Development And Training Act (MDTA)

While the federally assisted work and training programs are expected to continue for unemployed and underemployed people, there will be some changes made in 1974. Generally programs will be decentralized giving more responsibility to local communities. It is advisable that you check with your local state employment office to see what programs are currently open. There may be new opportunities in your state not in existence at the time of this writing.

The MDTA programs are for people who want to better themselves. The primary purpose of MDTA programs is to provide education and training to help unemployed and underemployed people get good paying jobs with good futures. It's a way of opening up new career opportunities to unemployed people who cannot reasonably be expected to obtain appropriate full-time employment without training. The other purpose of MDTA programs is to alleviate shortages in skilled occupations by providing the trainee with skills that are or will be in demand in the labor market. Over the years these closely related goals have guided the choice of occupations in which training is offered under MDTA.

The trainee not only receives specific training to perform his job skillfully, but he gets the needed support, guidance, and counseling required to improve his basic educational or personal problems.

Over 2,000,000 new enrollees a year participate in federally assisted work and training programs. Though most of these trainees are under 22 years of age, there are older workers, members of minority groups, and disadvantaged people. There are also programs for updating and upgrading occupational skills of employed workers who are interested in bettering themselves.

Training provided may be institutional (provided in either a public or private vocational or educational institution) using a classroom method of teaching; or on the job (OJT), which uses instruction combined with work at the jobsite; or in coupled projects which include both. On-the-job training (OJT) may be provided by employers, public and private agencies, trade associations, and other industrial and community groups.

The programs are administered by the U.S. Secretary of Labor and the Division of Manpower Development and Training together with the Bureau of Adult, Vocational and Technical Education, under the U.S. Office of Education, U.S. Department of Health, Education and Welfare.

The kinds of training you can get

The MDTA programs provide education and training opportunities in those occupations where you can reasonably expect to find employment. The programs for the most part are designed to meet the needs of the disadvantaged. This includes remedial training in the three Rs and even personal grooming if that's what is needed to make a person employable. In other words, basic education may be given to anyone who needs it in order to become employed or in order to profit from regular skills training.

Training may be for any job except those classified as professional occupations. Training is determined by job market surveys made by state employment services. Training can be full time (40 hours per week), part time, or merely upgrading of a person's present job.

What you can expect to learn

About 40 percent of all training under MDTA Institutional (classroom) programs is concentrated among these five high-demand occupations: health workers; practical nurses and nurses' aides; stenographers, typists and clerks; mechanics and machinery repairmen; and welders. However, the range of occupations offered shifts from time to time as demand for skilled labor shifts.

Training under state administered MDTA on-the-job programs is broader and includes numerous opportunities in construction, metal fabricating and machinery repair work. Actually it might include just about anything, depending upon where you live and what help the local industries need. There are programs such as the one sponsored by the book publishing industry to improve the job skills of present employees and give the skill training necessary for them to move up into better jobs within their own companies.

There are apprenticeship programs run for carpenters, plumbers, electrical workers, plasterers, auto mechanics, and other occupations, funded by grants from the U.S. Department of Labor and conducted or coordinated by unions and employers throughout the country. An extra effort is made to enlist the disadvantaged and minority group members in these programs.

Individuals may also be referred to ongoing programs in either public or private schools or skill centers. Arrangements can be made with private educational or training institutions when it is more economical or practical to do so. These schools may train either entire classes or individually referred persons who are then brought into the regular organized class groups.

About half of those trainees who complete their course find jobs in their chosen field, with the highest number of successfully employed trainees being those who got their training on the job.

Training allowances

Training allowances may be paid to trainees who satisfy certain requirements, in amounts equal to average weekly unemployment compensation payment in the state where the training is offered. Most enrollees are unemployed, in dead-end jobs, are underpaid, or require training for upgrading when they enter training. On the job trainees receive wages from their employers. Residents of Redevelopment Areas (under ARA) automatically qualify for training allowances. No training allowance will be paid to a high school dropout unless he has been out of school for a year or unless authorities determine he cannot benefit from regular school programs.

Who is eligible

Both men and women are eligible, with women making up about 40 percent of the persons enrolled. There are four categories of workers currently eligible for selection and referred to MDTA training:

1. Unemployed workers (includes members of farm families with less than $1,200 annual net family income).

2. Persons working less (or who have received notice that they will be working less) than full time in their industry or occupation.

3. Persons who have received notice that they will be unemployed because their skills are becoming obsolete.

4. Persons working below their skill capacity.

The highest priority is given to the disadvantaged (the poor, minority group members, dropouts, handicapped, welfare clients, and low-income farmers). A person may enter training at age 16, but isn't eligible for allowance benefits till age 17. Unemployed professionals may receive brief refresher courses. Inmates of correctional institutions may be provided MDTA education and training.

How to apply

If you are interested in applying for a MDTA program, see a counselor at your state employment service office. He will decide if you are eligible, and will describe the available programs to you. The counselor will help you pick a suitable vocational field and decide if you should undertake the training. He will also decide whether or not you will need to take any tests and what kind they should be, e.g., intelligence or manual dexterity. If you are to be referred to a program, the counselor will help you fill out the forms and request for allowance payments.

Once you are enrolled in a program, your counselor will continue to visit you and provide guidance and assistance should any problems arise. When your training is over, your counselor will help place you in a suitable paying job.

For more information, write:

U.S. Government Printing Office
Washington, D.C. 20402
Ask for: *The Federal Government As An Employer of the Unskilled and Undereducated,* 1972 CS 1.48:BRE 40 s/n 0600–00678, $.30.

Also contact:

Your state employment service office will give you the most up-to-date information on MDTA, including information on the types of skills currently being taught and where.

If Career Education Is for You, Start Here to Find the Right Occupation and the Right Place to Get Your Training

Guidance and Counseling

Choosing a career and selecting the proper type of training to prepare you for the career are two of the most important decisions you will ever be required to make.

Nearly everyone needs help (vocational guidance) during his school years. To be effective, the guidance counselor needs to consider your abilities in relation to current manpower needs as well as your personal needs and ambitions.

Good vocational guidance helps you with your vocational and other basic needs, assesses your vocational potentialities in relation to occupational possibilities, develops your life goals, sets up a plan of action toward your goal and then sets the plan in action. If you receive good counseling, you'll reduce your chances of failure and increase your chances of success in making the right vocational decisions. A trained guidance counselor can help you take into account factors you might otherwise overlook . . . things that don't seem important to you, but may be very important in your total career plan.

Your parents have a natural urge to make decisions for rather than with you. A wise parent will try to guide you, but leave the final decision to you.

Remember that most parents have hangups about their children's education and careers that tend to color their judgments. So you must consider your parents as people if you want to discuss your future with them in meaningful terms. Many parents, particularly those who haven't gone to college, have blind faith that attendance in such institutions will assure you future success. This may stand in the way of your choosing the education and career for which you might be best suited.

Your parents may simply not be aware of the changes that have taken place in jobs, careers, and education since the time when they went to school or entered their chosen fields of employment. So it's up to you to give them precise information on how the times have changed in terms of your career choices and the necessary preparation that might qualify you for them.

What a counselor will do for you

He'll test you, counsel you and help place you in a school, training program, or a job if you are ready.

Although methods of directing career-oriented students vary, most all educators agree that this type of student needs and usually receives highly individualized counseling.

"When a student states, 'I want to be an engineer,' he might mean anything from an auto mechanic to a Ph.D. in Nuclear Engineering," reports Joseph Van Ness, Head Counselor at Cortez High School, Phoenix, Arizona. "We put together for him his abilities and his aptitudes. And we're not reticent about pointing out both his weaknesses and strengths. We have literature from colleges and universities, as well as from institutes of technology and junior colleges that the student can use."

In some situations, the counselor may find that visits to various schools will aid the student in making a correct decision. "When we are discussing career possibilities with students," says Elizabeth Lockhart, guidance counselor at H. Grady Spruce High School, Dallas, Texas, "we offer them catalogs and other literature from schools that seem to fit their abilities and interests. We also feel it important that the student and his parents visit the institution before enrolling, to talk with faculty members and students."

Educators in this counseling survey made by Bell and Howell Schools pointed out another factor in counseling the career-oriented student: parental involvement.

Miss Lockhart reports, "The father of one of our students recently contacted me. He was disturbed when his son professed an interest in joining an institute of technology. The parents evidently wanted the boy to enter a liberal arts program in a college. But after they visited the institute of technology and discussed various programs with staff members, they agreed that their son would do well in this sort of situation, because of his interest in electronics."

How to tell if the counselor is competent

As to testing, counselors often use a variety

of tests in their work with students. If these tests are not administered and interpreted to the student by an expert, they are likely to be useless or worse. To describe these tests in detail would take several volumes. If you want counseling, put yourself in the hands of a professional who knows his trade, including the testing, and let him interpret your test results for you.

There are a number of ways of telling whether or not you are being advised by a competent counselor. A good counselor does more listening than talking, asks questions, avoids giving advice on the decisions to be made, seldom makes judgments on right and wrong, never pushes you toward one career or another, is more concerned with what you think and feel than with telling his own experiences, and lets you conduct the discussion at your own pace. He seldom uses psychological jargon. He won't tell a word of what you've said to others, including your parents, without your permission. He has at his fingertips or knows where to get the information you need on careers and how to get started. When he appraises your situation, he uses tests along with discussion to help you come to a decision. Testing alone is never adequate to give you direction to follow. These are just some of the ways of deciding if the counselor you are working with is a good one.

Where you can get help in choosing the right occupation and the right school

If you are thinking of taking some vocational training, but need some direction, advice, testing, or good ideas, there are many places you can look for guidance.

School guidance counselor. Ask for help from the guidance counselor in your high school. The counselor can direct your career choice as well as guide you to schools which offer training for the field of your choice. He is trained to assess your aptitudes, interests, and accomplishments and to relate this information to information about your occupational choice.

There is a hopeful new trend to high school counseling. School officials say the reason is the growing realization that too many counselors were interested only in college bound students. Job counseling now gets more emphasis at a Nashville Training school after a recent study showed "a large segment" of the students were taking jobs. In Philadelphia, eight of its twenty-five public high schools have added an extra "Job Bound" counselor to help students going to work directly after graduation. In Montgomery County, Maryland, at least one counselor in each high school is a specialist in vocational guidance. An expanded counseling effort in Cleveland inner-city schools boasts the placement rate for graduates to over 90 percent from 15 percent in 1966.

A word of warning about counselors: beware the counselor who is either obsessed with the notion of a college degree for all students, or who is not knowledgeable about vocational education opportunities beyond high school. If your conselor fits this description, find someone else. Don't be put off if you are sure you want vocational education and not a four-year baccalaureate degree.

State Employment office. The local office of your state employment service offers a broad range of job training and counseling services, probably through its Manpower Development and Trainng Program and its youth division. In many states the employment service will test anyone who walks in, then provide counseling and placement services in an effort to get you a job in an area which suits your aptitude and interest.

Each of the 2,000 local offices of the state employment services specializes in finding jobs for workers and workers for jobs. The state employment services are affiliated with the U.S. Training and Employment Service of the U.S. Department of Labor's Manpower Administration and constitute a federal-state partnership. Employment and related services are available without charge in every state.

Four basic services are provided to workers by the public employment service: 1) job information; 2) employment counseling; 3) referral to job training; and 4) job placement.

Job information: The personnel who staff the public employment service offices are familiar with their areas and thus know what kind of workers are employed in local industry, what jobs are available, what the hiring requirements and the opportunities for advancement are, and the wages that are paid. The staff conducts manpower surveys to determine the areas' available skills, training needs, and future occupational opportunities. Through the employment service network of offices, information is also available on job opportunities in other areas of the country.

Employment counseling: Employment counseling assists young people who are starting their careers as well as experienced workers who wish or need to change their occupation. The major purposes of employment counseling are to help people understand their actual and potential abilities, their interests, and their personal traits; to know the nature of occupations; and to make the best use of their capacities and preferences in the light of available job opportunities.

The employment counselor is specially trained and has access to a large store of occupational information.

Testing: Most local offices have available testing services which the counselor may use to assist him in appraising an individual's aptitudes, interests, and clerical and literacy skills.

United States Training and Employment Service aptitude tests are particularly helpful in relating applicant's potential abilities to the aptitude requirements of 62 broad occupational groupings and hundreds of specific occupations. A nonreading edition has also been developed for individuals with very limited education.

Referral to job training: Many individuals seek work for which they lack some qualifications. Sometimes the job requires basic education or a specific skill. Besides referring a jobseeker to a job, the public employment service may suggest training so the applicant can qualify or secure a better job.

Jobs and job requirements change. In today's fast-paced world, important considerations when selecting a vocation are the training required to perform the work and ways that training need can be met.

Job placement: A primary objective of the public employment service is to place workers in jobs. Regular contact is maintained with local employers to learn about their job openings. Requests are received from employers for many different kinds of workers. As a result, registered applicants have access to a variety of job vacancies with many employers, just as the employer has access to many applicants. This dual function eliminates "hit-or-miss" job hunting.

If job openings are not available locally, applicants may apply for employment elsewhere in the state, in another area, or even in a foreign country. Each state employment service prepares inventories of its hard-to-fill jobs so that other state employment services may refer local workers to out-of-area jobs for which they qualify. In addition, a national network of highly specialized professional placement offices operates within the employment service network to speed the matching of jobs and applicants in professional fields.

Special services for youth: In addition to all the previously mentioned services, the employment service performs two special efforts. 1) In the summer employment program, the employment service enlists the cooperation of business, government, and other groups to develop as many employment opportunities as possible for disadvantaged youth to provide valuable summer work experience and enable them to return to school in the fall; 2) The Cooperative School Program provides employment-related services to graduating seniors, school dropouts, and potential dropouts who desire to enter the labor market. Through this program they are provided employment counseling, testing, job development referral to jobs or training and followup services.

Special services for disadvantaged adults: Through its human resources development program, the employment service seeks to improve the employability of adults who are not in the

work force because of some social or cultural disadvantage. An important part of this program is "outreach" into slum areas.

Other special services: Individuals with mental or physical disabilities which constitute vocational handicaps are given special consideration by the employment service. Veterans also receive special services. Each local office has a veterans' employment representative who is informed about veterans' rights and benefits, and seeks to develop jobs for veterans.

Community manpower service: Jobseekers, employers, schools, civic groups, and public and private agencies concerned with manpower problems are invited to utilize the service of the public employment office in their community, and avail themselves of the job information in that office. The local office is listed in the phone book as an agency of the state government.

When you go to the employment service office, you will meet an employment counselor who works full time at helping people match their abilities and desires with suitable jobs. So, don't be surprised if he asks you what you like to do in your spare time, what your favorite and best (or worst) subjects in school are, and what kind of jobs you've held before.

He may also offer you the chance to take some aptitude tests that will help point out some of the skills you can learn. The employment counselor must know about you—both your acquired and your potential skills—to find the best job for you.

About 10 million people look for jobs each year through the local U.S. employment service offices and more than one million of them receive employment counseling in making a career choice or in referrals to suitable training.

The employment counselor wants to make sure you are qualified for the job before you go out on interviews. So he will tell you about the training programs that are available to you. Some are listed here:

The Neighborhood Youth Corps (NYC) provides part-time summer and full-time jobs for youth. In-school projects enable students to work after school and during the summer. For those who have left school, full-time programs of work and training are available. These projects give young people valuable work experience, training, counseling, and remedial education while they earn money.

Training programs under the Manpower Development and Training Act provide skills through classroom or on-the-job training, or both. At Manpower Training Skills Centers, you can receive counseling, basic education, prevocational training, communications skills, work orientation, skill training, and the necessary supportive services to prepare for a job in a variety of occupational areas. And training allowances may be given for up to 104 weeks to those who enroll in an MDTA program. See also pages 68-70.

The Job Corps offers skill training and basic and remedial education to young people who live in dormitories in residential centers. Other youth not enrolled in the Job Corps may receive the same comprehensive services on a nonresidential basis at these centers located in or near their communities.

Apprenticeship Programs in over 350 occupations teach young people a skill right on the job. An experienced craftsman supervises and instructs the apprentice, who also receives related classroom training. Apprentices earn good wages and, with satisfactory progress, they increase their earnings at fixed intervals. When the apprenticeship is completed, the worker—now a journeyman—receives the standard wages for his trade. See also pages 53-63.

Regular courses in reading and arithmetic, among others, are offered too. In some instances, you may receive medical, legal, or other services if you need them to get a job.

The employment service has set up special employment offices to provide coordinated and direct services for young people, 16 to 21. Most are called Youth Opportunity Centers (YOCs). There is at least one in every state. If there isn't a YOC near you, you can visit the Youth Unit of the local Employment service office. Both the YOCs and the other local employment service offices offer you the same comprehensive services in preparing for, getting, and keeping a good job. So, no matter which one you visit, you can be sure of meeting qualified people who will work with you to find "your" job; one with a good future and good pay; one to help you make the most of your working life.

Community Colleges. Vocational counselors are available in your city or community college. Contact the closest campus and ask to talk with the vocational counselor. Most of them will supply you with information on post-high school programs.

Community Centers. If you've lost contact with a school, there are counseling services offered by community centers and organizations to which you can turn. You can also learn about specialized training courses in your community from trade unions, private business, vocational rehabilitation centers, trade and technical schools, service organizations, public and private welfare groups, or the Veterans Administration office.

Apprenticeship Information Centers. The Labor Department supports Apprenticeship Information Centers in thirty-five cities. They conduct interviews and counsel applicants for apprenticeships, and refer prospects to openings. The nearest state training and employment service office also will assist you. Consult your telephone book for the number to call. You will be helped in choosing the trade best adapted to your interests and abilities and will get advice every step of the way to help you enter a training program.

Local Newspapers. You may also be able to get free career or school information from the public service department or school bureau of your local newspaper. Check the want ads or educational opportunities columns of the newspaper for offers of help.

Private Vocational Schools. Every private vocational school maintains an office specifically to provide individual career counseling and guidance to the entering student and help during his stay in the school. The office also helps secure part-time and summer jobs. The officers help the student assess realistically his career goals and long range plans. When the course is completed, the counselor assists in placement of the graduate in a full-time position in keeping with his education and training.

Private vocational schools are particuarly strong in the counseling and placement services they offer. All accredited private schools are required to operate free job placement departments. Many maintain permanent records of their alumni and help is always available. While the schools can't guarantee employment, they report 68 to 95 percent of their graduates go to work in the field for which they were trained.

Private Vocational Counselors. There is a growing number of private, fee-charging career counseling agencies. Some are affiliated with nonprofit organizations such as YMCA, the YMHA, and universities; others are profit-making ventures.

Some of the private agencies have been checked and certified as competent by the American Board of Counseling Services and are listed in the biennially revised *Directory of Counseling Services*, available in the counseling office of most schools. Those services which are not listed may or may not be reliable. They are less likely to be reliable if they advertise heavily; ask for a downpayment on the fee; offer guarantees of any sort; emphasize resume-writing and job placement; or lay great store on lengthy written reports based on test findings full of psychological jargon.

People in the Field. Ask people in the field of your choice for suggestions as to good schools. Where did your dentist's best assistant get her training? Employers can usually recommend schools from which they recruit students. Trade associations are good sources of information about specialized schools.

For details about specialized fields, the personnel director of a local hospital or board of education can provide information on how and where to receive training for jobs in their fields.

Veterans Administration. If you are a veteran, counseling help is available from the Veterans Administration to you, wives or husbands of veterans, and children of deceased or disabled veterans, and wives and children of servicemen missing in action or forcibly detained by a foreign country.

Occupational Information. There is often a great deal of occupational information available in college and community libraries—some of it good and some of it bad. There are real differences in authenticity and quality of materials. An occupational pamphlet that was once excellent may be hopelessly out-of-date. Important figures on how many people work in the field and how many are needed, may be misleading, just as the description of working conditions and necessary preparation may no longer be relevant. Look to see who is the sponsor or author of the material you are reading. Some materials are intended more for recruiting or advertising than for true, unbiased vocational guidance.

Because of the avalanche of materials from which to select, the National Vocational Guidance Association rates the value of what is available to help counselors, personnel workers, and librarians.

For more information, write:

B'nai B'rith Vocational Service
1640 Rhode Island Avenue, N.W.
Washington, D.C. 20036
Ask for: Sinick, Daniel. *You and Your Child's Career*, A guidance Handbook for Parents, Teachers and Counselors, $1.50.

International Association of Counseling Services, Inc.
1607 New Hampshire Avenue, N.W.
Washington, D.C. 20009
Ask for: *Directory of Counseling Services*, $3.00.

National Vocational Guidance Association
1607 New Hampshire Avenue, N.W.
Washington, D.C. 20009
Ask for: Knapp, Dale L. and Bedford, James H. *The Parent's Role in Career Development*, $.45.

Additional Reading:

Ginzberg, Eli. *Career Guidance: Who needs it; Who provides it; Who can improve it.* New York: McGraw-Hill Book Co., 1972. $7.95.

Vocational Testing

Before you pick an occupation, you should give some thought to your own interests, abilities, skills, likes, and dislikes. The scientific way to get to know yourself is by taking vocational preference tests.

Why use tests

If you don't know the field for which you are best suited, you can take tests to get an idea of where your abilities lie. You might think the easiest way for someone to find your interests in different types of work would be to ask you. But, answers to direct questions about interests are often unreliable, superficial, or unrealistic.

For after all, you probably don't have enough information about different jobs and can't really judge whether a particular job is for you or not. Your interest, or lack of interest, in a particular job may come from not knowing what the day-to-day work in the field really involves. You may also have a false picture of the whole occupation. The life of an average plumber is quite unlike anything you may have seen on TV or in the movies.

The result is that most of us are unable to know if we are really interested in a field till we have a chance to actually work in it, and by that time it may be too costly or wasteful to change jobs.

And so a more indirect and subtle way to find out where you belong is through tests which measure your interests, attitudes and aptitudes.

The major purpose of testing is to help you find out about yourself and to help others find out about you. In thinking about your career plans, you must realize there is no such thing as a bad job; there are only jobs that are wrong for you personally. The job may be perfect for your best friend, but absolutely terrible for you.

Vocational tests are a good way to learn more about yourself; and the more you know, the better your chances of making the right career choice.

What the tests are

There are several different types of tests used by psychologists and counselors. You may be given an aptitude test which measures a particular ability such as eye-hand coordination, or an intelligence test which shows your mental ability.

The tests take different forms. There are job sample tests where you are asked to do something similar to the work you are to perform on the job, e.g., in a stenographic test you take shorthand and then transcribe your notes into typed letters as you would on the job. There are written information tests where you show how much technical information you have in a particular field, e.g., welding. There are oral trade tests where you are asked a short series of questions about specialized trade knowledge, easy if you've ever worked in a particular type of job and know the jargon, but hard if you haven't.

Most of the tests you've taken up to now measure what you've learned in school. There are definite right and wrong answers. Vocational aptitude tests aren't really tests at all because there are no correct answers. You answer how you feel about the things asked. You'll have a series of choices about different activities and you specify which things you like to do and which you don't. When all the results are combined, these two kinds of tests will help tell you in which occupations you probably have enough ability and interest to succeed.

There are special aptitude tests specifically for use in vocational counseling to show how you stand in a number of traits. The tests give a separate score for each of several traits such as numerical aptitude, reasoning, mechanical, clerical, music, and artistic aptitudes.

Many of these vocational tests are used to select or classify people in industry, government (civil service), and the armed forces. They are often used in hiring workers in the skilled trades and in selecting apprentices. They can also be used for the transfer or promotion of workers, as they are quite likely to be acceptable to both labor and management as a basis for personnel decisions.

Here are two of the most commonly used tests. You may be asked to take others, perhaps more specialized ones or ones newly developed.

Strong Vocational Interest Blank (SVIB): when this test is used for high school students, the field or occupational group you will eventually enter can be predicted fairly well.

General Aptitude Test Battery (GATB): this test was developed by the United States Employment Service for used by employment counselors in state employment offices. It is actually a series of twelve tests using simple apparatus and paper and pencil. It takes two-and-a-half hours to complete. State employment service offices use it regularly in their counseling and job referral. This same test is also given by many other nonprofit counseling organizations and services.

What the tests tell you

There is no test which will answer positively that you will succeed in a particular occupation. But tests are an indicator reliable enough to pay attention to. They tell us a number of things, including what your underlying needs and values are, what kind of a person you are, or would like to become. Testing is a tool, but not a cure-all. One of the basic purposes of taking tests is to help you take stock of your experience and develop a deeper understanding of your assets and limitations in relation to the world of work.

People who work at the same occupation have certain common characteristics which make them different from people who work at other occupations. These differences in interests extend not only to things pertaining to the job, but also to schoolwork, hobbies, sports, types of plays or books enjoyed, and many other sides of life.

Therefore, the tests question your interests in familiar things. Analyzing the results, the counselor can help you determine if you have the qualifications for a particular occupation and how closely your likes and dislikes agree with those who already work in the field. When you are thinking about your choice of a career, you'll have to ask yourself if it's the kind of job you'd like to do; if you have the education and abilities the job requires; and if you are the kind of person who can succeed in this job.

Testing provides some of the answers to your questions. Results of studying careers of people who were tested in high school and years later tell us that many more people are happier and more successful in their jobs when they have entered a field that was most in line with their interests as shown on their tests.

How you can make best use of the results

Experts such as your guidance counselor or state employment service counselor will explain the results and help you interpret them.

The most important thing to remember is that tests can help you make a decision about your vocational choice. But there is no one test or group of tests yet devised which will tell you positively what career you should pursue.

Psychological and aptitude tests given by guidance counselors will reveal your strengths, weaknesses, and interests. They are indicators only; they do not give positively reliable information.

Be sure any test you take is administered and interpreted by a competent counselor or other expert. Otherwise you are wasting your time as the results will be worthless. (See page 71 for ways to decide if a counselor is competent).

Testing alone cannot give you all the answers. A good counselor will interpret the scores and study them along with information you give him plus your actual performance in various areas (academic record in school, after school jobs, etc.). Never let a counselor guide you using test results alone!

A career guidance counselor can be a valuable guide, but he isn't a miracle man. He can mislead you badly if you let him do all the work and supply all the answers. Before you are to see your counselor, do a little homework. Take stock of yourself and go prepared with a few ideas of occupations which possibly interest you.

Where you can go for vocational aptitude testing

Tests are given by many different organizations. You can go to the state employment services. They use the GATB; the NATB (Nonreading Aptitude Test Battery) for educationally disadvantaged people and the newest test, the BOLT (Basic Occupational Literacy Test) to assess the basic reading and arithmetic skills of disadvantaged people being considered for occupational training or placement.

Though budgets have been considerably cut back by the state employment services, you'll still find testing being done for Viet Nam veterans and school dropouts.

Other places you might try for testing are your school guidance office, local community and junior college, or community service agency.

Another place to turn is one of the private counseling services you'll find located in many parts of the country. These services are staffed with people who are usually well qualified to help with your school and career plans. Check the list of services approved by the International Association of Counseling Services, Inc., before making your choice. (See page 77 for where to write for directory).

After giving you aptitude and interest testing, the private counselor will then explain the results. They will show a range of aptitudes which the counselor then correlates with your interests to see where they overlap. The result is a selection or range of vocations he may suggest to you in a particular area, e.g., health fields.

The counselor may then recommend specific schools or types of training to pursue in getting ready to enter the suggested fields. He may give you a list of accredited schools which teach the range of occupations best suited to you personally.

Such a counseling service will cost from $50 to $200, depending on the amount of help and testing you need. If you want to find a private counseling service, look in the Yellow Pages of your phone book under "Educational Consultants" or "Vocational and Career Guidance."

The point of testing and consulting with a guidance counselor is to get to know yourself better. Only in that way will you be able to choose a career wisely.

For more information, write:

Business and Professional Women's Foundation
2012 Massachusetts Avenue, N.W.
Washington, D.C. 20036
Ask for: *Career Counseling: New Perspectives for Women and Girls.* 1972, $.50.

Engineers' Council for Professional Development
345 East 47th Street
New York, New York 10017
Ask for: *Do I have Engineering Aptitude?* (8-page questionnaire by A.P. Johnson), send stamped self-addressed envelope, free.

International Association of Counseling Services, Inc.
1607 New Hampshire Avenue, N.W.
Washington, D.C. 20009
Ask for: *Directory of Counseling Services,* $3.00.

Junior Engineering Technical Society (JETS)
345 East 47th Street
New York, New York 10017
Ask for: *National Engineering Aptitude Search,* free.

Choosing a School

When you are faced with making an occupational choice or a choice of school, you must decide honestly whether you are good enough to do what must be done to succeed in that particular occupation or school. You must honestly examine yourself and evaluate your own abilities, strengths, and weaknesses.

To learn what training to take, and where, consult a guidance counselor at your high school, state employment service, vocational rehabilitation center, community center, Veterans Administration office, or trade union. Read the education advertisements in your local newspapers; ask people in the field of your choice for suggestions of good schools. Where did your television repairman get his training? Employers can usually recommend schools from which they recruit students. Trade associations are good sources of information about specialized schools.

You'll find school guides and catalogs at your local high school guidance office or in nearly every library. They list thousands of schools which offer career and vocational training by state, by specific career, and type of school. (See also pp. 393-395 for a list of books to look for.)

Before making your final choice, write to those schools which interest you and ask for their catalogs and bulletins. Try to visit the schools you are considering for interviews with the president, dean, superintendent or admissions officer.

At any school you are considering talk to some of the students and instructors. Feel free to ask for names of graduates and employers. By all means, check the accredited status and job-placement assistance results. To find out whether a particular school is reputable, you can easily check with the Better Business Bureau or your local Chamber of Commerce to learn whether any complaints have been received against the school in the past.

When you are considering enrolling in a private vocational school, here are some special points to keep in mind.

Probably the best yardstick by which any private technical or trade school could be measured is its placement record. The first questions you or your counselor should ask about any private school are: Does the school graduate a reasonable number of its entering students? Are these students placed in jobs and can the school prove this? Do the school's graduates successfully advance once they are placed in jobs?

You must read between the lines to catch all the private vocational school's gimmicks. The broadcasting division of one school boasts a "directing faculty" of illustrious well-known radio and television stars. In fact, each of the stars' only contribution is one long-playing record of instruction to the student.

Some students select the institution they plan to attend after high school with less care than they would exercise in buying cars. There are differences in goods you buy, and there are just as many differences in education. It's not always easy to tell the difference between schools, but you must take time to investigate. Talk to several schools before making a decision.

Reputable schools encourage the kind of thorough investigation suggested here and will cooperate fully when you ask pertinent questions. Others will reply with high pressure salesmanship rather than solid, reliable information.

Not all schools or teachers are equally good. And it's not just a matter of cost. Comparison shop for your education as carefully as you would for a new car. In fact, shop more carefully. You may be able to trade in that lemon of a car; but you'll be stuck with your education for life.

Some problems are common to both colleges and vocational schools. And most students don't find out these shortcomings until it is too late.

Some vocational schools are woefully ill-equipped. The tools, machines, and textbooks they use or systems they teach are long out of date. Relevant job training means learning on up-to-date equipment.

How good are the teachers? Some vocational schools are safe harbors for professional dropouts who turn to teaching. And though they may have been top professionals in their time, they are sometimes out of touch with present day practices in their fields. Or, equally bad, they are teachers with no practical experience.

Avoid catch-all courses in colleges or vocational schools with titles like "mass communications" and "merchandising." Ask for what career a course in "graphic media" will prepare you. Question the practical background of the instructors and ask how recently they themselves have been employed and in what capacities.

If you are an art student, for example, beware of the school that gives its students a great deal of copying and very little creative and original work to do. Some private music, art, or dramatic schools are excellent; others are not so good. To check on the quality of various schools, write to the national association for schools in that particular specialty (like National Association of Schools of Music) and ask about the reputation and accreditation of the particular school that interests you. (See pages 10-14 for information on accreditation.)

Other schools promise to give aptitude tests, but don't mention that almost nobody fails their tests. And countless vocational school ads feature the phrase "V.A. Approved," implying that the Veterans Administration somehow oversees operations. All the phrase really means is that tuition is covered in part by the G.I. Bill for qualified veterans.

Many private vocational schools do everything they promise to do. But many do not. Under generally lenient state laws all too many engage in hard sell and promises of glamorous, high-paying jobs. Some schools have tuition rising to Ivy League heights and give poor training in return. High pressure and hard sell are frequent targets of complaints about vocational schools. In time of recession when jobs are scarce, people will snatch at straws and pay the high tuition costs in hopes of getting a better job.

The schools may mislead you. A TV commercial used by one computer school shows a handsome, white-smocked man walking around a computer room that he clearly supervises—implying that the students in its school will do the same. Potential students are never told that computer work isn't all glamour. Lots of its is just plain drudge work!

Pressure for stricter regulation of private vocational schools is growing, but truly effective supervision is all but impossible. The schools are generally so small and spread all across the country they are difficult to keep under control. (See pages 39-49 for more on private vocational schools.)

If you're considering enrolling in a home study course, protect yourself by asking the school to send you the names of former students and employees who have hired them in your locale. See what the students and employers think of the school.

Make sure you understand any contract provisions for cancellation and refunds of fees and tuition. This is particularly important because enrollments are frequently sold to finance companies. Students in most states have no legal recourse against the finance company even if the school is no good or, believe it or not, fails to open. This unfair consumer practice is changing, but to be sure, ask a lawyer what the facts are in your state (or, you can inquire at the nearest consumer protection agency).

Even if you attend a reputable school and finish the course, there's no guarantee that you will be able to find a job where you live, or that the course will be accepted by potential employers. It's best to spotcheck a few employers in advance to see if training by mail would qualify you as a beginner in their companies.

Along with the importance and improved status of the correspondence schools, however, has come an increase in the number of fraudulent operations. The Post Office Department says that prosecutions of correspondence schools for mail fraud have increased fourfold in the past three years.

Capitalizing on the nationwide stress on education and the good reputation of long-established institutions, con men have set up quickie learn-by-mail "schools" in states that have no regulations in this field or only minimal license requirements.

The problem confronting those who want to

take correspondence courses is how to avoid the fly-by-night school that takes the student's money and sends him wastepaper in return. The solution, unfortunately, is not as easy as it should be.

Legitimate institutions are making a real contribution to education. But the so-called "diploma mills" have tended to cloud the reputation of all correspondence courses.

To find out whether a particular home study school is reputable, you can check with the National Home Study Council's list or query the Better Business Bureau or Chamber of Commerce to learn whether any complaints have been received against the school. (See pages 49-52 for more information on home study schools.)

You'll get good training to prepare you for the career of your choice if you choose your school wisely and honestly. Do your investigation before you enroll to save yourself unnecessary problems.

200 Good Occupations
That Do Not Require College Degrees

If you're looking for a career that offers you a promising future with great rewards here's where to start your search. All of the occupations described in the following sections require some training beyond high school, but *none* requires a four-year bachelor's degree. Post high school education of some sort is your admission ticket. This is a directory of those occupations that offer the greatest opportunities for good-paying jobs in the 1970s. Only those fields that are growing or will need more workers are included. *These occupations need you now.*

Where will the jobs of tomorrow be? According to the Occupational Outlook Handbook, published by the United States Department of Labor, you can look at our country's industry as either goods-producing or service-producing. Most workers are in industries producing services such as education, health care, trade, repair and maintenance, government, transportation, banking and insurance. Less than half of our work force is involved in industries producing goods such as raising food crops, building, mining, and manufacturing of goods. We'll continue to have more jobs in the 1970s in service-producing industries than in goods-producing industries.

As our industries continue to grow, they will become more complex and more mechanized with the result that jobs will be even more specialized. The number of career possibilities is growing in some fields and shrinking in others. White-collar workers (professional, managerial, clerical and sales) now outnumber blue-collar workers (craftsmen, operators and laborers) and will continue to do so. The number of farm workers will continue to drop.

Growth will vary widely among occupations. Professional occupations will be the fastest growing. The next fastest growing group will be service workers, including men and women who maintain law and order, assist professional nurses in hospitals, give haircuts, serve food, and care for our homes. Clerical workers, including workers who operate computers and office machines, keep records, take dictation, and type are the next fastest growing group. The demand will be particularly strong for anyone qualified to handle jobs created by the change of clerical occupations from manual to electronically processed operations. But at the same time the use of electronic computing bookkeeping machines and other mechanical devices to do processing and repetitive work are expected to reduce the number of clerks employed in jobs such as filing, making up payrolls, keeping track of inventories, and billing customers.

Another fast growing group is sales workers. Then draftsmen and foremen come next, including carpenters, tool and die makers, instrument makers, all-round machinists, electricians and typesetters. Managers, officers, and proprietors are next with the demand greatest for salaried managers and the number of self-employed owners of small businesses dropping.

Semiskilled workers or operators are another fast growing group. In 1970 these workers made up the largest major occupational group of all along with workers assembling goods in factories, driving trucks and taxis, and operating machinery. Technological advances will continue to reduce employment for some types of jobs and increase it for others.

Laborers (except those in farming and mining) are the next group. These workers who lift and carry materials and tools will find little change in demand for their services.

The last group consists of farm workers, including farmers, farm managers, laborers, and foremen. The need for such workers will drop, partly because of continued improvement in farm technology. For example, with better fertilizers, seed and feed a farmer can increase his crop production without increasing the number of people he employs.

When you first think about an occupation, don't automatically rule one out just because it's not one of the fastest growing. There will always be some job openings in every category because of deaths, retirements, or other reasons. Replacement needs will be particularly large in occupations which now have a greater proportion of older and women workers.

Because most jobs are becoming more complex and require greater skills, employers will be looking for people who have more education. With a high school education accepted as a standard for American workers, employers are apt to take it for granted you have it and ask, "What else can you offer?" Employers want better trained workers to operate their complicated machinery. The more skill and education you have, the better position you will be in to qualify for a really good job. The number of young men and women from 16 to 34 years old entering the labor force in the 1970s is great, and so you'll face keen competition from a group who have more education on the average than new entrants to the labor force ever have before! With so much competition, if you don't have good job preparation, you'll find the going difficult in the years ahead.

Another point to remember is the less education and training a worker has the less chance he has for a steady job because layoffs come first, and last longest, for the worker with the least education. If you have acquired a skill or a good basic education, you have a better chance for steady interesting work and good wages.

Choosing A Career

A long time ago the famous Greek teacher Socrates said, "I am myself reminded we are not all alike; there are diversities of natures among us which are adapted to different occupations."

Actually choosing an occupation is a modern thing to do. In years gone by *you* didn't choose an occupation—you were expected to enter either your father's or one he chose for you. If you were truly daring, you ran away to sea, or became a soldier of fortune, or emigrated to a new world.

Career choice is truly an expression of your own personality and interests. There is a rich variety of choices open to you. Whatever you do select, you'll find your work and lifestyle are inevitably and completely intertwined.

Choosing an occupation is a very difficult and important thing to do. Your choice will give you a happy life, if it is suited to your ability and personal needs. Don't leave the choice to chance! Because of our country's rapid development and economic growth, you can't even count on being able to follow your parents' footsteps.

During the 1970s about 34 million young people will join the U.S. labor force. How you arrive at your career decision can mean the difference between professional fulfillment and a long series of sour work experiences leading to "job hopping" and unemployment.

The choice is enormous. There are now 30,000 different occupations, more than half of which didn't exist when your father was born. By the time your children are ready to start thinking about careers, there will be thousands of new occupations for them to consider.

Most studies of occupational interests of students show your ideas change constantly up to age 15. Your ideas sharpen rapidly from 15 to 20. Then change little from 20 on. By the time you are 35, your career ideas are virtually fixed for life.

Considering the stakes involved, you ought to be at least as careful in planning the next forty years of your life as you are in researching a paper for your history class. Don't make the mistake of basing your career decision on tired, worn stereotypes, misinformation, or just plain lack of information.

What Is the Difference Between a Job, an Occupation, and a Career?

An occupation is a collection of tasks you perform for pay. It is a particular set of jobs for which you are trained and at which you may spend the largest middle section of your life. A vocation is a specific occupation for which you are trained.

A career is a whole lifetime series of jobs and occupations. This includes jobs you have while you are a student and all the way through your life, perhaps even when you are living on an old age pension.

Through your working life you move up a career ladder—your personal pathway of advancement from one level to another.

You can see a career is a great deal different from just a job. If you're thinking only about "getting a job" when you finish school, you're saying all you are interested in is some kind of work with regular pay. A career has larger implications. It implies a life's work which interests you and for which you have received some special training and education.

Who Should Plan a Career?

It has always been assumed boys should plan their careers, but in the past few years it has become increasingly important for girls to spend just as much time as boys thinking about what they want to do. Almost half of all women over 16 are now in the work force—twice as many as in 1940. Nine out of ten girls will work sometime during their lives, but the career sights of too many are still limited and unrealistic. Most girls have a romantic image of life: school, marriage, a family. And living happily ever after. But this isn't the complete picture. A more accurate life-picture of the modern woman includes school, work and/or marriage, raising a family, sometimes continuing to work by either choice or necessity, and a return to work when the youngest child enters school. The average girl in high school today will eventually spend twenty-five years in paid work outside her home! This calls for serious planning and preparation now.

The two periods when women are most likely

to work are ages 20 to 24 and then again at 45 through 54.

This "split-level" characteristic of the working life of the American woman is the basic reason why girls' career plans should be made early. Girls in school should prepare for occupations in which they would like to work for the remainder of their lives, if necessary. It's wise for girls to choose careers that can be picked up again when they come back to the world of work as their children grow up. To be satisfied when they return to work, both psychologically and financially, girls should select fields that challenge their talents and help them to realize their full potential.

If college isn't possible financially, or isn't a wise choice, girls still can prepare for careers in many expanding fields such as health services and data processing. Or, why not become an apprentice? Why not a lady plumber, like "Cluny Brown," if that's your bent? The entire world of work is open to qualified women. Counselors, teachers, and parents need to help girls realize they have the ability and can be accepted.

There remains a shocking double standard in pay scales and promotion opportunities. Women have joined together in demanding a square deal in hiring, pay, and advancement. The courts are on their side with more and more ruling against laws or work rules that discriminate against women, including laws prohibiting laboring long hours and lifting heavy loads. Women are breaking down the myths of "man's work" and "woman's work," but the old stereotypes die slowly.

Some Things to Know about Different Occupations

Here are a few general suggestions to keep in mind as you consider different occupations. Jobs will be more plentiful in the service-producing industries than in those producing goods. Look for growing fields such as those dealing with ecology and the environment, rather than declining ones.

Carpentry will provide 40,000 new openings each year, many of them leading to wages of $12 an hour, including fringe benefits under unionized conditions. Plumbers will earn over $13 an hour. Both will fare better financially than many professional white-collar people. Mechanics and repairmen of many kinds are desperately needed and will be paid accordingly. Long-distance truck drivers will be in great demand. The best ones will rise to supervisory levels and command fine incomes.

But don't overlook the fact that even a stagnant or dying occupation may offer excellent lifetime opportunities for a small number of people simply because these fields tend to be ignored by most young men and women. Almost

unfillable openings develop as older workers retire. Some men with only a grammar school education have moved into high pay brackets because they are wise enough to master a craft few young men even consider, for example, fine jewelry engraving or furniture upholstering.

The range of occupations open to you gets bigger every year. You're no longer limited in your occupational choice to the community, state, or even the country in which you live. Not all the job breakthroughs have been made by women. Men, too, have been knocking down the sex barriers in jobs usually thought of as woman's work. They are becoming secretaries, telephone operators, nurses, and flight attendants.

The United States Department of Labor predicts a need for 65,000 engineering personnel by 1975 and this in turn means that from 130,000 to 200,000 supporting technicians will be needed.

An example of the change in need for workers from goods-making to services-producing industries is found in the rapidly expanding shipbuilding industry. The COM/CODE Corporation in Washington, D.C., was organized to sell know-how for computerized machines that automatically cut pieces of metal for ships. While this process reduced by half the need for unskilled and semiskilled workers, it generated nearly as many new service-type openings for marine engineers and analysts.

In the booming health field, we now need one professional to six paraprofessionals and the prediction is we'll need one to twelve shortly. This means we'll need 50,000 new physicians per year, 250,000 physicians assistants, the same number of family health workers, and some 25,000 clinical chemists and workers in many other health services.

What Are the Requirements For the Skilled Trades?

The greatest growing demand for craftsmen is in the building trades. There aren't enough apprentices and not enough students in vocational programs to meet the demand expected throughout the 1970s.

A marked movement of women into the crafts is underway, particularly into trades such as auto mechanic, baker, home appliance repairwoman, compositor and typesetter, business machine maintenance worker, decorator and window dresser, optician, lens grinder and polisher, tailor, and upholsterer. About one-third of the women in crafts jobs are foremen—twice the comparable proportion for men.

In the past, entry of girls into skilled jobs lagged because of a mistaken belief that there were great sex differences in aptitude and interests. Widespread use of aptitude and interest tests is correcting this belief as well as providing the means of identifying girls with potential for specific skilled occupations. In many communities these tests are now conducted by public schools, employers, and/or the public employment service offices. See pages 75-77 for more information on vocational testing.

The aptitudes required for a specific craft are well established. Certain requirements are unique to individual trades. Engraving, for example, requires a flair for drafting; tailoring requires an appreciation for style and design. Some requirements, however are common throughout the crafts.

The testing has shown that those aptitudes generally required in the skilled trades are for the most part found as often among girls as among boys. Such aptitudes include eye-hand coordination and finger and manual dexterity. Another common requirement is "form and space perception," the ability to see slight differences in shapes and shading of figures and in widths and lengths of line, and to visualize objects of two or three dimensions. This aptitude is found almost as frequently among girls as boys.

Other general requirements in all crafts include average to better-than-average ability to understand instructions and underlying principles, to reason, and to make judgments. In some crafts, average ability to comprehend meanings of words and ideas and to present information or ideas is essential; in others, considerably less-than-average ability is acceptable. As for numerical aptitudes, some crafts require above-average ability to perform arithmetic computations quickly and accurately, others require only average or less-than-average ability.

Physical requirements in many craft occupations create no problem to most girls. Levels of strength required in different jobs have been described in the U.S. Department of Labor's *Dictionary of Occupational Titles*, as follows.

"Sedentary" occupations involve lifting a maximum of ten pounds and occasional lifting and/or carrying small tools or articles. Examples of sedentary crafts are jeweler and camera repairman. Girls should have no trouble with the strength requirements of sedentary jobs.

"Light" strength requirements are those that involve the ability to lift a maximum of twenty pounds and frequent liftcarry of less than ten pounds, although many jobs in this group actually require less strength. Some jobs with "light" requirements are lens grinder, dispensing optician, electronic mechanic, office machine serviceman, radio repairman, electrical appliance repairman, and such automobile servicemen as speedometer repairman and the tune-up, carburetor, and front-end man. Girls should have no trouble with strength requirements in these occupations.

"Medium" strength requirements involve frequent liftcarry of less than twenty-five pounds and occasional lifts of a maximum of fifty pounds. Crafts in this category include television repairman, furniture upholsterer, and many machinist occupations. Some "medium" strengh jobs are within the physical capabilities of many girls. However, employment of women in work involving lifting of medium or heavier weights, such as required in many of the building trades, must conform with health and safety programs of individual states.

Generally, the crafts would be a good choice for you if you prefer working with techniques and machines to produce something tangible. You need to be able to find satisfaction in attaining set limits, tolerances, or standards for success in the crafts.

A fact of particular interest to girls, who may later move frequently because their husbands change jobs, is that skilled trade opportunities exist in every state and in almost every town.

Ten Things to Do Before You Make Your Choice

1. Don't make your final occupational decision until you have studied it from every possible angle. Learn all you can about the field you are considering by reading everything you can find on the occupation that interests you. Do this exploratory work *before* you start training for your chosen career.

2. Based on what you personally need—intellectually, socially, psychologically, financially—the best thing to do is make your own checklist when you are investigating occupations. Decide if a particular occupation measures up to your personal needs in all areas. How close does it come? Which of several choices comes closest?

3. Consult a qualified career guidance counselor for objective advice on your career plans. Make sure, however, the counselor spends enough time with you to gain a good insight into your particular situation and personal needs. See pages 71-75 for more on guidance and counseling.

4. Remember, two of the most important factors in choosing an occupation are to pick something you will enjoy and to pick something you are psychologically suited to handle. Take advantage of any psychological aptitude tests that are available. They may show you the type of work for which you are best suited.

5. Because everyone can do some things better than others, choose a field suited to your own particular abilities. Find out if there are any special mental, physical, or emotional qualifications necessary to succeed in the occupation you are considering. Are there any special mental qualities, such as the capacity for learning quickly and easily, imagination, originality, or good memory, essential in the vocation in which you are interested?

6. Make a point of discussing your career

plans with several people already established in the fields you are considering. You'll get a clearer picture of both favorable and unfavorable sides of the job, and a better understanding of the type of work involved.

7. Find out in detail about the actual work done in the vocation you are considering. Learn not only about the most common duties, or the few general ones usually thought of in connection with that occupation, but also try to learn precisely what is done during a typical day or week on the job. Are the same tasks done over and over again, or are they varied? What are the "sometime" duties of the job? What are those duties you would be called on to perform only once in awhile? Be sure you are aware of *all* the duties of the occupation which you are studying. It's the day-to-day experiences of a job that in the long run makes it agreeable or disagreeable.

8. If you can work summers or part-time in offices, laboratories or plants and talk to other workers about their jobs, so much the better.

9. Don't make the biggest mistake of all: allow your parents or teachers or counselors decide on an occupation for you.

10. Don't attach too much importance to what others may think of your choice of a vocation. You should take into account the effect of your work on your social standing, but don't overestimate it. There are types of work that are less crowded, more highly paid, and provide a higher standard of living than some of the white-collar jobs we generally think of as being so desirable.

The things that should influence you most in your choice of careers then, are high school courses in which you did well, reading about careers, friends and teachers in the field that interests you, and work experience in summer or part-time jobs.

Some Questions to Ask Yourself As You Make Your Career Choice

Once you have found out as much as you can about whatever careers interest you, ask yourself these questions:

If an occupation interests you, do you have the ability needed to do the job well? Just because a field interests you doesn't necessarily mean you will be good at the job. A girl may be intrigued with the idea of being an interior decorator, but if she has no feel for color or line, she'd be a poor designer, indeed. You must honestly measure your ability and personality against the requirements of several fields before you decide. Consider most seriously occupations using the skills and abilities you have or can develop; avoid occupations that require entirely different ones.

Are you willing to overlook the disadvan-

tages of the job, e.g., the work may be injurious to health, may keep a homelover away from home, or the hours of work may be very inconvenient.

Have you looked behind the scenes of what appears to be a very glamorous job to see what the disadvantages are? A model's life looks like a dream, but the discouragement, irregular employment, long hours of standing and posing may all be obstacles you couldn't take.

Does the vocation offer opportunities in the sections of the country you would like most to live? Are the working conditions pleasant for you? If the pace is fast, can you take it?

Does the occupation provide a standard of living, prestige, personal satisfaction, opportunities or whatever else is most important to you?

Will you like working with the type of people employed in this vocation?

Does the job offer as much salary, job security, and chance for advancement as you feel you'd like?

Are there opportunities for advancement?

If you want to climb the career ladder quickly, will you be able to do it?

Is it a kind of work of which you can be proud? Does it seem prestigious enough to you?

Does the occupation satisfy your desire to work with people, to work with ideas, or to work with things?

If you prefer to work on your own or under close supervision, can you in this job? Or if you prefer to work as part of a team, will you be able to do that?

Will the job offer enough challenge? Are you choosing this career just because it is glamorous?

Does the job offer as much freedom to come and go as you want?

Do you like the kind of work actually being done by people in this field?

Are there good training and educational opportunities in this field?

Would you be happy doing this for the rest of your life?

Finally, ask yourself very honestly if you have as good a chance to succeed as any other person would with your background and qualifications.

For more information, write:

American College Testing Program
ACT Publications
P.O.Box 168
Iowa City, Iowa 52240
Ask for: *Career Planning Program: Student's Booklet 1972–73.* $1.00.

American Vocational Association
1510 H Street, N.W.
Washington, D.C. 20005
Ask for: information on career selection and material on careers which interest you.

Chronicle Guidance Publications, Inc.
Moravia, New York 13118
Ask for: *1972–73 Guide to College Majors,* $4.50.

Institute for Research
537 S. Dearborn Street
Chicago, Illinois 60605
Ask for: *Here's Help on How to Select Your Career—How to Match Your Objectives with the Career and Job,* Careers Research No. 1, 1972.

National Vocational Guidance Association
1607 New Hampshire Avenue, N.W.
Washington, D.C. 20009
Ask for: Bryn, Delmont K., *Career Decision,* $.50.

U.S. Department of Labor
Bureau of Labor Statistics
Washington, D.C. 20212
Ask for: *Outdoors and Your Career,* 1972. free. (Describes outdoor opportunities—advantages and disadvantages of outdoor work and list of pamphlets on related occupations).

U.S. Department of Labor
Women's Bureau
Employment Standards Administration
Washington, D.C. 20210
Ask for: *Skilled Trades for Girls,* reprint from

Occupational Outlook Quarterly, December, 1967.

Also contact:

If an occupation interests you and you want to know more about it, you'll find a list of additional places to contact at the end of each description, starting on page 89.

More information and help is also available from these sources: public libraries, school libraries, guidance counselors and teachers, counselors at state employment services, employment and personnel offices at business establishments (names of local firms in a particular industry can be found in the yellow pages of your phone book or from your local Chamber of Commerce).

Trade unions, employers' associations, and professional societies and associations will send you free material describing jobs and training opportunities in their field.

Your state Department of Education will also supply job information and often lists of accredited schools offering training in the particular occupation that interests you. When you write to your state Department of Education, be sure you are very *specific* about what you are interested in since it will help them know exactly what information to send you.

Occupations

Aeronautics

The Job

For a career that's really sky-high, why not look at the airlines? The growth of airlines and air transportation has led to over half a million jobs, and nearly any interest or talent can be pursued through some kind of airline work. The variety of companies and positions is tremendous.

Scheduled airlines transport passengers, cargo, and mail. Supplemental airlines provide charter and nonscheduled flight services for passengers and cargo. General aviation includes a wide variety of activities in addition: business flying on company-owned aircraft; aerial application of insecticides, fertilizers and seed to crops, open land and forested areas; air taxi operations that deliver mail and light cargo to small airports on scheduled routes; industrial flying, which includes the inspection of pipe lines and power lines for breaks. Maintenance and repair of general aviation aircraft is performed at licensed repair stations.

Members of the civil aviation industry includes regulators and investigators from government agencies. These agencies are: the Federal Aviation Administration (FAA), which develops air safety regulations, inspects and tests planes and facilities, provides ground electronic guidance equipment and gives licensing tests to pilots, flight engineers, dispatchers, and aircraft mechanics; the Civil Aeronautics Board (CAB), which establishes policy on matters such as airline rates and routes; the National Transportation Safety Board (NTSB), which investigates aircraft accidents and other accidents involving death in the aeronautic industry.

Most of the 300,000 employees of scheduled airlines are involved with domestic service. The largest group of workers are specialized airline mechanics and other workers like carpenters, electricians, painters, welders, and metal platers who participate in aircraft maintenance.

The next largest group of employees for the scheduled airlines are traffic agents and clerks involved in servicing customers. Some of these jobs include ticket agent, reservations agent, traffic agent, and customer service representative.

About one-fifth of scheduled airline employees are involved with actual flight occupations. These include pilots, copilots, flight engineers and—the largest group—stewardesses and stewards.

Other employees of the scheduled airlines include cargo and freight handlers and custodial and other aircraft servicing personnel.

In the general aviation field, the majority of employees are mechanics and pilots, with administrators and clerks filling in most of the remaining jobs.

The government aviation agencies employ more than 50,000 people; most work in New York, California, Florida, Illinois and Texas. FAA workers are mainly involved in directing air traffic and in installing and maintaining the mechanical and electronic equipment used to control traffic. There are air traffic controllers and flight service station specialists. Many CAB workers are administrators and clerks who investigate accidents, promote air safety, supervise international air transportation and work with economic regulation of airlines.

What You Need Personally

Most jobs in aeronautics require good health, as the hours may be long and the work hard on body and mind. Some positions that have especially rigid physical examinations are flight engineer, pilot, and airtraffic controller. In addition, many of these jobs require dealing with the public, so a neat, attractive appearance, a pleasant manner, and tact and courtesy are important.

A sense of responsibility, attentiveness to detail, ability to work under pressure, and an understanding of mechanics are important for pilots, flight engineers, air traffic controllers, and airline mechanics.

What Education and Training You Need

The necessary training and education vary according to the job. Most airlines require at least a high school education, and for most jobs they prefer some college or post-high school training. To become a pilot, flight engineer, dispatcher, mechanic, or air traffic controller, you have to pass strict government licensing tests. The qualifications for licensing are specific and require at least two years of training or education.

For jobs in customer service as a steward, stewardess, or office worker, some college or experience in dealing with the public is preferred.

There are specialized schools which train people for skilled jobs in air travel, especially those that require licensing from the government. Airlines provide training programs for many jobs, and on-the-job training is given in all cases.

One other program to investigate is the Air Force ROTC, a college course of study designed to give you the necessary education to qualify for commission in the U.S. Air Force.

What the Occupation Has to Offer

There should be an increase in jobs in the aviation industry during the next decade, but the number of openings will vary according to occupation. There will be more planes in service in the years to come as economic growth, larger population, more economy-class passenger service, an increase in air cargo shipping, and an expansion of new uses for planes come into play.

Pilots and flight engineers—particularly the latter—will find some increase in employment with the scheduled airlines. The expected large growth of business flying and air taxi operations will provide additional opportunities for pilots, who will also find jobs in the field of aerial application.

Mechanics will discover openings with scheduled airlines, air taxi operations and, especially, in certified repair stations for general aviation. There should also be a large increase in employment opportunities with the scheduled airlines for stewardesses, ticket sales agents and baggage handlers.

Employment with government aviation agencies should grow moderately during the 1970s.

Aviation workers are, on the whole, well-paid and receive good benefits from employers. Many are also union members. An additional benefit to airline work is that you and your immediate family can fly nearly anywhere free or at greatly reduced prices.

Points to Consider Before Going into This Field

There are many advantages to working in this industry. Most jobs are steady, stable, and offer good salaries and benefits. The travel benefits are a particularly powerful incentive for many people. Most of the jobs are diverse, and few require as much as four years of college training. There are many challenging and responsible jobs in the field of aviation and many jobs that give an opportunity to help people.

The hours in the airlines industry can be highly irregular. Planes take off and land and people make reservations and buy tickets at every hour of the day and night. Most airlines personnel work on shifts and often find themselves working nights, weekends, and holidays. In those jobs that involve actual flying, many nights are spent away from home. Flight personnel may be away from home base a third of the time or more, but the FAA and the unions have stipulations for maximum monthly flying hours.

There are definite restrictions on who can enter many of these jobs. For instance, good health and mental sharpness are absolutely necessary for pilots, flight engineers, and air traffic controllers.

Men and women both are employed in large numbers in this industry, but there are almost no women in such positions as pilot, copilot, flight engineer, air traffic controller, or dispatcher; few men are stewards. Both men and women work in such areas as ticket sales.

For more information, write:

Information Retrieval Branch
Federal Aviation Administration Library
 HQ-630
Federal Aviation Administration
Washington, D.C. 20553
Ask for: list of FAA-approved training schools.

Professor of Air Force Aerospace Studies
AFROTC Dept. 157
Embry-Riddle Aero-University
Daytona Beach, Florida 32015
Ask for: description of Air Force ROTC program.

Also contact: personnel officers at the following
 Federal Aviation Regional Offices:

632 Sixth Avenue
Anchorage, Alaska 99501.

Box 90007
5641 West Manchester Avenue
Los Angeles, California 90009.

P. O. Box 20636
Atlanta, Georgia 30320.

P. O. Box 4009
Honolulu, Hawaii 96812.

601 East 12th Street
Kansas City, Missouri 64106.

Federal Building
John F. Kennedy International Airport
Jamaica, New York 11430.

P. O. Box 1689
Fort Worth, Texas 76101.

Additional reading:

World Aviation Directory, Washington, D.C:
American Aviation Publications, Inc., 1973
(lists airline officials with their addresses).

Official Aviation Guide, Chicago:
American Aviation Publishers. Monthly
(lists airline officials with their addresses).

Aircraft Mechanic

The Job

One of the most enormous and complex pieces of machinery today is the airplane. The size of its engines, the huge number of controls, the sophistication of the machinery make skilled maintenance and repair a constant and vital part of flying. Aircraft mechanics are responsible for this work. They make emergency repairs (line maintenance) or major repairs and periodic inspections of the plane's individual parts and sections. They often dismantle a complex component to replace worn or damaged parts; when the aircraft is reassembled, they make sure it is operating perfectly.

Line maintenance mechanics are generally all-around mechanics who are familiar with the engine's workings. They may receive instructions from the flight engineer on the engine's malfunction or may go over the aircraft themselves to find the problem. They make necessary adjustments or install new parts, from screws to an entirely new engine. Line mechanics are stationed at airports for regular inspection and repair of aircraft.

Maintenance base mechanics work in each commercial airline's huge maintenance headquarters. These mechanics may be specialized and trained to work on a certain part of each aircraft. Generally, they are responsible for modifying and overhauling commercial air fleets. They work at building, repairing, overhauling or manufacturing parts for air power plants or may work on radio equipment, electrical components, instruments, or mechanical systems. Some do welding, sheet metal work, or electroplating.

Aircraft mechanics employed in general aviation are responsible for maintenance and repair work on planes which are usually smaller and less complex than airlines carriers. Often a single mechanic does the complete servicing on a plane himself. Mechanics who work for supplemental airlines, air taxi operators and independent repair shops may also do overhaul work. Independent repair shops usually specialize in engine, instrument, or airframe overhaul.

Airline mechanics find most jobs in large cities with a lot of air traffic, such as New York, Chicago, Los Angeles, San Francisco or Miami. More than 50,000 mechanics are employed by the commercial airlines, half at maintenance bases, half at airports. Another 50,000 mechanics are employed by independent repair shops. Other mechanics work for supplemental airlines, air taxi firms, corporations with their own planes, the Air Force, the Navy, and the FAA.

What You Need Personally

As an aircraft mechanic you must be able to work with others as part of a team. You should have mechanical ability and be able to do detailed work. Manual dexterity, depth perception, and good eye-hand coordination are also important. You need to be strong enough to lift heavy parts and tools, agile and willing to work in high places. You will probably be required to pass a rigid physical exam, and in order to work in the United States you may be required to be a U.S. citizen.

What Education and Training You Need

Mechanics who do repair or maintenance work must be licensed by the FAA. They can receive either an airframe mechanic's license (to work on the plane's fuselage, coverage surface, landing gear, and control surfaces); a powerplant mechanic's license (to work on the plane's engine); an airframe and power-plant mechanic's license (to work on all parts of the plane); or an aircraft mechanic can be licensed as a repairman (authorized to make only special repairs).

To receive these licenses, applicants must pass written tests and demonstrate their ability to do specified work. In addition, at least 18 months' experience working with airframes or engines is needed for an airframe or power-plant license, and at least 30 months' experience working with both engines and airframes is needed for the combined airframe and power-plant license.

The larger airlines have three-to-four-year apprentice programs for potential mechanics. They usually expect trainees to be high school graduates, 20 to 30 years old, in good physical condition, with some background in mechanics. These training programs combine classroom instruction and on-the-job training. Men who have learned aircraft maintenance in the armed forces usually are given credit toward the program requirements.

Some mechanics prepare for licenses by graduating from FAA approved schools, usually private vocational schools. These schools offer full-time, eighteen-to-twenty-four-month programs, usually toward an associate degree. The programs have varied courses of study, leading to different positions, including aircraft maintenance. Applicants for these schools should be high school graduates or mature persons with armed forces or other related training. The courses of study combine classroom instruction and shop practice to give not only theoretical but also practical knowledge of repairing aircraft, engines and systems. Subjects of study include General Aeronautics, Aircraft Structures, Aircraft Systems, Electrical Laboratory, Aircraft Materials, Engineering Drawing, and many others. A degree course can cost from $1,800 to $3,000, but scholarships, veterans' benefits, and loans are available for these courses of study. The schools also provide placement services to help graduates find jobs after passing their FAA tests.

Some junior and community colleges and universities offer two-year programs that prepare students for the FAA examinations.

What the Occupation Has to Offer

There should be many good opportunities for aircraft mechanics in the years to come. Scheduled airlines are expected to increase the numbers of planes in flight, and growth is anticipated for general aviation flying. The latter will provide jobs both in general aviation services and in independent repair shops.

Earnings for mechanics are fairly good. Those employed by scheduled airlines have the highest salaries, averaging between $800 and $1100 a month. Mechanics working for other aeronautical firms generally earn a bit less. Mechanics who work for scheduled airlines are also usually union members.

There are many advancement opportunities for a skilled mechanic, especially if he is employed by the scheduled airlines. Most promotions require the passing of a test; the usual line of promotion is from mechanic to lead mechanic, inspector, lead inspector, shop foreman, and occasionally to higher supervisory and executive positions. To reach the higher positions, mechanics usually must have both airframe and power-plant ratings.

To qualify for a job as an FAA inspector, a mechanic must have airframe and power-plant ratings and must have broad experience in maintenance and overhaul work, including supervisory duties.

Mechanics are expected to provide their own hand tools in most jobs.

Points to Consider Before Going into This Field

A job as an aircraft mechanic promises to be a well-paid and stable one in the years to come. It offers a person with mechanical aptitude, but less than college training, an opportunity to get into a growing field. There are many chances for promotion and good salary rates. Because it is a skilled job, the position of aircraft mechanic carries some prestige in the industry.

Aircraft mechanics must often work in cramped, uncomfortable places. Although line mechanics usually work in hangars or indoor maintenance areas, they may often have to work outdoors, despite weather conditions. Some people are disturbed by the noise of aircraft engines. A potential aircraft mechanic must be in good physical and mental condition.

This is a man's field, although women are being encouraged to take up aeronautical studies. The strength requirements will eliminate many women from consideration for jobs as aircraft mechanics.

See pages 90-91 for places to write if you are interested in learning more about employment as an aircraft mechanic.

Airline Dispatcher

The Job

Airline dispatchers (also called flight superintendents) are airline employees who coordinate flight schedules and operations within an assigned area and make sure that all FAA, company flight and safety regulations are observed. Their work is performed from the standpoint of safety, efficiency, and economy.

The dispatcher first examines weather conditions to decide whether a flight can be made safely. Knowledge of weather is important in the performance of this job, and many dispatchers are meteorologists.

If there's any change in a flight's scheduled departure time, the dispatcher notifies the crew. He confers with the captain about the quantity of fuel needed for the flight, the best route and altitude at which to fly, total flying time, and

What Education and Training You Need

Airline dispatchers must receive an FAA dispatcher's certificate. To qualify to take the test, an applicant must have at least one year's supervised work with a certified dispatcher, or he must have completed a course of study in an FAA-approved private school or an airline training center. Applicants who have spent two of the previous three years in air traffic control work or in jobs like dispatch clerk or assistant dispatcher or in similar work in the armed forces may also qualify to take the test.

The FAA test is both written and oral. The four-hour written test covers federal aviation regulations, weather analysis, air navigation facilities, radio-procedures, and airport and airway traffic procedures. The three-to-five-hour oral examination gives the applicant a chance to interpret weather information and display his knowledge of landing and cruising speeds and other operational characteristics. He must also display familiarity with airline routes and navigational facilities.

Once the test is passed, dispatchers are given additional instruction at airline training centers to keep up with new flight procedures and new aircraft. Each year, the dispatcher flies with his airline over the portion of the system which he services to update his knowledge of routes and flight operations.

Assistant dispatcher jobs may not require certification, but airlines give preference to men who have had some experience in a related field or who have at least two years of college. College graduates with courses in mathematics or physics or with experience in flying, meteorology or business administration are considered top applicants. Promotions to assistant dispatcher can be made from ground operations staff such as dispatch clerks or radio operators.

alternate fields to use if landing conditions at the scheduled airport are bad. The dispatcher and captain must agree on all of these details before the flight can take off.

The dispatcher may also be responsible for record-keeping and for checking availability of aircraft and equipment, weight and balance of loaded cargo, the amount of time flown by each aircraft, and the number of hours flown by each crew member he works with at the station.

When a flight is in progress, the dispatcher plots the flight course based on regular radio reports from the captain and informs the captain of changing weather or other conditions which might affect his flight.

Assistant dispatchers help plot flight progress, secure weather information, and handle communications with aircraft.

Approximately 1200 to 1500 dispatchers work for the airlines, most are employed by the larger lines and work in the country's largest airports. Dispatchers usually work in a hangar or terminal office at the airport. Their duties are performed twenty-four hours a day.

What You Need Personally

You should be technically inclined. You must be able to communicate clearly and concisely with others, and you must be responsible and capable of making independent judgments. The job requires extreme dedication.

What the Occupation Has to Offer

The number of positions in this field should remain relatively stable over the next decade. The average age of working dispatchers is 45, so there will be a reasonable portion who will retire. Some new jobs will result from increased air traffic, the addition and extension of routes, and the extra difficulties in dispatching jet aircraft. However improved radio and telephone communications will offset this need for extra help to an extent.

Earnings for dispatchers vary. Beginners start at $700 a month. Experienced dispatchers earn from $1100 to $1900 a month.

Airline dispatchers may advance to jobs as operational planners or go into computer programming for long distance jet flights or move into various management positions where their pay may increase to $2000 a month.

Points to Consider Before Going into This Field

Airline dispatchers are able to perform responsible jobs at good salaries without college training. Although the tests are fairly stiff, the information can be mastered by someone with a talent and interest in mathematics, science, or mechanics. Airlines are selective in their choice of dispatchers. They tend to bring them up through the ranks rather than hire from the outside. It isn't an easy field to get into but job tenure is long and there's little job jumping. The commercial airlines offer good benefits for their employees.

One disadvantage to this job is the narrowness of the field. The job market simply is not very large, and there are not many dispatchers employed by each airline. The hours can also be irregular since each dispatching station must be covered twenty-four hours a day. The skills for this job are specialized and not particularly applicable to other positions.

Almost all dispatchers are men, although there are no restrictions against women in the field.

For more information, write:

Airline Dispatchers Association (AFL-CIO)
16219 142nd Avenue S.E.
Renton, Washington 98055.

Director of Flight Standards, FAA
800 Independence Avenue S.W.
Washington, D.C. 20590
Ask for: list of FAA approved schools which teach dispatching.

See also, pages 90-91.

Air Traffic Controller

The Job

When planes are stacked up over an airport or circling in the fog the man who guides them to safe landings is the air traffic controller. He advises pilots by radio so that aircraft move smoothly in or out of airports and avoid collisions. Those who control the traffic around airports are known as airport traffic controllers; those who guide planes between airports are called air-route controllers.

Airport traffic controllers work in airport control towers and give pilots in the area information on weather conditions and takeoff and landing instructions. They tell pilots which approaches and runways to use and when to change altitude. The controllers have to direct several planes at the same time and use a radar scope which shows the planes' locations. Instructions are given by remembering each plane's position and using numbers.

Airport traffic controllers keep records of all messages from planes and operate runway lights and other electronic equipment. They also send and receive information from air-route traffic control centers regarding flights over the airport.

Air-route traffic controllers, stationed at air traffic control centers, coordinate planes being flown on instruments. Pilots and dispatchers file written flight plans before taking off, and these help the air-route controller. He checks flight progress using radar and other electronic equipment and information received from planes and control centers to make sure aircraft are on course.

All air traffic controllers must keep in mind the weather, geography, amount of traffic and the size, speed, and other characteristics of each plane when giving instructions.

Almost 20,000 air traffic controllers work in this country, about half of them at airports. The others work in twenty-four control centers scattered along air routes.

What You Need Personally

Air traffic controllers must be in good physical condition and have a great deal of stamina. Applicants are given a rigid physical examination, which they must retake every year. Because the job involves responsibility for human lives, the air traffic controller must be alert, quick-thinking, and able to consider many different factors at once. He must be able to see and hear well and speak clearly and precisely.

What Education and Training You Need

To qualify as an air traffic controller, applicants must pass a tough series of federal civil service tests. A comprehensive physical test is given, and applicants also take a specially written test that measures their ability to learn and operate all the equipment used by an air traffic controller.

Those who pass the tests are given about nine

weeks of formal training to learn federal aviation regulations, radar and aircraft performance characteristics, and the fundamentals of the airway system.

Upon completion of the initial course, controllers qualify for a basic air traffic control certificate. They then work in an FAA control tower or center, receiving on-the-job training and classroom instruction to become familiar with specific traffic problems. It usually takes two or three years until they have sufficiently mastered the ability to apply procedures and use equipment under pressure and stress conditions before they actually work as controllers.

What the Occupation Has to Offer

There should be some increase in jobs for air traffic controllers in the 1970s. Although automated equipment is being developed for use in this area, the number of airport towers is expected to increase to handle the growing amount of airline traffic.

During the initial six-to-twelve-month training period, air traffic controllers earn about $578 per month. An experienced air traffic controller can earn between $872 and $1480 a month, depending on experience and the amount of traffic at the facility. Periodic wage increases are given to air traffic controllers, and additional pay is earned for night shifts and overtime. A chief controller in an area with a lot of traffic can earn more than $2,000 a month.

Air traffic controllers can advance to a chief controller's job, and, from there, to high management jobs or even administrative jobs in the FAA.

Points to Consider Before Going into This Field

Air traffic control is a stimulating and challenging field which offers good pay and steady employment. Vacations, sick leave, and other benefits are the same as those received by other federal employees.

The job is quite difficult, however, and the air traffic controller works under a lot of stress. Air traffic congestion is often serious; the controller must keep track of many things at once in order for airports and air traffic to function at all. Night work is often necessary, as is overtime during periods of heavy air traffic.

This job is only for those in top physical and mental condition because pressure is constant and the work nonstop.

For more information, write:

See pages 90-91 for places to write for further details on the work of air traffic controllers.
Department of Human Resources Development
Mail Control Unit
800 Capitol Mall
Sacramento, California 95814

Ask for: *Air Traffic Control Specialist (Controller)* No. 230, Free.

Flight Engineer

The Job

Flight engineers—also called second officers—are required by FAA regulations to be on all three- and four-engine and some two-engine jet aircraft. They are responsible for monitoring more than 100 instrument panels in the cockpit or flight deck, performing pre-takeoff inspections and assisting pilots in other ways.

A flight engineer performs a variety of jobs. About two hours before flight time, he makes an inspection of the exterior of the plane, checking the engines, tires, landing gear, brakes, and makes sure the fuel tanks have been filled properly. When cargo is loaded, he makes sure it is secure.

Inside the plane, he checks almost 200 items in the cockpit, passenger cabins, and any compartments where electrical equipment is located. He will then sometimes determine how much fuel the engines will consume per hundred miles of flight so that at any time during the flight he will know how much fuel is left on board.

Then the pilot, copilot, and flight engineer check all the instruments aboard the plane to make sure they are functioning properly. Once the plane is airborne, the flight engineer keeps a constant eye on the instruments to make sure the engines, airconditioning, pressurizing systems, electrical systems, oxygen flow, and many other things are working properly. He reports any difficulties to the pilot and helps with inflight repairs such as burned-out fuses. He also keeps records of engine performance and fuel consumption.

When the plane lands, the flight engineer makes sure that any mechanical problems are fixed, makes a post-flight inspection of the plane, and turns in his log on the flight.

Most of the 8500 U.S. flight engineers are employed by the major airlines; they are often based in the areas with the heaviest air traffic—New York, California, Florida, Illinois, or Texas.

What You Need Personally

The flight engineer has a very responsible job and must be dependable, thorough and accurate, attentive to details, quick-thinking, and able to cope with pressure. Because much of his work is with others, he should be cooperative.

Good eyesight and eye-hand coordination are essential to the performance of this job. The flight engineer must be in good physical condition, and most airlines prefer men between the ages of 21 and 35 who are from 5'6" to 6'4" tall.

What Education and Training You Need

Though a high school education is necessary for anyone who wants to be a flight engineer, most airlines prefer someone with at least two years of college. Courses in physical science, mathematics, and mechanical and electrical shop are helpful to potential flight engineers. Airlines also usually prefer that flight engineers have commercial pilots' licenses. Some airlines prefer men with maintenance backgrounds.

To become a flight engineer, you must be licensed by the FAA. There are several different ways to obtain this certification. Two years of training or three years of work experience in the maintenance, repair and overhaul of aircraft and engines—including at least six months training or a year of experience on four-engine piston and jet planes—will qualify an applicant to take the FAA tests. You can also qualify with at least 200 hours of flight time as a captain of a four-engine piston or jet plane or with 100 hours of experience as a flight engineer in the armed forces. Most flight engineers qualify by taking an FAA-approved course in ground and flight instruction at a private school or college.

Once an applicant has acquired the experience and training necessary to qualify for the certificate, he must take the necessary FAA tests. There is a rigid physical examination, which must be passed again every year. The FAA written test covers flight theory, engine and aircraft performance, fuel requirements, weather as it affects engine operation, and maintenance procedures. There is also a practical flight test on a four-engine plane, designed to show skill in performing pre-flight duties and normal and emergency inflight duties and procedures.

Once certified, most airlines give new flight engineers several weeks of additional training, which includes the use of simulators that dupli-cate the actual airplane instrument panels and reactions of all mechanisms.

Commercial pilots' certificates can be obtained through programs of private vocational schools, in military service, or from the Civil Air Patrol.

What the Occupation Has to Offer

As more heavy jet-powered planes come into use, there should be an increasing number of job opportunities for flight engineers. Air travel can be expected to increase, and more and more planes will be required to have flight engineers among their crews.

A beginning flight engineer earns about $650 a month, and his salary doubles after a year's probation. The average pay for an experienced flight engineer on a domestic run is $1702 a month, on international flights about $1920 a month. Flight engineers can earn as much as $3500 a month; earnings depend on the size, speed, and type of plane to which the engineer is assigned, the hours and miles he has flown, the length of his service, and the types of flights he has been on. Engineers are guaranteed a minimum monthly salary. Their flight time is restricted to 85 hours a month on domestic flights, 100 hours a month on international flights.

Advancement opportunities for flight engineers can be quite good; most airlines have seniority provisions, however. Examinations are required for any promotion. After a few years, a flight engineer with a pilot's license can advance to copilot and, after five or ten years more, to pilot. Flight engineers without pilot qualifications can advance to flight engineer positions on more desirable routes. If an engineer or pilot leaves his employer, he will have to start at the bottom of the job scale with another airline.

Points to Consider Before Going into This Field

There are many advantages to a flight engineer's job. The work is interesting, diverse, and responsible. It offers an opportunity to get into flying without getting all a pilot's credentials at once. The pay is good, the airline industry provides good benefits, and flight engineers and their families get to travel free or at large discounts. It is an emerging field; there should be plenty of job opportunities for flight engineers in the future.

There are some disadvantages to the job, however. It involves a great deal of responsibility and pressure, which not everyone can handle. Flight engineers work irregular hours; planes are taking off every hour and day of the year. About one-third of the time, the flight engineer spends the night away from home, although the airlines do provide accommodations. The work can also be dangerous when planes suffer from serious malfunctions.

The FAA criteria for applicants for this position are strict. Only those who are mentally alert and in top physical condition should consider becoming flight engineers. At this time all flight engineers are male, although discrimination against women should not last in the field.

For more information, write:

Airline Pilots' Association
1625 Massachusetts Avenue, N.W.
Washington, D.C. 20036.

Federal Aviation Administration
800 Independence Avenue, S.W.
Washington, D.C. 20590.

Flight Engineers' International Association
905 Sixteenth Street, N.W.
Washington, D.C. 20006.

National Aerospace Services Association
1725 DeSales Street, N.W.
Washington, D.C. 20036.

Additional reading:

Federal Aviation Regulations, Vol. 9;
Part 61 (Certificates: Pilots & Flight Instructors);
Part 63 (Flight Crew Members Other than Pilots);
Part 67 (Medical Standards & Certification; (all available from libraries, airports or FAA offices).

See also, pages 90-91 and pages 97-99.

Pilot and Copilot

The Job

The responsibility for flying a plane and safely transporting passengers and cargo lies with the pilot (or captain) and copilot. The pilot is basically responsible for operating controls and performing other necessary tasks to keep the plane on course and see that it is landed safely. He supervises the copilot, flight engineer, and flight attendants. The copilot, who is second in command, assists the captain in air-to-ground communications, monitoring flight and engine instruments, and in operating the plane's controls.

Both pilot and copilot have many duties to perform even before a plane takes off. They confer with a meteorologist about weather conditions, and with the airline dispatcher they set up a flight plan determining the route and altitudes which will give them the best weather and wind conditions for a fast, safe, and smooth flight. The flight plan then must be approved by FAA air traffic control personnel. The copilot actually plots the course to be flown and computes the flying time between various points. Before taking off, both men check to be sure the

plane's engines, various instruments, controls, and electronic and mechanical systems are working properly.

During the flight, the captain and copilot maintain radio contact with ground control stations to give information on their altitude, air speed, weather conditions, and other factors. The captain supervises flight navigation and keeps an eye on all the instruments before him. The copilot assists in these duties.

Before landing, the landing gear is rechecked and landing clearance is requested from air traffic personnel. When visibility is limited, the captain relies on instruments to land the plane. At the end of the flight, both pilot and copilot complete a flight report and file trip records.

Pilots who fly smaller planes sometimes perform minor maintenance and repair work on their aircraft or may act as hosts to their passengers.

Airlines employ check pilots who make at least two flights a year with each captain to be sure the pilots are maintaining their skills and following company and FAA regulations.

About half of the nation's 50,000 pilots and copilots are employed by the scheduled airlines and fly the large passenger planes. Other pilots fly for private corporations, for air taxi services, do crop dusting, patrolling, inspecting, aerial photography, or serve as flight instructors. The government employs about 2,500 pilots who examine applicants for pilots licenses, inspect navigation facilities along federal airways, test new planes, fight forest fires, and patrol national boundaries.

What You Need Personally

There are few careers where the physical demands are as strict as they are in flying. It is strongly urged that before you begin pilot training, you first have a physical examination and then get your first-class medical certificate from a local FAA medical examiner. Having this certificate and keeping it current is the key to earning a living in flying.

You must have excellent vision and hearing and quick reflexes. You must be alert, quick-thinking, and able to make judgments and perform under pressure. You must be able to take on responsibility, act independently, and have good leadership qualities.

Finally, you must be between the ages of 20 and 35, stand between 5'6" and 6'4", and weigh between 140 and 210 pounds.

What Education and Training You Need

Because other people's lives depend on a pilot's competence, educational and training requirements are quite strict. It takes time and is likely to be an expensive education. All airline applicants must be high school graduates. Studies in sciences, especially mathematics and physics, are suggested in addition to basic courses in social studies, history, economics, and political science. Some airlines require two years of college, and many prefer college graduates, particularly with degrees in aeronautical engineering or professional aviation. A few of the schools offering professional aviation degrees are Purdue University in Indiana, the University of Illinois, and Southeastern State College in Oklahoma.

To do any kind of commercial flying, pilots and copilots must have FAA licenses. Airline pilots must have an airline transport pilot's license, and those who are subject to FAA instrument flight regulations or who think they have to fly on instruments in bad weather must also have an instrument rating. Copilots and most pilots who work in general aviation must have a commercial airplane pilot's license. Pilots and copilots also must have a rating for the class and type of planes they can fly.

To obtain the knowledge, skills, and flight experience needed to become a pilot, you must either graduate from a private FAA-approved flying school or get the appropriate training in military service. Applicants with appropriate military flight training and experience have only to pass the FAA regulations test if they apply within a year after leaving the service. Graduation from the flying schools satisfies the flight experience requirements for licensing.

To obtain a commercial pilot's license, applicants must have at least 200 hours of flight experience. To obtain an airline transport pilot's license, applicants must be at least 23 years old and have 1500 hours of flight time during the previous eight years, including night flying and instrument flying time. To get an instrument rating, applicants must have at least 40 hours of instrument time, of which 20 must be in actual flight.

The FAA gives all applicants a strict physical examination, which must be taken every year. They also give a written test on the principles of safe flight operations, FAA regulations, navigation principles, radio operation, and meteorology. In addition, the pilot must take a practical test, demonstrating flying skill and technical competence.

Once a pilot is licensed by the FAA, he may have to log additional flying hours to pass the standards of the airlines. Airlines also require a pilot to obtain a restricted radio-telephone operator permit issued by the Federal Communications Commission, which allows the holder to operate the plane's radio.

Most scheduled airlines start new men as flight engineers, although they may begin as copilots. Often they are given intensive training courses lasting three weeks to three months in which they train on company planes. They also receive classroom instruction in flight theory, radio operation, meteorology, FAA regulations, and airline operations.

Because of the changes in technology regarding aircraft, pilots are given continuous training by the airlines, and are tested periodically by the FAA.

What the Occupation Has to Offer

The expected growth of airline traffic will open many new jobs for pilots. The greatest increase will probably be in general aviation jobs, particularly business flying, aerial application like crop dusting, airtaxi operations, and patrol and survey flying.

Pilots and copilots are well paid for their work. Their earnings vary, of course, depending on the type, size, and speed of the planes they fly, the number of hours and miles flown, and length of service. Captains and airline copilots with at least three years experience have guaranteed monthly minimum salaries; pilots are prohibited from flying more than 75 to 85 hours a month. Extra pay is received for night and international flights. Pilots employed by the scheduled airlines earn more than others. A copilot can earn up to $27,000 a year on domestic flights and over $30,000 a year in international flying. The average salary for a pilot on scheduled airlines' domestic flights is about $30,000 a year; for international flights it is about $37,000 a year. Some pilots earn more than $50,000 a year.

Most pilots are union members and have strict contracts governing flying time and other aspects of their jobs. They also receive all regular benefits from the airlines, including free or heavily discounted travel for themselves and their families.

A copilot can advance to a pilot's position as openings arise and the proper tests are passed. Seniority rules are in effect here, and it usually takes five to ten years to advance. A new pilot starts with smaller aircraft and is advanced, as there are openings, to larger aircraft.

Most airline captains spend their careers flying, but those with administrative talents can, if they are interested, advance to chief pilot, flight operations manager and other executive positions. Some plots go into business for themselves, operating flying schools or airtaxi or other services. Others work in administrative and inspection jobs in aircraft manufacturing or government aviation agencies.

Points to Consider Before Going into This Field

A pilot's job is interesting, responsible, challenging, and well-paid. It offers a man an opportunity to use all his faculties and to perform a difficult and skilled job. He works fairly independently, is assured of steady employment, and has a prestigious position. It's a job with the challenge of ever-present danger and uncertainty.

There are some disadvantages to this job. There is a lot of stress involved in being responsible for operating a plane and for the safety of its occupants. The pilot must be constantly alert and has to make decisions quickly. Pilots also have irregular hours and are often away from home overnight. Some pilots work for local airlines or for commercial flying services to get around that problem.

There are very few women employed as copilots or pilots, although there should be more opportunities for those who can meet the requirements in the years to come.

For more information, write:

Airline Pilots Association International
1625 Massachusetts Avenue, N.W.
Washington, D.C. 20036.

Department of Human Resources Development
Mail Control Unit
800 Capitol Mall
Sacramento, California 95814
Ask for: *Agricultural Aircraft Pilot* No. 290, Free.
Airline Pilot No. 374, Free.

See also pages 90-91.

Stewardess or Steward

The Job

If you're interested in a job without a nine-to-five routine, being a stewardess or steward—also known as a flight attendant—might be for you.

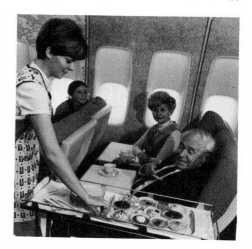

You'd be responsible for the comfort, well-being, and safety of passengers on commercial airline flights.

Before each flight, the stewardess attends a briefing meeting of the flight crew. Then she sees that the passenger cabin is in order and that all emergency and supply provisions are aboard. She also makes sure that food and beverages are in the galley. When passengers come aboard, she greets them, checks their tickets, directs them to their seats, and helps with luggage and coats. In some instances, she may sell tickets. She is a courteous hostess at all times.

When the plane is in the air, she checks seat belts, gives safety instructions, and distributes service items that people request. She answers passenger questions about flight and weather and keeps the flight cabin neat. She usually prepares, sells and serves beverages and usually heats and serves previously cooked meals.

One of the steward's and stewardess's most important responsibilities is to watch for and meet special passenger needs; he or she assists in the care of babies and small children, elderly people, and invalids.

At the end of the flight, the flight attendant makes preparations for landing and gives cordial farewells to the passengers. After the flight, he or she completes flight reports.

On international flights, the flight attendant also gives customs information and repeats instructions in an appropriate foreign language to help foreign passengers.

Most of the nation's 35,000 flight attendants are employed by domestic airlines and are stationed in all major cities in this country.

What You Need Personally

Personal qualities are of the utmost importance in this job, and airlines check carefully to see that their employees meet strict criteria. They are interested in young women—and in some cases young men—who are attractive, with neat appearances, nice complexions and teeth, and pleasant speaking voices.

The precise requirements vary for each airline, but generally airlines prefer female applicants between 20 and 27 years old, between 5'2" and 5'9" with weight not to exceed 140 pounds. Unmarried applicants are often preferred although married, divorced, or widowed persons may be considered. Good vision is a must.

The steward or stewardess must like people and enjoy helping them, be poised, have good posture, and be able to talk with anyone. She should be tactful and courteous and use intelligence and resourcefulness in handling on-the-job situations. Patience and a sense of humor are also important.

What Education and Training You Need

Flight attendants should be high school graduates and most airlines prefer that applicants have some college background or experience in dealing with the public. Applicants for international airlines should speak a second language. Applicants also have to pass a physical examination.

For those interested in a career as a stewardess or steward, the airlines suggest certain high school and college studies including psychology, English, public speaking, physiology, geography, hygiene, languages, first aid, nurses aid, nutrition or home economics, and other courses that will provide helpful background for dealing with a wide range of people.

Those applicants selected are sent to schools run by the individual airlines. The training courses usually run about five weeks, and transportation to training centers is sometimes offered. Room and board, but not salary, are provided during this period. These schools give classes in flight regulations and duties, company operations and schedules, emergency procedures and first aid, and personal grooming. Trainees for international flights are also given courses in passport and customs regulations. At the end of training, students practice under flight conditions.

There are private stewardesses' schools, but you should always check with the airline of your choice before attending such a school to be sure it meets the airline's requirements.

After completing training, stewardesses begin a six-month probationary period, working with experienced flight attendants and getting on-the-job experience.

What the Occupation Has to Offer

You can expect many openings for stewardesses in the 1970s. Airlines are scheduling more

flights, and more jumbo jets which require larger flight crews will be in service. There is a large turnover in these jobs; about 30 percent of all stewardesses resign each year. The airlines have difficulty finding enough young women to meet their high standards, despite the large number of applicants for the jobs.

Salaries for stewardesses vary, but most beginning stewardesses earn between $500 and $650 a month, depending on the airline and her hours of flying time. Stewardesses with more experience can earn $600 to $900 a month; those on international flights usually earn more than those on domestic flights.

Most stewardesses fly 75 to 80 hours a month. In addition to the usual benefits (most flight attendants are union members), stewardesses get quite a bit of time off, free visits to many places, and travel discounts for themselves and their immediate families.

Various advancement opportunities are available for a stewardess and they come quickly. A beginner can advance to first stewardess, purser, supervising stewardess, stewardess instructor, or recruiting representative. Men are more quickly advanced than women, despite the small percentage of men in the field.

Points to Consider Before Going into This Field

This job offers an opportunity to meet many people and to travel throughout the world. If you are an independent person with a desire to travel and a good attitude toward others, it can be ideal. A college education is not required, and the job offers an opportunity to develop poise and confidence while living a far from routine life.

Being a stewardess or steward is hard work. You have to be on your feet throughout most of a flight, and passengers can be difficult and demanding. No matter what the provocation, a flight attendant is expected to remain pleasant and efficient. The hours can also be difficult; flights take off at all times of the day and night, every day of the year. It is difficult to build any kind of stable home life because of the vagaries of flight schedules.

The restrictions on anyone wanting to become a steward or stewardess are stringent. The airlines check physical attributes carefully, and a bad complexion, ten extra pounds, or dirty hair may disqualify an applicant. College education is a plus, but not a necessity.

Most flight attendants are women, although a few stewards are employed, primarily on international flights. The airlines are now hiring more men who must meet essentially the same criteria as women but are more likely to be promoted when an opening occurs. It is expected that women will continue to hold the majority of positions as flight attendants.

For more information, write:

Department of Human Resources Development
Mail Control Unit
800 Capitol Mall
Sacramento, California 95814
Ask for: *Airline Stewardess* No. 79, Free.

See also, pages 90-91 for places to write for more details.

Traffic Agent and Clerk

The Job

The great number of flights and services offered by commercial airlines can be very confusing for passengers. To help them understand what the airlines have to offer, and to get people and cargo safely on and off planes, airlines employ a wide variety of traffic agents and clerks. These people sell flight tickets, reserve seats and cargo space, take care of the ground handling of planes, and answer passenger inquiries.

Reservation sales agents and clerks give customers information over the phone. They answer questions on schedules, fares, connecting flights, facilities and services. They also respond to inquiries about ground transportation, package tours, meal service, and related topics. Using computerized equipment, they check available seats on requested flights and make recommendations to callers. They make and confirm reservations through a computer.

Reservation control agents record reservations as they are made and report them to a central computer so that all offices know which seats are available on all flights. These employees do not deal with the public.

Ticket agents sell tickets and fill out ticket forms with such information as flight numbers and passengers' names and destinations. They check and weigh baggage and answer customer inquiries. Most ticket sales agents work in airports; others are in downtown airline offices.

Traffic representatives contact potential customers to promote greater use of airline services.

Passenger service representatives work in airports and in some city ticket offices answering customer inquiries, figuring fares, and arranging for special customer services. They help passengers acquire accommodations and transportation to and from the airport. They assist with boarding and baggage claims.

Operations or station agents are responsible for the ground handling of airplanes at their stations. They either supervise or assist in the loading and unloading of aircraft, check proper weight distribution of cargo, keep cargo lists, and keep records of numbers of passengers carried. They may also make arrival and departure announcements and prepare weather forms for pilots.

Most of these airline workers are employed by scheduled U.S. airlines; a few work for supplemental airlines or foreign carriers. Most work in airports or in downtown ticket offices.

What You Need Personally

The qualifications for these jobs vary, but since most require extensive public contact, you need an attractive appearance and a pleasant speaking voice. Reservation sales agents, particularly, are responsible for the first impression the airline makes. A pleasant, congenial and poised manner is important. If you are considering these jobs, you should enjoy working with people and be patient and be resourceful. Being able to think quickly and put your finger on necessary information is a plus.

What Education and Training You Need

High school graduation is required, and two or three years of college, or experience in a public-contact position is often necessary. For some jobs, like ticket sales or reservations agents, typing and neat handwriting are important qualifications. A good command of English is expected. For some jobs, business-school training may be substituted for previous experience.

Most airlines provide training of a week or more for these jobs. Additional on-the-job training is also given.

What the Occupation Has to Offer

These are good entry-level positions if you want to break into the field. There will be more openings in the next decade as more people travel by air. Some jobs, like reservation clerks will be affected by the use of more machines to record and process information. Most of these positions, however, are concerned with dealing with the public and will be little affected.

Reservations, ticket and passenger service agents normally start at $500 to $675 a month and can make as much as $600 to $900 a month. Station and operations agents start between $500 and $695 a month and can also make about $900 a month eventually. Many of these workers belong to unions, and all receive extensive benefits from the airlines, including insurance, paid vacations, and travel discounts.

Promotional opportunities exist for all these positions, but advances most often go to people with extra educational background. College courses in transportation will help in getting a higher grade job such as traffic representative. Some traffic agents and clerks are promoted to supervisory and managerial positions.

Points to Consider Before Going into This Field

If you are interested in getting into airlines work and lack specialized training, this is a good field. You can get satisfaction from helping people and handling their problems. Chances for inexpensive travel make work with the airlines especially attractive.

One disadvantage to these positions is that you must be willing to work rotating shifts and alternating days off. Airports are open twenty-four hours a day, and passengers contact the airlines at all hours. Someone must work at night, on weekends, and on holidays.

Women are not discriminated against in the majority of these jobs, although most operations agents are men.

For more information, write:

Airline Employees Association
5600 South Central Avenue
Chicago, Illinois 60638.

Department of Human Resources Development
Mail Control Unit
800 Capitol Mall
Sacramento, California 95814
Ask for: *Airline Ticket Agent, Airline Reservations Agent* No. 99, Free.

See also, pages 90-91.

Agriculture

The Job

One of the oldest occupations on earth is farming—and it is also one that has changed the most. Although we are eating more than ever, the number of people employed on farms has dropped more than 50 percent in the last twenty years; even fewer people are expected to be working on farms in years to come. Today's farmer can produce the same amount of crops as his grandfather did but in about five percent of the time! Every year, more of the 4 million people who work on farms are being employed on huge spreads that harvest massive amounts of food using the wide selection of available mechanical farming equipment. Fewer and fewer farmers are producing more and more farm products.

While farmers previously needed only general knowledge of working their lands and harvesting and selling crops, today's farmer has to be a scientist, a manager, a production man. The modern farmer is likely to have studied biology, engineering, soil science, agronomy, economics, and accounting.

Farms still come in all sizes and while all require an investment, some are more feasible than others. Some farmers borrow money to buy land, others rent out parcels of their land or have partners who provide most of the working capital. Whether you can afford to run your own farm or simply want agricultural work, there are plenty of opportunities to get started.

Most farms today are specialized in order to produce the most in the most efficient manner. If a farmer concentrates on one crop or several related crops and develops his knowledge and skill in this area, he has a better chance of increasing production. If his one crop should fail, however, he'll be wiped out.

One specialized type of farm found all over the country is the dairy farm. Dairy farms are in operation all year, seven days a week, and some dairy farmers grow crops in order to keep work forces fully occupied. Dairy farms that also grow crops may have to hire extra help at harvest time.

Dairy farming uses a lot of mechanical equipment and provides a variety of duties for the farmer. If he grows his own feed, the jobs are even more varied. Because work is evenly distributed throughout the year, his income is too; he is usually assured of steady money.

Some of the larger dairy farms employ dairy production technicians to help in the breeding or raising of cattle. Technicians may also work for the advisory services that the dairy farmer patronizes, giving him expert help where he needs it.

Earnings vary for dairy farmers, depending on the size and location of the operation and how much money the farmer owes on his land, stock, and machinery. In general, dairy farmers earn between $6,000 and $12,000 a year; the larger farms earn more.

A livestock farm or ranch is also specialized. Some farmers have general livestock farms, which offer more flexible schedules and usually fewer chores than dairy farms. For most of the year, the livestock farmer and his family can handle all the duties themselves; in peak periods they may hire extra help.

Most hog farmers have their own breeding stock. They raise the pigs they fatten for market. Cattle and sheep are usually bred and raised by Western ranchers, then fattened by other farmers for market. Large acreage is required to feed growing livestock, and most of the animals graze on public rangeland in the West, where ranchers spend much of the time out on the range managing the herds.

Livestock farms and ranches may also hire specialized technicians who have training in the care of animals, their feeding habits and the market. These technicians can also be employed by companies that service and supply the farmer. The livestock farmer's income is more sporadic than the dairy farmer's. On farms with limited acreage, income from a dairy herd will be higher usually than that of general livestock. A livestock farmer earns from $6,000 to $16,000 a year.

Poultry farms constitute a fairly small percentage of the nation's farms—less than 3 percent—although about one-third of other farms do raise some poultry. Poultry farmers may conentrate on egg production or on broiler production. Most of the larger egg farms are in the Southeast, Northeast, and California, and most broiler producers are found east of the Mississippi. There are also specialized turkey and duck producers.

Because poultry farmers devote all their energies to raising poultry, they usually don't take the time to also raise regular farm crops. Even though these farms are highly mechanized, skill in handling birds is most important for an aspiring poultry farmer.

Earnings for egg and broiler producers fluctuate every year. These farmers must make fairly high investments in their stock, so their profit margins are narrow. Many broiler producers stabilize their income by producing under contract. A financing agency—usually a feed-dealer—furnishes feed, chicks, and technical supervision. The grower provides buildings, equipment, and labor. He receives a certain amount of income per 1,000 birds marketed and perhaps a bonus for extra efficiency. The average poultry farmer earns about $6,000 a year.

Cash grain-growing (corn, wheat, and soybeans) offers a combination of working with crops and machinery. This work is good for people who don't want to work full days all year; cash grain-growing allows you to work long days with modern machinery during the periods of soil preparation, planting, and harvesting with more free time the rest of the year.

A few grain farmers also raise livestock, although most rely on the grain crops for their living. Bad weather and low prices can endanger income, but crop insurance and government price-support programs make this less of a problem today. Skilled technicians are also being trained to help the grain farmer, whether on his farm or in the service of a feed supply or research company. Incomes from cash grain-growing vary widely. Average yearly earnings might amount to $11,000.

Farms of every size grow cotton, tobacco, and peanuts. Most common in the Southeast and South Central states, cotton has also become a major crop for some growers in the West and Southwest. In fact, competition is such in the cotton market that many farmers have been forced to make large expenditures to diversify and enlarge their farms.

Because cotton, tobacco, and peanuts can be grown on one-man farms and on huge spreads, the yearly income ranges widely from $3,500 to $100,000 a year.

Specialty crops suitable to particular geographical areas include grapes, oranges, potatoes, sugarcane, and melons, among others. Exceptional skill is needed to farm these, and growers usually gain experience from working first for other specialty farmers. The crops also require expensive mechanized equipment. Most labor is done by seasonal workers. Earnings from such farms vary considerably, but keeping up on production and marketing methods will usually produce good returns.

The expanding recreational market has opened another source of income to farmers. Some farmers sell hunting or fishing rights on their land to individuals, form hunting clubs, or set up private campgrounds to accommodate the ever-increasing number of people looking for camping vacations. Other farmers take in vacationing family groups—usually from urban areas—in the summer or hunters in the winter. They may improve their ponds, stock them for fishing, and set up swimming and ice-skating areas. Old farm buildings can be converted into riding or horse-boarding stables, and dock areas can be used for private boats. Farmers may act as hunting guides or boat mechanics. On the average, farmers providing recreational activities on a part-time basis add about $1,500 a year to their incomes.

Fur farms, apiaries, greenhouses, nurseries, and flower farms are managed by people with very specific knowledge and equipment. These are high-risk operations, but can be very rewarding financially.

The specialized technicians mentioned earlier can train in virtually any area of farming. They find employment both on farms and with farm suppliers. Their jobs and training are discussed in detail later in the chapter, page 106.

Job opportunities in agriculture are available in the 22,000 cooperatives that serve rural residents. There are marketing and farm-supply cooperatives, rural electric telephone associations, rural credit unions, farm credit cooperatives, mutual irrigation and insurance associations and artificial breeding associations. Some are small local groups, others large regional cooperatives serving several states and employing several thousand workers. Many different types of occupations are available with cooperatives, including management positions and clerical positions, comparable to those in other businesses but requiring specialized farming knowledge. Some workers have marketing jobs with responsibility for harvesting, assembling, transporting, grading, storing, and selling raw products; or processing, packaging, selling, and distributing farm products to retail outlets. Cooperatives also hire personnel administrators, researchers, truck drivers, garage mechanics, and traffic managers.

Many farm supply positions are also available in petroleum refineries, feed mills, fertilizer manufacturing plants, or in supply centers. Farm service positions are diverse and include field men who advise farmers on soil, seeds, and fertilizer. they analyze soil tests and bulk feed. There are also deliverymen and machine operators who deliver supplies direct to farms, spread fertilizer, or haul farmers' products to market.

What You Need Personally

Qualities needed for a good farmer or farm worker depend on the job, but some things are always important. You should like the outdoors and be willing to be out in all kinds of weather. Physical stamina, and often strength, is important. An interest in farming, in making things grow, is equally vital. Farmers should have some interest in science, which is becoming increasingly important to their work. In order to be successful, a farmer must keep up with new developments, new products, and equipment.

What Education and Training You Need

Educational training for farmers varies considerably, but the increasing importance of scientific development means that the farmer needs all the background he can get. At least a high school education is recommended, including courses in mathematics, English, accounting, wood shop, and basic agriculture. There are many agricultural colleges, junior and community colleges, and technical schools that offer some agricultural training. Farmers may not want to take full-time college programs, but they should consider night-school courses or short courses at local agricultural schools. Courses could include land and soil management, crop and livestock production, new technology and equipment, financial management, farm planning, farm structures, construction, welding, livestock feeding, and management and record keeping.

You can also learn about agriculture from membership in the 4-H Club or Future Farmers of America or by working as a tenant farmer or hired worker on a successful farm. You should certainly work on a farm and get as much background as possible before considering buying a farm of your own.

What the Occupation Has to Offer

Although the numbers of farms are growing smaller, agriculture will continue to be important to the people of this country—we're not going to stop eating or using items produced on farms. There are opportunities in farming itself for people with knowledge and investment capital who are willing to work hard. People with a farming background and training can also look for jobs with cooperatives or with industries that supply products and services to the farmer.

A farmer has a risky living; his income is dependent on so many factors: the weather, the market, the competition, his debts. Other farm-related occupations offer steadier wages.

Points to Consider Before Going into This Field

There are many advantages in farming. The farmer gets the satisfaction of making things grow and viewing the fruits of his labors in tangible form. He works outdoors in an active occupation, and his work is never routine. He is performing a very necessary job.

Farm work does have its disadvantages, however. The hours can be long and the financial rewards meager or uncertain. Work is often strenuous, despite mechanization, and patience is needed. Medium- and large-sized farms pay very well, but they take a large investment for land and equipment. Even a small farm requires an investment, and the certainties of earning the money back are not always good.

For more information, write:

Department of Membership & Personnel Relations
American Meat Institute
59 East Van Buren Street
Chicago, Illinois 60605
Ask for: information on careers and training programs.

The Cooperative League of the USA
1828 L Street, N.W.
Washington, D. C. 20036.

Farmers Home Administration
U.S. Department of Agriculture
Washington, D.C. 20250
Ask for: information on systems of supervised credit combining credit facilities with extension teaching.

Superintendent of Documents
Government Printing Office
Washington, D.C. 20402
Ask for: *Agricultural Occupations* U.S. Department of Labor, $.20.

U.S. Department of Agriculture
Washington, D.C. 20250.

U.S. Department of Commerce
Washington, D.C. 20230.

Also contact:

State land-grant colleges or universities, county agricultural agents, the Future Farmers of America, 4-H Clubs.

Agricultural Technician

The Job

To grow and process the food we consume requires more than a single farmer or rancher and his forty acres. Most modern farms are huge specialized operations that require specially trained technicians to keep them running. There are specialists for all kinds of farms, each with duties relating to their particular kinds of operations.

One of the most generalized technicians is the agriculture business technician, or agribusiness technician. This new and expanding field offers jobs of many types. An agribusiness technician may work for a large farm, hiring, firing, and coordinating the duties of other personnel. Or he may work for a credit institution, soliciting business from farmers, appraising property, and organizing loans. A technician might also work for a food company or a feed and grain company, or he might be a salesman for a service such as aerial crop spraying. An agribusiness technician might also keep records for farmers by using data processing equipment. In all cases, he must combine a knowledge of business techniques with in-depth understanding of methods and problems of farming.

Dairy production technicians either operate or work for dairy farms, that breed and raise dairy cattle. Some work for businesses that service dairy farmers: keeping production records, working on artificial insemination, mixing feeds,

or selling supplies. This work requires a knowledge of science and business as well.

Farm-crop production technicians are involved with field crops such as grain and cotton that are grown for commercial purposes. This kind of farming has become increasingly scientific in recent years. A technician may work for a company that sells and services the farmer with such things as seed, fertilizer, or machinery. He may be involved in research, sales, or other functions of these firms. He may also be involved in the production end of the business; running the farm, taking charge of the machinery, or doing tests on fertilizers or other needed materials to see that they are doing the best possible job. Technicians are sometimes employed in the processing and distribution of farm-crop products; testing, grading, packaging, or transporting the goods.

Livestock production technicians are involved in the breeding, raising, and marketing of cattle, sheep, swine, and horses. These technicians work on a ranch or farm, for a feed company, or for a company that sells and/or services equipment to the farmer. This job calls for a combination of skills and knowledge that makes the technician a farm manager, geneticist, nutritionist, and physiologist.

An orchard and vineyard technician is also involved in a spreading and increasingly complex field. Fruits, nuts, and berries are now available all year and are used in fruit juices, wines, and canned and frozen goods. The technician may be involved in servicing and supplying the grower. He could be employed by an agricultural-chemical company, a nursery, a pest-control firm, an irrigation-equipment firm, or farm-machinery company. He does research, solves production problems, tells growers about the latest developments in the industry, and sells his company's products or services.

Some vineyard and orchard technicians work directly in the orchards; managing them for absentee growers or taking charge of soil and tissue tests. Technicians may also be involved in the processing and distribution of the product. In the laboratory, products are tested, quality controlled, graded, measured, and recorded. In the field, the technician would supervise the selecting and planting of seeds, weed and pest control, irrigation, harvesting, and product testing. Or he could do similar work for packers and canneries.

What You Need Personally

Certain qualities are important for work in any of these areas. You must enjoy the outdoors and take an interest and pleasure in watching things grow. Independent decisions are often called for, and self-discipline and reliability are needed.

Long, rigorous hours may be involved in

these jobs, so physical stamina is a must. You have to be attentive to details, observant, and able to keep neat, accurate records. Technicians must also be good communicators.

What Education and Training You Need

A high school education is preferred and sometimes required for these jobs. Courses in algebra, geometry, biology, chemistry, English, business mathematics, physics, vocational agriculture, and shop are all helpful. Membership in a 4-H Club or the Future Farmers of America is a good way to learn more about the work of agricultural technicians.

Some post-high school education is increasingly helpful in agricultural jobs. Agricultural or technical schools offer two-year programs that include courses in subjects such as agriculture, animal physiology, feeds and feeding, farm marketing. Some colleges have work-study programs, and many have placement services for graduates.

The beginning technician might get a job at a farm, ranch, or orchard, at a supply firm, or with other related businesses to polish his skills. Because of the continuing scientific and technicial developments in this field, it is important that you keep up with what is new and learn to apply it to your own business.

What the Occupation Has to Offer

The job outlook for these positions is good. Most of these jobs are relatively new, and the need for skilled workers outstrips the number of people trained to do the work. Openings should continue to increase, particularly for those with some advanced schooling. As farms and other agricultural businesses get larger and the food products we consume come from fewer and fewer places, the need for increased productivity grows. Technicians can play a major role in making modern techniques work.

Earnings for beginning technicians vary somewhat, depending on the employer and the fringe benefits associated with the job. In some cases, room and board are provided, which affects earnings. In general, earnings for beginning technicians with more than high school training are: agribusiness technicians, $7,500–$9,500 a year; dairy production technicians, $6,500–$8,000 a year; farm-crop production technicians, $7,000–$10,000 a year; orchard and vineyard technicians, $8,000–$9,000 a year.

Opportunities for advancement are also good in this field Some technicians hope to own their own farms or orchards some day; with experience and substantial capital, they may be able to do that. Orchard and vineyard technicians may become sales managers or farm managers. Livestock-production technicians may become livestock breeders, feed-lot managers, foremen, arti-

ficial-breeding distributors. Farm-crop production technicians can advance to managerial positions, as can dairy-production technicians. Agribusiness technicians may start their own businesses or work as independent agents, contracting their services to farmers.

Points to Consider Before Going into This Field

If you have a strong interest in farming and in all growing things but not enough capital or experience to start a place of your own, these jobs are ideal. They combine a chance to use your knowledge to improve crops and stock with an opportunity to provide better food for the nation. You can work outdoors, often independently, and have opportunities to keep up with all the latest scientific developments. The field is a new one and sure to continue growing in the years to come.

Because crops are seasonal, during planting and harvesting times, the hours for agricultural technicians can be long and rigorous. Livestock and dairy products may not be as seasonal, but there is still a lot of work at certain times. Weekend work is often required in agricultural occupations; there is usually compensating time off in slow seasons. Another disadvantage is weather or crops that have been destroyed by unexpected changes.

You must like the outdoors, have a strong interest in farming and/or animal-raising and be willing to work long and hard. But you can see the results of your work, and the rewards are good.

For more information, write:

American National Cattlemen's Association
1001 Lincoln Street, P.O. Box 569
Denver, Colorado 80201
Ask for: information on jobs as a cattleman.

See also, pages 105-106.

Blacksmith

The Job

We usually think of blacksmiths as nineteenth-century craftsmen busily shoeing horses, but today their work is much more diverse. They make and repair metal articles, such as machine parts and agricultural implements. They sharpen chisels, drills, and crowbars by heating and hammering edges. The blacksmith also shapes pieces of hot metal into new parts or tools; the process is called forging or fire-welding. The metal is heated in a special furnace called a forge, then placed on an anvil and shaped with presses and power hammers and finally finished with handtools like chisels and hammers.

After making or repairing a metal object, the

blacksmith may harden or temper it by heat treatment. To harden metal, he heats it to a high temperature in the forge, then cools it quickly in a water or an oil bath. To temper metal making it more durable, he heats it to a somewhat lower temperature and then lets it cool gradually. The blacksmith usually works on articles that must be made precisely, and he often uses precision measuring instruments.

Some blacksmiths still work on horseshoes. Today these men are called farriers. Ready-made horseshoes are available, but the farrier must still modify them to fit the individual horse, remove the old shoe, clean and trim the hoof and, very important, handle the horse during this whole procedure.

Most blacksmiths today are employed by industry to do maintenance and repair work. They are most frequently found working in steel, iron and machinery manufacturing, fabricated metal products, working with transportation equipment, working for railroads, in mining or with construction firms. Other blacksmiths have small shops where they repair farm implements, tools, and mechanical equipment and do welding, brazing, and tool sharpening.

Industrial blacksmiths work throughout the country but are found most often in Pennsylvania, Texas, California, Illinois, Ohio and New York. Farriers are found in all states, particularly around horse farms and race tracks.

What You Need Personally

You must be strong and in good physical condition to do this job. Do you like to work with your hands? Even with the increasing use of power tools, there is plenty of heavy work. Good eyesight and hearing are also important. A sense of timing and control are needed to make sure the proper amount of force is used on each blow. Judgment, imagination, and concentration also help. The blacksmiths who work with horses also need patience; they should, of course, like animals.

What Education and Training You Need

High school graduation is not necessary for this trade, but it is considered helpful. High school or vocational school courses in metalworking, mathematics, and blueprint reading are good backgrounds for the job.

Blacksmiths learn their work on the job, although some specific training can be obtained in the armed forces, through federal Manpower Development and Training Act programs, or in agricultural schools. Once hired, some blacksmiths learn their trade on-the-job by working up from helper to skilled worker. In some industrial firms, apprenticeship programs are available. These programs usually take three or four years, combining classroom training with on-the-job practice that includes training in blueprint-reading, proper use of tools and equipment, heat-treatment of metals, and forging methods including forge-welding. See page 52-63.

What the Occupation Has to Offer

There will probably be a decline in openings for industrial blacksmiths in the 1970s as their work can now be done by force shops and by other workmen. There will still be some jobs available each year, however, primarily to replace experienced workers who retire, die or change occupations. Because very few people enter the field, there are always openings for skilled farriers.

Earnings for blacksmiths vary; those who work in large industries usually earn between $3.50 and $5.00 an hour.

Points to Consider Before Going into This Field

Blacksmithing is challenging, independent work. Skill and judgment are required to perform the work properly, and satisfaction can be gained from a job well done. The training requirements for this job can all be satisfied on the job, so no investment in education is required.

There are some disadvantages to the work. It is strenuous, and the shops are usually hot and noisy. Many modern plants have improved these conditions, however. Blacksmiths can be subject to injury from the hot tools and metal, but safety precautions reduce this risk. Because of the strength required for this job, it is generally considered men's work, although a few women do practice the trade.

For more information, write:

International Brotherhood of Boilermakers, Iron Ship Builders
Blacksmiths, Forgers and Helpers
8th at State Avenue
Kansas City, Kansas 66101.

Landscaping and Nursery Work

The Job

In a world increasingly filled with concrete and buildings, flowers and plants give us touches of beauty, grace, and naturalness. If you enjoy working with things that grow, there are many jobs open within the landscape and nursery industries.

One area of job opportunity is as a grower. You can have a farm, greenhouse, flower shop, nursery, or garden center of any size. You can totally or partially grow plants and flowers to be sold either directly to the consumer, through a mail-order business, or to wholesalers or retailers. This work combines a knowledge of business with a specialized knowledge of horticulture. You must understand the proper uses of light and water, the effects of insects and weather on plants, and methods of grading and shipping along with other marketing information.

If you are a wholesaler, you usually offer a wide variety of flowers, plants, and supplies to smaller retail outlets. You need much the same knowledge as the grower, in addition to a clear understanding of marketing your products.

Nurseries and florist shops come in all shapes and sizes. Some are garden centers, which specialize in selling plants and various lawn and garden material like fertilizers and pesticides directly to consumers. Others emphasize house plants and flowers and do flower-arranging for customers. Some garden centers combine these activities.

Landscape nurseries usually sell, and sometimes grow, their own trees, shrubs, and plants. Landscapers have many additional duties, however. A landscaper may specialize in designing attractive plants and specifications for planting of home sites, playgrounds, business properties or other open spaces. Some landscapers are mainly involved in working out plans with customers; others are in charge of supervising the actual planting. Often a landscaper does all of these things and may also construct pools, terraces, or walks, or provide maintenance services such as tree-care, lawn-mowing and tree-spraying and pruning.

What You Need Personally

To be successful in these fields, you must enjoy making things grow and have a well-developed sense of beauty. Creativity, enjoyment of the outdoors and artistic talents are also helpful. Hard work and initiative are required for landscapers and nurserymen. An ability to apply knowledge and visualize how things will look when completed are important. Selling is often a part of the job, and you will have to be able to communicate with people and give them sound advice.

What the Occupation Has to Offer

The increasing urbanization of this country has led to a greater interest and concern for attractive open spaces. Proper land use and design, beautiful house plants and a generally more attractive and natural environment are increasingly important to Americans. Because of this, there should be good job opportunities in all phases of this industry. If you have more education and a greater understanding of the scientific and ecological aspects of your work, your chances for success will be improved. There is no ceiling on what you can earn in this field.

There are many opportunities for promotion in this industry. It is common for nurserymen or landscapers to go into business for themselves, whether as retail stores owners, landscape designers, contractors, or plant and flower growers.

Points to Consider Before Going into This Field

There are many advantages to this work. It offers you a chance to be creative and artistic and to be surrounded with things of beauty and, perhaps, to make things of even greater beauty that will bring pleasure to others. Much independent work is involved; there is a great deal of diversity and change. The field is open to both men and women.

For more information, write:

American Association of Nurserymen
835 Southern Building
1425 H Street, N.W.
Washington, D.C. 20005
Ask for: *Career Opportunities in the Nursery Industry*.

American Society for Horticultural Science
P.O. Box 109
St. Joseph, Michigan 49085
Ask for: *Horticulture: A Rewarding Career*.

Department of Human Resources Development
Mail Control Unit
800 Capitol Mall
Sacramento, California 95814
Ask for: *Ornamental Horticulturist* No. 396, Free.

National Landscape Association
832 Southern Building
Washington, D.C. 20005
Ask for: *Develop a Career as a Professional Landscape Expert.*

Society of American Florists
901 North Washington Street
Alexandria, Virginia 22314
Ask for: *Careers in the Floral Industry.*

Meatcutter

The Job

Packing houses and retail stores employ meatcutters to prepare meat, fish, and poultry for store purchase. Meatcutters are responsible for dividing animal carcasses into roasts, chops, steaks, and other serving portions. They once worked in grocery stores or ran their own butcher shops, but today the majority of meat is cut first in the packing houses before it's sent to your favorite supermarket for final portioning.

Meatcutters who work in packing houses are usually specialists; you could become a beef boner, trimmer, beef saw man, beef sider, ham boner, or loin puller.

The meatcutter works with various knives, cleavers, hand and power saws, scales, slicers, and other related equipment. To cut a beef carcass, the cutter divides it into halves with a band saw, then cuts each half between the ribs and saws through the backbone. He uses special saws to divide the quarters into major cuts, like rib or chuck, then uses a smaller butcher knife or boning knife to divide these cuts into retail cuts, such as rib roasts.

The meatcutter may then divide the retail cuts into individual portions using a butcher knife or slicer on boneless cuts and a bandsaw or cleaver on others. He removes bone chips, trims the meat, and grinds trimmings and less expensive cuts into hamburger. Some pieces of meat may also be rolled, tied, sewed, or skewered.

In retail stores, the meatcutter may also be responsible for weighing and wrapping meat and for putting it in the display case. Meat packages are usually wrapped with transparent wrap and marked with weight, date, and price.

There are other duties for meatcutters. They may pickle meat by pumping a brine solution into the arteries or may tenderize it by injecting an enzyme. In small shops, the meatcutter may also advise his customers on cuts and qualities of meat or even give out recipes or cooking advice.

There are almost 200,000 meatcutters employed in nearly every town and city in the country. Most work for retail stores, although the trend is toward more cutters working for meat packing plants.

What You Need Personally

To be a meatcutter you should be fairly strong, and, in some communities, you must have a health certificate. You need manual dexterity, good eye-hand coordination, form and depth perception, and color perception.

For the meatcutter who deals directly with customers, neatness, orderliness, and a pleasant personality are important. Being able to express things clearly will also help.

What Education and Training You Need

Most employers do not require high school graduation, but training in high school or a private meatcutting trade school is an asset. Some vocational schools offer meatcutting courses, and courses in food preparation, bookkeeping, arithmetic, and shop are helpful to the meatcutter.

More advanced courses are available at some meatcutting trade schools, and these will give the applicant a definite edge in employment. These schools give courses in handling and cutting all kinds of meat; they also teach students how to run cutting tests, figure yield, and determine selling prices and profits.

Most training for this work is acquired on the job. Many trainees work under experienced meatcutters to learn the different cuts and grades of meat and the proper use of tools and equipment. They learn to use scales, make counter displays, slice luncheon meats and cheese, wrap meat, and wait on customers.

The meatcutter must learn carcass breaking, boning and portion cutting, and master the use of all the necessary tools. Usually, these skills are taught in the general order in which they are performed. Meatcutters also learn to dress fish and poultry, roll and tie roasts, grind hamburger, prepare sausage, and cure and corn meat. In the latter stages of training, they may learn marketing operations like inventory control, meat buying, grading, and record-keeping.

Some meatcutters go through a two-to-three-year apprenticeship period, in which their on-the-job training is usually combined with some kind of classroom work. At the end of the training period, the apprentice is given a meat-cutting test in the presence of his employer and a union member. If he passes, he becomes a fully qualified meatcutter. Unemployed and underemployed workers who want to train for jobs in meatcutting can apply for such programs under the Manpower Development and Training Act in many cities.

What the Occupation Has to Offer

No particular growth in the number of jobs in this field is expected during the next ten years. Some openings will develop due to workers retiring, dying, or changing jobs: but automatic equipment will be used in many cases to do what meatcutters now do.

Most meatcutters are union members, and their wages are set by contract, although salaries vary depending on geographical areas. On the average, meatcutters earn between $3.45 and $4.56 an hour, with skilled workers making somewhat more.

The meatcutter has a number of opportunities for advancement. He may go from journeyman to first cutter, then to supervisor of his department. In retail stores, meatcutters who have taken outside courses in merchandising may become meat buyers or even store managers. Often meatcutters open their own markets.

Points to Consider Before Going into This Field

There are some advantages to this work. The working areas are usually modern and well-lighted and hours are regular. Meatcutters are assured of steady employment, and they can work anywhere in the country. The educational requirements for the job are few, the training period is relatively short and the opportunities for advancement are good for an ambitious person.

There are some disadvantages to the job, though. There is always a possibility of accidents because of the sharp instruments used in the work, although safety equipment reduces risk. There also may be unpleasant odors and sights and drastic changes of temperature going in and out of refrigerated areas. The work is always strenuous and exacting. Various jobs must be done in extreme heat or cold.

Almost all meatcutters are men, although some women work in related jobs in both packing houses and retail stores. With increasing mechanization, the work may become less strenuous, making it more feasible for women to be considered for jobs.

For more information, write:

Amalgamated Meat Cutters and Butcher Workmen of North America
2800 North Sheridan Road
Chicago, Illinois 60657.

Department of Membership & Personnel Relations
American Meat Institute
59 East Van Buren Street
Chicago, Illinois 60605
Ask for: *Opportunities for You,* and other information on jobs and training programs.

Also contact:

Local state employment offices for information about apprenticeships and training under the Manpower Development and Training Act; local unions; personnel offices of food chains or packing plants.

Art

There are many occupations open to talented people who like to draw, design, or otherwise create visual work. Some will earn their livings in the realm of fine art; others will find jobs which are commercially oriented.

An artist who paints, sculpts, or creates prints uses his media to express ideas and experiences. An established artist of this type may sometimes work on commission, but in most cases he's engaged in a long struggle to achieve recognition—and financial reward—for his work, which is labeled fine art and is thus distinguished from commercial work.

A related form of fine art is practiced by the artist-craftsman who works with clay, wood, silver, or other materials. The acceptance of a craftsman's work is often as unpredictable as the appeal a painter has to the buying public. Each sale involves the matching of individual tastes and to a certain extent depends on luck.

Most artists are involved in more commercial pursuits. Many commercial artists work in advertising agencies, publishing houses, or in a free-lance capacity. Advertising art involves designing and assembling illustration and lettering for ads, magazines, posters, etc. Some of the jobs for a commercial artist are letterer, layout artist, paste-up artist, illustrator, art director, book designer, magazine designer. There are also openings for package designers—who combine artistry with merchandising knowledge to design appealing wrappings and boxes—record jacket designers, greeting card artists, sign painters, and window trimmers.

Another area for artists is the world of fashion. Fashion designers create new styles of clothing; fashion illustrators sketch the clothes and accessories the designer creates and may also design packaging for these products. Artists who design fabrics and paper products for everything from clothing to wrapping paper can also be involved in the production and marketing of fashion.

Another type of artist is the cartoonist, who may be producing comic strips or comic books, editorial cartoons, instructional books or pamphlets.

Photographers have to combine their artistic talents with technical skills. They may be portrait photographers, may take pictures for ads or magazine articles, may specialize in aerial photography, or in motion picture photography. Some photographers work exclusively for specific companies, photographing their products and recording scientific or engineering developments.

Artists who go into industrial design work with manufacturers in designing different kinds of machines, packaging, displays, or buildings. Many industrial designers are specialists, working with one particular product or material.

Another popular career for artists is teaching. The art teacher is able to communicate his talent and love of art to students in public and private schools, colleges and universities, art centers, and museums. These jobs are often sought by painters or sculptors so that they may pursue their personal creative projects without worrying about money.

Artists who study art history may find careers in teaching or museum work. Others who also have administrative talents might run art schools or art centers. Still others go into art criticism, working for newspapers or art journals.

Art is a varied and infinitely changing field. As new means of communication evolve, new careers for the artist open up.

What You Need Personally

Creative talent is the most important thing for any aspiring artist to have. Without it, no other qualities will lead to success in the field. In addition, an artist must be original, patient, and hard-working. He needs a good color sense, manual dexterity, and some mechanical aptitude. The artist must be sensitive to people, their needs, motivations and tastes, and sometimes willing to place his clients' desires ahead of his own. A commercial artist or industrial designer in particular will need to be able to get along with people and communicate his ideas.

What Education and Training You Need

Some post-high school training is needed for most art jobs, but training should begin at an early age by experimenting with all kinds of art and developing a variety of skills.

Studies in art history are helpful to all artists, as are courses in the liberal arts. To communicate effectively, the artist should learn as much as possible about the world.

Most artists study in specialized art schools or in the art departments of colleges or universities. The length of study varies according to the profession and the degree of expertise the artist wishes to attain.

Commercial artists will study not only painting, drawing, and design, but also advertising design and production, lettering and typography and, increasingly, photography. Those aspiring to careers in fashion will take similar courses with an emphasis on the human figure and additional studies in fashion merchandising and fabric. Industrial designers will combine drawing and design courses with studies of engineering and architecture.

In general, art studies combine studio work with studies in theory, history, and general education. The student is encouraged to learn more about society, to increase his visual awareness and artistic skill and to develop creative thinking.

More and more frequently, the artist is expected to have a four-year college education, culminating in a degree (Bachelor of Fine Arts). There are some fields—cartooning, photography, and painting—where this is not as necessary, but the more training you have, the greater your chances of success in the pursuit of a career.

What the Occupation Has to Offer

Most fields of commercial art are expanding at a modest rate. Graphics are increasingly important in most media today, and creative artists are much in demand. The competition is heavy in all artistic fields, however, and talent and training are necessary for success.

There is no way to predict earnings for an artist. Commercial artists are quite well paid, and experienced, successful people in commercial art, industrial design, fashion, and photography can earn more than $20,000 a year. Many artists work in a free-lance capacity, however, which makes their incomes more variable and their potential higher. Income increases over the years as skills are learned and an artist's individual reputation grows.

Someone working in the fine arts will have a very unstable income, as it is more difficult to become known and get one's work into galleries where it can be sold. A successful painter or sculptor, however, can command thousands of dollars for his work.

All art fields are highly competitive, but talent and ambition usually assure success and promotion. In most art fields, the most successful practitioners are self-employed and name their own prices.

Points to Consider Before Going into This Field

For a talented, creative person, there is no more rewarding career than one in art. The work is visible and individual; and the artist who succeeds is highly rewarded in terms of recognition and money. Many artists are able to support themselves independently, often a strong draw for those of artistic temperament.

There are some drawbacks to a career in art. It takes a great deal of discipline and drive to create a career in this field. Those whose talent is only mediocre and whose desire to get ahead is low will fall by the wayside. An artist who does not reach the top of his profession may not receive very high rewards, and there is much time and frustration involved in attaining success. Anyone considering the field should give a long and objective look at both his talent and his dedication.

Women are found in all fields of art—although there are relatively few in industrial design. Because talent is the main criterion, female artists can be highly successful; but it should be noted that men are often favored in all artistic fields, except fashion. This situation has improved somewhat in recent years.

For more information, write:

National Association of Schools of Art
1 DuPont Circle N.W.
Washington, D.C. 20036
Ask for: list of accredited schools of art.

National Art Education Association
1201 16th Street, N.W.
Washington, D.C. 20036
Ask for: *Careers in Art*; and list of schools offering training in art.

Philadelphia College of Art
Broad and Pine Streets
Philadelphia, Pennsylvania 19102
Ask for: *Your Career in Art.*

University of Pennsylvania
Fine Arts Library
Philadelphia, Pennsylvania 19104
Ask for: *Your Career in Art.*

Additional reading:

Holden, Donald. *Art Career Guide.* New York: Watson-Guptill, 1961.

Cartoonist

The Job

Cartoons are condensed, simplified pictures and were drawn even in prehistoric times. By exaggerating human acts and attitudes, cartoons present events and ideas in a recognizable, universal way.

Today, cartoons poke fun at our life styles, and we chuckle at them in magazines, newspapers, and comic books. Over three-quarters of urban adults in this country read newspaper comics, and almost all children read comic books. Animated movies and television cartoons are just as popular. Industries, organizations, virtually anyone with a message to get across is finding out how effectively cartoons speak out.

A cartoonist works with a drawing board, a T square, triangles, brushes, pencils, pens, ink, and drawing paper. The comic-strip cartoonist combines his drawing and writing talents and usually has a continuing series of characters he must keep track of and keep consistent. The comic-book cartoonist works similarly, keeping characters and story lines simple, with an emphasis on humor.

Some cartoonists specialize in advertising and publicity. They work with newspapers, advertising agencies, and various other businesses. They combine artistic talent with their knowledge of sales and promotional techniques.

Some cartoonists specialize in doing sketch portraits, either working from real life or from photographs. Magazine cartoonists are often free-lance artists, who must have a universal sense of humor. The editorial cartoonist caricatures political events and public figures and has a special sense of perspective with regard to history and economics.

Book illustration is another field for the cartoonist. Most books illustrated by cartoons are published for children, and the artwork is more subtle and sophisticated than what is done for newspapers.

Movies and television offer still other jobs for the cartoonist. A motion picture cartoonist does cartoon drawings in a series of frames. Each frame is slightly different from the next and when the frames are photographed in sequence they show motion. A cartoonist animator does

ink drawings, colors them, and provides the background art against which the action sequences will appear. Television cartoonists should be able to do anything from a simple drawing to animated commercials. They need to be familiar with the technical aspects of television production as well as with cartooning artistry.

Cartoonists can work anywhere, but most work is done in well-lighted rooms at drawing boards.

What You Need Personally

The most important thing a cartoonist must have is the talent to draw characters with warmth and universal appeal. He needs to be imaginative, resourceful, and have a sense of humor. To be successful, a cartoonist must be ambitious, persevering, and highly motivated. He should be able to handle criticism and to get along with people. A cartoonist must be conscientious and able to sit for long hours at a drawing table. Because cartooning is often a hard field to break into, he should have patience and stick-to-itiveness.

What Education and Training You Need

No particular training is common to all cartoonists. Experience is one of the most important factors in developing cartooning skill. If you want to be a cartoonist, you should draw regularly, building your abilities both in conventional drawing and in cartooning. By studying the work of successful cartoonists and learning different drawing techniques, you'll find the best direction for your own style. A cartoonist must also be alert to people and to life situations. He will have to incorporate these into his work.

Formal education is helpful for a cartoonist and in some areas, such as animation cartooning, two or three years of art school training are considered essential. If no schools are immediately available, there are some good correspondence schools that offer helpful drawing courses. Check with an experienced cartoonist, your parents, and counselor before signing up for any school or correspondence course.

After completion of formal training, there are opportunities for apprenticeships in some areas of the industry. A cartoonist who is trying to develop a syndicated strip or some other type of free-lance work should start by submitting his work to various publications.

If you are interested in an apprenticeship, any formal art schooling you've had will be an asset. Some places, such as the Walt Disney studios, require two to three years of training in an art school before an apprentice is accepted. An apprenticeship lasts anywhere from nine months to three years.

What the Occupation Has to Offer

As the fields of advertising, industry, and education make greater use of cartoons, the variety and number of jobs for cartoonists should continue to grow.

For those trying to break into syndicated cartoon features, the job will be somewhat difficult. A cartoonist must be original and talented to be successful in this highly competitive area, and success usually comes slowly.

Because of the many different ways in which they are employed, cartoonists can earn virtually any amount of money. A salaried cartoonist can earn from $65 to $300 per week. A self-employed cartoonist usually earns between $100 and $500 a week, although his earnings are not always constant. Top-level cartoonists, like Charles Schulz of the "Peanuts" comic strip, can make unlimited amounts of money when their characters appear in syndicated strips, in books, on television, on napkins and sweat shirts and in any number of other places. Cartoonists are paid anywhere from $5 to $500 for piecework.

Promotion in cartooning is difficult to predict. Many of today's prominent cartoonists worked for years at low-paying jobs before hitting their strides and being discovered. A freelance cartoonist will have to continually prove himself to succeed.

In the motion picture industry, there are more clearly defined levels of work. An inker or painter may become an assistant animator and so on up the line.

Points to Consider Before Going into This Field

The cartoonist is an artist and, if successful, has an excellent opportunity to display his art and to entertain, educate, and influence people. Often, he is able to work independently, making his own hours (though they may be long) and working on projects that he has created.

Because talent is so important in cartooning, however, you should be sure you're good enough to have a chance at success. Because there's so much competition and even financial insecurity in this field, talent is vital.

There are no restrictions against women in this field; a talented woman has as much chance at success as a talented man.

For more information, write:

National Cartoonists Society
152 Colonial Parkway
Manhasset, New York 11030.

The Newspaper Comics Council, Inc.
260 Madison Avenue
New York, New York 10016
Ask for: Career Package, $.25.

Commercial Artist

The Job

Commercial artists create and execute the illustrations in advertisements, newspapers, magazines, on billboards, brochures, catalogs, and in television commercials. They design formats for magazines, prepare slides and filmstrips, do fashion and book illustrations, sketch and design greeting cards, design container labels, do technical drawings for industry, and do freehand and mechanical lettering. In short, they are responsible for all the graphics that brighten our daily lives but go largely unnoticed.

Often the work is produced by a team, supervised by an art director who develops the overall plan for an advertising campaign or editorial layout. The layout artist arranges what goes into the project, choosing color and other design elements and selecting and arranging illustrations, photography, and typography.

The finished product is produced by the layout man and other specialists. These include renderers, who make rough drawings; letterers, who design and execute the lettering either freehand or with mechanical aids; illustrators, whose drawings depict the finished format; paste-up and mechanical men, who cut and paste the needed artwork using various drafting tools.

In small offices, the art director and one or two others will do all these jobs. In larger office, the art director supervises a staff of several assistants and may also call on free-lance artists or outside art services.

A commercial artist must be able to take direction and understand that concepts are often dictated by a client. He must be familiar with different type faces and with the demands of the various media. He should be skilled in using different art techniques even if he specializes in only one.

Most commercial artists are employed by advertising agencies, commercial art studios, advertising departments of large companies, printing and publishing firms, textile companies, television and motion picture studios, or other business organizations. A few teach in art schools and others work free-lance.

Usually a free-lance artist works for some time in other capacities in order to build his skills and reputation. Then he solicits work from art editors until he is well established and clients begin to come to him. At that point he can usually specialize in his favorite type of work.

Of the 60,000 commercial artists currently employed, most are found in cities, like New York, Chicago, or San Francisco where publishing and advertising firms are headquartered.

What You Need Personally

Artistic talent and judgment are most important for a commercial artist. You must have imagination and originality and be able to visualize your ideas on paper. You should be able to do precise, detailed work, and work well under the pressure of deadlines. You should be resourceful and innovative, able to pick up ideas and learn from anything and anyone. An ability to get along with people is also important since the commercial artist frequently has to sell himself as well as his ideas. If you want to work in a free-lance capacity, you should also be organized and will need a good business head.

What Education and Training You Need

Specialized education in the fine arts and in commercial art techniques is essential to success in this field. Most art schools and colleges only accept applicants with a high school education, and high school studies in art plus samples of original work are usually required for admission.

The course of study for commercial artists usually takes two or three years. A certificate is awarded on graduation. In more and more cases, however, commercial artists are taking a four-year course for a Bachelor of Fine Arts degree. Some training in commercial art is also available from public vocational high schools and private home-study schools, but additional training is usually necessary to succeed in the field.

First-year art school students usually study fundamentals in art: perspective, design, color harmony, and composition. They learn to use pencil, pen and ink, crayon, and other media. After that, they go on to more specific studies, including advertising design, graphic design, drawing from life, lettering, illustration, and typography. Some knowledge of photography and printing production is also advantageous, and studies in business practice help. After schooling,

on-the-job training is required of all commercial artists.

What the Occupation Has to Offer

There should be some increase in jobs for commercial artists throughout the 1970s. A background of specialized training and a good portfolio will help in obtaining beginning jobs, for which there will be heavy competition. Visual advertising and an increased emphasis on the quality of all graphics should open more jobs in areas like packaging design, poster and window displays, and television. There should be greater demand for paste-up and mechanical artists. Designers, layout men and art directors will have tougher competition. As more skilled free-lance artists are used, there will be fewer staff positions created.

Inexperienced commercial artists start at $70 to $75 a week with high school education, $80 to $85 a week with two years of art training and $85 to $100 a week with four years of college. Some obviously talented artists may start at higher salaries and with some experience an artist can earn $125 to $175 a week or more. Art directors, designers, well-known free-lance illustrators and other artists in influential positions earn $15,000 to $20,000 a year and up.

Free-lance artists have a wide range in earnings, depending on the type of work and the artist's reputation. For example, a full-color figure with a background, $750. A full-color magazine cover may bring as much as $1,000 or $2,000. A free-lance paste-up artist gets $4 to $8 an hour, sometimes more. Free-lance artists are paid by the hour or a flat fee is agreed upon for an assignment.

A talented and ambitious artist can expect good promotions to administrative positions such as art director of a magazine or advertising agency, director of an art studio, head of a college art department.

Points to Consider Before Going into This Field

Commercial artists can find regular, salaried work in this creative field if they can be totally independent by doing free-lance work. They have the satisfaction of seeing their work displayed before a wide audience and can work in a variety of media. Competition in the field is exciting, and talent and originality bring high rewards. Commercial artists can work anywhere, and their work sometimes dramatically shapes modern living styles.

The stiff competition in this field is unappealing to some people. Others will not want to cope with the presence of meeting a firm deadline. Overtime work is common and many free-lance artists must work ten to twelve hours a day over a drawing board since their incomes tend to be irregular.

Women are frequently employed as commercial artists, but men have traditionally held the better jobs. Most women in the field are either involved in the fashion industry or are working as paste-up artists.

For more information, write:

Department of Human Resources Development
Mail Control Unit
800 Capitol Mall
Sacramento, California 95814
Ask for: *Artist, Animation* No. 215, Free. *Commercial Artist* No. 4, Free.

Society of Illustrators
128 East 63rd Street
New York, New York 10021.

Additional Reading:

Biegeleison, J. I., *Careers and Opportunities in Commercial Art.* New York: E. P. Dutton, 1963.

Fashion Designer

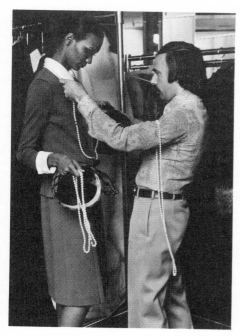

The Job

The fashion industry is exciting and continually changing. It offers an interesting career if you have an artistic bent, like clothes and fabrics, and are interested in a career that will give you an opportunity to create. The fashion designer is responsible for the original designs of new styles or even new types of clothing. Most designers have specialties—men's suits, women's dresses, children's clothes—although the work of some is more diversified. The designer must keep up with trends, consumer needs and whims in addition to studying art, history, and emerging fashion ideas.

A designer sketches his design ideas and presents his sketches to the management and sales staff of the company for approval. Sketches show not only the design but also the type of fabric, trim, and colors the designer recommends. In some cases, designers make an experimental garment in muslin from approved sketches.

In this country, the fashion industry is headquartered in New York, and most designers find jobs there. New manufacturing companies are springing up all over the country, particularly in Los Angeles, San Francisco, Miami, and Chicago.

What You Need Personally

A fashion designer should have artistic talent, particularly in sketching. You need to be creative, imaginative, original and capable of translating ideas into finished garments. Other important qualities for designers are a good sense of color, a knowledge of fabrics and an understanding of apparel-making procedures. You could learn this by working briefly at operative jobs such as machine sewing, draping, sample making and cutting. The designer must be interested in art and history and ever alert to the needs and interests of people.

What Education and Training You Need

Fashion designers usually have some post-high school training. There are schools that specialize in fashion careers, including design studies. Most of these programs are two years. Other designers receive their training on the job learning from experienced designers. Aspiring designers may be promoted from cutting or patternmaking jobs or may undergo apprenticeships. Young graduates will usually start as assistant designers with large firms.

There is an increasing tendency for apparel firms to recruit designers from colleges that offer specialized training in design. Some young people with background in designing may take jobs as designers with small firms and once their reputations have been established, transfer to jobs in larger, better-paying firms.

What the Occupation Has to Offer

With rising population and income, there should be more demand for clothing in the 1970s. Because Americans have more leisure time, they will probably be buying different types of clothing to fit their leisure activities. Increased income also seems to promote more frequent style changes, particularly as consumers become more style conscious. As fashion becomes more important in men's wear, a greater need for designers should exist in that area.

Earnings for fashion designers vary according to a designer's experience, the size of the company and its location. A beginning fashion designer with specialized education will usually earn from $85 to $150 a week, with most salaries falling within the $5,000 to $6,500 a year range.

Chances for promotion can be good for a designer, although a change of jobs may be necessary to achieve it. Some designers become world famous, operating their own firms and selling original designs for thousands of dollars.

Points to Consider Before Going into This Field

A fashion designer should have a good future if he or she is skilled and creative. The field is competitive, but someone with a good eye who is attentive to public taste can put such talents to work here. A successful designer can find respect, -money, and creative satisfaction in this job.

Talent is most important in this industry. Because competition is stiff, a designer must be continually alert to changes in the world of fashion and in what the public wants to buy. The fashion industry is also strongly affected by changes in the nation's economy, and in a recession there can be many layoffs.

A great many women are employed on most levels of the fashion industry, but there are many opportunities for men as well.

For more information, write:

Fashion Institute of Technology
State University of New York
227 West 27th Street
New York, New York 10001.

The Fashion Group, Inc.
9 Rockefeller Plaza
New York, New York 10020.

Also contact:
State Education Commissioners for lists of schools which teach fashion design.

Additional reading:

Is the Fashion Business Your Business? New York: Fairchild Publications (7 East 12th Street, New York, New York, 10003), rev. 1970.

Your Future in Fashion Design, New York: Richard Rosen, 1963. (Written for designing hopefuls by 15 famous members of the Fashion Group, Inc. and covering many sides of the fashion business.)

Industrial Designer

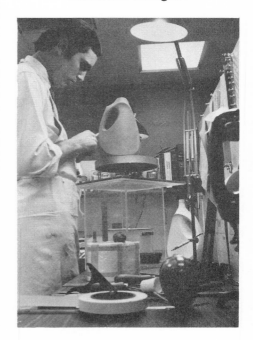

The Job

Above all else, industrial designers are creative. They combine artistic talents with knowledge of machines and production methods and awareness of public taste to create new products or improve the appearance and functional design of existing machine-made products. An industrial designer works on anything from dishpans to airplanes. He may specialize in one area or work on many different products.

Before he begins a project, the industrial designer researches the product he will redesign or similar products if he plans to create a novel item. He examines the way a particular object has been made and used and the ways it might be changed or improved. He surveys public acceptance of this product with regard to color, material and style.

The next step is to sketch possible designs based on his research and his own ideas. With sketches in hand, he discusses his proposals with his company's engineers, production supervisors and sales and market-research staffs. When they have agreed on the most suitable design, the designer makes a model, usually of clay so that it can be altered easily. The final or working model is usually made of the material that will be used in the actual product and is shown to the client for approval. If the model is approved the designer does carefully detailed drawings of it which are given to the engineering department to be put into production.

An industrial designer *must* be concerned with keeping the cost of his products down. To do this, he must be aware of production methods and plant equipment available for manufacture.

There are various types of related work an industrial designer may do. He may design containers and packages, create graphic designs for rugs or wallpaper, prepare display exhibits or design layouts for industrial fairs. Some will also design special commercial buildings, such as gasoline stations, or supermarkets.

The variety of an industrial designer's work usually depends on where he works. Most of the 10,000 industrial designers currently employed in the United States work for large manufacturing companies in large cities. Usually designers in such firms work exclusively on the products made by the employing company; senior designers in these firms are sometimes given freedom to work on long-range planning for products of the future. Other industrial designers are hired by design consulting firms or work on a free-lance basis, creating products for more than one manufacturer. A few others also work for architects or interior designers.

What You Need Personally

The industrial designer must have a combination of many skills and qualities. The most important asset you can have is creative ability, combined with some skill in drawing. You must also be practical and have an interest in mechanics. The work requires precision and independent judgment, as the product is often new. Thus, an industrial designer must be sensitive to and able to anticipate consumer needs, and translate such needs into an actual form.

An industrial designer must deal with people—both consumers and the members of other departments in his company—and most important, he must be able to communicate his ideas to them. His interest in people and their needs and desires tells him what motivates the public both socially and economically. A good business sense is a definite asset.

One of the major new fields for the industrial designer is in the area of social service. Here the design emphasis is on helping the individual improve his aptitudes or way of life in relation to a total society. Many designers have joined the government for work in underdeveloped countries as teachers. Many work in medical design for groups like the Peace Corps.

What Education and Training You Need

Virtually all industrial designers are high school graduates who then study industrial design studies in an art school, technical college, or art department of a university for at least three years, and more ideally four or five years. Some people go on to take masters' degrees in the subject. The Industrial Designers Society of America has a list of approved schools giving degrees in industrial design. The degree awarded is either Bachelor of Arts in art or Bachelor of Science in industrial design.

The course of study varies in different schools and the emphasis is not always the same. Because of the many types of knowledge required by the industrial designer, the curriculum includes courses in the areas of art, technology, science, business, and the humanities. Business courses have received increasing emphasis in recent years.

Usually half a student's courses are aimed at providing a broad background: marketing, sociology, history, etc. Other courses include speech, rhetoric, drafting, sketching, and model making. Courses more specific to the field deal with basic design, industrial design, and graphic design. Some of the things studied in the design courses might be color theory, spatial organization, abstract sculpture, and art structures. These courses include actual designing in studios with students making drawings and working models of clay, wood, and plaster.

Some schools also instruct students in the use of metalworking or woodworking machinery, and studies in basic engineering are often included also.

An industrial design graduate usually starts as an assistant, working on products that do not require structural changes and going on to more advanced work with increased experience.

What the Occupation Has to Offer

There should be a modest increase in jobs for industrial designers in the next years. Applicants with higher educational credentials will be most sought.

As things become obsolete more and more quickly, manufacturers will try to gain or regain their markets by creating new products and redesigning old ones. Small companies will probably hire industrial designers more often than in the past in order to compete with larger firms. The quality of our environment and our lives can be improved by industrial designers working with medical, social service, and ecological groups. Industrial design is a competitive field, however, and the state of the economy has a great effect on the demand.

Earnings for industrial designers depend on the employing company and its geographical location. An inexperienced industrial design graduate will earn from $125 to $175 a week. Consulting firms usually pay a little less to start and a lucrative industry like the automotive trade may pay a little more. Experienced industrial designers usually make from $8,000 to

$14,000 a year in manufacturing firms, with design managers earning from $20,000 to $35,000 a year.

A free-lance designer or consultant usually works on a fee or retainer basis, receiving a certain amount of money over a specified period of time from each company he works for. In addition, he sometimes gets royalties on his designs or participates in profit sharing. Free-lance designers or consultants earn anywhere from $200 to $20,000 for a design, and most consultants who are owners or partners in design firms make between $12,000 and $25,000 a year.

Chances for promotion are good for a talented industrial designer. In a manufacturing company, he can, with talent and effort, move from assistant designer to full designer to design project leader to design manager. Once he has established himself and built a reputation, an industrial designer can open his own consulting firm or perhaps teach industrial design at a college or university.

Points to Consider Before Going into This Field

Industrial design offers an opportunity to combine creative talent with practical, mechanical interests. For a person who likes to see the results of his work in concrete form, it is an ideal field. Industrial designers deal with people but must make many independent judgments. They are involved in an area of competition and are given plenty of chances to show their skills. Industrial design pays well and, if the designer works for a manufacturer, usually provides good benefits.

Because it is closely related to the health of the economy, industrial design is not a field of great job security. It also requires a long educational commitment. Independent designers, while having the benefits of that kind of work, also often have to work long hours with off-and-on income.

There are few women working in industrial design today, but their numbers are increasing slightly and will probably grow more in the future.

For more information, write:

Industrial Designers Society of America
60 West 55th Street
New York, New York 10019
Ask for: their book, $.50.

Interior designer

The Job

If you're looking for a job that's a marriage of art and business, interior design may be the place for you. The attractiveness and personality

of any room—whether in a home or a business office—is important to most of us. Interior designers and decorators plan and design rooms, homes, offices, and the interiors of whole buildings. They evaluate the space, perhaps working with architects if it is a new building. Then they figure out the best use of particular areas, and coordinate the selection and purchase of furniture, draperies, floor coverings, and accessories. All these must be selected with an eye to color, taste and practicality and with an emphasis on what the client wants.

Interior designers may specialize in residences or commercial buildings, or may do both. A decorator is more involved with particular rooms, while an interior designer may work on a whole office building or other establishment, even to laying out rooms within the building. In some cases, they may redesign the interiors of older buildings.

Interior designers frequently own or are employed by independent firms, which may sell some or all of the merchandise they work with. Some interior designers design furniture and/or accessories and arrange for their manufacture.

Department stores and furniture stores often have their own interior design departments, where designers or decorators help customers plan their decor, emphasizing merchandise available in the store.

The interior designer and decorator works directly with clients, whether individual or corporate, in order to understand what the taste and needs of the client are. The designer helps the client decide what will be done and at what price. Usually the designer will make a presentation to the client, including a cost estimate of furnishings, materials, transportation, labor and other incidentals. Along with that, the designer will submit floor plans, color charts, material samples, and photographs of furnishings. In many cases, the designer also will do sketches or other drawings showing what the finished room or building will look like. When the client accepts the proposal, the designer arranges to purchase the furnishings and other materials and hires and supervises the craftsmen—painters, cabinetmakers, or carpet layers—who will complete the job.

Over 15,000 people work in this field, sometimes on a part-time basis. Although many work for independent firms, large department and furniture stores are creating more such positions. Other places that employ interior designers and decorators are architectural firms, furniture and textile manufacturers, antique dealers, hotel chains, theaters, magazines in the field, and other large corporations. Movie and television studios hire interior decorators as set designers.

What You Need Personally

This is an excellent field in which to combine creative ability and a knack for business. You need artistic talent, good taste, a good color sense and a great deal of knowledge about your field. Because you are always dealing with people—and their taste and ideas may be different from yours—tact, pleasant manners and an ability to compromise are absolutely necessary. You need physical stamina to keep up with the pace of the work, and good judgment in both a business and personal sense.

What Education and Training You Need

Formal, post-high school education is a must in this field. Most employers look for graduates of three-year accredited, full-time interior design or art schools or four-year college graduates with a major in interior design or decorating. Correspondence or home-study courses are not considered adequate formal education. Be sure to pick your school carefully.

The course of study is wide ranging, including principles of design, history of art, freehand and mechanical drawing, painting, architecture as it relates to interiors, design of furniture and exhibitions, study of materials like woods, metals, plastics, and fabrics. Other studies could include salesmanship, business procedures and other business courses, and history of furnishings, art, and antiques. Many designers after graduation join the National Society of Interior Designers or the American Institute of Interior Designers.

New design graduates, no matter where they go to work, will have to go through on-the-job training—almost an apprenticeship. At least three to five years work experience is needed to be considered a professional designer, one to three years before advancing to decorator. Trainees might perform office duties, cataloging, research, matching materials or work as stockroom assistants. Beginners who don't get trainee jobs

may work selling fabric or furnishings and graduate to a trainee job.

What the Occupation Has to Offer

The increasing population, availability of spending money and the growing use of decorators by middle-class families and commercial establishments should create a good job market in the 1970s for qualified decorators and designers. More department and furniture stores will also hire decorators and designers, but talent and education will be important.

Earnings for these jobs vary a great deal. A trainee with formal schooling in the field will earn anywhere from $75 to $125 a week, depending on his background and his employer. Salaries will increase slowly as the trainee gains experience.

Designers or decorators may earn straight salaries, salaries plus 5 to 10 percent commissions on sales or straight commissions of as much as one-third on sales. Incomes vary considerably, running from $5,000 to $24,000 a year. Famous designers and decorators may earn as much as $100,000 a year.

Promotion comes slowly in this field: experience is required to build a reputation. A person with talent who works hard will move up. Design department head and interior furnishings coordinator are two of the available positions in stores and design firms. In many cases, a designer or decorator will open his own firm.

Points to Consider Before Going into This Field

This is a good field for someone who is creative, likes working with people and has a head for business. You get to see the results of your work and get to apply your talents to a wide variety of projects. The pay can be very good for a talented person, with fame and recognition coming to the top decorators and designers.

The work has some disadvantages, though, particularly dealing with difficult clients, who may change their minds or complain about costs or just have poor taste. The hours can be long and erratic, especially if you have your own business. There is a lot of leg work involved in searching for the right fabrics and furniture. Employment fluctuates as the economy is good or bad.

There are no restrictions against women in this field. In fact, about half the people employed in this area are women. The majority of interior decorators are women; most interior designers are men.

For more information, write:

National Society of Interior Designers
315 East 62nd Street
New York, New York 10021

Ask for: *Interior Design: Student Career Guide,* send self-addressed stamped No. 10 envelope.

National Home Fashions League, Inc.
767 Lexington Avenue
New York, New York 10021.
Ask for: *Your Career in Home Furnishings*

Additional Reading:

Greer, Michael, *Your Future in Interior Design.* New York: Arco Publishing Co., 1971.

Photographer

The Job

Photography is often considered a glamorous profession and some photographers do in fact travel throughout the world, photographing news events, fashion models, or breathtaking scenery. Photographers do portraits, photograph weddings and other parties, and take pictures for advertising and magazine articles.

Many skills are needed in photography, and a specialist will have to call on extra talents. A good portrait photographer, for example, must be able to take pictures that express the individual personality, are attractive and natural looking.

Photographers work with a variety of still and motion-picture cameras, which may have telephoto wide-angle or other special lenses and light filters. Photographers use many kinds of film and must know which filter and speed of film is appropriate for each type of picture, lighting condition, and camera. If pictures are taken inside or in the dark, the photographer sometimes uses elaborate lighting equipment.

Most photographers are also familiar with chemical and mechanical processes needed to develop, enlarge and print pictures. A photographer who works independently or in a small shop will often do this work himself; in a larger studio, special technicians are responsible.

Photographers, whether still or movie (few people are expert in both) need to be able to direct the use of makeup and props and must be able to arrange their subjects against a setting for best effect. This requires some knowledge of art and design.

Most professional photographers specialize in a particular area that often defines how or where they work. Portrait photographers usually work in their own studios, occasionally in people's homes. Commercial photographers take pictures for use in advertising or related use of the media. An industrial photographer works for one company, shooting for company publications and advertising. He may also take motion pictures of workers on the job and of operating machinery; these can be used to improve work or production methods. Press photographers, who seek out news events like illustrative photographers are also specialists. Some photographers specialize in aerial photography, in educational photography or in science and engineering photography. One of the newest specialties is biomedical communications photography—the photographing of medical developments and treatments for textbooks and other teaching aids. Still other photographers are employed as teachers; as representatives of photoequipment manufacturers; as photographic-equipment salesmen; or as the producers and cameramen for documentary films. A free-lance photographer may select any of the above specialties.

About half the working photographers are employed in commercial studios—either in business for themselves or as employees. The country's 65,000 photographers are found throughout the United States but most are in heavily populated states: New York, California, Pennsylvania, Ohio, and Illinois.

What You Need Personally

A photographer should have an artist's eye, combined with imagination and originality. You should have manual dexterity, good eyesight, good color distinction, and good taste. You need patience, a pleasant personality, and the ability to put people at ease. For press photographs, a knowledge of news values and the ability to act quickly are important. A sense of timing and physical agility help too.

What Education and Training You Need

There's more to it than just asking someone to say "cheese!" Many photographers learn their trade by working under a professional photographer for two or three years in a commercial studio. The trainee usually starts in the darkroom, learning to develop, print, and enlarge film. He may also set up lights and cameras and otherwise help the photographer.

Photographers can also take courses from trade schools, technical schools, colleges, universities, and correspondence schools. Almost every state has schools that teach photography, and some schools offer a four-year degree program in the subject. A college program will usually combine photography courses with studies in liberal arts. A few schools offer a master's degree in specialties like color photography. There are also some schools that offer two-year programs for an associate degree.

Art-school design courses can be useful to a photographer. Some people learn photographic skills in the armed forces. Others are trained in three-year apprenticeship programs in photographic studios.

Special training is required for scientific photography, which calls for background in science and engineering. Extra training will naturally be required for photographers working in similar areas of specific knowledge.

What the Occupation Has to Offer

The employment outlook is best for those trained in color work but good for all highly trained and skilled photographers. It is a competitive field, and the more talent and knowledge the aspiring photographer has, the surer he is to succeed.

There should be more openings in industrial photography in the 1970s than in either portrait or commercial work, though portrait and commercial work are easier to get into. Photographers are being used increasingly frequently in research and development as audio-visual aids become more popular. Microfilming, which reduces large quantities of file material to 16mm film for easier storage and access, offers additional jobs to people with photographic talent. Photographers with well-developed skills have promising futures in scientific and engineering photography, photo-journalism, and other technical fields.

Photographers' earnings vary considerably according to experience and type of work. Beginning photographers may earn between $125 and $140 a week. An inexperienced newspaper photographer earns from $95 to $200 a week, depending on the size of the newspaper. Photographers with from four to six years of experience earn between $165 and $290 a week on newspapers.

Photographers with a science and engineering background start earning between $9,000 and $10,000 a year. In the federal government, photographers' salaries start between $5,800 and $9,880 a year and increase to between $6,500 and $14,000 with experience. A few earn even more.

Photographers in business for themselves usually have higher incomes, but their work is irregular and it takes time to build a reputation.

There are really no limitations on what a skilled photographer can earn. A well-known photographer who names his own price may receive as much as $2,000 for a shot that appears on a magazine cover.

Points to Consider Before Going into This Field

Photography is a good career for someone with talent and artistry who wants independence and a chance to be creative. It will not be affected adversely by advancing technology. In fact, new developments in photo equipment and developing processes continually increase the quality of photographs and cut the time needed to take and process them. Much photography is done independently, and it is up to the individual to create his own opportunities.

While photographers employed in salaried jobs usually work normal hours and receive benefits, those who are in business for themselves frequently work long and hard hours with no paid vacations or company-sponsored health insurance. You may do very well one year and flop the next. Expenses are high and photographers frequently have to travel.

The majority of professional photographers are men, although there are some women who are very successful in this field. As a rule, there is no particular discrimination against any minority group unless an individual editor or art director has prejudices. Examples of prejudice in the hiring of photographers have decreased over the past few years.

For more information, write:

Brooks Institute School of Photography
2190 Alston Road
Santa Barbara, California 93108.

Department of Human Resources Development
Mail Control Unit
800 Capitol Mall
Sacramento, California 95814
Ask for: *Photographer* No. 51, Free.

Consumer Markets Division
Eastman Kodak Company
Rochester, New York 14650
Ask for: *Photography in Your Future*, and other booklets on job opportunities and training programs.

Master Photo Dealers and Finishers Association
603 Lansing Avenue
Jackson, Michigan 49202.

Professional Photographers of America, Inc.
1090 Executive Way
Oak Leaf Common
Des Plaines, Illinois 60018.

The Society of Photographers in Communications (ASMP)
60 East 42nd Street
New York, New York 10017
Ask for: ASMP Membership Directory ($2.50).

The Automotive Industry

The automotive industry is one of the most important in the United States, accounting for nearly one out of every six jobs in the American economy. When you recognize that there are 90 million automobiles on the road in this country, that about 10 million new cars are sold annualy, and that Americans drive nearly a *trillion* miles a year, you realize we are talking about a huge and vital industry.

A key part of the industry is the retail business: selling and servicing automobiles and trucks. Dealerships are an important part of every American community. A single sale can range from a compact car for an individual family, to a fleet of cars for a large corporation, to a gigantic diesel truck. And nearly every new motor vehicle sale involves the trade-in of a used vehicle. Servicing ranges from simple adjustments to a major overhaul.

To serve the vast automotive market, there are about 34,000 franchised new-car dealers and 27,000 new-truck dealers in the United States, nearly all of whom provide service as well as sales. When other automotive businesses—such as auto-supply stores and repair shops—are added, the number of retail automotive operations in the U. S. totals more than 800,000.

Since automotive outlets are found in just about every city and town, the prospective employee can find work virtually anywhere he wants to live. This section will discuss job opportunities in retail dealerships primarily.

While sales is the basic business of an automobile franchise, service and parts replacement is more than just a sideline. Most dealerships employ many more people in service than in sales, and devote far more physical space to it. The dealership includes an accounting department, a secretarial staff, and often specialists in financing and automotive insurance, since these are important services for the purchaser.

Because the selling and servicing of motor vehicles has become such an essential component of modern life, the retail automotive business offers real job stability. The industry is expected to continue growing vigorously, and opportunities for advancement are bright. It is estimated that as many as 50,000 new trained mechanics a year for the next 10 years will be needed to keep up with the exploding car population. Many free training programs are available, both from automobile manufacturers and from individual dealers. As a mechanic or salesman, you may be sent to be trained by top-flight instructors in the latest automotive developments and sales techniques. Training and experience in the automotive field is valuable if you enter the armed forces since it could qualify you for the same kind of job in the service and better your chances for promotion.

The person who eventually wants to run his own automotive dealership would do well to start at the ground floor with an existing dealer. Many dealers began their careers in sales, many others in service.

The automotive dealer generally holds one of the most important and respected positions in the community. He is a combination of businessman, financial expert, automotive authority, sales executive, and community leader. The foundation of his position is his intimate knowledge of automobiles and this comes only from years of experience in the retail automotive business.

For more information, write:

National Automobile Dealers Association
2000 K. Street, N.W.
Washington, D.C. 20006.

Ryder Schools, Inc.
2701 South Bayshore Drive
Miami, Florida 33133.

Automobile Mechanic

The Job

The automobile mechanic is responsible for keeping the nation's cars in good operating condition. Given the American driver's great dependence on his automobile, it is an enormous responsibility. The customer depends on his mechanic for safe, dependable transportation. The dealer depends on his mechanics to maintain the reputation and success of his business by keeping his customers well-satisfied.

The automobile mechanic performs preventive maintenance (spotting trouble *before* it occurs), diagnoses breakdowns, and makes repairs. Preventive maintenance is one of the mechanic's most important responsibilities. He often follows a checklist to be sure he examines all important parts of the car. He may then decide whether to replace worn parts, or whether to simply clean and adjust them.

To diagnose a mechanical or electrical failure, the mechanic first obtains a description of the problem from the owner. If the cause is not immediately apparent, he may inspect or listen to the motor or test-drive the car. He usually has at his disposal a variety of modern testing devices, such as motor analyzers, spark-plug testers, and compression gauges. The ability to make an accurate diagnosis in a minimum amount of time is one of the mechanic's most valuable skills and requires analytical ability as well as a thorough knowledge of a car's operation. Many skilled mechanics consider diagnosing hard-to-find troubles one of their most challenging and satisfying duties.

Once the problem is diagnosed, the mechanic makes the repairs, using a wide range of tools and equipment. As the modern automobile has grown more complex, the tools have become more sophisticated. Examples are wheel-alignment machines and headlight aimers. Mechanics also consult repair manuals and parts catalogs, since different makes of automobiles require different parts and adjustments.

The growing complexity of the automobile has led to specialization among mechanics. There are automatic-transmission specialists, tune-up men, air-conditioning specialists, front-end mechanics, and brake mechanics. However,

specialists with sound basic skills also may perform general automobile repair work.

Most of the more than 600,000 automobile mechanics employed in 1970 worked for automobile dealers, independent automotive repair shops, and service stations. Others were employed by government agencies, taxicab and auto-leasing companies, and other organizations that maintain and repair their own cars. Some mechanics are also employed by automobile manufacturers to make final adjustments and repairs at the end of the assembly line. A small number are employed by department stores that have automotive service departments.

Working conditions for mechanics have much improved in recent years. With the increasing emphasis on customer service, mechanics usually work in modern facilities with the latest equipment. The newest and most advanced tools make their work easier, cleaner, and faster. Neat uniforms are often a part of the job, as are clean, well-lighted, well-ventilated work areas and locker rooms.

What You Need Personally

If you are mechanically inclined and like to tinker with cars, you're off to a good start. On-the-job experience is important. Beginners usually start as helpers, lubrication men, or gas-station attendants. They gradually acquire the necessary knowledge and skills by working with experienced mechanics.

You'll need strength and manual dexterity to handle the tools and equipment. A pleasing personality will help you get along with customers. You must be able to work independently.

Completion of high school is an advantage in obtaining an entry mechanic's job because to most employers it indicates that you can finish a job and have potential for advancement.

What Education and Training You Need

To begin, a high school diploma and interest in automobiles is usually sufficient, although courses in automotive mechanics, manual training, and shop are helpful, as are courses in mathematics, chemistry, physics, English, and speech.

Once your on-the-job experience has begun, most training authorities recommend a three-to-four-year formal apprenticeship program as the best way to become an all-round mechanic. These programs include both on-the-job training and related classroom instruction in nearly all phases of automobile repair. Other specialties take less time to learn; a few take more.

Training programs for unemployed and underemployed workers seeking entry jobs as automobile mechanics are available in many cities under provisions of the Manpower Development and Training Act. These programs, up to a year long, stress basic maintenance and repair work.

Training also is available from the major automobile manufacturers and from private technical schools.

What the Occupation Has to Offer

As the number of cars in use in the United States increases, employment of automobile mechanics will increase with it. Employment opportunities are also expected to grow because of a greater number of automobiles equipped with exhaust emission control devices, air-conditioning and other features that increase maintenance requirements.

Because there are many degrees of skill among auto mechanics, there is considerable room for advancement. A trainee or helper can look forward to becoming a light repair mechanic, usually dealing with routine maintenance on newer cars. The next step is heavy repair mechanic, dealing with all aspects of engine, transmission, differential and electrical service. Specialization might come next or advancement to repair shop foreman, where you assign, supervise and inspect service work. Top rung on the ladder is service manager, a highly responsible position combining sales, administrative and technical duties. The service manager is one of the key executives in a typical auto dealership.

Skilled automobile mechanics in 1973 earned in straight-time hourly pay an average of over $6.00 an hour. Inexperienced beginners or helpers generally earned half or a third of that. Frequent overtime pay adds to your income.

A large proportion of experienced mechanics are paid a commission, usually about 50 percent of the labor cost charged to the customer. This way, the mechanic's earnings can increase according to the amount of work he is assigned, and how fast he completes it. No qualified auto mechanic will ever be out of work.

Points to Consider Before Going into This Field

Working conditions are generally good for the automobile mechanic, although older shops do not have all the frills of the new and more modern facilities. Though the mechanic's job is continually being made more interesting and less strenuous by the introduction of many labor-saving tools, it still requires frequent work with dirty and greasy parts, working in awkward positions, and lifting heavy objects. Nevertheless, the automobile mechanic has the satisfaction of knowing he is performing a vital service for his customers who depend upon him for the proper functioning of their cars.

For more information, write:

Automotive Service Industry Association
230 North Michigan Avenue
Chicago, Illinois 60601

Ask for: list of accredited schools and home study courses.

Department of Human Resources Development
Mail Control Unit
800 Capitol Mall
Sacramento, California 95814
Ask for: *Automobile Mechanic* No. 24, Free.

Independent Garage Owners of America, Inc.
4001 Warren Boulevard
Hillside, Illinois 60162.

Also contact:

Local automobile dealers and repair shops can provide specific information about work opportunities. Your state employment service can be a source of information about the Manpower Development and Training Act, apprenticeships, and other programs that provide training opportunities. Locals of the unions to which mechanics belong (i.e., United Auto Workers) will also give you information about apprenticeships.

Automobile Body Repairman

The Job

A top body repairman is a true craftsman, and after a look at today's highly styled and gracefully curved automobiles, it's easy to see why. Reshaping any area of the body surface or restoring any part of the handsome interiors calls for unusual skills.

As a body repairman, you must be able to take care of almost any kind of damage that can occur to metal, trim or upholstery, and bring the car back to its original condition. Because no two jobs are apt to be alike, you must use your head as well as your hands. There is plenty of room for honest craftsmanship.

The job will vary from year to year as auto models change. New methods of repair must be learned to keep up with new metals, plastics and fibers, with changes in body styling, interior design, finish, hardware and fittings. The job never lacks variety. Automobile body repairmen usually work by themselves with only general directions from foremen. Sometimes they have assistants.

Typical repairs include straightening bent auto frames, removing dents from fenders and body panels, welding torn metal, and replacing badly damaged parts. A supervisor determines which parts are to be restored or replaced and estimates the time the repairs should take.

The body repairman works with a wide variety of tools: a prying bar or hydraulic jack to push out large dents; a small anvil and hammer to smooth small dents and creases; pick hammers and punches to remove pits and dimples from the metal. Removing badly damaged sections might call for a pneumatic metal-cutting gun or an acetylene torch. Solder or plastic are used to fill small dents that cannot be worked out of the metal.

After being restored to its original shape, the repair surface is sanded in preparation for painting. In most shops the painting is done by trained automobile painters, although many small shops employ workers who are both body repairmen and painters.

Besides having a broad knowledge of automobile construction and repair techniques, the repairman must also utilize appropriate methods for each job. Most of the 100,000 body repairman employed in 1970 worked either in shops that specialize in automobile body repairs and painting or in the service departments of automobile and truck dealers. Other opportunities exist with organizations that maintain their own fleets of vehicles, such as trucking companies, government agencies, and vehicle manufacturers.

What You Need Personally

Interest in automobiles and good manual and mechanical skills are the prime requirements. People interested in body repair work should be in good physical condition and have good eye-hand coordination.

Automobile repairmen usually are required to own their handtools, but power tools are usually furnished by the employer. Many of these craftsmen have a few hundred dollars invested in tools. Beginners are expected to accumulate tools as they learn their trade.

What Education and Training You Need

Most body repairmen learn the trade on-the-job. Helpers begin by assisting body repairmen in simpler tasks, then gradually learn how to remove small dents and make other minor repairs. Generally three to four years of on-the-job training is necessary. A three-to-four-year formal apprenticeship program is thought to be the best way for young men to learn this trade. These programs include both on-the-job and related classroom instruction.

Training programs for unemployed and underemployed workers for entry level automobile body repairmen jobs are available in many cities under provisions of the Manpower Development and Training Act. Lasting up to a year, these programs stress the fundamentals of the jobs, and should be followed by on-the-job or apprenticeship training.

Courses in automobile body repair, offered by a relatively small number of high schools, vocational schools, and private vocational schools, provide helpful experience, as do courses in automobile mechanics. Most body repairmen find their work challenging and take pride in being able to restore damaged automobiles.

What the Occupation Has to Offer

Employment of body repairmen is expected to increase moderately during the 1970s. As automobile traffic continues to grow, body repair will probably become an increasingly important part of an automobile dealer's business. As the number of body repairmen increases, there will be greater demand for experienced men to supervise body repair service.

This rise in job opportunities will be offset somewhat by developments that will increase the efficiency of body repairmen. For example, there is a growing practice of replacing rather than repairing damaged parts, and the use of plastics for filling dents along with improved tools make it possible for workers to finish jobs in less time.

In 1969, body repairmen averaged straight-time earnings of $5.51 per hour. Overtime work is common. Skilled body men earn between two and three times as much as inexperienced helpers and trainees. Many experienced body man are paid a commission, usually about 50 percent of the labor cost charged to the customer. The more skilled you are and the faster you work, the more you earn.

Points to Consider Before Going into This Field

Two of the attractions of body repair work are the personal satisfaction of seeing the finished results of your work and the opportunity to work largely on your own, with only general directions from foremen. The work is slightly hazardous, although safety measures have greatly improved. Body repairmen often work in awkward or cramped positions, and much of their work is strenuous and dirty.

Although the finished product often is one of great beauty, the typical automobile repair shop is noisy and dusty because of the hammering, sanding, and painting. Most shops are well ventilated, but often the odor of paint is noticeable.

For more information, write:

Automotive Service Industry Association
230 North Michigan Avenue
Chicago, Illinois 60601.

Independent Garage Owners of America, Inc.
4001 Warren Boulevard
Hillside, Illinois 60162.

Also contact:

Local employers, unions, and state employment services are good sources of information about specific employment opportunities for body repairmen. The state employment service also may be a source of information about the Manpower Development and Training Act, apprenticeships and other programs which provide training opportunities.

Automobile Service Advisor

The Job

As the middleman between customers and mechanics in a busy service department, the automobile service advisor has one of the most important public-relations jobs in an automobile dealership. Customers look to him for solutions to their automotive problems. The mechanics look to him for an equitable flow of work and for assistance and guidance in making repairs.

The service advisor is usually the only person the customer deals with when an automobile is brought in for repairs or maintenance. He confers with the customer to determine service requirements and arranges for a mechanic to perform this work.

For a routine checkup, the advisor merely writes the customer's request on a repair order. When the customer complains of mechanical or electrical difficulties, the advisor tries to learn more about the problem and may test drive the automobile. He writes a brief description of the symptoms on the repair order to help the mechanic locate the trouble. He also determines whether or not repairs are covered by a factory warranty on the automobile.

The service advisor tells customers which repairs are needed and estimates their approximate cost and how long the work will take. He may advise on the necessity of having work done by pointing out that it will assure improved performance, safer operation and prevent more serious problems later on.

In some shops the service advisor gives the repair order to the shop dispatcher, who in turn computes the cost of repairs and assigns the job to a mechanic. Otherwise the advisor himself computes the cost of the job. The mechanic brings his questions about the job to the service advisor, and after the mechanic has completed the job, the advisor may again test drive the automobile to be sure the problem has been corrected.

When the customer returns for his car, the advisor answers his questions, explains the repairs and charges and settles any complaints about the cost or quality of the work done.

Most of the 20,000 automobile service advisors in the United States are employed by large automobile dealerships. Although they work in the same shop as mechanics, their jobs are less strenuous.

What You Need Personally

The automobile service advisor must combine a good technical background in automotive service with the ability to deal with people smoothly and tactfully. It helps to be a good listener with a pleasing personality. Most employers prefer high school graduates over 21 years of age who have had work experience in automobile repairs or related activities.

What Education and Training You Need

Service advisors are trained on the job under the guidance of experienced service advisors and the service manager. In many shops, the trainee's first assignment is to assist the service department dispatcher or cashier. By working with the dispatcher he learns how repair orders are routed through the shop, how long it takes to complete specific jobs, and how to figure repair costs. From the cashier he learns the cost of different repairs. He also learns how experienced service advisors handle customer complaints.

The beginner usually can become a qualified service advisor in one or two years, although it may take longer if his duties include estimating automobile body repairs. In addition to on-the-job training, some advisor trainees attend formal training programs conducted by automobile manufacturers.

Employers usually promote young persons from within their own organizations when vacancies arise. Some firms, however, prefer to hire qualified automobile mechanics who then join the organization as service advisors. In either case, employers look for applicants who are neat, courteous, even-tempered, attentive listeners, and good conversationalists. High school and vocational school courses in automobile mechanics, commercial arithmetic, salesmanship, public speaking, and English are helpful to young people interested in becoming service advisors.

What the Occupation Has to Offer

The increased complexity of automobile repairs and greater emphasis on service among auto dealers spells an increase in demand for automobile service advisors in the years ahead. While opportunities are now limited to larger dealerships, smaller dealers who presently do not employ service advisors are expected to hire them as their volume of service work increases.

According to a survey in late 1969, service advisors had straight-time hourly earnings averaging $4.38 per hour. Many advisors are paid a salary plus commission, with the commission based on both the cost of repairs and the price of accessories sold.

Service advisors with supervisory ability may advance to shop foremen or to service managers. Some service advisors open their own automobile repair shops.

Points to Consider Before Going into This Field

The automobile service advisor performs no repairs but rather spends most of his time in contact with customers. The peak hours—early morning when customers drop off their cars and late afternoon when they pick them up—can be extremely hectic. Occasionally an advisor must deal with a disgruntled customer but this is part of the challenge of a job that involves dealing with the public. Service advisors stand most of the time and may be outdoors in all kinds of weather, yet the work isn't physically strenuous. It's the service advisor's job to make the customer feel his car is in good hands.

For more information, write:

Automotive Service Industry Association
230 North Michigan Avenue
Chicago, Illinois 60601.

Independent Garage Owners of America, Inc.
4001 Warren Boulevard
Hillside, Illinois 60162.

Also contact:
Local automotive dealers, repair shops, state employment services.

Automobile Parts Counterman

The Job

Automotive accessories and parts replacement is big business. In recent years, sales have reached $8 billion a year, more than the annual retail sales of all furniture and home-furnishings stores in the country.

The parts counterman is in the retailing business: stocking, selling, and reordering thousands of different items. Parts countermen are employed both by parts wholesalers and by franchised automobile dealers. Those employed by wholesalers sell automotive parts to independent repair shops, self-employed mechanics, service station operators, and do-it-yourselfers. The counterman at a dealership usually sells parts only for the particular makes of automobiles and trucks sold by his employer. He supplies the parts to mechanics employed by the dealer and to independent garages and service stations in the area needing factory parts.

A parts counterman identifies the item the customer needs—often only from a general description—and locates it in the stockroom. By knowing parts catalogs and the layout of the stockroom he can find any one of several thousand items reasonably quickly. If a customer needs a part that is not stocked, the parts counterman can suggest one that is interchangeable, place a special order, or refer the customer elsewhere.

The parts counterman determines the prices of parts from price lists, receives cash payment or charges the customer's account, fills out sales receipts and when necessary packages the item. In addition, the counterman keeps catalogs and price lists current, orders parts to replenish stock, unpacks and shelves incoming shipments, maintains sales records, and takes inventory. He may also repair some parts.

What You Need Personally

An aptitude for selling is useful, since much of the job calls for dealing with a variety of customers. It's helpful if you are neat, friendly, and tactful. In addition, the counterman should be familiar with the various parts of an automobile and should have an aptitude for working with numbers. A good memory and the ability to write legibly and concentrate on details also are desirable qualifications.

What Education and Training You Need

High school or vocational school courses in automobile mechanics, commercial arithmetic, salesmanship, and bookkeeping are helpful if you are interested in becoming a parts counterman. Experience in a service station or automobile repair shop or working on cars as a hobby is also good. Employers generally prefer high school graduates.

Most countermen learn the trade through informal on-the-job training. Trainees gradually learn the different types of parts, the use of catalogs and price lists, and the layout of the stockroom. Although trainees may wait on customers after a few months' experience, generally about two years are required to become a qualified parts counterman.

Training programs for unemployed and underemployed workers for entry jobs as parts countermen are in operation in several cities under the Manpower Development and Training Act.

What the Occupation Has to Offer

Demand for parts countermen will continue to increase moderately, because the variety of parts to be sold is growing. Automobile manufacturers are producing a greater selection of makes, models, and optional equipment. As a result, dealers and wholesalers are selling a larger variety of parts. Trucking companies and bus lines hire parts countermen to man their stockrooms and dispense parts to the mechanics who repair their own fleets.

In late 1969 (the most recent figures available), automobile parts countermen earned an average straight-time hourly wage of $3.40. Overtime and working half a day on Saturday are common.

As for advancement, parts countermen who have supervisory and business management ability may become parts department or store managers. Others may become outside salesmen for wholesalers and distributors. Some parts countermen establish their own automobile parts stores. Some become automobile or truck salesmen.

Points to Consider Before Going into This Field

The job requires both selling skill and automotive knowledge and is a good vantage point from which to learn the workings of an automobile dealership. Experienced parts department managers are increasingly in demand and earn

salaries comparable to service and sales managers.

This work is not strenuous, though much of the day is spent standing or walking. There is occasional pressure or tension when you are waiting on several customers at one time and the phone keeps ringing. It's a job for a man who has an orderly mind and gives attention to detail.

For more information, write:

Automotive Service Industry Association
230 North Michigan Avenue
Chicago, Illinois 60601.

Department of Human Resources Development
Mail Control Unit
800 Capitol Mall
Sacramento, California 95814
Ask for: *Automobile Parts Man* No. 237, Free.

National Automotive Parts Association Inc.
10400 W. Higgins
Rosemont, Illinois 60018.

Also contact:

Local automotive dealers, parts wholesalers.

Automobile Salesman

The Job

An automobile salesman's job is to persuade people to buy the make of automobile he is selling. Most salesmen are employed by new-car dealers and sell both new and used automobiles. Others specialize in either new or used cars.

The salesman spends much of his time waiting on customers in the showroom or on a used-car lot, determining the kinds of cars they want by asking questions and by making encouraging comments about cars on display. Some customers are interested primarily in economy and ease of operation, others in styling and performance. The salesman's challenge is to emphasize the points that satisfy the customer and stimulate his willingness to buy. This is often done by inviting the customer to test-drive the automobile.

Because an automobile represents a considerable investment, the salesman must convince the customer he is making a wise decision. One measure of a successful automobile salesman is his ability to overcome the customer's hesitancy. Since closing the order frequently is difficult for beginning salesmen, experienced salesmen or sales managers step in and help when a closing seems likely.

Salesmen may quote tentative prices and trade-in allowances when talking to customers, but these figures usually must be approved by the sales manager. Salesmen may also arrange financing and insurance for the cars they sell and will take care of registering the car and obtaining license plates.

Before delivery of the new car, the salesman makes sure it has been properly serviced and is properly equipped. Key to a salesman's success is "repeat" business. Satisfied customers may return to a particular salesman to buy a second car or to trade in the car they bought initially. So customer satisfaction and followup by the salesman are most important.

While many cars are bought by customers who literally walk into a showroom off the street, most cars are sold by salesman who find and sell potential customers on their particular automobile makes and models. A major part of the automobile salesman's job is to obtain leads from sources such as auto registration records, dealer records, service station and parking lot operators, and others whose work brings them into frequent contact with the driving public. The salesman then contacts these prospects by mail or phone.

What You Need Personally

Automobile salesmen must be tactful, well-groomed, able to express themselves well, make good impressions on customers. Initiative and aggressiveness are important: the more prospective customers a salesman approaches, the greater the number of sales he makes. Because the salesman may go for several days, even weeks, without making a sale, he needs self-confidence and determination to get through these low periods. Patience and persistence are important qualities.

What Education and Training You Need

Most beginning salesmen are trained on the job by sales managers and more experienced salesmen. Larger dealerships may also provide several days of classroom training in such areas as finding and following up on customer leads, making sales presentations, and closing sales. Training programs are also offered by automobile manufacturers.

A high school diploma is usually the minimum educational requirement for a beginning automobile salesman, and most have had some additional education. Courses in public speaking, commercial arithmetic, English, business law, psychology, and salesmanship provide a good background for automobile selling. Previous sales experience or work requiring contact with the public is helpful.

Most beginning salesmen are in their middle to late 20s and 21 is generally considered the minimum age.

What the Occupation Has to Offer

With the number of automobiles in the United States expected to increase over the years, opportunities for automobile salesmen will also increase. Your income will depend directly on your selling ability. If you're good, you'll make a good living.

Most salesmen are paid a commission based on the selling price of a car or the gross profit realized by the dealer. A salesman may also receive commissions when he arranges financing and insurance for the customer. To protect the salesman from year-to-year fluctuations in car sales, most dealers pay a small base salary in addition to commissions. Dealers may guarantee beginners a modest income for a few weeks or months. Thereafter they are paid on the same basis as experienced salesmen. Automobile salesmen had average weekly earnings of $193 in 1969, generally higher in high-volume dealerships.

Many dealers furnish their salesmen with demonstrator cars free of charge. Others make cars available to their salesmen at a substantial discount.

The successful automobile salesman with managerial ability may advance to sales manager or general manager of a dealership and may eventually open his own dealership or become a partner in an existing one.

Points to Consider Before Going into This Field

Because earnings are largely on a commission basis, the capable and energetic salesmen can make a handsome living. However, auto sales do fluctuate periodically, and even the best salesman's earnings will suffer somewhat in lean periods. You must be able to live with these alternating periods of high income and then drought.

Most prospective automobile buyers shop in the evening or on weekends (including Sunday), so the salesman must adjust his work schedule accordingly. It's a fairly stable job for those who are suited to the field: those who can talk persuasively and convince a potential buyer to choose the car the salesman is pushing.

For more information, write:

National Automobile Dealers Association
2000 K Street, N.W.
Washington, D.C. 20006.

Also contact:
Local automobile dealers, state employment offices.

Business

When you hear the word "business," do you think of retail stores, manufacturing companies, banking and investment firms, and corporations involved in construction? If you do, you are right. Those operations are a conspicuous part of the business world. You should also keep in mind, however, that opportunities for business-men and businesswomen to join companies which offer services, rather than goods, to their customers are becoming quite common. Health service agencies—hospitals, nursing homes, soci-eties devoted to discovering causes and cures for diseases like cancer and multiple sclerosis—need to utilize sound business practices. Architects, engineers, theatrical producers, even gas station owners need the assistance and advice of ac-countants and bookkeepers, bankers, and often public relations experts.

If any of the jobs described in this section appeal to you, be sure to look into jobs described in other sections of this book as well. You may find that combining business knowledge with other skills and interests, will pay off in great personal achievement and satisfaction.

Every business office directs the actions of all business and consumer services, industries and professions, while at the same time offering its white-collar workers the opportunity to move up to positions of greater responsibility.

Skilled, conscientious business employees will be in great demand in the next decade. The job opportunities, chances for advancement, and salaries offered should match those in any of the most lucrative professions. It's up to each indi-vidual to gain the experience and knowledge that will enable him to take advantage of these op-portunities.

Business skills are as useful at home as in the office. Being aware of the value of careful budg-eting can save you dollars weekly. You will be relieved to be able to prepare your own income tax reports and your improved ability to commu-nicate with salesmen and manufacturers, and should eliminate many consumer headaches. Of course, clubs and volunteer organizations will welcome your skills and want to take advantage of them.

Business skills can be helpful in many profes-sions. The ability to type is a necessity to most writers. Reporters benefit greatly from the ability to take shorthand. Even artists would often be better off if they had at least a basic knowledge of bookkeeping and budget planning.

Preparation for employment in the world of business can be anything from a good business program in high school to getting a university doctorate in business. In between, there are courses offered in community and junior col-leges, private vocational schools, cooperative work-study programs. There are home-study courses, industry training programs, programs for the handicapped and many more. No matter where you live, or what your personal or finan-cial circumstances, you'll be able to locate places to get the training needed for this field.

As you look through the following job de-scriptions, keep an open mind. It's been said that half the jobs which will be available in ten years don't even exist today. Perhaps you will create one of them!

Accounting

The Job

Remember Bob Cratchit? Perched on a high stool at a tall, narrow desk, he labored from dawn to dusk in bad light with a quill pen, keeping track of both Ebenezer Scrooge's money and the number of shovels of coal that went into a tiny stove. The firm of Marley and Scrooge in Dickens' *A Christmas Carol* obviously had more money than heat, for Bob had to wrap himself in a shawl and wear tattered gloves to keep his fingers warm enough to move the pen.

Modern accounting has come a long way since the days of Bob Cratchit in terms of working conditions and tools, although accountants must still be able to account for every penny received or spent by the organizations for which they work.

Technically, a bookkeeper keeps the books in which the organization's income and expenditures are recorded. The accountant interprets these figures for management. In actual practice, there may be very little difference between the two—especially in a small firm.

Accountants may work in a variety of places. In government, the accountant can be involved solely with the receipt and expenditure of taxes and other federal income or his work might involve checking—or auditing—the records of firms that do business with the government. A management accountant works for a private firm, keeping track of all kinds of financial records, including sales, purchases, payrolls, taxes paid and due, social security payments. The work is a vital part of every business and of most service organizations, including doctors' and lawyers' offices.

In small offices, general bookkeeping duties are often part of other secretarial or clerical duties, while complicated work, such as estimating and filing tax returns, may be turned over to an independent accounting firm, referred to as a public accountant. A public accountant may be a one- or two-person office or a fairly large company handling the accounts of numerous small companies that do not need or prefer not to have their own accounting services. If a public accountant meets the educational requirements, gains the experience required by the laws of his state and passes the required state examination, he becomes a certified public accountant (CPA). Certification is official recognition of his skill and judgment. He is usually employed on a fee- or retainer-basis and performs a variety of auditing duties.

What You Need Personally

Most important in the accounting field is an ability to work in great detail with complete accuracy. Even in the use of computers and other electronic equipment, 100 percent accuracy is required in preparation of basic information. Diligence and patience in pursuit of missing figures are absolute musts. Most jobs require at least some understanding of tax laws and other regulations which govern the specific field in which you are employed. It will help if you have a keen analytic mind, a genuine respect for figures and accuracy, ability to keep confidential the secrets of employers or clients.

What Education and Training You Need

Many jobs in the accounting field are available to young people right out of high school if they have had at least one year, and preferably two years, of high school bookkeeping. Also required is the ability to use adding machines and calculators. Good typing is an asset since reports with lengthy columns of figures are often required. Knowledge of basic economics, business English, and general office procedure is also helpful.

While opportunities in the field are good, educational requirements are increasing. Regardless of how much high school training you have received, if you have an accounting career in mind, it is wise to take at least two years of training beyond high school. There are many junior college courses in accounting. Private business schools and correspondence schools also offer suitable courses in this field. Plan to continue to take courses whenever possible beyond your basic education if you wish to take the best advantage of opportunities for advancement in accounting. Major positions require a college degree and often a master degree in accounting.

The Internal Revenue Service also has positions for two-year college graduates. If you have completed two years of study in a college or junior college, business school, or technical institute, you may qualify as a Revenue Representative or a Tax Fraud Investigative Aide. If your two years of study included six semester hours in the study of business, economics, accounting, finance, law, or other related subjects you may qualify as an Internal Revenue Aide.

What the Occupation Has to Offer

The accounting field is rapidly expanding. Increasing awareness on the part of nonprofit organizations and small businesses of their needs for accounting services is a major factor in opening new jobs. Complex and changing tax laws, the demand for detailed financial statements to stockholders and the public along with general changes in business management are creating new demands for bookkeeping and accounting services.

While demand for college graduates will be greatest, opportunities are still expected to be good for all those with ability and special training. Computers and other data processing equipment are coming into greater use in accounting, so knowledge of these related fields is a great asset.

Salaries reported in the period of 1968–70 ranged from $90 to $125 a week for beginners with little training. Starting salaries for junior accountants averaged about $8,500 a year. Salaries of $12,000 to $15,000 are not uncommon, and this is one field where the more education you have, the higher your salary and the greater your chances for advancement.

Points to Consider Before Going into This Field

Because of widespread demand for accounting services of various types great flexibility is available in your choice of the kind of organization for which you work, the area of the country and the type of community you live in. Working conditions are generally good. Fringe benefits depend on the organizations for which you work.

Bookkeepers and accountants, especially those working for private firms dealing in auditing and tax work, are required to put in a great deal of overtime work at tax reporting time, at the close of each twelve-month financial or fiscal year. You may be required to travel a good deal when you first begin work.

The greatest restrictions are those imposed by failure to improve one's skills through continuing education. At one time, the accounting field was mostly for men, but opportunities for women are improving each year.

For more information, write:

Association of Independent Schools and Colleges
1730 M Street, N.W.
Washington, D.C. 20036
Ask for: *Accounting for Your Future.*

Personnel Division
Internal Revenue Service
Washington, D.C. 20224
Ask for: *Co-op and the IRS* (pamphlet describing the cooperative education program of the IRS); and ask for other job and training information.

Banking

The Job

Today, banks touch the lives of almost all of us. Your family probably pays bills by check, has a savings account, may have received a mortgage from a bank to buy a home or may have borrowed money to pay for a car or a major appliance.

More people have savings and checking accounts now than ever before. Many banks offer free checking accounts to teen-agers, and even newborn infants may have savings accounts, started by a loving relative.

There are a number of jobs available in the banking field.

Tellers: When you enter the bank, the staff member you are most likely to meet first is a teller. These people receive and pay money and record the transactions, stamp loan payments, and exchange coins for folding money.

After banking hours, tellers count cash on hand, list the currency-received tickets on a settlement sheet, and balance the day's accounts. They also sort checks and deposit slips and do other similar tasks. Approximately 150,000 tellers were employed in the United States in 1970. A considerable number worked part time; nearly nine out of ten were women.

Clerks: Some clerks in banking institutions do work quite similar to clerical jobs in other businesses. Many banks also employ clerks to sort customers' checks, to total deposits and withdrawals, and to prepare monthly statements for mailing. Other clerks act as bookkeepers. They keep track of each depositor's current balance, compute interest charges or payments, post investment transactions, and prepare documents for transmittal to other banks.

Office Workers: Banks employ a variety of office workers, including secretaries and clerks who are not directly involved in handling money.

Data Processing: Much of the work done in banking institutions is handled by automated equipment. Small banks may send work to a data processing center; very large banks, on the other hand, often process data for other business firms or for local government bodies.

What You Need Personally

In hiring personnel, banks look for at least a high school diploma, some experience in clerical work, maturity and neatness. With those who will meet the public—such as tellers—tact, courtesy, and a generally pleasing personality are especially important. Having discretion is an important characteristic of all banking personnel, since the customer must feel confident that his financial transactions will not become gossip. You should be able to accept the responsibility of handling large amounts of money. Tellers and other banking personnel must meet the standards of the bank's bonding company because they must be bonded before handling money. Naturally, anyone entering banking must enjoy working with figures.

What Education and Training You Need

Educational qualifications are flexible. Positions as tellers, clerks, and secretaries are often available to young people out of high school. Specialized courses in bookkeeping and accounting are important for getting better jobs.

Many banks help employees to get additional education through special courses given for bank employees either at the bank or elsewhere and paid for by the bank. You can earn while you learn to prepare for a better job. Colleges and universities offer one-term courses and seminars, which are extremely helpful for advancement. Banking associations also sponsor educational programs, and these may be paid for in total or in part by an employee's bank. The American Institute of Banking offers courses in cities across the country and also has correspondence courses available for bank employees.

A review of educational requirements for bookkeepers and accountants will give you a more detailed picture of the background desirable among applicants for banking positions.

New tellers usually observe experienced workers for a few days before doing the work themselves under close supervision. Training may last from a few days to three weeks or longer. A beginner usually starts as a commercial teller; in large banks, which have a separate savings teller's cage, he may start as a savings teller.

After gaining experience, a competent teller in a large bank may advance to head teller and eventually to bank officer if he has had some college or specialized training offered by the banking industry.

Many banks refund tuition fees when their employees complete a course of study. Few industries offer better promotional prospects through educational opportunities and on-the-job training than banks.

What the Occupation Has to Offer

A moderate rise in the number of bank positions is expected throughout the 1970s. New jobs result from general employment and business growth. Jobs become available as employees retire or stop working for other reasons or leave the banking business to enter other fields.

In 1969, a survey by the Bureau of Labor Statistics showed clerical salaries in banks to range between $70 and $130 a week, with men earning slightly more than women. Tabulating machine operators earned as much as $130 a week. A 1970 report showed nonsupervisory workers, including tellers, averaged about $100 a week. Advancement and salary increase depend on experience, individual ability, and the degree of training an employee has received—including special courses that may be bank-assisted financially. The banking professional believes in promoting from within whenever possible.

Points to Consider Before Going into This Field

Banking employees usually have very good working conditions. Generally, bank work is done in modern, clean, well-lighted, and air-conditioned offices. Hours are generally less than forty hours a week and legal bank closings ensure holidays. Most banks offer some form of profit sharing or bonuses to employees and provide sick leave. Vacations increase from two weeks after one year to as much as a full month after twenty to twenty-five years. Group plans provide life and health insurance and retirement income. Some banks also give free services to employees in the form of no-charge checking accounts and safe deposit boxes. Some banks have evening hours. Banking employment tends to remain stable during times of uncertainty in the general employment market.

Bear in mind that, other than for top officers, work will vary little from one day to the next, and total accuracy is required. Customers are not amused by mistakes in handling of their money, no matter how entertaining the story about the error may be.

Banking positions are available in local or neighborhood banks dealing directly with the public, in central offices of large bank chains, in the Federal Reserve Banks (which act as the bank for the commercial banks), in foreign exchange firms, in clearing-house associations, in check-cashing agencies, and in other organizations that do work related to finance.

Both men and women are welcome as bank employees, with women holding about two-thirds of all bank jobs in 1970. Women with ability and training are given responsible management positions in banks. There are many opportunities for minorities, particularly in urban centers.

For more information, write:

The American Bankers Association
90 Park Avenue
New York, New York 10016.

National Association of Bank-Women, Inc.
111 E. Wacker Drive
Chicago, Illinois 60601.

Also contact:
Local banks, state banker's associations.

Hotel-Motel Industry

The Job

America is a mobile society. Living for at least a day or two in a hotel or motel is perfectly normal for many of us. Commercial hotels, motels, and tourist courts cater to traveling businessmen, people attending conventions, and thousands of people who move from one part of the country to another. Residential hotels are temporary—or sometimes permanent—homes usually for single people. Many resort hotels, motels, and tourist courts operate only during the vacation or sports seasons in their areas.

Most of these establishments have rather complicated business operations, creating a rising need for specially trained people. The maintenance of rooms involves maids, porters, linen-room attendants, switchboard operators, and frequently room service. The hotel or motel might also employ receptionists, reservations clerks, bookkeepers and coffee-shop workers. You may find an elaborate restaurant, full recreational areas, newsstands, gift shops, even laundry and valet service for your traveling convenience. Some establishments provide clerks to handle travel or theatre tickets and a baby-sitter service! Restaurants, ballrooms, and gift shops are often open to the public as well as to hotel or motel guests.

Many hotel and motel jobs require little or no formal training. The larger establishments have trained supervisory personnel to run various parts of the overall operation.

What You Need Personally

Courtesy is a byword for almost every successful hotel-motel employee. Prompt service is important, especially where travelers are involved. Patience is absolutely necessary when confronting guests who make difficult demands, crying children, and noisy parties in rooms. A neat appearance and a pleasant way of speaking are important to all people who meet the public in their jobs.

What Education and Training You Need

Many of the less skilled jobs do not require special hotel training. Turnover, in hotel restaurants is likely to be high, but these jobs may offer a foot in the door. Various clerical jobs also offer a good start in this field. Experience counts a lot in the hotel-motel industry, and the more special training and education you have, the faster you'll progress.

Among the jobs that require special training, but do not require a college degree, are the following:

Housekeepers and Assistants: These are basically supervisory personnel, although in medium-sized hotels and motels housekeepers and assistants may also lend a hand with some of the housekeeping. They will supervise the housekeeping staff; prepare the budget for their department; report to the manager on the condition of the rooms (need for repairs and suggested improvements); purchase or help purchase supplies; and supervise decorating or redecorating of rooms. In very large hotels, the executive housekeepers may have specialized areas of responsibility.

Experience and training are important in obtaining a supervisory job. An increasing number of special courses are being offered by junior and community colleges and private vocational schools. Some are summer courses, some are given in the evening. The Educational Institute of the American Hotel and Motel Association offers home-study and classroom courses. Knowledge of housekeeping procedures, personnel management, budget preparation, interior decorating and the use and care of equipment and fabrics are particular assets. Experienced housekeepers can also find jobs in hospitals, clubs, college dormitories, and a variety of welfare institutions.

Clerks: Clerks in small hotels and motels may handle a wide variety of responsibility from sorting mail to keeping track of room vacancies and accepting reservations. In larger hotels and motels, each clerk has specialized duties.

Desk or Room Clerks greet guests, assign rooms (if a specific reservation has not been made), give information about services available and see that registration cards are properly filled out.

Reservation clerks keep track of room assignments and reservations, keep forms indicating when rooms are closed for repairs or renovation and keep other hotel personnel—such as housekeeping employees—informed about changes in occupancy of rooms.

Key, mail, and information clerks fill such jobs in large hotels as described by their titles.

Floor supervisors or clerks handle distribution of mail and perform other incidental duties for a specific floor.

Some of these basic jobs, such as mail or key clerk, are open to high school graduates. In addition to possessing the general personal qualifications, you will find that having taken typing and bookkeeping courses will make you stand out as an applicant. Clerks hired for night shifts are often assigned bookkeeping jobs.

Both on-the-job training and specialized courses are important for advancement to top clerk positions, some of which carry quite a bit of responsibility. Home-study courses, such as those sponsored by the Educational Institute of the American Hotel and Motel Association can contribute a great deal to your advancement.

Hotel Managers and assistants: These are among the top managerial positions which will be found in a branch of a hotel chain or in an independent hotel or motel. Four-year college educations, specializing in hotel and restaurant management, are increasingly important to applicants. Some junior colleges also offer helpful courses in this field. The hotel field is one in which experience is emphasized, so you may be able to combine day study with evening experience or vice versa. Some hotels financially assist promising employees with their formal studies.

What the Occupation Has to Offer

As Americans have become more travel-minded, both in business and for pleasure, the hotel-motel field has expanded tremendously. The employment outlook for the 1970s appears very good for the field in general.

The higher up the ladder you go, the more important both your own capabilities and your formal training become. Even a very large hotel will have only one manager, though he may have several assistants. Most hotels promote their employees from within. So if you have ability, you are assured of steady work.

Earnings vary tremendously, depending on the section of the country in which you work, the size of the hotel or motel, local or organizational tipping practices, and the strength of unions. Salaries are generally comparable to similar jobs in other industries, meaning that college graduate trainees and lower-level supervisory personnel earn salaries in the general range of $10,000 a year. You may get special pay for evening hours, and some employees receive free meals during working hours.

What is an advantage to one person is often a disadvantage to another. Remember, hotel-motel work is always a twenty-four-hour-a-day operation, seven days a week. Many jobs require odd hours with work on weekends and holidays. This is unattractive to some people, but if you are trying to attend school and work at the same time, you may find a special opportunity in this field. Hotels and motels in resort areas usually hire extra help during vacation and holiday seasons.

The more important the job is, the fewer openings there are, so you may find advancement to higher positions difficult simply because no vacancies exist. However, hotel-type jobs are also available in hospitals, school dormitories, private clubs, and similar institutions. If you do rise to managerial responsibility, you'll discover that hotel and motel chains frequently transfer experienced personnel to supervise new operations or establish hotels and motels in new locations. If you are flexible about where you live, you may find this both challenging and exciting.

Both men and women find employment on just about every level of hotel work.

For more information, write:

Council on Hotel, Restaurant, and Institutional Education
1522 K Street, N.W.
Washington, D.C. 20005
Ask for: *Directory of Schools Scholarships Directory* $.50.

National Executive Housekeeper Association, Inc.
c/o Miss Alberta J. Wetherholt
Business and Professional Building
Second Avenue
Gallipolis, Ohio 45631.

Insurance industry

The Job

Insurance companies sell policies that offer the buyer financial protection against some kind of loss. Life Insurance pays to a person's survivors money to compensate for financial problems resulting from the death of the insured person. Health and accident insurance pays money to compensate for the cost of hospital and medical bills. Property insurance covers loss of or damage to property such as houses, cars, or other personal possessions. Liability insurance protects against lawsuits in the event of damage

Investigators can work for insurance companies or adjusting organizations, or they can go into business for themselves. In most insurance companies there is ample opportunity to move upward to supervisory positions.

Claims Examiner: His work is closely related to that of the adjuster. Examiners deal more frequently with life, accident, and disability insurance; the adjuster works primarily with property and liability policies. Besides verifying a claim and approving its payment, a claims examiner also maintains records and prepares claims reports.

Either an examiner or an adjuster may be required to undertake a good deal of field work, traveling to the site of an accident or fire, to look into the extent of damage, the way in which the incident occurred and the other factors that have a bearing on the liability of the firm.

Underwriters: It is the job of the underwriter to evaluate the risks his company takes in issuing an insurance policy. He analyzes statements in the customer's application for insurance, reviews safety reports, studies actuarial reports (which give figures on the degree of risk involved under the circumstances described). He determines the premium rate for each policy his company issues and may determine that an extra risk calls for an increase in cost to the policyholder.

When working in an area not covered by rule or precedent, however, an underwriter must exercise personal judgment. If he is too conservative in appraising risks, his company may lose business to a competitor. On the other hand, if his underwriting actions are too liberal, his firm may have to pay too many claims in the future.

What You Need Personally

Interest in figures and statistics, coupled with ability to search out detail, are important traits for insurance workers. The ability to be tactful but firm, and to speak and write clearly are important in your contacts with clients. Habits of keen observation are vital in this work as you gather all the facts relating to a claim and weigh them together in making a decision. Claims adjusters and examiners should enjoy moving about for much of the work takes place outside the office.

What Education and Training You Need

A college degree is becoming more important in this field, but a generally good educational background along with expertise in some related field is acceptable to many firms. For example, an experienced auto repairman may qualify as an adjuster in cases involving auto damage. A background in business or accounting would be important to an adjuster working on business-loss claims. New adjusters generally begin working with simple claims and are supervised by an

or injury to another person. The latter two are usually handled together.

Depending on the policy, insurance may include retirement funds, disability payments, education of children, and income protection.

Information on work of the insurance agent will be found on pp. 337-339. When most people think of insurance work, the agent is the person they have in mind. Though agents are the best known, they are least in number in the industry; well over half of all insurance employees are in jobs other than that of insurance agent.

Duties performed by secretaries, clerks, typists, and bookkeepers are similar in the insurance field to those performed by the same workers in other fields. For more information on these jobs check the Index.

Claims Adjuster: The claims adjuster has an action-packed responsibility, says the Insurance Information Institute. He hurries to scenes of accidents, fires, and other disasters, determines if losses or damages are covered by the claimant's policy, inspects damaged or destroyed property and estimates the costs of repair or replacement. He then works out a settlement satisfactory to all concerned.

Claims adjusters are often specialists in handling property, claims arising from auto accidents, claims of home owners, or claims of business firms and public institutions.

The work of an adjuster frequently involves honest differences of opinion on the part of the company and the policyholder. So, to be effective, the adjuster must be tactful and patient and show good judgment in dealing with many kinds of people in difficult situations.

experienced adjuster. An adjuster who lacks college training will be slower in advancing to senior or supervisory positions. You probably will have to be 20 or 21 years old before you are accepted for work.

For nearly every job in insurance there is on-the-job training. In addition, the home offices offer courses so that you can improve your general skills. For example, if you get a job as a file clerk and would like to learn how to type, you could probably take a typing course right at the office after work, for which the company would pay. Courses offered by the various companies cover almost every office skill—shorthand, bookkeeping, accounting—and, in addition, companies often will pay for courses taken at night school or nearby colleges. All insurance companies ask is that you earn a reasonable grade in the course before you are reimbursed for its cost.

Many insurance companies and adjustment firms offer a combination of on-the-job training and home-study courses to prepare new employees for work as adjusters. The Insurance Institute of America offers a six-semester program leading to a diploma in Insurance Loss and Claims Adjusting. The diploma is given after the applicant passes six national examinations, which can be prepared for with home-study, through company or public classes or through college courses in insurance. The College of Insurance in New York City offers a professional Certificate in Insurance Adjusting.

Positions as claims examiners are often available to people with high-school educations who have experience in clerical work or some college training. The more education you have beyond high school, the higher your starting position can be. College graduates do have an edge.

The employee who has a high school education begins in a clerical job, perhaps as a claims processor in a group-life or health department. College graduates, or those having two years or more of college training, may begin work as junior claims examiners. Although courses in insurance, economics, or other business subjects are helpful, a major in almost any college field is adequate preparation. A college-trained employee can look forward to promotion to senior claims representative or claims examiner after a year or more; high-school graduates usually need several years' experience before advancing to one of these positions. Advancement to most supervisory claims examiner jobs demands a college education, although experience can sometimes be substituted for a part of the work leading to a college degree. The employee who lacks formal college training generally advances at a slower rate.

As is true of the adjuster, ability to communicate clearly with people of many types and levels of education is important. Attention to detail and mathematical ability are both important. This isn't a good job choice for a person who overlooks details or who has a poor memory for facts.

Underwriters' jobs are being filled more and more by college graduates. Those with less than a college degree are able to obtain these positions but find advancement is limited. A combination of on-the-job training and home-study courses or special classes taken at home, in the office, in schools or at local colleges is part of the learning program for underwriters. Many firms assist with the cost of these courses for their employees and offer salary increases as incentives. You will need good analytic ability, good judgment, as well as creativity and drive when seeking information about a claim.

What the Occupation Has to Offer

The most rapid growth during the 1970s is expected to be in jobs for claims adjusters, with moderate growth of underwriters' positions, and very little growth for examiners.

Trainees' salaries usually start at about $7,000. Generally speaking, salaries for all three cateogries of insurance employees with some years experience run from $10,000 to $15,000. While supervisory personnel earn higher salaries (over $15,000), there is keen competition for such posts. Promotions depend upon your performance in handling claims. All along the ladder of employment, additional education and training are important in seeking promotion. You should plan to continue taking many special courses if you choose a career in the insurance field and wish to continue to advance.

Points to Consider Before Going into This Field

Insurance offices are usually pleasant places in which to work. It can be a satisfying career for a young man or woman who is patient with details and who enjoys relating and evaluating facts. The young person who dislikes being tied to a desk and prefers working with people should consider other career fields. In addition to powers of analysis and good judgment, an underwriter must be imaginative and aggressive, especially when need arises to obtain additional information from outside sources.

Most underwriters have desk jobs that require no unusual physical activity and work in pleasant, quiet surroundings. Some underwriters may work irregular hours when traveling to advise field personnel, when attending underwriting seminars or at times of peak load in policy applications. Since relatively few underwriting decisions are reviewed at a higher level, the underwriter holds a job of considerable responsibility.

Examiners usually work a 35–40-hour week with only occasional times out of the office.

Adjusters do not work at desks. They must be physically fit since their work involves driving from one place to another, spending a good deal of time out of doors, walking about, climbing stairs. Adjusters often work long and unusual hours—in the evening or on weekends in order to interview witnesses and persons making claims at their convenience. You may have seen insurance ads which promise twenty-four-hour service; it is the adjuster who makes this possible by calling on a witness or policyholder on very short notice. People who like regular hours are well advised to forget about a job as an insurance adjuster.

While most jobs as adjusters and underwriters are held by men, half of the claim examiners are women. There is no real reason why a woman with equal capability and training cannot obtain any position in the insurance industry. Insurance is for people who like to deal with things precisely and to see the results of their efforts often. It is for those interested in job security.

Insurance firms also employ all varieties of clerical, secretarial, accounting and purchasing personnel, and other businessmen and businesswomen. Positions of this type may well provide entry into specialized insurance jobs.

For more information, write:

Department of Human Resources Development
Mail Control Unit
800 Capitol Mall
Sacramento, California 95814
Ask for: *Claims Adjuster (Insurance)* No. 67. Free.

Educational Division
Institute of Life Insurance
277 Park Avenue
New York, New York 10017.

Insurance Information Institute
110 William Street
New York, New York 10038
Ask for: *Careers in Property and Liability Insurance.* Free.

Also contact for programs for the training of adjusters:

General Adjustment Bureau
123 William Street
New York, New York 10038.

Insurance Institute of America
270 Bryn Mawr Avenue
Bryn Mawr, Pennsylvania 19010.

Legal Assistant

The Job

The nicest part of being a lawyer on television is that you can spend your entire career

brilliantly investigating and arguing cases. In real life, however, it could be said that all Perry Mason and no drudgery makes a feeble case in court.

Any practicing lawyer will tell you that a great percentage of his time is spent in the library of his law office or in consulting official records of a town, city, or state. Large law firms often assign this research to new lawyers, but the attorney in a one- or two-member firm finds many of his or her hours are spent finding the basis on which to build a case rather than in the more commonly known elements of the practice of law.

Each year that passes adds to the abundance of precedents, prior cases, and court decisions that could apply to any one case. The American Bar Association, recognizing this problem, recommends the training and employment of legal assistants. This is quite a new field and can be expected to grow as attorneys become increasingly aware of the value of specially trained lay assistants, who can effectively relieve the fully trained attorney of time-consuming background work.

The ABA's Special Committee on Legal Assistants recognizes three possible levels of aides.

Legal Secretary: The legal secretary must be able to perform all the normal secretarial tasks. (See pp. 156-158.) In addition, he or she must have a knowledge of legal terminology, be prepared to handle fee and disbursement sheets and know how to prepare proper documents for real estate, probate, corporate, tax, civil or criminal litigation, and family or domestic relations cases. Simple bookkeeping is usually part of the job. The Bar Association recommends that legal secretarial training be taken at the junior or community college level, rather than at a vocational-technical school, if career advancement is sought. This is because colleges that grant degrees do not always give credit for courses taken in vocational-technical schools.

Legal Assistant: This job includes the ability to apply knowledge of the law and legal procedures by helping lawyers do their research, by the modification of new procedures and techniques, by preparing or interpreting legal documents, by selecting and compiling technical information from digests and encyclopedias, and by analyzing and following procedural problems that involve making independent decisions.

Legal Administrator: In addition to all of the above, the legal administrator must be trained to plan and assist in the installation of fairly complex office equipment, to advise about the operation and maintenance of such equipment, and to plan operations involving the best use of manpower, materials, money, and equipment.

Generally speaking, law offices are pleasant places to work, There is always a great deal of person-to-person contact, whether with other employees and members of the firm or with clients. Hours may be longer than average and some weekend work may be involved. Holidays are usually good.

In addition to working in independent law firms, legal staff members sometimes find themselves employed in legal departments of large corporations. Government on all levels has need for legal staffs. The city or corporate counsel who handles civil cases needs assistance as do criminal divisions of city government which handle prosecutions and public-defender law cases.

What You Need Personally

You need an agreeable personality, you should enjoy paying attention to detail, you must be willing to become totally in sympathy with your client's point of view, and you will, of course, display great discretion in all your dealings.

What Education and Training You Need

The legal secretarial course is a post-high school course and may be one or two years, with the two-year course preferable. Legal assistant formal training is recommended as a two-year course also. It is given in both junior colleges and universities. The legal administrator course is proposed as a four-year course. Since the ABA's recommended curriculum for the two latter courses is identical for the first two years, you could go back later to study for Legal Administrator once you've completed the two-year assistants' course.

What the Occupation Has to Offer

Despite the less exciting aspects of doing legal research, the law profession is a challenging and stimulating one. The employment outlook for legal secretaries is usually good, at least in part because of marriages and accompanying retirement of young women in those jobs. The positions of legal assistant and legal administrator are new, but jobs can be expected to increase.

It's too early to give a good analysis of earnings, except to say that salaries in legal offices are usually good.

Advancement is not dramatic because one cannot move from legal assistant or administrator to attorney without a great deal of additional education. However, as the field expands, you may find jobs developing such as "chief assistant," the supervisor of several assistants in a large law firm. You may also find similar development in governmental operations.

Points to Consider Before Going into This Field

Because this field is new, you will be going into relatively unexplored territory. You may well expect to become exposed to the world of politics, since so many lawyers are involved in politics and so many politicians are lawyers. A crackerjack legal assistant may be just what a newly elected government official needs too. On the other hand, if going into a new, untested field sounds a little frightening, this is not for you. There should certainly be equal employment opportunities as either legal assistants or legal administrators for both men and women (the girls have pretty well taken over the secretarial field).

For more information, write:

Information Service
American Bar Association
1155 East 60th Street
Chicago, Illinois 60637.

As of late 1972, the ABA had not formally approved or accredited any courses. Ask for their curriculum guide and follow it closely.

National Association of Legal Secretaries
Legal Assistant Section
3005 East Skelly Drive, Suite 120
Tulsa, Oklahoma 74105

Also contact:
Local colleges and universities.

Personnel

The Job

Finding the right people to fill jobs for the company is the task of the personnel department. This matching of the correct man or woman to the available job—and the task of keeping good people working for the company—is one of the most important parts of any company operation.

Personnel workers are involved in recruiting and hiring the staff, including interviewing applicants. They advise employees about working conditions, benefits and problems, deal with discipline, classify jobs, plan wage and salary

scales, and help develop safety programs. They often supervise employee orientation, on-the-job advanced training, and administer various employee benefit programs.

The size of the department depends on the size of the firm and may range from a one- or two-man department to a rather large staff with a number of specialists. Almost every business firm and government agency has some form of personnel department. There are also a number of independent personnel firms, dealing in management consultation and management-employee relations or acting as employment agencies.

Most personnel work is desk work with regular hours and generally good working conditions.

What You Need Personally

Can you speak and write clearly? These are important qualities for people interested in careers in personnel. You also need a talent for working with people of all levels of intelligence and experience. You must be able to see both the employer's point of view and that of the employee. You should like detailed work and be pleasantly persuasive.

What Education and Training You Need

As is true in so many professions, a college degree is virtually a mandatory requirement for top personnel jobs. However, there are well-paying jobs available for those with less than a four-year college education.

Wage and salary analysts, for example, have need for college courses in this specific area of personnel work, both a beginner's course and an advanced course for a total of six credits over two semesters. If you are interested in this field, you should contact your local junior college or

university and see if they offer courses in wage and salary analysis.

Large companies often have people on the personnel staff who do nothing but interview prospective employees and those within the company who wish to advance to higher positions. Here, experience is the most important qualification, and you can work your way into an interviewer's position from another position in the department.

A time-study analyst often starts as an apprentice and is trained on the job. Many companies fill positions in their personnel departments by transferring talented employees from other departments in the company. A large number of the people now in personnel work who are not college graduates entered the field in this manner.

What the Occupation Has to Offer

Personnel is still a growing field. The importance of good employee relations is being recognized more and more by both large and small firms. The larger the firm, the better your chance of obtaining work without a lengthy educational background and experience in the field. Small companies are more dependent on having a wide range of knowledge and skill available from one person. A larger firm is more likely to have specialized jobs available.

Salaries are comparable to those paid for similar work in other fields, but are not exceptionally high. A trainee will earn from $6,000 to $8,000 a year with experience. Directors of personnel work earn between $12,500 and $22,000.

It is possible to work your way up to an important personnel position without a full four-year degree, but this is difficult to do. Usually employees who advance without the degree have rounded out their practical experience with evening courses at the college level.

Points to Consider Before Going into This Field

If you have a real feeling for people, personnel work can be especially stimulating and rewarding. You can find great satisfaction in having a direct hand in the improvement of working conditions and wages for large numbers of people. Since the personnel department is responsible for carrying out work regulations, you should expect to be called upon to set an example.

It is extremely embarrassing to the personnel director if his staff members abuse company regulations, fail to dress in business-like clothes, or are found to be careless about safety regulations. After all, the personnel department is the place where most new employees get their first impressions of the firm. Your employer will expect those impressions to be good.

Both men and women are welcome in personnel work, and many women hold responsible jobs in the field. If a company employs more men than women as workers, that tendency will probably be reflected in the personnel department staff. Similarly, firms with very large numbers of women on the staff will probably lean toward hiring women in their personnel departments.

For more information, write:

American Personnel and Guidance Association
1607 New Hampshire Avenue, N.W.
Washington, D.C. 20009.

International Association of Personnel Women
358 Fifth Avenue
New York, New York 10001.

Purchasing Agent

The Job

The Purchasing Department of a company has the job of buying the supplies the company needs, seeing they are obtained at the best possible prices, making sure they arrive on time, storing them properly, and replacing them when the stock begins to run low.

All this sounds rather routine, but in today's complicated world, purchasing can be a challenging occupation. The men, and sometimes women, in charge of buying supplies are no longer limited to dealing with supply sources in the immediate area. Modern transportation methods—trucking, shipping, railroads, and air freight—make available to the head of the purchasing department a world-wide market from which to make selections. Companies are also no longer content to depend on one supplier for an indefinite period and entertain competitive bids. The head of purchasing, regardless of his title, has a responsible and important position.

While small companies may combine purchasing responsibilites with other duties, such as those of the business manager, firms of medium size and larger firms in virtually every field maintain some kind of purchasing office. Manufacturing firms, hospitals, advertising agencies, publishing firms, school sytems, and government—all must have competent personnel who handle the purchase of raw materials, a wide variety of office supplies, the items used in keeping the company or organization running from day to day. Even in firms that employ specialists to purchase wholesale goods for resale to customers (such as a department store that hires buyers of clothing and other merchandise), a purchasing department must obtain and supply to the staff hundreds of items used in running the business.

Working conditions are generally good, with most staff people in purchasing working regularly scheduled hours, except during inventory when overtime may be required. If stockroom or storeroom work is part of the purchasing department operation, you should keep in mind that work in these areas often involves fairly heavy labor and that stock shelves are never elegant.

Generally speaking, you will find the following jobs within the framework of the purchasing field:

Clerks: These jobs are often filled by women and are frequently regarded by both employee and employer as permanent positions for the employee. Untrained young people, usually men, may be placed in these positions to receive basic training in the field in preparation for advancement. Clerical duties include typing purchase orders, correspondence with vendors, maintaining vendor lists, filing requisitions and other documents, maintaining a library of catalogues from vendors, and in some companies keeping inventory records.

Traffic Managers: Supervision of traffic operations includes providing shipping costs to buyers so they have an accurate picture of total costs, obtaining special equipment where needed, routing and tracing incoming shipments, checking and approving transportation bills for payment, handling claims and adjustments on damaged shipments. The traffic supervisor also negotiates for special prices and shipping arrangements and advises the purchasing manager of shipping methods to be used. Large firms have specialists to handle these responsibilities, but smaller firms welcome purchasing department employees with special skill and training in these areas.

Expediter: This job involves follow-up on orders to see that they are delivered promptly. In small companies, follow-up or "tickler" file is maintained to make sure deliveries are coming as promised. In larger firms the expediter would be in direct contact with the vendor, possibly even with the firm from which the vendor, in turn, buys his supplies.

Buyer: The buyer has a wide variety of responsibilities for the purchase of materials and supplies. He will check requisitions, confer with departments about requirements, suggest cost-saving substitutes, follow-up on orders, seek quotations from suppliers, interview salesmen, and arrange for manufacture of special equipment according to his firm's own specifications. Buyers are often called upon to visit the plants where supplies are manufactured.

Purchasing Agent: Purchasing agents often have two responsibilities—doing a certain amount of buying on their own and supervising the work of other buyers. In smaller companies, the purchasing agent is the principal buyer for the firm, possibly its only buyer.

Manager of Purchases: The executive in this position will be responsible for establishing purchasing policies in line with other company policies, organizing the department for efficient operation and personnel training, seeking adequate sources of supply, arranging for purchase contracts, supervising both purchasing and traffic operations (where these two are separate departments), working on budget development and cost control and forecasting supply and price trends.

What You Need Personally

Obviously, if you are interested in any of the several jobs in the purchasing field, you must be good at mathematics, have a good memory for specifications, be able to handle detail, and work well with other people. Since purchasing personnel spend great amounts of company money, you must have the highest personal integrity. Dependability in following through on orders is extremely important. You will need initiative, the ability to seek new sources of supply and effective solutions to sudden problems. During inventory times or during periods of rapid expansion, you may be called upon to work long hours under considerable pressure. An industrious nature is an integral part of the character of purchasing staff personnel. The abilities to cooperate with other department heads, use tact in dealing with company personnel and salesmen, and a sense of values are all important personality traits for men and women in purchasing.

What Education and Training You Need

The higher up the purchasing ladder you go, the more important a college degree becomes. However, many purchasing agents and buyers have worked their way into these positions without formal college education. Some companies prefer experience with the company and select purchasing workers from among their own personnel, whether or not they have the recommended college education. You may have to start at the bottom, as a stock clerk for example, but it is possible for a talented and industrious person to work his or her way up in the field. Some companies even maintain training programs of their own for purchasing personnel, no matter how much previous training or education they've had.

Educational programs are available from extension divisions of universities. Courses are also sponsored by purchasing agents' associations and by management associations. Willingness to spend both time and money on evening courses in various subjects related to purchasing will certainly help you advance in the field.

What the Occupation Has to Offer

Purchasing is receiving increasing recognition for its importance in both the business world and in service or nonprofit organizations. New trends, such as use of data processing to reduce paper work, are part of the picture for the future. Opportunity for employment is generally good, particularly within the governmental and institutional fields. Advancement often takes place within the company, not just within the department itself but at times to good positions in other departments. Recent salaries ranged from $6,000 to $15,000 for buyers and from $12,000 to $25,000 for purchasing agents or managers. The specific salaries depend on both the size of the company and the part of the country in which the firm is located.

Points to Consider Before Going into This Field

Both men and women are welcome in purchasing, although about 90 percent of employees are men now. People in purchasing have the opportunity to obtain at least a modest knowledge of the operations of many different departments within a company. Problems encountered in obtaining supplies, especially at periods of rapid expansion or when financial difficulties make cost control more important than ever, can be both challenging and frustrating.

For more information, write:

Department of Human Resources Development
Mail Control Unit
800 Capitol Mall
Sacramento, California 95814
Ask for: *Purchasing Agent*, No. 266. Free.

National Association of Purchasing Management, Inc.
11 Park Place
New York, New York 10007
Attn: Professional Activities
Ask for: *Your Career in Purchasing Management* (free). *Purchasing as a Career.* ($0.50).

Clerical Occupations

The Job

Over 13 million people are concerned with "paper work." Their jobs range from unskilled messengers or file clerks to supervisory positions requiring quite a few skills and much training. Every kind of business, large or small, employs clerical help. Many clerical workers work part time, a growing trend in this field.

The duties of clerical workers vary according to job. The largest group—about 20 percent—are secretaries, stenographers, and typists. The duties of a *secretary* are incredibly varied, but usually at least include taking dictation, typing letters, reports and other material, filing, and answering and making phone calls.

File clerks maintain files of correspondence, reports, invoices, etc. They sometimes establish filing systems and have to be sure that materials are up-to-date, accounted for, and returned to files after being borrowed.

Mail clerks open, sort, and deliver incoming mail, pick up, sort, seal and stamp outgoing mail, and operate the various machines needed for these tasks.

General office clerks do all kinds of tasks, including filing, handling mail, running duplicating equipment and entering information in record books.

Receptionists greet callers in the office and direct them to the proper person. They also make appointments and frequently operate switchboards or perform other office duties.

Office machine operators handle many different machines. In large offices, an operator will usually only work with one or two. These machines include bookkeeping machines, billing machines, keypunch machines, duplicating machines, and addressing machines.

Telephone switchboard operators connect interoffice calls, answer and relay incoming calls and help staff members with outgoing calls.

Cashiers and bookkeeping workers are in charge of handling the company's money. The cashier receives money from customers, makes change and often keeps track of the day's receipts. Bookkeepers enter financial records in ledgers, prepare statements, balance bank accounts, and do many other tasks that help keep the firm's finances in order.

Shipping and receiving clerks and *stock clerks* are responsible for seeing that materials are accurately received by, sent out by, and inventoried by the company.

In many cases, these jobs are combined or the division of responsibility is varied.

What You Need Personally

There are some qualities that are important for all office workers. In every case, the clerical worker must be able to get along with and work with other people. This quality is more important in some jobs than others (receptionists, for instance) but is necessary for all of them.

Clerical workers should also be dependable, accurate, and able to work under pressure. Interest in work and ability to stick with a job are also important. Workers who operate machines should have some mechanical aptitude and manual dexterity.

What Education and Training You Need

Most clerical jobs require a high school education and a basic knowledge of spelling, grammar, and arithmetic. Other qualifications change according to the job. Knowledge of typing, business arithmetic and general business procedures are helpful in most jobs. Bookkeeping and stenographic skills are necessary for many jobs, and being able to operate business machines is helpful.

It is increasingly advantageous for the clerical worker to have additional business training, available from technical schools, junior and four-year colleges, home-study courses, and private business schools. There are more than 200 junior colleges that offer courses in business. The more training, the greater the opportunity for the worker.

All companies provide on-the-job training for clerical workers. Training usually lasts no longer than a few weeks and is principally designed to familiarize the worker with the techniques and equipment used by the particular firm.

What the Occupation Has to Offer

Clerical jobs should be more plentiful in the 1970s as companies find themselves with more paperwork to do. There is also a high turnover in this field, creating new job openings.

Technological advances will cut down the number of clerical openings in some areas as new machines are developed to handle routine work. Operators for these machines will be needed so the job market should not be severely affected.

Some clerical jobs are not at all affected by automation: secretaries, receptionists, bookkeeping clerks, telephone operators and shipping or receiving clerks. These job opportunities should increase.

Earnings among clerical workers vary considerably depending on type of job, amount of experience, employer, and geographical location. Men generally are paid more than women for the same job.

Opportunities for promotion are often good for clerical workers who take additional outside training and who perform well on the job. Post-high school courses in colleges or business schools are recommended if you wish to advance. You can work up to managerial positions in your field, because companies usually prefer making promotions from within the company, rewarding those who have shown reliability and initiative on the job.

Points to Consider Before Going into This Field

Most clerical workers work in pleasant, modern offices, have regular hours, and company benefits. Entry-level clerical jobs require little investment of time or money in special training and can be used if you are ambitious and hard-working as the first step to a business career. Clerical jobs are available anywhere and usually provide steady and stable employment.

Clerical jobs are not recommended for people who don't like to sit all day, although some positions, notably shipping and receiving and stock clerks, are more active. There is an element of confinement to working in an office. All these jobs involve pressure at least part of the time, and a person has to be able to perform his duties without getting rattled. There is a certain amount of routine to an office job.

Another disadvantage to clerical jobs is that they rarely pay very high salaries and can prove to be dead ends for people who don't take additional courses of study in their fields.

About 70 percent of clerical workers are women and, in fact, they account for almost 100 percent in some jobs. Most men are employed as shipping or receiving clerks, stock clerks or, more occasionally, as bookkeepers or machine operators. Men who do work in clerical positions usually are paid more and promoted more easily than are women. Most companies still find it difficult to promote female clerical workers, but new laws and increasing recognition of the ine-

qualities of present policy should change that in the new few years.

For more information, write:

American Council on Education
1785 Massachusetts Avenue, N.W.
Washington, D.C. 20036
Ask for: *American Junior Colleges.*

Association of Independent Colleges and Schools
1730 M Street, N.W.
Washington, D.C. 20036
Ask for: *Directory of Accredited Institutions*, Free. *Don't Overlook the Business College*, Free. *The Job's the Thing*, Free.

National Business Education Association
1201 Sixteenth Street, N.W.
Washington, D.C. 20036
Ask for: *Careers in Business*, $1.00, 1972.

National Home Study Council
1601 18th Street, N.W.
Washington, D.C. 20009
Ask for: *Directory of Accredited Private Home Study Schools.*

Superintendent of Documents
U.S. Government Printing Office
Washington, D.C. 20402
Ask for: *Job Guide for Young Workers*, $1.50.

Bookkeeper

The Job

Keeping track of money spent or earned is as old as money itself. One of the most important responsibilities in any business is the recording and handling of the company's money. In many offices these records are handled by members of an occupation that acquired its name, "bookkeeping," in the Middle Ages from the bound volumes in which transactions were generally entered.

Systematic and up-to-date financial records are vital to the success and efficiency of any company. Bookkeepers record day-to-day business transactions in journals, ledgers, and other accounting forms. They also prepare regular income statements that show all monies received and paid out and to whom. Profits and losses must be recorded and receipts prepared.

The duties of a bookkeeper vary according to the size and type of office. Most small firms have one general bookkeeper. He or she usually works with an adding machine or calculator and sometimes a check-writing machine. Duties include balancing books, posting ledgers, and doing reports on all financial transactions. The bookkeeper usually reconciles the bank statement and checkbook, calculates wages of employees, and makes up paychecks. Other duties may include sending out monthly statements to customers, making bank deposits or taking telephone orders. In many small offices, the bookkeeper also serves as cashier, answers phone calls, handles the mail, does the filing, and does credit work.

In a larger company, you'll find several workers under the supervision of the accountant or head bookkeeper. In these offices, bookkeeping and accounting clerks will usually be responsible for one or two specific types of bookkeeping work. One person may handle accounts payable, for example; another may handle accounts receivable or prepare income statements. Others may handle more routine tasks such as recording and posting items by hand. The bookkeeping machine operator may work with a machine that handles only one kind of data, or may work with something more complex. Division of responsibility usually depends on the amount of training and experience a worker has.

There are more than 1,300,000 bookkeeping workers in this country, most of whom do general bookkeeping or accounting. They are found all over the country at work in every kind of business, including retail stores, banks, insurance companies, and manufacturing firms.

What You Need Personally

If you want to be a bookkeeper, you should enjoy working with numbers and be good at it. You need good powers of concentration and should like detailed work. Small mistakes can have a large effect in this field, so the bookkeeper should be a careful and accurate worker, orderly and systematic. Because much financial information is confidential, the bookkeeper should be dependable and trustworthy.

Bookkeepers often have to work with others and should have pleasant and agreeable natures. The increasing number of bookkeeping machines make manual dexterity an asset for this job. Good eyesight is also an asset.

What Education and Training You Need

Employers prefer applicants who finished high school and took courses in business arithmetic, bookkeeping, typing, and use of office machines. Any other business courses are considered an asset.

Many companies look for people who have had some post-high school training, either in a business school, a junior or community college, a technical school, or through a correspondence course. This extra training is usually required for advancement in the field. By taking college accounting courses for a degree, bookkeepers can become accountants. (See section on accountants, pages 133-135.)

Many large companies provide on-the-job training in bookkeeping operations, and in any job the beginning bookkeeper is likely to start with routine work and progress to more complex duties.

What the Occupation Has to Offer

You can expect a slight increase in bookkeeping jobs during the next few years. Economic prosperity will create more jobs, but these will be counteracted to some extent by technological developments. Posting machines, punchcard machines, electronic computers and other machines can do a quick and accurate job of processing bookkeeping data. Workers will still be required to run these machines, and the increasingly complex tax regulations in this country will continue to make detailed record keeping essential.

Earnings for bookkeepers vary by city and industry. Larger companies in metropolitan areas and public utilities tend to pay more. A beginning bookkeeping machine operator earns an average of $85 to $100 a week; more experienced machine operators average about $115. Beginning accounting clerks make about $110 a week, and more experienced clerks make between $112 and $145 a week.

Opportunities for advancement are good for bookkeepers with skill and training. There is a high rate of turnover in the field, and it is important to keep up on technological advances relating to bookkeeping. Usually extra training is needed for advancement, but the bookkeeper may move on to head of the department, office manager, accountant, or auditor.

Points to Consider Before Going into This Field

There are many advantages to a career in bookkeeping. It is an easy occupation to train for, because bookkeepers are found in every industry and instruction is available in almost any kind of school. Jobs exist in any location; they are usually stable. Bookkeepers work in pleasant, modern surroundings and are provided with an opportunity to learn about business. A beginning bookkeeping job is a good stepping-stone to positions with greater responsibility and higher salaries, such as accountant or auditor.

The most frequent complaint about this work is that you must sit in one place for long periods of time, bending over books, and using your eyes a great deal. Eyestrain is a common complaint of bookkeepers. In large offices where each worker has a single task, the job may sometimes seem monotonous.

There are no restrictions for employment in this field. It is, in fact, a good profession for a person with some physical handicap other than eye or hand difficulties.

About 90 percent of all bookkeeping workers are women; there is no discrimination in this field.

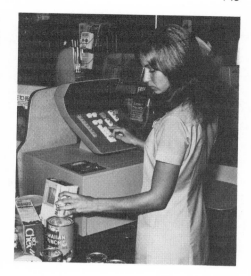

For more information, write:

Association of Independent Colleges and Schools
1730 M Street, N.W.
Washington, D.C. 20036
Ask for: *Accounting for your Future*, Free.

Also contact:
Vocational education divisions of state education departments for lists of accredited schools offering bookkeeping courses.

See also: page 147.

Cashier

The Job

The cashier's job is familiar to most people. Most of us have dealt directly with one in a school cafeteria or at a grocery store. Cashiers are employed by many different kinds of businesses and are known by various job titles. In general, they are responsible for accepting money from customers, making change, and giving out receipts for payment. Other duties may include keeping records of each day's transactions, preparing bank deposits, or paying out cash or checks for company expenses. In some cases, cashiers make out paychecks or sales tax reports.

Most cashiers use cash registers in their work to list and total individual purchases and print a record of the amount of sales. Others use accounting machines, adding machines or change-dispensing machines.

The specific duties of a cashier depend on the type of job. A theater cashier will collect money, operate a ticket-dispensing machine, and answer phone inquiries. A restaurant cashier may handle reservations, type menus, or be responsible for the candy and cigarette counter. In a hotel or motel, duties may include recording charges for telephone and other services utilized by the guest and notifying the room clerk when guests check out. Cashiers in supermarkets or food service stores—also known as check-out clerks or checkers—may also pack groceries, stock shelves, and mark prices on items in the store.

The cashier's job is an important one because he or she handles a great deal of money and is responsible for making sure it is all there at the end of a day. The cashier is often the employer's main bridge with customers, so the job involves some public relations as well.

Most of the country's 850,000 cashiers work in cities and heavily populated suburban areas, but there are jobs in even the smallest towns. About three-fourths of all cashiers work in grocery, drug, and other retail stores.

What You Need Personally

As a cashier, you must be accurate, quick, and enjoy working with numbers. At busy times, there is a great deal of pressure, so you must be able to do your work, make correct change, and move customers through quickly without getting rattled. Manual dexterity and good eye-hand coordination are important for a cashier. Because of the amounts of money involved, the cashier must be honest and reliable.

As your company's representative to the public, you ought to like people and have a pleasant and courteous manner. You should be neat and able to handle situations with customers tactfully.

What Education and Training You Need

For a beginning cashier job, most companies prefer to hire high school graduates who are at least 18 years old. Skill in arithmetic is helpful, and courses in business arithmetic, bookkeeping, typing, and other business subjects are an asset. Some business organizations and schools offer short courses in operating a cash register and in other cashier duties.

Most companies give on-the-job training to cashiers during which they work under a more experienced employee's supervision. Some large companies give a brief period of classroom instruction to all new employees.

Occasionally, employers look for cashiers with special skills or business experience, like typing or selling, to fit the needs of the job.

What the Occupation Has to Offer

There should be some increase in cashiers' jobs during the 1970s as the expanding economy creates a need for more retail operations. Self-service operations are becoming more and more common, making more cashiers' jobs. The turnover in the field is also high; a lot of women working as cashiers return to their families after a relatively short period of time. Mechanical equipment like vending machines and change-making machines will offset some of the newly created jobs.

Many cashiers work part-time, and this trend should continue. Cashiers with typing, bookkeeping or other skills should compete in the job market.

Earnings for this job vary according to type of business, experience and geographical location. In many cases, beginning cashiers start at the minimum wage. Experienced cashiers or those belonging to a union make between $2 and $3 an hour. Supermarket cashiers may earn more than $100 a week. Restaurant cashiers usually make less than others, but often receive one or two free meals a day. Most places that employ cashiers provide paid vacations and sick leave in addition to insurance benefits. Retail outlets frequently offer discounts to their employees.

Promotional opportunities vary for cashiers. In small companies, particularly, there is often no position to which you can advance. But the job does offer an opportunity to learn about business in general and the employer's business in particular, and a job well done could lead to a more responsible clerical position. Chain stores frequently make promotions from within the organization and there are possibilities to advance to department manager or store manager. Promotion is more likely if you take time to learn about the business and take courses in marketing, merchandising and other studies concerned with the running of a business.

Points to Consider Before Going into This Field

A cashier's job affords an opportunity for getting into business and learning the ropes without specialized training. For someone who is quick with figures and likes working with people, it can be a pleasant job.

One disadvantage to the job is that it is often necessary to work on holidays, weekends, late afternoons and evenings. At rush hours, the work can be hectic. In many jobs, the cashier must stand for hours at a time.

To a large extent, this job is what the individual makes of it; it can be used as a first step toward a more responsible position, or it can become a dead end.

About 90 percent of the cashiers in this country are women, but there is no particular discrimination against men for this job.

For more information, write:

National Association of Retail Grocers
360 North Michigan Avenue
Chicago, Illinois 60601
Ask for: *What Every Clerk Should Know Checker's Manual.*

See also: page 147.

File Clerk

The Job

Filing is actually arranging and keeping records in such an organized way that you can find them when you need them. Business today is very complex, and laws governing taxes and other areas of government regulation have made it necessary to keep careful records. Most businesses find it necessary to refer to past correspondence or paperwork in transacting current business. It is most important to be able to find records and correspondence quickly, and many businesses, particularly large ones, employ file clerks to keep all this material accurate, up to date, and properly located. Smaller firms may combine this responsibility with that of the typist or secretary.

The file clerk's duties depend on the type of business she works for, but there are certain things she is always expected to do. Correspondence, orders, and other forms are collected from their sources and arranged in a systematic way. Then the papers are filed in a particular order. The file clerk keeps track of entering and removing material and seeing that everything is up-to-date and in proper sequence. At the end of the year, the file clerk often supervises the transfer of material to another place to make room for the new year's paper work.

Things are extremely systematized in large offices; the file clerk may use some type of automatic sorting device to assist in the work. There are often codes to learn in using these machines. As a space-saver, many companies put old records on microfilm, and the file clerk must arrange material for this purpose.

In a small office, the file clerk will often have to set up a system for record-keeping, one which is easily understood, and which is carefully followed. The clerk must then determine where in the filing system the correspondence and records go.

The type of material filed varies according to company. In a bank, for instance, the clerk may file deposit or withdrawal slips or loan records. A file clerk for a magazine would file subscriptions, pictures and clippings, among other material.

The file clerk's job is important because lost or misplaced material can be quite costly in terms of time or even money. To avoid having materials disappear, the clerk usually keeps careful records of who takes materials in and out of the files and must be sure that things are returned.

About 170,000 file clerks are currently employed; 75 percent work for finance, insurance, real estate, and manufacturing companies.

What You Need Personally

If you are considering becoming a file clerk, you should be an orderly person with a liking for detail. You'll need to use judgment, read rapidly, and make decisions easily. Accuracy and speed are important to the best performance of this job. A good memory helps. You have to be dependable and discreet, as confidential information often passes through your hands. An understanding of filing processes and good spelling ability are also important.

Because you are dealing with a variety of people in the office all day, a file clerk should be neat and have a pleasant appearance and manner. You should be able to get along with people and handle criticism or complaints without getting flustered. Patience is needed when looking for lost material.

What Education and Training You Need

Most companies expect a file clerk to have a high school education, and high school studies in business subjects are quite helpful. The most useful courses would cover clerical or office practice, general business, typewriting, bookkeeping, and record keeping. Some schools have programs whereby the student spends half a day in school and half a day getting on-the-job work experience during the senior year. If you haven't taken these courses in high school, they can be taken at private business schools or in adult education classes.

On-the-job training is given to any beginning file clerk and usually involves spending from a few days to a few months getting familiar with the filing system used in that company. Experience is rarely required for this job.

What the Occupation Has to Offer

There are always job openings for file clerks, because they perform a function necessary in any office and because there is a fairly high job turnover. If you have no extra training beyond high school business courses, you can begin a career in this way. Most offices have pleasant working conditions, good hours, and many benefits.

In the future, filing jobs will be influenced by automation as machines are developed to do much of the work. File clerks will still be needed, but the job will be less routine and the clerk will need other abilities. Automation will have most effect in large companies.

Earnings vary according to size and type of company and location. Most file clerks start at about $70 to $80 a week and may make $80 to $100 with some experience.

A job as file clerk can be a steppingstone to bigger things for a person who works hard and develops other skills while on the job. Large companies may offer promotions to filing supervisor, but usually the file clerk advances by moving to another company. Developing skills in typing, shorthand, and use of office machines with this in mind is your best guarantee for the future.

Points to Consider Before Going into This Field

A file clerk can get a job anywhere and usually with no specific training. The working atmosphere is generally pleasant, and a hard worker can use the job to move into higher paying and more complex positions.

A disadvantage to filing is that it's often boring and routine and offers little chance for original thinking. It can be a dead end for anyone who fails to take additional training. Almost all file clerks are women.

For more information:
See page 147 for for places to write for more details about clerical occupations.

Office Machine Operator

The Job

It's less than 100 years since the sale of the first typewriter, and yet there is an office machine available for almost every clerical task you can name. Modern business offices use many machines to help them run operations more quickly and efficiently and employees are needed to run these machines. Machines range from simple devices that open letters to complex computerized electrical equipment. The duties of an office machine operator depend on the type of machine she or he operates.

The billing machine operator uses a machine to prepare statements, bills, and invoices for customers. The machines type, add up, and itemize customer accounts. By pressing the machine's lettered and numbered keys, the operator transcribes information such as the customer's name and address, items purchased or services rendered, the amounts of money involved, discounts or finance charges. The machine does all the calculating.

Bookkeeping machine operators record the daily transactions of a business on an electric machine. By pressing the keys, the operator prepares customer invoices, enters totals and net amounts on office bookkeeping forms, prepares periodic trial balances, and enters other statistical data.

Adding machine operators use an electric or manually operated machine to add, subtract, multiply or divide groups of numbers to perform computations.

Calculating machines and comptometers do similar work, but are more complex. They not only do basic arithmetic figuring, but also figure square roots, percentages, and check their own computations. They may be used to figure payrolls, compute bank interest payments, calculate research correlations, inventories, balance sheets, or other kinds of statistical reports.

A keypunch or tabulating machine operator runs a machine designed to record large quantities of accounting and statistical information. In processing the information, it is inserted through punch cards and the machine counts the items on the cards, makes calculations, and prints the results on the appropriate forms.

A sorting machine operator runs punch cards through a machine that sorts them according to punched holes and puts them in order.

A number of different machines are involved in preparing and handling mail. An addressing machine prints names and addresses on envelopes, forms or company literature. Embossed plates or stencils are fed into the machine, which then does the addressing work. The operator keeps plates on file, making any necessary changes or corrections. There are also machines that open incoming mail and other machines that fold enclosures and/or insert them in envelopes, seal and stamp them.

Most offices have duplicating machines that reproduce copies of typed, printed, or handwritten matter. There are a number of different types of machines used for this, some of which are relatively simple and are used by many different office employees. In larger offices, the machines may be more complex, able to make thousands of copies at a time and may have full-time operators. The operator may have to produce a master copy by stencil or other means and then make sure the correct number of copies are made in readable form.

The duties of an office machine operator vary considerably. In large offices, the operator usually uses only one or two machines. In a small office, the operator may operate a variety of machines, or machine operation may be combined with other office duties.

The nation's 365,000 office machine operators, not including computer operators, are employed in virtually every kind of company, and are most often found in large firms with a lot of paper work. About one-third work for manufacturing firms. Other large employers are banks, insurance companies, government agencies, wholesale and retail firms. Some office machine operators work for independent service centers which have a variety of office equipment and contract to do work for small firms which don't have such machines.

What You Need Personally

As a machine operator, you should be quick, accurate and mechanically adept. You need to have good manual dexterity, good eye-hand coordination and good vision. If you're going to work with bookkeeping or calculating machines, you should have mathematical experience. The machine operator should be patient, because the work can be monotonous. Thoroughness is important and a pleasant and easy-going personality helps.

What Education and Training You Need

Most employers require a high school education for all but the most routine jobs. Some vocational high schools give courses in machine operation. Private business schools also give courses in machine operation, and additional training is available in some junior colleges. Special schools for calculating and key-punch training are found in many places, and employers often pay for such schooling. A knowledge of business arithmetic and typing is often helpful.

On-the-job training is usually given to office machine operators. The amount of time needed to learn the job varies by machine—it may take only a few days to learn to run a duplicating machine or a few weeks to learn a calculating machine.

What the Occupation Has to Offer

There should be a moderate increase in jobs for office machine operators in the 1970s. As new equipment is introduced, new operators will be needed to run it. More companies will start using machines to deal with a growing volume of work. There is a high turnover in this field, making many new jobs available by people leaving the job market or going into other occupations. Some of this job growth will be offset by increasing automation.

Earnings for office machine operators vary considerably depending on the complexity of the machine and the experience of the operator. A keypunch operator makes between $83 and $120 a week; a bookkeeping machine operator from $90 to $115; a comptometer operator $97 to $115; a tabulating machine operator from $90 to $125; a billing machine operator from $92 to $127.

The opportunities for promotion are limited for most machine operators. If skilled, they may advance from a simple to a more complex machine or to a supervisory position. With additional training in business studies, a machine operator may move into a clerical or bookkeeping position.

Points to Consider Before Going into This Field

Most office machine operators work in comfortable offices, and the work is not strenuous.

Machine operators usually work for companies that offer steady employment, and they receive all the normal benefits. Not too much training is required for most of these jobs; they provide a good way to enter business.

One disadvantage to the work is that it can be monotonous. Most machines are noisy, although workers get accustomed to the sound fairly quickly. Because of the noise, machine operators are often segregated from the rest of the office. Another drawback is that many machine operating jobs do not lead easily to better positions unless you have additional business training.

About three-quarters of all office machine operators are women, although there is no discrimination against men for this work. Men who do work in this field are often paid more than women.

For more information, write:

U.S. Office of Education
Division of Vocational and Technical Education
Washington, D.C. 20202

See also: page 147.

Receptionist

The Job

A receptionist is the first person a client, customer, or patient meets on entering an office, and first impressions can be crucial. The receptionist finds out the caller's name and the nature of his business and directs him to the appropriate person. In many offices, the receptionist keeps records of the name of the caller, time of call, nature of business, and the person to whom he was referred. She may also be in charge of making future appointments.

Receptionists' duties vary according to the kind of business. In a hospital the receptionist may direct the patient to the proper waiting room or actually be an admissions clerk. In this case, she greets the patient and writes down information about him—name of doctor, ailment, method of payment to the hospital. She also holds personal property while the patient is in the hospital and may collect deposits on bills.

The receptionist assigns the patient to the appropriate ward or room, and when he is dismissed, enters the time of discharge and other information on his card.

In a doctor's office, the receptionist makes appointments, sends out statements and keeps payment records, in addition to greeting the patients and making them comfortable. In a beauty shop, the receptionist arranges appointments and may show the customer to the operator's booth. In a large defense plant, the receptionist may provide the caller with an identification card and see that he has an escort to take him to the proper office.

In small offices, receptionists can be called on to perform many different duties. They often operate the office switchboard and handle incoming and outgoing phone calls. Other duties include typing, sorting and opening mail, filing or keeping books, or petty cash accounts.

The nation's 350,000 receptionists are employed all over the country in almost every kind of business establishment. Over half are employed by physicians, attorneys and other professional people. Others work in hospitals, educational institutions, banks, insurance companies, real estate offices, manufacturing firms, and beauty shops.

What You Need Personally

The receptionist represents her employer to the public, so personal characteristics are very important. A pleasant disposition and well-groomed appearance are essential. A nice speaking voice and the ability to listen and communicate well are also important. Courtesy, poise, tact, patience, and dependability are considered vital for a good receptionist, who should, of course, like people.

Because what you say and do reflect on your company, you should make a point of learning as much as possible about your company and use judgment in giving information to visitors. It helps to have a good memory for names, faces, and pertinent information about regular callers.

What Education and Training You Need

Employers require a high school education for receptionists, and one out of five have some college training. Knowledge of typing, bookkeeping, and business practices is helpful, and a good command of English and spelling are needed. In many offices, knowing how to operate a switchboard is necessary for the job, but on-the-job training is usually provided.

What the Occupation Has to Offer

There should be an increase in jobs for receptionists. Automation will have no effect on this job. Competition is keen for these positions, as both young applicants and more experienced workers apply for openings. The applicant with some business knowledge and training will have an edge.

Earnings for receptionists vary according to the type of business and the part of the country. In general, receptionists earn more in the West and less in the South. Salary levels also differ depending on experience and other duties performed on the job. On the average, receptionists earn between $85 and $135 a week, with the higher salaries usually going to those with experience who also operate switchboards.

Promotional opportunities for receptionists are generally few, especially in small companies. A competent receptionist who acquires additional business training can, however, advance to a job as secretary, administrative assistant or cashier.

Points to Consider Before Going into This Field

Receptionist work has a lot of advantages for the person who enjoys working with others. She meets many different people and the work is rarely routine. The receptionist is constantly having to use judgment in handling new situations that develop, and her attitude is important to the company's image. Working conditions are usually very pleasant for receptionists, most of whom work in attractive, modern offices in a spacious area.

This job is not for anyone who has trouble meeting people or who is unable to handle rudeness or pressure. A receptionist has to keep her head at all times and remain pleasant and courteous no matter how much pressure is put upon her. Another drawback to the job is that it is not always easy to advance to a better position.

Almost all receptionists are women. The few men in this field are mainly employed by hospitals, manufacturing companies, and banks. Those few men in the field generally have better chances for promotion than do women. (See also page 147 for details about clerical occupations such as receptionist.)

Shipping and Receiving Clerk

The Job

In order for modern businesses to keep track of the large amount of goods and materials they handle, a variety of workers must be employed. Shipping and receiving clerks handle the paper work connected with the shipment and receipt of goods. In small companies, the same person usually keeps records of all shipments sent out and received by his employer. In larger firms, there are often separate departments with a number of clerical and supervisory employees.

There are about 380,000 shipping and receiv-

ing clerks. About two-thirds of them work for manufacturing firms; the remaining one-third work for wholesale houses or retail stores. Their jobs vary according to the kind and size of company, but there are some general responsibilities.

A shipping clerk checks his company's shipments before they go out to be sure that orders have been filled correctly; he prepares invoices and other shipping forms, looks up freight and postal rates, records the weight and cost of each shipment, and makes sure the shipment is addressed properly. It is important that the materials being shipped reach the customer by the least expensive and most appropriate way and that they arrive by the date promised. The shipping clerk must also do what he can to be sure the shipment arrives at its destination in good condition.

Shipping clerks keep records of all details associated with each shipment. They sometimes requisition the requested merchandise from the stockroom, wrap and pack it, and direct its loading onto trucks.

Receiving clerks handle similar details when shipments reach their destination. They check the shipment received against the original order and the accompanying bill of lading or invoice to be sure that they have received what was ordered. They also make sure the merchandise has arrived in good condition. All information on incoming shipments and their condition must be recorded carefully, as the company's knowledge of their inventory—and thus their efficient operation—depends on the accuracy of these records. When shipments are damaged or lost, receiving clerks handle the appropriate paper work. Often they also route shipments to the proper department of the company or the proper place in the stockroom.

In small companies, these duties of shipping and receiving clerks are often combined into one job.

What You Need Personally

As a shipping or receiving clerk, you should be neat, orderly and systematic because of the number and importance of records to be kept. A good memory is also helpful. You should be responsible and attentive with an even temper for the times when orders are changed at the last minute. Because physical work is sometimes involved, you need good health and at least average strength.

The job requires dealing with people all day—truck drivers, salesmen, and others. Having a pleasant personality helps.

What Education and Training You Need

Most firms prefer high school graduates for these positions. Useful high school studies include mathematics, typing, and other business subjects. A knowledge of geography is also helpful in discovering where a place is located and computing rates and arranging shipments. Legible handwriting is very important.

Once hired—and preference in jobs is often given to people who gained experience during summers and other school vacations—the beginning shipping or receiving clerk receives on-the-job training supervised by an experienced worker. The clerk learns about the regulations for shipping, including the ones applying to merchandise shipped to or from foreign countries. He also learns special methods of handling fragile materials or other specific kinds of merchandise.

The beginner is expected to become familiar with his company's products and methods. By handling routine work, such as checking addresses, attaching labels and checking items included in shipments, the clerk starts to learn the names, places, and procedures used. As experience grows, the clerk will be given more duties requiring independent judgment—such as handling problems caused by damaged merchandise or supervising other workers.

What the Occupation Has to Offer

Shipping and receiving clerks should find a modest increase in jobs during the next few years. More goods will be distributed as the population and income grow. However, warehouse operations should become more efficient in the years to come as moving belts and other laborsaving equipment are installed and as faster methods of record keeping are developed. This will be particularly true in larger companies.

Earnings vary for shipping and receiving clerks depending mainly on the parts of the country where they work. On the average, they earn somewhat more than $3.00 an hour, and most receive paid holidays and vacations, insurance and other fringe benefits. Many companies, particularly wholesale and retail establishments, offer employees a 10 to 20 percent discount on merchandise.

Opportunities for promotion are good for

someone who is ambitious and uses this job to learn the details of the company's products and procedures. The shipping or receiving clerk can advance to foreman or supervisor of his department, which may lead to various other jobs. For further advance, studies in transportation and business are recommended. With this added training, the clerk might eventually advance to warehouse manager, purchasing agent, industrial traffic manager, or into a sales position.

Points to Consider Before Going into This Field

Work in shipping and receiving has many advantages. It is steady and available in virtually any town or city. With no advanced training, it provides a good entry position into the world of business; a person with ambition can make his performance on the job the key to advancement. There are few others jobs with a better chance for future advancement, because you get a good over-all view of your company and learn of the job openings.

There are some disadvantages to this job. Warehouses may be drafty and cold, and the clerk may have to stand for long periods of time at work. Checking cartons also requires bending, stooping, and stretching. Some night work and overtime is usually necessary in this job, and there is quite a lot of pressure at these times; the materials or merchandise are usually needed immediately, and the work has to be done as quickly—but accurately—as possible.

There are no real restrictions for this job; as long as a person is healthy, alert and accurate, the job has a great deal to offer.

Over 85 percent of all shipping and receiving clerks are men. This is mainly because most firms expect their clerks to handle fairly heavy packages. See also page 147 for places to write for more details and clerical occupations.

Stenographer and Secretary

The Job

Literally, a secretary is a "keeper of secrets," but actually she is much more than that. There are few jobs which offer as wide a variety of tasks as does secretarial work.

In the early 1970s 218 million persons were employed in occupations requiring stenographic skills. Though more than 95 percent were women, this is an area of employment more men ought to consider; the opportunities for them are growing.

Stenographers are responsible for taking dictation from one or more people and transcribing letters, memorandums, or reports, on a typewriter. In small businesses, stenographers may be called upon to answer telephones, serve as recep-

tionists or operate duplicators, calculators, and similar office machines. Most work done by stenographers is fairly routine. Some stenographers who specialize in shorthand reporting become court reporters; they usually take their notes by machine.

In addition to taking dictation and transcribing, a secretary may be asked to compose routine letters herself. She is given more responsibility when meeting office visitors and screening telephone calls. Sometimes the secretary handles personal financial records or compiles statistical data for reports. She is usually responsible for the executive's files (and perhaps for all the files if the business is small), for scheduling work time and appointments, and for maintaining attractive surroundings.

The title "executive secretary" is often given to a top executive's secretary who has responsibilities resembling those of an assistant.

Stenographers and secretaries are employed by organizations of every size and type. A few—chiefly public stenographers and some reporting stenographers—are self-employed.

Working conditions for secretaries are usually good. The modern office is well lighted, comfortable, and pleasant. The confidential nature of the work performed makes you feel a part of the organization and a member of the team. Secretaries have one of the highest prestige positions for women in business, and they exercise more responsibility and initiative than is permitted in many other office jobs.

What You Need Personally

Promptness, neatness, a pleasant and friendly manner and an attractive personal appearance are desirable for all office workers. For responsible secretarial positions, discretion, good judgment, loyalty, initiative, the ability to make decisions and a well-modulated voice are important. You need to be versatile and adaptable to many different work situations.

The relationship between employer and secretary should be one of mutual trust and respect;

if you're considering a career in the secretarial field, analyze your own personality to be sure you can be loyal and discreet.

What Education and Training You Need

To prepare yourself for a career in this field, you need a good basic education and specialized training. Graduation from high school is essential for almost any job. Specialized training can be found in daytime and evening courses in high schools, vocational-technical schools, private business schools, correspondence courses, and two- or four-year colleges. Stenographic instruction in high school may give you enough background to get your first job, but you should plan to continue your education while you work if you want to advance further, With the current upgrading of secretarial positions, some college education is becoming increasingly important, especially for those jobs which are trainee positions for higher level positions.

The federal government sponsors training programs for unemployed and underemployed workers for entry positions as stenographers under provisions of the Manpower Development and Training Act. Associate degrees in secretarial studies are conferred by a great number of junior and community colleges and some private business schools.

Some courses that train for stenographic work are limited to shorthand and typing and can be completed in a few months. In other courses, which usually last longer, students learn additional office skills, general business practices, and office conduct. Some courses offer intensive training to prepare students for stenographic reporting or for legal, technical, or medical-dental secretarial work.

Many companies have a need for secretaries, receptionists, and clerical workers who can speak a language other than English, especially in urban areas which have large numbers of residents who speak primarily Spanish, Italian, or other languages. If you have basic skills in another language, you may find that improving them will be a great asset, both in job-seeking and in career advancement.

Costs and length of training vary greatly, depending on the field you wish to enter and the level of achievement on which you have set your sights. Some secretarial schools offer both one- and two-year courses.

A number of community and junior colleges offer two-year secretarial programs which include courses in economics, management, marketing, business law, accounting, business correspondence, and a wide range of related subjects. There are secretarial scholarships available from the National Secretaries Association and the National Legal Secretaries Association.

What the Occupation Has to Offer

Job opportunities through the 1970s will be good. The increased paper work in modern business will lead to a rapid expansion in the employment of secretaries and stenographers. The increasing use of dictating, duplicating, and other office machines will undoubtedly continue, but technological changes of this kind won't greatly affect the growth of employment in these occupations. Turnover and replacement among stenographic workers is high, because many young women leave to care for their families.

Employment opportunities for men trained in the secretarial skills are expected to be excellent for the next several years. Employers in finance, insurance, real estate, and transportation industries often prefer male secretaries. Most of the court reporting stenographers are men. Because the number of men preparing for secretarial work is small, their opportunities for employment are that much better. The promotional opportunities for male secretaries to managerial positions are excellent.

In 1970, general stenographers in metropolitan areas surveyed by the Bureau of Labor Statistics earned average salaries of $461 a month. Salaries earned by senior and technical stenographers working in metropolitan areas averaged $526 a month.

The salaries earned by individuals included in the survey varied considerably because of differences in their location, the industries where they were employed and their relative experience. The earnings of reporting stenographers generally are considerably higher than those of other stenographic workers.

The same survey found salaries of secretaries ranged from $522 a month to $679, depending on where they worked, for whom they worked, and how much experience and responsibility they had. A woman given the title of secretary may actually be an administrative assistant and earn as much as $1,000 a month, while a high school graduate of a vocational office occupation program may have a stenographic position that pays $300 a month.

Capable and well-trained stenographers and secretaries have excellent opportunities for advancement. Many stenographers advance to better paying positions as secretaries; others, who acquire the necessary speed through experience or additional training, may become reporting stenographers. Both stenographers and secretaries eventually can be promoted to jobs such as administrative assistant, office supervisor, executive secretary.

Experienced secretaries may, with further preparation, apply to take the Certified Professional Secretary's examination. The National Secretaries Association awards CPS certificates to those who successfully pass its difficult and comprehensive tests. CPS certificates attest to extensive business background, outstanding personal characteristics, and superior secretarial proficiency.

Points to Consider Before Going into This Field

What happens to career jobs if they are interrupted by a young woman taking time off to raise a family? In some fields, a career is greatly retarded by a long absence from the profession. In secretarial work, you can almost always return after a simple review of your office skills. No matter where you may want to move or are required to move because of family responsibilities, there are usually jobs available.

The working relationship between employer and secretary is one which is satisfying to many women who don't seek prominence for themselves, but who enjoy helping someone else succeed at his or her job. The secretary's unique contribution is her ability to understand her employer's business, his way of thinking and acting and his personality. Some people regard this subordinate role as a distinct disadvantage of secretaryship; it ought to be considered before you go into this field.

For more information, write:

National Shorthand Reporters Association
25 West Main Street
Madison, Wisconsin 53703
Ask for: information on jobs and training in shorthand reporting.

The Institute for Certifying Secretaries
616 East 63rd Street
Kansas City, Missouri 64110
Ask for: information on becoming a certified professional secretary.

National Association of Legal Secretaries
3005 East Skelly Drive
Suite 120
Tulsa, Oklahoma 74105
Ask for: information on becoming a legal secretary.

See also: page 147.

Stock Clerk

The Job

Stock clerks are employed by many different kinds of businesses to take charge of storerooms, stockrooms, and keep records. The duties of a stock clerk depend on the kind and size of business in which he works. In smaller firms, he performs the functions of receiving clerk, shipping clerk, and inventory clerk; in a larger firm, his duties may be narrower.

Stock clerks usually receive and unpack incoming merchandise and material and check the items to be sure the right quantity has been

received and that none are damaged. Clerks make any minor adjustments or repairs that are necessary, report damaged or spoiled goods, and process the papers necessary for obtaining replacements or credit.

Stock clerks store received materials in their appropriate places and sometimes are asked to organize and mark the items so that they can be easily located. They keep records of all items entering or leaving the stockroom and may also prepare inventory reports showing how much is in stock. Inventory reports can be kept up through a perpetual inventory system or might be put together by taking periodic physical inventories. Stock clerks sometimes order supplies; and label, pack, or address goods for delivery.

Some stock clerks perform very specific duties for their particular firms. A cellarman at a hotel or restaurant receives and inspects incoming beverages like wine and liquor, separates them by class, and stores them in temperature-controlled rooms.

A film library clerk stores and issues motion picture films and keeps a catalog on them.

A salvage clerk sorts and stores unserviceable equipment to be disposed of, reclaimed, or sold.

A zoo commissary man is responsible for determining the amount of food and medical supplies needed daily for the animals and for ordering and delivering those supplies.

About half a million stock clerks are employed in this country; most work for manufacturing, wholesale, and retail companies. They also work for mail-order houses, airlines, government agencies, hospitals, transportation companies. Most stock clerks work in metropolitan areas.

What You Need Personally

A stock clerk should be in good physical condition with stamina, good health, and at least average strength. You are likely to be on your feet all day and will often have to lift things and climb around. Good eyesight and good hearing are relevant qualifications for this job.

An orderly and accurate person with an inclination for mathematics and detailed work makes a good stock clerk. Another necessary quality is the ability to get along with people.

Because you are handling goods of considerable value, the stock clerk must be responsible and honest. In jobs involving the handling of jewelry, liquor or drugs, stock clerks are often bonded.

What Education and Training You Need

Most employers prefer that stock clerks be high school graduates, and they look for skill in reading, writing, mathematics, typing, and filing. Training for the position is conducted on the job. For the first few weeks, workers do simple jobs like counting and marking stock, then they progress to learning to keep records, take inventories and order supplies.

What the Occupation Has to Offer

There should be a slight increase in jobs for stock clerks during the 1970s. Most openings will come as a result of workers retiring or leaving the job. Technological developments in computers that control inventories and other areas of stock work will limit the number of new jobs.

Wages for stock clerks usually range from $92 to $125 a week in metropolitan areas, with men earning more than women. Experienced workers with greater responsibility have greater earnings.

Advancement opportunities are good for a hard-working stock clerk. In a small firm, he may become an assistant buyer or purchasing agent or could be promoted to a sales position. In a larger firm, he could be promoted to invoice clerk, stock control clerk, or merchandise supply man. He may supervise a group of clerks or become head of the stock department.

Usually promotion goes to workers who demonstrate ability, hard work, and initiative. Night-school studies in merchandising, accounting and other related topics are an asset to advancement.

Points to Consider Before Going into This Field

For an ambitious person with physical stamina, a stock clerk's job can provide a good entry into business. It requires no specialized training or schooling, and hours are usually regular. The opportunity to learn many different business techniques and procedures is very much a part of this job.

Work as a stock clerk is strenuous, and some stock rooms are damp or drafty. Stock clerks are on their feet most of the day and have to do a lot of bending, lifting and climbing. There is usually a great competition for these jobs.

About 20 percent of stock clerks are women, but opportunities are fairly equal except in industries that involve heavy merchandise. Women are usually paid less than men, however, and are less likely to be promoted. (See also page 147 for places to write for more details about clerical occupations.)

Telephone Operator

The Job

Although today many telephone calls can be made without assistance, there are still times we need help from an operator. Many telephone company operators specialize in a particular type of call, such as local or long distance. Operators may be asked for emergency numbers or for directory assistance information. They may give dialing instructions and rates, or arrange conference calls. Other operators place long distance calls, overseas, or marine calls.

Operators either work at switchboards in telephone company central offices or at private branch exchange (PBX) switchboards. Switchboards are either operated by inserting and removing plugs attached to boards or with push-button or dial console machinery.

Most operators in the telephone company central offices are long-distance operators. The operator requests and receives information from the caller and the person he is calling, prepares tickets on calls, and computes charges for them. If the call is person-to-person, the operator must locate the person being called; if it is collect, she must make sure that charges are being accepted. She notes the time the call begins and ends. The long-distance operator is often asked to provide callers with various kinds of information.

The telephone company also employs directory assistance operators. These operators sit at desks with local directories and newly listed numbers. They also have lists of emergency numbers and of numbers for hotels, large businesses, and schools that are frequently requested.

PBX operators work at switchboards that serve business offices or other establishments. They connect interoffice calls, answer and relay outside calls, and help other employees in placing outside calls. In smaller businesses where the volume of calls is not too heavy, the operator may perform other duties such as receptionist or information clerk.

There are about 420,000 telephone operators, more than half employed by telephone companies. Most of the operators are employed in heavily populated areas; about one-fifth of them in the New York, Chicago and Los Angeles metropolitan areas. PBX operators are most often employed by manufacturing plants, hospitals, schools and department stores.

What You Need Personally

Because being a telephone operator means dealing continually with people, it is important that you be patient, stable, courteous, and have a good sense of humor. You should have a pleasant speaking voice and be able to express yourself clearly. Operators should also be good listeners and be able to analyze the often incomplete information they are given.

Most phone companies require operators to pass a physical examination, because good health and regular attendance are important to the job. Eye-hand coordination, manual dexterity and good eyesight and hearing are all important for a telephone operator. You should be able to read quickly, have a good memory, and be able to sit still for long periods of time. The most important quality for operators, however, is wanting to help and being able to get along with and communicate with the public.

What Education and Training You Need

A high school education is required for most operators' jobs; the applicant should have a good background in English and arithmetic. Good spelling and legible handwriting are important. For jobs at office switchboards, knowledge of typing and other office work is helpful.

Most operators are trained on the job. At the telephone company, there is a period of programmed instruction that takes one to three weeks. Trainees practice simulated calls and learn the procedures used to handle calls. They are then assigned to the regular operating force where they learn other specifics of the job while working.

PBX operators have a shorter training period. They are instructed by a supervisor within the company or by a representative of the telephone company.

What the Occupation Has to Offer

The number of jobs in this area should increase moderately over the next few years. Turnover is high because many operators are young women who leave to raise families. The volume of phone calls is expected to increase, but direct dialing and other types of automation should offset that area of growth.

The job outlook for PBX operators should be somewhat greater. Their jobs are not as greatly affected by technological development, and more companies are expected to use PBX services in the years to come.

Earnings for telephone company operators vary; they are highest in the Pacific States. Trainees average $2.16 an hour and experienced operators in nonsupervisory positions average $2.74 an hour.

PBX operators have great variation in pay, depending on the type of businesses that employ them and the places where they work. Earnings are highest in the West and lowest in the South. Public utilities pay a substantially higher salary than retail or service businesses. In general, a PBX operator averages between $91 and $113 a week.

Both kinds of operators frequently have to work odd shifts, nights, holidays, and weekends. Pay is higher for work during these hours.

Opportunities for promotion within the telephone company are good, especially if you have other business skills. An operator may be promoted to service assistant, central office supervisor or chief operator. Some operators are promoted to clerical jobs. Large firms offer similar opportunities for PBX operators, but in small companies there is less room for advancement.

Points to Consider Before Going into This Field

Telephone operators are offered a good chance at a steady job with a minimum of training and good benefits. They usually have no trouble finding employment. For someone who enjoys dealing with people, it is a good job to consider. Operators usually work in modern, comfortable offices.

One disadvantage to this job is the odd hours often required. This affects telephone company operators and PBX operators who may work for hotels or hospitals or other institutions that have to be open twenty-four hours a day. Operators have to sit for long periods of time in a somewhat confining position, and the work can be tiring.

Almost all telephone operators are women, although the telephone companies are beginning to hire men for these positions.

For more information, write:

Telephone Operator Booklet
State of California

Department of Human Resources Development
800 Capitol Mall
Sacramento, California 95814
Ask for: *Telephone Operator* No. 54, Free.

See also: page 147.

Also contact:
local telephone companies; unions representing telephone workers.

Typist

The Job

Practically every business employs typists to put into presentable form all the letters, reports, manuscripts, bills, messages, statements, legal briefs, and newspaper, television, and advertising copy that is generated every day. Using a standard or an electric typewriter, the typist applies her skills as quickly and accurately as possible.

There are many different jobs in which the emphasis is on typing. In addition, there are various kinds of jobs where typing is a needed skill, if not the one most used. Beginners in this field, sometimes called junior typists, work on routine tasks like addressing envelopes, typing headings on form letters, or copying directly from typed or handwritten drafts. Senior typists do work that requires more independent judgment and very accurate typing; they work on complicated statistical tables, combine and rearrange materials from several different sources, copy from rough drafts or prepare master copies of material to be reproduced by photographic processes.

Clerk-typists spend half to three-quarters of their time typing reports, addresses, bills, copying from a rough draft, cutting simple stencils, or setting up simple tabulations. Clerk-typists may also distribute mail, file, or operate other simple machines.

General and technical typists spend about three-quarters of their time typing and doing work similar to the clerk-typists. In addition, they may copy more complex statistics or type routine forms. They also type legal briefs or reports using technical language.

A dictating machine typist spends most of her time transcribing material from the dictating machine, and may also be expected to maintain the machine and proofread her typed copy.

There are certain specialty typists who operate either typewriters or specialized machines with similar keyboards, such as computing billing machines, teletype machines and Varitype machines. A Recordak-projector operator copies data projected onto a small screen onto a typewriter or billing machine. She chooses the correct film from the file, runs it through a projector, types a copy and gives it to the person requesting it. A tape perforator operator uses a specially equipped electric typewriter to transfer coded instructions to magnetic or paper tapes for use in electronic computers.

Other typists have special duties and job titles, such as policy writers in insurance companies, waybill clerks in railroad offices, and mortgage clerks in banks. Some typists specialize in foreign language typing.

All typists should know how to use their machines, clean them, and change ribbons. They should be able to type at least 40 to 55 words a minute.

In a small office, a typist may do many of the above duties. In larger offices, she is more likely to spend all her time at one task.

What You Need Personally

As a typist you should be neat and accurate. Untidy or careless work is unacceptable. You should be able to concentrate despite noises and people around you. A typist needs some manual dexterity to operate her machine, and good hearing is important for a transcription typist.

A typist should be dependable, alert and willing, and must be able to work efficiently at times when there is pressure. Most typing jobs include some contact with other people, whether the public, employers, or other employees, so a typist should have a pleasant disposition.

What Education and Training You Need

Most employers prefer applicants for typist positions to be high school graduates with some business training in typing and in the use of other office machines. Applicants usually are required to take typing tests and should be able to type at least 40 words per minute. The tests check both speed and accuracy. A typist should also have mastery of spelling, punctuation, grammar and vocabulary. Any additional knowledge—proofreading skills, use of dictating machines and so forth—will be helpful in getting a job.

Training opportunities for this work are available in the business courses of all high schools. In addition, there are many private business schools, junior and community colleges that teach office procedures. The federal government has training programs for typist positions under the Manpower Development and Training Act.

What the Occupation Has to Offer

Virtually every business employs typists, and the turnover in the field is fairly high. Typists can be well assured of employment no matter where they may live. Routine typing will be increasingly taken over by machine, however, and the greatest demand in the future will be for specialized typists and for those who can combine typing with other office skills.

Typists' salaries vary a great deal, depending on type of industry and location of the firm. A beginning typist may start at about $4,600 a year and make up to $5,580 a year.

The opportunities for promotion are good for a typist, particularly if she has other skills. Large offices offer more opportunities for advancement, because they usually have a greater variety of typing positions available. Seniority is a factor in many of these promotions. A junior typist can be promoted to a senior typist or a clerk typist. A clerk typist can be promoted to a technical typist. With training in shorthand, a typist could be promoted to secretary.

Points to Consider Before Going into This Field

A typist job is a good way to get into business. Opportunities for advancement and greater pay are there for the typist who increases her skills and works hard. The job requires little investment of time or money for training. Most typists work in pleasant offices with regular hours, and the jobs offer opportunities to meet people. Typing jobs are available all over the country, in every town and city and in every kind of business. Over half of the 700,000 typists in the country work for manufacturing firms, banks, insurance companies and federal, state and local government agencies.

One disadvantage to the typist's job is that it requires sitting in one place for long periods of time. The work necessitates using the eyes constantly; eyestrain is not uncommon. Most offices are fairly noisy, but it doesn't seem to disturb most office workers.

Only about 5 percent of typists are men, who usually feel the work is too low paying for them. In some instances, they get further training to work as secretaries, or court reporters. Financial, real estate, and insurance companies often prefer men for some kinds of typing.

See also page 147 for places to write for more details about clerical occupations. Information on training programs available under the Manpower Development and Training Act is available from your state employment service.

Communications

The art of communications is as old as man himself. The early grunts of the cavemen, the world-famed drawings on walls of caves once inhabited by prehistoric man, even the designs lovingly painted on ancient pieces of pottery, now broken and time-faded, are all symbols of man's never ending urge to transmit information.

As man became more civilized, his awareness not only of the people around him but of generations yet to come, led him to look for better ways of setting things down in a permanent record.

From the earliest discoveries of papermaking techniques, through the invention of movable type, to the development of electronic marvels which enable us to talk to men on the moon, we prove that we keep trying to speed up and make more permanent reports of life in our time—no matter how good or bad times may be.

Today we have so many ways to communicate they would stagger the minds of the prehistoric cave artists. Imagination has created endless ways to deliver messages: newspapers, books, magazines, pamphlets, flyers, posters, radio, television, theatre program ads, billboards, catalogues, even the inside flaps of envelopes and the reverse sides of tickets to theatrical events and ballgames.

The major divisions of the communications field are advertising, editorial (news writing), and business production. The skills needed here are represented in some form or another in the various media. The media include primarily newspapers, radio, television, magazines, book publishing, and public relations. Many jobs require more than one skill.

When you consider all of the possible combinations, you realize that communications is a field which not only touches our lives daily but plays an important role in virtually every other field.

Jobs in communications offer exciting possibilities if you have the training and the skill they require.

For more information, write:

Public Relations Service
National Association of Broadcasters
1771 N Street, N.W.
Washington, D. C. 20006
Ask for: *Careers in Radio; Careers in Television;* free. *Broadcast Education,* $5.00, (1972 list of radio-television programs in American colleges and universities, including 2-year colleges), and other information on careers in broadcasting.

Television Information Service
745 Fifth Avenue
New York, New York 10022
Ask for: General information about broadcasting and broadcasting training.

American Women in Radio and Television Inc.
1321 Connecticut Avenue, N.W.
Washington, D. C. 20036
Ask for: *Careers for Women in Broadcasting.* (Includes description of jobs and schools offering training.)

Advertising

The Job

Advertising's the means by which buyers and sellers of goods or services are brought together. You certainly have been exposed to this field. You have seen advertisements on television, in magazines and newspapers, on billboards, and have heard many ads on radio. Even a simple poster in a store window announcing an amateur theatrical event or a church supper is advertising. Usually, the seller pays for the advertisement, which is designed to attract the attention of a buyer. In other instances, you will see that a buyer has placed an ad. The most common example of the latter is the "help wanted" sections of newspapers, where employers state the kinds of services they wish to purchase from people who will become their employees.

Few fields offer as many different kinds of jobs as you'll find in advertising. While many of these jobs—such as copywriter or account executive—nearly always require a college degree, there are openings that call for a combination of special talent and specialized training not necessarily acquired in college. Advertising workers

include executives responsible for the planning and overall supervision of ad campaigns, copywriters who write the text of advertisements, artists who prepare the illustrations, and layout specialists who put copy and illustrations together. The advertising profession also includes administrative and technical workers responsible for the satisfactory reproduction of ads and salesmen, who sell advertising space in publications or time on radio and television programs. In a small advertising organization, one person may handle all these tasks. Large organizations employ specialists for research, copywriting, and layout work.

If you enter the advertising field, you may be employed by the company which is doing the selling (such as a department store), you could work for an advertising agency which handles advertising planning and placement for the seller or you could find a job on a newspaper, a magazine, or in a radio or television station which sells space or time to the advertiser.

What You Need Personally

This field is for people who enjoy a frequently frantic pace. You must be interested in people and what makes them tick. Whether you are writing a description of a product, supplying illustrations or planning the design—or layout—of an advertisement, your ability to figure out what will catch the buyer's eye or ear, hold his attention and arouse his interest enough to encourage him to buy the product or service is most important. Being able to write clearly and correctly is essential. You must be able to get along with a variety of people. You should be able to stay cool under pressure, remembering that when things aren't going as they should, tempers sometimes get short.

What Education and Training You Need

There are no set requirements, but most employers who hire advertising trainees prefer college graduates having liberal arts training or majors in advertising, marketing, journalism, or business administration. Nevertheless, some successful advertising people have started in such varied occupations as engineering, teaching, chemistry, art, or sales. If you have artistic talent in particular, you should consider advertising, where good jobs are available for illustrators, photographers, and layout artists. Many art schools offer special courses aimed at preparing young people for this work.

If you are planning to enter advertising, try to get some experience in copywriting or related work with your school publications and, if possible, through summer jobs connected with marketing research services. If you decide to attend a junior college or vocational school, you'll find many that offer associate degree courses for advertising students.

When it's time to look for a job, most beginners start as assistants in research or production work or as space or time buyers. A few begin as junior copywriters. One of the best avenues of entrance to advertising for women is through advertising departments in retail stores.

What the Occupation Has to Offer

The employment outlook in the advertising field is generally good. Although the competition for all jobs is always difficult, it is a thriving field in general; advancement is rapid for workers with ability. Earnings are usually good with salaries for beginners starting at $6,500 and going up rapidly. With competition stiff for promotions, a positive personality and strong drive are important assets—in addition to talent and training. Since there are advertisers across the land and advertising agencies in almost every city of any size, there is great diversification available in choosing a section of the country in which you wish to work and live.

A fairly new development in the field is the moving of medium sized advertising agencies from cities to suburban communities where many executives live. In addition, the growing sensitivity of small stores and companies toward their needs for professional advertising services has opened a new field for small agencies serving suburban or semirural areas.

Points to Consider Before Going into This Field

There is great excitement involved in development of an advertising campaign, followed by great satisfaction when the campaign is successful. Of course, you have the extra satisfaction of seeing your own handiwork on the printed page, on television, or on a billboard or sign. Flexibility of places to live and work, excellent salary potential and the opportunity to meet and work with stimulating people are all assets in the field.

If you are anxious to accept these advantages, you must also be prepared to consider the disadvantages. Job security is nearly always a problem. there are great pressures in developing an advertising campaign and, the higher you go, the greater the risks are that if an account is lost, you may lose your job as a result. Working hours are sometimes irregular, because deadlines must be met.

The advertising field is wide open to both men and women and to people of all ethnic backgrounds.

For more information, write:

American Advertising Federation
1225 Connecticut Avenue, N. W.
Washington, D. C. 20036

The Women's Advertising Club of Chicago
400 West Madison Street
Chicago, Illinois 60606
Ask for: *111 Jobs for Women in Advertising,* $1.00.

Association of Industrial Advertisers, Inc.
Education Committee
41 East 42nd Street
New York, New York 10017
Ask for: *Industrial Advertising Careers.*

See also: page 163.

Newspaper Reporter

The Job

In a world where every day sees an incredible range of events, changes and developments, one of the most exciting and challenging occupations is that of the newspaper reporter. The reporter covers every kind of newsworthy event and writes about it for daily or weekly newspapers. He may interview people, review public records, attend news happenings and do research. Some reporters work on general assignments and others are given a particular "beat," such as police, town hall, or education.

Reporters must be well-educated and generally well-informed. They must be able to interview, write, analyze, and interpret news either in their specific field or on a wide range of subjects. Reporters who work on small newspapers usually cover all the local news and may also take photographs, write headlines, lay out inside pages, write editorials, and even solicit advertisements.

After getting a story the reporter may either go back to the office to write the story himself, or may phone it in to a rewrite man. A reporter also spends a good deal of his time going over background material for stories, and researching articles and records of the past, since accuracy is vital in his job.

About 39,000 newspaper reporters are at work in this country, most employed by daily newspapers. Others work for weekly papers, press services, and newspaper syndicates. They are employed all over the country, in every size town and city.

What You Need Personally

Many different kinds of people are successful newspaper reporters, but one trait is common to all—curiosity. You must want to know what happened, and why, what people were involved, and be willing to seek out information. A reporter needs persistence, initiative, resourcefulness, and a good memory. You must be able to work under pressure and have the physical stamina needed for an often fast-paced and pressured life.

Being able to get along with and communicate with people are most important on this job. You need cooperation and information from people in the news, and then you need to communicate it, clearly, so that others understand it.

To be a good reporter, you must be interested in everything, not just the subject you're writing about. The more knowledge and interest you bring to a job, the better your stories will be.

What Education and Training You Need

A newspaper reporter must be able to write well and type well, but there are many ways of getting the necessary training and experience. Newspapers are increasingly looking for college graduates with either a bachelor's or even a master's degree.

An aspiring reporter can begin early, even in high school, to prepare for this career. Some high schools offer journalism courses, and most have school newspapers or other publications that offer valuable experience. Local papers often hire high school students to report on school events for their papers. In school, English courses are, of course, important, and part-time jobs relating to news work can be helpful.

Many papers prefer to hire graduates of journalism schools, but some find a degree in liberal arts equally desirable. Some high school graduates do go directly into this field, but usually become writers for small papers, and remain there.

In college, journalism students take liberal arts courses in English, sociology, political science, economics, history, psychology and speech. If you want to specialize in a particular area, like science, take as many courses as you can in that field, too.

Specific journalism courses, usually taken during the junior and senior years, include reporting, copyreading, editing, feature writing, and the history of journalism.

Some 250 junior colleges also offer programs that are usually transferable to four-year journalism schools if you want to continue. These prepare you directly for work on a weekly or small daily newspaper.

During college, the journalism student should try to get as much writing experience as possible, perhaps working on the school paper.

Other opportunities for studying journalism are provided by the Armed Forces and by summer internships on newspapers.

If you need financial help, various scholarships, loans and other financial aid programs are offered by The Newspaper Fund, Inc., and other sources. (See page 166.)

Once out of college, the newspaper reporter may start as a general assignment reporter for a small paper or as copy editor for a large paper. Beginning reporters usually cover small local events, write obituaries, etc., and are promoted to cover more important developments as they gain experience.

What the Occupation Has to Offer

There should be many job openings for newspaper reporters during the 1970s. Despite the failures of some major newspapers in recent years, the newspaper business is continuing to grow, and good reporters are important. There will be stiff competition for positions on the larger city dailies, but openings on smaller papers should continue to be available. Mass communication is increasingly important in this country, and a good reporter has many opportunities for success.

Earnings for newspaper reporters vary considerably, depending on the size of the paper and the amount of experience of the reporter and whether the reporters for your paper are members of the American Newspaper Guild (a union which negotiates contracts). In general, inexperienced reporters start somewhere between $90 and $140 a week, with most salaries falling somewhere in between. More experienced reporters usually earn between $170 and $230 a week, although some top reporters may earn over $300 a week. Reporters are almost always given paid vacations, insurance benefits, and pension plans.

A newspaper reporter has many varied opportunities for advancement. He may move up from a small paper to a larger one or to a press service. Some become columnists, correspondents, editors, publishers, or newspaper executives. Other newspaper reporters transfer to similar, but often better paying jobs, such as writing for magazines, or preparing copy for radio and television news reporters.

Points to Consider Before Going into This Field

There are many advantages to this profession. The reporter gets diversity and constant change covering each day's news. He is in on what is happening, contributing a useful, and often vital service to his community. He gets to produce something tangible, and to exercise creativity, initiative, independent judgment. The work is often prestigious, and gives the reporter a chance to meet many people, often famous and important ones. There are many opportunities for a good reporter to expand his options and move on to other interesting fields.

There are, however, some disadvantages to the work. Because of the nature of news, the reporter must have a great deal of physical stamina, nonstop work ability, writing talent, curiosity, persistence, and the ability to work under pressure.

Over thirty-five percent of all newspaper reporters are women, and their numbers can be expected to increase. Formerly women were hired for and kept on the "women's pages," reporting on fashion, recipes, and weddings. Today, women are moving out into all areas of reporting.

For more information, write:

The Newspaper Fund, Inc.
Box 300
Princeton, N.J. 08540

Ask for: job opportunities information and financial aid sources; and schools which offer training.

American Newspaper Guild
Research Department
1126 16th Street, N.W.
Washington, D.C. 20036
Ask for: information on union wage rates.

American Newspaper Publishers Association Foundation
11600 Sunrise Valley Drive
Reston, Virginia 22070
Ask for: *Your Future in Daily Newspapers.*

American Council on Education for Journalism
School of Journalism
University of Missouri
Columbia, Missouri 65201
Ask for: Information on journalism opportunities.

Sigma Delta Chi
Professional Journalistic Society
35 East Wacker Drive
Chicago, Illinois 60601
Ask for: *The Big Story: ten questions and answers about the booming career field of journalism and communication*; and list of recommended readings for careers in journalism.

See also: page 163.

Public Relations Worker

The Job

The public relations field is that part of any organization which is involved "in building and maintaining sound and productive relations with special publics such as customers, employees, or stockholders, and with the public at large, so as to adapt itself to its environment and interpret itself to society." That at least is what the dictionary says. Cynics call it "free advertising" or "fence mending."

There's some truth in both points of view. Public relations (PR) is one of the least clearly defined fields in the entire communications world. All organizations want the world to think well of them. In general, it's the PR worker's job to make this happen by building a good public image for his employer.

In the 1970s, public relations has moved far out of the limited field of "free advertising" for the individual or corporation client. PR people are charged with a wide variety of responsibilities concerning the welfare of the client's customers as well as with the client, personally.

Corporate public relations, the liaison between a company and the people with which it deals, includes not only business and industry, but most of the service organizations. PR staffs work for hospitals, national health organizations, local, state and federal governments, private and public school systems, even religious bodies.

The job, most generally, is that of maintaining communications between the organization and the audience or public it serves. This can, and often does, involve both the external public, which means anyone who reads newspapers and magazines, and the internal public, which includes the employees, boards of trustee, immediate customers or clients and other corporations with whom the company has direct dealings.

For the service organization, which cannot subscribe to paid advertising for ethical reasons, public relations becomes the only means of communicating information about the organization, its services and growth. Business and industry use public relations in addition to advertising. Some major organizations, both business or service, have separate employee relations staffs; in other firms, this is part of the overall public relations program.

There are eight areas in which public relations personnel are involved.

Writing is a major responsibility of PR. including preparation of news releases about personnel changes, new programs, and other organization activities. Publication of a corporate news letter or newspaper may also be part of the job. Some are designed for employees, others are mailed to donors, stockholders, customers, and other special groups. Depending on the kind of company, writing can also include radio and television, copy, annual reports, technical material, special flyers and brochures.

Editing may also be the job of the writer, especially in a small company or office.

Placement is the art of finding the right publication for your article. In some instances the local newspapers and radio stations are the only available outlets. In others, trade publications, magazines aimed at members of a particular profession, and consumer magazines are suitable showcases.

Promotion utilizes special events such as convention exhibits, open houses, anniversary or "grand openings" and similar occasions to publicize the company and its services or products.

Speaking is often the job of top management and the PR staff may be involved only in preparation of the text. Sometimes however, members of the public relations staff must deliver speeches. This is particularly true when the PR department is responsible for community relations and must establish a permanent favorable relationship with various groups and organizations in the community. The PR staff looks for meetings and other events at which they provide a speaker, planning and making the speeches themselves.

Production of printed material requires some knowledge of art and layout for brochures, reports, news letters, etc. Sometimes the PR staff is entirely responsible for this, otherwise there may be a company art department to do the work, or an outside firm may be hired. In either case, the PR staff must be skilled enough to supervise and approve the art work and design.

Programming includes the overall, top-level planning of the entire PR program. The needs of the firm, means of meeting those needs and the schedule for each activity must be determined. This approach is most often found in large companies; smaller firms tend to "play it by ear," meeting the needs as they arise.

Advertising, even when actually carried out by a separate department, must often be carefully coordinated with public relations plans. In some small firms, the public relations and advertising director are the same person. More often, there are two separate operations that must be directed toward the same goal.

A public relations man or woman may work for one firm or may work for an independent advertising or public relations company which has a number of clients. In this case he or she may be assigned exclusively to one large client or may have several small accounts. The third form of employment is as an independent public relations representative or consultant. The free-lance PR man or woman may employ a small staff of aides and clerical workers and may work on either a "retainer" or single job work basis.

Working conditions are usually fairly good, especially when the PR staff is expected to meet the public, face to face, in its own office. In fact working conditions can be plush if the firm wishes the world to believe it is a really first-class outfit. In any case, most companies realize that the PR staff needs good lighting, functional desks and files, comfortable chairs, electric typewriters, pleasant atmosphere, and reasonable quiet to function.

What You Need Personally

The job of public relations, regardless of its form, is basically handling people. Since PR people often get the job of dealing with irate customers, you must be able to keep your cool and stay sympathetic, even after the fifth time you hear the same story. You must be pleasant even on rainy days. You must also be ready to ward off unreasonable demands from your "publics" without angering them further. You should be skilled in the art of saying "no" nicely and of compromising. Being creative, imaginative, well organized, able to verbalize, and full of ideas for promoting your company will help too.

What Education and Training You Need

Since public relations is yet to be clearly defined and since there are so many fields into which a PR person can go, it is difficult to specify educational requirements. A good solid background in writing skills is basic. Special courses in various aspects of public relations, especially in typography and layout are important. Industrial firms looking for someone to do semitechnical writing are often more interested in specific education within the field, than courses in public relations.

Generally, a solid liberal arts background with emphasis on journalism and public relations courses is most desirable. Some colleges do offer courses and degrees in public relations. A college degree is becoming more and more important, although many of today's public relations executives do not have this formal training. A young person with two years of formal training and initiative may find his or her way into the field through working first for a newspaper—the common background of many PR people. Young women with junior college liberal arts education and secretarial skills may find secretarial jobs are an opening wedge. If you are interested in public relations, you must plan, however, on continuing your education with evening courses, for advancement may be highly dependent on obtaining advanced education. Jobs in the public service or nonprofit agency fields are probably more readily available to nondegree applicants than are those in industry and business. Most companies will give you additional on-the-job training once you are hired.

What the Occupation Has to Offer

This has been a rapidly expanding field in recent years, as more and more businesses and nonprofit organizations became aware of the need for a public relations or public information staff. Expansion is expected to continue though not as rapidly, with the new thrust of consumer protection and consumer "right to know" adding new importance to public relations in many fields.

Starting salaries for PR trainees ranged from $4,600 to $7,000 in 1970, and with a few years experience from $9,000 to $13,000 a year. Executive salaries in business and industry are high ($25,000 to $50,000 a year or more) but so is the competition. Salaries in nonprofit fields and for lower level jobs are usually good, but not outstanding. Directors of PR of medium-sized firms earned from $14,000 to $25,000 in 1970. Business conditions affect the number of PR workers, for example, when business is good, there are lots of jobs, but in times of recession, the public relations staff is often the first to be cut. It is therefore a fairly unstable field. If job security is what you are looking for, this may not be a good choice.

Points to Consider Before Going into This Field

The public relations job is seldom routine and there is tremendous personal satisfaction to be gained from a successful campaign. There is great opportunity to work with different types of people, and to tackle and solve a variety of problems. The field offers an excellent outlet for creative talent.

Unfortunately, public relations is not always well understood. The name is still interchanged with "press agent" by some of the public and sometimes other staff members of the firm. Companies attempt to correct this by using designations such as "public information" or "communications department." Since duties are so varied, this latter title is a good description of the job.

Even employers sometimes do not fully understand the public relations job and these staff members are often among the first to be fired when the employer is in financial difficulty. The ability to find new employment has a great deal to do with the geography of the nation. In the northeast, for example, the availability of qualified people outstrips the demand, making it very hard indeed to find employment when the economy dips.

Women hold almost as many important public relations jobs as men, particularly in the nonprofit field.

For more information, write:

Career Information Service
Public Relations Society of America
845 Third Avenue
New York, New York 10022
Ask for: *An Occupational Guide to Public Relations*; American colleges offering degrees and Courses in public relations.

See also: page 163.

Broadcast Technician

The Job

Technicians in the broadcasting industry are responsible for all of the wide variety of electronic equipment necessary for radio or television transmissions.

They set up the equipment, operate it and keep it in working order. In the studio itself, they operate microphones, lights, sound effects devices, various recording devices, film projectors, and television cameras. Separated from the studio by soundproof walls and glass is the control room in which technicians run the equipment that controls the quality of sound and picture. It is in this booth that the switch is made from one camera to another, from one "set" to another, or from one "on the scene" broadcast to another.

Small radio and television stations give their technicians a variety of jobs to perform. As is true in many industries, the larger the station, the more specialized a technician's job may be.

A transmitter technician keeps check on outgoing broadcast signals and takes care of correct operation of the transmitter. A maintenance technician sets up, maintains and repairs broadcasting equipment. The audio control technician is responsible for sound pickup controls. A video control technician is concerned with total quality of television pictures. The lighting technician is responsible for proper lighting in television broadcasts. Work involved in picking up broadcast material from outside the studio is the job of the field technician. The recording technician is in charge of sound equipment; the video tape recording technician handles electronic tape on which pictures are recorded for later television transmission.

Much of this work, of course, takes place inside a radio or television studio. However, many technicians are deeply involved in prerecording of special interviews, commercials, and other segments of radio and television programs which are prerecorded—often in special studios where no "live" broadcasts take place. The broadcasting networks and very large stations have special field or location crews that are almost exclusively involved in work outside the studio, covering for example floods, fires, press conferences by government officials, the arrivals of VIPs and other major news stories. Field crews are also vital to documentaries and interviews that are recorded outside the studio. The time involved in preparation of these special segments and programs is always much greater than the time taken by the broadcast. Some of these "location" assignments require many hours of preparatory work; in almost all cases much more material is recorded than is ever broadcast.

Working conditions vary greatly, depending in part on the size of the station. A technician who does all inside work at the studio has quite a different life from the technician who must race to a fire in the middle of a freezing winter night.

What You Need Personally

Flexibility and a talent for working efficiently and accurately under sudden great pressure are important assets in the broadcasting industry. In the news department in particular, quick reaction is important, since major news stories are no respecters of coffee breaks and news editors always want the story, in full, by the next deadline. Even routine schedules may be abruptly interrupted by a sudden news development and technicians must be prepared to handle changing situations smoothly and at a moment's notice.

Technicians who go into the field must be able to maneuver equipment into inadequate spaces, often unobtrusively so the subject of a news story or interview does not become unduly distracted by the cameras, lights, and recorders. Ingenuity is necessary when either the "geography" of a field assignment or the reaction of the subjects is unfavorable.

What Education and Training You Need

The most basic background for a broadcast technician is a Radiotelephone First Class Operator license, issued by the Federal Communications Commission. Federal law requires this license for anyone involved in operating a transmitter and some stations demand this qualification from all their broadcast technicians. (Information on requirements for these licenses is available from the FCC, Washington, D.C. 20036.)

In high school, you should have courses in algebra, trigonometry, and physics as part of your general background. Work in operating an amateur radio station is very good training. Electronics courses given by a technical school are very helpful; look for a school that gives courses especially designed to prepare you for obtaining an FCC First Class license.

While a college degree is becoming more and more important for top-level supervisory jobs, you still have an advantage if you study at the junior college or post-high school technical level. Since electronics is a rapidly changing field, you should be prepared to keep up with new developments and should look for means of continuing to add to your technical education even after you find your first job.

What the Occupation Has to Offer

There is tremendous variety in the broadcasting field, both in sizes of stations and in the kinds of places in which you may live. There are home town radio stations all over the nation, small city television stations abound and major cities can be counted on to have competing radio and television companies. There are radio stations of varying sizes all over the world. While television stations are somewhat more limited in number, new facilities are still being developed here and abroad.

Small stations in small communities tend to employ very few technicians and openings are most likely to become available as talented technicians move on to greener pastures in larger cities. Some increase in total jobs available will come from new stations going on the air in the 1970s; other openings will occur as people now in these jobs retire.

Earnings are dependent on the size of the station, the area it serves, whether you are working in a radio or a television station and your individual experience. In large stations, you would work a 37- to 40-hour week, with overtime beyond that limit. Smaller stations require more frequent overtime. Network technicians are often called on to work for many hours without interruption when they are covering fast-breaking major news stories.

Advancement depends on your individual length of experience and the capability you have to offer. Your basic salary may increase either through your personal negotiations or through benefit of union contracts. Advancement to a more important job occurs when the person who has that job leaves it.

Points to Consider Before Going into This Field

In this field you can take great pride in doing an outstanding job with lights, camera, sound effects, or switching from one camera or microphone to another. The drama of getting a late story, getting it well, and getting it in time is stimulating, satisfying, and exhausting.

You must be prepared to cope with any kind of emergency from a defective piece of equipment to a rush assignment. Pressure is part of the job.

There has been some problem with minority hiring by the networks, but a special technical training school has been set up for blacks and the opportunities for jobs should be better in the next ten years.

The field is, at present, almost exclusively a man's world, probably because women have not made much effort to obtain the required technical education. At least one major television station in the east received publicity in 1972 for its appointment of a female cameraman. There is no reason why a qualified woman cannot obtain a good job in the field, but she should be prepared to work harder in order to have her ability recognized.

For more information, write:

Department of Human Resources Development
Mail Control Unit
800 Capitol Mall
Sacramento, California 95814
Ask for: *Broadcast Technicians (Television)* No. 359, Free.

Also contact:

If you are interested in the field, you may be able to get information and advice from the staff of your local station (especially if you live in a small city or town). Check also with your local college, university or technical school.

See also: page 163.

Radio and Television Announcer

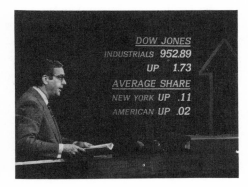

DOW JONES
INDUSTRIALS 952.89
UP 1.73
AVERAGE SHARE
NEW YORK UP .11
AMERICAN UP .02

The Job

Radio and television announcers are in charge of reading or introducing commercial messages from advertisers, introducing shows, and reporting sports programs "live." They sometimes conduct interviews with people currently in the news or act as disc jockeys. In small stations, they may also write both commercial and news copy, and perform other nonspeaking tasks. Some announcers serve as masters of ceremonies, but by that time may have a new title as a radio or television personality.

What You Need Personally

A good, clear speaking voice is the first requirement for an announcer on either radio or television. Also included are excellent pronunciation, correct English, and a good sense of timing in delivery of the spoken word.

Special knowledge of sports, music, and current events adds to your capability and provides better opportunity for both employment and advancement. In television, of course, personal appearance is important, although a glamorous appearance is not the asset it once was. Announcers must both look and sound believable. Listeners or viewers have to think you mean it when you give a commercial message. Filmed commercial messages on television are usually dramatized using professional actors and actresses or celebrities to play roles. The announcer, however, often introduces or wraps up the message.

What Education and Training You Need

High school courses in dramatics and public speaking are helpful general background for announcers. Also you can work on your school radio station if you have one. Major cities often have foreign language radio stations, so fluency in languages such as Italian, Spanish, German, or French is helpful in these areas.

Some private vocational schools offer specialized training for announcers and you will also find courses at community and junior colleges. Liberal arts courses are an asset if you want to be a disc jockey or broadcast personality. Since the first job is easier to obtain in a small station, you should obtain an FCC Radiotelephone First Class Operator license (see page 170). You must audition for all announcing jobs.

What the Occupation Has to Offer

Good announcers have a wide range of choice in terms of geography and career future. Many well-known radio and television stars began as announcers or disc jockeys in small stations in suburban areas or small cities and then moved up to better paying jobs in larger communities. There is great competition for the major jobs on networks however, and personality is as important as specific ability in this area. Employment opportunities will rise moderately through the 1970s.

More than eighty percent of all employed staff announcers work in radio, so it is easier to get entry level jobs at radio stations. Earnings depend in part on the section of the country in which a station is located and the size of the station, but generally range from $100 to $300 a week for staff announcers. Personalities may earn anywhere from $20,000 a year up to well over $50,000. Many announcers earn extra fees taping commercials. For the beginner, however, these tasks are usually part of the total job. Only as experience increases and your popularity among your listeners or viewers grows, can you expect to add to your salary with special fees.

Points to Consider Before Going into This Field

Flexibility of employment is one of the main advantages of the field. Announcers receive satisfaction from becoming well known in the area serviced by their stations. And announcing is a good springboard to other jobs in the broadcasting business.

However the field is not stable, stations change personnel and policies often, and job insecurity is a definite disadvantage in this field. Hours are seldom 9 a.m. to 5 p.m., since radio and television stations are often on the air twenty-four hours a day. New announcers will most likely be blessed with the night shift.

Most announcers are men, probably a holdover from the early days of radio when the broadcast signal was not dependable and the male voice was judged better able to project through static and transmission problems. Women are believed to be less likely to want lonely night shift jobs and many people still argue that the female voice is less pleasant sounding over the airwaves. This, of course, has not prevented women from becoming top radio and television stars in soap operas, situation comedies, and dramatic series. The higher pitched tones of the female voice remain an obstacle to employment. However there are some women in announcing jobs, particularly individual and specialty type programs such as interview and women's news shows, and commercials aimed at women.

For more information, write:

American Federation of Television & Radio Artists
1350 Avenue of the Americas
New York, New York 10019

Department of Human Resources Development
Mail Control Unit
800 Capitol Mall
Sacramento, California 95814
Ask for: *Radio and Television Announcer* No. 390, Free.

See also: pages 163 and 172-174.

Radio and Television Journalist

The Job

The news department of a radio or TV station is similar to, and yet different from, the newsroom of a newspaper. Both employ reporters, and television stations have their photographers (cameramen). Radio and television stations are now making more frequent use of editorials—the official position of the management of station or newspaper—and they have commentators who are roughly similar to the columnists of a newspaper.

When radio and, later, television, came into serious existence, most of the newspeople hired came from the newspaper field. If newspapermen were very courageous (or foolhardy, depending on your point of view), and if they could enunciate especially clearly, they took a chance on radio. Later the more daring tried television.

Somewhere along the line the former newspaperman became a well-paid broadcaster, and radio-television journalism came into its own.

Much of the work is the same. A reporter (with or without tape recorder or camera) is assigned to a story. It may be a news story such as a strike, fire, or press conference, or it may be a feature story such as the opening of an art show. Or it may be a documentary, perhaps an indepth study of a person or event of major interest.

The radio or television reporter has the benefit of sight and sound, to either supplement or replace his spoken word. He must, however, work very quickly, for the attention span of the viewer-listener is appreciably shorter than that of the reader. In addition, the reader of a paper who is interrupted by the doorbell, telephone, or crying baby can pick up his newspaper, book, or magazine later on and continue. The broadcaster who has lost the audience has lost it forever. The broadcast journalist must, therefore, be especially sensitive to the impact of his words, the speed of his delivery, and the attention-holding value of his sounds and pictures.

Broadcast journalists in very small cities and towns may do the great majority of their work in the studio. Local personalities may come to them for interviews, and telephone contacts may play a major role. In larger cities, reporters go more into the field for on-the-spot coverage. Major stations, as is true of major newspapers, assign their own men and women to foreign posts, instead of depending entirely on wire services.

Radio and television stations, as well as newspapers, use wire services, including remote oral reports as well as typed copy. Many stations belong to national news networks. Wire services and network operations are also major employers of broadcast journalists and assign their staffs to offices throughout the nation and the world.

Working conditions vary. If you were the only member of the news department in a small station, your work would be almost exclusively indoors, conducting interviews, getting your news by telephone or off the wires. As one of many reporters for a large station, you might get very wet in a flood, even shot at on a foreign battlefield. Your ability to take risks and accept assignments will be a major factor in your career development. You will be faced with odd shifts and holiday and weekend work for most of your career.

What You Need Personally

Much of the ultimate success of a journalist lies in his or her ability to feel a story. You must understand the business, the importance of deadlines, how to write (or report verbally) a story in a short time. But the most successful journalists—in newspapers, radio or television—have a kind of sixth sense for seeking out the hidden part of a story, for evaluating claims by opposing factions, for instinctively knowing that a story will be more important tomorrow than it is today.

Coupled with this is a personal ability to ask the tough questions without driving away the target of the question. When you see a television interview by a top newsman, listen carefully to his questions and watch the response of the person he is interviewing. Why wasn't he thrown out of the room? Why wasn't the door slammed in his face? Because he is an important newsman? Perhaps. But the reason he is an important newsman may well be because he always knew how to keep the other fellow talking.

What Education and Training You Need

A college degree is playing a more important role in broadcast journalism now than in the past. Certainly a liberal arts education through the junior college level is fairly basic and special training in writing, public speaking, and related fields are important. "On the air" experience in a high school or college radio station is good training. People with specialized backgrounds in such fields as science, economics, politics, and literature are finding more opportunity to use this knowledge in the increasingly specialized broadcasting field.

What the Occupation Has to Offer

Broadcast journalists are among the highest paid members of the industry, but don't expect to start out at $25,000 a year. It takes time, energy, and talent to get there. With increasing specialization, more time spent on newscasts and documentaries, more on-the-spot coverage, and the use of communications satellites, this field has increasing variety and additional need for special knowledge and skills. The journalistic side of broadcasting is expanding.

Advancement is possible from reporter to newswriter to chief writer to "anchor man" or principal commentator or news director. The latter require the most talent, experience, and general education.

Points to Consider Before Going into This Field

While some radio-television reporters in small stations find life fairly routine, most people in this field find excitement and challenge in getting a story. As mentioned, salaries can be excellent, and travel can be a regular part of the job for experienced, capable people.

However there is tension and pressure much of the time. That attractive travel proposition can be inconvenient, and a real handicap to family or social life. Another disadvantage is irregularity of hours. News stories are not respectful of social commitments or dinner hours.

There is a great deal of hard work, fast thinking and expenditure of energy required in all aspects of radio-television broadcasting. Today, there are fewer restrictions. A good speaking voice is important, as is a good appearance, but extremes in either are no longer needed or desired. Knowledge and ability to project personality have assumed greater importance. While both radio and television reporting, at least on the air, were once exclusively male jobs, women are being heard and seen more and more in serious news reporting roles. There are also more jobs open to members of minority groups.

For more information, write:

Sigma Delta Chi
Professional Journalistic Society
35 E. Wacker Drive
Chicago, Illinois 60601

Ask for: *Mike and Camera: A Broadcasting Career for You?*

National Association of Broadcasters
1771 N Street, N.W.
Washington, D.C. 20036
Ask for: *Broadcasting the News,* and their radio and TV careers pamphlets.

See also: pages 163 and 171.

Radio and Television Production Worker

The Job

In addition to the radio and television jobs described under broadcasting technicians, announcers, and journalists, there are a number of jobs in the production end of the field.

Some, such as those in the business or financial management areas require a college degree. Other jobs can be filled by people with either a junior college education or special training.

The programming department is in charge of scheduling daily and weekly shows, assigning personnel to cover special events and providing general services. It also hires announcers, entertainers, etc., for special jobs.

The traffic manager is responsible for keeping a record of broadcast time which can be sold to advertisers.

The continuity director is in charge of the writing and editing of all scripts. He may have an assistant or writer who prepares material for announcers.

Announcers on some stations do nothing but present prepared material for advertisers, introductory material at the start of a show, or credits at the conclusion. Others may be involved in some technical work.

Program assistants aid the director or producer in carrying out program plans. (Jobs as directors or producers require a good deal of

formal education and much experience, as a rule.)

Musicians are sometimes employed on a one show basis. Others are employed full time by the station. A thorough musical background is, of course, mandatory for this work. Musical directors, with a great deal of formal training and experience, supervise all music activities.

The studio supervisor plans and arranges setting up of scenery and props. The floor manager or stage manager plans and directs actors' positions and movements in accordance with the director's instructions. Training in the theatrical field is helpful in this area.

Floormen set up props, hold cue cards (sometimes known as "idiot cards"), and perform other nonskilled jobs. This is often the opening job for a new man in the production department.

Makeup artists see that performers are properly made up for television cameras.

Scenic designers plan and design sets for television shows, including backgrounds, furniture, draperies and props for dramatic, news, "talk," and quiz shows. A background in art and design is important in this job.

Sales and management jobs in broadcasting stations are very similar to those on newspapers, magazines and other communications media. *(See pages 163-165.)*

What You Need Personally

All broadcasting field positions require accuracy and attention to detail. You must be resourceful to meet demands for last-minute changes and must be ready to work under great pressure at times.

What Education and Training You Need

It is obvious that some of the jobs do not require any special training. Some are similar in demand to clerical positions. Others, such as make-up artist or scene designer, require special training. Many junior colleges offer courses in drama and theatrical production. There are also special schools devoted almost exclusively to classes in theatrical training. Generally speaking, the top jobs in broadcasting, including producing and directing and assisting positions do require a college degree, or its equivalent in solid background and experience.

What the Occupation Has to Offer

As in every other field, there will be a certain number of jobs created through retirement, death, or relocation of personnel. In addition, opening of some new radio and television stations will add new jobs. Cable television (CATV) is a fairly new development, the impact of which has not yet been fully felt in the field. Use of closed circuit television in industry and education is increasing, thereby expanding the potential for employment in independent firms making films for these specialized consumers. All of these facts add up to moderate growth through the 1970s.

Competition is always keen, even with new jobs opening up, partly because of the great attraction this glamorous field has for young people.

A 1970 survey showed that the average earnings for nonsupervisory personnel was about $145 a week for an average of a little over 38 hours a week. As is usually true, salaries in large cities are better than in rural areas, and major networks, stations, and independent production firms pay better than small stations or producers.

Advancement depends on availability of jobs, on individual training and talent, and experience in the field.

Points to Consider Before Going into This Field

Jobs in the communications field appear to be exciting. Much of the time they are, whether you are handling a top news story, which has just broken, or meeting the daily challenges of the profession. However, along with the excitement is a great deal of old-fashioned hard work, pressure, and planning. Nerves can become frayed, if not fractured, under pressure of things going awry. Be prepared for shows of temperament, long irregular hours, and changes of plans.

Women make up almost one-fourth of broadcasting staff employment. Many women use a secretarial job as a good entry position if they are interested in moving up to programming or administrative work.

For more information:

See page 163.

Conservation

The Job

In our rush toward urbanization and industrialization, we have too frequently neglected our most valuable resources: forests, range lands, water, and wildlife. Only in recent years have we become aware of the damage that is being done. And we have just begun a dramatic effort to correct this damage and to prevent further waste. Such an enormous task has called for the creation of many jobs and the development of new skills. The conservatists' purpose is to protect, develop, and manage our natural resources. Because there are so many opportunities to work in conservation and because new occupations are being continually created, a complete picture of this vast job market cannot be presented here. Instead, we will discuss what's available now in the field of conservation for anyone with less than four years of college education.

Any conservation career requires an interest in nature and in preserving it, in addition to specialized skills and knowledge.

One group of conservation workers is known as *natural resource managers.* These people are concerned with analyzing problems and devising programs to deal with pollution and waste. They keep track of the resources in their territories and cooperate with other people in the field for best results.

The *fish and game warden* is one of these specialists. His main concern is to enforce the laws that protect the creatures in his territory. He is on the go much of the time, enforcing laws, investigating violations, and arresting violators. By teaching sportsmen how to use their equipment properly and explaining the laws, he tries to benefit both man and nature. Safety rules are very important to his job; he tries to be sure hunters and fishermen know all about them. The warden also collects information on the health, availability and homes of the fish and animals in his area.

Another conservation worker is the *range manager,* who has duties connected with the proper use and improvement of our country's one billion acres of rangeland. Sometimes he plans and directs range improvements or may inspect or monitor the land in his territory to be sure it is being properly used. Other duties include determining livestock grazing patterns, examining seeding and planting methods, restoring or developing methods, fire protection and pest control.

A closely related job is that of the *watershed manager,* who is responsible for the country's reservoirs and aqueducts. The water so necessary to us all is maintained by the manager, who monitors and controls the levels and regulates its flow rate both in everyday use and in flood control and irrigation. He also regulates the machinery in the affiliated hydroelectric plants. One of his most important duties is to control the daily chemical content of water purification processes. The watershed manager is also in charge of caring for the land area from which the water flows. He patrols this area, inspecting equipment and checking for animal damage or trespassing.

While the three workers mentioned above are usually employed by the federal or state government, the *wildlife manager* works for private game preserves. As our animal population grows smaller and smaller, its preservation has become a matter of major concern to conservationists. The wildlife manager plans the planting of preserves, taking into consideration the animals' eating habits and their natural forms of protection. He also plans and oversees the construction of water sources for the animals. One of the most important responsibilities of the wildlife manager is to keep a regular count of all animals in the preserve and determine the number of animals permitted to be killed during a hunting season without threatening a species with extinction. Predicting a proper balance of nature is not an easy task.

Another group of conservation workers is *monitors and inspectors*. They are the ones who see to it that all our theories are being properly applied to nature and that they are working. This work requires careful attention to detail and offers an ever-increasing number of jobs both with the government and with industry.

Environmental inspectors usually specialize in one area of our environment and use a variety of chemical and mechanical tests to determine its purity. They investigate air, water, land, solid waste, industrial pollutants, noise and pesticides. The inspector is supported by laws which regulate the amount of pollution that is acceptable; by taking samples and analyzing them, the inspector can check adherence to the law. He can recommend changes or call for prosecution of violators.

Food and drug inspectors inspect all the different businesses that sell, process, handle, and store the products we buy to make sure they conform to the laws regulating quality, purity, and sanitation. They may inspect the building, the employees or the goods, and can recommend penalties for breaking the law. These inspectors must have in-depth knowledge of the substances they are dealing with and use many specialized kinds of equipment to determine the qualities of the goods they inspect.

Related to the food and drug inspector is the *health inspector*. He makes sure that the places that handle and sell food are meeting standards of cleanliness, safety, and food quality. He reports violations of regulations and works closely with people like public health nurses and engineers to help prevent outbreaks of disease.

One of the conservation employees most involved with new scientific development is the *nuclear inspector*. He inspects the construction, employees, and environment around nuclear plants to make sure that the radiation level is safe and that nuclear waste products are not excessive. These inspectors use sophisticated detection instruments to check radiation; they make recommendations when they consider levels to be unsafe.

Another fast-growing job is that of the *conservation technician*. With the increasing complexity of our world, assistants for highly educated professionals are often needed. Technicians usually have taken some special post-high school training for their specific field so that they can work closely with professionals. They need background in both mathematics and science for these jobs.

The *biological technician* assists a biologist in studying plants, animal and human tissues, microorganisms and marine life. He studies the relationship between the living thing and its environment and may breed organisms for study. Behavior, diseases and the effects of pollution are all investigated in this work.

Environmental technicians work in the laboratory and in the field to try to preserve and increase the purity of the environment. Using a great deal of sophisticated equipment, these workers sample, analyze, and study the environment and recommend possible solutions to our problems. One area in which they are critically needed is population management. This involves doing population research and developing methods to help manage and control the world's expanding birth rates.

Food technicians participate in the many aspects of growing, processing, and marketing foods. They research new sources of food, improved production methods, better use of current resources, and better packaging and delivery processes. They may inspect food for flavor, nutritional value, and appearance.

Another technician involved with the pollution problem is the *health technician*. He studies environmental problems as they pertain to our health and to disease. Some of these technicians specialize in industrial health and are mainly concerned with the safety conditions and toxicity of the air in factories. Laboratory technicians in this field research and analyze existing environmental health hazards.

The *horticultural technician* is directly involved with the raising and care of flowers, shrubs, and trees. With the ever-increasing presence of concrete in our society, greens have become more desirable, not just for beauty but also for oxygen and noise reduction. Some technicians are involved in physically working with plants, others with designing planting areas and floral arrangements (see separate section of the book on Landscaping and Nursery Work, pages 109-110).

Land use technicians specialize in rural and urban planning and assist professionals in finding the best use for existing land, in enforcing zoning regulations and in solving problems of urban blight. They may investigate violations of land use and zoning regulations and review applications for building and land use.

Nuclear technicians assist nuclear engineers, particularly in laboratory work, on testing nuclear waste disposal, developing helpful machines and equipment and checking plant and environment for radiation.

Physical science technicians work closely with physical scientists and engineers on problems in different areas. They may deal with electronics, mathematics, astronomy, geology, geophysics, meteorology, engineering, minerals, and noise. They try to find ways of preventing pollution and conserving natural resources.

The *resource conservation technician* works in forests, parks and recreation areas, assisting the land management official. He surveys, constructs, and maintains recreational areas and monitors and cares for wildlife. He tries to prevent the waste of natural resources and encourage their best use.

Still another conservation group is the *testers and analysts,* who usually work for government agencies. The *environmental tester* or analyst checks the purity of air, water, or soil by using various mechanical and chemical tests. He investigates how well control devices work and makes suggestions on how to improve them.

The *mechanical tester* may be a test engine evaluator checking sound and emission pollution from engines. The automobile mechanic fits into this cateogry as he must analyze and repair car engines so they run but give off fewer pollutants. Other mechanical testers check noise pollution in engines.

In order for conservation techniques and operations to be put into use, many *operations workers* are employed. Operators, foremen, and controllers set up, start, adjust, operate, and stop the various machines used in conservation and check for needed repairs and adjustments. They provide the muscle to make the conservation program work. Most workers in this area have specialized responsibilities relating to the machine or system they operate.

The *dump and solid waste disposal operator* operates various equipment that collects and processes solid waste. He dispatches trucks and organizes collection. As recycling becomes more prevalent, his job will undergo many changes.

The *incinerator foreman* runs the equipment that burns refuse and directs the workers who are under him. Using the incinerator properly is important to keep air pollution down. The *incinerator operator,* whom he supervises, directs other employees in feeding materials into the incinerator and is responsible for keeping controls adjusted for constant temperature. He may also repair equipment and handle disposal of ashes and dumping.

The *power plant operator* operates all the equipment that provides us with our various forms of power. He regulates speed, voltage, and turbines; makes notes and reports any equipment problems.

An increasingly urgent job is that of the *recycling operator.* He may determine what materials should be salvaged and instruct other workers in how to sort, store, and redistribute them. Where large objects have to be taken apart, he will check the parts for either repair or salvage.

The *water or sewer systems foreman* supervises the workers who install, maintain, repair and service our water distribution and sewage systems. He is responsible for efficient service and for meeting environmental standards.

The *waste water treatment plant operator* is directly concerned with recycling water and removing and disposing of solid waste. His work is very important in dealing with water pollution and promoting conservation. Among his duties are operation of various kinds of special equipment, reading and recording meters, sampling materials, and maintaining records of operation.

Water treatment plant operators are responsible for providing us with pure water. They read, record, and maintain the correct chemical balance in the water.

What You Need Personally

The qualifications for all these jobs vary considerably, but an interest in the improvement of our environment and the protection of our natural resources is most important. You should be observant, accurate, and attentive to detail for these jobs, and dependability is a must. You should be oriented toward public service, because so much of your work will be with your community. Most of these jobs require working closely with others. Being able to get along with people and communicating well are important.

A lot of conservation jobs are performed partially or entirely outdoors, so good physical health and stamina are needed. You'll need to be versatile—able to work at a remote outpost one week and appear before a tour meeting the next.

What Education and Training You Need

Requirements depend on the job, but a high school education is an asset, and even a necessity, in most cases. Natural resource managers usually need post-high school training, the more the better because of the wide range and amount of responsibility in their work. Studies in all areas of science, ecology, mathematics, and management are desirable.

Inspectors and monitors need some special training as well as on-the-job experience.

Technicians are often able to take specialized post-high school courses designed specially for their fields. These one- to three-year courses are offered by technical colleges, private vocational schools, junior and community colleges, and in the military service. In general, scientific, mathematical, and engineering studies will be most useful.

Testers and analyzers also usually have some post-high school training. Their course of study would include mathematics, physics, and chemistry.

Operators and foremen sometimes take post-high school studies and in other cases learn their work on the job or in apprentice programs. In this field, the more background the better the chances for success.

What the Occupation Has to Offer

The employment outlook for all conservation jobs is extremely good. As our concern with the environment grows and our related technology is developed, skilled workers will be in increasing demand in all areas. If you have solid training in any field mentioned here, and the many more that will appear in the years to come, you will be assured of steady employment.

Earnings for conservation workers depend on the job done and the experience of the worker. Natural resource managers will probably start at about $5,000 a year or slightly more. Inspectors and monitors earn between $6,000 and $7,000 and may make $10,000 a year or more. Technicians usually start at about $5,000 or $6,000 and with experience make about $10,000. Testers and analysts usually start at $6,000 or $7,000 a year.

Opportunities for promotion are good in all these jobs for workers who are diligent, responsible, and keep up on new developments in their field. This is particularly important in conservation, which is an area where changes and improvements are a regular occurrence.

Technician jobs are among the fastest growing, particularly for people with post-high school training in life science, engineering, drafting, and the physical sciences. Most technicians work for private industry.

Points to Consider Before Going into This Field

There are many advantages to conservation work. You have a chance to do something worthwhile, improving the world in which we live. The results of your work are often visible, giving you a real feeling of satisfaction. Many of these jobs involve outdoor work and are ideal for people who enjoy nature, particularly since you are contributing to nature's preservation and improvement.

Although most of these jobs require some post-high school training, it need not always be extensive. You can get into a rapidly expanding field fairly easily and grow with the field.

There are a few disadvantages to these jobs. You may have to work outdoors in weather that is pretty unpleasant. Or, the work may have to be done in places that are remote. Some tasks can be fairly monotonous, too, as in routine sampling and testing.

For more information, write:

American Association of Community and Junior Colleges
1 Dupont Circle, N.W.
Washington, D.C. 20036
Ask for: *Environmental Education in the Community College.*

American Fisheries Society
Fifteenth Street at New York Avenue, N.W.
Washington, D.C. 20005
Ask for: fisheries management information.

Department of Human Resources Development
Mail Control Unit
800 Capitol Mall
Sacramento, California 95814

Ask for: *Fish and Wildlife Assistant,* No. 447, Free.

Environmental Protection Agency
1626 K Street, N.W.
Washington, D.C. 20460
Ask for: *Working Towards a Better Environment—Some Career Choices* and *Information on Careers in Water Pollution Control.*

National Sanitation Foundation
P.O. Box 1468
Ann Arbor, Michigan 48106

National Wildlife Federation
1412 16th Street, N.W.
Washington, D.C. 20036
Ask for: Wildlife conservation and management information.

Superintendent of Documents
U.S. Government Printing Office
Washington, D.C. 20006
Ask for: *Career Education in the Environment* U.S. Office of Education, Division of Vocational and Technical Education, 1972. HE 5.6/2: EN 8/2 $3.00, paper.

Vocational Guidance Manuals
235 East 45th Street
New York, New York 10017
Ask for: *Opportunities in Environmental Careers,* $5.75.

The Wildlife Society
Suite 5–176
3900 Wisconsin Avenue, N.W.
Washington, D.C. 20016
Ask for: wildlife conservation and management information

Additional Reading:

Arnold, Walter M., *Career Opportunities: Ecology, Conservation, and Environmental Control.* Chicago: Doubleday Ferguson Publishing Co., 1971.

Day, Albert M., *Making a Living in Conservation: A Guide to Outdoor Careers.* Harrisburg: Stackpole Books, 1971.

Dodd, Ed., *Careers for the 70s: Conservation.* New York: Crowell-Collier Press (866 Third Avenue, New York 10022). 1971. $4.95.

Fish Culture Technician

The Job

Fish are among the creatures most affected by the upsets industry has caused in the environment. Fish culture technicians are at work to help make sure there are enough fishes for food, sport and collecting. In general, these specialists are involved in hatching fish eggs, raising or buying young fish, and selling fish.

These technicians may be employed in a variety of places. Some work for fish hatcheries,

the largest branch of fish culture. Here, they raise and spawn brood fish, care for the eggs, feed the young, clean the ponds, and keep the grounds and equipment properly maintained. One of their most important responsibilities is to keep accurate records on all the stages of fish development.

These workers are also employed as fish wildlife conservation technicians. They help biologists and are involved in gathering data, keeping records, and working to improve the natural habitats of fish. Technicians and biologists try to adjust natural fish populations to suit the needs and habits of people; so often a lot of travel is required.

Some technicians are employed in experimental biology laboratories. Here they help biologists both in the field and in the lab in various kinds of research pertaining to fish. They may, for instance, test foods or evaluate tags and marks on fish.

What You Need Personally

A fish culture technician must like the outdoors; he is likely to spend at least half his time there. He should be able to work well with his hands, be interested in fish and be alert to the environent. Because so much observation and record keeping is involved, he should be neat, accurate, and meticulous. Technicians should be able to get along well with others and communicate clearly.

What Education and Training You Need

A high school education is necessary for this job. Courses in biology, chemistry, physics, mathematics, and English are recommended. Legible handwriting and typing skills are important.

In addition to high school, most employers prefer applicants who have had two years of college-level study in the field. Some schools offer two-year programs with an associate degree in fish technology or biological science and often have fish hatcheries in the schools for practical experience. There are many areas of study vital to doing well at this job: fish anatomy and classification, relationship between fishes and their environment, and use of laboratory equipment. For some jobs in this field, you'll be asked to take physical examinations and/or civil service tests.

What the Occupation Has to Offer

The outlook for job openings in this field is very good. It is a relatively new and growing concern. Fishes are much in demand for food, for sport and for home aquariums, and the technician is needed to raise the use, preserve their habitats, and research fish-related matters.

Earnings vary for these technicians. In general, a beginning technician with a two-year degree can expect to start at $8,000 to $9,000 a year. With experience, he may make as much as $12,000 a year, and he also receives regular fringe benefits. He is sometimes provided with low-cost housing.

Chances for advancement should exist in this field, although it is so new that it is difficult to tell. A technician who works hard and keeps up with changes in technology might advance to fish hatchery manager, fisheries management specialist, owner of a fish farm, or senior conservation technician.

Points to Consider Before Going into This Field

This field has many advantages for a person whose interests lie in conservation. The work is interesting and diverse and makes many valuable contributions to the community and to conservation efforts. Salaries are good, and because the field is so new, opportunities should continue to expand in the years to come.

There are some disadvantages however. The hours can be very long, and some work will have to be done outdoors no matter what the weather. Some people also have trouble getting used to the constant overpowering odor of fish.

For more information, write:
Sport Fishery Research Foundation
Suite 503
719 13th Street, N.W.
Washington, D.C. 20005

Forestry Aid And Forestry Technician

The Job

Two important jobs contributing to our efforts to preserve trees and public lands are that of the forestry aid and, on a somewhat higher job level, the forestry technician.

Forestry aids perform a wide variety of duties and assist foresters and rangers in their work. Some of the many tasks they perform are scaling logs, marking trees, collecting and recording information on tree heights, diameters, and mortality. They assist in installing, maintaining, and keeping records of rain gauges, stream-flow recorders and soil moisture measuring instruments, and help road survey crews.

If there is a forest fire, the aids lead fire-fighting crews, take inventory of burned areas and plant new trees to replace those burned. They also offer fire-prevention instruction to those using the forests. In forested areas that are also public parks, they provide information to the public, enforce regulations and regulate campgrounds.

Forestry technicians are involved in supervising timber sales, recreation-area use, and road-building crews that make timber accessible for cutting. They also may work on fire-fighting crews and do work to prevent soil erosion. They work on plant and insect control projects and may also give guided tours, operate camp-grounds, and patrol roads.

Over 11,000 persons are employed in these jobs; about half work for the federal government, often in the heavily forested Western states. Other employers are lumber, logging, and paper milling companies, tree nurseries, and forestation projects.

What You Need Personally

You must enjoy the outdoors and have a feeling for nature to work in these jobs. Physical stamina, and sometimes strength, is needed. You should be able to work without direct supervision.

As a forestry aid, you will spend a lot of time dealing with other people—work crews and the public—so a pleasant disposition and appearance are essential.

What Education and Training You Need

A high school education is an asset for these positions, but not necessarily required. In order to work for the government, you must pass a civil service test. An aid must have at least one year's experience, or a high school education and some post-high school training or job experience. A technician must have at least two years of general experience and one year of specialized experience or two years of college-level studies in this area.

There are a number of ways to get the specific training for forestry work. Various technical schools and colleges give courses specifically designed for forestry careers. In addition, the Forest Service has two training centers used to give employees further education and training in their field.

Specialized courses for forest aids include forest mensuration, wood utilization, and silviculture (methods of growing and improving forest crops). Students also learn drafting, surveying, report writing, and first aid and may live in a camp operated by the school to gain practical experience.

What the Occupation Has to Offer

People are demanding more scientific management of forest land and water supplies and more recreational facilities. Forestry aids will be needed to assist professional workers in all these areas. More of the routine jobs now being done by foresters will be handled in the future by aids. In addition, private industry is expected to hire more trained people to help apply scientific forestry practices. In all, the job outlook for forestry aids, particularly those with some post-high school education, is very good.

Starting salaries for forestry aids working for the federal government are usually $5,166 to $5,688 a year; beginning technicians earn $6,544. Earnings can go as high as $14,000 a year. Although there are no statistics for workers employed by private industry, it is expected that earnings are about the same.

Opportunities for advancement are good, particularly for workers with some extra educational background. The more scientific studies you have taken, the better your chances for promotion. In federal work, advancement requires taking further civil service examinations.

Points to Consider Before Going into This Field

There are many advantages to working as a forestry aid or technician. You are offered a good entry-level job into the world of conservation work, doing many different jobs every day and learning continually. The work is not usually routine and often involves independent thinking and decision making. For people who enjoy being out of doors in natural surroundings, this is a great opportunity. In addition, you are making a real contribution to society.

The work does have some disadvantages. Working outdoors means being out in all kinds of weather and in dangerous situations like floods and fires. The hours may be long and the work very strenuous and tiring. Some work areas are remote, cutting the aid off from the civilized world and most other people.

To do this work, you must be in good physical condition, mentally alert and able to apply a wide range of knowledge to what you do. There are no regulations against women being employed in these jobs, but the work is considered strenuous.

For more information, write:

Education Division
American Forest Institute
1619 Massachusetts Avenue, N.W.
Washington, D.C. 20036
Ask for: information on careers in forestry.

Robert A. Holcombe, Manager
Wood Technology
National Forest Products Association
1619 Massachusetts Avenue, N.W.
Washington, D.C. 20036
Ask for: *Opportunities Unlimited*, and list of schools offering courses in forestry.

Department of the Interior
Career Employment
National Parks Service
Washington, D.C. 20240
Ask for: *Careers in the National Parks Service.*

National Recreation & Park Association
1700 Pennsylvania Avenue, N.W.
Washington, D.C. 20006.

Society of American Foresters
1010 16th Street, N.W.
Washington, D.C. 20036
Ask for: List of schools offering forestry training.

Society of Wood Science and Technology
P. O. Box 5062
Madison, Wisconsin 53705.

Superintendent of Documents
Government Printing Office
Washington, D.C. 20402
Ask for: Miscellaneous publication 843, *A Job with the Forest Service—A guide to non-professional employment, $.15.*
Women in the Forest Service. 1972 Rev. A 1.38:1058/3–S/N 0100-02641. $.10.

U.S. Department of Agriculture
U.S. Forest Service
Division of Information and Education
Washington, D.C. 20250
Ask for: information on employment in the U.S. Forest Service; *So You Want to Be a Forester.*

Laboratory Animal Care Technician

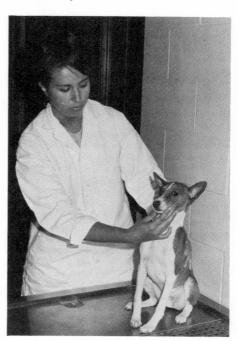

The Job

If you like animals and have an interest in science, this may be a good field for you. Some technicians work for pharmaceutical companies with animals the companies keep for the purpose of testing drugs and chemicals. The technician maintains and cares for the animals, conducts experiments under the direction of the research staff, watches the results of the experiments and keeps records. In some cases, autopsies are made and analyzed.

Medical schools and research centers are employing growing numbers of these specialists to assist them in their work on disease. The technician may supervise the animal caretakers, purchase animals for the laboratory, arrange for their housing, and care and keep records on them. This requires a thorough knowledge of the animals, their habits, their relationship with their environment, and their food. In some cases, specialized research is done in hospitals under the supervision of an experienced doctor in the field. The technician assists in these studies of topics such as blood, microbiology, tissues, genetics, cancer, and immunity. Work in these areas requires specialized study.

Technicians are also employed in the offices of veterinarians. These technicans keep admission records, are responsible for the care and supervision of animals boarding there, administer some medicines and treat minor wounds, sterilize equipment and help prepare for surgery, give anaesthetics, and take and develop X-rays.

Still another area for the laboratory animal care technician is working for a company that grows, sells and ships experimental animals to the medical research centers and pharmaceutical companies mentioned earlier. This requires a thorough knowledge of animals in order to produce and raise disease-free specimens.

What You Need Personally

The most important quality for this job is to like and have a feeling for animals—but still maintain a realistic attitude toward what might, and probably will, happen to them and why.

You should also be clean and neat, have some manual dexterity, have highly developed powers of observation, and skill in record keeping.

What Education and Training You Need

A high school education is mandatory for this job. Studies in algebra, chemistry, biology, and English will be helpful. A further two years of study in a junior or community college or technical institute is highly recommended. Some schools have courses leading to an associate degree in laboratory animal care technology. Education is very important to this job, because much of the work is technical and detailed and requires comprehensive background.

What the Occupation Has to Offer

Sophisticated research has become very important today. Skilled assistance is vital in all the areas where technicians are hired. They are considered specialists. This is a relatively new job category and should see great growth in the years to come.

Although earnings vary, most beginning technicians start at between $7,000 and $8,500 a year. They may, with experience, make as much as $12,000 a year. Various fringe benefits are also available to technicians, in addition to the usual insurance, and paid vacations. In some cases, housing is provided at little or no cost. Technicians who work for medical schools often get tuition benefits.

Advancement opportunities are also good. The technician may go on to become a research science assistant, a microbiologist, or an animal breeder.

Points to Consider Before Going into This Field

There are many advantages in this field. The work is interesting, diverse, and regular. Hours are good, except in veterinary offices, and working areas are usually pleasant. The worker is well-paid, has opportunities for advancement and is able to feel he is making a contribution to humanity.

For people who are especially fond of animals, work for a veterinarian would be most advisable. Some people suffer terrible conflicts working with animals in research laboratories, torn between the fate of the animals and the good that is being accomplished in research. If you think you would have such a conflict but are interested in the field, aim for a veterinarian's office.

This field is equally suited to women as well as men.

For more information, write:

Board of Schools of Medical Technology of the American Society of Clinical Pathologists and American Society of Medical Technologists
2100 West Harrison Street
Chicago, Illinois 60612.

Council on Medical Education of the American Medical Association
535 North Dearborn Street
Chicago, Illinois 60610.

Wastewater Treatment Plant Operators (Sewage Plant Operators)

The Job

Wastewater treatment plant operators protect the country's water resources by controlling water pollution through removal of domestic and industrial wastes. Because clean water is necessary for the health and recreational enjoyment of our growing population, and for the existence of

fish and other wildlife, this industry is essential and one which is growing.

Domestic and industrial waste is carried by water through sewers and arrives at treatment plants in a diluted state. As a waste treatment plant operator, you control equipment and facilities to remove waste materials or make them harmless to humans and animal and fish life. (Frequently such things as boards, sticks, sand, rags and grit are present in the wastewater.) By operating and maintaining pumps, piping, and valves that connect the collection system to the wastewater treatment facility, you move the wastewater through various treatment processes.

As an operator you would be responsible for reading meters and gages and entering information on log sheets. You might monitor meters that record the volume of flow of wastewater into a plant or read gages that measure the level of water in a well and supply the information needed to decide upon normal pump action. You might also operate screening devices for removing large objects, make minor repairs on valves, pumps, and other equipment, sample wastewater at various stages of treatment for laboratory analysis and test and correct the level of chlorine in the water. You might lubricate equipment and hose walls and tanks to break up sludge. In your work you would use tools such as wrenches, pliers, hammers, and other handtools.

Occasionally you might have to work under emergency conditions; for example, in the event of a pump breakdown that causes flooding of the station, you might make emergency repairs or locate the trouble and report it to a supervisor.

Your duties depend on the size and complexity of the treatment plant in which you work. In a smaller plant you might be responsible for the entire system, including making repairs, filling out forms, handling complaints, patrolling, and doing chores such as painting and cutting grass.

In a large plant, duties are performed by staff members who range in experience from a helper, who performs housekeeping jobs, to the chief operator, who supervises the entire operation.

Out of some 30,000 wastewater treatment plant operators in 1970, about 4,000 worked in industrial treatment plants, 25,000 in municipal plants throughout the nation and 1,000 in federal installations.

Because pollution control is continuous, operators work in shifts, and in an emergency operators work overtime. When working outdoors the operator is exposed to all kinds of weather, and may be exposed to hazardous conditions, dust, and toxic fumes in the atmosphere as well as noise from electrical motors, pumps, and gas engines. Odor is kept to a minimum by the use of chlorine.

Many plants are modern, have good lighting, clean washrooms equipped with showers, and a lunch room for employees. Plant sites are usually landscaped. For the most part tanks are open, but the pipes and sludge digestion tanks are covered or beneath the ground.

What You Need Personally

In order to be a wastewater treatment plant operator you must be agile since you will have to climb up and down ladders and move easily around heavy machinery. You also need the physical stamina to work outdoors in all kinds of weather.

What Education and Training You Need

Entry jobs usually do not require specific training, and most operators learn on the job. As a new worker under the direction of an operator, you learn by helping in routine tasks such as recording meter readings, taking samples of wastewater and sludge, and doing simple maintenance work. You are also expected to do cleaning jobs and maintain plant equipment and property.

Many operators are trained in programs approved under the provisions of the Manpower Development and Training Act. Employers usually prefer them to have a high school diploma or its equivalent. An operator should also have some mechanical aptitude and be able to perform simple calculations.

Some treatment operators, especially in large municipalities, are covered by civil service regulations and may be required to pass written examinations testing knowledge of elementary mathematics, mechanical aptitude, and general intelligence.

Most state water-pollution control agencies offer some short term courses to improve the operator's skill. These courses cover principles of sludge digestion, odors and their control, chlorination, sedimentation, biological oxidation, and flow measurements. Some operators take advantage of correspondence courses; some large municipalities pay part of the tuition for courses leading to a college degree in science or engineering.

Although a chief operator of a large and complex plant is expected to have a bachelor's degree in science or engineering, a high school diploma or its equivalent and sufficient experience can qualify you for the position of chief operator of a small or medium-sized plant.

A limited number of operators may become technicians, employed by state or local water-pollution control agencies to collect and prepare water and biological samples for laboratory examination. However, some technical-vocational school or junior college training is usually preferred for technician jobs. (See pp. 229-231.) Some operators become consulting engineers.

At St. Cloud (Minnesota) Area Vocational-Technical School, there is a new two-year, college-level course in Water, Wastewater Technology, aimed at meeting the increasing demand for paraprofessional personnel in this field. In addition to on-the-job training at the St. Cloud Water Utilities Department, the students, who must have graduated from high school or have equivalent educational credits, receive technical training in physical sciences, biological sciences, water technology, waste treatment, sanitation, environment sciences and use of equipment. Related courses are given in technical mathematics, drafting, safety, surveying, communication skills, technical reporting, economics, contracts-codes, accounting, and government and industrial organizations.

All but three states have certification programs designed to improve plant operations and improve employees' positions. Twenty-seven states (California, Connecticut, Delaware, Georgia, Illinois, Indiana, Iowa, Kentucky, Maine, Maryland, Michigan, Montana, New Hampshire, New Jersey, New York, North Carolina, Ohio, Oklahoma, Pennsylvania, South Carolina, South Dakota, Texas, Virginia, West Virginia, and Wisconsin) have adopted mandatory certification laws requiring examination of operators and certification of their competence to supervise the operation of treatment plants. Besides requiring supervisors to be certified, these states encourage other operators to become certified. Twenty-two states have voluntary certification programs, and municipalities in these states are urged to employ certified operators.

A typical licensing program might have four classifications. A Class I operator (to correspond with a Class I plant serving a population of less than 2,000) might be required to demonstrate general knowledge of treatment operations by passing a written examination, by completing a year of field experience and by proving he is a high school graduate.

A class IV operator, however (corresponding to a Class IV plant serving a population of over 40,000) might need a college degree or a two-year degree in science or engineering along with five years of experience at a Class III plant (two years of which were in positions of responsibility) and specific knowledge of the entire field, demonstrated through a written examination.

What the Occupation Has to Offer

Employment of operators in this field is expected to rise rapidly through the 1970s, mostly as a result of the construction of new treatment plants to process an increasing amount of domestic and industrial wastewater. Another reason for employment growth will be the expansion of plants to include advanced treatment in order to cope more efficiently with water pollution. In 1968, 9 out of 10 communities had treatment plants. By 1980 almost all communities are expected to have these services.

Earnings (from a survey covering a number of municipalities) ranged from about $5,000 to $11,000 a year in early 1971. Foremen earned up to $12,000 and chief operators as much as $22,000. Salaries for trainees were about 80 percent of the operators' salaries in most cities. Operators may be promoted to foremen and chief operators.

Points to Consider Before Going into This Field

Fringe benefits provided for plant operators are usually similar to those received by other municipal and civil service employees. Many operators receive paid vacations and holidays, overtime, shift differential pay, sick leave, paid life insurance, paid hospitalization, and retirement benefits.

For more information, write:

Department of Human Resources Development
Mail Control Unit
800 Capitol Mall
Sacramento, California 95814
Ask for: *Water treatment Plant Operator*, No. 443, Free.

Water Pollution Control Federation
3900 Wisconsin Avenue, N.W.
Washington, D.C. 20016.

Also contact:
local and state water pollution control agencies.

See also: page 179.

Construction Industry

The Job

The construction industry is a brawny, hearty giant of a field that employs more than three million skilled workers. They erect towering skyscrapers and bridges and construct highways. Any major structure built in the United States employs one or more of the different types of craftsmen in the construction industry. Most of the work is done by journeymen who are assisted in their jobs by apprentices, laborers, and helpers. There are three general classifications into which most journeymen fall: mechanical, structural, and finishing.

Mechanical journeymen are plumbers, pipe fitters, millwrights, electricians, sheet metal workers, and elevator constructors.

The structural journeymen are operating engineers, rodmen, boilermakers, riggers, reinforcing iron workers, ornamental iron workers, structural iron workers, carpenters, stone masons, bricklayers, blocklayers, and concrete or cement masons.

The finishing journeymen of the construction industry are gypsum board applicators, glazers, lathers, terrazzo workers, tile setters, painters, paperhangers, carpet layers, roofers, asbestos workers, and siding applicators.

The duties of these journeymen are varied, yet the work of each contributes to the building.

What You Need Personally

Prospective construction workers should enjoy working with their hands and their heads. You should be able to read blueprints, measure, and do simple math. Manual dexterity and a desire to create are requirements throughout the construction industry. You must be at least 16, 17, or 18 years old depending on the trade, and be healthy and willing to work out of doors. Some trades in the construction industry require above average physical strength and anyone with a major physical handicap is usually discouraged. Although a high school education is not required in all fields, it is strongly recommended. Individual trades have their own personal requirements, for example, structural steel workers cannot be afraid of heights since they work high above the ground on narrow beams and girders.

One way to feel out a career in the construction industry is to take a summer job as a helper. After two months of working, you should know whether or not you enjoy the trade.

What Education and Training You Need

Although many men acquire the necessary skills of their trade by working alongside skilled craftsmen, some type of formal training is usually recommended.

The most popular way of entering a trade in the construction industry is through an apprenticeship program. Apprenticeships usually last for three or four years with the apprentice being paid while he trains. In most cases the apprentice starts earning at least 50 percent of the hourly rate paid journeymen in his field. This percentage increases regularly until the apprentice becomes a journeyman. Apprentices receive on-the-job training and are required to participate in classroom instruction as well. In most cases classroom instruction is held one night a week.

To be eligible for apprenticeship applicants must usually be at least 17 years old and in good physical condition. In some trades a high school education or its equivalent is required.

Most apprenticeship programs are jointly run by the local union office and local contractors. In some cases apprenticeship is formal and agreements are registered with the State Apprenticeship Committee of the U.S. Department of Labor's Bureau of Apprenticeship and Training. (See pages 52-63 for more information.)

You will find other institutions which offer education for entry into the construction industry such as vocational schools, technical institutes, junior and community colleges, four year colleges and correspondence schools. In many cases educational programs offered by these schools enable you to enter the construction industry at a higher position. Most of the schools offering these courses are eligible for state and federal student loan programs.

There are two-year programs in civil engineering or construction technology. They prepare students in the basic fundamentals of construction techniques, materials, surveying, cost estimating, office and business procedures, and planning of construction work. After graduation you will be able to qualify for work as junior field engineer, layout man, draftsman, detailer, product representative, and estimator in the various phases of the construction industry.

What the Occupation Has to Offer

The construction industry, which by dollar volume is the largest business in the United States, is supposed to double by 1975 and keep on growing. There are acute labor shortages almost everywhere, making jobs readily available throughout the United States.

Journeymen in the construction industry are highly paid craftsmen. Union members earned a minimum average of $6.54 per hour in 1970. Also a great deal of overtime work is available in most building trades.

Skilled workers of the construction industry can advance to become foremen, superintendents, contract estimators, or trade school instructors. There is also an excellent opportunity in many trades for people with enough ambition to start their own contracting business.

Points to Consider Before Going into This Field

There are many advantages to working in the construction industry. Journeymen of building trades earn high hourly wages, receive union benefits, and enjoy job availability.

The main disadvantages are the general working conditions and slow advancement in some cases. You will have to work outdoors in all kinds of weather, possibly in dusty, wet, or dirty areas. You may have to work at moderate or great heights, and risk of injury is always present.

Physical and personal restrictions keep many people out of the construction industry. Careful thought should be given to the requirements of the trade in which you are interested.

Although at the present time there are not many women in the construction industry, things are changing. In 1972 the National Association of Women in Construction had a membership of 5,600 and has a full-scale program to help women qualify for responsible positions in management.

For more information, write:

Associated General Contractors of America
1957 E Street, N.W.
Washington, D.C. 20006
Ask for: information on apprenticeships and careers in construction.

General Building Contractors Association, Inc.
Suite 1212
2 Penn Center Plaza
Philadelphia, Pennsylvania 19102
Ask for: *Construction: Building Your Future.*

National Association of Home Builders
National Housing Center
1625 L Street, N.W.
Washington, D.C. 20036
Ask for: information on apprenticeships and careers in construction.

National Association of Women in Construction
1000 Vermont Avenue, N.W.
Washington, D.C. 20005
Ask for: *Operation Woman Power.*

Also contact:

For information about jobs in your area contact your local trade association; nearest office or state apprenticeship agency (or the Bureau of Apprenticeship and Training, U.S. Department of Labor, Washington, D.C. 20210); local state employment service office; local vocational schools; State Director of Vocational Education; local unions, local contractors (listed as "Contractors" in yellow pages of telephone book); and local joint union-management apprenticeship committee.

When you are applying for a job, go in person. Ask for an apprentice job, a trainee job, or a helper job.

Asbestos and Insulating Worker

The Job

It is the job of asbestos and insulation workers to check the flow of heat or cold by applying special retarding materials to exposed surfaces. An example of this process is the insulation of buildings. For example, in the winter the insulation in a building keeps heat inside the building, thereby keeping the building warm. In the summer this same insulation blocks heat from the outside, keeping the building cooler. Workers in this field insulate buildings, boilers, stills and tanks, furnaces, hot or cold air ducts and pipes, steam generators, and refrigerated cars. Men in the insulation field work mainly with hand tools, but power equipment is becoming more and more common.

Most insulation and asbestos workers are employed in the construction of new buildings. Maintenance is also a very large field and workers may find employment in chemical plants, atomic energy plants, and petroleum refineries. Also companies that have extensive power, heat, or refrigeration facilities may need insulation workers.

What You Need Personally

If you are thinking of entering the insulation and asbestos field, you should have good mechanical aptitude and manual dexterity. Because of the nature of the work, agility and physical coordination are very important and you must be willing to work in high places. Because the many different skilled tradesmen of the construction industry must work together, it is important for people entering this field to be able to get along with fellow workers.

What Education and Training You Need

The majority of asbestos and insulation workers learn their trade through "improvership" programs. These programs are similar to the apprenticeship programs found in some of the other skilled trades. You should be between 18 and 30, in good health, and have a high school education or its equivalent. Courses offered in most high schools that would be helpful are algebra, geometry, wood or metal working, and mechanical drawing. Unlike the apprenticeship of other trades, improvership programs for asbestos and insulation workers usually do not have related classroom instruction. The programs last four years, spent in on-the-job training. Trainees are assigned to assist experienced workers and in this way acquire the necessary skills of the trade. At the beginning of your four-year improvership, as a trainee you receive 50 percent of the hourly earnings of a journeyman in this field. This percentage increases by 10 percent every year until you are earning 80 percent of a journeyman's hourly rate. At the end of the four-year program you must pass a test which measures the amount of knowledge and ability you have acquired. On passing this test, you become a journeyman and are entitled to all benefits.

The easiest way to join an improvership program is through the local branch of the International Association of Heat and Frost Insulators and Asbestos Workers. In some rural areas there might not be a local union branch. If this is the case, contact a local insulation contractor. You might also work as a trainee with a plumber who does insulation work in heating, and gain basic knowledge here.

What the Occupation Has to Offer

Asbestos and insulation workers share the common construction industry benefits of good pay, union benefits, and job availability.

Employment in this field is supposed to increase moderately throughout the 1970s. Since the asbestos and insulation field is still in its infancy, technological advances may open up new areas of employment. One such field is sound conditioning. However, along with technological advances that open up new areas of employment, are advances that increase productivity, thereby reducing the number of people required.

Asbestos and insulation workers earned an average of $6.69 per hour in 1970, fifteen cents more per hour than the average of the other skilled tradesmen in the industry.

There are two ways of advancing in the asbestos and insulation field. The first way is to become a foreman, a superintendent, or an estimator. These jobs are available while working under an insulation contractor and many times promotion is based on seniority. The second way is to start an insulation contracting business. People who start their own asbestos and insulation business have usually spent time working for other contractors first.

Points to Consider Before Going into This Field

There are many advantages in the field of asbestos and insulation work. Workers earn more per hour than most other skilled tradesmen in the construction industry and jobs are available everywhere.

The occupational disadvantages of the asbestos and insulation field are the same as in most other skilled construction work. Exposure to seasonal temperatures and weather conditions, possibly in unheated buildings, a great deal of time spent standing, stooping, and kneeling, working in tight or cramped quarters, and possible dirty or damp working sites are among them. There is always risk of injury and seasonal layoffs are frequent.

Restrictions in this field of work are mostly physical or personal ones. People with major physical handicaps or with objections to the working conditions should not enter the field.

Almost all workers are men.

For more information:

See page 187 for places to write for details.

Bricklayer

The Job

Bricklaying is not an easy job. It is a skill dating back to the ancient Romans and the basic concepts and skills have remained virtually the same for hundreds of years. The development of machines to mix mortar, power elevators, and tools are the only modern refinements of this ancient trade.

Bricklayers (or brickmasons) construct walls, chimneys, fireplaces, partitions, and buildings. They also do special fire and refractory brickwork for glass and steel companies.

A bricklayer's first step is to spread a layer of mortar. Next he applies a full cross-joint of mortar to one side of the brick in place, and a full cross-joint of mortar to the brick he is going to place. After positioning the brick he taps it into place with the trowel and scrapes off excess mortar. When a line of bricks is completed in this manner, he stretches a horizontal line (gauge or course line) to be sure his work is properly aligned. Once a section is completed he finishes

the joints between bricks with special tools to get a uniform look. You must be able to read and follow blueprints in this trade.

Though bricklayers work mainly on new construction projects, they also do alteration, repair, and maintenance work. In addition, manufacturers who use furnaces or kilns need bricklayers' skills.

What You Need Personally

A man who is thinking of being a bricklayer must be physically strong, with no major physical handicaps. Bricklayers often have to do heavy lifting. At times they work with cement blocks that weigh thirty or thirty-five pounds. Also at times they are exposed to bad weather and cramped working quarters. Manual dexterity, good eyesight, and the willingness to do hard work are essential personal qualifications.

What Education and Training You Need

Many men have reached journeyman status in this field by working as helpers and acquiring the necessary skills. But prospective bricklayers who complete apprenticeship programs usually are better qualified and get better jobs. To be eligible for apprenticeship applicants must be over 17 years of age and in good physical health. A high school education or its equivalent is desirable and proficiency in arithmetic is an

asset. In some areas of the country prospective apprentices must take introductory classes at a vocational school before on-the-job apprenticeship training begins. This preliminary training is brief, its purpose to introduce the apprentice to the types of tools and materials used on the job. Apprenticeship programs are run by local bricklayers' unions and usually last three years. During this three-year program, apprentices receive 6,000 hours of on-the-job training and are required to participate in related classroom instruction, usually held at vocational schools, one or two nights a week. To join an apprenticeship program get in touch with your local bricklayers' union. (See pages 52-63 for more information.)

What the Occupation Has to Offer

A job as a bricklayer offers good pay and union benefits. Employment opportunities are expected to increase rapidly throughout the 1970s.

Although general job availability is expected to increase throughout the 1970s, if you are interested in this field of work, check local job markets. Most bricklaying is done in city areas and employment in rural districts may be limited. Local unions control the number of apprenticeships offered, thereby making sure that the job market is not flooded with skilled workers.

In 1970 the average bricklayer earned $6.77 per hour. This is twenty-three cents more than the average hourly earnings of the other skilled trades in the construction industry. This high hourly rate may be deceiving since bricklayers do not work as steadily as some other skilled trades during winter months.

Bricklayers with enough initiative may become foremen, general foremen, superintendents, and ultimately private contractors.

Points to Consider Before Going into This Field

Bricklaying is a trade for a strong person who likes strenuous, active work. The advantages of this job are the same as those of other skilled construction trades, high pay and union benefits among them. However, local job availability may be limited. Also the seasonal nature of the job affects income. Building activity slows in winter and during rain or other storms.

Because of strength requirements this is a job held exclusively by men.

For more information, write:

Bricklayers, Masons and Plasterers' International Union of America
815 15th Street, N.W.
Washington, D.C. 20005
Ask for: *The Bricklayer and his Union.*

Brick Institute of America
Mason Relations Department
1750 Old Meadow Road
McLean, Virginia 22101
Ask for: *Bricklaying as a Vocation.*

See also: page 187 for other places to write for details.

Carpenter

The Job

Carpentry is one of the most versatile and interesting jobs in the construction industry. It is the largest group of building trade workers. Journeymen in this field are skilled craftsmen who work predominately with wood. Carpenters using hand and power tools participate in almost every phase of the construction process. Just a few of the carpenter's many jobs include erecting frameworks; sheathing; studding; building stairs; laying floors; erecting scaffolding; building temporary construction site offices; installing linoleum, and making concrete pouring forms.

Because of the many different types of work, carpenters often become specialists in certain areas. These man may specialize in such things as installing millwork or laying hardwood floors.

There are many avenues of employment open to carpenters. Contractors and homebuilders are the main employers, but work in alteration, remodeling, and building repair is also available. A large number of carpenters are employed by government agencies and as maintenance men in private industry.

What You Need Personally

Since there are so many different aspects to the field of carpentry, if you are interested in this type of work you should be willing to spend many years learning your trade. Good manual dexterity and arithmetic ability are essential personal qualifications. You need to have a good sense of balance and the ability to work in high places. Because much of a carpenter's work is finish work (such as paneling and cabinets), you need to be patient and willing to devote time and energy to a well-finished project.

What Education and Training You Need

Completion of an apprenticeship program is generally the most accepted way of becoming a carpenter. There are many workers who have acquired carpentry skills without apprenticeship training but keeping abreast of modern technological innovations is difficult for them. Carpenters with apprenticeship backgrounds are preferred and generally get better jobs. Prospective carpenter apprentices must be between 17 and 27 years old and in good health. Although it is not usually required, a high school education or its equivalent is desirable.

Apprenticeship programs are conducted by local carpentry union offices. These programs usually consist of four years of on-the-job training (8,000 hours) and 144 hours of related classroom instruction. (See pp. 52-63 for more information.)

What the Occupation Has to Offer

Carpenters are among the most respected members of the construction industry. The personal satisfaction of playing a major part in a business of many skilled tradesmen is rewarding.

Carpenters are in demand everywhere and are not being trained fast enough to fill the need. Tens of thousands of carpentry jobs will be available in the 1970s. Retirements and deaths alone yield twenty thousand jobs per year. However, technological innovations and more efficient equipment continue to limit employment growth somewhat, and because of modernization carpenters' duties are constantly changing.

Unionized carpenters earned on an average $6.42 per hour in 1970. The average rate earned by the other journeymen in the construction industry was $6.54 per hour.

Advancement opportunities in the carpentry field are good. Carpenters may become foremen or advance to general construction foremen. More carpenters become general construction foremen than members of the other skilled trades, because they are usually involved with a greater part of the total construction process. A large proportion of carpenters are self-employed. These men do work on their own or hire other journeymen and become contractors.

Points to Consider Before Going into This Field

Working conditions in the carpentry field are much like those in other areas of the construction industry. However, carpenters do risk injuries from falls or contact with rough and sharp materials. Proper training in the use of power tools and other equipment greatly reduces potential injuries. You do not need unusual physical strength to be a carpenter. However, good health is required since a great deal of a carpenter's time is spent on his feet, climbing, and squatting. A large proportion of carpentry work is done outside and workers are subject to seasonal temperatures and weather conditions.

Carpenters earn good pay, receive union benefits and have a wide range of jobs from which to choose. They are involved in more of the total construction process than most other skilled tradesmen and therefore work more often. There are more types of carpentry and skills than one man can learn in a lifetime. Carpenters can, therefore, continue to learn and advance throughout their careers.

As in most other construction jobs almost all carpenters are men. This trend may change in the future especially in the field of finished and ornamental carpentry.

For more information, write:

Department of Human Resources Development
Mail Control Unit
800 Capitol Mall
Sacramento, California 95814
Ask for: *Carpenter, Carpenter Apprentice.* No. 169, Free.

United Brotherhood of Carpenters & Joiners of America
101 Constitution Avenue, N.W.
Washington, D.C. 20001.

See also: page 187 for other places to write for more details.

Cement Mason

The Job

Cement masons are responsible for all the cement work you see around you every day. They work on a wide variety of jobs from patio building to dam construction. They prepare the site, pour and finish by leveling, smoothing, and shaping surfaces of freshly poured concrete. A cement mason must know the characteristics of concrete and other materials and the effects of heat, cold, and wind on the curing of these mixtures to prevent defects.

Cement masons are employed mainly on large building and highway projects. Most often they work for general contractors or a concrete contractor or for municipal public works departments, public utilities or manufacturing firms. Cement masons may also be self-employed, doing small cement jobs such as driveways or patios.

What You Need Personally

Cement masons must bend, kneel, and stoop since a good deal of their work is done at ground level. As in most construction industry jobs, cement masonry is somewhat physically demanding. A large percentage of a cement mason's work is done outdoors. He is therefore subjected to seasonal temperatures and conditions.

Anyone thinking of taking a job in the field should be in good physical condition and enjoy working outdoors. Manual dexterity and pride in one's work are also valuable assets to cement masons.

What Education and Training You Need

A high school education is not a necessity for a job as a cement mason. Apprenticeship is one way of entering the field. This can be arranged either through your local union office or your local contractor and lasts three years. It requires 6,000 hours of on-the-job training plus related classroom instruction. On-the-job training provides the future cement mason with a basic knowledge of the skills required, while classroom instruction includes mathematics, science, blueprint reading, architectural drawing, estimating materials and costs, and knowledge of local building regulations. You do not have to be a high school graduate or attend an apprenticeship program to become a cement mason. Many men acquire cement masonry skills by working as a laborer and assisting a journeyman. (See pp. 52-63 for more information.)

What the Occupation Has to Offer

The need for cement masons is growing in this country. This is one of the jobs in the construction industry where there is almost always an opening. Journeymen in this field averaged $6.02 per hour in 1970. This is in comparison with the $6.54 per hour earned by journeymen in other building trades. Cement masons can advance to foremen, estimators or may start their own concrete contracting business.

Points to Consider Before Going into This Field

The advantages of being a cement mason are generally the same as in any skilled construction job. Although not paid the highest wages in the construction industry, cement masons earn good hourly pay. Overtime work at extra rate is common. They also enjoy union benefits, and excellent job availability which is this field's greatest advantage.

Cement masons work outdoors in all kinds of weather. Much of their time is spent stooping, kneeling, and bending. This coupled with occupational heavy labor may be a disadvantage to anyone not in good physical condition.

There is limited room for advancement as a cement mason, and jobs are held entirely by men.

For more information, write:

Bricklayers, Masons and Plasterers' International Union of America
815 15th Street, N.W.
Washington, D.C. 20005.

Operative Plasterers' and Cement Masons' International Association of the United States and Canada
1125 17th Street, N.W.
Washington, D.C. 20036.

See also: page 187 for other places to write for more details.

Electrician—Construction

The Job

Electricians are among the most respected workers in the construction industry. These men lay out, put together, install and test all of the electrical work used on any type of building project. Construction electricians are responsible for all of the heat, light, power, air conditioning, and refrigeration found in building projects throughout the world. The installation and connection of electrical machinery, controls, and signal equipment are also duties of the construction electrician. They have to follow blueprints and specifications when installing electrical components. In addition to other duties, construction

electricians must follow nation, state, county, and municipal wiring regulations.

About 95 percent of the electricians engaged in the construction industry are unionized. They are in demand and employed throughout the world, though most of the jobs are in cities. Construction electricians work for electrical contractors, for government, for private industry or are self-employed electricians doing small jobs.

What You Need Personally

As in any construction oriented job you should be willing to do physically strenuous work. Good mechanical aptitude and above average finger dexterity are also useful assets. Normal color vision is important because different types of wires are recognized by their color schemes. Last but not least, a sense of responsibility and pride in your work is very important. Faulty wiring may result in fire and even death.

What Education and Training You Need

A high school diploma is desirable. Take as many math courses as you can in high school. Problems dealing with fractions, decimals, and angles confront electricians every day. The reading of blueprints is essential and if available, courses in drafting and mechanical drawing should be taken. Science courses such as physics will also be helpful, and wood and metal shop classes should be taken since they teach proper handling of many of the tools you will one day be using.

Training to become an electrician is obtained mostly through an apprenticeship program. This program usually takes 8,000 hours of on-the-job training (four years). In addition, 144 hours of classroom work is required every year. (See pp. 52-63 for more information.)

What the Occupation Has to Offer

Construction electricians are in growing demand throughout the world. Jobs in this field are also available because experienced men are always moving into other related fields. Many men, after being construction electricians for several years, become electrical contractors or go to work for private companies.

Hourly wages of electricians are among the highest in the construction industry. Because electricians are affected less by seasonal changes in temperature and weather conditions, they work more of the year than many other skilled tradesmen. Union hourly wages for electricians average $6.82 per hour. This average is twenty-eight cents an hour higher than the averages of other journeymen in the construction business.

Experienced construction electricians can move easily into other fields. Many become maintenance electricians for large companies and corporations. Skillful journeymen move up to foremen and then to superintendents. Advanced construction electricians may also go into business for themselves as electrical contractors.

Points to Consider Before Going into This Field

The advantages of a construction electrician job are many. Good pay, union benefits, and job availability are just a few.

There is a certain amount of danger in this as in any other construction job. But while injuries do occur, the percentage is lower than that of most other construction trades. Construction electricians at times may be exposed to dirty, hot, cold, windy, humid, or dusty working conditions. People in this field may work indoors or outdoors, though the majority of the work is done indoors. A good deal of walking and crawling in cramped quarters is required, and electricians must also be alert and aware of safety precautions to prevent cuts from sharp tools, falls from ladders or other high places, or electrical shocks and burns.

Almost all of the electrician jobs in the construction industry are held by men. Women may find openings in the future.

For more information, write:

International Brotherhood of Electrical Workers
1200 15th Street, N.W.
Washington, D.C. 20005.

See also: page 187 for other places to write for more details.

Elevator Constructor

The Job

If you have ever ridden the elevator to the top of the Empire State Building you may have wondered how that marvelous piece of lifting machinery got there? Elevator constructors, or elevator mechanics as they are sometimes called, perform a very important and highly skilled function in the construction industry. It is their job to assemble, install, and maintain elevators, dumbwaiters, escalators, and similar equipment. The men in this field work with modern apparatus in both new and old buildings. Because of the rapid innovations and improvements in the field, maintenance and alteration are very important parts of this work.

To be an elevator constructor you need the skills of an electrician, ironworker, carpenter, painter, sheet metal worker, plumber, and pipefitter.

There are an estimated fourteen thousand elevator constructors employed in the United States. Almost fifteen hundred jobs were available last year with elevator manufacturers. Other elevator constructors were employed by small local contractors, who dealt mainly in repair and maintenance. Large private businesses and the government also employ many elevator constructors every year. Jobs as elevator inspectors are also available through municipal and governmental agencies.

What You Need Personally

To be an elevator constructor you must be in good physical condition. You must also be able to work at heights and in closed cramped working quarters. If you have claustrophobia you had better forget this line of work. Being mechanically inclined and taking pride in your work are valuable assets. In this field like many others in the construction industry careless or sloppy work may result in injury or death. You will need to take responsibility for your part of a tough job.

What Education and Training You Need

Training in the field of elevator construction is relatively informal. On-the-job training is the most common way of reaching journeymanship.

Prospective elevator constructors must be at least 18 years old, in good physical condition, and have a high school education. Two years of continuous on-the-job training plus six months experience at a factory of a major elevator firm is usually necessary to become a journeyman. During this time the prospective elevator constructor works as a helper-trainee and usually goes to vocational school at night. After a period of at least two years training the helper-trainee must pass a test given by a joint examining board, which consists of three representatives of the local union and three representatives of the employer. Passing this test, which deals with all the basic information of the trade, enables the helper-trainee to become a full-fledged elevator constructor.

Some states require licensing and registration of all elevator constructors. During the first six months helper-trainees are on probation. At this time they receive 50 percent of the hourly wages earned by a journeyman. This percentage increases as the trainee gets more experience.

What the Occupation Has to Offer

Employment opportunities for elevator constructors will probably increase through the 1970s. Technological advances in elevator and escalator design are partly responsible for providing more employment since they necessitate the modernization of old facilities.

Hourly wages and annual earnings are high in the field of elevator construction. Minimum hourly rates for union members averaged $6.65 in 1970. This is eleven cents an hour more than the average journeyman receives in other skilled trades.

Advancing elevator constructors may become foremen, supervisors, or estimators. The latter estimate the amount of money a project will cost and submit it to the contractor who adds it to his other estimates and bids on the jobs being offered. The elevator constructor may also work as a salesman for a company that sells elevators and equipment. Elevator design is a field open to college graduates with degrees in electrical or mechanical engineering.

Points to Consider Before Going into This Field

In the field of elevator construction the advantages are many. Good pay, fringe benefits, regular hours, steady work, and job availability are just a few. In addition little time is lost because of seasonal layoffs.

The main disadvantages of this field are the exposure to height and at times cramped working quarters. Elevator constructors work both indoors and out. They may have to carry heavy equipment or parts though most heavy work is done by helpers. Exposure to the elements and awkward working positions are also part of elevator construction.

The only restrictions in this field are personal ones such as acrophobia and claustrophobia.

At present elevator construction is not a field for women.

For more information, write:

International Union of Elevator Constructors
12 South 125th Street
Room 1515
Philadelphia, Pennsylvania 19107

For information on job opportunities, contact elevator manufacturers; elevator constructors; or a local of the International Union of Elevator Constructors.

See page: 187 for other places to write for more details.

Floor Covering Installer

The Job

The job of floor covering installer (floor covering mechanic, floor layer) has many specialties. Men in this field may have one or all of the skills to qualify them as asphalt tile installers; carpet installers; linoleum installers; mosaic wood parquet layers; marble setters; vinyl asbestos tile layers or terrazzo workers. All of these men perform the same function of installing, repairing and replacing floor coverings.

The duties of the floor covering installer usually fall into two categories, preparing and installing. In preparing the floor the worker sands, fills in cracks, and at times precovers the floor with plywood. After making sure that the floor is free of dust or dirt he is ready to cover it. In covering, the installer measures carefully, cuts the required amount of covering and lays it out. It is then properly aligned and secured. Floor covering installers must know when to use certain kinds of coverings and by what means to secure them.

Most floor covering installers are employed by flooring contractors. These contractors usually handle commercial, industrial, or residential contracts. They may also specialize in certain types of coverings such as mosaic wood parquet. There are many job opportunities available with local retail floor covering stores, home alteration contractors and repair contractors, furniture and department stores.

What You Need Personally

As a floor covering installer you must be at least eighteen years old, in good physical condition, of average strength and have good manual dexterity. You should also have no physical disabilities that affect the knees or back. Good color vision and pattern-matching ability is also an asset. As in all of the other jobs in construction industry, you should have initiative and dependability. A neat appearance and a pleasant businesslike manner are important because you will be working in the customer's home or office.

What Education and Training You Need

A high school education, while not required, makes it easier to become a floor covering installer. Equally if not more important is good manual dexterity. How good a floor covering installer you become depends on how well you work with your hands. Many men in this trade have acquired floor covering skills by working alongside journeymen or acting as helpers. There are also many home-study programs, trade school and manufacturer programs to help prospective floor covering installers. Inquire at several firms about their training programs before becoming a trainee.

The most common way of entering this trade is through apprenticeship programs. These vary in length depending on the requirements of the local union. Some programs last three years (6,000 hours) while others may take four years (8,000 hours). An apprentice's time is spent in on-the-job training and taking related classroom courses. These usually include: mathematics, interpretation of architectural drawings; planning and layout of floor covering installations; and the care and maintenance of the tools used in the field. (See pages 52-63 for more information.)

What the Occupation Has to Offer

Job opportunities are expected to increase rapidly throughout the 1970s. In addition to continual expansion of the construction industry, new floor coverings are being developed with a greater variety of uses. Most of the jobs in this field are found in and around cities. If you are interested in this line of work but live in a rural area, check your local job market. The best job opportunities are expected to be for installers with good all-around training in the installation of resilient tile and sheet goods or carpeting.

Workers earn between $3.50 and $7.00 per hour. Earnings vary within different areas depending on the amount of skill and specialization of the worker.

Experienced floor covering installers may become foremen, salesmen, estimators, or installation managers. People with enough initiative and business sense may start their own contracting businesses.

Points to Consider Before Going into This Field

Good pay, union benefits, and job availability are just a few of the advantages of being a floor covering installer. Work is usually done during the daytime, but occasionally at night or on weekends.

Working conditions in the field are better than those of most other skilled trades in the construction industry. Almost all of the work in this field is done in heated buildings and there is little risk of injury except to back and knees. Although there are some heavy materials to carry, equipment is usually provided to make this job easier.

The only disadvantages are physical or personal. If you lack the personal or physical requirements listed earlier, then another line of work would be more advisable.

Women are usually discouraged from entering this field.

For more information, write:

Department of Human Resources Development
Mail Control Unit
800 Capitol Mall
Sacramento, California 95814
Ask for: *Floor Covering Installer*, No. 383, Free.

National Association of Floor Covering Installers
4301 Connecticut Avenue
Washington, D.C. 20008.

Public Relations and Public Affairs Department
Room 135
Armstrong Cork Company
Lancaster, Pennsylvania 17604
Ask for: *Your Opportunity as a Professional Flooring Craftsman*, Free.

Additional reading:

Van Nostrand and Reinhold Co., 450 West 33rd Street New York 10001, *The Essentials of Modern Carpet Installation*. $6.50.

For information on floor covering, apprenticeships, or other work opportunities, contact local floor contractors or floor covering retailers; a local union of the United Brotherhood of Carpenters and Joiners of America (in eastern states); a local union of the International Brotherhood of Painters and Allied Trades (in western states) or any of the places listed in the introduction to this section.

See also: page 187 for other places to write for more details.

Glazier

The Job

When you look through the window, you're looking at the work of a glazier. In the construction industry glaziers are responsible for the sizing, cutting, fitting, and setting of all glass products into openings of all kinds. They may work with window glass, preassembled stained glass, mirrors or leaded glass panels. Basically, glaziers perform two types of glass setting. The

first and most common is the installation of glass in windows and doors. First he measures and cuts the glass. Then he prepares the bed (window frame, door frame, etc.) with putty and sets in the glass. Next he secures the glass, usually with metal triangles or wire clips. Finally he putties the outside to keep out moisture.

The second type of glass work is the installation of structural glass. This type of glass is used as decoration for ceilings, walls, building fronts, and partitions. The glazier in this operation applies a mastic cement to the supportive backing and presses the structural glass into place. Glaziers are also responsible for mirror and shower or bathtub enclosure work.

Most glaziers are employed by glazing contractors, where they work on new construction, modernization, alteration, and the replacement of broken glass. There are also employment opportunities with government agencies and large businesses. In addition, glaziers are employed by shipbuilders, furniture companies, automobile manufacturers, mirror manufacturers, and factories that install glass in sash doors and other items.

What You Need Personally

Prospective glaziers should be patient and careful workers. Good manual dexterity and the ability to align things by eye are also important assets. This job requires a good deal of freedom of movement and anyone with major physical impairments should look for another line of work.

What Education and Training You Need

Although many men have acquired glazier skills by working alongside skilled tradesmen, the successful completion of an apprenticeship program is the easiest way to enter this field. These programs consist of three years (6,000 hours) of on-the-job training and 432 hours of related classroom courses. These courses cover

such things as: safety, first aid, blueprint reading, and scaffolding. To qualify for apprenticeship, you must be at least eighteen years old and have a high school education or its equivalent. High school classes in mathematics and shop would be helpful for basic knowledge and tool familiarity. (See pages 52-63 for more information.)

What the Occupation Has to Offer

The 1970s promise rapid increase in jobs for glaziers. Glaziers belonging to unions earned an hourly rate averaging $6.08 in 1970. This is compared to a $6.54 average for journeymen in the other building trades.

Skilled glaziers may advance to foremen or superintendents, or may start their own contracting business.

Points to Consider Before Going into This Field

The advantages of this field are the same as any highly unionized building trade. Good pay, union benefits, and job availability are just a few.

Working conditions for glaziers are much like others in the construction industry. Some glaziers are exposed to seasonal weather conditions and temperature, and all risk occupational injuries. These, such as cuts from broken glass and sharp tools, are minimized by safety precautions. Since this is a highly unionized field, as are the other trades in the construction industry, working conditions are generally good.

The glazier field is relatively small and although, nationally, job availability is good, you should check local job markets. As in the other construction trades, women are not usually employed as glaziers. However, we may see an increase in female glaziers in the future.

For more information, write:

Department of Human Resources Development
Mail Control Unit
800 Capitol Mall
Sacramento, California 95814
Ask for: *Glazier (Construction)*, No. 104, Free.

International Brotherhood of Painters & Allied Trades
1750 New York Avenue, N.W.
Washington, D.C. 20006.

For further information on apprenticeships or job opportunities contact local glazing contractors or general contractors; a local of the International Brotherhood of Painters and Allied Trades; or sources listed in the Introduction to this section.

See also page 187 for other places to write for more details.

Lather

The Job

Lathing is an ancient trade going back to the Egyptians who plastered on reeds, very much like our modern process of lathing and plastering. It is the job of lathers to install lath, which is the supportive backing onto which stucco, plaster, or concrete material is applied. Lath is usually made of metal or gypsum although at one time it was made exclusively of wood. The first step in installing lath is the building of a framework or "furring" as it is called. This furring is attached to the structural framework of the building. The lather then cuts the lath to the desired sizes and secures it. The installation of lath varies depending on the area being covered. For instance, columns, curved walls, and stairways require different methods of lathing.

Lathers also do reinforcement work. For this they usually use wire mesh which is flexible and easy to work with. Reinforcement work is done on all corners and inside angles.

Most lathers work for lathing and plastering contractors. Their time is spent working on new buildings, or doing alteration and modernization work.

What You Need Personally

Lathing is hard physical work and prospective lathers should be of average strength and in good physical condition. Manual and finger dex-

terity is also essential. As a lather you are often under pressure because of plastering deadlines and if you go into this field you will have to work well with fellow craftsmen. You need to know how to handle many materials and tools. You also need to be able to accept responsibility.

What Education and Training You Need

Many men acquire lathing skills by working with experienced journeymen. Most training authorities agree however, that the easiest way to enter this field is by the successful completion of at least two years of apprenticeship. To be eligible for an apprenticeship program, you must be at least sixteen years old and in good physical condition. Although a high school education is not required it is suggested. Applicants are often given aptitude tests to see if they have the personal qualifications it takes to be a good lather. Related classroom courses in such things as blueprint reading and mathematics are also a part of the apprenticeship program. You may have to pass exams every six months to retain your apprenticeship. (See pages 52-63 for more information.)

What the Occupation Has to Offer

The employment outlook for a lather is very good throughout the 1970s. Modern technology is also developing new plasters with a wider variety of uses which will result in a greater need for lathers.

Unionized lathers earned an average of $6.44 per hour in 1970. This is compared to an average hourly earning of $6.54 for journeymen throughout the construction industry. Lathers can advance to foremen, superintendents, estimators, or contractors. Experience is required, and further education may prove helpful for lathers who hope to advance.

Points to Consider Before Going into This Field

Lathers enjoy the general advantages of a job in the construction industry including good pay, union benefits, and job availability. Working conditions are usually good, and so are the opportunities for advancement.

New materials and techniques are making the job easier. Injuries are kept low and working conditions good by safety programs and union standards. In the past, lathers worked mainly indoors. However, the modern look of many buildings requires exterior lath work, which subjects the lather to greater injury risks and inclement weather.

Lathers are required to do physically strenuous work. Because of this, men with major physical impairments or below average strength are discouraged. Women are also discouraged because of the physical nature of the work.

For more information, write:

International Association of Wall and Ceiling Contractors
20 E Street, N.W.
Washington, D.C. 20005.

National Bureau for Lathing and Plastering
938 K Street, N.W.
Washington, D.C. 20001.

Wood, Wire and Metal Lathers International Union
6530 New Hampshire Avenue
Takoma Park, Maryland 20012.

For information on apprenticeships or other job opportunities, contact a local lathing contractor; a local of the Wood, Wire and Metal Lathers; International Union; or the places listed on page 187.

Marble Setter, Tile Setter, Terrazzo Worker

The Job

Marble setters, tile layers, and terrazzo workers use materials and skills dating back to the days of the Bible. Some of the greatest buildings of all time have been built using these materials and skills.

Marble setters work with marble, terrazzo panels, artificial marble, and structural glass. First they prepare the supportive backing, apply different types of adhesives, and set the materials they are working with in position. Next they tap the marble (or whatever material they are working with) into proper alignment, and wait for the adhesive to dry. At times they must brace their work to hold it in position while the adhesive dries. Marble setters do very little cutting since most of their materials come already cut to size.

Tile setters apply thin tiles made of baked clay, stone, or other materials to ceilings, walls, and floors. Like marble setters their job consists

mainly of preparing the supportive backing, setting and aligning the material they work with. To the supportive backing, tile setters lay a "setting bed." This is basically a cement mixture to which a bonding agent is applied to secure the tile. Tile setters must be skilled in the chipping and cutting of tile to produce a uniform appearance in irregular areas and corners.

Marble chips mixed with cement produce the ornamental yet durable effect known as terrazzo used mainly on floors. The first step in terrazzo work is to lay a base of concrete mortar. Next the terrazzo worker applies the marble chips and allows for drying. After thorough drying he grinds and polishes the surface to make it smooth. Metal strips and molds are used to produce varied colors and pattern effects.

Marble setters, tile layers and terrazzo workers usually have helpers and/or apprentices to assist them with their work.

Men in these fields work mainly in new construction. For this reason city areas offer the best chances for employment. The largest number of terrazzo workers are employed in California and Florida, which are noted for the terrazzo work in their buildings.

What You Need Personally

To work in this field you must be in good physical condition and have average eyesight, with or without glasses. You must be patient and have the ability to get along with other workers. A good mathematical aptitude and a love of working with your hands are also very important assets.

What Education and Training You Need

While many marble setters, tile layers, and terrazzo workers have acquired their skills by working alongside journeymen in their fields, apprenticeship programs are the easiest way to enter the trade.

To become an apprentice you must be at least seventeen years old. Although a high school education is not a prerequisite it is highly desirable. Programs usually last three years and consist of 6,000 hours of on-the-job training and related classroom instruction, including such subjects as blueprint reading and basic mathematics. (See pages 52-63 for more information.)

What the Occupation Has to Offer

Employment opportunities for marble setters are expected to remain steady throughout the 1970s. Opportunities are expected to increase mildly for tile setters and rapidly for terrazzo workers. However, local job markets should be checked before entering any of these trades.

Average hourly earnings in 1970 for journeymen in these fields were $6.46 for terrazzo workers, $6.29 for marble setters, and $6.08 for tile setters. These rates are eight cents, twenty-six cents, and forty-six cents lower than the average hourly earnings of other skilled craftsmen in the building trade. However, hourly rates may be deceiving because men in these fields work more of the year than many other craftsmen and therefore their annual earnings may be higher.

Skilled men in these fields may become foremen or start their own contracting business.

Points to Consider Before Going into This Field

The advantages of being a marble setter, tile layer, or terrazzo worker are basically the same—good pay, job availability, and union benefits.

Marble setters, tile layers, and terrazzo workers work both indoors and outdoors. Since a good deal of their work is done inside buildings they work more of the year than most of the other craftsmen in the construction industry. Men in these fields are constantly kneeling, bending, twisting, and reaching. Often work is done high above ground on a scaffold, or in cramped, dusty areas. They are subject to occupational injuries such as falls, cuts, and muscle strains, but these are minimized by safety precautions.

Women are not usually employed in these trades but exceptions have been made.

For more information, write:

Bricklayers, Masons and Plasterers' International Union of America
815 15th Street, N.W.
Washington, D.C. 20005.

International Association of Marble, Slate and Stone Polishers, Rubbers and Sawyers, Tile and Marble Setters' Helpers and Marble and Mosaic and Terrazzo Workers' Helpers
821 15th Street, N.W.
Washington, D.C. 20005.

National Terrazzo and Mosaic Association, Inc.
716 Church Street
Alexandria, Virginia 22314.

Marble Institute of America
1984 Chain Bridge Road
McLean, Virginia 22101.

For information on apprenticeships or job opportunities contact your local tile, terrazzo, and marble setting contractors; locals of the unions listed above; or places listed in the Introduction, page 187.

Operating Engineer

The Job

Operating engineers, or construction machinery operators as they are sometimes called, operate, maintain and repair power-driven construc-

tion machinery such as cranes, bulldozers, derricks, piledrivers, and tractors. They may operate one or several different types. The more machines an operator can handle the more jobs he will be eligible for. Because of the many different types of machines in this field, the duties of operating engineers are varied. The amount of skill needed ranges from relatively little to operate an earth-boring machine to a great deal required to operate a crane.

Machines are used to excavate for building basements and foundations, to hoist large quantities of materials, to move large amounts of earth on highway or dam projects, and to drive piles to support bridges.

There were over 300,000 operating engineers employed throughout the United States in 1970. The majority of these men worked on large scale building projects such as highways, dams, and airports. Many operating engineers were also employed by manufacturers, utility companies, state and local highway departments, and mines. Relatively few were self-employed. Those who were, usually owned their own machine and did small contract work.

Operating engineers work outdoors and are exposed to seasonal weather conditions and temperatures. Cold weather may cause work to slow down in winter months. The operation of bulldozers and other types of equipment that shake and jolt the operator can be physically tiring. The work may take you to remote areas where highways and big projects such as dams are being built.

What You Need Personally

Although great physical strength is not required, operating engineers must be in good physical condition and have good eye-hand-foot coordination. Since you work almost exclusively outside, you should appreciate and enjoy the outdoors. A great deal of responsibility goes along with this job since equipment is very expensive and the work important.

What Education and Training You Need

There are three ways to become an operating engineer. The first is to act as an oiler, repairing and maintaining the machinery and assisting the operating engineer in many ways. After several years of experience assistants may be taught operation of the machinery. The oiler may eventually become a journeyman.

The second way is to take courses in construction machinery operation at private vocation or technical schools. Courses run from three to six weeks and are expensive—they cost between $1,000 and $1,500. Students attending accredited schools offering such courses are usually eligible for state and federal student loans. If you should decide to attend a heavy equipment school, write to the Office of Vocational Education of the Department of Health, Education and Welfare, or the Veterans' Administration (both in Washington, D.C.), to see if the particular school is properly accredited. It will also help you to compare the costs and facilities of various schools.

The third and most popular way to enter this field is through the successful completion of an apprenticeship program. Prospective apprentices must be at least eighteen years old, in good physical condition, and have a high school education or its equivalent.

Apprenticeship programs require three years of on-the-job training (6,000 hours). In addition, 144 hours of related classroom instruction is taken each year. Classroom instruction includes reading grade plans, elements of physics and electricity, automotive maintenance and welding. (See pages 52-63 for more information.)

What the Occupation Has to Offer

Employment is expected to increase rapidly for operating engineers throughout the 1970s. Since there are so many different types of operating engineers the wages vary considerably. The more difficult the machine is to operate the higher the hourly wage. Crane operators who are generally acknowledged as the highest paid earned as high as $8.35 minimum hourly wages.

Points to Consider Before Going into This Field

The advantages of being an operating engineer are many. Operating engineers receive high hourly wages, enjoy union benefits, and experience widespread job availability. Men in this field may learn to operate two or more types of machinery and thereby increase their employment opportunities and annual income.

The main disadvantages of this field are subjection to seasonal weather conditions and the general lack of advancement possibilities.

There are a few women in this field, but if you wish to enter it is best to have a job promise before you sign up for training.

For more information, write:

International Union of Operating Engineers
1125 17th Street, N.W.
Washington, D.C. 20036

National School of Heavy Equipment Operations
P.O. Box 8520
Charlotte, North Carolina 28208

For information on apprenticeship or job opportunities contact: your local general contractor; a local of the International Union of Operating Engineers; or places listed on page 187.

Painter and Paperhanger

The Job

Although painting and paperhanging are separate skills, many craftsmen learn to do both. The methods of preparation and application are different, but both jobs are concerned with covering walls and other building surfaces.

The painter begins this job by preparing the surface of the area on which he is going to work. On some new jobs preparation work is not necessary except possibly for a primer coat. Older surfaces may require scraping off old paint, filling nail holes, or sandpapering rough surfaces. After the preparation work, paint, varnish, enamel, lacquer, or stain may be applied.

A painter works with a variety of tools. He must know how to use brushes, rollers, and spray gun applicators; in addition he must have a knowledge of paints. He must also know how to erect and work on different types of scaffolding.

Before wallpaper can be hung, the paperhanger must also prepare the surface of the area on which he intends to work. New or clean surfaces are prepared by applying "sizing" to the surface area. Sizing fills in the porous surfaces of such materials as plaster, and offers a better backing for the wallpaper. On older surfaces the paperhanger may have to remove layers of old wallpaper and on occasion do minor plaster repair work. He then measures the surface and cuts the wallpaper to the exact size. It takes a good deal of skill for the paperhanger to match patterns on corners adjoining pieces of wallpaper. The next step is the application of paste to the back of the paper. He then positions the wallpaper and works out all the air bubbles from underneath. A wide variety of specialized tools helps the paperhanger throughout the process. He may also work with fabric, vinyl, or other materials.

Most painters and paperhangers work for contractors on new construction sites, on alteration, repair, or modernization work. Substantial numbers are also employed by hotels, shipyards, utility companies, manufacturing firms, government agencies, schools, and large businesses. Craftsmen working for business concerns such as hotels may be expected to do both painting and paperhanging.

What You Need Personally

If you want to be a painter or paperhanger, you need to be in good physical condition, have good eye-hand coordination, good color discrimination, and manual dexterity. Painting is active and strenuous work. You particularly need strong arms because much of the work is done with arms raised overhead. To advance in either of these fields you must be able to get along with fellow craftsmen. If you are dependable, enjoy seeing a job done well, you will be successful and assured of steady employment.

What Education and Training You Need

It is easier to become a journeyman in either of these two fields without the completion of an apprenticeship program than in most of the other skilled trades in the construction industry. Acting as helper or handyman to an experienced craftsmen is the usual procedure here. Although many workers have learned their skills this way, apprenticeship programs are still considered the best way to learn painting and paperhanging.

To be eligible for apprenticeship, applicants must be at least sixteen and in good physical condition. Although a high school education is not required it is a definite asset. Apprenticeship programs last three years with 6,000 hours of on-the-job training, in addition to 144 hours of related classroom instruction given annually. An apprentice may study such subjects as color harmony, estimating costs, and paint chemistry. (See pages 52-63 for more information.)

What the Occupation Has to Offer

In 1970 there were 385,000 painters and 5,000 paperhangers employed in the United States. Many of these craftsmen although technically called painters or paperhangers performed duties of both jobs. Employment for painters is expected to increase rapidly throughout the 1970s. Moderate employment increases for paperhangers are projected during this time. The craftsman who can both paint and hang paper can look forward to better employment opportunities than the one limited to a single function. The more trained and versatile he is, the more likely his chances for steady employment.

Union hourly minimum wages averaged $5.95 and $6.02 an hour for painters and paperhangers in 1970, less than the average minimum hourly rate of other journeymen in the construction industry. Painters and paperhangers generally work throughout the year and although their hourly rate may be lower than some of the other journeymen in the construction industry, their annual earnings may be higher.

They may advance to become foremen, estimators or supervisors, or they may start their own contracting business.

Points to Consider Before Going into This Field

Painters and paperhangers enjoy good pay, union benefits, and job availability. They also work under better conditions than many other craftsmen in the construction industry. Apprenticeship is not as necessary in these fields as it is in others.

The disadvantages of being a painter or paperhanger are few. Physical and personal requirements must be met and anyone who is allergic to paint or varnish fumes is discouraged. Also workers must stand for long periods of time and risk injuries such as falling from ladders and scaffolding.

Maintenance painters usually have steady work, but others have periods of unemployment, particularly during the winter or in time of business recession.

Women have been employed as painters and paperhangers but usually on less strenuous jobs such as interior work. The physical strain of construction site work in these fields severely limits the number employed.

For more information, write:

International Brotherhood of Painters and Allied Trades
1750 New York Avenue, N.W.
Washington, D.C. 20006.

National Joint Painting and Decorating Apprenticeship and Training Committee
1750 New York Avenue, N.W.
Washington, D.C. 20006
Ask for: *Opportunity in the Painting, Decorating*

and Coating Trade, 1972, Free (opportunities for apprenticeships).

Painting and Decorating Contractors Association of America
7223 Lee Highway
Falls Church, Virginia 22046
Ask for: job opportunities and apprenticeship information.

Also contact:
For information on apprenticeships or other job opportunities contact: local paint and decorator contractors; a local of the International Brotherhood of Painters and Allied Trades; or sources listed in the Introduction to this section, page 187.

Plasterer

The Job

Early man used to put clay on the inside walls of his hut to make them smoother and to keep himself warm. Today we apply plaster and cement plaster to both indoor and outdoor walls and ceilings for much the same reasons. When working indoors plasterers usually apply three coats. These are known as the scratch coat, the brown coat, and the finish coat. The first one, the scratch coat, is applied directly to the lath. (Lath is the supportive backing installed by lathers, to which plaster readily adheres.) After this coat is applied the plasterer scratches it with a special raking tool. This rake produces furrows which helps the brown coat to stick. The scratch coat is allowed to dry for several days and then the brown coat is applied. It is during the application of the brown coat that the plasterer makes sure that the angles and corners are level. A special wooden float is then used to rough up the undercoat and provide greater adhesion for the finished coat. After being allowed to dry for several days the surface is ready for the finish coat. The finish coat is applied in small amounts because it dries very quickly. The surface is smoothed out, and after it dries the finish coat becomes very hard and durable.

In exterior plaster work (often known as stucco) the plasterer uses a mixture of portland cement and sand. This base mixture is applied to some type of lathing and is then allowed to dry. The finishing plaster is usually made of white cement and sand or a patented finishing material.

Some plasterers with specialized skills do complicated, ornamental plaster work. These ornamental plasterers may cast cornices or moldings and must be able to follow blueprints and other instructions. They may also do restoration work on such historical buildings as the White House.

Plasterers work on new construction sites, do alteration or modernization work, or plaster repair and maintenance work in older buildings.

What You Need Personally

As a prospective plasterer you should be in good health, have good manual dexterity and physical agility and be of average intelligence. You must be able to get along with fellow workers. Although not a requirement, artistic ability is a definite asset. Since plastering is strenuous work and much of a plasterer's day is spent standing, bending and stooping, people with major physical handicaps are discouraged.

What Education and Training You Need

Although many plasterers have acquired their skills by working alongside skilled journeymen, the most accepted way of entering this field is the successful completion of an apprenticeship program. Depending on the area of the country, apprenticeship programs usually last for three or four years, 6,000 to 8,000 hours. This time consists mainly of on-the-job training and includes an additional 144 hours of related classroom instruction annually in such things as blueprint-reading and mathematics. To be eligible for apprenticeship programs applicants must be over seventeen years old. (See pages 52-63 for more information.)

What the Occupation Has to Offer

In 1970 there were an estimated 35,000 plasterers employed in this country. This figure is supposed to increase slowly throughout the next ten years.

In 1970 plasterers belonging to unions earned an average minimum of $6.35 per hour. This is nineteen cents less than the average minimum hourly earnings of the other skilled craftsmen in the construction industry.

Advancement opportunities are good. A skilled plasterer may become a crew leader, foreman or superintendant, or start his own plaster contracting business.

Points to Consider Before Going into This Field

Among the many advantages enjoyed by plasterers are good pay, good working conditions, and union benefits. Plasterers also have a better chance of advancement than many of the other skilled tradesmen.

Physical and personal restrictions are the main disadvantages of this field. Exterior work requires fairly moderate weather and temperature conditions and in many areas this may shorten the work season.

Working conditions are generally good. Although plasterers work both indoors and outdoors, weather and temperature conditions must be good before they can do their job. A few of the occupation hazards in this field are falls from ladders or scaffolding; inhalation of harmful dust particles, and in some cases burns. However, these hazards are kept at a minimum by safety practices and protective equipment. Plasterers also spend a great deal of their time walking, bending, or stooping.

Yearly wages are slightly lower than other skilled workers because most plasterers work only nine months a year and about half work eleven or more months a year. Also since most of the jobs in this field are found in urban areas, if you live in a rural area, it is best to check local job markets.

Because of the physical restrictions women are usually discouraged from entering this line of work.

For more information, write:

Bricklayers, Masons and Plasterers' International Union of America
815 15th Street, N.W.
Washington, D.C. 20005.

International Association of Wall and Ceiling Contractors
20 E Street, N.W.
Washington, D.C. 20005.

National Bureau of Lathing and Plastering
938 K Street, N.W.
Washington, D.C. 20001.

National Plastering Industry's Joint Apprenticeship Trust Fund
National Headquarters
1000 Vermont Avenue, N.W.
Washington, D.C. 20005
Ask for: apprenticeship information.

Also contact:
for information about apprenticeships or other job opportunities, contact your local plastering contractor; locals of the union listed below, or places listed in the Introduction to this section, page 187.

Operative Plasterers' and Cement Masons' International Associaton of the United States and Canada
1125 17th Street, N.W.
Washington, D.C. 20036

Plumber and Pipefitter

The Job

Plumbing is an ancient skill. It goes way back to the early Egyptians who used lead pipes to carry water and drainage into and out of buildings. Today, plumbers and pipefitters are craftsmen who install pipe systems that carry water, steam, air, or other liquids or gases necessary for sanitation, industrial production, and other uses. They also alter and repair existing pipe systems and install plumbing fixtures, appliances, and heating and refrigerating units.

The work of the pipefitter differs from that of the plumber mainly in its location and in the variety and size of the pipes used. The plumber works in residential and commercial buildings; the pipefitter is generally employed by a large industry such as an oil refinery, refrigeration plant or defense establishment where more complex systems of piping are used.

Although plumbing and pipefitting are sometimes considered to be a single trade, journeymen can specialize in either craft, particularly in large cities. Water, gas and waste disposal systems, especially those connected to public utility systems, are installed by plumbers. These installations are made in residential and commercial buildings, schools, industrial plants and other structures. In homes, for example, plumbers initially "rough in" (install) the pipe system as the building progresses. During the final construction stages, they install the heating and air-conditioning units and connect radiators, water heaters and plumbing fixtures, such as bathtubs and sinks.

Pipefitters install both high and low-pressure pipes that carry hot water, steam, and other liquids and gases, especially those in industrial and commercial buildings and defense establishments, such as missile launching and testing sites. Pipefitters, for example, install ammonia-carrying pipelines in refrigeration plants, complex pipe systems in oil refineries and chemical and food-processing plants and pipelines for carrying compressed air and industrial gases in many types of industrial establishments.

Both plumbers and pipefitters use a variety of skills when installing pipe systems. They bend pipe and weld, braze, calk, solder, or thread joints. After a pipe system is installed, the plumber or pipefitter tests for leaks by filling the pipes with liquid or gas under pressure.

Plumbers and pipefitters use wrenches, reamers, drills, braces and bits, hammers, chisels, saws, and other hand tools. Power machines often are used to cut, bend, and thread pipes. Hand-operated hydraulic pipe benders are also used. Plumbers and pipefitters all use gas or acetylene torches and welding, soldering, and brazing equipment in their work.

What You Need Personally

To be a good, successful plumber or pipefitter, you should like to work out and solve a variety of problems. You shouldn't object to being called out during evenings, weekends, or holidays to perform your job. As in most service occupations, you'll need to get along well with all kinds of people.

As a plumber you should be able to work well by yourself or perhaps direct the work of helpers, and you should like the company of those workers in the other construction trades.

What Education and Training You Need

Most training authorities, including the national joint labor-management apprenticeship committees for the plumbing and pipefitting industries, recommend a formal five-year apprenticeship for plumbers or for pipefitters as the best way to learn all aspects of the trade. A large number of plumbers and pipefitters, however, have acquired their skills informally by working for several years with craftsmen, by observing and receiving instruction from them. Many of these workers have gained some knowledge of their craft by also taking trade- or correspondence-school courses.

Apprentice applicants generally are required to be between 16 and 25 and in good physical condition. They are often required to take aptitude tests, particularly to determine whether they have the high degree of mechanical aptitude required in this field.

As an apprentice you receive classroom instruction in subjects such as drafting and blueprint reading, mathematics applicable to layout work, applied physics and chemistry and local building codes and regulations that apply to the trade.

To obtain a journeyman's license, which some communities require, you must pass a special examination to demonstrate knowledge of the trade and of the local building codes (see pages 52-63).

If you cannot gain acceptance or if the apprenticeship program is filled, you may decide to enter the field as an on-the-job trainee. In this case, you usually contact a plumbing contractor directly and begin work as a helper.

What the Occupation Has to Offer

Employment in this field is expected to rise rapidly through the 1970s, partly because of the increase in construction activity. Most plumbers and pipefitters are employed by plumbing contractors in new construction activity, mainly at the construction site. A substantial proportion of plumbers are self-employed or work for plumbing contractors doing repairs, alteration, or modernization.

Technological developments are expected to limit growth in the number of jobs for plumbers and pipefitters. For example, prefabricated plumbing assemblies can now be installed as a unit, reducing the amount of on-site plumbing required. Packaged gas vents also are available. Vent pipe sections come in standardized lengths that can be fastened together by locking joint bands, thus eliminating cementing operations.

Some builders are preassembling their own waste, vent, and other systems components. This work—usually performed by the employers' regular crew in well-equipped shops set up near building sites—can be performed during inclement weather or other "slow" periods.

Union minimum hourly wages for plumbers and pipefitters averaged $7.01 and $6.93 per hour respectively in 1970 according to a national survey of building trades workers in sixty-eight cities. At the same time, the average hourly rate for all journeymen in the building trades was $6.54. Among individual cities surveyed, the union minimum hourly wage rates for plumbers ranged from $5.00 in Norfolk, Virginia, to $9.42 in Oakland, California.

Annual earnings of workers in this field are among the highest in the building trades, because plumbing and pipefitting are affected less by seasonal factors than are most other building crafts.

Points to Consider Before Going into This Field

The work of plumbers and pipefitters is active and sometimes strenuous; they must stand for prolonged periods and occasionally work in cramped or uncomfortable positions.

Workers in this trade risk the danger of falls from ladders, cuts from sharp tools and burns from hot pipes or steam. The number of injuries per million man-hours worked by employees of plumbing, heating, and air-conditioning contractors in the contract construction industry has been lower than that for the contract construction industry as a whole but higher than the average for production workers in manufacturing industries.

Most plumbers and pipefitters have a regular 40-hour workweek with extra pay for overtime. Unlike most of the other building trades, this field is affected very little by seasonal factors.

For more information, write:

Department of Human Resources Development
Mail Control Unit
800 Capitol Mall
Sacramento, California 95814
Ask for: *Plumber, Plumber Apprentice*, pamphlet No. 173, Free.

National Association of Plumbing-Heating-Cooling Contractors
1016 20th Street, N.W.
Washington, D.C. 20036.

United Association of Journeymen and Apprentices of the Plumbing and Pipefitting Industry of the United States and Canada
901 Massachusetts Avenue, N.W.
Washington, D.C. 20001.

Also contact:
Plumbing, heating and air-conditioning contrac-

tors; locals of the United Association of Journeymen and Apprentices of the Plumbing and Pipefitting Industry of the United States and Canada; joint-union-management apprenticeship committees; offices of state apprenticeship agencies; the Bureau of Apprenticeship and Training, U.S. Department of Labor in Washington, D.C.; state employment services for information on the Manpower Development and Training Act, apprenticeships and other training programs in your area; employment services which give aptitude tests and screen applicants for training programs.

Roofer

The Job

Everyone wants a roof over his head, and that's the job of the roofer. He puts roofing, wood shingles, asphalt, slate, and other materials on the roofs of buildings. He also dampproofs and waterproofs such structures as swimming pools, tanks, and concrete walls.

Most of today's roofing employs composition roofing material, and can be broken down into level roofing and pitched roofing. On level roofs, the first step is to coat the area with a layer of hot asphalt or coal tar pitch. Next, a strip of asphalt or tar-impregnated felt is rolled over the bed of hot asphalt or coal tar pitch. This process is repeated two or three times. To finish, roof gravel or asphalt is applied to help withstand weather conditions. On pitched roofs, asphalt shingles and roll roofing materials are applied in an overlapping manner and then are secured to the house with nails or roofing cement.

Roofers also work with metal, tile, slate and wood roofing materials. These materials are attached to the roof bed with nails, roofing cement, and solder.

In the waterproofing process, the roofer prepares the surface of the structure and applies a coat of waterproofing compound. He may also

nail some type of waterproof fabric to the surface. In dampproofing he usually applies tar or asphalt to the surface of the structure to keep dampness out.

Most roofers are employed by roofing contractors. The majority of their work is done on new construction, although they also do alteration, maintenance, and repair work. They are also employed by government agencies and businesses large enough to support their own roofing department. Many roofers start their own businesses.

What You Need Personally

You must be physically strong because this work is strenuous. Since much of your time is spent stooping, squatting, or bending, you must also have flexible muscles and joints. Roofers often work high above the ground and anyone with a fear of heights should look for another field. Roofers often work in very hot or very cold weather. If you have sensitive skin and are easily wind- or sunburned, this is not a good area for you.

What Education and Training You Need

Although many men in this field have acquired their skills by working alongside journeymen, apprenticeship programs are the best way to learn the trade. Most apprenticeship programs consist of three years of on-the-job training and related classroom instruction. In the classroom the apprentice studies such subjects as blueprint reading and mathematics. Classroom instruction is usually held one night a week throughout the program. To be eligible, applicants must be at least 18 years old and in good physical condition. A high school education or its equivalent is not a prerequisite, but is a definite asset. (See pages 52-63 for more information.)

What the Occupation Has to Offer

The employment outlook for roofers is expected to be good throughout the 1970s. Growth of the industry should produce several thousand jobs every year.

Union hourly wages among composition roofers averaged $6.17 in 1970. This is compared to the $6.54 hourly average of other journeymen in the construction industry. Slate and tile roofers earned on the average of thirty-six cents less per hour than composition roofers.

Journeymen in this field may advance to become foremen or superintendents. Ambitious roofers may also start their own businesses. In some cases roofers may use the skills they have learned and branch out to become coppersmiths, tinsmiths, and carpenters.

Points to Consider Before Going into This Field

Roofers enjoy the many advantages prevalent throughout the construction industry—good pay, job availability, and union benefits.

The disadvantage of a job as a roofer in concerned with working conditions, including such things as exposure to the elements and injury risks. However, these are common throughout the construction industry.

There is limited opportunity for advancement in this field. Because of physical requirements women are usually discouraged.

For more information, write:

National Roofing Contractors Association
1515 North Harlem Avenue
Oak Park, Illinois 60302.

United Slate, Tile and Composition Roofers,
Damp and Waterproof Workers Association
1125 17th Street, N.W.
Washington, D.C. 20036.

Also contact:

For information on apprenticeships or other job opportunities, contact your local roofing contractors, a local of the United Slate, Tile and Composition Roofers, Damp and Waterproof Workers Association; or places listed in the Introduction to this section, page 187.

Sheet Metal Worker

The Job

Sheet metal workers construct and install building products made of sheet metal, fiberglass, and plastic. The first step in their job is to study printed instructions or blueprints. Then they lay out the pattern and cut the material according to pattern specifications. In many cases there are layout specialists whose job is to lay out materials. These men have assemblers working under them who cut and fabricate the material. The material is then assembled with rivets, screws, or bolts, by the sheet metal work-

ers using a wide variety of hand and power tools. Most sheet metal workers employed in the construction industry work on the fabrication and installation of ducts. These ducts are used in ventilating, heating, and air-conditioning systems. Siding, roofing, partition and storefront work are among the many other jobs of sheet metal workers.

They are employed by heating, refrigeration, and air-conditioning installation companies; building or roofing contractors, and governmental agencies and large businesses that do their own sheet metal work; custom kitchen equipment businesses; aircraft, shipbuilding, and railroad industries.

What You Need Personally

Sheet metal men must do neat and accurate work, and for this reason, manual dexterity and good eyesight are required. Good physical condition, agility, steady nerves, and sense of balance are important. Mechanical aptitude and the ability to get along with fellow workers are also good assets.

What Education and Training You Need

Many journeymen in the sheet metal trade have acquired their skills as helpers. However, most experts recommend a four-year apprenticeship program. It is important to know all aspects of the trade. These programs produce well-rounded journeymen whose chances of employment are much better than those of workers who have picked up skills as a helper. Prospective apprentices must be at least seventeen years old. A high school education or its equivalent is required. Apprenticeship programs consist mainly of 8,000 hours of on-the-job training (4 years). In addition, apprentices receive related classroom instruction which includes such subjects as blueprint reading and mathematics. (See pages 52-63 for more information.)

What the Occupation Has to Offer

In 1970 there were an estimated 60,000 sheet metal workers employed in the United States. Job openings are expected to increase rapidly for the next ten years. This anticipated growth is partly a result of an increase in the construction industry, and partly because of the increase in the use of air-conditioning.

Most of the men in this field are employed in and around large cities. Urban areas in warm climates may have larger job markets because of the increasing use of air-conditioning systems.

Sheet metal workers are among the highest paid skilled craftsmen in the construction industry. In 1970 they earned an average of $6.75 an hour. This is twenty-one cents an hour higher than the average hourly earnings of other journeymen in the building trades.

Sheet metal workers may advance to become foremen, or superintendents, or go on to form their own contracting businesses.

Points to Consider Before Going into This Field

Sheet metal workers enjoy better job availability and receive higher hourly wages than most of the other skilled craftsmen in the construction industry.

Working conditions in this trade vary greatly. As a sheet metal man working for a custom kitchen business, you will probably work under better conditions than a man installing gutters. Since a good deal of sheet metal work is done outdoors, you are often exposed to seasonal weather conditions and temperatures. You are also exposed to occupational injuries such as falls, cuts, and sprains. However the number of injuries is kept low by safety practices and equipment. You may also have to work in high places or in cramped quarters. Some seasonal layoffs occur for outdoor work.

Because of the physical requirements women are not frequently employed as sheet metal workers.

For more information, write:

Department of Human Resources Development
Mail Control Unit
800 Capitol Mall
Sacramento, California 95814
Ask for: *Sheet-Metal Worker, Aircraft*, No. 28. Free *Sheet-Metal Worker, Sheet-Metal Worker Apprentice* No. 49, Free.

Sheet Metal and Air Conditioning Contractors' National Association
1611 North Kent Street
Arlington, Virginia 22209.

Sheet Metal Workers' International Association
1750 New York Avenue, N.W.
Washington, D.C. 20006

Also contact:

For information on apprenticeships and other job opportunities contact your local sheet metal contractors or heating, refrigeration, or air-conditioning contractor; or a local of the Sheet Metal Workers' International Association, or places listed in the Introduction to this section, page 187.

Stone Mason

The Job

Wherever you go in the world you find evidence of the artistic ability of stone masons; the great buildings of ancient Rome, the cathedrals of Europe, and monuments of our own like the Washington Monument in the nation's capi-

tal. Stone masons are responsible for all exterior stone work on buildings or other structures. Two types of stone are used, natural and artificial. Natural includes stones like granite, marble, limestone and sandstone while artificial ones are made from cement or other masonry materials.

Much of a stonemason's time is spent setting "cutstone." This is stone that has been precut and numbered to tell him where it belongs. The stonemason follows a diagram and positions the stone in its alloted place. When working with large stones a mason may have to rely on a derrickman to lift them into position. The stonemason then applies mortar and makes sure the stone is in proper alignment. After finishing the joints the stonemason moves on to another stone.

In their work stonemasons use trowels, mallets, hammers, chisels, pneumatic tools, and abrasive saws. When they have to cut the stone they use a special hammer or an abrasive saw.

Stonemasons may become specialists, working in such areas as curbsetting, granite setting, flagsetting, veneer, or alberene stone work. They are employed mostly on the construction of expensive commercial, public, and residential buildings. Because of this, whether expensive buildings are built in a particular area and whether stone is available dictate whether a stonemason will find a job.

What You Need Personally

Anyone interested in becoming a stonemason should be in good physical condition and have stamina. Manual dexterity and good eyesight and the ability to understand and follow directions are also essential personal requirements. In addition you should be able to make rough sketches and drawings. You need to be well-coordinated, systematic, and orderly. You must respect neatness and accuracy. Your mistakes will be clearly visible.

What Education and Training You Need

Although many stonemasons have acquired their skills by working alongside skilled craftsmen, the easiest way is to serve as an apprentice.

Apprenticeship programs last three years, 6,000 hours. This time is spent receiving on-the-job training and participating in related classroom instruction. On-the-job training enables the apprentice to practice the basic skills, while classroom instruction covers such subjects as sketching, the characteristics of concrete, stone and mortar and safety procedures. (See pages 52-63 for more information.)

What the Occupation Has to Offer

The employment opportunities for beginning stonemasons will not be as good as for most of the other skilled construction tradesmen throughout the 1970s. Little increase is expected in this field and death and retirement will be depended on to yield most of the new jobs. The main reason for the low employment increase rate is that modern architectural design does not depend as heavily on stonemasonry as did architectural designs of the past. Before you enter this field, carefully check into present and proposed local job markets.

In 1970 stonemasons who were union members averaged a minimum hourly wage of $6.73. This is nineteen cents an hour higher than the average minimum hourly rate paid journeymen in other fields of the construction industry. This high hourly rate may be deceiving, since stonemasons may work fewer months of the year than other craftsmen.

Advancement in this field is the same as in most other construction jobs. Stonemasons may advance to become foremen, estimators, or superintendents. In addition a small percentage of them go on to start their own contracting businesses.

Points to Consider Before Going into This Field

The advantages of being a stonemason are many—good pay, union benefits, and the chance to learn a time-honored skilled trade.

Work as a stonemason is strenuous and involves lifting heavy materials. You will be exposed to seasonal weather and temperatures. In addition you run the risk of certain occupational injuries but these are kept minimal by safety precautions and equipment.

It is mainly because of the physical requirements that women are discouraged from this line of work.

For more information, write:

Bricklayers, Masons and Plasterers' International Union of America
815 15th Street, N.W.
Washington, D.C. 20005.

Also contact:
For information about apprenticeships and other job opportunities, contact your local bricklaying contractors; a local of the Bricklayers, Masons and Plasterers' International Union of America; or the places listed in the Introduction to this section, page 187.

Structural, Ornamental, and Reinforcing Ironworker, Rigger, and Machine Mover

The Job

In this day of giant skyscrapers and bridges, we depend on steel framework and the men who are skilled craftsmen in this field. There are four separate trades that require the skills of ironworkers: structural, ornamental, and reinforcing ironwork, rigging and machine moving. It is not uncommon for an ironworker to be proficient in the skills of two or more of these trades.

Structural ironworkers erect the steel framework of buildings and other structures. They position steel beams and girders that are held in place by hoists and then secure them. Structural ironworkers who are working on a large project may specialize in a certain area of their trade such as welding or bolting.

Riggers and machine movers set up and rig hoisting equipment that is used to erect and dismantle steel frameworks and to move heavy construction machinery and equipment. They do this by studying what has to be moved and selecting the proper rigging to move it. Then they rig the object and attach the rigging to the hoist. Next they help the hoist operator move the load using hand signals and other directions. Riggers and machine movers must know the capabilities of the various hoisting and lifting devices.

The ornamental ironworker installs a variety of metal fixtures to building surfaces such as catwalks, floor gratings, stairways, ladders, doors, window sashes, screens, grilles, and balconies. Ornamental ironworkers employ various kinds of metals which they usually attach by welding or bolting.

Placing steel bars in concrete forms, to reinforce concrete structures, is the job of reinforcing ironworkers. Carefully following verbal or written instructions they place and connect steel bars in concrete forms in such a way that each bar bears the proper structural load. Reinforcing ironworkers may also work with wire mesh which they cut, bend, and shape into the intended form.

Most ironworkers are employed by building contractors, steel erection contractors, or ornamental contractors. They work in crews on the construction of large building projects, dams, bridges and in any other construction process where vast quantities of concrete are being used. They may also find employment with governmental agencies, large industries, or public utilities.

Ironworkers risk injury from falls and are subjected to seasonal weather conditions and temperatures. They may also have to drive long distances to job sites.

What You Need Personally

Above average strength and agility are required of anyone who wishes to become an ironworker. The materials used are very heavy and the work is often done on narrow footing. You must have a good sense of balance and no fear of heights. Good eyesight without glasses and good eye-hand-foot coordination are also very important. In addition you must be able to work from blueprints and carry out complicated oral instructions.

What Education and Training You Need

Although some men have acquired skills by working as helpers, the completion of an apprenticeship program is the easiest way to become a good ironworker. You must be at least eighteen years old and in good physical condition. A high school education is not required but is a valuable asset. Apprenticeship programs usually last three years or 6,000 hours. Apprentices receive on-the-job training plus an additional 144 hours of related classroom instruction annually. Classroom instruction includes subjects such as blueprint reading and mathematics. Apprenticeship programs for ironworkers are not as localized as programs for the other craftsmen in the construction industry. It is not unusual for a single apprenticeship program for ironworkers to cover an entire state. (See pages 52-63 for more information.)

What the Occupation Has to Offer

Employment opportunities for ironworkers are expected to increase rapidly throughout the 1970s. Qualified ironworkers should have no difficulty finding employment.

Ironworkers who were union members earned an average minimum hourly rate of $6.72 in 1970. This is eighteen cents an hour higher than the average minimum hourly rate paid other journeymen in the construction industry. Ironworkers with the proper qualifications and initiative may advance to foremen or superintendents.

Points to Consider Before Going into This Field

A few of the advantages of being an ironworker are good pay, union benefits, and job availability. As an ironworker you may also branch out and learn more than one trade. By doing this you can be even better assured of employment.

However, the work is usually outdoors, and often in high places, such as on scaffolds, hanging stages, or open steel framework high above ground or water. Workers are exposed to heat, cold, sun, and constant loud noises from riveting guns and other construction operations. There are some hazards, but modern safety equipment has reduced accidents to a bare minimum. In fact, the safety record in this field is better than in many trades because of the special training given.

As with other outdoor construction trades, you will lose time because of weather conditions. You may also have to spend a considerable amount of time traveling because there isn't enough local work. Because of physical requirements women are not employed as ironworkers.

For more information, write:

Department of Human Resources Development
Mail Control Unit
800 Capitol Mall
Sacramento, California 95814
Ask for: *Structural Steel Worker, Structural Steel Worker Apprentice* No. 115, Free.

Also contact:

For information about apprenticeships or other work opportunities in this field contact: your local general contractors; a local of the International Association of Bridge, Structural and Ornamental Iron Workers; or places listed on page 187.

Surveyor

The Job

Before any construction project is started, the surveyor does his job. He establishes land boundries, collects information for maps, charts, or plates, and measures and locates elevations, points, contours, and lines in or near the earth's surface. There are many different types of surveying: topographic, hydrographic, geodetic, aerial, and magnetic. Surveyors usually work in parties ranging from three to six people, consisting of a party chief, instrumentman, rodman, chairman, and notekeeper. The party chief is responsible for the work of the party and must know how to do all of the other jobs. The instrumentman sets up and takes readings on the instruments. The rodman holds a graduated rod that measures elevation. The chairman measures

horizontal and slope distances with various instruments, while the notekeeper records the findings of the other members of the party. Notekeepers may also be called upon to draw sketches of the terrain. In addition to doing field work the party chief must also draw maps, prepare reports, and work with project and field engineers.

In 1970 there were an estimated 50,000 surveyors employed in the United States. One-third of these were employed by state and federal agencies. Some of the agencies in the federal government that employ a large number of surveyors are the U.S. Geological Survey and Bureau of Land Management, the Agriculture Department's Forest Service, and the Army Corps of Engineers. State and local urban planning and redevelopment agencies and highway departments also employ many surveyors. In addition, they may find employment with construction companies, engineering and architectural consulting firms, or in the crude petroleum or natural gas industries.

Surveyors work exclusively outdoors. Because of this they are exposed to seasonal weather conditions. They are not usually subject to injuries, but when working around construction sites protective clothing should be worn. This includes boots, steel helmets, and brightly colored jackets.

What You Need Personally

Anyone interested in a job as a surveyor should enjoy computational and outdoor work. Good eyesight is a very important personal requirement. This includes normal near- and far-vision and color discrimination. You should be in good physical condition and have good hand-eye coordination and finger dexterity. Because surveyors work in parties, the ability to get along well with your fellow workers is also very important. Leadership qualities are often necessary to direct the work of a party. Attention to detail and good mathematical ability will also help.

What Education and Training You Need

A high school education or its equivalent is required before you can enter the field of surveying. High school courses in algebra, geometry, trigonometry, calculus, drafting, and mechanical drawing will be great assets to you. As a prospective surveyor with a high school education you start out as rodman and may work your way up to party chief. This is usually the most difficult way to become a surveyor and post-secondary schooling is recommended if you wish to advance rapidly in this field. There are post-secondary curriculums offered in surveying through correspondence schools, technical schools, junior and community colleges and vocational schools. These programs usually run from one to three years and will prepare you to start out as an instrumentman in the surveying party.

Land surveyors must be licensed in the United States. These are the surveyors who are responsible for the setting of boundaries. To become licensed you must have four to eight years of experience and pass a written examination established by your own state. If the surveyor has had some post-secondary schooling, the amount of experience required is usually lowered.

What the Occupation Has to Offer

The employment outlook is good for surveyors throughout the 1970s because of the development of our rural areas and the construction and improvement of our nation's highways.

Party chiefs employed by the federal government earned starting salaries of between $7,300 and $8,100 a year in 1970, with experienced party chiefs earning between $8,000 and $11,000 and some surveyors in higher positions earning in excess of $12,000 a year.

Advancement in the field of surveying is usually achieved by starting out as a rodman and working your way up to party chief. In addition, a small number of surveyors branch out and start their own surveying businesses.

Points to Consider Before Going into This Field

A job as surveyor has many advantages. You learn a useful and stimulating trade and receive a high annual income. You also enjoy company fringe benefits and good working conditions.

Remember, however, that the work is active and sometimes strenuous. You'll have to stand, walk, or climb with heavy pieces of equipment.

In 1970 only five percent of the surveyors in the United States were women because the work is so strenuous.

For more information, write:

American Society of Photogrammetry
105 North Virginia Avenue
Falls Church, Virginia 22046
Ask for: general information on careers in photogrammetry.

American Congress on Surveying and Mapping
Woodward Building
733 15th Street, N.W.
Washington, D.C. 20005

Ask for: *Careers in Surveying and Mapping*; and lists of schools offering training programs.

Also contact:

Look for local information in your telephone yellow pages under "Surveyors ... Land." See also page 187 for other places to write for more details.

Data Processing

Few technological advances have had as rapid and dramatic an impact on our society as the computer. First put into use less than twenty-five years ago, there are now more than 100,000 of these data-processing systems in use the world over, the majority of them in the United States. Computers were conceived originally as giant calculators for the solution of complex scientific problems. Today they play a major role in virtually every field of human endeavor—science, industry, business, education, medicine, space exploration, national defense, government, the list is endless.

In our immediate personal lives, computers keep track of automobile registrations, credit-card charges, magazine subscriptions, telephone bills, tuition costs—even our birth certificates and school test scores. Monitoring air and water pollution? Analyzing great literary works of the past? Calculating the proper feed mix for beef cattle or the proper color blend for house paints? All are being done today with the help of computers.

As you might expect, an industry that has grown as rapidly and pervasively as data processing has created hundreds of thousands of new jobs. And as the demand for computers continues to increase, so does the demand for qualified people to enter the field.

There are many different careers associated with computers. While most require a college education, several are within the reach of high school graduates who take additional, specialized training. Two of these—computer operator and computer programmer—are described in this section. Other careers requiring less than a college education for participation such as the jobs of engineers and technicians who build, test, install and maintain computers are described on pages 220-222 and pages 239-240.

Three national bodies, all in Washington, D.C., which accredit private computer schools are:

The Accrediting Commission of the National Association of Trade and Technical Schools

The Accrediting Commission for Business Schools

The Accrediting Commission of the National Home Study Council

For more information, write:

The American Association of Community and Junior Colleges
1 Dupont Circle
Washington, D.C. 20036
Ask for: Directory of junior colleges offering data processing courses.

American Federation of Information Processing Societies
210 Summit Avenue
Montvale, New Jersey 07645.

Business Equipment Manufacturers Association
1828 L Street, N.W.
Washington, D.C. 20006.

Data Processing Management Association
505 Busse Highway
Park Ridge, Illinois 60068.

Additional Reading:

Englebardt, Stanley L. *Careers in Data Processing*, New York: Lothrop, Lee & Shepard Co., 1969.

Nussbaum, Martin, *Opportunities in Electronic Data Processing*, New York: Vocational Guidance Manual, 1972. $4.95.

Programmer

The Job

A programmer is a skilled professional who devises a detailed plan for solving a particular problem with a computer. The plan is based on work prepared by a highly skilled expert called a systems analyst, who analyzes the problem at hand, the data available, and the capabilities of the computer to be used. The analyst then formulates a general approach to solving the problem. At this point the problem is turned over to the programmer.

The programmer creates a series of coded step-by-step instructions called a program, which causes the computer to perform the desired operations. The programmer employs one of many computer languages that may use English words or phrases or common mathematical expressions to communicate with the computer.

The programmer then checks his program—a process called debugging—by making several trial runs with his program on the computer.

Programming is intellectually rewarding but painstaking work. Programs to solve large and complex problems can take months or even years to create and debug, and the program steps can fill several volumes.

Programmers often work as a team, with responsibilities divided according to the skill and experience of the individuals. Many programming jobs require college degrees. Those that do not require a degree are generally called junior programmer or coder.

While computer operators usually work in data-processing centers—attractive, brightly lit, modern surroundings—the programmer divides his time among the computer center (where he tests his programs), his own private work area (where he does the actual program writing or coding), and in some cases the location of the source of the problem he is trying to solve. For example, if he is working on a payroll problem he will spend some time with accounting people. If he is writing a program to regulate the flow of work through a manufacturing plant he may spend some time on the plant floor to get a first-hand feeling for the problem.

What You Need Personally

A prerequisite for success in the computer field is precision and a logical mind. If you enjoy working puzzles, you are likely to enjoy the work demanded by data-processing positions. Strong qualifications would include the ability to work with and through people, to grasp a situation quickly, to analyze a problem objectively, to think creatively, to work under pressure, to organize and interpret information, and to make logical decisions. Patience, perseverance, and ingenuity are particularly desirable qualities.

What Education and Training You Need

Education is fundamental to a career in data processing: the more education the better. But a high school education coupled with some additional technical training can be sufficient for a computer operator or an entry-level programmer. Training on specific machines as they are introduced, either on the job or at the manufacturer's plant, is a continuing necessity.

Many two-year colleges now offer an Associate of Arts degree in data processing and computer programming. Some offer a uniform curriculum developed by the U.S. Office of Education. It is directed toward the business uses of computers, and enables the graduate to apply programming techniques to a defined problem with a minimum of supervision. In the final semester, the student must carry a major project through to completion.

For those who cannot attend college, many technical and trade schools offer good courses in computers. A large number of the schools are publicly supported, and vocational-training programs are offered by the school systems in most metropolitan areas. These usually provide training equal to that available from private business or data-processing schools at a much lower cost.

While there are many good private data-processing schools, the glamour of computers and the critical shortage of trained personnel have spawned some private schools of questionable ethics which provide poor training and charge very high fees. The prospective student should do some careful checking before enrolling in any private school, including a call to the local Better Business Bureau or state employment service. In general, you should be wary of schools using extravagant or misleading advertising, high-pressure salesmen, and pie-in-the-sky promises. Avoid a school that tries to pressure you into signing a contract immediately. Be wary of schools that do not require an aptitude test or whose test is so short or simple as to make its value seem questionable. Be skeptical of any school whose courses are so short that they appear unrealistic when compared to training required by companies in your area. Schools that promise high-paying jobs upon graduation should also be suspect.

What the Occupation Has to Offer

As the number of computers rises to meet the growing demand for data processing, many thousands of new jobs will become available each year through the 1970s.

Although most computer jobs are concentrated in metropolitan areas, openings exist wherever a computer is in use. Most programmers and operators are employed by large business organizations and government agencies. In addition, a growing number are employed by computer manufacturers and independent service firms which furnish computer and programming services to clients on a fee basis.

Salaries in the computer field are above average, reflecting the skills required and the shortage of qualified people. A 1970–71 survey by the Bureau of Labor Statistics showed average salary ranges of $148 to $226 per week for junior programmers. These tend to be entry-level positions, however, and the long-term prospects are considerably brighter for those who demonstrate the aptitude and determination to advance.

Junior programmers can move to higher levels of responsibility within the programming profession, eventually becoming systems analysts who specialize in certain uses of computers such as scientific or business applications. In the case of either operators or programmers, eventual supervisory positions with salaries of $20,000 per year and more are possible.

One of the virtues of a career in computers is that advancement is based on merit and merit alone. The work is so demanding and the shortage of skilled people so serious that advancement is readily available to those who earn it.

Points to Consider Before Going into This Field

Computer jobs can be among the most challenging and satisfying anywhere. They are not only financially and intellectually rewarding, but also the operator or programmer often has the added satisfaction of knowing he or she is working on something important. Solutions to some problems may mean survival for a business, success for a space mission, a breakthrough for a research project, or a forward step in medicine or education. The computer professional often works close to the frontier of human knowledge. Job security is another plus. Places of employment usually are modern offices, well-lighted, and air-conditioned.

But not everyone is suited for a career in data processing. The intellectual demands are considerable, and many interested applicants will not have the aptitude for computer work. Even those with aptitude may lack the enthusiasm for education, dedication, and responsibility that are critical to success. The information-professional must often stretch his imagination and intelligence to the limit and pay religious attention to detail and logic.

Those who do fit the bill will find a career virtually free of social barriers. Women, minority members, the young and the old have all achieved great success in data processing. It's performance that counts.

For more information, write:

Association for Computing Machinery
1133 Avenue of the Americas
New York, New York 10036.

Additional Reading:
Davis, Sidney. *Your Future in Computer Programming.*(revised) New York: Arco Publishing Co. 1971.

Electronic Computer Operator

The Job

A computer operator is the man or woman you see working at data processing centers pushing buttons, feeding punched cards to the computer, and in many ways supervising the operations of the system.

Computer operators usually serve an apprenticeship during which their main duties are inserting punched cards, mounting magnetic tape reels and keeping high-speed printers filled with blank forms. More experienced operators have responsibility for actually running the computer—determining the correct setup, starting the operation, and investigating any difficulties in the operation of the system. The operator holds a position of considerable responsibility since mistakes and stoppages can be time-consuming and costly. When the control panel lights indicate that the machine has stopped, the operator must investigate and correct the stoppage or call a maintenance engineer. He also keeps a log of work done by the computer and prepares reports on its use.

What Education and Training You Need

Employers require a high school education, and many of them prefer some college or technical school background. A college degree is helpful if you plan to progress into programming or systems analysis.

Employers often transfer operators of tabulating and bookkeeping machines to newly installed electronic computers, but other computer operators are recruited from the outside. Many private employers give tests to measure an applicant's aptitude, especially his ability to reason logically.

Beginners usually receive training after they are hired. The training of auxiliary equipment operators may require a few weeks, that of console operators somewhat longer. Console operators usually attend classes to learn to mount tapes, operate the console, and must become sufficiently familiar with the equipment to be able to trace mechanical failures. Their training is supplemented by further instruction on the job.

What the Occupation Has to Offer

The use of electronic data processing equipment will continue to grow rapidly. Thousands of operators will be needed to fill new jobs, both in firms having their own computer installations and in service centers that rent computer time to businessmen.

Equipment changes that are expected in computers may produce changes in job requirements for console and auxiliary equipment operators. Because of advances in technology, much of the equipment in use today is far less complex to operate than computers of the early 1950s and 1960s; future changes may bring further simplification. As a result, newcomers to this field may find it easier to qualify for the openings available than have applicants in the past.

A 1970–71 survey by the Bureau of Labor Statistics showed average salary ranges of $125 to $205 per week for computer operators. But salaries of over $300 are not unusual for skilled console operators.

Points to Consider Before Going into This Field

Computer operators can advance to positions as supervisors of operations, programmers, and managers of data processing centers. Operators of electronic computer systems generally work the same number of weekly hours and are allowed the same holidays, vacations, and other benefits as most office employees. Since many computers are operated on a two- or three-shift basis, scheduled hours for some console and auxiliary equipment operators include late evening or night work.

Because electronic computers must be housed where temperature is carefully controlled, operators work in air-conditioned rooms. A disadvantage of their working environment is the high level of noise generated by the operation of computer consoles and other equipment.

For more information, write:

Association for Computing Machinery
1133 Avenue of the Americas
New York, New York 10036.

See also: Programmer, pages 212-214.

Electric Power, Electronics Manufacturing, Telephone Industry

The increasing use of electric power in the United States requires a large number of workers to produce electricity, develop markets for it, and distribute it to the consumer. The electric power companies in this country employ over half a million people in every job capacity you can name and at every income level. Most utility jobs are in urban areas with many large industrial users, although there are power companies almost anywhere in the country.

About ten percent of electrical utility workers are directly involved in generating electricity, twenty percent in the transmission and distribution of power to customers, twenty percent in maintenance and repair work, thirty percent in clerical and administrative positions, ten percent in customer service and ten percent in scientific, engineering, and other technical jobs. (You'll find separate sections on transmission and distribution jobs and customer service jobs on following pages).

Maintenance jobs may include skilled workers such as electricians, instrument repairmen, maintenance mechanics, machinists, pipe fitters, and boilermakers.

Engineers and technical workers fill a great many important positions in the electric power industry. They plan installations of new transmission and distribution systems, plant additions, and interconnections of power systems. They test equipment efficiency, supervise construction, select plant sites and types of fuel. They also help customers make the best use of electrical power.

This industry requires large numbers of office workers such as typists, stenographers, bookkeepers, accounting clerks, and others, although many billing operations are now being done by computer. Administrative employees include accountants, personnel officers, purchasing agents, and lawyers.

Because of the possible danger in working with electrical wires and components, the industry is very safety conscious, makes a great effort to offer good working conditions to its employees, and has a low accident rate.

Our growing population and a continued trend toward electric power for use in heating and in running machinery will keep the industry expanding in the 1970s. All job areas will have some openings, but increased mechanization will limit the number of new openings.

While the number of substation operators will probably decline due to more use of automation, more maintenance and repair craftsmen will probably be needed to service the complex machinery being used. Jobs involving repair and maintenance of distribution and transmission lines should remain stable, as increased mechanization is offset by the need for more work crews to service new power customers.

Administrative personnel needs should increase somewhat, and the increased use of electronic data processors in the office should be offset by the high turnover in clerical employees.

Earnings in the electric power industry are generally good; in 1970, nonsupervisory employees averaged $4.21 per hour. Many of the workers are union members.

Because electricity must be supplied all day every day, some employees work alternate shifts, receiving from four to twenty-six and a half cents an hour more on the evening shift, and six to thirty-nine and a half cents an hour more on the night shift than on the day shift. Overtime work is also often called for, particularly in times of emergency like floods or storms. Such work is usually paid at time and a half. Benefits for workers are quite substantial, including vacations, paid holidays, insurance and retirement plans.

Opportunities for advancement exist wherever supervisory jobs need to be filled.

Electric power companies offer a chance to work in a field of steady economic growth and steady work. Some job openings exist in every area, which offer stability and liberal benefits as inducements.

Because of a lack of expansion in the number of jobs, however, advancement is usually limited to filling the job of someone who has retired, died, or changed positions. There is usually sufficient turnover to provide advancement for a good worker.

Women have mainly been limited to non-technical office jobs but with proper training there is no reason why engineering or other jobs should not be open to them.

For further information, write:

Edison Electric Institute
90 Park Avenue
New York, New York 10016.

International Brotherhood of Electrical Workers
1200 15th Street NW
Washington, D. C. 20005.

Also contact:

For information about jobs, contact your local electric utility companies; industry trade associations; or the local offices of unions which have electric utility workers among their membership.

Transmission and Distribution Workers

The Job

When you switch on your television set, you are relying on a job done by your local power company employees who control the flow of electricity to us and who construct and maintain the power lines used for transmission.

Load dispatchers, also known as system operators or power dispatchers, control the flow of electricity throughout the area serviced by the power company. The load dispatcher's room is dominated by a pilot board with a complete map of the transmission system so that he can check conditions throughout the system at a glance. He

controls all plant equipment used to generate electricity and send it through the system. He instructs switchboard operators at generating plants and substations and tells them when to use or turn off additional boilers and generators. He must anticipate power needs in the area and be prepared to direct any emergencies. He may also be in charge of interconnection with other systems, and directing transfer of current between systems when necessary.

Substation operators, under directions from the load dispatcher, direct the flow of current out of their stations by means of a switchboard. They must be sure the demands of users are met by the right amount of electricity. Instruments on the board register the amount of power flowing through each line and the substation operator connects or breaks the flow of current with levers that control the circuit breakers. Substation operators also make sure all equipment is in good working condition.

Linemen construct, install, maintain, and repair the power lines that carry electricity from the power plant to the consumer. They often receive emergency calls to splice or replace broken wires and cables or to replace other damaged equipment. Most work from trucks with pneumatic lifts that take them to the tops of power poles. In some companies, linemen specialize in certain types of work, such as high voltage lines.

Troublemen are linemen who are part of special crews that handle emergency calls. They must know the company's transmission and distribution network thoroughly to locate and fix the source of trouble.

Groundmen dig pole holes and assist linemen in putting up the wooden poles that carry the distribution lines. They also help to raise and attach the wires and cables and other equipment.

Cable splicers install and repair single and multiple conductor insulated cables on utility poles and towers, and underground. They join and insulate cables and splice conductors. Their job mostly involves repairing and maintaining cables, checking the cable insulation and changing the layout of cable systems. They must know the arrangements of the wiring system.

Jobs exist throughout the country for any of these skilled workers. Most power plants are well-lit and ventilated, and load dispatchers and substation operations have pleasant working conditions. Linemen, groundmen, and troublemen work outside in all kinds of weather, while cable splicers work mostly underground, in somewhat cramped quarters.

What You Need Personally

Substation operators and load dispatchers should be mentally alert, clearheaded, and precise. Good eyesight and coordination are required, and an interest in technical and scientific areas is important.

The same qualities are helpful for linemen, groundmen, troublemen, and cable splicers. People in these occupations should also have physical stamina, strength, agility, steady nerves, good balance, and no fear of heights.

What Education and Training You Need

A high school diploma or equivalent is usually required for substation operators, and courses in science, mathematics, and shop will be helpful. Some college or technical school training is an asset. Most power companies offer on-the-job training. They expect workers to begin at the bottom of the ladder and then become junior operators. On-the-job training takes three to seven years.

Load dispatchers are promoted from the ranks of senior switchboard or substation operators and must show a knowledge of the entire utility system. About seven to ten years experience as a senior switchboard or substation operator is required for a load dispatcher.

Skilled linemen usually spend about four years in on-the-job training, sometimes with a formal apprenticeship program. This formal program, which may have a written agreement worked out with the labor union, combines training with classroom instruction in such subjects as blueprint reading, elementary electrical theory, electrical codes and methods of transmitting electrical currents. (See pages 52-63 for more details.)

Both formal and informal training programs move the worker from simple assistant duties through more complex responsibilities until he can operate as an independent. The informal training program does not include classroom study.

A groundman requires less knowledge and skill and his training lasts a shorter time. A skilled lineman can work up to troubleman.

Cable splicers also have on-the-job training, usually lasting about four years. They, too, progress from simpler to more complex and independent tasks.

What the Occupation Has to Offer

Modest increases in employment opportunities in the power industry are expected during the 1970s. Most openings will, however, come from the need to replace experienced workers who retire, die, or change jobs. Automation and mechanization will prevent great increases in the number of these jobs. Most substations will be able to operate largely by remote control. More mechanized equipment is being used to construct and maintain power lines, cutting the growth in groundman, lineman, and troubleman positions. However, new power customers will require more work crews, offsetting the improved technology. Some increase in the demand for cable splicers is expected, due to the increased use of underground power lines.

Earnings for transmission and distribution workers vary around the country, but average earnings for 1970 are as follows: groundman, $3.50 an hour; lineman, $5.05; troubleman, $5.27, substation operator, $4.63; and load dispatcher, $5.75

Most electric utility workers belong to unions and receive substantial benefits and paid holidays.

Promotions in all these positions depend on the availability of openings in a particular company, but, as indicated, substation operators receive top consideration for load dispatcher positions, and groundmen can become linemen or troublemen.

Points to Consider Before Going into This Field

As a member of this industry you will be making a substantial contribution to the community by helping to provide and maintain the electrical services so vital to the working of every home, business, or institution. If you enjoy being outdoors and also want a job that requires thinking and learning, a lineman is a good position.

If you are considering these jobs keep in mind, however, that the importance of the continued flow of power to our society makes speed and accuracy on the job of utmost importance. Mistakes can be costly and time-consuming. Anyone not sure of his physical stamina would be better off at one of the indoor jobs. However, while substation operators and load dispatchers work more comfortably indoors, they do have to be continually alert and accurate.

Although there is no reason women could not be substation operators, they have not generally been employed for such positions. A woman with sufficient physical strength and stamina could also do the outdoor jobs, and a few have started in these formerly all-male occupations.

See: page 217 for places to write for more details.

Electrical Technician

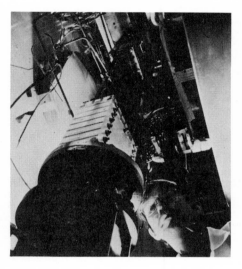

The Job

An electrical technician can work in a variety of positions involving electrical power distribution and the design and manufacture of electrical equipment. He uses testing equipment, hand tools, drafting instruments and slide rule. Many specialties are open to him within his field, and within a particular company. About 75 percent are employed by private industry.

If an electrical technician chooses to work for an electric power company, his responsibilities will include testing power equipment with instruments such as ammeters, phase meters, galvanometers, and oscilloscopes, and gathering the information needed by electrical engineers to insure that equipment meets specifications. He may also be involved in the planning, construction supervising, installing, and operating of power generator plants. With his knowledge of test equipment and procedures, he can do maintenance work on power station equipment or assist engineers in researching and developing new equipment processes or procedures. Other possible jobs for the electrical technician in this

industry are installation, estimation, inspection, sales, and field service work.

Transportation is another area in which electrical technicians are employed. Railroads use electrical generators to drive their motors and electric signal systems. Ships also use electrical generators, and automobile and aircraft engines use electrical power for starting, ignition, and lighting. Defense industries, making aircraft, missile systems, etc., often employ electrical technicians.

Lighting for homes, offices, factories, and streets also requires the services of electrical technicians for installation, distribution of power, and maintenance. Airports, marinas, theatres, and other specialized areas all require special controls and materials for their lighting.

Electrical technicians are frequently hired by firms which manufacture electrical devices and components. They may work in research and development, design, or prototype assembly and testing. They may also test or install industrial electronics equipment. They often take on practical engineering responsibilities that free the engineer for more theoretical tasks.

The communication field is still another which provides jobs for electrical technicians, and the new field of lasers should bring new opportunities

The electrical technician usually works in modern, air-conditioned offices with up-to-date machinery and environmentally controlled laboratories. He may be asked to travel occasionally to install or maintain equipment.

What You Need Personally

You should be accurate, analytical, and creative, with an ability to communicate clearly verbally and on paper. You must be willing to apply yourself and be able to make independent judgments. Because you often supervise, you must like and be able to get along with others. To work in a defense industry, you must be a citizen and able to obtain security clearance.

Because the job combines thinking and doing, ideally you should enjoy doing labwork and applying it practically. To use the tools and laboratory equipment needed for the job, you should be able to work well with your hands. An understanding of machines and devices and how they work is also helpful.

What Education and Training You Need

Electrical technicians are usually graduates of a two or three year program in electrical technology at a technical institute, junior or community college, or private vocational school. These programs lead to an associate degree in science, planned science, or in engineering. The studies are essentially similar to those taken by electrical engineers, but on a less theoretical level.

Electrical technology programs usually accept a C average in high school grades, and expect students to be in the top half of their graduating classes. Strong interest and high performance in science and math are important for this occupation, and a mechanical aptitude test is recommended. High school preparation should include one-and-a-half years of algebra, one year each of geometry, physics, chemistry, and drafting or mechanical drawing, a half year of trigonometry, and three years of English. Biology, slide rule, and social sciences are also helpful.

The course of study in electrical technology is quite broad. First year courses cover basic mathematics, science, electricity, social science, and English. The second year concentrates on principles and theory of electricity and their applications to power systems and control and protective devices. The courses are practical and intensive, with about three-fourths of the time devoted to lectures and the rest to lab work.

Some technical institutes have recently introduced accredited four year programs toward a bachelor of engineering technology degree in order to make it easier for a graduate electrical technician to continue his or her education and become a graduate electrical engineer. The first two years are the same as the associate program; the last two involve further study of electrical technology.

What the Occupation Has to Offer

The employment outlook for electrical technicians is very good. The electrical industry shows tremendous growth because electric power is so essential to our way of life. The U. S. Department of Labor has projected a need for 80,000 new technicians per year for the next few years, plus 32,000 yearly to replace those who retire, die, or change jobs. The schools are not graduating qualified technicians fast enough to meet the demand.

Electrical technicians with an associate degree earned an average of $650 per month in 1969. Experienced technicians average $14,000 per year or more. The electrical industry offers good insurance and retirement benefits, in addition to paid holidays and vacations.

Chances for advancement to supervisory positions are very good, especially if you take advantage of training programs offered in the industry. Promotions go to those who show drive and good performance, and who continue to learn new developments in the field.

Points to Consider Before Going into This Field

For someone who likes math and science, who enjoys figuring things out and making them work, a career as electrical technician is very promising. It offers diversified work and a chance to use your knowledge in many areas. The field is continually expanding and shows no signs of a slowdown.

Another advantage is that although similar to electrical engineering, the course of study is shorter and less expensive. The job offers a fair starting salary and a good chance for advancement.

Anyone who does not have facility for mathematical and scientific concepts, or who doesn't feel capable of exercising independent judgments, should think twice before entering this field.

Although at this time only one percent of electrical technicians are women, those whose interests lie in this direction are encouraged to pursue the career.

For more information:
See: pages 231-232 for places to write for more details.

Electronics Manufacturing

The Job

Electronic devices and instruments are used in the United States to run everything from alarm clocks to televisions to missiles.

In order to produce the vast number of instruments needed over one million workers are employed in manufacturing operations in jobs ranging from engineers and scientists to unskilled plant workers.

About half of the electronic products in this country are produced for the government, about a third for industry, and about a seventh for consumer products. The remaining small percentage takes in components.

About half the workers in the electronics industry are employed in plants, the other half have white-collar jobs.

Engineers and scientists are well-represented in electronic manufacturing, particularly in plants making military and space equipment. Electronic engineers are usually involved in research and development, although they also work as design engineers, in quality control, in sales, and in the field. Mechanical engineers work in product development, in tool and equipment design and as plant engineers. Industrial engineers work on production, or in improving efficiency or methods. Other engineers in the industry include chemical, metallurgical, and ceramic.

Physicists are also involved in electronics manufacturing, as are chemists and metallurgists, mathematicians and statisticians, and industrial designers.

Technicians—electronics technicians, draftsmen, engineering aides, lab technicians, and mathematical assistants—are often involved in research and development, testing and customer service. Draftsmen are also included in the field, particularly in military and space equipment areas. Technical writers are needed to work with engineers in the preparation of training and technical manuals, catalogs, project reports, and proposals. They are assisted by specifications writers and technical illustrators.

About twenty percent of electronics workers are in administrative or clerical jobs. These include purchasing agents, sales executives, market researchers, personnel workers, advertising personnel, clerks, secretaries, typists and the growing number of employees who operate electronic equipment that processes payroll, inventory, costs, sales, and other information.

The large number of electronics workers in the actual manufacturing are involved with assembling, inspecting, testing, machining, fabricating, processing, and maintenance. The largest group here are assemblers, most of whom are semiskilled and work with hand tools following diagrams and models. Some are involved in very precise work in which operations must be carried out within a thousandth of an inch. In some cases, they operate the machines that do the assembly work. Hand assemblers may repeat a single motion over and over or may totally assemble a particular component.

Another group includes those who operate machine tools and power machines. Toolmakers and diemakers are among them.

Fabricating workers are mainly found in plants making industrial products. They may include sheetmetal workers, glass blowers, punch press operators, blanking machine operators, lathe operators, spot welders, coil winders, and crystal grinders.

Another relatively small group includes the processing workers. They are electroplaters, tinners, anodizers, and silk screen printers. They may coat parts with metal, oil or plastic, treat parts to prevent corrosion or operate machines that insulate components. Some operate furnaces, ovens, or kilns that harden ceramics, bake on coatings, and eliminate contamination.

Testing and inspection are crucial to electronic production, and these processes are done throughout the manufacturing process. Testing jobs are usually quite specific and may require a great deal of experience.

Another important group are those employed in maintenance. They are responsible for the proper performance of machinery and equipment and most are specialists in certain types of machines or systems.

Other workers include parts changers, who replace defective parts, forklift operators, and truck drivers.

What You Need Personally

Most all the jobs in this field require precision and an interest in how things work.

What Education and Training You Need

Each type of job requires something different. Engineering jobs are almost always filled by graduates of engineering colleges, some with advanced degrees. Sometimes engineering assistants or electronics technicians without college degrees are promoted to these positions if they have taken advanced electronics programs in night school.

Mathematicians and scientists have college degrees, with master's degrees preferred.

Technicians need specialized training, usually obtained from a vocation or technical school or Armed Forces program. Some receive their training through a three or four year apprenticeship. Apprentices should have a high school education including courses in mathematics and science. Training includes learning job skills and studying such subjects as basic electronics theory, mathematics, drafting, and reading of schematic diagrams. Technicians must have an understanding of technical writing and good eye-hand coordination and manual dexterity. If they do final testing with radio transmitting equipment, they must hold licenses from the Federal Communications Commission.

Laboratory technicians, engineering and scientific aides and mathematical assistants frequently have a few years of college training. Others are promoted from lower assistant positions.

Draftsmen usually study at a trade or technical school and are sometimes given on-the-job training during this period. Their studies include basic electronic theory and circuits and the reading of electronic schematic diagrams.

Technical writers must combine a talent for writing with an interest in technical training. They usually have college degrees in English or engineering.

Tool and die makers, machinists, pipefitters, and other craftsmen usually learn their trades through a four or five year apprenticeship program. Others are promoted through the ranks or take courses at vocational schools.

Plant workers are usually required to have a high school diploma and must pass aptitude tests for their jobs. They are provided with on-the-job training and usually need good vision, color perception, manual dexterity, and patience.

What the Occupation Has to Offer

Electronics manufacturing is a growing field and is expected to continue expanding. It is affected by defense spending and suffers setbacks whenever federal budgets are cut. Industrial and consumer products will continue to increase, however.

Technological improvements and increased mechanization in the electronics industry will mean that increase in jobs will be somewhat less than the growth in the industry as a whole. Skilled maintenance personnel and engineers, scientists and technicians will find more openings than semiskilled workers.

Earnings for electronics workers vary by type of product produced, geographic location, skill level, length of service, and amount of overtime. Overtime work receives high pay in this industry. Vacations, paid holidays, insurance and pension plans are common. Many workers are union members.

The average hourly earnings of a plant worker in the electronics industry is $3.36 per hour.

Because of the size and diversity of most manufacturing operations, there is plenty of opportunity for advancement in all areas and types of jobs. Usually outside study is helpful when you are trying for promotion.

Points to Consider Before Going into This Field

Electronics manufacturing is a growing field. Most companies offer unlimited opportunities for skilled technicians or craftsmen and a chance to put knowledge and skill to good use.

Jobs involved in the manufacturing process itself may not be quite as promising, as they become more mechanized. There is still a need for people to operate the machines, however, and to do the precision jobs that a machine cannot do. Because this work can be tedious, it is not recommended if you are an especially active person. In an effort to combat this problem,

many plants are making work areas more pleasant, and are providing recreational facilities and other "extras" for employees.

Women are heavily employed in this industry. Most are assemblers or office workers, but there are no restrictions against women in other jobs.

For more information, write:

Electronic Industries Association
2001 Eye Street, N.W.
Washington, D. C. 20006.

Telephone Industry

The Job

Alexander Graham Bell really started something when he invented the telephone. We now have more than 120 million telephones in use in this country, and the telephone industry employs nearly one million people to provide this service. As new means of communication are developed, telephone companies are continually increasing their services to the public and employing more people. In addition to providing telephone services, the companies also build and maintain cable and radio relay systems, including those used by broadcasting stations. They also operate the teletype and private wire services which are leased to business and government offices.

Over eighty percent of the nation's telephones are owned by the Bell System, the rest belong to nearly 1900 smaller independent phone companies. Telephone jobs are found in every city and town in the country, but almost three-fifths of them are in the ten states with the most phones: California, New York, Pennsylvania, Illinois, Ohio, Texas, Michigan, New Jersey, Florida, and Massachusetts.

The telephone system employs many different types of skilled workers: craftsmen who install, repair, and maintain telephones, cables, switching equipment, and message systems; construction workers who place, splice, and maintain telephone wires and cables; installers and repairmen who place, maintain and repair telephones and private branch exchanges (PBX) in homes and businesses; and central office craftsmen who test, maintain, and repair equipment in central offices. Central office equipment is usually installed by employees of the equipment manufacturers, although a few work for phone companies.

What Education and Training You Need

Phone company employees are required to have a high school education or its equivalent, and other training varies according to the position. The less complex jobs do not require extra schooling, but some technical school studies in electronics are helpful. Technical and scientific jobs require additional schooling.

Generally, the telephone company provides on-the-job training for its employees in all categories. In many cases training is an on-going process, as new developments in communications technology require adding to or changing job requirements.

What the Occupation Has to Offer

Total employment in the telephone industry is expected to increase moderately in all categories. Service is expected to grow, but more sophisticated technology will limit job growth. More telephones will undoubtedly come into use, creating a demand for more installers, repairmen, and central office craftsmen. The use of electronic switching systems will make repair and installation simpler, however.

Earnings in the telephone industry depend on the type of job, length of service, and wage rates in the area. Generally, wage rates are highest in the Pacific and Middle Atlantic states and lowest in the southeast. More than two-thirds of industry workers are union members, mainly operators and craftsmen. Their wage increases are governed by pay scales. In general, employees start at the minimum wage for the particular job, and advancement to the maximum rate takes four to six years and involves ten to fourteen pay grades. Extra pay is allotted for overtime, Sunday, holiday, and emergency work, and usually for night shifts.

At last survey, central office craftsmen averaged from $3.46 to $4.38 an hour and installers and repairmen earned up to $4 an hour. Line-men and splicers averaged about $3.25 an hour.

Fringe benefits are quite good in the telephone industry including paid holidays and vacations, and insurance and retirement benefits. Vacation is based on length of service and can be as much as five weeks per year for someone who has been with the company twenty-five years or more. The telephone industry also has a very good safety record in all areas.

Chances for advancement are good. Most positions lead to higher ones as skills are increased. Supervisory jobs exist in all areas.

Points to Consider Before Going into This Field

The telephone industry can be expected to expand and to offer steady employment at wage scales that increase with the economy. Good benefits are provided, and there is sufficient diversity of jobs for almost any type of interest. Telephone companies are located all over the country, providing employment no matter where you live.

More than half of all workers are women, most of whom are employed as telephone operators or clerks. Jobs involving installation, repair, and maintenance of telephone equipment have usually been filled by men, but some women have been hired in these areas and more can be expected.

For more information, write:

Communication Workers of America
1925 K Street N.W.
Washington, D.C. 20006.

International Brotherhood of Electrical Workers
1200 15th Street N.W.
Washington, D.C. 20005.

United States Independent Telephone Association
438 Pennsylvania Building
Washington, D.C. 20004.

Also contact:

For information about jobs contact your local telephone company or local unions with telephone workers among their membership.

Central Office Installer And Craftsmen

The Job

Without properly installed and maintained equipment, we would have no telephone system. The telephone companies' local central offices are the nerve centers of the system. All telephone calls go through the network of equipment maintained in these offices.

Central office equipment installers set up the complex switching and dialing equipment, some-

work at special switchboards that have electrical testing instruments that test for, locate, and analyze trouble spots. If repairs are needed on a breakdown outside the central office, they direct the outside repair crews. If the trouble is inside, they inform and direct the central office repairmen.

What You Need Personally

Central office installers and craftsmen should have manual dexterity, good eyesight, and an aptitude for reading diagrams and blueprints, and working mechanically. They cannot be color blind because wires are color coded. Since teamwork is essential, they should be able to work with others. They should also be flexible enough to adapt to technology changes. A background in electricity and electronics is important.

What Education and Training You Need

At least a high school or vocational school education is required for either central office installers or craftsmen.

Installers often have some college training, especially in engineering. They are given mechanical aptitude tests and physical examinations before hiring.

times installing an entire new central office, or simply adding or replacing equipment in an existing facility. They assemble, wire, adjust, and test the equipment.

Most of the nation's 22,000 central office installers work for the manufacturers of the equipment rather than telephone companies. A few do work directly for the phone companies, and some are employed by private contractors. Installers are usually assigned to areas that cover several states. To install a central office switchboard in a small town may take only two or three workers while a large job may employ hundreds.

Central office craftsmen test, maintain, and repair the mechanical, electrical, and electronic switching equipment in the central office. They try to locate potential trouble before service is affected. Over 92,000 telephone company employees are employed in this type of work.

The lowest level job is frameman. This position involves running, connecting, and disconnecting wires according to plans prepared by line assigners. He joins customer telephone lines with dialing equipment which serves as the connecting link to other phones.

Central office repairmen, or switchmen, maintain and repair switching equipment and automatic message accounting systems. They locate and repair trouble on customers' lines in central office equipment as reported by testboardmen and check switches and relays in the equipment.

Testboardmen check customers' lines to find the cause of breakdowns or interference. They

Installers receive on-the-job training combined with classroom instruction. A few weeks of classes include instruction in basic installation methods before job training begins. On-the-job training continues throughout the career of the installer, and it takes several years to qualify as a skilled worker. To keep up with new technology, additional courses are given periodically on new techniques and skills.

Central office craftsmen should have some basic knowledge of electricity and electronics in addition to high school education. Some technical training beyond high school or in the armed services can be helpful and may allow you to start work at better than an entry level position.

Most telephone companies give on-the-job training and classroom instruction to new central office craftsmen. They may begin by assisting experienced framemen and work up. The telephone company gives periodic instruction to central office craftsmen to keep them abreast of new developments and instruct them on how to work with new equipment.

What the Occupation Has to Offer

Job opportunities for central office installers and craftsmen are expected to increase moderately in the next few years. Installers are particularly vulnerable to the fluctuations in the economy; when business is good, more phone systems are added, more sophisticated equipment installed. As their work gets increasingly complex, they are required to keep up with all new developments.

Central office craftsmen will be needed in the years to come as more telephone service and data communications systems are demanded by the public. Technological developments like automatic testing devices and electronic switching will offset some of this job increase, however.

Central office installers' earnings vary according to geographical area. In 1970, one contract provided $2.50–$2.69 an hour for inexperienced installers, giving periodic increases that, after six years, paid the installer $4–$4.82 an hour. Installers also get time-and-a-half for overtime, double time for Sundays and holidays, and travel and expense allowances. Most equipment installers are union members and receive paid holidays, vacations, etc.

Central office craftsmen are usually well-paid, with earnings varying according to locale and length of service. Testboardmen average $3.80–$4.38 an hour, repairmen $346–$3.81 an hour. Overtime and off-hour work schedules are common, and these pay more.

Promotions are available to all these workers. Installers may advance to engineering assistant jobs, particularly if they have some post-high school technical training. Framemen can work up to repairman or testboardman, and supervisory positions in all these areas offer more pay.

Points to Consider Before Going into This Field

The telephone industry is expanding its services and technology. Skilled craftsmen who keep up on developments can expect a good future with a company.

See: page 223 for places to write for more details.

Telephone and PBX Installer and Repairman

The Job

Telephones and PBX (private branch exchange) systems are installed for the customer and repaired on his property by telephone and PBX installers and repairmen or servicemen. These men are the largest group of telephone craftsmen with over 100,000 currently employed. Traveling to customers' homes and offices in trucks equipped with telephone tools and supplies, they install new phone equipment or make requested changes on existing facilities. They may install a PBX system in an office or add an extension phone in a private home. Some phone companies have different men installing and repairing, while others combine the jobs.

Telephone installers install and remove telephones, employing outside service wires. PBX installers specialize in more complex switchboard installations, connecting wires from termi-

nals to switchboards and testing connections. Sometimes they also set up equipment for radio and television broadcasts, mobile radio-telephones, and teletypewriters.

Telephone repairmen, assisted by testboardmen in the central office, track down the trouble in customer equipment and make the needed repairs to restore proper service. PBX repairmen go through similar procedures on PBX systems and also maintain associated equipment like batteries, relays, and power plants.

Telephone and PBX installers and repairmen work indoors and outdoors, often having to climb poles to place and repair phone wires in all kinds of weather. When major breakdowns occur, they may have to work extra hours.

What You Need Personally

Jobs are sometimes filled by promoting workers from within the ranks of the telephone company. Important personal qualities are a neat appearance, the ability to make a good impression and to get along with and communicate with people. A good driving record is also required.

You need manual dexterity for the job, and good vision (either with glasses or without). An aptitude for mechanical work and reading diagrams and blueprints is also important. Because communications technology is always advancing, installers and repairmen have to be quick enough to adapt to changes. A repairman must be a good pole climber.

What Education and Training You Need

A high school or vocational school education is required. The telephone company will usually give aptitude tests to assure that the candidate has some natural ability for the mechanics of the work. The company provides on-the-job training and classroom instruction. The classes are equipped with telephone poles, lines and cables, terminal boxes, and models of typical houses to simulateworking conditions. Trainees spend a few weeks installing telephones and making connections to service wires in these classes and then continue their training by watching and assisting experienced workers in the field.

What the Occupation Has to Offer

As the demand for telephones and PBX and CENTREX systems continues to grow, the number of jobs in this area will increase. Other job openings will be created by workers retiring, dying, or leaving the industry.

There will be more use of specialized and complex phone equipment in the years to come, providing more work for installers and repairmen. The employment increase will, however, be limited by the new technology that has increased the efficiency of installers and repairmen. Improved designs for telephone instruments, wires and cables all cut installation and repair time.

Earnings for these craftsmen vary from city to city; most are covered by union contracts. The average rate for PBX repairmen is about $4 per hour, for telephone and PBX installers somewhat less. Union contracts call for automatic pay raises each year you work for the phone company.

Installers and repairmen are sometimes promoted from linemen, and later advance to PBX installer or repairman.

Points to Consider Before Going into This Field

The telephone company is a growing industry, offering steady work with good benefits. With improved technology, more phone systems can be expected to be installed in a more sophisticated manner. If you work as an installer or repairman you will get an opportunity to keep up on developments in technology and continue to add to your skills.

If you do not like working out of doors, you should not consider work as an installer or repairman.

See: page 223 for places to write for more details.

Lineman and Cable Splicer

The Job

The wires and cables that connect the nation's millions of telephones and switchboards to the telephone companies' central offices are con-structed and maintained by over 44,000 linemen, cable splicers, and their assistants.

Linemen construct new telephone lines by erecting telephone poles, then climbing the poles to attach the cables. Some telephone lines run underground and are also installed by these workers. Construction linemen work in crews of two to five men and a foreman supervises several crews.

Linemen also make emergency repairs and do routine maintenance. They periodically inspect sections of lines and make minor repairs and line changes.

After the lines have been placed, cable splicers complete the line connections. They work on aerial platforms, in manholes, or in basements of large commercial buildings. Individual wires within the cable are connected by matching wire colors. When lines have to be changed, they rearrange pairs of wires within a cable. At each splice, they wrap insulation around the wires and seal the joint or cover the splice. They also repair cables and do preventive maintenance to avoid service interruptions.

Linemen and cable splicers work out-of-doors in every kind of weather and are often exposed to danger from height and high voltage.

What You Need Personally

These jobs require physical stamina and some strength. Candidates should like the out-of-doors and enjoy working with their hands. Manual dexterity, mechanical aptitude, agility, good balance, and steady nerves are important. Good vision and the ability to distinguish colors are also required. Quick-wittedness, dependability, and cooperation with others are also good traits. A lineman is a pole climber.

What Education and Training You Need

A high school or vocational school education is necessary for these jobs, and a knowledge of the basic principles of electricity is helpful. Aptitude tests are often given and physical examinations are quite thorough because of the strenuous nature of the work.

Telephone training and experience in the armed forces will often give an applicant preference in job openings.

Telephone companies provide training programs for these positions, which include classroom instruction and on-the-job training. Trainees practice with telephone apparatus and are taught climbing skills. Then they are assigned to crews with experienced workers. Continued training is provided in order to keep up with technological changes.

What the Occupation Has to Offer

Only moderate increases in these jobs is expected, despite the growth of the telephone industry. Cable splicers, particularly, are finding that new technological developments are making their jobs easier, limiting the need for more help. The number of linemen is expected to remain stable.

Earnings for linemen and cable splicers vary according to length of service and geographical location. When last surveyed, linemen earned from $2.51-$3.33 an hour, cable splicers from $3.43-$4.02 an hour. Most of these jobs are covered by union contracts and include higher pay for overtime and emergency work, paid vacations and holidays, and insurance and retirement benefits.

Promotions to supervisor or foreman are open to linemen and cable splicers.

Points to Consider Before Going into This Field

These are strenuous and demanding jobs, offering a good career to those who enjoy working out-of-doors and working with their hands. Because of the physical nature of the work, however, it is basically a young man's job, and workers are often transferred to less demanding work as they get older. Top physical condition is mandatory, and if you question your stamina, you'd better think twice about such a job.

Because of the physical nature of the work, women have not held these jobs.

See: page 223 for places to write for more details.

Engineering and Science Technology

The Job

Missiles, dishwashers, heart pacemakers, air-conditioning, are but a few of the results of modern technology, a field that is advancing at an explosive rate.

Within the last decade a new occupational group of specialists, known as engineering and science technicians, has been created to meet the needs of our increasingly complex industrial process, and the expansion of research and development.

Most of our technical achievements are due to the efforts of not one person, but a team including engineers, scientists, technicians, and skilled craftsmen.

As an engineering and science technician you will hold the unique position of liaison—the link—between the engineer or scientist and the craftsman. You are the vital tie in this three-way team translating ideas, plans, and specifications of the engineer into practical application which become the working plans the craftsman follows. In short, you turn theory into results.

As a technician you differ from the engineer because your background is more specialized and you use technical skills to support your work, though you may work closely with him through every aspect of the job. You differ from the craftsman, too, because you have scientific and mathematical knowledge and specific education or training in some phase of technology.

Technicians work alongside engineers and scientists in a great variety of industries and at all stages of production—from the origin of the idea to the completion of the project. In many cases technicians perform tasks that would otherwise have to be done by engineers and scientists.

As a technician you can consider yourself the "man Friday" of the technical world. Your training will make you competent to work with the engineer at the design, development, or research level of an industry. You may work on production, operation or control. Or you may be involved in such operations as installation, maintenance, or sales, or a combination of these.

For many jobs you may need to be familiar with one or more skilled trades, though you may not need the ability to perform as a craftsman. Some jobs demand an extensive knowledge of industrial equipment and processes. Others require the use of electronic and mechanical instruments, laboratory apparatus, drafting instruments, and an understanding of tools and machinery. For most jobs you should be able to use handbooks and computing devices like the slide rule or calculating machines.

The fields of work open to the technician are numerous, and the variety of jobs within each field is extensive. For instance, you might work with engineers in building the pilot system for a new chemical or textile process, or help lay out new manufacturing plants and offices to assure the most efficient flow of men, materials and paperwork. You might supervise actual manufacturing operations, or sell specialized equipment to meet a customer's technical requirements. Or, using a scientist's or engineer's design and rough notes, you might draw plans for a control system.

Some 650,000 engineering and science technicians were employed in 1970. (This figure does not include draftsmen and surveyors.) Seven out of ten (almost 460,000) were employed by private industry. Electrical equipment, chemicals, machine, and aerospace were the industries that employed the largest number of technicians. In the nonmanufacturing category the communications industry and engineering and architectural firms employed large numbers also.

The United States federal government employed 85,000 technicians, chiefly as engineering aids and technicians, electronics technicians, equipment specialists, cartographic aids, meteorological technicians, and physical science technicians. The largest number worked for the department of Defense. Most others were employed by the Department of Transportation, Agriculture, Interior and Commerce.

State government agencies employed 50,000, local governments about 12,000 and the remainder were employed by colleges and universities, mostly in university-operated research institutes, and by nonprofit organizations.

Because engineering and science technology is such a broad field and is at the heart of so many industries, as a technician your choice of places of employment is almost limitless. Technicians are used in industries such as air-conditioning, mining, food processing, oil, ceramics and aeronautics, just to mention a few.

Working conditions vary with each industry employing technicians. Generally, however, surroundings are modern, clean and comfortable. Because of the nature of the work, tools and equipment are usually up-to-date and often the best available.

What You Need Personally

You will make a good engineering and science technician if you have the desire to turn ideas and theories into actual results.

You should be creative and resourceful. For although technicians work with scientists and engineers, frequently they work independently.

You should enjoy mathematics and physical science. And you should have a healthy intellectual curiosity combined with the ability to use machinery, although you need not be a craftsman.

You should like people and be able to work with them since you will often supervise the work of others.

One of the most important traits of the technician is the ability to communicate clearly and accurately with scientists, engineers, and shopmen alike. It is this special talent—the ability to translate from theory to working plan that makes the technician so valuable to his society.

What Education and Training You Need

You can study to become an engineering or science technician in a variety of educational institutions, or you can get your training on the job. But most employers look for people who have had some specialized training and today a growing number of jobs require post-high school training.

Formal training is offered in over 500 institutions in the United States. Most of these schools require a high school diploma or its equivalent.

You can study to become a technician at technical institutes (colleges which specialize in engineering technology), junior and community colleges, area technical-vocational schools, and extension divisions of colleges and universities. Courses are also taught in technical and technical-vocational high schools.

Engineering and science and engineering technology programs offer you a planned sequence of college-level courses leading to an associate degree, a certificate, or a diploma in the field of engineering technology. Courses run two to three years, but two years is the most common length of time. (See page 24 for information on the degrees offered.) It is sometimes possible to transfer or go on for a four-year college degree with credit being given for courses you've taken to become a technician. Check this with your school.

You can also qualify for a technician's job through a combination of work experience and formal courses taken part-time in a post-high school or correspondence school, or through training and experience you receive while serving in the armed forces.

Training for some occupations, like tool designing and electronic technology can be obtained through a formal apprenticeship.

Some large corporations conduct training programs to meet their own special needs for technically trained personnel. There are also some special purpose institutions that concentrate on a single field, such as electronics.

Because there is such a wide variety of educational institutions offering technical training today, and such a difference in the level of training offered, you should select your school carefully. The school you choose must be accredited. (See pages 10-14 for more information and pages 77-79 for help in choosing a school.)

You will find that some programs prepare you for a particular service common to many different industries, like instrumentation for example. While other courses of study train you to be a technician in one specific industry, like aviation technology.

These programs, in any case, are "self-contained" or "terminal" meaning they prepare you for immediate employment in specialized fields of industry and science.

Technical institutes offer two- and three-year programs. These are usually designed to prepare you for a specific job or a cluster of related jobs. These programs are highly practical and shorter than four-year professional engineering courses. For while you get intensive training, you get less of the theoretical and general education the engineer gets.

Some of these schools and some junior and community colleges, offer cooperative programs in which you spend part of your time in school and part in employment related to your training.

It may take more than two years to complete this kind of program, but you can finance your tuition expenses this way. Most technical institutes conduct both day and evening sessions and operate all year long as well.

Many junior and community colleges offer two-year technical programs, and often these are planned around the employment needs of the industries in their particular localities.

Area vocational-technical schools are public post-secondary schools, set up in central locations so they can serve students from surrounding areas. Their requirements are usually similar to those of other institutions. They, too, specialize in fields in which technicians are most needed in the area.

Be careful not to confuse an engineering technology program with a pre-engineering program or with a vocational training program. The pre-engineering program is the freshman and sophomore years of the four-year engineering college. It does not offer you the immediate career training provided by the engineering technology program. The vocational training program emphasizes mechanical and manual skills rather than college-level subject matter you will receive in the program designed for the engineering technician.

You should start applying early to particular institutions for catalogues and applications for technology programs because courses vary as well as entrance requirements.

Not everyone can get into technical education programs. You must have taken the proper courses in high school and be judged well qualified for the tough schedule ahead of you.

If possible start early in high school (ideally in the 10th or 11th grade) to take the courses that will best prepare you for a college-level engineering technical program. A typical high school program would include the following: English, at least 3 preferably 4 units; Mathematics, 2 units in algebra and 1 in plane geometry (intermediate algebra and trigonometry are also desirable and sometimes required); Physical science, at least 1 unit in chemistry or physics with laboratory work. Some institutions also require some drafting and electrical or mechanical shop. Mathematics and physical science are the foundation of all branches of engineering technology. You should include as many of these courses as possible.

Because many interested students lack enough preparation for admission, some technical schools offer a pretechnical post-high school program in high school level science, mathematics, and communications arts. You may enter this special program before you are fully accepted into the regular technical course.

For information on state or community schools see your high school counselor. Also, the local office of your state employment service may be able to help you pick your special field through vocational testing.

The cost of your education will vary with your choice of school. It will also depend on whether you live at home or in a dormitory. At some schools, technology programs cost little more than the price of your books and supplies, while some college fees can run as high as $5,000 a year. You can find out about an institution's schedule of fees by sending for its catalogue.

Some colleges charge different fees for local and for out-of-state students, and some charge for special services like student activity fees, medical fees, and laboratory fees. Also at most schools you buy your own books and supplies, though some furnish or rent them.

You can almost always find the means to get an engineering technology education. If you don't think you have enough money to attend the college of your choice, check its catalogue to find out about its financial aid programs and how to apply for help. The catalogue will usually tell you about scholarships and other means of assistance. (See pages, 14-24 for more information on getting financial aid.)

There are several typical aid programs. The straight scholarship requires only that you maintain your marks at a certain level. There are two types of scholarships those awarded on a basis of high school grades, and those awarded to deserving but financially needy students.

A loan is another means of aid. This must usually be paid after graduation, but it will enable you to attend school full time without having to do outside work.

Many schools have cooperative programs under which you may attend school one term and work in industry the next. This plan has the advantage of giving you practical experience in a job related to your schooling. It also builds contacts which might be useful to you after graduation.

Some engineering technology programs offer evening classes, which allows you to carry a full-time job while you go to school. This type of program can take twice as long to complete. Once you complete the course at an accredited school, you will be certified. The Institute for Certification of Engineering Technicians (ICET), sponsored by the National Society of Professional Engineers, certifies engineering technicians in these classifications: associate engineering technician, engineering technician, and senior engineering technician. Many engineering technicians who have been certified by the ICET are members of the American Society of Certified Engineering Technicians, their own professional society.

The Civil Service Commission is revising its standards for classification of engineering technicians. Proposals include acceptance of certification by ICET as evidence of required education and experience. This adds to the evidence that industry, education, and government are placing more importance on the role of the engineering technician in the national economy.

What the Occupation Has to Offer

Opportunities for employment for engineering and science technicians are expected to be excellent throughout the next ten years. The greatest demand will be for graduates of post-high school technical programs.

As a technician you will find the law of supply and demand working in your favor. Government studies show we need five technicians for each engineer (varying slightly for each field), but we are graduating only *one* technician for each engineer, which is resulting in a critical shortage. The Bureau of Labor Statistics indicates that by 1975 the employment demand for technicians will be 1,235,000. At the present rate of graduation, less than 50,000 a year, there will be a shortage of 160,000 technicians by 1975. These figures would indicate that employment opportunities not only exist now, but will increase in the future. These increased needs are the result of industry expansion and the complexity of modern technology. As the number of engineers and scientists grows, the need for technicians increases.

The trend toward automation of industrial processes, as well as the growth of new areas of work like oceanographic exploration, environmental control, and urban development will probably add to present demands for technicians. Growth in research and development expenditures of industry and government are also expected to increase, although at a slower rate than during the 1960s.

Bear in mind, however, that expenditures for defense and space programs will affect the demand for certain types of technical personnel because a large number of technicians are engaged in work related to the defense and space programs.

As a technician your earnings will depend on your education, technical specialty, personal ability, work experience, and the amount of responsibility you are given. The type of company you work for, and its location in the country will also be important factors. However, if you are well trained you can expect a good starting salary as soon as you graduate, and increases as you move to higher positions.

In 1970, starting salaries in industry for technicians with associate degrees ranged from about $6,500 to $8,300. For technicians with responsible positions, salaries averaged about $11,000, with 25 percent earning over $11,900 and some in the $14,000 range. Federal government agencies in 1970 paid beginning engineers between $5,212 and $6,548, depending on the job and the applicant's education.

It has been estimated that a technician can expect to earn about $100,000 more in his lifetime than an untrained or semitrained worker.

Points to Consider Before Going into This Field

One of the advantages of this kind of career is the broad range of opportunities it offers in a wide variety of fields, including private industry, government, education, and the military.

More and more the technician is coming into his own, and his job is being recognized as indispensable. Professional engineering societies, realizing the importance of a well-qualified technician, are concerning themselves with the quality of his education.

The shortage of well-trained men and women in the field and the satisfaction of being a member of a professional group, which is motivated and respected, makes engineering and science technology a rewarding career.

Women should find growing employment opportunities in this field. While most technicians' jobs have traditionally been held by men, these traditions are beginning to break down. In 1968 about 11 percent of all engineering and science technicians were women. The proportion varies with the occupation within a field. At present women work mostly in designing jobs, in chemical and laboratory work, and in computation and other jobs requiring the use of mathematics.

But a recent study of high school seniors found that for three boys with engineering aptitude there were two girls with similar engineering ability, and these women are being encouraged to follow their interests and aptitudes.

For more information, write:

Accrediting Commission for Business Schools
Association of Independent Colleges and Schools
1730 M Street, N.W.
Washington, D.C. 20036
Ask for: Directory of accredited schools.

American Society for Engineering Education
Suite 400
One Dupont Circle
Washington, D.C. 20036
Ask for: *The Engineering Technician*, $.50.

Careers
Washington, D.C. 20202
Ask for: *25 Technical Careers You Can Learn in Two Years or Less.*

Education Division
American Institute of Physics
P. O. Box 617
Stony Brook, New York 17790

Ask for: information on the role physics plays in the education of engineering technicians.

Engineers' Council for Professional Development
345 East 47th Street
New York, New York 10017
Ask for: Directory of accredited schools
New Careers in Engineering Technology, $.25.
Sources of Engineering Technology Career Information, $.25. (Both are especially helpful publications and highly recommended for all technician jobs.)

National Association of Trade and Technical Schools
2021 L Street, N.W.
Washington, D.C. 20009
Ask for: Directory of accredited schools.

National Council of Technical Schools
1835 K Street, N.W.
Washington, D.C. 20006
Ask for: *Directory of Technical Institute Courses* Engineering Technology Careers, Publication No. 1065.

National Home Study Council
1601 18th Street, N.W.
Washington, D.C. 20009
Ask for: Directory of accredited home study or correspondence schools.

Occupational Educational Project
American Association of Community and Junior Colleges
One Dupont Circle
Washington, D.C. 20036
Ask for: *Directory of Accredited Schools.*

Scientific Manpower Commission
2101 Constitution Avenue, N.W.
Washington, D.C. 20418
Ask for: *Search*, science engineering and related career hints, 1971, $1.00.
Test Yourself for Science, booklet to test your interest in various fields of science, $1.00.

U.S. Department of Health, Education and Welfare
Office of Education
Division of Higher Education and/or Division of Vocational and Technical Education
Washington, D.C. 20202
Ask for: information on training opportunities.

Also contact:
For more information about approved schools within your state, ask your state department of education at the state capital.

Aerospace and Aeronautical Technician

The Job

The aerospace/aeronautical industry has captured the imagination of man as no other

field has. The technician can choose from three separate but related areas of work. Space exploration, the newest, includes work not only concerned with manned flight, but also communications satellites and weather.

The second area, air transportation, grows every year as commercial passenger and freight travel continues to rise. The use of private aircraft and the development and use of helicopters adds more jobs.

The last one, development and production of aircraft, spacecraft, and missiles comes under manufacturing. New techniques and equipment make this a highly complex industry, and one that is heavily involved in research and development.

You may choose from a wide variety of positions. For example as an aircraft weights technician you determine the weight and balance of aircraft on the basis of its design and materials. As an aircraft systems test technician you test and evaluate hydraulic, pneumatic, and electrical systems. As a jet power plant technician you operate, inspect, and evaluate power plant equipment.

As you gain more experience you can take on advance positions such as aerodynamics technician. Here you work with engineers using advanced wind tunnels and instrumentation to create standards for safe vehicles.

If you have a flair for writing, the opportunities are excellent in this field. You can outline work to be done, make progress reports, create procedure sheets, reference bulletins, sales and service brochures for men in the field, and make presentations to customers.

Because technical advances in this field are so rapid, laboratories, research and engineering departments, and manufacturing plants are modern, clean, and usually temperature controlled. Tools, equipment, and the material you work with are the most up-to-date.

What Education and Training You Need

In addition to the regular course of study, your program should include such subjects as analytic mechanics, strength of materials, thermodynamics, aerodynamics, aircraft structure, aircraft power plant, and the art of technical expression. (See pp. 229-231 for complete details on the technical education required for entry into this field.)

What the Occupation Has to Offer

The number of jobs available in this field is closely tied to federal spending for space and defense needs. Before you start your training, it would be a good idea to talk with several people in the industry to see what the prospects are expected to be at the particular time you will be looking for a job.

See: Engineering and Science Technology, pages 228-232 for more complete information.

For more information, write:

Office of Public Affairs
National Aeronautics and Space Administration
Washington, D.C. 20546
Ask for: latest publications list and bibliography.

Additional reading:

Levine, Sol. *Your Future in NASA:* New York, Arco. 1971.

Air-Conditioning, Heating and Refrigerating Technician

The Job

Air-conditioning, heating, and refrigeration deal with the control of temperature, humidity, and the circulation and cleanliness of air, which adds up to the control of the environment in which we live. All three grow increasingly important to the modern way of life, and offer a wide range of careers.

These systems require equipment for changing temperature, and duct-work or piping for the distribution of hot or cold air, hot water or steam or refrigerating fluid.

As a technician in this multimillion dollar industry you can become a specialist in one of these three. You can concentrate on research and development, or design layouts for heating, cooling, or refrigerating systems.

In the manufacturing end, you can assist engineers and scientists in research and engineering departments. Or you may be involved in actually designing systems of air-conditioning, heating, or refrigeration for particular offices, homes, or stores and in preparing instructions for installation.

Other typical jobs include devising methods for testing equipment, or analyzing production methods. Or you may be a control specialist, heat-pump specialist, or installation supervisor.

You may also be employed by an equipment manufacturer for sales work. Here you work with contractors who design and install systems, and supply them with information on such things as installation, maintenance, cost of operation and expected performance of equipment.

After you have had enough experience you may wish to become a dealer and contractor yourself, selling, installing, and servicing equipment.

What Education and Training You Need

Air conditioning, heating and refrigeration is a complex technology. You should include in your course of study college algebra, engineering graphics, computer programming, engineering fundamentals, materials processing, the physics of mechanics, geometry, and calculus. (See pages 229-231 for complete details on the technical education required for entry into this field.)

Technical studies should include such subjects as refrigeration, air-conditioning design and application, electric motors and controls, kinetic theory, heat transfer mechanisms and thermodynamics. (See also pages 305-307.)

What the Occupation Has to Offer

Because people prefer comfortable surroundings, temperature control is accepted as standard in most stores, hospitals, theaters, offices, restaurants, and is fact increasing in private homes.

Air transportation as we know it is not possible without environmental control. Precise control is also required for the production of foods, chemicals, drugs, medicines, as well as the manufacture of precision instruments, computers, and components used in aerospace machines, to mention a few.

Refrigeration continues to increase with the growing popularity of frozen foods. The new science of cryogenics is developing rapidly, making medical advances with applications of computer and space technology.

The heating industry grows yearly with the development of new methods and material. As a result of all this, the need for personnel trained in this field is expected to be great.

See: Engineering and Science Technology, pages 228-232 for more complete information.

Architectural Technician

The Job

The profession of architecture is as old as civilization itself. Its first function was utilitarian—shelter and defense. But as civilization has become more complex and more diverse, the architect's work has broadened considerably.

Today, in fact, architecture is not a single discipline, but a blend of many. The architect must be part creative artist, part engineer, and part businessman with a healthy interest in education, political and social science, urban planning—and even data processing.

The great majority of architects are in private practice, often as owners or partners in their own firms. They generally see a project through from start to finish—from the first meeting with the client, through design and working drawings, then on-site supervision while the building is going up. Others work for larger firms, where they have the opportunity to work on a variety of projects over a shorter period of time. Still others work for government agencies, such as the U.S. Army Corps of Engineers. Architects and architectural firms can be found, or are needed, in virtually every U.S. city with a population of 50,000 or more. Some specialize in the design of

certain types of buildings—hospitals, for example, or factories. Most architects will take on projects of almost any size, from a private home or a small school to a giant skyscraper complex or even an entire section of a city.

Nor is architecture confined to the design and construction of buildings. Modern architects concern themselves with transportation systems, recreational facilies, parks, interior design, and the availability of fresh air and clean water for entire urban areas. The architect, in short, is concerned with the total physical environment in which people live, work, and play.

Architecture is a relatively small profession. Somewhat more than 30,000 are practicing in the United States today. Yet because of the increasing diversity and complexity of their work, it is estimated that approximately 127,000 supportive or backup people are needed.

These are the *architectural technicians.*

The range of jobs available to the architectural technician is as broad as the field of architecture itself. The technician may be engaged in the drafting of drawings; in the estimating of job costs; in the search for and acquisition of architectural information; in the preparation of graphic materials—proposals, brochures, displays; in the building of models; in the writing of specifications for a construction job; in the data processing required to plan complex projects; and in the reproduction—via blueprint, photography, and microfilm—of architectural documents.

What You Need Personally

The architectural technician, like the architect himself, must be intelligent. He or she must be concerned and motivated about our physical environment. And they should possess some inherent mathematical, artistic, or manual skill. Architecture is a highly rewarding field, but a demanding one as well. But you must be willing to invest in the time, study, and self-development required.

What Education and Training You Need

In recognition of the growing demand for architectural technicians, the American Institute of Architects (AIA) has proposed a comprehensive program for training people entering the field.

The foundation of the program is a solid high school education, including successful completion of algebra, plane geometry, trigonometry, English, social studies, and physical science.

This is followed by four years of architectural training—two years full-time developing technical skills at a technical or junior college, followed by two years of continuing education and on-the-job training with an architectural firm. You receive an Associate in Applied Science degree.

Once you have the degree, you are equipped for either a paraprofessional job in architecture or transfer to a university for work toward a bachelor's degree.

There are 250 two-year colleges and private vocational schools in every section of the country offering programs in architecture. A graduate technician who successfully meets all the AIA requirements will receive certification. (See pages 229-231 for complete details on the technical education required for entry into this field.)

What the Occupation Has to Offer

It's been estimated that by the year 2000 this country will need twice its present number of homes, factories, and office buildings. Less than thirty years to duplicate 200 years of construction.

That statistic alone should spell out the opportunities available for architectural technicians.

The opportunity exists in every part of the country, in large firms and small, in government bureaus, and in such related fields as construction, landscape architecture, interior design, building supplies, furniture manufacture and engineering.

Through the required employment experience, graduates of the two-year program will have an opportunity to decide if they wish to remain in architecture, or move into other engineering fields.

The technician joining an architectural firm typically will begin at the lower levels of the office, but advancement is limited only by his own ability and motivation. A strong commitment to continuing education is an important ingredient in his success.

A vital point to consider is that this new training program doesn't easily permit its graduates to go on to become full-fledged architects at a later date. Architectural training is considered a terminal program rather than a transfer program. So be sure you want to remain a technician rather than a professional before enrolling in a technician program. If you're not sure, you'd be wise to enroll in a transfer program. If you don't understand the difference, ask your school counselor to explain before you enroll in any institution.

See: Engineering and Science Technology, pages 228-232 for more complete information.

For more information, write:

The American Institute of Architects
1735 New York Avenue, N.W.
Washington, D.C. 20006
Ask for: information on careers as an architectural technician, on the training required, and a directory of two-year colleges offering architectural programs.

Building Construction Engineering Technician

The Job

Building construction engineering technicians deal with the actual construction of houses, stores, shopping complexes, schools, factories, public buildings, as well as other projects. In addition to new construction, they also answer the constant need for upkeep, repair, and modernization of buildings that already exist.

You might work as a foreman, supervisor, superintendent, or inspector. Or you might choose to become a manufacturer's representative and sell construction equipment, building materials, and supplies.

While construction and architectural firms employ the greatest number of technicians in this field, other allied businesses like realtors, lumber dealers, building and loan associations, and property management firms also hire technicians.

You may also want to consider the possibility of eventually owning your own business as a construction contractor, with housing, business, and industrial work open to you.

This field is so broad that occupations within it vary as far as working conditions are concerned. Occupations involving planning are based in an office, although there will be many opportunities for contact with outsiders and trips in the field.

Jobs in construction will demand more physical energy and are subject to weather conditions and occasional overtime. If you like outdoor work, this field should appeal to you.

What You Need Personally

You need imagination and ingenuity for both the indoor and outdoor jobs connected with this field. You should enjoy work that is challenging and is not repetitive.

What Education and Training You Need

You will need to study structure and use of materials, know architectural forms and concepts, and thoroughly understand types of construction. You should be skilled in drafting and be able to read and interpret blueprints easily.

You will need to know office practices, accounting, business systems, and estimating. A knowledge of computer programming will be of value in order to understand "critical path" in construction. (See pp. 229-231 for complete details on the technical education required for entry into this field.)

What the Occupation Has to Offer

Shelter is a necessity of life. If you think of it in relation to our increasing population and its needs, you will understand why building is one of America's largest industries.

The construction industry, unlike others which may concentrate in one area, is nationwide and offers employment nearly everywhere. This includes small rural areas as well as large cities so that you can usually find opportunities in your own community.

The industry is a large, complex, stable and growing one. Population growth and shifts increase this business by creating needs for housing developments, industrial expansion, relocation and urban renewal. Add to this all the reconstruction which goes on yearly due to such things as fire, modernization, modification, upkeep and repairs of existing buildings.

Income varies with the kind of work you do, your experience and the amount of responsibility you are given.

See: Engineering and Science Technology, pages 228-232 for more complete information.

Ceramic Technician

The Job

Ceramic technology is one of the principal fields in the study of materials, their behavior, application, and use. The ceramic technician is concerned with the development of ceramic ma-

terials and their production in commercial quantities at desirable costs. Part of the challenge of this field is the selection of the best material for a specific need.

About 90 percent of the known elements are used to make ceramic products. All of them have the earth as their common origin. But ceramic technology is no longer limited to the combinations of atoms and structures found in nature. Developments in the physics and chemistry of the solid state, applications of heat processes, and the past decade of basic research have given us such things as computer memory cores, miniaturized circuits, components of aircraft, space vehicles, and deep-sea submersibles. They have also given us human bone and teeth replacements, filters to reduce pollution and structural parts for nuclear reactors, among many others.

If you are trained in ceramic technology you can find opportunities in basic research, new product development, technical sales and production and management. (See pp. 229-231 for complete details on the technical education required for entry into this field.)

The universal use of ceramic products makes every major company in the world a potential employer of personnel trained in ceramic technology. The industry itself is growing so rapidly that over one-third of the sales of five years from now will be from products that are not yet available.

See: Engineering and Science Technology, pages 228-232 for more complete information.

For more information, write:

American Ceramic Society
65 Ceramic Drive
Columbus, Ohio 43214

Ask for: *Career Opportunities in Ceramic Engineering* and list of schools offering courses in ceramic technology.

Chemical Technician

The Job

Because the chemical industry supplies raw materials to almost every other industry, it is one of the most rapidly growing fields in the country.

Technicians work mostly with chemists and chemical engineers in the development, production, and sale of chemicals and related products and equipment.

The largest number of technicians are employed in research and development, helping to create new products like fabrics, metals, plastics, alloys, ceramics, fuels, pharmaceuticals, and insecticides.

The industry is so broad that technicians frequently become specialists in one industry, like food processing or in a particular area like quality control.

Technicians make chemical tests of materials to determine whether they meet specifications, or whether certain substances are present, and if so in what quantity.

As a technician you might perform experiments to determine the characteristics of substances such as the specific gravity and ash content of oil. You might analyze steel for carbon, phosphorus, and sulfur content, or water for the amount of silica, iron, and calcium present. In a research or testing laboratory you will use such apparatus and instruments as dilatometers, analytical balances, and centrifuges.

Besides being employed for laboratory work, technicians are sometimes hired to supervise operations in the production of chemical products, and as technical salesmen of chemicals and chemical equipment.

Chemical technicians work in a large number of industries ranging all the way from aerospace to zinc production. Any list would be incomplete, but here are a few of the fields where your technical services would be needed: petroleum refining; automobile manufacturing; power production; criminalistics; publishing; fermentation industries; water and sewage treatment; banking and finance; cosmetics; foods; paints; agriculture; textiles; heavy chemicals; fine chemicals; petrochemicals; explosives; and pest control.

What You Need Personally

You should like the practical aspects of science and mathematics, especially laboratory work. And you should like working with people.

What Education and Training You Need

A typical program for a chemical technician might include twenty-eight units of chemistry core, twenty-four units of related subjects like physics, mathematics, and communications, with emphasis on one field such as chemical engineering, industrial chemistry, materials science, radiation science, biological science or electronics and instrumentation.

Tuition to institutions offering these programs range from no tuition at all to over $1,000 a year. Most employers prefer graduates of two-year chemical technology programs. See pages 229-231 for complete details on the technical education required for entry into this field.

What the Occupation Has to Offer

There are some 70,000 chemical technicians working today. Manpower experts figure we have only half a technician for each science or chemical engineer, where we should have two. With only 600 to 800 graduates a year, there is a shortage of technicians.

The graduate of a chemical technical program can find good employment almost anywhere in the country or abroad if he or she wishes.

Salaries of chemical technicians who have completed a two-year program are excellent, and raises are substantial as you gain experience.

Average starting salaries run between $6,300 and $8,700 a year, but this figure varies depending on the school you attended and the area in which you are working. After eight years of experience, an average graduate was receiving just over $10,000 a year in 1971, but technicians who excel in the field can earn as high as $16,000.

In chemicals you will find that this is one technical specialty that is as much a woman's field as a man's. (One out of eight workers in the entire industry is a woman.)

See: Engineering and Science Technology, pages 228-232 for more complete information.

For more information, write:

American Chemical Society
1155 Sixteenth Street, N.W.
Washington, D.C. 20036
Ask for: *A Different Career in Chemistry*, October, 1968, pp.18 ff. *Career Opportunities in Chemistry*. Chemistry, March 1971, p.18 ff, and ask for a list of colleges offering programs in chemical technology.

Manufacturing Chemists Association
1825 Connecticut Avenue, N.W.
Washington, D.C. 20009
Ask for: *A Bright Future for You as a Chemical Engineer.*

Also contact:

Further information is available from the public relations department of industrial chemical companies.

Civil Engineering Technician

The Job

Civil engineering includes the planning, design, and construction of highways, railroads, bridges, airports, dams, harbor facilities, viaducts, pipelines, and irrigation systems. It is concerned also with control of the flow of water and its uses for flood protection, power generation, and recreation.

Civil engineering is one of the broadest areas in the field of engineering because its work is coordinated with so many other fields. As a technician on a construction project in the planning steps you might help estimate costs, prepare specifications for materials, survey or do designing or drafting work.

In the building stage you might assist a contractor or superintendent in scheduling work

and in inspecting, using blueprints and specifications.

You might work as an estimator, supervisor, photogrammer, preparing maps and charts from aerial photos or a specifications writer. You might assist a city engineer in the layout and construction of streets, sewers, water mains. You might help in planning and zoning, or prepare traffic studies.

As a surveyor you might run lines to establish boundaries and elevations, subdivide land using the transit, level and other surveying instruments or you might prepare maps. As a highway technician you might run surveys, prepare plans and estimates and supervise the construction and maintenance of roads.

Because this is such a broad field, opportunity lies across the entire country, where slum clearance, water shortages, traffic congestion, urban development, waste pollution, among many other problems, need action. There is also opportunity to work abroad, especially in underdeveloped nations.

What You Need Personally

Civil engineering offers the technician interesting job opportunities at every turn. The professional will appeal to you if you are adventurous, have stamina, like outdoor work, physical activity, and travel, sometimes to faraway places.

What Education and Training You Need

As a civil engineering technician you must have a variety of special skills and be trained in special techniques particularly in areas like hydraulics, structures, field surveying, traffic control, computations and the fundamentals of construction. (See pages 229-231 for complete details on the technical education required for entry into this field.)

You should be skilled in the use of surveying instruments, in engineering graphics and in the knowledge of the composition, properties, and use of structural material.

Your studies should stress such subjects as mathematics, physics, chemistry, calculus, surveying, statics and dynamics, soil mechanics, fluid mechanics, elementary structural design and the fundaments of engineering construction. Courses in industrial commerce, business, and economics are necessary. And a knowledge of computer programming is helpful.

What the Occupation Has to Offer

Civil engineering continues to grow as the country grows. With travel at an all-time peak, construction can hardly keep pace with our needs. Development of natural resources adds further to the demand for technicians in this field both here and aborad.

Both income and the chance for advancement in the field are excellent.

See: Engineering and Science Technology, pages 228-232 for more complete information.

Computer Technician

The Job

Computer technology, one of the major fields in electronics engineering, has become so important to industry, science, and to our daily living, that it warrants a category of its own.

A computer is basically an electronic brain which is part of a system composed also of other machines such as high-speed printers and magnetic tapes. Today computers do everything from placing our phone calls to controlling automated factory processes.

As a computer technician your job is to keep these systems, made up of electronic parts and miles of wire, running smoothly. In order to do this you must service machines regularly, oiling, adjusting, and cleaning parts, and checking equipment for loose connections, etc. In case of breakdown, you must know how to find the cause and repair it. You use such things as oscilloscopes, ohmmeters, voltmeters, wirestrippers, pliers, and soldering equipment.

You may also install new machines, test them, and make all adjustments for new customers. After much experience you may wish to specialize in one particular computer system, or even in one model, or in one specific type of repair. This kind of specialization, however, usually requires advanced training.

You will use repair manuals for the equipment you service, and must not only be familiar with them, but must keep up with new information issued from computer manufacturers, too. In this field you may also keep your own books, so to speak, ordering parts, keeping inventory, recording repairs and expenses.

What You Need Personally

In order to be a computer technician you need to have good vision because you work with small parts. And you need normal color perception because wires are color coded. Normal hearing is also a requirement because machine breakdowns are sometimes detected by sound.

A pleasant manner is an asset, as well as the ability to cope with other people, since you will be dealing with customers. Last, but by no means least, you should be resourceful and able to work independently with little or no supervision.

What Education and Training You Need

If you wish to become an electronics technician you should begin in high school to take courses in mathematics and physics. If your high school offers programs in computer programming and electronics you should, of course, take advantage of them. Beyond this, most companies require one or two years in a post-high school course with emphasis on electronics or electrical engineering. Technical institutes or junior colleges offering technical programs are ideal training. Or you may get your training in a computer school. The armed forces also offers a good program in basic electronics.

A trainee who is just beginning, usually spends three to six months in a company training center learning theory, computer mathematics, etc. This is accompanied by on-the-job training which usually spans one to two years.

Even when formal education is finished, whether at a technical institute or in a company school, the experienced computer technician must attend training sessions from time to time to keep abreast of changes and improve skills. Advanced technicians may also want to specialize in such fields as systems analysis or programming. (See pp. 229-231 for complete details on the technical education required for entry into this field.)

What the Occupation Has to Offer

Employment in this field is expected to increase rapidly in the next ten years. It is estimated that there will be some thousand new jobs open annually. Industry, business, and government will be using more and more computers, and it is expected that many new uses will be found for them.

Salaries for computer trainees ranged from about $126 to $145 a week in 1971, while experienced technicians averaged between $205 and $305 a week.

A technician with experience and good ability may advance to become a technical specialist. This work involves more difficult repairs, and sometimes includes involvement with design procedures for maintenance.

A transfer to another company may require retraining and possibly a loss of seniority.

Points to Consider Before Going into This Field

As a computer technician you may have to work overtime and on weekends to make emergency repairs. (Technicians often work on a rotating basis, days one week and nights the next.)

Employers usually offer life and health insurance, sick leave, and retirement plans. They also assume travel expenses and advanced education costs.

See: Engineering and Science Technology, pages 228-231 for more complete information.

For more information, write:

American Federation of Information Processing Societies, Inc.
210 Summit Avenue
Montvale, New Jersey 07645
Ask for: information on careers in computer maintenance.

Institute of Electrical and Electronic Engineers
345 East 47th Street
New York, New York 10017
Ask for: information on careers in computer maintenance.

Also contact:
For further information on training and job opportunities, contact the personnel and service departments of computer manufacturers and other firms employing computer technicians.
See also: pages 212-215.

Draftsman

The Job

An object which is to be produced or manufactured begins as an idea in someone's head. Before it can be produced, detailed drawings are needed that have the exact physical dimensions and specifications of the object and all its parts.

Draftsmen draw these plans, translating the ideas, rough sketches, specifications, and calculations of engineers, architects, and designers into working plans.

As a draftsman you may have to calculate the strength, reliability, and cost of materials. You may have to describe what materials and processes the craftsmen are to use on a particular job.

You will use instruments such as compasses, dividers, protractors, templates, and triangles as well as machines that do combinations of jobs

which other devices do. You may use engineering handbooks, tables, and slide rules to help you solve technical problems. You may also have to translate blueprints into three-dimensional drawings.

Draftsmen are often classified according to the type of work they do or what responsibilities they have. Senior draftsmen use the preliminary information provided by engineers and architects to prepare design layouts (drawings of the object to be built, made to scale).

Detailers make drawings of each part shown on the layout, giving dimensions, material and any other information necessary to make the detailed drawing clear and complete.

Checkers carefully examine drawings for errors in computing or in recording dimensions and specifications. Draftsmen, called tracers, make corrections and prepare drawings for reproduction by tracing them on transparent cloth, paper, or plastic film. The initial job classification will depend on the amount of formal training you have.

An estimated 310,000 draftsmen were employed in 1970. About nine out of ten were employed in private industry. The manufacturing industries that employ large numbers are those making machinery, electrical equipment, transportation equipment, and fabricated metal products. In the nonmanufacturing category, engineering and architectural consulting firms, construction companies, and public utilities employed large numbers.

Over 20,000 draftsmen worked for federal, state, and local governments in 1970. The federal government used the large majority for the departments of Army, Navy, and Air Force. Draftsmen for state and local governments worked mostly for highway and public works departments. Several thousand were employed by colleges and universities and by nonprofit organizations.

What You Need Personally

Drafting work requires good vision, uncorrected or corrected, eye-hand coordination and manual dexterity. You should also have imagination and a certain amount of creative drive.

It is helpful if you have the ability to visualize objects in three dimensions, as well as the ability to do freehand. Although these two are not usually requirements, they are very helpful in some specialized fields.

What Education and Training You Need

In addition, you need a thorough background and knowledge of drafting and design techniques, as well as mathematics and the basic sciences. Since you probably will specialize in a particular field, you should be well versed in the practical aspects of your chosen area. For instance, if you wish to be a mechanical draftsman you will need to study mechanics, shop operations, and the principles of gears, among other things. If you wish to specialize in architectural drafting you should be familiar with the principles of construction, the properties of building materials, wiring, lighting, and heating.

No matter what your specialty, technical training is essential if you are planning a career in drafting technology. The work is so important and complex that companies select with great care the personnel in this field. (See pp. 229-231 for complete details on the technical education required for entry into this field.)

What the Occupation Has to Offer

Employment opportunities are expected to be favorable through the 1970s. Your prospects will be best if you are technically well trained. The employment of draftsmen is expected to rise rapidly as a result of the increasingly complex design problems of modern products and processes. Also, draftsmen will be needed as supporting personnel as engineering and scientific occupations continue to increase. (Photoreproduction of drawings and the use of electronic drafting equipment and computers are eliminating some jobs, however. This situation will probably reduce the need for some less skilled draftsman.)

In private industry, beginning draftsmen earned about $470 a month in 1970 according to a Bureau of Labor Statistics survey. As you gain experience you may move up to a higher level with a substantial increase in earnings, with senior draftsmen averaging about $800 a month. Most earned about $700 a month.

Beginning pay in the federal civil service in 1970 for trainee-draftsmen with a high school education was $380 a month. But for those with technical training or experience salary was higher. The majority of experienced draftsmen working for the federal government earned between $600 and $740 a month.

As you gain skill you can advance to higher positions. You can also become an independent designer. Some draftsmen who take engineering and mathematics courses transfer to engineering positions.

Points to Consider Before Going into This Field

Since draftsmen are on the ground floor, so to speak, they are in a position to gain knowledge and develop skills for advancement to such positions as inspectors, sales engineers, architectural assistants, technical report writers, installation technicians, and supervisors.

Four percent of the draftsmen employed in 1970 were women.

See: Engineering and Science Technology, pages 228-232 for more complete information.

For more information, write:

American Federation of Technical Engineers
1126 16th Street, N.W.
Washington, D.C. 20036.

Drug Technician

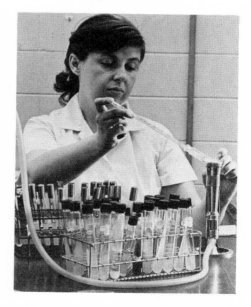

The Job

Twentieth-century science has created a supply of drugs undreamed of in the past. More than 10,000 prescription drugs alone are available to every physician today. The American drug industry spends a higher proportion of its funds for research than any other industry in the country and has risen to a position of worldwide prominence.

A large pharmaceutical firm may test 2,000

substances a year and spend millions of dollars to develop one new drug. But the research has paid off by resulting in the control of many diseases like pneumonia, malaria, cardiovascular disease and even some forms of cancer. Hormones relieve the pain and crippling effects of arthritis and other diseases. Tranquilizers help to reduce the afflictions of mental illness. And vaccines reduce the toll of diseases like polio, whooping cough and measles. The drug industry looks to its scientific and technical personnel to carry out its vast research programs.

About one out of every five employees in the industry is a scientist, engineer or technician, a far greater proportion than in most other industries. While the majority research and develop new drugs, others work to streamline production methods and improve quality control.

Technicians represent over one-fifth of the industry's scientific and technical personnel. Laboratory tests play an important part in the detection and diagnosis of a disease and in the discovery of medicines.

Laboratory technicians perform these tests under the direction of scientists in such areas as bacteriology, microbiology, virology (the study of viruses), cytology (analysis of blood cells) and nuclear medical technology (the use of radioactive isotopes to help detect diseases).

About three-fourths of the industry's workers are employed in six states: New Jersey; New York; Indiana; Pennsylvania; Illinois; and Michigan. Large plants are located in: Indianapolis, Indiana; Chicago, Illinois; Nutley and Rahway, New Jersey; Philadelphia, Pennsylvania; Detroit and Kalamazoo, Michigan; and Pearl River, New York.

Working conditions in drug plants are generally better than in other fields of manufacturing. Because of the danger of contaminating drugs, much emphasis is placed on keeping equipment and work areas clean. Plants are usually air-conditioned, well lighted and quiet. Ventilation systems protect workers from dust, fumes and disagreeable odors.

Special precautions are taken to protect the relatively small number of employees who work with diseased cultures and poisonous chemicals. Most jobs require little physical effort, and the frequency of injuries in drug manufacturing has been about half the average for all manufacturing industries in recent years.

What Education and Training You Need

As a technician in the drug industry you may qualify for your position in a number of ways. Many technicians enter the field with a high school diploma and advance to jobs of greater responsibility after they acquire experience and additional formal education.

However, companies prefer to hire men and women who are graduates of technical institutes or junior colleges, or those who have completed college courses in chemistry, biology, mathematics or engineering.

In many companies, inexperienced workers begin as laboratory helpers performing routine jobs such as cleaning and arranging bottles, test tubes and other equipment.

The experience required for higher levels of technician jobs varies from company to company. Usually one year of experience is required for assistant technician jobs, three years for technicians, six years for senior technicians, and ten years for technical associates. Some companies require senior technicians and technical associates to complete job-related college courses. (See pp. 229-231 for complete details the technical education required for entry into this field.)

What the Occupation Has to Offer

Drug manufacturing employment is expected to grow rapidly through the 1970s. The demand for drug products will be the result of increased population, particularly in the numbers of older people and children. Greater personal incomes, a rise in health consciousness, the growth of hospitalization and medical care programs and the discovery of new drugs will also add to this demand.

While the industry's employment will not increase as rapidly as the demand for drugs because of improved methods of production, the need for technicians will increase faster than many other occupational groups in this field because of the continued growth in research and development.

The following tabulations, based on information from one of the country's largest drug manufacturers in 1969, will give you some ranges in weekly earnings for technicians: beginning technicians, $111 to $158.77; laboratory technician I, $116.77 to $168.69; laboratory technician II, $123.69 to $193.15; laboratory technician III, $130.62 to $215.31; technical associate, $130.62 to $241.15.

Points to Consider Before Going into This Field

Many employees work in plants that operate around the clock, three shifts a day, seven days a week. In most plants workers receive extra pay when assigned to second or third shifts. They receive premium pay for working over 40 hours a week. And most of the industry's workers have year-round employment because the field is not seasonal.

Paid vacations and holidays are common, and most workers receive insurance and pension benefits, paid in part by their employers. These benefits include life, sickness, accident, hospitalization and surgical insurance. Employee stock purchase plans are in effect in many firms.

See: Engineering and Science Technology, pages 228-232 for more complete information.

For more information, write:

National Pharmaceutical Council, Inc.
1030 15th Street, N.W.
Washington, D.C. 20005
Ask for: information on careers in drug technology.

Pharmaceutical Manufacturers Association
1155 Fifteenth Street, N.W.
Washington, D.C. 20005
Ask for: information on careers in drug technology.

For further information contact the personnel departments of drug manufacturing companies and ask for information on careers in drug technology.

Electronics Engineering Techician

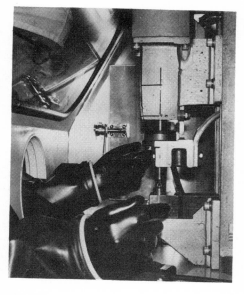

The Job

Electronics engineering technology is a new science which has created one of the giants of industry. Radio, television, radar, sonar, missile and spacecraft guidance, and computers are just a few of the fields it encompasses.

The solid-state transistor is another major achievement in this age of electronics. So are tunnel diodes, thin-film memories, electron microscopes, ultrasonic oscillators, super-conductors, all magnetic circuitry, and facsimile transmitters. Electronic systems and instruments have opened new eras in therapy, and in medical treatment and research.

In electronic controls, electronic switching, telemetering, servo systems, computers, etc., mechanical devices are combined with electronic circuitry to perform at amazing speeds. This area of specialization requires a combination of electronic and mechanical skills.

Electronics is altering methods of business and industry, and has opened up whole new fields in science and education. The computer alone is making daily changes in our lives, doing everything from controlling automated processes in industry, to issuing your bank statement.

Because this field is so broad, technicians usually become specialists in one area, for instance communications. Often they go further and specialize in a subdivision of the area, like radio or television. They may also specialize in a particular aspect of industrial electronics, for instance induction or dielectric heating, servomechanisms, automation controls, or ultrasonics.

As an electronics engineering technician your specialty will be solving problems, particularly those related to design, production, maintenance, installation, or servicing of electronic equipment.

You may convey a design engineer's ideas into preliminary "breadboard" or trial models that will be evaluated before the final design is made and production begins. Or you may debug each unit during the final assembly and checkout stage.

Field engineering was once the job of the graduate engineer. Today, as a technician, you may perform this function, installing complicated instrumentation systems and making them work. You may also serve as technical sales or field representative for a manufacturer. Or you may work as a technical writer, preparing service manuals and reference materials.

When a malfunction occurs in data processing equipment, you may be the troubleshooter who isolates the problem and corrects it to minimize a customer's loss of time. You may operate, maintain, and troubleshoot the complicated communications equipment in a TV or radio station. Or you may work as a serviceman for home entertainment equipment such as radio and television receivers, sound systems, and tape recorders.

Any field which does not include electronics today, will probably do so in the near future. As an electronics technician you may be employed anywhere around the world installing, operating, and maintaining equipment from computers to TV broadcasting and receiving units. You may help develop products used in aerospace programs, medical research, automated manufacturing processes, electronic data processing, television, appliances and in fact practically anything that contains a transistor or has a button to push. The field is almost limitless in regard to places where you may be employed. It includes everything from industrial plants, broadcast studios, and research laboratories, to missile launching sites.

What Education and Training You Need

The course designed for the electronics technician usually tries to give the student practical electronics know-how and mathematical ability to develop, for instance, electronic circuits common to instrumentation, servomechanisms, automation systems, and television receivers. Mathematics and circuit calculations are usually stressed too.

Advances in electronics are rapid and complex, requiring a great deal of know-how from the electronics technician. A sound grounding in the fundamentals of this technology is a must. As a prospective student you would do well to investigate the academic standing and industry recognition of any school you are considering before you enroll. (See pp. 229-231 for complete details on the technical education required for entry into this field.)

What the Occupation Has to Offer

Electronic applications have progressed at a rate which few other branches of applied science can equal, and more skilled engineering technicians are needed in every phase of this field. The law of supply and demand will work in your favor, whether you are a man or a woman. You'll find jobs waiting for you if you are a qualified graduate of an accredited school.

See: Engineering and Science Technology, pages 228-232 for more complete information.
See also: Computer Technician, pp. 239-240; Data Processing, pp. 212-215; and Electronics Manufacturing, pp. 220-222.

Fluid Power Engineering Technician

The Job

Fluid power is used to push, pull, rotate, regulate or drive the mechanisms of modern life, by generating, controlling, and applying smooth, effective power of pumped and compressed fluids like oil and water.

French scientist Blaise Pascal was the first to demonstrate that pressure exerted anywhere on a confined fluid is transmitted, undiminished, in all directions, acting with equal force on all equal areas. The principles of fluid mechanics resulted in the development of industrial hydraulics, industrial pneumatics, and similar technologies.

With World War II, a new dynamic or "systems" approach evolved, and fluid power be-

came a new and promising field of engineering technology. Fluid power products range all the way from highly sophisticated servo-controlled drives to packings. They include such things as high pressure piston pumps, cylinders, control valving for air and liquid applications, and van and gear pumps.

Fluid power has made the modern construction equipment industry possible. Power transmission and control problems of machinery like power shovels, dump trucks, and self-loading scrapers would have been difficult to solve without fluid power.

Machinery and machine tool industries also use fluid power. Electro-hydraulic servosystems are used on mill and lathe tracers. Fluid power techniques have been applied in many clamping devices, transfer devices used for loading or unloading machines, feed mechanisms, and air motor drives, as well as in bailing presses, die casting, and injection molding machines.

The principles of fluid power are found in many industrial areas, insuring the smooth functioning of billions of dollars worth of appliances, equipment, and machines in manufacturing, national defense, building projects, transportation, agriculture, and even in peoples homes and garages.

As a technician in this field you might work as a laboratory technician, production supervisor, field service technician, or design and development technician.

As a design technician, for instance, you would sketch designs and prepare drawings for the development of fluid components and systems. In field service you would install and maintain fluid power systems or serve as a manufacturer's representative. You might also work as a fluid power technician, inspecting, operating and servicing fluid power equipment in various industrial applications. With added experience you might become a laboratory supervisor or a research technician.

What Education and Training You Need

If you wish to specialize in fluid power technology, your studies will include fluid mechanics, circuit analysis, industrial pneumatics, hydraulic components, hydraulic circuits, analytical techniques in fluid power, advanced hydraulic circuits, and systems and problems in fluid power. (See pp. 229-231 for complete details on the technical education required for entry into this field.)

What the Occupation Has to Offer

The needs of the nation for more power and increased production, with reduced costs and less waste, require greater use of fluid power. Continuing advances and refinements in automation and design simplifications will lead to the development of new applications for fluid power. As a result, the demand for fluid power technicians to fulfill specialized jobs in research, development, testing, production, and operation is increasing.

See: Engineering and Science Technology, pages 228-232 for more complete information.

Food Processing Technician

The Job

Almost all of the food we eat today is processed by industrial companies. Food processing technicians are a small but important group employed by these firms.

As a technician you may assist food scientists

in research and development, and in the quality assurance laboratories of these plants. Or you may work as an assistant supervisor in operations related to production, such as processing, packaging, and sanitary maintenance and waste disposal.

As a technician your title may vary from plant to plant and responsibilities may overlap within these positions, depending on where you work. You may be a laboratory or quality assurance technician, a physical science aide, a plant facilities technician, a biological aide, a laboratory analyst or a research and development technician.

In research and development you assist food scientists in improving food products, creating new ones and developing and improving processes which are part of the production. Your duties might include such things as weighing out ingredients, doing microbiological tests and chemical analysis. You might also set up panels for organoleptic tests that judge taste, smell, and sight.

You also gather and store samples for testing, operate and maintain laboratory equipment, and experiment with new methods for testing. You may be required to make formal reports on experiments, tests, and other projects. You use such instruments as balances, spectrophotometers (to measure color intensity), autoclaves (to sterilize), microscopes and cryoscopes (to determine the freezing point of liquids.)

In the quality assurance laboratory you conduct chemical, physical, and bacteriological tests on raw ingredients and on finished products to make sure they conform to government and industry standards. You may also make brand comparisons, fill sample orders, check samples which are received against product reports or shipping manifests. You use equipment such as incubators, refractometers (to measure heat), centrifuges (to separate particles of substances), torsion balances, color comparison charts and pH meters (to determine the degree of acidity).

In production operations you assist in the supervision of the overall processing of food production. You work with fieldmen to make sure you have a steady flow of products from the farm to the plant. You inspect raw materials to make sure they are suitable for processing and that they are stored under the right temperatures.

You may also recommend ways to improve production methods, performance of equipment, and quality of the product, or ways to increase efficiency through working conditions.

You may supervise packaging; or be involved with sanitation in all areas of the plant. You may identify bacterial problems on the line or elsewhere in the plant, recommend solutions, and direct cleaning crews.

About 3,400 food processing technicians were employed in the food processing industry in

1970. They are employed in most states and by all major food industries. The states which employ the largest number of technicians are those that have the heaviest concentration of food processing workers. They are California, Illinois, Pennsylvania, Texas, Ohio, New Jersey, Wisconsin, Michigan, Iowa, and New York.

Technicians are also employed by state and federal government food inspection agencies, food brokers, and supermarket chains. And some work in related businesses where their specialized training is needed, such as food packaging companies, food warehousing and transportation companies and manufacturers of food processing equipment.

What You Need Personally

Because the quality of processed food may affect many people, you should be a person who can work to exacting standards, and one who is dependable. You should be able to get along with and work well with other people because the food processing technician usually works as part of a team.

What Education and Training You Need

Post-high school technical training is required for a growing number of food processing technician jobs. Laboratory technicians in the dairy industry must meet licensing requirements in most states. These vary, but generally they include a written test. Some states require that you demonstrate your capabilities.

To prepare for study at a technical institute, you should begin in high school by taking one year each of biology and chemistry. English and social science are also important. (Some post-high school institutions, however, will admit you on the basis of successful work experience in the food industry and on the recommendation of your employer.)

In a technical institute a typical course would include chemistry, microbiology, mathematics, and specialized courses in food processing, quality control, packaging, plant and environmental sanitation, and technical report writing. Accounting, economics, and English may be offered as elective courses.

Curriculums vary among schools offering food science technology programs. Some are geared toward an individual food processing industry, like the dairy industry. Many two-year programs require work experience between the first and second years.

Many students from various fields of science who have not completed all the requirements for a bachelor's degree are able to qualify as technicians in this field after they get some additional technical training and experience. (See pages 229-231 for complete details on technical education required for entry into this field.)

What the Occupation Has to Offer

Employment opportunities for the food processing technician are expected to be favorable through the 1970s, with the highest demand for graduates of post-high school technical training programs.

The demand for technicians is caused partly by the public's desire for more convenience foods, and the need for this type of product by food service companies. Also, the complexity of new food products and the processes which they require all create the need for more technicians to assist food scientists and management personnel in areas like production planning, technical sales work, and warehouse management. As quality and safety standards rise, the need for technicians will be critical in quality assurance areas. Also many smaller processing firms that have not used the aid of technicians before, are expected to require their services in the future.

A technician's earnings generally depend on his or her education, ability, and experience. The type of firm you work for, your duties, and geographic location will be factors.

Government statistics, based on limited data, set salaries for beginning food processing technicians at $7,000 in 1970.

As a technician you can look forward to an increase in your earnings as you gain experience and advance to higher positions. You may begin your career at a lower level supervisory job and, depending on training, ability, and experience you can work up to the mid-management level. As a food technician in a laboratory you may be assigned more demanding jobs as you gain experience and may advance to other positions such as salesman, purchasing agent, or fieldman.

See: Engineering and Science Technology, pages 228-232 for more complete information.

Industrial Engineering Technician

The Job

As industry grows more complex the smooth flow of men, materials, and products becomes more important. Industrial technicians (also called production technicians) assist engineers on all problems involving efficient use of manpower, materials, and machines they use in mass production.

In your work as a technician you might prepare layouts of machinery and equipment, plan work flow, and make analyses of production costs to eliminate unnecessary expense. You might assist in time and motion studies, which lead to changes in tools and equipment and the organization of operations.

As a production planner you would make

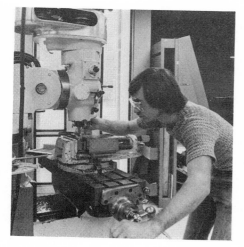

schedules, estimate rate and cost of production, maintain production cost, and control record systems.

In your field you must know how to eliminate waste in motion and materials, control quality, evaluate jobs and personnel requirements, and in general oversee all the operations that allow men and machines to operate efficiently and profitably.

Your work will bring you in contact with people from all phases of manufacturing—from executives and engineers to on-the-job workers. Here you will need to combine your technical training with your ability to deal in human relations.

The experience you gain can equip you to specialize later on in such fields as industrial safety, materials handling, setting job standards, or interviewing, testing, and training personnel.

What You Need Personally

If you want to be an industrial engineering technician you should have a sound aptitude for mathematics, drawing, and science. You should be interested in efficiency, in quality and cost control, and in personnel.

You should be able to express yourself in writing as well as orally. And you should be able to deal with groups of people, as well as individuals, at all levels of industry.

What Education and Training You Need

Industrial engineering technicians are offered subjects like statistics and quality control, budgeting and accounting, time and motion study, process and production planning, linear programming, plant layout and materials handling, operations research, and industrial engineering. You should include some social science and industrial psychology in your course of study.

(See pp. 229-231 for complete details on the technical education required for entry into this field.)

See: Engineering and Science Technology, pages 228-232 for more complete information.

Instrumentation Technician

The Job

Instrumentation technology grew out of the introduction of more and more automatic controls and precision measuring devices in manufacturing operations. In industrial plants and laboratories, instruments are used to record data, to control and regulate the operation of machinery, and to measure time, weight, temperature, speeds of moving parts, mixtures, volume, flow, strain, and pressure.

Technicians with special training in instrumentation or training chiefly in electronics, mechanics or hydraulics, work with the engineers and scientists who develop these complex devices, and with those who use them for research and development.

What Education and Training You Need

See pp. 229-231 for complete details on the technical education required for entry into this field.

What the Occupation Has to Offer

Because instruments and controls are the tools of automation, the demand for trained technicians increases as more manufacturing processes are done automatically.

Automatic measuring instruments and allied control devices are found in every phase of business, industry, and defense. Just a few of the

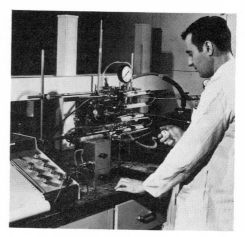

fields in which you could find employment as an instrumentation technician would include aviation, pulp- and paper-making, oil refining, food processing, flood control, development of atomic energy, meteorology, metals processing, and sugar refining.

See: Engineering and Science Technology, pages 228-232 for more complete information.

Mechanical Engineering Technician

The Job

Mechanical engineering technology is the applied science of designing, producing, testing, installing, and operating machines, equipment, instruments, and devices. This broad field covers many other technologies such as automotive, diesel, tool design, machine design, and production design.

It involves the tooling required to manufacture a product economically. Also it involves machines operated by steam, gas, or electricity, and machines that use power or produce power from coal, gas, oil, or nuclear fuels.

As a mechanical technician you will be trained to visualize data from blueprints, diagrams, or even sketches and verbal information, in two- or three-dimensional forms.

You may assist an engineering team in decisions involving design, materials, tooling and fabrication methods for a particular project. Or you may test the performance and endurance of mechanically or electrically propelled devices, and determine weight, stress and strain of components. In this instance you might select, arrange, and connect as well as calibrate your test equipment and measuring instruments. After this, you might record your results and prepare a test report.

You might be an estimator, computing the cost of labor, material, equipment and installation in preparing bids for metal fabrication and steel work. Or, with some experience you might work as a die designer, or a metals-processing technician, specifying methods of processing metals for the best design results. Or you might work as an equipment or machinery salesman, selling complex machine tools and other large pieces of equipment, using your technical knowledge to best serve your customers.

A better known specialty, often included under mechanical engineering is tool designing. In this field you design tools and devices for the mass production of manufactured articles. You make sketches of the designs for cutting tools, jigs, dies, special fixtures and other attachments used in machine operations. You may also make the detailed drawings, or supervise others in making them. You also redesign tools to make them more efficient.

Mechanical engineering technology figures heavily in industrial plants and manufacturing concerns of every size and type in the country. And many of these companies and corporations have overseas plants.

What Education and Training You Need

Other than a well-rounded preparation in engineering fundamentals, other special subjects might include mechanics, power systems, materials circuits, and industrial organization. (See pp. 229-231 for complete details on the technical education required for entry into this field.)

What the Occupation Has to Offer

The aptitude and training of a mechanical technician usually covers a wide variety of skills and talents, keeping him or her in demand in our increasingly complex industrial setup. Skills in this field are required to make everything from mechanical pencils to missiles, and from nuts and bolts to cars and ships.

See: Engineering and Science Technology, pages 228-232 for more complete information.

Metallurgical Engineering Technician

The Job

Metal is the essential working substance of modern industry. Metallurgical engineering technology is concerned with the processing and production, the physical properties, and the use of metals and alloys. It involves the study of why metals and other materials behave as they do, how their behavior is affected by environment and how it can be changed.

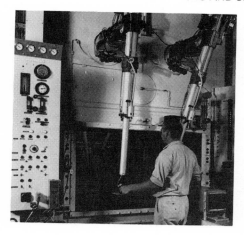

The technician in this field studies what materials are made of all the way down to the atom. He finds out how these atoms are made to assume definite positions in a crystalline structure, and how individual crystals are built up to form the final shape. He learns what changes in structure will affect the behavior. He uses forces such as heat and pressure to re-form material to suit requirements. His field can range from the production of 200-ton castings down to the growth of a single crystal "whisker." He is the one on whom all the other technologies rely to furnish them with the materials they need.

Technicians perform a wide variety of functions depending on whether they are working in areas of research or manufacturing and depending upon the industry in which they are employed. As a technician you may test the mechanical properties of materials, make chemical and spectrographic analyses of material, develop manufacturing processes, examine and photograph the microscopic structure of materials by use of optical and electron microscopes, make X-ray analyses, make calculations and write reports, to mention just a few.

As a technician you will find employment in plants, in foundries, in metallurgical control laboratories and in research and development laboratories.

The metalworking industry employs by far the largest number of people in metallurgical technology. Other employers include: automotive and mechanical equipment; electrical machinery and equipment; aerospace and components; chemical, drugs, and allied products; electronics and instruments; petroleum and allied products; and construction and building materials. Although these are the larger employers, this technology is used in almost every industry including food, paper, marine, and utility industries, etc.

What You Need Personally

In order to best succeed in this field you should be able to reason clearly and understand abstract ideas. You should be alert and observing with a good memory and a relatively long span of attention. Originality and inventiveness are also helpful.

What Education and Training You Need

Like the other technologies, the complexities of metallurgy require a good deal of technical training. Essential courses include subjects like mathematics, chemistry, physics, engineering graphics, engineering fundamentals, and materials processing. Special technical courses might include such subjects as physical metallurgy, heat treating, metallurgical design, nonferrous metallurgy, welding and foundry work. Courses in speech, social science and industrial organization might also be included. (See pp. 229-231 for complete details on the technical education required for entry into this field.)

What the Occupation Has to Offer

Metallurgical engineering technicians are in great demand and short supply. More than 2,000 new technicians trained in materials technology are needed every year.

Metalworking is by far the largest industry in the nation. It accounts for nearly half of all manufacturing activities in the country, and more significantly, it is growing. In 1967 sales amounted to $115 billion. It is estimated that by 1980 sales will exceed $300 billion. The tremendous size and scope of this field means you can work in almost any type of plant, on almost any type of product, in almost any geographic area.

Points to Consider Before Going into This Field

There are many metallurgical and materials engineering functions well suited to the talents of both women and men. Metallurgy is more and more becoming an air-conditioned office or laboratory-type profession. Women have demonstrated excellence in many areas of metallurgy and materials science. Opportunities here are many and varied for anyone who is interested in this type of work.

See: Engineering and Science Technology, pages 228-232 for more complete information.

For more information, write:

Office of Career Development
American Society for Metals
Metals Park, Ohio 44073
Ask for: information on careers in metallurgy.

Nuclear Atomic Technician

The Job

Atomic energy, that source of tremendous heat and radiation that made the atomic bomb a reality, is more and more being utilized for peaceful purposes. This energy, more accurately called nuclear energy, may be produced through several processes, but the most important are fission and fusion.

Fission is the splitting of the uranium or plutonium nucleus under neutron bombardment. When neutrons emitted from this fission process bombard other nuclei, further fission takes place, and under proper conditions results in a "chain" reaction. This reaction liberates energy which, if controlled, can be converted into useful power.

In fusion, energy is released by combining the nuclei of two light atoms into a heavier atom. The detonation of atomic bombs is an application of the explosive release of enormous amounts of atomic energy. For applications other than for weapons, the release of energy must be carefully controlled so that it proceeds at a manageable rate.

Controlled fission is the essential feature of a nuclear reactor. The reactor, which is a furnace, requires fuel to operate. The principal source for reactor fuel is uranium 235.

The federal government supports most of the basic atomic energy activities, with the Atomic Energy Commission (AEC) directing its atomic energy programs, and regulating the use of nuclear materials by private organizations.

AEC-owned laboratories, uranium processing plants, nuclear reactors and weapons manufacturing plants are contracted with private organizations. In their own installations, private firms are engaged in many types of atomic energy activities, except development and production of military weapons and certain nuclear fuel processing operations.

A great deal of research and development is done in this field, much of it by AEC-owned laboratories and by universities and colleges, other nonprofit organizations, and industrial firms under AEC contracts.

Much research and industrial work is required for the production and application of this energy. Industrial processes include: mining; milling and refining uranium-bearing ore; production of nuclear fuels; manufacture of nuclear reactors, components, and nuclear instruments; production of special materials for use in reactors; design, engineering and construction of nuclear facilities; operation and maintenance of nuclear reactors; disposal of radioactive wastes; processing and packaging of radioisotopes; production of nuclear weapons; and research and development work.

All of these activities are carried on in plants in several different industries, as well as in laboratories. Much of the work (like mining, manufacture of heat transfer equipment and construction of facilities) is similar to nonatomic engineering work. Other work, such as manufacture of the fuels needed to run reactors, is unique to this field.

There are more engineers, scientists, technicians, and craftsmen in this field than in most others because much of the work is still in the research and development stage.

A large number of technicians assist in this research as well as in designing and testing equipment and materials. They include draftsmen, electronics, instrument, chemical and other engineering and physical science technicians, and radiation monitors.

As a technician in this highly specialized field you may work in radiation safety, radiation instrumentation, reactor operations and controls, instrument repair and maintenance, or in a chemical laboratory.

The jobs are many and varied. You may engage in anything from stacking lead bricks around a source of radiation in order to form a protective shield, to performing medical therapy for treatment of diseases with radiation and radioisotopes.

As a radiation monitor (also called a health-physics technician) you usually work under the supervision of a health physicist. You employ special instruments to monitor work areas and equipment to detect radioactive contamination. You take soil, water, and air samples frequently to determine the radiation level. You might also collect and analyze the radiation detectors worn by other workers.

You inform your supervisor when a worker's exposure to radiation approaches the maximum limit, and you recommend work stoppage in potentially unsafe areas. You calculate the amount of time personnel may work in contaminated areas. In addition you may give instruction in radiation safety procedures, and prescribe special clothing for workers entering radiation zones.

As a hot-cell technician you operate remote-controlled equipment to test radioactive materials that are placed in hot cells. (These are rooms enclosed with radiation shielding materials, such as lead and concrete.) You perform standard chemical and metallurgical operations with radioactive materials by controlling "slave manipulators" (mechanical devices that act as a pair of arms and hands) from outside the cell, and observing through the cell window. The above are just a few of the jobs open to you.

More than half of all the workers in nuclear energy are employed in government-owned facilities.

The working conditions in instrument and auxiliary equipment manufacturing, in uranium mining and milling, and in facilities construction are similar to those in nonnuclear energy activities—except for the radiation safety precautions which must be taken. In other activities, in which the major portion of personnel is employed, conditions are very good. Buildings are well lighted and ventilated. Equipment is modern, and often the most advanced of its kind. Only a small portion of employees work in areas where direct radiation hazards exist. In these areas shielding, automatic alarm systems, and clothing give ample protection to workers. In some instances, plants are located in remote areas.

Extensive safeguards and operating practices ensure the health and safety of workers and the AEC and its contractors have an excellent safety record. The AEC inspects nuclear facilities to insure compliance with their safety requirements, and continuing effort is made to provide better standards.

What You Need Personally

Nuclear technology is an exacting field. In order to succeed in it you should be able to follow directions to the letter. You should have manual dexterity and be well coordinated in general. You should be a person who gives attention to detail for your work will probably require precision. You should be a generally careful person since, even though radiation is controlled under strict safety regulations, a nuclear laboratory contains equipment which is highly complicated, often fragile, and sometimes dangerous as in the case of high voltage amplifiers.

What Education and Training You Need

In addition to a sound technical background including mathematics, physics, chemistry, electronics, and electrical circuits and machines, special subjects might include nuclear physics and instrumentation, radioisotopes and reactor principles, thermodynamics, and physical metallurgy.

Another candidate for a technical position in this field might be the student with one or two years of college background in engineering and science.

A good deal of on-the-job training is necessary in this field because different specialized techniques are required for different projects. A solid technical education will make the technician more versatile in moving from assignment to assignment.

The Atomic Energy Commission, at its contractor-operated facilities, supports on-the-job and specialized training programs to help prepare technicians for this field.

Some jobs, like radiation monitor, require a high school education with emphasis on special subjects, in this case mathematics, physics and chemistry, plus on-the-job training. The hot-cell technician has the same requirements, with emphasis on mechanical experience. (See pages 229-231 for complete details on the technical education required for entry into this field.)

What the Occupation Has to Offer

Employment opportunities for trained nuclear technician is expected to be very good through the 1970s. Increased use of nuclear reactors in electric power generating stations, expansion of the "Plowshare" program to develop peaceful uses for nuclear explosive, in programs, to further develop radioisotope technology are a few of the contributing factors. Use of nuclear reactors for propulsion of surface ships is also growing. And the reactors are being used in conjunction with such projects as desalting sea water.

Earnings vary widely with the employer and the background and training of the technician. Base pay ranges from about $5,600 to $9,800 annually. But these are only averages. A technician's salary advances according to increased skill and top pay can go much higher.

Points to Consider Before Going into This Field

Many large organizations offer technicians the opportunity to study for degrees in engineering or science if they wish to continue their education.

If you handle classified data (restricted for reasons of national security) or if you work on classified projects in the nuclear energy field, you must have a security clearance, based on an investigation of your character, loyalty, and associations.

Physical strength is not required in the field of nuclear technology. Although fewer women than men are employed, the field has good possibilities for women and most organizations are willing to hire them.

See: Engineering and Science Technology, pages 228-232 for more complete information.

For more information, write:

Department of Human Resources Development
Mail Control Unit
800 Capitol Mall
Sacramento, California 95814
Ask for: *Nuclear Technician* No. 379, Free.

Division of Nuclear Education and Training
U.S. Atomic Energy Commission
Washington, D.C. 20545
Ask for: *Careers in Atomic Energy. Educational Programs and Facilities in Nuclear Science and Engineering. Nuclear Engineering in Your Future.*

Division of Personnel
U.S. Atomic Energy Commission
Washington, D.C. 20545
Ask for: *Opportunities for Challenging Careers.*

Edison Electric Institute
90 Park Avenue
New York, New York 10016
Ask for: information on careers as a nuclear technician.

Ocean Technician

The Job

Oceanography is the scientific study of all aspects of the oceans, their boundaries and their contents, according to the National Academy of Science. While it is still a relatively small field,

the vast untapped resources of the seas make it a natural area for future research and development.

The search for off-shore oil, improvement of harbors, prevention of pollution, underseas exploration to study tides and currents, or the development of sea fauna and flora to feed the hungry are only a few of the fields in this science.

As an ocean technician you might collect sea samples, analyze them, conduct various tests, monitor equipment or work in a hatchery tending fish or shellfish, among many other things.

A number of government agencies employ civilians in a variety of oceanographic or marine-related jobs. They are The Naval Oceanographic Office, and the Coast and Geodetic Survey (both of the federal government's Environmental Science Services Administration (ESSA); Office of Naval Research; Bureau of Commercial Fisheries; the Coast Guard; the Maritime Administration; and the Geological Survey of the Department of the Interior. Some districts of the Army Corps of Engineers, and the Corps' Coastal Engineering Research Center also employ marine specialists.

Many leading firms have oceanographic divisions, including some involved in aerospace. And a few, like Ocean Science and Engineering located near Washington, D.C., and Alpine Geophysical in New Jersey, are involved mostly with ocean developments.

What Education and Training You Need

If you are planning a career as an ocean technician you should include as much math and science in your high school course as possible.

In anticipation of the country's future need for ocean engineers and technicians, Congress created the National Sea Grant Program which, among other things has partly financed the University of Rhode Island's Marine Affairs program. (See pp. 229-231 for complete details on the technical education required for entry into this field.)

What the Occupation Has to Offer

Though this field is a small one at present, it is generally agreed that its possibilities for the future are unlimited. Mining and aquaculture (a kind of farming under the sea in which fish are raised, pastured in fertile areas, and rounded up for market, among other things) are two of the experiments going on right now which may create whole new industries and new resources for mankind.

A recent survey shows a present need for three technicians for each ocean scientist.

As a technician you can expect a salary anywhere from $450 to $500 up to $1,000 a month depending on your specialty, schooling, and experience.

Points to Consider Before Going into This Field

If you are considering this field it might be wise to remember that collecting data is often a repetitive job. In addition, most research vessels are small and quarters can be cramped, especially on an extended cruise. These points may be overridden, however, by the anticipation of new discoveries, and the sense of accomplishment which can accompany this kind of work.

See: Engineering and Science Technology, pages 228-232 for more complete information.

For more information, write:

International Oceanographic Foundation
10 Rickenbacker Causeway
Miami, Florida 33149
Ask for: *Training and Careers in Marine Science.*

Marine Technology Society
1730 M Street, N.W.
Washington, D.C. 20036
Ask for: Pennington, Howard, *The New Ocean Explorers*, $5.95. *The Oceans and You*, $3.00.

National Oceanography Association
1900 L Street, N.W.
Washington, D.C. 20036
Ask for: career information (free), schools which offer courses (free), scholarships and grants ($.50). Enclose stamped, self-addressed large envelope with request.

Vocational Guidance Manuals
235 E. 45th Street
New York, New York 10017
Ask for: *Opportunities in Oceanographic Careers*, $1.95.

Paper Technician

The Job

The paper industry, producing many different kinds of papers and paperboard products, is highly mechanized. Manufacturing plants are engaged in one or more of three different operations. They are the production of pulp (the basic ingredient of paper) from wood, reused fibers, or other raw materials; the manufacture of paper or paperboard (thick paper) from pulp; or the conversion of rolls of paper or paperboard into other products.

Because of the complex processes and equipment used, this industry employs many professional and technical workers. Testing is a typical job of a paper technician, and it carries such titles as laboratory technician, paper tester, pulp tester, paper inspector, and chemical analyst.

Under these titles you would work in the plant laboratory, using chemicals and testing equipment. You might assist professional engineers and chemists in research and development

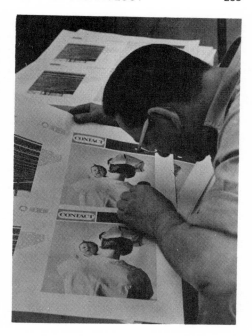

activities. Depending on your education and experience you might perform anything from simple routine tests to highly skilled technical or analytical work.

Workers in this industry are located throughout the country, but about half are employed in the following eight states: New York, Pennsylvania, Ohio, Illinois, Wisconsin, Massachusetts, New Jersey, and California.

Most pulp and papermaking jobs do not require strenuous physical effort. Some employees, however, work in hot, humid, and noisy areas. They may also be exposed to disagreeable odors from chemicals used in the papermaking process. However, pulp and papermaking companies have made intensive efforts recently to improve working conditions.

What Education and Training You Need

It should be noted that in this field while generally no specialized education is required for technicians, some employers do prefer to hire those who have had training in a technical institute or junior college. Otherwise, training is usually given on the job. (See pp. 229-231 for complete details on the technical education required for entry into this field.)

What the Occupation Has to Offer

Although business is expected to increase as a result of population growth and expansion in the 1970s, employment will increase at a slower rate because of more efficient laborsaving machinery and automatic control equipment.

The numbers of engineers, scientists, technicians, and skilled workers are expected to increase faster than other occupational groups. And more scientific and technical personnel will be needed as research and development activities increase.

See: Engineering and Science Technology, pages 228-232 for more complete information.

For more information, write:

American Paper Institute
260 Madison Avenue
New York, New York 10016.

Robert A. Holcombe, Manager
Wood Technology
National Forest Products Association
1619 Massachusetts Avenue, N.W.
Washington, D.C. 20036
Ask for: *Opportunities Unlimited*, and list of schools offering courses in forest products industry.

National Paper Box Manufacturers Association, Inc.
121 North Broad Street
Philadelphia, Pennsylvania 19107.

Paper Industry Management Association
2570 Devon Avenue
Des Plaines, Illinois 60018.

Graphic Communications (Printing) Industry

The Job

Communications is one of the basic industries of our modern world, and one of the major means of communications is printing. More than one million workers are involved in the art of printing, using a wide range of techniques in many varied jobs.

The printing process is basically a way of transferring ink impressions of words, numerals, symbols, photographs, and art to paper, metal, and other materials. Printing, or graphic communication, is used in such things as newspapers, magazines, books, advertising matter, business forms, greeting cards, and gift wrapping. Newspaper printing and publishing companies alone employ almost 400,000 persons. Commercial or job printing establishments employ about 355,000 workers. These shops produce advertising matter, letterheads, business cards, calendars, catalogs, labels, maps, and pamphlets, in addition to a limited run of newspapers, books, and magazines. About half of them employ less than 100 people. Printing jobs can be found in almost any town or city in the country.

The most common methods of printing are letterpress, lithography or offset press, gravure, flexography, and screen printing. Each method requires specialized skills and has certain advantages. In all methods, a surface of metal, wood, linoleum or other material is prepared so that part of it can be covered with ink which is then transferred to a sheet of paper or other material that is pressed against the prepared surface.

In relief printing, usually letterpress, the printing surface stands up from the rest of the printing plate area. Ink is rolled over the raised surface and paper is then pressed against it. Other methods in this kind of printing are linoleum and wood block printing, relief engraving on metal and plastic, and flexography in which a flexible rubber plate and quick-drying fluid inks are used. The latter is most commonly used to print on plastic films, foil bags, milk containers, and bread and candy wrappers.

In lithography, or offset printing, the plate surface is smooth, and both image and nonimage areas are on the same level. The image areas are coated with a substance to which greasy printing ink will adhere. The plate is moistened with water before each inking so only the image areas will take up the ink. The inked image is transferred to a rubber blanket and then offset to the printing surface. Virtually anything can be printed by this method. In gravure printing the image is etched into the surface of the printing plate. The whole surface is covered with ink and then wiped off so ink is left only in the etched areas. Paper or other material is pressed against the surface and the ink is lifted out and appears on the paper.

Screen printing is a method in which ink or other materials like paint are forced, by a flexible blade, through a stencil mounted on a finely woven screen. The shape of the stencil openings determines the design to be printed. This can be used on irregular and cylindrical surfaces, and on paper, wood, textiles or any other surface.

We need craftsmen for all the different kinds of printing. Some specialize in just one type, and usually in one specific process.

The largest group of craftsmen are those who work in the composing room. This group of 185,000 includes hand compositors, typesetting machine operators, makeup men, tape-perforating machine operators, and proofreaders. Other skilled workers in this field are printing pressmen, lithographic craftsmen (cameramen, artists, strippers, platemakers, and pressmen), bookbinders, photoengravers, electrotypers, and stereotypers.

Maintenance machinists, who are responsible for adjusting and repairing machinery such as printing presses, bindery equipment, and typesetting machines, are also frequently employed in large printing plants.

Other employees include semiskilled assistants to printing craftsmen, executives, salesmen, accountants, engineers, stenographers, and clerks. Mailroom workers are employed by most printing plants. To keep up with increasingly sophisticated technology, new positions are being created, such as the production technician, who sees that specific standards are met on each printing job.

What You Need Personally

Although qualifications vary according to the job, there are certain ones that almost all graphic communications workers need: manual dexterity, good eyesight, and color determination: and at least average physical strength and stamina.

Mental alertness, precision, neatness, patience, and the ability to work quickly and accurately are also important. An artistic sense is helpful in some jobs, as is a knowledge of language.

What Education and Training You Need

Again, requirements for jobs vary according to the particular skill. Education is always an asset. Many high schools, vocational schools, technical institutes and colleges offer courses of study directly related to graphic communications. A high school education is frequently considered desirable by employers, and studies in English (spelling, grammar, and punctuation), basic mathematics, chemistry, physics, and electronics are very helpful. Scholarships and financial assistance are available for some post-high school courses of study.

Most skills are acquired on-the-job. Some people are hired as helpers and gradually master skills while they work. In other cases, trainees enter apprenticeship programs. These programs are required in some unionized shops in order to become a skilled journeyman. Apprentices are often chosen from the helpers already at work in the shops. Mechanical aptitude and industriousness are important qualifications here.

Most apprentice programs are registered with the government and include a specific agreement. During the period covered, the apprentice learns his trade through a combination of classroom study and on-the-job practice. Most apprenticeships in this field last four to six years, and include general instruction in methods of the industry, and specific instruction in the job for which the trainee is preparing. (See pages 52-63.)

What the Occupation Has to Offer

Graphic communications is an expanding field and is being utilized in a growing number of ways. Printed materials are being used increasingly for the distribution of information, packaging, advertising, and other industrial and commercial purposes. This growth, however, will not produce as many new jobs as might be expected because of the increasing use of mechanical equipment, which makes the printing process faster and more efficient.

Some jobs will be affected more than others by technology. Compositors and bookbinders, for instance, will probably see some decrease in jobs, while lithographic craftsmen will find more job openings as the use of lithographic printing grows.

Earnings for workers in the printing industry are generally high, although they vary according to job, skill, experience, and geographic locale.

Most printing trades workers are covered by union-management agreements which set minimum wage rates. In general, compositors make at least $5.00 an hour, and bookbinders, just under $5.00. The minimum hourly wage for electrotypers is almost $5.00; for stereotypers, somewhat less. Pressmen may make anywhere from $4.50 to $5.00 an hour minimum: photoengravers, $5.56: and mailers $4.50. Many in this field work night shifts, particularly on newspapers, and receive higher pay. Overtime is also paid for weekend or holiday work.

If you're ambitious and can master the skills needed in your shop, you may become a supervisor. You may also open your own shop.

Points to Consider Before Going into This Field

As a worker in this field, you will be skilled and financially rewarded accordingly. Most of your job training is received while working, and there are opportunities for advancement. The work is not particularly strenuous or dangerous, and many of the jobs are sufficiently diversified to alleviate boredom. Jobs are available all over the country, and the work is usually steady.

There are some disadvantages, however. Printing shops can be noisy and some workers are on their feet all day. There are often deadline pressures, creating a strain on everyone. Nevertheless pressure cannot be allowed to affect the quality of work. You'll probably be required to work some night shifts. And some skills are in less demand in our increasingly technological world.

Women are employed in these jobs, but usually on lower semiskilled levels.

For more information, write:

American Newspaper Publishers Association
11600 Sunrise Valley Drive
Reston, Virginia 22070.

Education Council of the Graphic Arts Industry
Graphic Arts Technical Council
4615 Forbes Avenue
Pittsburgh, Pennsylvania 15213.

Graphic Arts International Union
1900 L Street N.W.
Washington, D.C. 20036
Ask for: information about careers and training.

International Typographic Composition Association
2233 Wisconsin Avenue N.W.
Washington, D.C. 20007
Ask for: job and training information.

Lithographers and Photoengravers International Union
233 West 49th Street
New York, New York 10019
Ask for: job and training information.

Also contact:

For information on apprenticeships and other types of training apply directly to printing companies in your area; to local unions and employer associations in the printing industry; or to your state employment service.

Bookbinder and Related Workers

The Job

When the printed pages of a book or magazine stay together rather than falling in a disorganized pile at your feet, it's because a skilled bookbinder has been at work. Many printed items—books, magazines, pamphlets, business forms, and calendars—have to be folded, sewed, stapled, or bound by a bookbinder after they leave the printing shops.

There are several different kinds of binderies. Edition and pamphlet binderies bind books, magazines, and pamphlets printed in large quantities. Trade or job binderies do bindery work on contract for printers, publishers, or other customers. Blankbook or looseleaf binderies bind various types of blank books such as ledgers and accounting and bookkeeping volumes, in addition to looseleaf binders and looseleaf-type bound books.

The most complex form is edition binding. This is used to make large numbers of books from big, flat printed sheets of paper. The first step is to fold the printed sheets into one unit or more, called "signatures," so the pages will be in the right order. Then, any illustrations that have been printed separately are inserted. The signatures are then gathered and assembled in order and sewn together. The signatures are then shaped with power presses and trimming machines, and the spines are reinforced with glued fabric strips. The covers are glued or pasted onto the body of the book, and then various finishing operations are completed. Finally the books are wrapped in paper jackets and are ready for shipment. Many different machines are used in this process.

In large shops, skilled bookbinders are responsible for just a few operations, employing complicated machines. Most journeymen have had experience in all the processes. In large shops, other less skilled bindery workers or bindery hands do assembly line work.

Of the nation's 30,000 bookbinders, most work in shops mainly involved in the bookbinding process. Some also work in the bindery departments of large book, periodical, and commercial printing plants, and large libraries.

What You Need Personally

You need some mechanical aptitude, manual dexterity, and eye-hand coordination to be a bookbinder.

What Education and Training You Need

Skilled bookbinders usually go through a four or five year apprenticeship period to qualify as journeymen. You should be eighteen years old and have a high school education. On-the-job training is combined with classroom instruction during the apprenticeship period, and you learn to assemble signatures, renovate old, worn bindings, and use various binding machines like punches and folders.

The apprenticeship training varies depending on the type of bookbinding plant in which you are employed. In places that bind large numbers of books on a mass production basis, machine methods are used. In a few shops, fine hand binding is still done, including artistic designing and decorating of leather covers. (See pages 52-63.)

The less skilled bindery occupations also have a training period ranging anywhere from a few months to two years.

What the Occupation Has to Offer

During the 1970s, there should be a few hundred openings in this field yearly, mainly as a result of experienced workers retiring, dying, or transferring to other jobs. There is a high turnover among bindery hands, and most job openings result from this. On the whole, increasing mechanization will cut down on the number of people needed in this field.

Most skilled bookbinders and bindery hands are union members, and their contracts specify minimum hourly wage rates. Skilled workers average a little less than $5.00 an hour, and bindery hands about $3.00 an hour. Both receive fringe benefits.

Points to Consider Before Going into This Field

Bindery work has the advantage of being clean and not particularly strenuous. One disadvantage is that the number of workers in the field is is declining, Also the tasks done by bindery hands can be monotonous.

Women are frequently employed, but almost exclusively as bindery hands, and usually they do not progress to become skilled bookbinders. There are apprenticeship programs for women in union shops lasting two years.

For more information, write:

Department of Human Resources Development
Mail Control Unit
800 Capitol Mall
Sacramento, California 95814
Ask for: *Bookbinder and Bindery Woman (Bookbinder Apprentice and Bindery Woman Apprentice)* No. 214, Free.

International Brotherhood of Bookbinders
1612 K Street N.W.
Washington, D.C. 20016

See also: pages 256-257.

Composing Room Worker

The Job

When a completed manuscript is ready to become a book, newspaper, or magazine, it goes first to the composing room. Here the copy is set in type, either by machine or hand, proofed and checked for errors, and assembled and prepared for the pressroom.

Many skilled workers are employed in the composing room, each one well-trained for his craft. In a small shop, workers may be expected to do most or all of these jobs, but in large shops, responsibilities are divided.

The compositor, or typesetter, sets type by hand for work that requires especially fine composition, or for small jobs where machine setting is unnecessary. To handset type, the compositor reads from the manuscript copy and sets each

line of type in a "composing stick," which holds the type in place. He does this letter by letter, and when the stick is full he slides the completed lines onto a shallow metal tray called a "galley." The compositor has to work fast; be sure all the lines are even and be attentive to spacing.

A typographer, or type director, plans the printing job with customers. He is an expert on the hundreds of available typefaces and their best use in designing the material to be printed. The mark-up man does similar work, spelling out instructions for typesetting so that it will be done the most efficient way.

There are various kinds of typesetting machines which work semiautomatically and are much faster than hand setting. These machine operators are also specialists.

The linotype operator works with a keyboard machine and, reading from copy clipped to a board, selects from among the ninety keys to put the words together. The letters, in forms of metal molds called matrices, assemble into lines of words, and at the end of each line, the operator touches a lever to make the machine cast the line of type into a solid metal strip called a slug. The slugs are put in a galley and later assembled into type forms which make either printing impressions or plates. In small plants, the machine operators also maintain and repair the machines.

Monotype keyboard operators work with machines that have four times as many keys as the linotype. The machine produces a perforated paper tape that is fed into the casting machine. These machines are often used for complicated statistical material.

The monotype caster operates a machine that automatically casts and assembles type guided by perforations in the paper tape prepared by the keyboard machine. It forms one letter at a time and corrections can be made by hand without redoing the whole line.

Phototypesetting machine operators work with a machine that uses a photographic process that produces a film or photographic paper print of the type rather than a metal slug. Some of these machines have keys and others are fed paper tapes.

Phototypesetting also involves a knowledge of photography and darkroom procedures in order to develop the film on which the type has been photographed. The operator may also assemble the film into pages.

Typesetting machine operators also use typewriter-like machines to set "cold type' on paper. These machines automatically space letters and lines.

The paste-makeup man assembles and pastes cold type on layout sheets. This procedure is often used for newspaper display advertising or for the text copy of small newspapers.

Computer typesetting is becoming more common today, although relatively few plants have it at this time. It is certain to become more widely used in the future and will require some computer knowledge.

Proofreaders check all the type set in the composing room against the original manuscript to eliminate typographical and grammatical errors.

Other workers in larger plants include bankmen, who assemble type into galleys and make trial proofs; makeup men, who assemble type and photoengravings in page forms; and stonehands, who arrange the pages in proper sequence.

About 185,000 craftsmen are employed in these jobs. They work for newspaper plants, commercial printing shops, book and periodical printing plants, typographic composition firms, advertising agencies, and advertising departments of large firms.

What You Need Personally

For this work, you need good vision and something of an eye for artistic design. Good manual dexterity and eye-hand coordination are also important. You should have some stamina and stability, because deadlines are common in this business and pressures can mount.

What Education and Training You Need

A high school education is necessary for this field, with printing and typing courses as good background. A knowledge of photography and electronics is becoming more useful as the typesetting equipment gets more sophisticated.

The exact qualifications vary from job to job. Some workers learn their skills from on-the-job training or from courses in trade school. Apprenticeship is a common way to learn the trade, however.

Tape-perforating machine operators, for instance, must be expert typists. This is a skill they can learn in high school or business school. Their training, which takes about a year, includes learning how to operate the machine and becoming familiar with printing terms and measurements.

Apprentices are frequently selected from among the helpers in the shop. Most programs take five or six years, although they can be shortened by as much as two years if you have had specific schooling or experience, or show a natural talent for the trade.

An apprenticeship program for compositors includes learning elementary hand composition, page makeup, lockup, lineup, and proofreading. After mastering this, the apprentice gets intensive training in one or more specialized fields, like operating a typesetting machine, as well as specialized work in hand and photocomposition. Apprentices are frequently expected to attend night classes to increase general literacy. (See pages 52-63 for more details.)

What the Occupation Has to Offer

Composing room occupations will be significantly affected by technological advances during the 1970s, although there should be some job openings. Automatically operated typesetting machines are more common, and computers will be coming into greater use in this field, making it necessary for workers to broaden their skills. Phototypesetting, for instance, will be used to a greater extent so photographic skills will be more important in the years to come. Some knowledge of electronics will also be useful in the operation of new machines.

Wages for composing room employees vary depending on the firm and on the geographical area. The average minimum hourly wage is somewhere around $5 for day shifts. Many compositors are union members, and benefits are good.

Opportunities for advancement are good for the worker who develops skills with advancing technology. He can move to different, more difficult jobs in the shop, and may even open his own shop.

Points to Consider Before Going into This Field

There are many job opportunities for compositors, and technology should serve to change, rather than eliminate jobs in the future. Many different skills, aptitudes and interests can come into play in this field, and you can get satisfaction from seeing the results of your work. Jobs are steady, and available in any part of the country.

While newer plants are clean and often air-conditioned, some older ones may be hot and very noisy. Although most machine work is done sitting down, hand compositors may have to stand for long periods of time. Work often has to be done on night shifts. However, extra pay is provided.

There are few restrictions on people who wish to go into this kind of work, as long as their vision and skills are sufficient. Some handicapped persons, such as the deaf, can do well at these jobs.

Composing room employees have traditionally been men, but opportunities for women are starting to open up with the introduction of photographic procedures and the increased need for designers.

For more information, write:

Department of Human Resources Development
Mail Control Unit
800 Capitol Mall
Sacramento, California 95814
Ask for: *Composing Room Occupations* No. 86, Free.

See also: pages 256-257.

Electrotyper and Stereotyper

The Job

The books, magazines, and newspapers we read go through many steps between the time the words are put down by the writer and the time we sit down to read them. One of the important people in this process is the electrotyper or stereotyper, who makes duplicate press plates from which written material is letterpress printed. These plates, which are made from metal type forms, are necessary because so many copies of a volume must be printed, that single plates are just not enough. If an especially large edition of a book is printed, several plates must be used to replace the ones that become too worn to print clearly. Duplicate plates also allow printers to use several presses at the same time and speed up printing, especially important for newspapers. Many big plants use rotary presses. These require curved plates, which electrotypers or stereotypers make from flat type forms.

To make a duplicate curved metal plate, the electrotyper goes through a series of steps. A wax or plastic mold of the type form is made and coated with special chemical solutions. Then it is suspended in an electrolytic solution containing metal, which leaves a metallic shell on the coated mold. The shell is stripped from the mold, backed with metal or plastic, and carefully finished.

Stereotypers have an easier and less expensive process to go through, but the plate is not as fine or durable. The stereotyper makes molds or mats of papier-mâché, which are placed on the type form and covered with a cork blanket and sheet of fiberboard. The covered form is run under heavy power driven steel rollers to impress the type and photoengravings on the mat. Then the mat is placed in a stereotype casting machine which casts a composition lead plate on the mold. Stereotype plates are often cast in automatic machines, particularly in larger printing plants.

Journeymen in this trade must know how to handle all related tasks, but in larger plants, workers usually do only one phase of the work, such as casting, molding, finishing, or blocking.

Most electrotypers work in large plants that print magazines and books. Stereotypers usually work in newspaper plants, although some work in commercial printing plants. Some workers in both areas are employed by independent service shops which do contract work for printing firms.

What Education and Training You Need

The most common way to learn these trades is through an apprenticeship program. You should be at least eighteen years old and most employers prefer that you are a high school graduate or equivalent. High school courses in chemistry and mechanically related studies are helpful. Physical examinations and aptitude tests are frequently given.

Electrotyping and stereotyping are entirely different processes, so training programs do not overlap. Apprenticeship usually lasts about five or six years and includes classroom instruction on related technical areas and on-the-job training that covers all phases of the job. (See pages 52-63.)

What the Occupation Has to Offer

There will continue to be some openings in this field during the next ten years, but most will be to fill vacancies caused by the retirements, deaths, or job transfers of experienced workers. Although more books, magazines, and newspapers will probably be printed, automation will significantly reduce the number of workers required. Automatic plate casting eliminates many of the steps currently used to make plates. Plastic and rubber plates are being made more frequently outside of the electrotyping and stereotyping shops. Also, more publishers are turning to offset printing, which does not require this type of plate.

Earnings for electrotypers and stereotypers vary around the country, but almost all are union members, and their contracts specify minimum wages. Electrotypers' minimum wage rates average almost $5.00 an hour, and although stereotypers have more variation, the average is about the same. Both receive the usual fringe benefits. Overtime and night shift workers earn additional pay.

Opportunities for promotion are limited for these workers because their duties are so specialized. They can, however, become supervisors.

Points to Consider Before Going into This Field

Work is available on a steady year-round basis, and workers receive good wages. Most printing plants are fairly modern and increased automation has eliminated much of the heavy lifting.

One disadvantage is that automation will reduce the number of these jobs in the years to come. Although it doesn't appear that electrotypers and stereotypers will be phased out, there will probably be fewer openings as time goes on.

For more information, write:

International Association of Electrotypers and Stereotypers
758 Leader Building
Cleveland, Ohio 44114

International Stereotypers' and Electrotypers' Union of North America
10 South LaSalle Street
Chicago, Illinois 60603

See also: page 256-257.

Lithographic Worker

The Job

The incredible amount of printed material we are exposed to daily is a mixture of black and white pictures, copy, reproductions and a dazzling variety of colors. Much of this is produced by lithography, or offset printing, a fast growing process. Lithography is especially desirable when you want to reproduce photographs, drawings,

or paintings, because the rubber blanket which transfers the image from the plate to the printing surface allows great flexibility in the types of paper which can be used. Books, magazines, newspapers, calendars, maps, catalogs, posters, labels and folding cartons are all printed by this process.

There are several operations in lithography, and each one requires a special group of skilled workers. First the cameraman photographs the copy. He is usually either a line cameraman, who photographs black and white; a halftone cameraman, also a black and white photographer; or a color separation photographer.

After the negatives are made they frequently need retouching to lighten or darken certain parts. This is handled by the lithographic artist, who uses chemicals, dyes and special tools to make corrections by sharpening or reshaping images on the negatives. These artists must be adept in at least one of the various retouching methods and may be known as dot etchers, retouchers or letterers.

The next man in the process is the stripper, who makes layouts on glass, paper or film. Working on layout sheets called flats or strip up, he arranges and pastes film or prints of type, pictures and art work. Photographic impressions of the layout sheet are made for the lithographic press plates.

The platemaking department then takes over the process. The platemaker exposes press plates to the photographic films made by the cameramen and corrected by the artists. He may cover the surface of the metal plate with a coat of photosensitive chemicals, or the photosensitive layer may be applied before it reaches him. He then exposes the sensitized plate through the negative or positive to strong arc lights in a vacuum printing frame. When many of the same images are to be exposed on one plate, however, the operation is done in a photocomposing machine, and the plate is developed and chemically treated to bring out the image.

The lithographic pressman puts the plate on the press, adjusts the pressure, cares for and adjusts the rubber blanket which takes the impression from the plates and transfers it to the paper, adjusts water and ink rollers, mixes inks and operates the presses. In larger plants, the pressman is assisted by press feeders and helpers.

What You Need Personally

You should be in reasonably good physical condition for any of these jobs, have good vision and color determination and manual dexterity. Precision, reliability and careful attention to detail are also important. An artistic sense is helpful, especially for the stripper and lithographic artist.

What Education and Training You Need

High school or vocational school education is recommended for these jobs, and courses in mathematics, chemistry, physics, art, and photography are helpful. Most people get into this trade by serving an apprenticeship. For this you must be at least eighteen years old, and may be required to take an aptitude test. (See pages 52-63.)

The apprenticeship usually lasts four or five years, and you learn all lithographic operations, with an emphasis on the specific area in which you want to attain journeyman status. The Lithographers and Photoengravers International union in many cities offers classes which apprentices may be required to take, and which are also open to journeymen who want to improve or update their skills.

Courses of advanced study leading to careers in lithography are also offered by some technical institutes and colleges. The Educational Council of the Graphic Arts Industry has a National Scholarship Trust Fund which offers scholarships to qualified young people interested in this type of study. (See page 256.)

What the Occupation Has to Offer

There should be some increase in jobs in the lithographic industry in the next decade. Offset printing is expected to grow in popularity and the number of fields in which it is used will increase. Commercial printing firms and small and medium size newspaper publishers will use more of these presses, and the increased use of color, photographs and drawings in printed matter will also help the growth of lithography. All this expansion will be somewhat offset by the new technological developments however, and will affect new workers in the field.

Earnings for workers in this industry vary for each specific occupation, the amount of experience, the type and size of equipment, and the part of the country in which the worker is employed. These workers are usually union members, and most have union contract minimum hourly wage rates set for their jobs. Cameramen or artists have minimum wages ranging from $3.71 to over $6 an hour. Plate makers' minimums are about the same. The widest wage range is that of pressmen—anywhere from $3 to over $8 an hour—resulting from the variety of sizes and types of presses in use. All receive fringe benefits.

Lithographic workers can advance by becoming experts in their specialty and by learning as much as possible about the industry in general, and their company in particular. Possible growth positions would include department head, production chief and plant supervisor. Large lithographic plants have estimators who must calculate what any job will cost, taking into consideration production time, wages, cost of paper, etc. The industry also has many sales representatives who sell the lithographic process and product.

Points to Consider Before Going into This Field

Offset printing is a growing field, and will continue to require skilled workers to perform its operations. Although the industry will be affected by mechanization, jobs will be altered rather than eliminated. In this industry, you have a chance to develop a skill and to do work that is challenging, interesting, and which pays well. The hours are usually regular, the working conditions fairly clean and pleasant, and physical strain is at a minimum.

For more information, write:

International Printing Pressmen and Assistants Union
of North America
1730 Rhode Island Avenue, N.W.
Washington, D.C. 20036.

National Association of Photo-Lithographers
230 West 41st Street
New York, New York 10036.

See also: pages 256-257.

Photoengraver

The Job

When books or magazines include photographs, artwork or other material that cannot be set in type, a special process is needed to make the metal printing plates. Photoengravers then make special metal printing plates on which the printing surfaces stand out in relief above the

shops. The country's printing centers—New York, Chicago, Philadelphia, and Los Angeles—are the location for most of these jobs.

Gravure photoengravers work mostly for the few large firms that specialize in this work. A few also work for large newspaper and commercial plants. The main locations for these jobs are New York, Pennsylvania, Illinois, and Kentucky.

What You Need Personally

One of the most important qualifications you can have for this job is good eyesight. There is a lot of detail work and clear vision and good color discrimination are needed. You also have to be able to do close, fine work with infinite concentration and patience to see that the job is done right.

nonprinting spaces, as do the letters and the accompanying type. Gravure photoengravers are a specialized kind of photoengravers; they make gravure plates in which the image is etched below the surface to reproduce pictures and type.

When photoengraving plates are made for letterpress printing, one man may do the whole job, or a group of skilled specialists may each perform a particular operation. Large shops usually employ different specialists, including cameramen, printers, etchers, finishers, routers, blockers, and proofers.

The first operation is performed by the cameraman, who photographs the material to be reproduced. A plate, known as a halftone plate, is then made from this photograph. Plates made from line drawings are called line plates. After the cameraman develops the negative, the printer prints the image on a metal plate by coating it with a light-sensitive solution and then exposing it and the negative to arc lights. The image areas are protected by chemicals. The etcher then places the plate in an acid bath which etches away the nonimage areas and leaves the image areas standing out in relief.

High quality book or magazine photoengravings require more careful finishing than those for newspapers. In these instances, the finisher inspects and touches up the plate with handtools and the router cuts the metal away from the nonprinting part to prevent it from touching the inking rollers during printing. The blocker then mounts the engraving on a base that will make it reach the right height and the proofer prints a sample copy on a proof press.

The gravure photoengraving process is very similar, except that the image areas, rather than the background, are etched away.

There are about 17,000 photoengravers, most of whom work in commercial service shops that specialize in making photoengravings for others. Other places that employ photoengravers are newspaper and rotogravure shops, book and periodical shops, and the U. S. Government Printing Office. Some craftsmen have their own

What Education and Training You Need

The best way to get into this field is through an apprenticeship. Applicants must be eighteen years old, and most employers prefer that you have a high school education or its equivalent. Courses in chemistry, physics, and art are good background.

The usual apprenticeship period is five years, but may be shortened if you have previous experience in the field. The program combines on-the-job training with at least 800 hours of classroom instruction. The apprentice learns to use and care for the tools needed in the trade, is taught to cut and square negatives, make combination plates, inspect negatives for defects, mix chemicals, sensitize metal, and operate the various machines used for photoengraving. (See pages 52-63.)

What the Occupation Has to Offer

There should be a few hundred openings in this field during the next decade to replace experienced workers who retire, die, or transfer to other occupations. On the whole, however, there will be a decline in the number of workers needed because electronics, improved photographic equipment, and the use of offset printing (which doesn't need photoengravings) will limit the number of people needed for these jobs.

Earnings for photoengravers are quite high. The average minimum wage rate is almost $6 an hour, and higher rates are paid for overtime and night shifts. Most photoengravers are union members and they receive all the usual fringe benefits.

The opportunities for advancement for photoengravers are limited other than promotion to supervisory positions.

Points to Consider Before Going into This Field

There are various advantages to working as a photoengraver. You will be a skilled craftsman, doing work that demands attention. The wages are very good, and the training is all done on the job. The work is not physically strenuous and working conditions are generally good.

The main disadvantage is that the field is a shrinking rather than an expanding one.

For more information, write:

American Photoplatemakers Association
166 West Van Buren Street
Chicago, Illinois 60604
Ask for: information on a career as a photoengraver.

See also: pages 256-257.

Printing Pressman and Assistant

The Job

The final and actual job of printing a book, magazine, or newspaper is handled in the pressroom. It is here that all the previous processes take shape to make up the printed pages with which we are familiar.

Printing pressmen prepare or "makeready" type forms and press plates for final printing. They are also responsible for tending the presses while they are in operation.

The makeready process is aimed at making sure printing impressions are distinct and uniform, a task that is both delicate and difficult. Some of the methods used to assure uniformity and clarity include placing pieces of paper of exactly the right thickness under low areas of the press plate to level them, and attaching pieces of tissue paper to the surface of the cylinder or flat platen which makes the impression. There are other adjustments that have to be made. Margins must be controlled for instance, and the ink flowing to the inking roller regulated. In some shops pressmen also oil and clean the presses and make minor repairs.

In the larger pressrooms, the pressmen have assistants and helpers. Press assistants feed sheets of paper into the presses and help operate the larger and more complicated rotary presses. Assistants who mainly feed paper are usually called press feeders.

A pressman's work varies according to the kind and size of presses used in his particular shop. In small commercial shops, the presses are usually small and fairly simple. Paper is fed into them by hand. Large newspaper, magazine and book printing plants, on the other hand, have huge web-rotary presses. Big rolls of paper, as much as fifty inches wide, are fed into the presses. The paper is printed on both sides by means of a series of cylinders, and then the press cuts, assembles and folds the pages. When the printing is finished, the press counts the finished newspaper sections which come off the press ready to mail. A crew of pressmen and assistants are needed to attend to all these operations, and they work under the direction of a pressman-in-charge.

What You Need Personally

You should have an aptitude for mechanics to do this job because it requires making adjustments and repairs on the press. For color press work, which is being used more every year, you should be able to visualize color. Physical stamina, and in some cases, strength, is also needed, because pressmen have to stand for long periods of time and sometimes have to lift heavy type forms and press plates.

What Education and Training You Need

Some vocational schools offer courses that are helpful to a potential pressman. In general, the work is learned through an apprenticeship. Most companies select apprentices from among the helpers in the pressroom, usually after they have worked there for two or three years. They prefer a high school education or its equivalent, and courses in chemistry and physics are considered useful.

An apprenticeship program usually combines classroom study and on-the-job training. The length of training varies. In commercial shops, the apprenticeship period is two years for press assistants and four years for pressmen. In newspaper pressrooms, it is five years. To operate a web press usually requires a five-year apprenticeship. On-the-job training includes learning to care for pressroom equipment, makeready, running the job, press tending and maintenance, and working with different kinds of ink and paper. (See pages 52-63.)

What the Occupation Has to Offer

Every year sees more printed materials coming off the presses, and this will cause some increase in jobs for pressmen during the 1970s. Other jobs will be available because of the retirement, death, or change of occupation of older workers. The job growth will be somewhat offset, however, by the use of newer and more efficient printing presses.

Earnings for pressmen vary according to the kind of press operated, the type of printing plant and the geographical area. Most pressmen are union members and minimum hourly wages are in effect for these jobs. The minimum wage for pressman-in-charge at a newspaper is $5.24 an hour; for a newspaper pressman, $4.94; for book and job platen pressmen, $4.46; for book and job press assistants and feeders, $4.26. When pressmen have to work night shifts, particularly for newspapers, their pay is higher. Pressmen and assistants also receive fringe benefits like insurance, retirement, paid holidays, vacations, and sick leave.

There are some opportunities for advancement for pressmen in a large shop from a helper to journeyman to pressman-in-charge.

Points to Consider Before Going into This Field

Pressmen have the advantage of having a skilled trade that is unlikely to become obsolete. Even the modern automated presses require skilled workmen to attend to them. The work pays fairly well, is steady, and doesn't require post-high school education.

The job does have some disadvantages, however. All those presses make a lot of noise, and some pressmen feel it necessary to wear ear protectors. The machinery can prove hazardous if not approached cautiously. Because of deadlines that must be met, there can be a lot of pressure on the job, and night shifts are not infrequent. Pressmen sometimes have to lift heavy type forms and printing press plates.

For more information, write:

International Printing Pressmen & Assistants
    Union of North America
1730 Rhode Island Avenue, N. W.
Washington, D. C. 20036
Ask for: career and training information.

See also: page 256-257.

Health Services

When the general field of health is mentioned, our minds may turn first to Marcus Welby or Dr. Kildare, but the real scene is far broader than a hospital setting and the cast much more diversified than the physicians, nurses, and dentists. Out of every 100 health workers, only 9 are physicians. All together there are more than 200 other different occupations that fall under the umbrella of allied health fields.

Health is our nation's third largest industry. In 1970 it employed more than 3.5 million people, and medical services are expanding rapidly. The past twenty years have seen a rapid rise in the number of people working in health care, with the most marked increase among the *paramedical* groups—those technicians and assistants who provide vital help and free the professionals from certain routine duties so that they in turn can devote themselves to those tasks requiring more advanced skills. By 1975, we will need twenty-five allied health workers for each practicing physician. We now have 334,000 licensed physicians.

Hospitals, of course, employ large numbers of health workers but they are not the only places which do. Jobs are also available in clinics, laboratories, pharmacies, nursing homes, industrial plants, public agencies, mental health centers, schools, offices, and homes. The field employs large numbers of women, especially as registered nurses, licensed practical nurses, assistants and technicians, and there are many opportunities for women to work part time or return to their occupation when their families are grown.

People trained in health related occupations can generally find work in all parts of the country and overseas as well. Although populated and prosperous areas may offer more varied opportunities, sometimes there can be a surplus of people trained for certain specialties in these locales, while other rural communities may desperately need health workers of every type.

The training for some of the fields described in this section can be obtained on-the-job, but more often special schooling in hospitals, vocational or technical institutions, or junior or community colleges is required. Entrance requirements, certification and registration for health occupations are becoming increasingly standardized by national professional organizations, so that the people employed in these areas may enjoy recognition and status, even though the training period may be relatively short. Some of the allied health fields are so new they have not been in existence as long as the average high school senior, and formalized training programs are still in development stages.

Few college students in other fields can look forward to summer work in their chosen occupation, but Allied Health students at Central YMCA Community College in Chicago, for instance, are expected to intern at local hospitals during their summer vacations. This is part of the clinic plus classroom plan that makes the health program so versatile.

Central YMCA Community College is just one of dozens of such schools awarding Associate of Arts Degrees in Science, which qualify people to enter the health professions as paraprofessionals or specialist technicians, with recognized standing after only two years of work. Each curriculum, for example the one for inhalation therapist, combines a liberal arts and science education with hospital internship. During the first year, students spend three days at the college and two at the hospital each week. During the summer months and second year, all training is given at the hospital.

Because of the urgent need for more health workers, many educational institutions, health organizations, and state and federal government programs are either free or offer financial aid in the form of scholarships and loans. (See pages 14-24 for more details.)

As the population grows and more government funds are devoted to health care and coverage, related occupations should continue to expand throughout the 1970s. The field is undergoing constant change, and factors such as national health insurance will have an influence on manpower requirements in the future. Present needs vary considerably, depending on location and economic climate. In many areas there is a severe shortage of health workers but not enough money to hire more.

The general employment outlook, however, is

highly favorable, especially for those who obtain the recommended training. Most paramedical fields are open to both men and women.

In addition to a generally healthy job forecast a health field career is well worth investigating if you are looking for an opportunity to be of service to others, and to feel an active involvement with your work. There is a special satisfaction in most health occupations, even those jobs requiring relatively little training, in which you work as part of a team whose goal is sounder bodies and minds, and longer happier lives. In the past it has been difficult to advance in the health field without a great deal of additional education, but this condition may change as personnel practices become more flexible. There can also be demands on your time and energy, but to those working in health professions, the rewards far outweigh the disadvantages.

This section on health services is divided into the following groups: dental services; eye care; medical laboratory worker; medical office assistant; nursing; radiologic technologist; rehabilitation; and other jobs in hospitals. These are just some of the promising areas in the allied health field. Because new career categories are opening up all the time, you would be wise to ask about new fields which may offer even better job opportunities in your community.

For more information, write:

American Hospital Association
840 N. Lake Shore Drive
Chicago, Illinois 60611
Ask for: information on health and hospital occupations; names and addresses of the health career information service in your area; *Careers That Count: Educational Programs in the Health Field* (lists educational programs in 27 health technology areas); *Today's Hospital . . . Career Center for America's Youth*; *State and Metropolitan Hospital Associations and Health Career programs.*

American Medical Association
535 N. Dearborn Street
Chicago, Illinois 60610
Ask for: *Horizons Unlimited* (a handbook describing rewarding career opportunities in medicine and allied fields).

Association of Schools of Allied Health Professions
One Dupont Circle
Suite 300
Washington, D. C. 20036.

Your local Blue Cross Plan Offices
Ask for: *The Hospital People* (An illustrated booklet on a variety of hospital jobs).

National Chicano Health Organization
1709 W. 8th Street
Suite 807
Los Angeles, California 90017

Ask for: information on recruiting Chicanos for health services field.

National Health Council
1740 Broadway
New York, New York 10019
Ask for: *Where to get Health Career Information,* 1972, Free.

U. S. Department of Health, Education and Welfare
Public Health Service
National Institute of Health,
Bureau of Health Manpower Education
Division of Manpower Intelligence
9000 Rockville Pike
Bethesda, Maryland 20014
Ask for: *Summary of Training: Physcian Support Personnel,* 1973, Free. (composite listing of training programs for physician support personnel).

Superintendent of Documents
U. S. Government Printing Office
Washington, D. C. 20402
Ask for: *Health Careers Guidebook,* 1972. L1.8:H 34/972 S/N 2900–00158, $2.25. *Allied Health Education Programs in Junior Colleges,* American Association of Junior Colleges and U. S. Department of Health, Education & Welfare, $3.00.

Health Careers Information

Government Agencies (Compiled by American Hospital Association). The following is a list of selected federal agencies that provide information on health careers. Information is also available from state agencies such as the board of education and its divisions, department of public health, and state employment services.

U. S. Atomic Energy Commission
Division of Technical Information Extension
P. O. Box 62
Oak Ridge, Tennessee 37839
Ask for: information on health-related nuclear science and atomic medicine careers.

Bureau of Labor Statistics
U. S. Department of Labor
Washington, D. C. 20210
Ask for: pamphlets on over 100 health careers reprinted from *Occupational Outlook Reports.*

U. S. Civil Service Commission
Bureau of Recruiting and Examining
Washington D. C. 20415
Ask for: information on health careers in government.

National Institute of Mental Health
Public Information Office
5600 Fishers Lane
Rockville, Maryland 20852
Ask for: information on careers in mental health.

Office of Education
U. S. Department of Health, Education and Welfare

400 Maryland Avenue, S. W.
Washington, D. C. 20202
Ask for: material on vocational and technical
   education opportunities.

Personnel Office
Food and Drug Administration
U. S. Department of Health, Education and
   Welfare
Washington, D. C. 20204
Ask for: information on food and drug inspec-
   tors.

Public Health Service
Bureau of Health Manpower Education
National Institutes of Health
Information Office
9000 Rockville Pike
Bethesda, Maryland 20014
Ask for: general information on health careers.

U. S. Public Health Service
Office of Personnel
Office of Surgeon General
9000 Rockville Pike, NBOC No. 2
Bethesda, Maryland 20014
Ask for: information on careers in public health
   such as nurse, physician, dentist, etc.

U. S. Public Health Service
Office of Public Inquiries
Bethesda, Maryland 20034
Ask for: information on careers in the public
   health service.

Veterans Administration
VA Forms and Publications Depot
2625 Shirlington Road
Arlington, Virginia 22206
Ask for: information on health careers with the
   V. A.

Vocational Rehabilitation Administration
U. S. Department of Health, Education and
   Welfare
Washington, D. C. 20201
Ask for: information on vocational rehabilita-
   tion counselors.

For information on health careers in the
armed forces, write to the recruitment offices of
the appropriate service branch in Washington,
D. C. or to your local recruitment office.

Additional reading:

Lee, Essie E. *Careers in the Health Field.* New
   York: Julian Messner, 1972, $4.79.

Ogden, Ruth F. and Wenberg, Bruness G. (Eds.).
   Introduction to Health Professions. St. Louis;
   C. V. Mosby Co., 1972.

Dental Services: Dental Assistant

The Job

The dental assistant is the dentist's "right-
hand man"—helping him in the examination

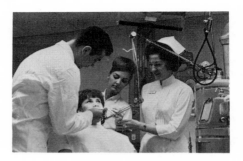

and treatment of patients. The assistant may
greet the patient, make him comfortable and
prepare him for treatment, get out his records,
give the dentist the proper instruments as he
works, keep the patient's mouth clear, prepare
materials for impressions, process X-ray film,
and sterilize and care for instruments.

Besides these "chairside" duties, assistants
also perform simple technical work, such as
making casts from impressions. Some manage
the dentist's office as well, arranging appointments, keeping records, ordering materials, and
handling billing and payments.

The extent of the assistant's responsibilities
varies depending on training, the size of the
dentist's staff, and the state regulations, but an
assistant does *not* perform any actual work in the
patient's mouth, as a dental hygienist does. The
Council on Dental Education of the American
Dental Association has defined the functions of
the dental assistant as (1) operatory chairside
assisting, (2) reception and secretarial duties,
and (3) dental laboratory technical work. In
some offices, the same person handles all these
tasks, while in others they may be divided among
two or three individuals.

Most dental assistants work in private offices,
either for a single dentist or a group. Some are
also employed in dental schools, hospital dental
departments, state and local public health departments, or private clinics. And there are also
opportunities for dental assistants to work in
specialty practice, hospital or government service, education or the armed forces.

Approximately 100,000 people worked in this
field in 1970, practically all of them women.
About one out of six worked on a part-time
basis.

Assistants generally work a 40-hour week,
including Saturdays. Most dental offices are
pleasant, attractive places, conveniently located.

What You Need Personally

Because the assistant is the liaison between
the dentist and the patient, it's important that
she like people and they like her. She should
have a cheerful pleasant disposition and should
also be able to handle children if they constitute
a large part of the dentist's practice. Also impor-

tant are good physical and mental health, manual dexterity, professional attitude, tact, thoroughness, enthusiasm, and a pleasing voice.

What Education and Training You Need

Although most dental assistants have heretofore learned their skills on the job, an increasing number are now entering the field through formal post-high school dental assisting programs. The Council on Dental Education of the American Dental Association now accredits about 170 such programs, some of them supported by federal legislation.

Most of these courses are offered in junior or community colleges, correspondence courses, or vocational or technical schools. More than two-thirds of them consist of one academic year leading to a certificate or diploma. Graduates of two-year college programs earn an associate degree, and their course work includes one year of liberal arts and another year of special training. Students are taught dental, biological and social sciences; English; business; and chairside and laboratory skills. Trainees also get practical experience in offices, clinics, or dental schools. You must be a high school graduate, and some programs also require a typing or business course.

Graduates of approved programs can take an examination given by the American Dental Assistants Association and after meeting certain experience requirements become Certified Dental Assistants. Such certification is seldom necessary for employment, but it does prove you are qualified and may insure you a better salary. There are a limited number of scholarships available for students interested in becoming dental assistants.

What the Occupation Has to Offer

By 1980 the need for dental assistants may reach 150,000, an increase of 50 percent over present levels. People are becoming much more aware of the importance of dental care, and more of them are able to pay for dental services. As a result, there is now a shortage of dentists, and trained workers (dental paraprofessionals) are needed to free the dentist for professional tasks.

Earnings for assistants usually relate directly to community standards for office and secretarial workers. Weekly salaries for those working in private dental offices in 1970 ranged from $75 to $150 depending largely on education, experience, and responsibilities, as well as how long the assistant had worked for the same dentist. Specialists and those with very busy practices tend to pay more but also demand more experienced assistants.

Advancement opportunities are limited. However, the American Dental Assistants Association does offer many continuing education courses for those who are certified, so that they may upgrade their skills and keep up with new developments in the field. Also, some assistants, with further study, go on to become dental hygienists.

Points to Consider Before Going into This Field

The dental assistant can generally find work in most parts of the country, although there are many more dentists in highly populated areas. The job provides excellent opportunities for married women, working conditions are pleasant and duties are varied. An assistant who has worked for the same dentist over a long period of time may feel a real sense of importance both to him and to his patients.

For more information, write:

American Dental Assistants Association
211 East Chicago Avenue
Chicago, Illinois 60611
Ask for: information about career opportunities; scholarships; accredited programs; and requirements for certification.

Division of Career Guidance
American Council on Dental Education Association
211 East Chicago Avenue
Chicago, Illinois 60611
Ask for: list of accredited dental assisting programs.

Division of Dental Health
Public Health Service
U. S. Department of Health, Education and Welfare
Washington, D. C. 20201
Ask for: information on opportunities for dental assistants.

See also: pages 267-268

Dental Services: Dental Laboratory Technician

The Job

A dental laboratory technician may never see the people for whom his work is intended. Dentists used to make most appliances, dentures (artificial teeth), crowns, and bridges themselves. But today they turn most of these construction assignments over to laboratory technicians, giving the dentist more time to work directly with patients.

Most technicians work in commercial dental laboratories that serve a large number of dentists. These laboratories usually employ from five to ten people, though some are much larger.

in this field, and some post-high school institutions have one or two-year programs, combining formal training with supervised work in a laboratory. There are about thirty two-year programs which include both academic and laboratory instruction and lead to an Associate of Art degree. However, even with courses in the field, most technicians must also show evidence of actual work experience in order to be considered qualified. A number of scholarships for study at schools accredited by the American Dental Association are available through grants to the American Fund for Dental Education.

What the Occupation Has to Offer

This relatively new field offers very good job prospects for the 1970s, both through replacement of present workers and expansion of the entire dental care field. As more dentists are delegating work to paradental employees, the need for laboratory workers should continue to grow. Predictions are that dentists will hire more technicians as part of their office staffs as well as utilize commercial laboratories.

The starting salary for trainee technicians is about $75 for a 40-hour week, but technicians with experience can earn up to $150, and master technicians with managerial experience are paid as much as $300 a week.

Advancement opportunities are good, and many technicians have gone on to start their own businesses or become salesmen or technical representatives for dental equipment firms.

Points to Consider Before Going into This Field

This work requires precise and painstaking craftsmanship, and while it is highly satisfying to those who enjoy working with their hands, it can be tedious to others. It's an attractive, challenging, and well-paying field for those who are able to acquire the necessary skills.

Eighty percent of all laboratory technicians are men, but women are welcome, especially in the larger commercial laboratories.

Other technicians work directly for an individual dentist or a group dental practice.

There are more than 35,000 technicians in the United States and approximately 7,000 laboratories, many of them small privately owned businesses.

In making an appliance the technician may form a hard plaster model from the impression of the patient's mouth taken by the dentist. He also may make metal casting for dentures, finish and polish the dentures, construct metal or porcelain crowns or inlays, make bridges of gold or other metals, and build appliances to correct abnormalities such as cleft palates or orthodontic problems.

Trainees are usually given fairly simple tasks such as mixing and pouring plaster into molds. The more skill and experience you have, the more complex is the work you do. Some technicians perform all kinds of laboratory work, while others, especially those in large labs, specialize in certain operations. All technicians use the specialized equipment of their craft in doing their jobs.

What You Need Personally

You should have good vision and color perception and should like detailed work. Because working in a dental laboratory is not strenuous, handicapped workers can perform many of the tasks provided they have good use of hands and fingers. Young people who have taken courses in art, ceramics, metalworking, plastics, and sciences such as chemistry and physiology are preferred candidates for training.

What Education and Training You Need

There are no special entrance requirements for dental laboratory work, but a high school diploma is usually a minimum qualification. Most technicians learn their skills on-the-job in a commercial laboratory, dental office, or hospital which offers dental services. Training generally takes three to four years, depending on ability, previous experience, and the range of skills being learned.

A few vocational high schools offer courses

For more information, write:

American Fund for Dental Education
211 East Chicago Ave.
Chicago, Illinois 60611
Ask for: scholarship information.

Council on Dental Education
American Dental Association
211 East Chicago Ave.
Chicago, Illinois 60611
Ask for: career information and list of accredited programs.

The Dental Laboratory Conference
1918 Pine Street
Philadelphia, Pennsylvania 19103
Ask for: information on apprenticeship programs

National Association of Certified Dental Laboratories, Inc.
3801 Mt. Vernon Avenue
Alexandria, Virginia 22305
Ask for: career information and requirements for certification.

See also: pages 267-268.

Dental Services: Dental Hygienist

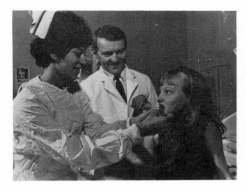

The Job

When you make a visit to the dentist, the chances are good that the first person who treats you will be the dental hygienist rather than the dentist himself. Usually a woman, she will "clean" your teeth, removing stains and deposits, and apply decay resisting agents. She may also record your dental history, prepare diagnostic tests for the dentist's interpretation, take and develop dental X-ray films, sterilize instruments, mix filling compounds, and act as a chairside assistant to the dentist.

Hygienists who work in school systems help promote dental health by examining children's teeth and reporting findings to parents. They also give instructions on correct care and brushing and sometimes help to develop educational programs on dental health.

About 16,000 dental hygienists were employed in 1970, most of them in private dental offices. However an increasing number of hygienists are participating in community health programs and school dental educational programs, and opportunities also exist in hospital dental clinics and clinics for the physically or mentally handicapped. Many hygienists work part time for several different dentists.

What You Need Personally

Besides the ability to master necessary skills, the hygienist must have a knack for putting the patient at ease. She should enjoy working with

people and have a cheerful pleasant personality. Good health, manual dexterity, and the stamina to spend long hours standing are also important.

What Education and Training You Need

Dental hygienists must pass an examination to be licensed in the state in which they wish to practice. In all states except Alabama, eligibility for a license depends on graduation from an accredited school of dental hygiene. There are more than 100 such schools in the United States, most of them providing a two-year certificate or associate degree program.

These courses are given in community and junior colleges, technical and vocational schools, including many private schools. Some are reliable, others are not. Before enrolling in a private school, consult dentists and your state department of education and board of dental examiners to find out if the school is reliable.

If you wish to be a hygienist in a private dental office, completion of such a program is generally adequate preparation. Admission to these schools requires a high school diploma and may require some courses in science. The curriculum usually consists of courses in basic sciences, dental sciences, and liberal arts. Laboratory work and clinical experience are also included in most cases. Specific admission requirements should be obtained directly from each school. Some schools ask applicants to take the Dental Hygiene Aptitude Test given by the American Dental Hygienists' Association. This is a test which measures numerical ability, general background in science and the humanities, and ability to comprehend scientific information.

The Association suggests that students contact the financial aid office of the school they plan to attend for information on scholarships and state and federal loan funds. Special scholarships are offered by the Association itself, but they are not available to first-year students.

What the Occupation Has to Offer

By 1980 employment requirements for dental hygienists are expected to reach 33,500, an increase of more than 100 percent above the 16,000 now working, and demand is growing in other countries also. With a rising population, increased concern for proper dental care, expansion of educational programs, and increasing emphasis on preventive dentistry, this need for many more hygienists is not surprising.

Earnings vary with the employer, the area, and the education and experience of the individual hygienist. Salaries for graduates of two-year programs—the great majority of hygienists—averaged about $6,000 to $7,000 a year in 1970.

This is not a field in which you can advance in the sense of moving up in your work, but it is an excellent occupation to which women can return when family responsibilities lessen. It also provides excellent opportunities for part-time work. The hygienist is a responsible and respected member of the dental field, whose services are becoming more valued all the time.

Points to Consider Before Going into This Field

The dental hygienist has the advantage of belonging to a licensed group whose members must fulfill specific requirements. Although there is a set routine in many of the tasks she performs, her day is made up of a procession of different patients with different problems. A great deal of her job satisfaction depends on a good working relationship with the dentist or dentists in her office.

Hygienists are almost exclusively women and this situation will probably continue.

For more information, write:

Division of Educational Services
American Dental Hygienists' Association
211 East Chicago Avenue
Chicago, Illinois 60611
Ask for: information about the aptitude test, educational programs, admission requirements, and scholarships.

State Board of Dental Examiners in your state.

National Board of Dental Examiners
211 East Chicago Avenue
Chicago, Illinois 60611
Ask for: information on licensing requirements.

See also: pages 267-268.

Eye Care: Optometric Assistant

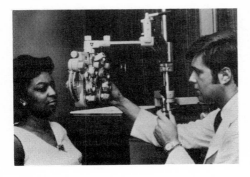

The Job

Optometric assistants help optometrists perform a variety of tasks. They may assist in eye examinations, prepare the patients and measure them for pupillary distance and bridge width. They may aid the patient in selecting eyeglass frames and adjust the finished glasses. They may also work in the laboratory, modifying glasses or

contact lenses to assure proper fit. Some assistants keep an inventory of materials, care for instruments, keep records, and schedule appointments.

Most assistants work for optometrists in private practice, but some are employed by optical instrument makers, health clinics, or government agencies. Since optometrists are located primarily in highly populated areas, the job opportunities for their assistants are also found in those locations.

What You Need Personally

If you are planning to enter this field, you should have manual dexterity and good visual color perception. Your duties put you in direct contact with patients—similar to the medical or dental assistant—and therefore neatness, courtesy, tact, and a pleasing personality are definite assets.

What Education and Training You Need

Most assistants are trained on-the-job by optometrists, but a few vocational and technical schools do offer courses in this occupation. Admission to these programs requires a high school diploma or its equivalent and some courses in mathematics and office procedure.

To be an optometric assistant you must learn the physiology and anatomy of the human eye; corrective eye exercises; how to measure, fit, and prepare lenses; how to select and adjust glasses; and other details of the profession. Such programs include some training in office management and clinical experience under the supervision of a practicing optometrist.

There is an effort to get more qualified people into this field; the State of New York (SUNY) State College of Optometry, for example, is offering three new programs for the training of optometric assisting personnel: 1. Optometric Assistant (Community Eye Health Aide), a 12-month certificate program, prepares the student to function as an extension of the professional. An aide might help in the home by counseling on eye care, such as the proper use of visual aids; interview clients and families; do administrative work such as maintenance of files and clinic records; identify eye-care needs of neighborhood families; work in an agency with an eye-care research program. 2. Optometric Assistant (Clinical), a 15-month certificate program, prepares the student to perform technical skills. This assistant may work in an eye-care center, clinic, hospital, public health institution, as well as in private and group practices. Skills such as color vision testing, visual skills testing, lensometry, prescription verification, and frame selection will be developed. 3. Optometric Technician (Clinical), a 2-year AAS degree program, prepares the student to work as an assistant to the optometrist in the office. The technician may perform initial history taking, routine visual acuity measurements, contact lens modification, instruct patients in contact lens insertion and removal, as well as perform those tasks done by either or both of the assistants' duties. The college provides counseling, both preadmission and during the course of programs, to help students select the particular program best suited to his or her needs and desires.

What the Occupation Has to Offer

With increasing recognition of the importance of good vision and a growing population with large numbers of older people, there will be a continuing demand for optometrists and those who aid them. However, this is not a field that is expected to grow as dramatically as some others in the health area.

Inexperienced assistants earn between $80 and $100 a week and those with experience earn $125 to $160. Most work a 40-hour week, but this schedule often includes Saturdays. Assistants who have an associate degree from a two-year junior or community college can advance to the position of optometric technician.

Points to Consider Before Going into This Field

The work of an optometric assistant is similar in some ways to that of a medical or dental assistant, but the specific duties are different. For those with a special interest in vision problems and their correction, this occupation should have appeal.

There is not much opportunity for advancement, and employment is generally restricted to urban and suburban locations.

Most of the 5,000 optometric assistants in the country are women.

For more information, write:

American Optometric Association
7000 Chippewa St.
St. Louis, Missouri 63119.

Assisting Optometric Personnel Programs
State College of Optometry
122 East 25th Street
New York, New York 10010.

See also: pages 267-268.

Eye Care: Dispensing Optician and Optical Mechanic

The Job

A dispensing optician works in a retail optical establishment, fitting and adjusting glasses and helping the customer select proper frames.

He does not prescribe glasses as an optometrist does. In some states, opticians also fit contact lenses, a procedure requiring special skill and patience.

An optical mechanic (or optical laboratory technician) actually makes the glasses, grinding and polishing the lenses to the specifications of the prescription and assembling them in frames. The mechanics who grind lenses are called "surfacers" and they use precision instruments to convert standard, mass-produced lenses into what is called for in the work order. The finisher or "benchman" marks and cuts the lenses and smooths the edges to fit the frame and then assembles the parts into the finished glasses.

What You Need Personally

An optician deals directly with the public, so he should have tact and a pleasant personality. On the other hand the ability to do precision work combined with good vision and manual dexterity are important for the optical mechanic.

What Education and Training You Need

Most people in these occupations learned their skills on-the-job, although the training may take several years. Trainees or apprentices in optical mechanics begin with simple operations and progress to more complicated tasks as their skills improve. It usually takes about three years to gain experience in all phases of eyeglass production, after which the mechanic may go on to specialize in surfacing or bench work.

Training for the optician is becoming more formalized, with several junior and community colleges now offering two-year courses leading to an associate degree. There are also vocational schools which have nine-month courses in optical mechanics, and some optical firms have four to five-year apprenticeship programs. (See pages 52-63.

Workers in both areas should be high school graduates who have studied the basic sciences. Some background in mathematics and mechanical drawing is also helpful. State regulations on licensing in these fields vary considerably.

What the Occupation Has to Offer

Extensive growth in these fields is not expected in the near future, but there are opportunities in both areas, especially for those who complete degree or apprenticeship programs. Optical mechanics earn from $2.50 to $4.25 an hour depending on experience, and opticians earn about 15 to 25 percent more. Mechanics may advance to foremen, with a 20 percent increase in pay. Many opticians go on to own their own businesses.

Points to Consider Before Going into This Field

Nearly all optical mechanics are men, but a small number of women have become dispensing opticians. Restrictions on the specific duties which can be performed vary state by state, and working conditions for mechanics may be governed by union-management contracts.

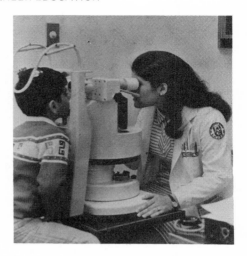

For more information, write:

American Board of Opticianry
821 Eggert Road
Buffalo, New York 14226.

Guild of Prescription Opticians of America, Inc.
1250 Connecticut Avenue, N. W.
Washington, D. C. 20036.
Ask for: list of schools offering programs in this field.

International Union of Electrical, Radio and Machine Workers
1126 16th Street, N. W.
Washington, D. C. 20036.

Optical Wholesalers Association
6935 Wisconsin Avenue
Washington, D. C. 20015
Ask for: job information and training programs; and Stimson, Russell L. *Opportunities in Opticianry* New York: Vocational Guidance Manuals, 1971. $1.95.

See also: pages 267-268.

Orthoptic Technician

The Job

The orthoptist has a highly specialized job in the field of eye improvement: a therapist who helps youngsters or adults overcome the handicap of crossed eyes. An orthoptist works under the supervision of an ophthalmologist (a doctor of medicine who specializes in diseases of the eye) or a group of ophthalmologists in a clinic, office, hospital, or medical center.

As a trained technician, the orthoptist teaches the patient certain exercises which help his eyes to work together as they should.

As an orthoptist you will probably see four-teen or fifteen patients a day, spending half an hour with each. Working with one child at a time in a quiet, relaxed atmosphere, you might see a patient once or twice a week for one to three months. During this time, the patient is also doing exercises at home under the guidance of the orthoptist. It's part of your responsibility to be sure the home exercises are being done properly and are giving the hoped for results.

What You Need Personally

Since much of an orthoptist's work is done with children, you must be able to win the confidence of both the child and his parents. You must be a patient, understanding person, with a liking for people. A neat appearance, general good health and good eyesight are also important. It'll help if you are emotionally mature and have scientific curiosity.

What Education and Training You Need

Before you can study orthoptics, you must be at least 20 years old, and must have completed two years of college or comparable education. A college degree is specified by at least one training school.

Orthoptic technician programs are offered in hospital training centers and universities across the country. To get your special training, you may go directly to one of the schools giving a year's training in orthoptics, or you can be placed in a training center for a ten- to twelve-month period of practical work under the supervision of a certified orthoptist, combining this with the basic two-month course offered by the American Orthoptic Council.

A certificate is issued by the American Orthoptic Council to qualified students who successfully pass an examination given by the Council. There is no legal requirement to obtain such certification, but more than 95 percent of all medically trained orthoptists are certified.

What the Occupation Has to Offer

The acute shortage of orthoptists in the United States and Canada assures virtually every one trained in this field of employment immediately after graduation. Since the orthoptist usually functions as an assistant to the ophthalmologist, you will work chiefly in cities where eye specialists are located. Orthoptists may also be needed in specialized hospitals and clinics. Earnings vary in different communities, but the starting salary of a certified orthoptist is usually around $400 a month.

Points to Consider Before Going into This Field

Hospitals, clinics, and ophthalmologists' offices are clean and pleasant places in which to work. Although home exercises are frequently prescribed for patients, orthoptists are not required to make home visits. Since many orthoptic patients are children, orthoptists usually work on Saturdays and choose another day off during the week.

Though men are not excluded from this field, most orthoptists are women. This is a field with a satisfying and continuing need for intelligent, enthusiastic people to apply standard techniques and devise new ones to help patients in need.

For more information, write:

American Academy of Ophthalmology and Otolaryngology
15 Second Street, S. W.
Rochester, Minnesota 55901
Ask for: information on training programs and American Association of Certified Orthoptists and American Orthoptic Council.

American Orthoptic Council
555 University Avenue
Toronto Canada, M5 G1X8

Delta Gamma Foundation
3250 Riverside Drive
Columbus, Ohio 43221
Ask for: information on scholarships.

Medical Laboratory Worker

The Job

Workers in modern medical laboratories perform tests which can be vital in the detection and treatment of diseases. Their work is accomplished with the help of a variety of highly technical and precise equipment including microscopes, analyzers, spectrophotometers, and gas chromatographs.

Different levels of workers are needed to staff

a medical laboratory, and there are job opportunities for many kinds of people with varying degrees of training and experience from the pathologist, who is a physician, on down.

Two newer categories of laboratory workers provide starting and intermediate levels of responsibility in this group. One is the certified laboratory assistant, and the other is the medical laboratory technician. Other relatively recent and specialized additions to the laboratory staff include the cytotechnologist and the histologic technician.

Just as a medical technologist works under a pathologist and carries out laboratory routines, these new workers also help relieve more highly trained personnel of routine duties.

A certified laboratory assistant works in all areas of laboratory science. Specific tasks might include collecting blood specimens, grouping and typing blood, analyzing blood and body fluids, preparing and staining slides and making microscopic examinations of samples. As an assistant you have learned your skills in a one-year approved program and passed a national certifying examination.

The medical laboratory technician has an associate degree or its equivalent and has been trained to perform more complicated procedures than the assistant. This is a relatively new profession whose members serve as a bridge between the lab assistant and the professional technologist.

Cytotechnologists specialize in screening samples under the microscope to detect early warning signs of cancer. They are employed in pathology laboratories after completing a one-year training program.

Histologic technicians are trained over a one-year period to cut and stain tissues which the pathologist examines for malignant or questionable cells.

What You Need Personally

Working in a medical laboratory requires a high degree of accuracy, reliability, and serious dedication. You should be able to work under pressure. Neatness and manual dexterity are also desirable traits.

What Education and Training You Need

Because of the complicated and rapidly changing nature of occupations within a medical laboratory, those who are interested should carefully examine the training programs available.

The certified laboratory assistant (CLA) must be a graduate of an accredited high school or have a certificate of equivalency and should preferably have shown some interest and ability in science or mathematics. CLA programs approved by the American Medical Association are now in operation in about 225 locations throughout the country. They take one year to complete and include at least 100 hours of classroom instruction plus at least 40 hours of laboratory experience.

Most CLA programs are offered in hospitals, but some are available in vocational and technical schools, community colleges, and military bases. Many charge little or no tuition, and several offer scholarships or financial aid. Graduates who complete these programs are eligible to take the registry examination and add the letters CLA to their names if they pass.

Medical laboratory technicians must have an associate degree from an accredited junior or community college program, including supervised clinical experience in a laboratory. Such programs are now being developed under guidelines from the American Medical Association. The curriculum includes general education and laboratory sciences.

Cytotechnologists must have two years of college and a year of training in one of the nearly 100 approved schools. Histologic technicians need a high school diploma and must complete a one-year hospital or junior college course, which will lead to examination and certification. Most of these schools charge little or no tuition and many offer scholarships or financial aid.

What the Occupation Has to Offer

Career opportunities in the medical laboratory are among the most varied and challenging in the entire health field. Laboratory workers include both men and women, young and old. There are job opportunities here for the handicapped, too.

Chances of advancement are excellent with additional training. Salaries tend to follow the career ladder with assistants earning the least. Their salaries range between $6,000 and $7,000 a year. Laboratory technicians average between $7,000–$8,000; and cytotechnologists with experience earn between $7,000 and $10,000.

Points to Consider Before Going into This Field

Availability of jobs and opportunity for advancement are among the advantages in this kind of health work. However the atmosphere of a laboratory is specialized, and not for everyone. It is a good idea to get some exposure to this type of work, equipment, and surroundings before committing yourself to training. In the past, technicians and assistants have been primarily women, but more men are entering the field.

For more information, write:

American Medical Technologists
710 Higgins Road
Park Ridge, Illinois 60068
Ask for: information about technician training
    programs offered in private schools.

Registry of Medical Technologists
American Society of Clinical Pathologists
Box 4872
Chicago, Illinois 60680
Ask for: Career opportunities programs available and scholarship information.

American Society of Medical Technologists
Suite 1600, Hermann Professional Building
Houston, Texas 77025
Ask for: career opportunities, programs available and scholarship information.

See also: pages 267-268.

Medical Office Assistant

The Job

A medical assistant is just what the name implies—one who helps a physician in the examination and treatment of patients as well as in the paperwork that is part of a medical practice. In the medical end the assistant may perform laboratory tests, arrange hospital admissions etc., and the clerical end may keep records, fill out insurance forms, send out bills and record payments, schedule appointments, and handle correspondence. The assistant may also be responsible for general office maintenance, supplies, and instruments.

There were 175,000 medical assistants working in 1970. Jobs in this field vary widely depending on the office, size of staff, and type of practice. Most assistants, however, function as a link between physician and patient to relieve the doctor of administrative duties so that he may concentrate on diagnosis and treatment. Some work in hospitals and medical clinics as well.

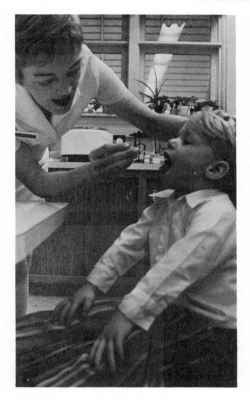

What You Need Personally

As a medical assistant you should be able to get along well with people. Often you are the first person the patient or prospective patient contacts. You can help create a positive impression and ease some of the anxieties that often accompany a visit to the doctor. Assistants also need to be accurate, thorough, and dependable in following up the many medical and clerical details involved in the job.

What Education and Training You Need

In the past, most medical assistants were trained on-the-job by individual physicians to meet their particular needs. Today, however, most doctors are too busy to provide such training, and assistants are formally trained in special programs.

A number of junior and community colleges and vocational-technical schools offer such training. The Council on Medical Education of the American Medical Association, in cooperation with the American Association of Medical Assistants, has outlined the essentials of approved programs in detail. College programs take two years and offer an associate degree with a broad foundation in office and medical skills, including a period of experience in a doctor's office. Other schools provide one-year programs that also combine academic courses and clinical work.

Medical assistants who meet the national organization's qualifications may receive certification. Candidates must be high school graduates currently employed and have three years of experience. Exceptions are made for those who hold an associate degree, in which case one year of experience is sufficient. A written examination is given, which is composed of three divisions. A passing mark in the first two divisions is needed for certification as an administrative medical assistant; in the first and third divisions to be a clinical medical assistant; and in all three divisions for dual certification (administrative and clinical). Such certification is not a prerequisite for membership in the AAMA, nor is it a license to work in the field, but it does mark the holder as a well-qualified worker.

What the Occupation Has to Offer

With a nationwide shortage of physicians and nurses, many more medical assistants will be needed in the years ahead. The growing stream of paperwork flowing through a doctor's office also adds to the demand for qualified help. Opportunities should be especially good for graduates of two-year college programs.

Assistants' salaries reflect the prevailing scale for office workers with comparable training. Average national weekly salaries in 1970 ranged from $90 to $125 for inexperienced assistants and from $125 to $160 for those with experience.

Advancement is somewhat limited, but increased experience and skill usually mean increased responsibilities and higher pay. A top-notch assistant can be an invaluable asset to a busy physician, and such a person is often well rewarded in the satisfaction of performing essential and humanitarian services.

Points to Consider Before Going into This Field

As in other jobs in the health field, a medical assistant can experience a real sense of pride in the work. Jobs are widely available with a minimum of training, and skills can be updated through experience or continuing education. A woman with a family can return to this work with little difficulty and sometimes on a part-time basis.

Some feel the hours are a disadvantage, because they can be irregular and often include Saturdays or evenings. However, equivalent time off is given during the week.

Almost all medical assistants are women, but there is no reason why men cannot enter the field.

For more information, write:

American Association of Medical Assistants
One East Wacker Drive
Chicago, Illinois 60601
Ask for: information on accredited programs, scholarships and loans, and certification.

See also: pages 267-268.

Nursing: Licensed Practical Nurse

The Job

There are many aspects of caring for an ill person that do not require the specialized training of a physician or a registered nurse. Often these services to the convalescent, the handicapped, or the aged are provided by licensed practical nurses (LPN).

In hospitals they offer bedside care, such as changing dressings, bathing patients, taking and recording temperatures and blood pressures, assisting in examinations, and helping in the delivery and care of newborn infants. In private homes they take care of patients' personal needs, comfort, and well-being as well as provide specific care directed by the doctor. In offices and clinics they assist physicians in preparing patients for examinations and recording information.

Because of the special personal association the practical nurse has with the patient, she is frequently the individual the ill person feels closest to and remembers afterward.

There are openings for the LPNs throughout the country and overseas through service in the Army or the Peace Corps. Of the approximately 370,000 practical nurses employed in 1970, more than half worked in hospitals. Most of the others were employed by nursing homes, clinics, sanitoriums, doctors' offices, public health agencies, and welfare or religious organizations. Some were self-employed, either in patients' homes or hospitals. Those who work in homes generally are on duty for 8- or 12-hour periods and go home at night. However, some do live in the home and are on duty around the clock.

What You Need Personally

A practical nurse should have a sincere concern for others and a deep desire to be of service. You need a good deal of physical stamina and emotional stability, because working with the sick, and especially with the handicapped or chronically ill, can be difficult and demanding. You often have to perform the most menial tasks, and a general cheerful disposition is invaluable. As part of the health care team, the LPN must be able to take directions and follow them carefully.

What Education and Training You Need

Until recently anyone could call herself a practical nurse, but now all states have licensing laws.

In 1970 about 1,250 state approved programs offered training in practical nursing; more than half of them were given in public schools as part of vocational or adult education programs. Many community and junior colleges, hospitals, health agencies, and private institutions also provide such training.

Most of the programs take one year to complete and include both classroom study and practical experience. The course work includes nursing principles, first aid, nutrition, anatomy and physiology, psychology, pharmacology, and community health. Students are then given an opportunity to apply their skills in hospitals under supervision and learn by doing.

Admission to these programs usually requires only two years of high school or its equivalent. Some states however accept people who have completed eighth or ninth grade, while others require a high school diploma. Only those who complete a state approved course may receive state licensing.

The age range for admission is from 17 to 50, with applicants over 50 considered on an individual basis. Tuition in most schools is low, ranging from a maximum of about $500 to free admission. Many offer scholarships or loans, and inquiries about financial aid should be made to individual schools. The National Association for Practical Nurse Education and Service (NAPNES) also has a scholarship program that is available to needy students already enrolled in programs. You cannot become a LPN through correspondence courses.

What the Occupation Has to Offer

As part of the increase in health services, there will be a growing need for more practical nurses. Paraprofessionals are being utilized more and more in all areas of medical care, and LPNs are already in very short supply. Opportunities for part-time work should continue to be good.

Earnings for practical nurses in hospitals and medical schools average about $110 a week;

increases are often given after specified periods of service and fringe benefits are generally provided. Pay varies with location and type of duty, but LPNs tend to earn about three-fourths of what RN's do in the same setting.

Although the usual work week is 40 hours, this may include some night, holiday, or weekend duty. Without additional training advancement is limited. However, sometimes practical nurses can take advantage of in-service programs to prepare for more specialized areas such as rehabilitation work.

Points to Consider Before Going into This Field

Certainly a great advantage of practical nursing is the relatively short and inexpensive training period; another is the fact that work opportunities are widespread and offer so much choice. You can move from state to state once you have your license, and age and race are not barriers to employment. Part-time opportunities are excellent, so that married women with families may work on flexible schedules.

While practical nursing can offer personal satisfactions, you should keep in mind that much of the work is taxing. And because your rank is low in the health hierarchy, you may be taking orders from several different people.

Most LPNs are women, but the field has begun to attract some men in recent years.

For more information, write:

National Association for Practical Nurse Education & Service
1465 Broadway
New York, N. Y. 10036
Ask for: information on training programs.
See also: pages 267-268.

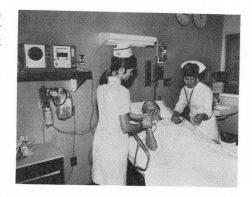

tion, and promotes health and safety within the firm.

Even hospital staff nurses often specialize in areas such as pediatrics (working with children), operating room (surgical) or geriatrics (the elderly). Others supervise auxiliary workers, such as practical nurses or aides. Some RNs are private duty nurses who give individual care to single patients who need constant attention.

Approximately 700,000 registered nurses were employed in the U. S. in 1970, and the projected national need is for 1,000,000 by 1975. More than one-fourth of the nurses currently employed work on a part-time basis.

What You Need Personally

As nurse you are constantly being called upon to demonstrate your competence. You must be intelligent, alert, and possess good judgment and a strong sense of responsibility. Nursing education programs, even the shortest, require good study habits and concentration.

Those who wish to enter nursing should also have sympathy and understanding of others, a desire to serve, and a sense of humor. Good health is essential; a physical examination is required for all training programs.

It's important to have a clear understanding of what nursing is and what it is not. Joining a Future Nurses club or working as a volunteer or aide in a hospital can be helpful in giving you a realistic picture of the profession.

What Education and Training You Need

If your career goals don't include four years of college, there are two- and three-year nursing programs.

Most two-year courses are offered in junior or community colleges, and graduates earn an associate degree. Major emphasis here is on nursing theory and practice, and includes some general education and science courses.

The two- and three-year programs which give you a diploma in nursing are offered at hospital or independent schools of nursing. The curricu-

Nursing: Registered Nurse

The Job

Registered nurses (RN) share the general aim of caring for the sick and promoting health, but they work in a wide variety of jobs and settings. We usually think first of nurses employed in hospitals and clinics, but there are many others working in health agencies, schools, industry, doctors' offices, nursing schools, and private homes. Government also offers a selection of jobs to trained nurses.

Wherever she works, the image of "the woman in white" is a familiar one to most people because she plays a role in most of our lives. Students know the school nurse, who is concerned with the general health of the student body. Workers have contact with the industrial or occupational health nurse who provides emergency care to employees of a particular organiza-

lum is similar, but more opportunity is provided for practical experience because of direct hospital affiliation.

Admission to all programs requires a high school degree but some schools require class standing in the top one-third or one-half. Other requirements vary greatly. Minimum age is usually 17 and maximum is 35, but many schools take students up to age 50. Entrance tests are required, and personal traits and character may also be considerations. Nursing is a very popular career choice, so admission to certain programs may be very competitive.

While tuition in public junior or community colleges is low, private institutions fees are higher. Diploma programs in nursing schools are generally low in cost, but all charge some tuition. Scholarships and low interest loans are available under Title II of the Health Manpower Act of 1968. The Nurse Training Act also provides funds for tuition and fees and an allowance for nurses who seek advanced training in the field.

What the Occupation Has to Offer

The demand for RNs is steadily increasing. With new emphasis on outside of the conventional hospital, health care, more nurses will be needed to serve patients in community health centers, clinics, public agencies, doctors' offices, and occupational settings.

Nursing also offers increasing opportunities for specialization in such areas as mental health therapy, rehabilitation work and anesthetics. There is also a growing trend toward nurses getting additional training to become midwives or physicians' associates.

Nursing used to be considered a stepchild in the health career family because earnings were low in relation to training and responsibilities. But this is no longer true. Nurses' salaries have doubled during the last ten years, and a beginning RN now receives a starting salary of at least $700 to $750 a month in populated urban areas. New York City municipal hospital salaries now start at over $10,000 a year for a fixed 40-hour week.

In 1970 salaries for industrial nurses averaged $147 a week, and fees for private duty nurses ranged between $26 and $44 for an eight-hour shift. Most hospital nurses earn extra pay for night duty and receive health and retirement benefits, several paid holidays, and at least two weeks of paid vacation after one year of service.

There are many avenues for advancement in nursing, including specialization, supervision, teaching, and administration.

Points to Consider Before Going into This Field

Once you become an RN you have a wide selection of duties and work settings. Women who choose nursing find they have a lifetime career because not only do they have the opportunity to work on a part-time basis but can apply their training to a home and family situation as well.

Nursing is still difficult and demanding work. But enrollments in nursing programs have risen because nursing is where the action in medicine is and the nurse has a chance to work with patients and practice independently.

For more information, write:

American Association of Industrial Nurses, Inc.
79 Madison Avenue
New York, New York 10016
Ask for: information on occupational health nursing.

For details on becoming a nurse-anesthetist, write:

American Association of Nurse Anesthetists
111 East Wacker Drive
Suite 929
Chicago, Illinois 60601

American Nurses' Association, Inc.
2420 Pershing Road
Kansas City, Missouri 64108
Ask for: list of nursing careers material.

B'nai B'rith Career and Counseling Service
1640 Rhode Island Avenue, N. W.
Washington, D. C. 20036
Ask for: *A Career in Nursing*, $1.00.

Division of Nursing
Bureau of Health, Manpower Education
U. S. Department of Health, Education and Welfare
9000 Rockville Pike
Bethesda, Maryland 20014
Ask for: *YOU-IN: Making It in Nursing*, Free.

Additional Reading:

Facts About Nursing.
American Nurses' Association, Inc.
2420 Pershing Road
Kansas City, Missouri 64108. $5.75.

See also: pages 267-268.

Nursing: Physician's Associate

The Job

Nurses and medical assistants have for years been performing tasks in order to relieve physicians of routine tasks. There still remain, however, many other duties to be performed by people less extensively trained than doctors. In a recent but fast growing trend, programs have been springing up around the country to train such paramedical personnel. If you're interested in functioning at a patient-care level higher than that of a nurse but lower than a doctor, you

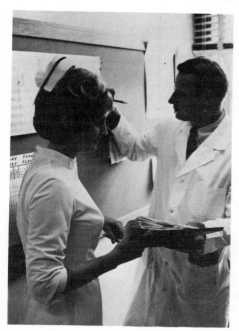

What Education and Training You Need

This field is still in the formative stages, and programs vary in caliber, scope, and length. Most of them fall into one of three categories:

(1) The broad based physician's associate programs generally take two years and lead to a certificate or an associate degree. (As in RN training, there are also four-year programs leading to a bachelor's degree.) Much of the course work is similar to that in a medical school, and you may be taking some classes with medical students.

(2) MEDEX programs last about fifteen months, divided into three months of class work and twelve months of a "preceptorship" working with a doctor. This program is designed especially for ex-military medical corpsmen.

(3) Specialty programs in surgery, pediatrics, orthopedics, cardiac care, etc., range in length from several weeks to a year.

Because there is such a wide range of programs, the entrance requirements vary greatly.

What the Occupation Has to Offer

Opportunity seems to be wide-open in this infant field where demand far exceeds present supply. Salaries vary depending on training and experience, but the graduates of Duke University's pioneer program have more job offers than they can handle, some of them paying $10,000 a year or more.

One can advance by improving one's skills and specialty. The field also offers an opportunity for upgrading or advancement for people in lower allied health jobs, such as LPN or RN. It is also particularly appealing to former military medical corpsmen.

Points to Consider Before Going into This Field

If you decide to become a PA, you're getting in on the ground floor of what is proving to be an exciting and challenging occupation. However, because the field is so new, it has not yet been able to establish the precise standards of training and certification which prevail in many health jobs. State laws vary widely, and there are still legal questions as to the licensing of PAs and their liability in malpractice suits. It also may be too soon to evaluate what resistance the PA might encounter from both doctors and patients if the occupation greatly expands.

The field is open to both men and women.

For more information, write:

American Academy of Physicians' Associates
Room 356, 2150 Pennsylvania Avenue
Washington, D. C. 20037
Ask for: career information, accredited program, and financial aid information.

See also: pages 267-268.

might investigate becoming a physician's associate.

Physician's associates, as additions to the health team, work in a variety of ways—from taking patient histories and blood pressures to dressing wounds, applying casts, giving injections, and taking electrocardiograms, and white blood cell counts. Some of them are trained only to perform in certain areas such as surgery, obstetrics, or pediatrics and work only under the direction of physicians in those fields.

The concept of the physician's associate, or PA is still so new that only a small number of persons are employed under the title. The first training program got under way in 1965 at the Duke University Medical Center, and since that time more than 50 other programs have been established, many of them at other medical schools.

What You Need Personally

Physician's associates were known first as physician's assistants; some are still called health practitioners or paramedics. But whatever the title, the person working in this capacity must have a high degree of intelligence, be dedicated and thorough. He or she should have the same qualities that are desirable in a nurse or a physician. The major difference here is that requirements for entrance into training programs are less stringent and the programs are shorter.

Radiologic Technologist

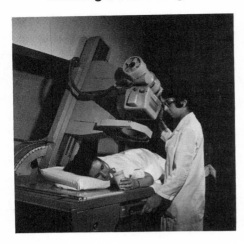

The Job

Radiologic technologists are the extra hands of the radiologist, the physician who specializes in the use of X rays. They assist him in taking the actual X ray and in administering X ray therapy under professional supervision.

In taking X rays, the radiologic or X-ray technologist prepares the chemical mixture which a patient swallows in order to make certain organs show up more clearly on the plates. He or she uses protection devices and techniques to safeguard against radiation hazards. Technologists may also be responsible for scheduling X-ray examinations and treatments, and for keeping patients' records.

Some technologists now work in the new field of nuclear medicine, in which radioactive isotopes are used in diagnosis and treatment. These techniques permit the viewing of organs that cannot be seen by X rays and are used in the treatment of thyroid conditions and certain forms of leukemia.

Technologists, some 80,000 of them, work in the X-ray departments of hospitals, clinics or laboratories, in government health agencies, public school systems, or physicians' or dentists' offices.

What You Need Personally

Good health, good judgment, and stamina are essentials for the X-ray technologist. You must be able to work rapidly and accurately, sometimes under pressure. You should also be the kind of person who can deal sympathetically and tactfully with various types of patients.

What Education and Training You Need

Most approved schools of radiologic technology are in hospitals or medical schools affiliated with hospitals, because an essential part of the curriculum is practical experience. Most programs take two years to complete. Some vocational and technical schools and some junior colleges also offer programs and provide experience at nearby hospitals.

About 1,200 schools of X-ray technology are approved by the American Medical Association, and only graduates of approved schools are eligible to take registering examinations in this specialty. Tuition ranges from nothing to $500 per year; some schools provide room and board and pay a salary for students on call during their second year.

You must be a high school graduate to enroll, preferably with a background in math, science, and typing. X-ray technology courses usually include anatomy, physiology, physics, radiation protection, nursing procedures, X-ray therapy, darkroom chemistry and technique, radiographic positioning and exposure, and equipment maintenance.

Successful completion of the certifying examination results in registration with the American Registry of Radiologic Technologists. This listing will be an asset in obtaining more highly rated positions. Certification in nuclear medicine technology requires an additional year of combined work-study experience.

What the Occupation Has to Offer

Use of X-ray equipment is continually increasing, so the demand for trained technologists should continue to rise. Jobs are available all over the country, but a shortage of trained personnel is especially acute in communities with small hospitals.

Earnings vary with location, and salaries in industry and civil service tend to be somewhat higher than in hospitals. New graduates of AMA-approved schools employed by the federal government received annual pay of about $6,000 in 1970. Earnings increase proportionately with experience and can reach $10,000–$15,000 a year.

Some technologists in large X-ray departments can advance to chief X-ray technicians or qualify as instructors who teach techniques to beginners.

Points to Consider Before Going into This Field

This field offers job security and the opportunity to contribute to the improved health of large numbers of patients. Working conditions are pleasant and hours are regular. There is opportunity for travel, both in the U. S. and abroad, since your skill can be utilized anywhere.

Even with modern precautions, however, some people are still concerned about the hazards of radiation equipment and dislike working with it.

Approximately two-thirds of X-ray technologists are women, and the ratio is expected to remain about the same.

For more information, write:

Publications Department
American College of Radiology
20 North Wacker Drive
Chicago, Illinois 60606

American Medical Association
Department of Allied Health Professions & Services
535 North Dearborn
Chicago, Illinois 60610
Ask for: list of approved schools.

The American Registry of Radiologic Technologists
2600 Wayzata Boulevard
Minneapolis, Minnesota 55405
Ask for: information about registration.

American Society of Radiologic Technologists
645 North Michigan Avenue
Chicago, Illinois 60611
Ask for: list of approved schools; career information.

Society of Nuclear Medical Technologists
1201 Waukegan Road
Glenview, Illinois 60025
Ask for: information about nuclear medicine.

Technical Education Record Centers
44 Brattle Street
Cambridge, Massachusetts 02138
Ask for: information about nuclear medical technologist and Biomedical Equipment Technician.

See also: pages 267-268.

Rehabilitation: Occupational Therapy Assistant

The Job

The aim of occupational therapy is to design and carry out projects to help increase a patient's self-suffiency through a variety of vocational, educational, and recreational activities. Occupational therapists help rehabilitate patients who are physically or mentally disabled; occupational therapy assistants help therapists accomplish this goal.

Occupational therapy promotes health through purposeful activities that require the physical and/or mental involvement of those being treated. Services vary widely—from helping a child develop muscle dexterity by molding clay, to teaching an accident victim how to shave himself, to instructing a convalescent in the use of a printing press.

The OT assistant sometimes works with individual patients and sometimes with groups. She may function under the close supervision of a therapist or work quite independently. Responsibilities may include such things as ordering, preparing, and maintaining equipment and supplies as well as keeping patient records and assisting with special orthopedic devices.

Most of the 6,000 OT assistants employed in 1970 were women working in the occupational therapy departments of general and specialized hospitals. Some also worked in homes for the aged, rehabilitation centers, nursing homes, schools for the handicapped or mentally retarded, and out-patient clinics.

What You Need Personally

There is a strong one-to-one relationship in occupational therapy, and would-be assistants should like people, be warm and relate to them well. Physical and mental health are important factors, because the work is sometimes strenuous and emotionally tiring. You needn't be a skilled artist or craftsman, but you should be able to work with materials, tools, and simple mechanical equipment. You need to be versatile and keep up with new developments; you need to be determined and patient because progress can be painfully slow.

What Education and Training You Need

As in other paramedical fields, there is an increasing emphasis on approved training programs for OT assistants. In the past many assistants trained on the job under professional therapists, but the American Occupational Therapy Association has now established standards for certification of assistants. About one-third of those now employed are qualified to add the initials COTA (Certified Occupational Therapy Assistant) to their names.

To become certified you must be a high school graduate who has completed one of three kinds of training programs: (1) an associate degree program in an accredited junior or community college, usually requiring two years; (2) a one-year program in an approved educational institution; or (3) a twenty- twenty-five week program in a hospital or community agency.

Each of these programs includes a minimum of two months of supervised practical experience as well as courses in physical disability, mental illness, growth and development, therapeutic skills and crafts, and the structure and function of the human body.

What the Occupation Has to Offer

As the need for professional occupational therapists grows, there will be a corresponding need for assistants, especially for those with certification. Many community agencies, public health programs, and special organizations serving the handicapped are making more use of occupational therapy in their rehabilitative programs. Children with learning disabilities, returning war veterans, drug addicts are among those who benefit from the help of occupational therapy workers.

Certified assistants receive higher starting salaries than inexperienced beginners. Experienced assistants earn from $125 to $150 a week. A five-day, 40 hour week is normal, with the possibility of some evening or week-end assignments.

Points to Consider Before Going into This Field

A job in occupational therapy can bring much personal satisfaction because of the constructive, purposeful nature of the work. Teaching an injured man to dress himself or a handicapped child to paint a picture can bring substantial inner rewards.

On the other hand, OT assistants must face difficult and even tragic situations involving the aged and the ill, and not everyone is suited to such challenges.

Most OTs and assistants are women, but there's no reason men can't enter the field. Occupational therapy is an excellent field for women to return to, often on a part-time basis, as their children grow older.

For more information, write:

American Occupational Therapy Association
6000 Executive Boulevard
Rockville, Maryland 20852
Ask for: career information and programs.

See also: pages 267-268.

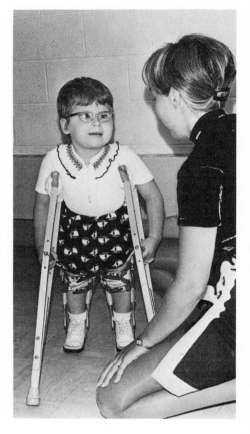

Rehabilitation: Physical Therapy Assistant

The Job

As a result of the skills of the physical therapist, an accident victim can be helped to walk again, a child with cerebral palsy can learn to use his limbs and attend school, and a person who has suffered a stroke can regain the use of an arm and return to work. Physical therapy is one of the fastest growing areas of the allied health field. Working under the direction of a physician, the physical therapist (PT) helps in the rehabilitation of people with injuries or diseases which have affected their muscles, nerves, joints, or bones. Through therapeutic exercise and massage, and applications of heat, water, light, and electricity these patients can often be aided in overcoming their disabilities.

Physical therapy assistants help the therapist carry out these activities. They perform tests to determine proper treatment, position patients, use special equipment, and report results. Assist-

ants may also aid patients to dress and undress, remove and replace braces or splints, and may transport patients to and from treatment areas. Sometimes they assist in the fitting of artificial limbs and the instruction on how to use these prosthetic devices. PT assistants are responsible for the care and maintenance of physical therapy equipment and the clerical record keeping involved.

Most of the 10,000 assistants employed in 1970 worked in the PT departments of general and specialized hospitals. Others worked in rehabilitation centers, nursing homes, schools for crippled children, offices, clinics, and government health agencies.

What You Need Personally

Anyone working in physical therapy should be in good physical and mental health. Unusual strength is not necessary, but a certain amount of manual dexterity and body coordination is helpful. You also need to be sincere and warm in order to establish positive and pleasant relationships with disabled patients for long-term periods.

What Education and Training You Need

Until recently most PT assistants got their training through on-the-job programs in hospitals and other health care facilities. Programs varied in content and length, but those enrolled were usually high school graduates with some science background. Some assistants learned their skills in vocational, technical, or adult education programs. Today, however, an increasing proportion are being trained in two-year college courses. These programs lead to an associate degree, and include biological, physical, and social sciences; humanities; technical courses in physical therapy; and clinical experience. The American Physical Therapy Association recommends these junior college programs, and their graduates receive preference in employment.

There are various sources of financial aid in this field, including the federal government, and a list of scholarship and loan programs is available from their national organization (see p. 285 for address).

What the Occupation Has to Offer

A growing public awareness of the importance of rehabilitation services has led to expansion of physical therapy facilities, and an increased need for personnel trained in this area. Job openings should continue to be numerous for PT assistants, and especially for those with associate degrees.

Average weekly salaries range from $80 to $110 for inexperienced assistants and from $110 to $150 for those with experience. If you have graduated from a college program, your earnings will be higher.

You can advance by getting a bachelor's degree, and obtaining certification as a physical therapist.

Points to Consider Before Going into This Field

This can be an extremely satisfying area of work because you can often see patients improve right before your eyes. There can be discouraging moments, of course, but the constructive nature of the work appeals to many who wish to be of service.

Part-time opportunities are open to family women, but this is a field which has attracted both men and women and they participate on an equal basis.

For more information, write:

American Physical Therapy Association
1156 Fifteenth Street, N. W.
Washington, D. C. 20008

Ask for: information on programs, and financial aid.

Registry of Medical Rehabilitation Therapists and Specialists.
4975 Judy Lynn
Memphis, Tennessee 38118
Ask for: registered career information.

See also: pages 267-268.

Other Jobs in Hospitals: Hospital Attendant

The Job

For those who wish to be directly involved in the field of health care and want to work in a hospital setting, there are some jobs open to both men and women with a minimum of training.

Hospital attendants work under the direction of registered and licensed practical nurses to make patients more comfortable. Women in these jobs are usually called nursing aides, nursing assistants, auxiliary nursing workers, or—in mental hospitals—psychiatric aides. Men are most often called orderlies.

Duties may include answering patients' bell calls, making beds, feeding, bathing, and dressing patients, giving massages, taking temperatures, and assisting patients in getting out of bed and in walking. Orderlies also wheel patients to other rooms and transport and set up equipment.

Another kind of hospital attendant is the central service technician; his chief responsibilities are the cleaning and sterilizing of instruments, supplies and equipment; the assembling and processing of treatment and procedure trays; and the receiving and storing of replacement supplies.

What You Need Personally

Nursing aides and orderlies work directly with patients and should have an interest in people and an ability to get along with them even in difficult situations. A desire to be of service, a sense of responsibility and attention to details, are helpful qualities. Service technicians also need manual dexterity. Good physical health is important for all those engaged in hospital work.

What Education and Training You Need

Most of the training here is provided in on-the-job hospital programs lasting about three months. A high school education is preferred but not always required. Volunteer and temporary jobs often provide helpful experience. The training for central service technicians is longer and more technical. Some of these programs are now offered in trade and vocational schools.

What the Occupation Has to Offer

These jobs offer little opportunity for advancement without further training, but for those who wish to work in a hospital with a minimum of training, they provide an entrance into the health field. Weekly earnings averaged about $80 a week in 1970. Some hospitals provide free room and board or meals at cost plus uniforms and laundry service. Service technicians can be promoted to senior or chief technicians and eventually to supervisors. Aides and orderlies can train further and become practical nurses, inhalation therapists, or X-ray technicians.

Points to Consider Before Going into This Field

Work at these fairly menial jobs can help you decide whether you like hospital work and wish to consider further training.

For more information, write:

Division of Careers & Recruitment
American Hospital Association
840 North Lake Shore Drive
Chicago, Illinois 60611
Ask for: career and training information.

See also: pages 267-268.

Other Jobs in Hospitals: Dietetic Technician and Dietetic Assistant

The Job

The titles of dietetic technician and dietetic assistant were first defined by the American Dietetic Association in 1970. Both job classifications are examples of the growing trend in the allied health fields to subdivide and distribute duties within a professional area so that the most highly trained person in a specialty is able to delegate routine-type tasks to those with appropriate training for those jobs.

The professional dietitian is aided by the dietetic technician either in helping to provide and assess food service management or nutritional care services. So there are really two kinds of technicians—one trained in food service and the other in nutritional care. The first type is involved in such activities as planning menus; developing and testing products; procuring and storing food, supplies, and equipment; selecting, training, and scheduling employees; maintaining quality control and sanitation and safety standards; and preparing budget data.

The technician with a background in nutritional care on the other hand gets the diet history of patients and relates their needs to a registered dietitian. She also implements the care plan developed by the dietitian by helping the patient select his menu, planning a diet for home use, and following up through home visits. In some cases the technician may teach classes in formula preparation or food purchasing, develop teaching materials, and maintain a variety of product and resource files.

The dietetic assistant (previously called food service supervisor) may work under the supervision of a dietitian, dietetic technician, or other administrator. She helps provide food service supervision and nutritional care services, but her duties vary greatly depending on the size of the institution and the responsibilities of the nutrition staff.

What You Need Personally

People entering the fields of dietetics and nutrition need physical stamina and an ability to get along well with others. For them food is both a science and an art, and they should have talents in both areas.

What Education and Training You Need

More than 70 approved dietetic assistant programs are now offered in vocational-technical schools and junior and community colleges throughout the country. Some programs are also available by correspondence. All courses combine classroom work and field experience and usually require one year of part-time study. Applicants should have a high school diploma or its equivalent.

Training programs for dietetic technicians have still not received final approval by the American Dietetic Association, but they can supply you with a list of those programs which have been given potential approval. All are offered in junior or community colleges and award an associate degree.

What the Occupation Has to Offer

It's difficult to evaluate the employment outlook for fields which are so new, but it seems safe to assume that the rapidly expanding health field and severe shortage of trained dietitians should result in excellent opportunities for these para-professionals.

Salaries will be similar to those of assistant and technician jobs in the health area in your particular community. Opportunities for advancement will be limited without further training. An assistant, with further study, however, can become a technician.

Points to Consider Before Going into This Field

A notable advantage of working in dietetics is the reward of feeling needed and performing a useful service in a positive and constructive way.

Working conditions are generally pleasant, and the newness of these classifications may add to their appeal.

As in many assisting health jobs, dietetics, and nutrition have always been primarily female territory.

For more information, write:

Coordinator, Education of Supportive Personnel
American Dietetic Association
620 North Michigan Avenue
Chicago, Illinois 60611
Ask for: information on career, program approval and schools offering programs.

See also: pages 267-268.

Other Jobs in Hospitals: EEG Technician

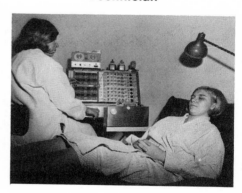

The Job

Electroencephalographic (EEG) technicians are important members of the hospital staff. They help diagnose brain disease and infection through a device which detects and records a patient's brain waves.

The technician attaches electrodes to the patient's head, which in turn lead to the electroencephalography machine, a complex apparatus which registers the brain's electrical currents on a graph. The procedure is safe and painless and is especially helpful in diagnosing epilepsy and brain tumors and in assessing damage and recovery after strokes.

Physicians and specially trained personnel interpret the EEG results, not the technician, but the technician does observe the patient's behavior and must be able to recognize abnormal wave patterns that indicate a condition requiring immediate medical attention.

Technicians also schedule appointments, keep patient records, and make minor repairs and adjustments in order to keep the equipment in good operating order.

EEG technicians work mostly in the neurology departments of hospitals. Some however, are employed in physicians' offices, private clinics, and state and federal institutions.

What You Need Personally

If you're considering becoming an EEG technician, you should be mature and emotionally stable in order to deal with the patients who must be tested. The prospective technician also needs manual dexterity, good vision, and an aptitude for working with relatively complicated equipment.

What Education and Training You Need

The minimum educational requirement for an EEG technician is a high school diploma. Courses in the physical and social sciences are particularly helpful in understanding patients' mental and physical conditions.

Most EEG technicians learn their skills during on-the-job training, which lasts from three to six months. They work under the guidance of a neurologist or electroencephalographer and a senior technician.

Some technicians also take formal training programs at hospitals, colleges and universities. In 1970 there were fifteen such programs in the U. S., ranging in length from three months to one year. Some schools require two years of college for entrance into the program, while others require only a high school education. One university offers a two-year associate degree program. Students take courses such as physiology and anatomy, electronics and instrumentation, and are also given clinical experience.

What the Occupation Has to Offer

Job opportunities for EEG technicians are excellent and should continue to be good throughout the 1970s. In 1971 more than 1,900 hospitals provided EEG service, and an estimated 3,000 technicians were employed. As advances in medical technology continue, the horizons for the trained technician should expand even further. One new application of the EEG is pinpointing the time body functions stop, a step necessary for vital organ transplants.

EEG technicians generally work a 40-hour week with little overtime or weekend duty. In 1971 starting annual salary ranged from $4,800 to $6,000. Technicians in the federal government can earn as much as $9,881 yearly, and some senior technicians earn between $10,000 and $12,000.

To upgrade professional standards, the American Board of Registration of Electroencephalographic Technologists periodically gives a written and oral examination. Those EEG technicians who meet the experience requirements and successfully complete the exam may become registered. Although you do not need registration for employment, it does substantiate your qualifications and makes it easier to obtain better jobs.

In large hospitals, the technician may advance to senior or chief EEG technician, supervising and instructing others.

Points to Consider Before Going into This Field

An EEG technician fulfills an important function and can feel a real sense of pride in her work. Most of these workers are women, but there are no restrictions against men entering the field. The relatively short training period and availability of jobs combine to make this an attractive allied health occupation.

For more information, write:

American Hospital Association
840 North Lake Shore Drive
Chicago, Illinois 60611
Ask for: career information.

American Society of Electroencephalographic Technologists
University of Iowa, Division of EEG
500 Newton Road
Iowa City, Iowa 52240
Ask for: information on registration.

You can also ask about employment and training programs at your local hospital.

See also: pages 267-268.

Other Jobs in Hospitals: EKG Technician

The Job

The electrocardiograph (EKG) machine records heart actions in the form of a graph which is used to help diagnose heart disease and record the progress of heart patients. Some physicians order electrocardiograms as routine diagnostic procedures for patients over a certain age.

The EKG technician takes and processes these electrocardiograms at the doctor's request. Electrodes are attached to the patient's chest, arms and legs, and the recorded tracings create a chart of the heart action on a continuous roll of paper. The technician then clips and mounts the resulting "picture" for analysis by a physician qualified in cardiology. The test may be given in a doctor's office, hospital laboratory, or at the patient's bedside.

While taking the electrocardiogram, the technician must be able to recognize and correct interference or errors, as well as significant deviations from the norm which might call for the doctor's attention. She may direct mild exercises for the patient in order to measure their effect on

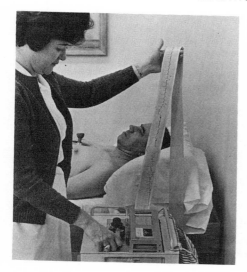

the heart muscle for a second graph. She may also make photocardiograms which record the sounds of the heart valves and the blood passing through them. In addition to these jobs, the technician's schedule may include typing the diagnoses charts, caring for equipment, and maintaining patient files.

What You Need Personally

EKG technicians work directly with patients who may be ill or apprehensive, so a sympathetic cheerful personality is helpful. You also need to be able to follow detailed instructions, react quickly in emergencies, and work harmoniously with other members of the health team. Mechanical aptitude is an asset in understanding the machinery and knowing when it is functioning properly.

What Education and Training You Need

An EKG technician should be a high school graduate, preferably with some courses in the physical sciences. Training is generally given on the job by a senior technician or a cardiologist and can last as long as three months. Some institutions provide tuition assistance or free courses.

A few colleges and hospital affiliated universities offer EKG courses lasting several months, and manufacturers of electrocardiographs often provide instruction in the operation of their own equipment.

What the Occupation Has to Offer

As physicians rely upon electrocardiograms more and more for diagnosis and for monitoring patients under intensive care, job opportunities

for EKG technicians should continue to be excellent.

Most of the 10,000 technicians employed in 1970 worked in the cardiology departments of large hospitals. Others had jobs in small hospitals, clinics, and doctors' offices on full or part-time bases.

Those working in hospitals received average monthly salaries of about $470 in 1970, but some earned as much as $950. Technicians receive the same fringe benefits as other hospital personnel and generally work a 40-hour week which may include some duty on Saturday.

Opportunities for advancement are limited, although some EKG technicians are promoted to senior technician or supervisor.

Points to Consider Before Going into This Field

If you enjoy working directly with patients in performing a vital service, you might well enjoy the job of EKG technician. Both men and women work in this field, although the large majority are women, many of whom like the flexibility of being able to work part time.

Training is relatively short and inexpensive, and job opportunities are plentiful. With additional training, technicians can become junior vascular-cardio technicians.

For more information, write:

American Hospital Association
840 North Lake Shore Drive
Chicago, Illinois 60611
Ask for: career information

You can also contact your local hospital for information on employment opportunities and training programs.

See also: pages 267-268.

Other Jobs in Hospitals: Inhalation Therapist

The Job

Inhalation therapists are "life-support specialists" who have been trained to aid the physician in restoring the heart-lung system to a normal function. Their treatments of respiratory problems range from giving relief to patients with chronic asthma or emphysema to giving emergency care in cases of heart failure, stroke, drowning, hemorrhage, and shock.

If a patient is unable to breathe for more than four minutes, his brain tissue will be affected, and after nine minutes his heart will stop. So the therapist must work quickly in many cases to aid the breathing process through oxygen administering apparatus, aerosols, and medical gases.

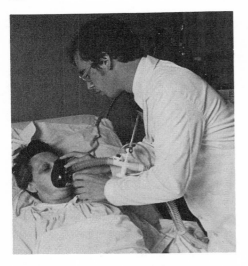

The techniques of inhalation therapy are also used for diagnostic purposes, such as helping to secure lung secretions samples for cancer diagnosis.

Some therapists instruct doctors and nurses in the use of inhalation equipment or explain to patients and their families how the equipment may be used at home. They're also responsible for making minor adjustments and repairs on equipment, keeping complete and accurate records, and preparing charges to be added to patients' accounts.

Most of the 10,000 therapists are now employed work in hospitals, but some work for oxygen equipment rental companies, ambulance services, and nursing homes.

What You Need Personally

A young person planning to enter this field should have the ability to work directly with severely ill patients and understand their physical and psychological needs. You should have good judgment, patience, and tact, and enough mechanical ability to understand the equipment used. You should be able to follow directions carefully and be able to give clear instructions to others.

What Education and Training You Need

Until the mid-1960s most inhalation therapists received all their training on the job by taking a one-year program under the direction of the hospital's chief therapist and medical supervisor. It's still possible to enter the field via that route, but the trend today is toward formal accredited training.

The American Association for Inhalation Therapy states that a therapist must have a high school education, be a graduate of a qualified school of inhalation therapy, and have clinical experience. Those having only on-the-job training may qualify for the lesser title of inhalation therapy technician but they are encouraged to go on further in their training by enrolling in an approved program.

Most are two-year programs offered at the junior college level, and are designed to prepare graduates for a certifying examination. To be eligible for the certification test, an applicant must either have graduated from an approved program on the associate degree level, or have completed an approved one-year program plus one year of supervised clinical experience or have a high school education plus two years of experience.

The technician can study even further and become a registered therapist. You must have two years of college and clinical experience before you can take the required oral and written examination to receive this rating.

There are several scholarships and fellowships available for people who wish to enter this field or take advanced training.

What the Occupation Has to Offer

Most hospitals are short of personnel in inhalation therapy, and as new uses are developed for their services, the demand should be even greater. As the occupation evolves and expands, there will also be a need for better trained persons in supervisory capacities.

Advancement opportunities are good because technicians can become therapists; and therapists can move up to positions as assistant chiefs, chief therapists, or instructors of inhalation therapy.

The average national monthly salary for hospital therapists in 1970 was about $550, with top earnings going as high as $830. Average yearly salaries for those employed by the federal government were between $4,125 and $5,212, but some earned as much as $10,000.

Therapists usually work a 40-hour week, but special duty may be required at night and on weekends since most hospitals need round-the-clock coverage in this vital area.

Points to Consider Before Going into This Field

Inhalation therapy is a relatively new and fast growing career field. It offers satisfying and well-paying work to men and women who are prepared to get the technical training and accept the serious responsibilities involved. However, it does demand personal qualities of coolness under stress and careful consideration of safety precautions.

Until recently almost all therapists were men, probably because of the need to handle heavy cylinders of oxygen. Now that oxygen is piped directly into hospitals, physical strength is no longer necessary, and more women are entering the field.

For more information, write:

American Association for Respiratory Therapy
7411 Hines Place
Dallas, Texas 75235
Ask for: career information; certification; schools offering programs; scholarships.

You can also contact your local hospital for employment and training information.

See also: pages 267-268.

Other Jobs in Hospitals: Medical Record Technician

The Job

A medical record technician works in the medical record department of a hospital, clinic, or nursing home. The duties are the preparing, analyzing, and preserving of the many kinds health information needed by the patients, hospitals, and public.

Included in this ever-growing bank of information are case histories, examination findings, test reports, and physicians' and nurses' notes. Access to these records is necessary not only for diagnosis and treatment by doctors, but also for insurance claims, legal actions, research and evaluation, and training.

It's the job of the technician to type and file these permanent reports, review them for completeness and accuracy, assist the medical staff by preparing special studies and tabulating data for research. In larger departments, technicians may work under the supervision of a medical records librarian or administrator, but in smaller departments may be in charge of the whole operation.

What You Need Personally

You need a capacity for detail in medical records work, thoroughness, and accuracy in dealing with various kinds of technical information. Because medical records are confidential, you must exercise judgment in processing and releasing information. A pleasant personality and the ability to work well with other members of the hospital staff are also important assets.

What Education and Training You Need

A high school diploma will qualify you for entrance into a one- or two-year approved course for medical record technicians. Subjects include anatomy, physiology, medical terminology, medical record science, and statistics.

Practical experience is provided in a medical record department. Many junior or community colleges offer programs in this field which lead to an associate degree. Student loans are available through the Foundation of Record Education of the American Medical Record Association.

After completing one of the approved programs, you may take a national accreditation examination given once a year by the Association. Successful candidates may add the initials ART after their names as proof of competence. The Association also offers a correspondence course for home study, and graduates are eligible to take the same examination. Tuition runs about $425.00

What the Occupation Has to Offer

The job prospects in this field are excellent and should continue to be so for the period ahead. The growing volume and complexity of hospital records, especially with the increase in private and public health insurance, should lead to an ongoing demand for trained personnel.

Most of the available jobs are in hospitals, but some technicians are employed in clinics, research centers, nursing homes, medical departments of insurance companies and industrial firms, and local and state health departments.

Salaries vary with the size and location of the employer and the scope of the technician's duties. However, medical record technicians tend to earn more than general office workers, and experience and accreditation can lead to better jobs and higher salaries.

With additional training, it is possible to advance to medical records administrator or librarian.

Points to Consider Before Going into This Field

This is a growing occupation which combines interesting work with an opportunity for service. Most technicians are women, but there is no reason why men cannot enter the field. In fact the increasing use of computers to store and retrieve medical information will probably attract more male applicants who enjoy working with electronic equipment.

For more information, write:

Academic Department
American Medical Record Association
875 North Michigan Avenue
Chicago, Illinois 60611
Ask for: list of accredited schools, programs, student loans, accrediting exam, and career information.

See also: pages 267-268.

Other Jobs in Hospitals: Surgical Technician

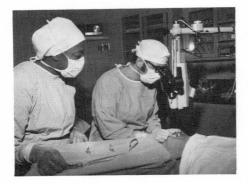

The Job

The surgical technician (also called an operating room technician) works in the operating room under the supervision of registered nurses in assisting surgeons and anesthesiologists. Duties might include transporting patients to the operating room and helping to position them on the operating table, obtaining the necessary instruments and equipment, and preparing patients by washing, shaving, and disinfecting the area where the surgeon will be operating.

As the operation proceeds, the technician provides valuable extra hands to aid the surgical team by passing instruments and supplies, preparing specimens for testing, applying dressings, and operating sterilizers and diagnostic equipment.

When the operation is over, the technician helps transport the patient to the recovery room and aids nurses in preparing the operating room for the surgery that is to follow.

About 25,000 surgical technicians are employed in hospitals all over the country. Most of them are women, although male technicians are found in the armed forces in larger numbers.

What You Need Personally

You should be skilled at working with your hands if you wish to become a surgical technician because instruments and equipment must be handled with ease and speed. You should also be neat and orderly and have a high degree of emotional stability in order to face the daily routine of the operating room. Surgery is teamwork, and the technician must play her part calmly and efficiently.

What Education and Training You Need

Applicants for technician jobs may have to pass aptitude tests and physical examinations. They usually need a high school diploma or its equivalent in order to be accepted in a hospital training program. Preference may also be given to those people with experience as attendants, nurses aides, or practical nurses. The armed forces trains surgical technicians in their medic programs.

On-the-job training in hospitals varies in length from six weeks to one year, depending on the trainee's qualifications and the type of program. As in many other health fields, there is a growing trend toward hiring people who have completed a one- or two-year junior or community college program. These programs are now offered in about 25 colleges and include classroom courses in the basic sciences such as anatomy, physiology and microbiology; care and safety of patients during surgery; use of anesthetic agents; nursing procedures and post-operative care; principles of operating techniques and handling of special drugs and equipment. This academic training is supplemented by supervised clinical experience.

What the Occupation Has to Offer

A growing population and expanding health care programs are resulting in more surgery being performed, and therefore a need for more surgical technicians. As more duties are turned over to these workers, registered nurses are able to devote themselves to other duties.

Job opportunities should continue to be excellent for technicians, especially those with experience. Weekly salaries in 1970 ranged from $75 to $140 for new technicians, with junior college graduates receiving higher pay. Experienced technicians may earn from $95 to $180 a week, again depending on qualifications and responsibilities.

Points to Consider Before Going into This Field

Becoming a surgical technician commits you to a field of work where your services are truly needed, and which offers you good job security.

Trained technicians can utilize their skills in operating rooms in all parts of the country.

Not everyone is suited to this sort of work. Those thinking of entering the field might do well to consider working as a volunteer or aide to get some on-the-scene exposure to the operating room environment.

For more information, write:

Association of Operating Room Technicians, Inc.
Suite 101
1100 West Littleton Boulevard
Littleton, Colorado 80120

Ask for: job information, training programs, and certification information.

See also: pages 267-268.

Machining Occupations

The Job

Most industrial products are either produced by machines made of metal parts, or are composed of separate metal parts. To produce these and parts products, industry employs over a million workers in skilled and semiskilled jobs to work with machine tools. A machine tool is a power-driven machine that holds a piece of metal and cuts or shapes it. Some common machine tools are lathes, which turn and shape metal against a sharp cutting tool; grinding machines, which smooth metal parts with abrasive wheels; driving machines, which make holes; boring machines, which enlarge holes; milling machines, which remove excess metal; shapers, planers, and broachers, which produce flat surfaces.

Machining workers must be very accurate, as they often produce parts that must meet very precise dimensions. They often follow directions from a blueprint or drawing and use precision measuring instruments to check the accuracy of their work.

Some of the larger job categories in this field are machine tool operators, who may be skilled or semiskilled and usually operate only one kind of machine tool; tool and die makers who make special dies or devices for particular jobs; instrument makers who produce metal instrument parts for precision instruments; and setup men, who adjust machine tools for semiskilled operators.

Machinists are employed in every state and city, but more than half work in California, Ohio, New York, Michigan, Illinois, and Pennsylvania.

Most machinists are employed in metalworking industries, transportation industries, fabricated metal products and electrical machinery and equipment industries. Others are employed in repair and maintenance shops.

Some of the largest employers of machinists are the companies that produce motor vehicles and equipment. In their large assembly plants, they employ many machine tool operators, tool and die makers, punch press workers and welders. Other related occupations in the automotive industry are foundry workers, forge shop employees, assembly workers, inspectors, metal finishers, sprayers, and polishers.

What You Need Personally

Most machining occupations require that you be in good physical condition with good use of fingers and hands, good vision, and good eye-hand coordination. Depth and distance judgment are also important.

The qualifications vary from job to job, depending on the complexity, but in general, you must be dependable, patient, and careful. Accuracy is vital. In more complex occupations, such as tool and die making, you must be able to apply various kinds of mathematical figures and knowledge to the particular job on which you are working.

What Education and Training You Need

Applicants with a high school education and some background in mathematics and mechanical studies are preferred for these jobs. In some cases, employers look for workers who have had some post-high school training from a technical institute, or perhaps a government training program.

On-the-job training is most important for these jobs, and training periods can vary, depending on the skill required. It usually only takes a few months to learn a semiskilled machine tool operator's work, but most other jobs take longer. Formal apprenticeships are common, and involve four years of combined on-the-job training and classroom instruction. Classroom studies include mathematics, blueprint reading, and other subjects directly related to the particular trade. On the job, the trainee works with experienced men, learning how to use the necessary tools and how to make the decisions needed to do accurate, skilled work.

It is not unusual for machining workers to continue to learn while they work in order to move up in their fields. Studies of electronics and hydraulics are helpful. Some manufacturers and unions also provide programs to keep workers up to date on new technology in their field.

What the Occupation Has to Offer

The need for more machined products will grow as our economy grows. Cars, appliances, and industrial equipment will all be in demand, creating jobs for machining workers. The job outlook will be affected by automation, however. New tools will increase worker output. Numerically controlled machine tools will be especially significant since these tools can be set automatically for dimensions, tolerances, cutter shapes, sizes, paths, and sequences. All this will be coded and will set the machine with punch cards, cutting down the number of jobs for semiskilled workers. The more complex jobs will continue to grow moderately.

The automotive industry is a good example of the effects of automation, since it is using computerized machines already for machining and assembly operations. These changes have meant a slight decrease in jobs in these areas and a greater emphasis on technical and research positions.

Earnings for machining jobs vary greatly according to skill, type of business, and area. The automotive industry is one of the higher paying, and their machine tool operators average between $3.55 and $4.75 an hour. Tool and die makers in this industry earn between $4.32 and $4.91; by comparison, automative assemblers earn between $3.03 and $3.60, and inspectors $3.38 to $3.67.

In general, machining workers earn between $3 and $5 an hour, and receive extra pay for overtime or weekend work. Benefits are usually very good, particularly in the automotive industry, covering paid holidays, vacations, sick leave, health insurance, and retirement benefits. Most machining workers are unionized.

Different kinds of promotional opportunities are open to the machinist. Less skilled workers, such as machine tool operators, can advance to tool and die makers or all-round machinists. Any workers with proven skill can advance to foreman. With specialized training, some move on to jobs such as tool and die designer, instrument technician, and programmer. Others open their own machine shops.

Points to Consider Before Going into This Field

Machining offers steady, well-paid work without requiring expensive training. You can continue to develop your skills and graduate to more complex jobs. The industries that hire you are not likely to go out of business, and you will be assured of work as long as you keep developing your skills and advancing in technology. Machinists usually work regular hours at a job that is not too strenuous.

There are some disadvantages, however. You will have to be on your feet most of the day. There can be danger from cutting edges or flying metal if you do not observe safety regulations carefully, and plants are usually noisy. Some jobs can be very repetitive when identical parts are being produced over and over again. This is not true in the more complex jobs like instrument making or tool and die making.

Some women are employed in machining trades, but they are usually semiskilled workers. Up until now there has been little advancement potential for women in this field.

For more information, write:

Automobile Manufacturers Association Inc.
320 New Center Building
Detroit, Michigan 48202
Ask for: information on careers in machining
    trades.

National Machine Tool Builders Association
7901 W. Park Drive
McLean, Virginia 22101
Ask for: information on careers in machine tool
    industry.

Manager, Training
National Tool Die and Precision Machining
    Association
9300 Livingston Road
Washington, D. C. 20022

Ask for: information on apprenticeships for tool
    and die makers.

For apprenticeship information, apply at the local offices of the following unions:

International Association of Machinists and
    Aerospace Workers
1300 Connecticut Avenue, NW
Washington, D. C. 20036

International Union, United Automobile, Aero-
    space and
Agricultural Implement Workers of America
8000 East Jefferson Avenue
Detroit, Michigan 48214

International Union of Electrical Radio and
    Machine Workers
1126 16th Street NW
Washington, D. C. 20036

International Brotherhood of Electrical Workers
1125 15th Street, NW
Washington, D. C. 20005

Also contact:

You may also contact your local state employment office for free aptitude testing if you are interested in being an all-round machinist or a tool and die maker. They will also offer information about employers with apprenticeship programs or training available under the Manpower Development and Training Act.

All-Round Machinist

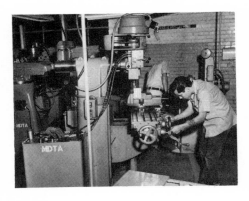

The Job

One of the most varied jobs in the machine shop is that of the all-round machinist. He is a skilled worker who can set up and use a wide range of machines such as lathes, planers, shapers, milling machines, and grinders. With these machines he can make dies, machines, and gauges, or repair them. By understanding his tools and the properties of the metal he works with, he can take a block of metal and shape it into a very precise and intricate machine part.

The all-round machinist often works on different machines during the day, plus an assortment of hand tools. He frequently may have to switch from making one product to another.

To plan a job, the machinist studies blueprints and specifications in order to select the tools and materials the job requires. Then he plans the cutting and finishing operations and sets up the machines in order to make the finished product meet specifications. He often uses precision measuring instruments such as calipers and micrometers to check the accuracy of his work down to millionths of an inch. After the machine operations are completed, he may use files and scrapers to finish the job, then put finished parts together with wrenches and screwdrivers. He may also "heat treat" cutting tools and parts to improve machinability.

If an all-round machinist is involved with making or repairing metal parts of machines and equipment, he will sometimes have to adjust and test parts he has made or repaired. He needs a knowledge of mechanical principles for this part of his job.

Some machinists, in plants that produce large numbers of metal products, specialize in putting specifications on metal to guide machine tool operators.

All-round machinists are employed in virtually every town and city and in a wide range of industries. Most work for firms that produce machinery, including electrical transportation equipment, fabricated metal products, and primary metals. Other employers include railroads, chemical industries, food processing companies, textile industries, and the federal government.

What You Need Personally

An interest in and an understanding of things mechanical are important if you want to be an all-round machinist. You'll need to apply intelligence, judgment, and precision to your work with blueprints, measurements, and machinery. Some amount of coordination and finger dexterity is necessary, and good hearing is important in judging whether the machine is running properly.

A machinist works with many people and should be able to get along with them. He must be able to work independently in solving problems and making work-related decisions.

What Education and Training You Need

Most companies prefer machinists who are high school graduates with backgrounds in algebra, geometry, trigonometry, drafting, physics, and shop courses. Other helpful courses are blueprint reading, shop mechanics, and courses that use precision measuring devices.

Extra training will help both the aspiring and the experienced machinist. Courses in mathematics and electronics and in general machining operations are offered by high schools, vocational schools, technical schools, and correspondence schools. If you are already employed, the company may pay for these studies to help you learn to use more complex machinery. Companies that make equipment also provide training in the electrical, hydraulic, and mechanical aspects of machine and control systems.

Some machinists get to their positions by working through a variety of other machining trades over a period of years. However, most experts agree that the best way to become an all-round machinist is through a four-year apprenticeship program. These programs usually involve a formal written agreement that specifies that the apprentice will get an opportunity to learn all kinds of machining techniques and will receive periodic wage increases during the program. In some cases, employers are improving programs so that a hardworking apprentice can get through it in three years.

A four-year apprentice program involves about 8,000 hours of shop training and 570 hours of classroom instruction. The classroom studies include blueprint reading, mechanical drawing, shop mathematics, and shop practices. The shop training teaches the apprentice how to use different kinds of machine tools and how to do hand operations like filing, chipping, and riveting. (See also pages 52-63.)

One of the new developments in this trade is

on-the-job training for up-and-coming machinists already employed in the shop. What makes it new is a formalized structure similar to the apprentice programs, but without some of the apprentice requirements.

What the Occupation Has to Offer

The demand for all-round machinists should increase moderately in the next decade, depending on the national economy. The more skilled the machinist, the more his services will be in demand. Maintenance shops, which repair the increasingly complex machinery used by today's factories, will show growth in these jobs.

Wages for machinists vary, but compare well with those of other skilled factory workers. Their earnings vary in different geographical locations, but in general, they earn somewhere between $3 and $5 an hour. They receive more for overtime, and many are union members.

Chances for advancement are good. Machinists often become foremen or take on other supervisory positions. With additional training, they can become tool and die makers, instrument makers, technicians, tooling engineers, or machine programmers. Some machinists open their own machine shops.

Points to Consider Before Going into This Field

The machinist is a skilled worker who has a place in many industries. His work is usually steady and available in any location. An all-round machinist works independently and has an opportunity to use a variety of different skills. His hours are regular and his wages and benefits better than average.

If a machinist is not alert, he may sustain injuries from machines or flying metal parts. However, shops have many safety regulations and usually require the wearing of safety glasses and other equipment to eliminate these hazards.

For more information:

See page 295.

Instrument Maker

The Job

Automation often eliminates jobs, but it also can create new occupations. One job that has grown with technology is that of the instrument maker, also known as experimental machinist or modelmaker. Instrument makers work with engineers and scientists in the designing and perfecting of sophisticated instruments used in production, research, development, and testing. They also modify existing instruments for special purposes. Some of the results of their work include instruments that regulate heat, measure dis-

tances, control industrial processes, and record earthquakes. They make mechanical instrument parts or models ranging from simple gears to complicated navigational system parts for guided missiles.

The instrument maker is a craftsman who usually translates the ideas of engineers or designers, although he sometimes devises the ideas himself. In making parts, he can work from rough sketches, detailed blueprints, or verbal suggestions from other staff members. He prepares designs and sketches and suggests materials to be used, type of construction, and the best way to produce the instrument. Often they must work on very delicate parts that must not vary from specifications by more than ten millionths of an inch. They also work with many different materials including plastics and all kinds of metals, and must be familiar with all their properties.

The instrument maker uses a wide variety of tools, including measuring devices like micrometers and calipers; and gauges are always important. He also works with machine tools like engine lathes and drill presses and with hand tools like wrenches, files, and chisels.

He may work on every phase of the instrument construction, making and assembling parts and testing finished instruments for proper operation. In large shops or in operations that include electrical or electronic components, however, electronic specialists usually make various parts of the instrument.

Instrument makers are employed largely by instrument manufacturing firms, research and development laboratories, and the federal government. Most work in or around large cities, particularly New York, Chicago, Los Angeles, Boston, Philadelphia, Washington, Detroit, Buffalo, Cleveland, and Rochester.

What You Need Personally

Because of the precise nature of the work, you must have better than average skill in working with your hands. Your vision and attention must be suited for fine, close, detailed work. You should be interested in mechanics, and understand mathematics, chemistry, physics, and mechanical drawing.

You must be mentally alert, conscientious, and able to visualize parts in relation to the whole. You often work alone, so you need initiative, resourcefulness, and stick-to-itiveness. You must be able to make decisions on your own, and communicate your ideas to others.

What Education and Training You Need

A high school diploma or equivalent is necessary in this field. Important studies for the instrument maker are algebra, geometry, trigonometry, science, physics, chemistry, mechanical drawing, and machine shop.

Most employers prefer applicants who have completed a two-year technical course, particularly in mechanics or electronics. For some of the higher level and professional positions, a college degree in engineering or science is required.

Apprenticeship programs, lasting four or five years, are common in this field. They usually combine about 8,000 hours of shop training with about 570 hours of classroom instruction. The classroom instruction includes courses in mathematics, physics, chemistry, electronics, blueprint reading, and fundamental instrument design. A basic knowledge of mechanical principles is also covered. In the shop, the apprentice learns to use machine tools, hand tools, and measuring instruments. He first works on routine tasks, observing more experienced workers, and gradually learns how to approach and solve the problems himself. (See also pages 52-63.)

Some instrument makers are selected from among the machinists or skilled machine tool operators in a company. They usually need one or two years of shop experience in instrument making to qualify as skilled craftsmen.

What the Occupation Has to Offer

There should be an increasing number of job opportunities for instrument makers in the next decade. Instruments are being used in more kinds of manufacturing processes and research and development work, and both mass-produced and custom instruments will be in greater demand. Among the industries that will be using more instruments are aerospace, marine science, biomedical science, metal, pulp and paper, power, transportation, chemical, petroleum, and instrument manufacturing. New precision instruments will be needed, too, as a result of research being carried out by private organizations, universities, government agencies, and manufacturers.

Instrument makers are considered skilled craftsmen and their earnings compare well with other skilled metalworkers. For a standard work week, most instrument makers earn between $3.50 and $5.30 an hour. Most of these positions offer benefits of insurance, paid holidays and vacations, sick leave, etc.; and many instrument makers are union members.

Opportunities for advancement are good for those who go beyond high school training. It usually takes up to ten years to become a highly skilled instrument maker. If you study machine design or instrument technology you may advance to a technician's job, or may become a supervisor.

Points to Consider Before Going into This Field

The instrument maker is a skilled worker in a field that will grow with increasingly sophisticated technology. The work is challenging and gives you the opportunity to produce something yourself. Because you work on your own and have highly developed skills, you have prestige in your plant. You work independently in clean, well-lighted, comfortable, usually quiet, work areas. The hours are almost always regular, and you are able to sit for many of your tasks. Although training for the job takes a few years, it is usually done on-the-job, so there is no financial investment involved, and you can take additional courses at night.

There are few disadvantages to this job. The high speed machines do present some safety hazards, but you can overcome this by being alert and observing safety regulations. Most firms require the wearing of special glasses, aprons and short-sleeved clothing, and prohibit the wearing of neckties.

There are very few women employed in this field, but there is no reason why women who meet the qualifications for the job cannot become instrument makers.

For more information, write:

Recorder-Controller Section
Scientific Apparatus Makers Association
370 Lexington Avenue
New York, New York 10017
Ask for: Career and Training information.

Instrument Society of America
400 Stanwix Street
Pittsburgh, Pennsylvania 15222
Ask for: *A Rewarding Technical Career in Instrumentation Awaits You*, $.50.

See also: page 295.

Machine Tool Operator

The Job

Manufacturing today is so complex that many different kinds of workers are needed to

produce goods. In the metalworking trades, the largest group is machine tool operators.

Machine tools are stationary power-driven machines. They hold the metal that is to be cut, shaved, grinded or drilled. Some of the more common of these are engine lathes, turret lathes, grinding machines, drilling machines, milling machines, screw machines, shapers, and planers. Machine tool operators use these tools to shape metal to exact dimensions.

There are many degrees of skill found among machine tool operators. Some specialize in one type of machine tool while others can operate several. They usually have job titles relating to the machine they operate. Some are semiskilled and do the simple, repetitive operations that are easily learned. Others are skilled and perform a variety of complex operations.

A semiskilled worker operates a machine tool on which the speeds and operation sequence have been set by a more skilled employee. He places the rough metal stock in the machine and makes sure it is operating properly. He uses simple gauges to measure the work. Some semiskilled operators can make minor adjustments in their machines, but usually they go to their supervisors for assistance.

A skilled machine tool operator usually works on a single type of machine. He plans and sets up the correct sequence of operations based on information from blueprints or layouts. He adjusts speed and other controls and selects the proper cutting tools or instruments for the operation.

A skilled operator must know how to use all the special attachments for his machine in order to make any changes in the setup. When the work is completed, he checks to make sure it meets specifications by using various precision instruments.

Machine tool operators are employed all over the country and in many different kinds of businesses. The states with the largest number are New York, Pennsylvania, Ohio, Illinois, California, and Michigan. Most semiskilled operators are employed by plants that manufacture large numbers of units for such products as fabricated metal products and automobiles. Skilled operators may also work in production shops or in maintenance departments, toolrooms, and job shops. Some work for automotive machine shops where they rebuild parts.

What You Need Personally

You should have some mechanical aptitude, manual dexterity, and good eye-hand coordination. You should be attentive, accurate, and careful, as well as responsible.

What Education and Training You Need

Although high school education is not necessary for these jobs, most employers prefer it, especially for apprenticeship programs. Useful studies in high school include industrial arts, machine shop, woodworking, and sheet-metal shop. A basic knowledge of mathematics and blueprint reading is also helpful.

Additional training can be obtained from a trade school, vocational school, technical school, or correspondence school. You should consult with your employer about such courses, some of whom will even pay part or all of the tuition costs for courses they approve.

Machine tool operators usually learn their specific skills on the job. Some companies have formal apprentice programs and others have short formal training programs to acquaint new workers with their machines and operations. Length of training varies with the worker. It usually takes a few months to learn a semiskilled job, and from one-and-a-half to two years to become a skilled operator.

A beginner usually starts by watching a skilled operator, and when he starts to use a machine, he is closely supervised. He learns to use measuring instruments, read blueprints, operate a machine tool, and make computations.

What the Occupation Has to Offer

The number of openings for machine shop operators should remain relatively constant during the next decade. Although metalworking should continue to grow as an industry, most openings will be to replace workers who have retired, died, or transferred to other jobs. The reason is that technology has developed automatic machine tools that increase each worker's output and require less work on the part of the operator. Semiskilled workers will be mainly affected by this automation.

Earnings for machine tool operators vary a great deal depending on the area in which they work. Most make between $3.33 and $4.87 an hour. They receive more money for overtime and night work, and most companies provide insurance, paid vacations and other benefits. Most operators belong to unions.

There are various opportunities for advancement for machine tool operators. Semiskilled operators can increase their knowledge and become skilled operators. Skilled operators can advance to jobs as all-round machinists, tool and die makers, foremen, set-up men, or machine programmers. These jobs require extra knowledge and training, and workers who study on their own time will be the most likely to advance.

Points to Consider Before Going into This Field

Machine tool operators have steady work that is available in most locales. The work does not require a financial investment in training and you are allowed to learn and advance on the job, while getting paid. Opportunities for promotion are good for the worker who continues to learn and keep up with technological developments.

Machine shops may be dirty and noisy and the worker is on his feet all day. There is some danger from machines, but safety clothing and goggles are usually worn and accidents are not too frequent. Because machine operations are repeated over and over, the work can be monotonous. Some jobs may become obsolete and the unskilled worker is advised to learn additional skills.

There are some women employed in these jobs, but they are almost always semiskilled operators. Since the work isn't strenuous, there is a chance that more opportunities will open up to women in the future.

For more information:

See page 295.

Setup Man

The Job

Many of the goods manufactured today are composed of complex parts—gears, shafts, cams, wheels, etc. To make anything from an electric drill to a jet plane requires the use of many different kinds of machines to cut and shape the metal. One of the most important workers in this area of manufacturing is the setup man, or machine tool job setter, who adjusts and otherwise gets machine tools ready for use by semiskilled workers.

A setup man may work with only one or two kinds of machines, or with a variety of different ones. He sets up machine tools such as lathes, milling machines, boring machines and generating and finishing machines for other workers. He runs off the first pieces from the machine to check his settings, changes worn cutting tools and adjusts speeds and feed rates. He may also set up machines like welders or flame-cutting machines, and may instruct new workers on how to use them and how to check the accuracy of the work.

Machine shops may turn out only a few specialized parts or may produce many identical pieces, so settings have to be precise.

To determine machine settings, the setup man works with drawings, blueprints, written specifications, or job layouts. From these he can determine the operating speeds, tooling and operation sequence, and the rate at which material is to be fed into the machines. He then selects and installs the proper cutting or other tools and adjusts guides, stops, and controls. To make these settings, he uses a variety of precision tools. With a micrometer he measures to thinnesses of one ten-thousandth of an inch. He uses thread gauges to see that screws are properly turned out, and calipers to make sure preset measurements stay precise. He also uses inside, outside, and depth gauges to make sure tolerances are holding.

In order to set up machines, he must be familiar with the characteristics of all the metals he works with, such as how fast and how deep each can be cut. He also has to know how each machine works. Once he has completed his job, he may have to make later adjustments to keep production standard.

Most setup men work in factories that manufacture fabricated metal products, transportation equipment, and machinery. They are most often employed by large companies whose machinery is run by semiskilled machine tool operators.

What You Need Personally

In this job you must be attentive to detail and be thorough in your work. You must be able to cope with many different problems at once and apply your knowledge to different situations. Your memory and judgment should be good.

The most important personal quality is the ability to communicate: to explain the job to other workers is necessary in order to get the work done properly.

What Education and Training You Need

The setup man must first be a skilled machine tool operator or all-round machinist and able to operate one or more kinds of machine tools. He must be able to read blueprints and make computations.

This job usually requires a union apprenticeship program. These programs are open to high school graduates, usually with a background in mathematics (up to beginning trigonometry), machine shop, and metal shop. Any construction hobbies like model building, radio work, and automobile repairing are also helpful.

Trade schools can be useful in areas like mathematics and introduction to machining, but apprenticeship is preferred. (See pages 52-63.)

Apprenticeship programs last four years and cover each aspect of the trade. At the end of the apprenticeship, you can choose a specialty, such as setup man, and move into a position when an opening occurs. Openings for setup men are usually filled by promoting a man already working in the shop.

What the Occupation Has to Offer

There should be some increase in jobs for setup men in the next decade as metalworking industries expand. However, there will probably be some difference in the duties of the setup man in the future. Increased mechanization may mean he will only have to preset tools and instruct operators, with the computing no longer necessary. As a result, the setup man of the future should have a basic knowledge of electronics, and continue to develop and modernize his skills. If he does so, he should have no trouble finding employment.

Earnings for setup men vary according to geographic location and place of work. A skilled setup man makes more than other machinists, usually between $3 and $5 an hour. Most setup men work regular hours and receive extra money for overtime and night work. Benefits are good for machinists, and most are union members.

There are good chances for advancement. The setup man is a skilled worker and knows a lot about his company's work. Many setup men are promoted to foreman, as they are already experienced supervisors. Other jobs, such as parts programmer, are also closely related to the work of the setup man. If he takes night courses at a trade school or technical college, his chances to move up are even better.

Points to Consider Before Going into This Field

There are many advantages to a setup man's job. He is a skilled worker, with supervisory functions, and his job has status and a good rate of pay. No outside training beyond high school is required to get an apprenticeship in the trade, and chances for advancement are good. Because of the diversity and challenge of the work, it rarely becomes routine. Difficult jobs give him a chance to show off his skills. Setup men usually work regular hours, and because of their specialized skills are rarely laid off.

Remember however, that the setup man is on his feet all day, and machine shops can be noisy. Good safety habits are a must, because sharp cutting instruments are the setup man's stock in trade.

Virtually all setup men are male.

For more information:
See page 295.

Tool and Die Maker

The Job

Tool and die makers are among the most skilled and important craftsmen involved in mass-production metalworking industries. Toolmakers produce the devices, known as jigs and fixtures, that hold the metal while it is being shaved, stamped or drilled. They also make gauges and measuring devices that are used in the manufacturing of precision metal parts. Die makers make dies, which are metal forms used in stamping and forging operations to shape metal. They also make metal molds used in die-casting and in molding plastics.

Other duties of tool and die makers include helping to design the tools and dies they will later produce, and repairing worn or damaged dies, gauges, jigs, and fixtures.

Tool and die makers must have a broad knowledge of maching operations and be able to operate all kinds of machines. They do a great deal of precision handwork, often to extremely close tolerances, and are deeply involved in the use of mathematics and blueprint reading. All the metals and alloys used in these industries are employed by these workers, and they must know the relevant properties of all of them.

Tool and die makers work with machines such as lathes, drill presses, shapers, grinders, and milling machines. They also use saws, heat-treating instruments and files.

Tool and die makers are employed in many different industries. They are most often found in plants that produce manufactured products, construction equipment, and farm machinery. Transportation equipment industries are also major employers. They may also work in small tool and die jobbing shops or in plants that manufacture electrical machinery and fabricated metal products.

What You Need Personally

You do very precise work in this field, so you need mechanical ability and manual dexterity. You must be patient and meticulous. You must also be able to make calculations and use judgment.

What Education and Training You Need

This occupation requires a combination of skill, formal education, and experience. Most employers prefer graduates of high school or trade school who have had some studies in mathematics, physics, and mechanical drawing. With this background, some skilled machine tool operators or machinists take additional specific on-the-job training and qualify as tool and die makers.

The recommended method is to go through an apprenticeship program. Apprentices should be between eighteen and twenty-five years old and have graduated from high school or vocation school. They serve four or five years apprenticeships that combine classroom instruction with on-the-job training. The first sixteen weeks of the program are spent in school and include 240 hours of classroom studies and 320 hours of machine operation. Trainees then enter a thirty-six week on-the-job training period. Following that, they spend the next three years of apprenticeship increasing their skills. In some cases, trainees can receive an allowance from the government during the sixteen weeks of schooling, with wages paid by the company for the rest of the apprenticeship period.

Classroom training for an apprentice includes shop mathematics, shop theory, mechanical drawing, tool designing, blueprint reading, elementary physics, metallurgy, elementary economics, and elements of tool and die design. At least 144 hours a year are devoted to classroom studies during apprenticeship.

On-the-job training teaches the apprentice how to use such machines as the drill press, milling machine, lathe, and grinder, plus handtools used to fit and assemble mechanical equipment. Heat-treating and other metalworking processes and inspection work are also included in training. (See also pages 52-63.)

After the apprenticeship program is completed, it may take another few years to master the most complex tool and die operations.

What the Occupation Has to Offer

There should be only a moderate increase in job openings for tool and die makers in the 1970s because of the increasing use of electrical-discharge and numerical control machines to do part of the work. These machines do not need as many of the special tools, jigs, and fixtures that tool and die makers produce, and also make the production of tools and dies faster and more efficient.

Earnings for tool and die makers vary in different geographical areas, but in general they are reasonably well-paid. Their earnings usually range anywhere from $3.45 to over $5 an hour, and they receive insurance, paid vacations and holidays, and other benefits. Many are union members.

There are some advancement opportunities for tool and die makers, particularly those with more training. They often move up to supervisory and administrative jobs in their companies. Others become tool designers or may open their own tool and die shops.

Points to Consider Before Going into This Field

There are many advantages to a career as a tool and die maker. You need no financial investment in your training, but you do acquire a skill that is recognized and in demand. Because skills and knowledge are specialized and acquired over a period of years, employers are reluctant to lay off such workers. You can go anywhere in the country with these skills and, because you are familiar with so many machines and operations, you can also get jobs as a machinist or instrument maker.

Other advantages to this trade are that the hours are regular, the work is independent and creative, and there is no physical strain involved.

For more information, write:

Department of Human Resources Development
Mail Control Unit
800 Capitol Mall
Sacramento, California 95814
Ask for: *Tool and Die Maker* No. 15, Free.

See also: page 295.

Mechanics and Repairmen

The Job

If you're only happy when you're tinkering with a broken appliance or repairing a sputtering motor, why not look into careers in the field of mechanics? Office machines, automated factory equipment, televisions, cars, furnaces and so many other products of modern technology that make our lives more comfortable all have to be serviced from time to time. In an increasingly mechanized world, mechanics and repairmen make up one of the fastest growing occupational groups.

There are almost 3 million of these important workers. In the United States the largest group (approximately 840,000) are automotive mechanics who work on cars, trucks, buses, or body repair (see pages 125-127).

Other large groups of more than 100,000 workers each include appliance servicemen, industrial-machinery repairmen, business-machine servicemen, aircraft mechanics, and television and radio service technicians. The responsibilities in these jobs vary. Appliance servicemen work for either small repair shops or the service departments of dealers and distributors. They fix anything from toasters to refrigerators, the larger items in the customers' homes, the smaller items in the shop (see pages 307-309).

Industrial-machinery repairmen are specialists found in most large manufacturing plants (see pp. 314-316). Aircraft mechanics are licensed specialists who work on anything from a private plane to a jumbo jet (see pages 91-92). Television and radio service technicians (see pp. 320-322) work for small repair shops or for distributors; they often work on sets in customers' homes. Business-machine servicemen (see pp. 309-311) work in large offices, maintaining and repairing typewriters, calculators, copiers and similar equipment; in some cases they will repair machines brought to their shops.

Air-conditioning, refrigeration, and heating mechanics (see pp. 305-307) work on heating and cooling equipment for homes and large companies. They may work for dealers, contractors, or public utilities. Instrument repairmen maintain and repair the precision instruments used by industry (see pp. 316-317). Maintenance electricians work in factories, office buildings and other large concerns which utilize a lot of electrical equipment (see pp. 317-319). Other specialists are farm-equipment mechanics, millwrights, vending-machine mechanics, watch repairmen, electric-sign servicemen (refer to those headings in this section).

Almost 30 percent of mechanics and repairmen work for the manufacturing industries. About 20 percent work for retail firms, another 20 percent for service shops. The remaining 30 percent work in the transportation, construction, and public utilities industries or for the government.

All states employ mechanics and repairmen, but about half the jobs are found in the most populous states: California, New York, Pennsylvania, Texas, Illinois, Ohio, Michigan, and New Jersey.

What You Need Personally

If you want to be a mechanic or repairman, you should display some mechanical aptitude and manual dexterity. Good vision is usually important. Some of these occupations—such as millwright—require good physical condition and agility; others, like watch repairman, are not particularly physically strenuous.

A mechanic or repairman often has to work cooperatively with other members of a maintenance group or customers so should be patient and reliable. He may also work independently and without supervision.

What Education and Training You Need

A high school education is always desirable for these jobs and is sometimes required, particularly for apprentice positions. Courses in mathematics, chemistry, physics, blueprint reading, and machine shop are a good background. The applicant who has had some experience in his chosen trade—for instance, an aspiring television serviceman who has operated a ham radio set—will have an edge.

Post-high school training in specific aspects of mechanics is available for most trades and is always combined with on-the-job training. Vocational technical schools, community and junior colleges, correspondence schools and the armed forces will provide good training opportunities. Some private schools also train for special jobs. The federal government sponsors programs under the Manpower Development and Training Act in many trades, including television and appliance repair.

Formal apprenticeships usually last four years and include job practice as well as classroom instruction. Depending on the trade, a training period of from a few months to four or five years is needed before a worker becomes skilled. Most trades require that even experienced workers keep up with technological developments in their fields.

What the Occupation Has to Offer

As we become more affluent and businesses grow with the economy, we will be using more of the products. Repairmen and mechanics should have a secure future. Some of the workers who will find the most job openings in the next ten years are automobile mechanics, business-machine servicemen, maintenance electricians, appliance servicemen, aircraft mechanics, industrial-machinery repairmen, instrument repairmen, and television and radio service technicians. As machinery becomes more complex, it will be increasingly important for these workers to have some advanced schooling and to keep abreast of changes in their fields.

Earnings in this field vary widely, depending on type of work, length of experience, employer and area employed. In all cases, it takes a few years for workers to move to the upper pay brackets. Some salary ranges are: TV-radio serviceman, $120–$300 a week; maintenance electrician, $108–$174 a week; automobile mechanic, $138–$184 a week; air-conditioning, refrigeration and heating mechanic, $130–$280 a week; business-machine serviceman, $100–$288 a week. Many mechanics and repairmen are self-employed; their incomes can be much higher.

Mechanics and repairmen have a variety of opportunities for promotion. Appliance servicemen, TV-radio servicemen and automobile mechanics can go into business for themselves. Mechanics and repairmen who work for larger companies can advance to foreman, service manager, supervisor, maintenance manager. Others may take additional training to move on to more highly technical jobs.

Points to Consider Before Going into This Field

This field offers a good future for a person with mechanical talents. We'll continue to see many job openings all over the country, and workers are usually well-paid with advancement opportunities available to the skilled and ambitious person. The work is diverse and involves independent analysis and decision making. It is rarely dangerous but does offer daily challenge.

There are a few disadvantages to the work. Mechanics and repairmen work odd hours if emergency repairs are needed and sometimes must work in awkward and uncomfortable positions for long periods of time. The work can be dirty or the environment unpleasant. Some jobs have restrictions that pertain to physical condition, vision or amount of education and training.

Though women are rarely found in any of these jobs, there is no reason why they can't qualify. Women are slowly breaking into fields like television repair which do not require great strength, and several schools are establishing courses in auto mechanics for women.

Air-Conditioning, Refrigeration and Heating Mechanic

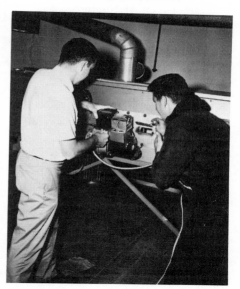

The Job

If we want to be warm in the winter and cool in the summer—at home, at work, and in school—we need heating and air-conditioning units. Many additional units are used in manufacturing processes which require artifically created temperatures, not to mention those purchased for refrigerating food products and medicines. The men who install, maintain, and repair these systems are specialists—air-conditioning, refrigeration, and heating mechanics. Some operate in large commercial installations; others work on smaller home units.

Air-conditioning and refrigeration mechanics

install and repair anything from portable room air-conditioners to central-plant air-conditioning or refrigeration systems. When setting up a system, the mechanic follows blueprints or other manufacturer's instructions and installs motors, compressors, absorption equipment and evaporators. He connects tubing to different units and connects all the equipment with an electrical power source. Once the unit is installed, he charges the system with the proper amount of refrigerant. Usually several hours are required to adjust a large unit for proper operation, but the mechanic never leaves until he is certain the system is working properly.

When an air-conditioning or refrigeration unit breaks down, a mechanic is called to diagnose the problem and repair it. He will usually check for leaks, inspect thermostats, check the electrical system, lubricate moving parts, and replenish the liquid refrigerant. He must understand control circuit diagrams and be able to use electrical testing instruments. He also works with electric drills, pipe cutters and benders, acetylene torches, hammers, screwdrivers, and pliers.

Furnace installers, or heating-equipment installers, use blueprints or other instructions to install oil or gas heating units. When the heating units are in place, they install fuel pipes, air ducts, pumps, and other equipment. They then connect electrical controls and wiring and make sure the units are working properly.

Oil-burner mechanics usually work during the fall and winter, repairing oil burners and heating systems. They check thermostats, controls and other parts to determine why the burners aren't working properly and replace faulty parts. Major repairs are done in the shop. During the spring and summer, the mechanic services heating units, cleaning them out and replacing parts.

Gas-burner mechanics perform similar functions, diagnosing what is wrong with gas heating systems and making necessary repairs and adjustments. They also work on hot-water heaters or stoves, and during the summer those employed by utility companies inspect and repair gas meters.

About 115,000 air-conditioning, refrigeration, and heating mechanics are currently employed. They work for dealers and contractors who specialize in selling and servicing such equipment or for construction companies, fuel-oil dealers, and gas utility companies.

A few operate on a free-lance basis. New York, Texas, California, Pennsylvania, Ohio, and Illinois have the greatest concentrations of these workers, but mechanics, of course, are needed throughout the country.

What You Need Personally

Mechanics should have a good understanding of how things work and an interest in puzzling out unusual complications. Because they work with their hands, they should have adequate finger dexterity, motor coordination, and sufficient physical strength to lift heavy equipment.

What Education and Training You Need

Employers frequently prefer high school graduates who have taken courses in mathematics, physics, and blueprint reading. Many vocational and public high schools offer special courses in this trade in cooperation with local employers, the Air-Conditioning and Refrigeration Institute and the National Oil Fuel Institute. Shop training in mechanical skills is combined with classroom instruction in these two- to three-year courses. Training programs are also available under the Manpower Development and Training Act, but on-the-job training is still always required.

Formal apprenticeship programs are recommended for those entering this field. These programs combine classroom instruction and on-the-job training and take from four to five years. Apprentices study mathematics, blueprint reading, electrical controls and other subjects, and learn to install and repair all types of air-conditioning, refrigeration, and heating systems (see pages 52-63).

If you want more advanced educational training to become an air-conditioning, heating, or refrigeration technician, some technical institues offer two- or three-year programs with an associate in science degree that will prepare students for jobs in research, design, production, or sales (see pp. 233-234).

New technological developments make it important for all mechanics in this field, new or experienced, to keep informed of progress. Manufacturers often conduct training courses for this purpose.

What the Occupation Has to Offer

There should be many openings in this field in the next decade, with qualified mechanics having especially good opportunities. Many more houses, offices, schools and other buildings are using air conditioning, and more refrigeration equipment will probably be needed to produce, store, and market food and other perishables.

Furnace installers and gas-and oil-burner mechanics will have some increase in jobs, but more and more homes and businesses are using electrical heat. Equipment for electrical heating systems is installed and maintained by electricians.

Earnings for these mechanics vary. Many factors are taken into consideration in determining salaries, such as size and location of employer, work performed, etc. Unionized mechanics usually make higher salaries and receive more benefits than non-union workers. Mechanics who work on large commercial equipment earn more than those who work on home units. Generally speaking, hourly rates for skilled mechanics range from about $3.25 to $7 an hour, with experienced mechanics making two or three times more than beginners. Mechanics who can work on both heating and air-conditioning equipment usually make more than those who specialize.

Opportunities for advancement in this field are rather limited. Inexperienced mechanics can naturally earn more money and do more complex work as they improve their skills, and some mechanics will go into business for themselves. As mentioned earlier, mechanics who complete technical school programs may be able to go into other areas of the industry or progress to become technicians.

Points to Consider Before Going into This Field

Air-conditioning, refrigeration, and heating mechanics can make quite a lot of money without having to invest in expensive training. Their skills should continue to be needed in the years to come, particularly in air-conditioning and refrigeration. Most mechanics work fairly regular hours and receive insurance and paid-holiday benefits.

There are some disadvantages to this work. It can be seasonal, although employers usually try to keep workers employed all year long. During seasonal peaks, you may have to put in long hours; overtime is paid. The work can sometimes be strenuous and dirty and servicemen may have to endure temperature changes while they work. Burns or electric shocks can also be suffered.

For more information, write:

American Gas Association, Inc.
1515 Wilson Boulevard
Arlington, Virginia 22209
Ask for: information on training programs for gas-burner mechanics.

American Society of Heating, Refrigeration and Air Conditioning Engineers
345 East 47th Street
New York, New York 10017

Director of Manpower Development
Air Conditioning and Refrigeration Institute
1815 North Fort Myer Drive
Arlington, Virginia 22209
Ask for: list of schools offering training programs.

Refrigeration Service Engineers Society
2720 Des Plaines Avenue
Des Plaines, Illinois 60018

Appliance Serviceman

The Job

Less than one hundred years ago, electricity as we know it was unheard of. Yet today, our homes are filled with electrical appliances we can hardly imagine living without. Every year sees wondrous electrical inventions soon to be taken for granted.

To install, inspect, repair, and rebuild this wide range of appliances, a whole new job category has emerged: the appliance serviceman. The serviceman may work on all kinds of appliances or may specialize in one or two—washing machines or dishwashers, for instance. If he works in a shop, he will usually repair small appliances (toasters, hair dryers, etc.) or specialize in one type or brand of large appliance. Other servicemen work in the repair departments of factories and repair and rebuild the appliances produced by their companies. They may do one special task or an entire repair job.

Most servicemen who repair major home appliances come to the customer's home. If the repair is major, the serviceman may take the appliance to his shop or return it to the manufacturer. Smaller appliances are usually brought to the repair shop by the customer, fixed by the repairman, and picked up by the customer.

Some servicemen are employed by utility companies to restore service and make minor repairs and adjustments or to recommend specific kinds of repairmen for the faulty appliances.

When servicing an appliance, a repairman first asks how the appliance performed when it was operating properly. He then checks for odd noises; overheating or broken, worn, or loose parts; faulty power lines and connections. Servicemen carry testing devices, such as ammeters, voltmeters, and vacuum and pressure gauges for these purposes. Once the problem has been determined, necessary parts are replaced using hand tools, such as screwdrivers and pliers.

Servicemen also answer questions and complaints from customers and will often advise them on the proper use of their appliances. They usually keep records of parts used and hours worked on each repair job.

Of the nation's 220,000 appliance repairmen most work for independent repair shops or service departments of department and appliance stores. The remaining men work for appliance manufacturers or utility companies.

What You Need Personally

An appliance serviceman should have an understanding of mechanics and electrical theory. He should display manual dexterity, patience and attention to detail. Average physical strength and good eyesight are also needed in the job.

One of the most important qualities for an appliance serviceman is the ability to communicate with people. The serviceman meets many different customers and is often his employer's only customer contact, so the impression he makes is important. He should be able to express himself well in explaining the functions and malfunctions of appliances and should be honest and tactful.

What Education and Training You Need

Many employers prefer applicants who have graduated from high schools or vocational high schools and have had courses in mathematics, science, and electricity. Courses in public speaking, mechanical drawing, and electrical shop would also be helpful. In some places, employers and high schools cooperate to combine part-time work in appliance repair shops with related school studies.

Additional courses of study are available in evening high school or trade school classes, from technical school programs, from correspondence courses or from manufacturer training courses.

In most cases, appliance servicemen learn skills on the job. Workers begin as helpers and are sometimes given classroom instruction in appliance repair as part of their training. Even after they become experienced, servicemen are often urged to take additional training (often on company time) to become familiar with new appliances.

The inexperienced repairman spends his first few months helping on installations, driving service trucks or other relatively routine operations. He learns to use electricity-measuring equipment and must understand electronics and wiring, in addition to remembering the specifics of repairing different appliances.

Trainees receive close supervision for six to eighteen months, after which they can usually repair small simple electric or gas appliances. It takes about three years' experience to become qualified to repair complicated electrical appliances.

What the Occupation Has to Offer

There should be a great increase in appliance repair jobs during the 1970s, as people have more money to spend and new appliances are introduced. Servicing the increasing number of coin-operated washing machines and dry cleaners will also open jobs. Some of the employment growth will be offset by improvements in manufacturing, but jobs should still be plentiful.

Wages for appliance repairmen are hard to estimate. In general, inexperienced workers start at $2 to $3 an hour, and experienced servicemen can make more than $5 an hour. In most cases, repairmen receive extra pay for overtime, paid vacations, sick leave, insurance, and other employee benefits.

If an appliance serviceman works in a large repair shop or service center, he may be promoted to foreman, assistant service manager, or service manager. Knowledge of bookkeeping and business is helpful for these promotions. If he works for a manufacturer, he may become an instructor to new servicemen or a technical writer who prepares service manuals. In some cases, servicemen are promoted to managerial positions. Experienced servicemen with business knowledge and investment funds can go into business for themselves.

Points to Consider Before Going into This Field

There are many advantages to working as an appliance serviceman. The work can be done in any locale and is rewarded by good wages and benefits. There should continue to be a demand for repairmen in the years to come, increasing with new technology. Repairmen work regular hours in a relatively safe profession. Of great importance to many people, the serviceman works independently and without supervision. He must make decisions and gets the credit for a job well done.

There are also disadvantages to the job. To get at large appliances, servicemen may have to work in uncomfortable positions or dirty places. They have to bend and stoop and sometimes must lift heavy appliances while installing them or taking them away for repair. There is no reason why a woman couldn't do these jobs; nevertheless women are rarely found in this field.

For more information, write:

Association of Home Appliance Manufacturers
20 North Wacker Drive
Chicago, Illinois 60606

Department of Human Resources Development
Mail Control Unit
800 Capitol Mall
Sacramento, California 95814

Ask for: *Household Appliance Repairman* No. 161, Free.

National Appliance and Radio-TV Dealers Association
318 West Randolph Street
Chicago, Illinois 60601

Also contact:

Appliance repair shops; appliance dealers; gas and electric utility companies and appliance manufacturers; state employment offices for information on training available through the Manpower Development and Training Act; vocational schools which offer courses in appliance servicing and electronics.

Business-Machine Serviceman

The Job

Every day another type of electronic equipment is developed: machines to record and process transactions, duplicate and mail information, or otherwise make office work more efficient. Some of the more common office machines are typewriters, adding and calculating machines, cash registers, electronic computers and other data-processing machines, dictating and transcribing machines, mailing, duplicating and copying machines, and microfilm equipment. Because of the electronic complexity of this equipment and its increasing use, we need more and more people trained to install, service and repair it.

Most office-machine repairs are done in the customer's office. Servicemen usually make routine service calls—perhaps twice a year—to inspect, clean, and adjust the machines. They also give machine operators instructions on better use of the machines, and respond to emergency repair calls. If a machine cannot be fixed at the office, they take it to the manufacturer's service department for a major repair or overhaul. In their work, servicemen use hand tools like screwdrivers and wrenches, plus gauges, meters, and testing equipment.

Servicemen may also have sales reponsibilities. They frequently sell preventive maintenance contracts for machine servicing on a regular basis and may sell supplies that are used with particular machines.

Most servicemen are employed by the service departments of business-machine manufacturers and may specialize in one or two machines or work on the whole line produced by the manufacturer. Each serviceman has regular customers in a particular geographical area. Other servicemen work for small, independent repair shops and maintain and repair a variety of brands. Such servicemen might specialize in a particular type of machine, such as the typewriter, but other servicemen have work that is more varied.

The most widely used business machines are typewriters; about 19,000 typewriter servicemen work on them. Most servicemen work on both manual and electric typewriters and in many cases maintain and repair more complex machines, such as tape-fed automatic typewriters and interchangeable-typeface machines, which require extra training.

About 5,000 servicemen work on adding machines; some of these workers also repair calculators and about 10,000 servicemen work primarily on calculating machines, and another 4,000 specialize in cash registers. These machines are of varying complexity, so servicemen are usually employed by the manufacturers of the equipment.

Accounting-bookkeeping machines are more complex than most other office machines; more than 2,500 servicemen specialize in them. These machines have to be set with special controls or programs, and the workers who do this are usually employed by the machine manufacturers.

The most skilled of the office-machine repairmen work on data-processing equipment. These 30,000 workers need a good electronic background to service machines that usually include highly sophisticated computer systems.

Dictating-machine servicemen require a knowledge of electronics and mechanics. Most of the 700 men who specialize in this work are employed by business-equipment manufacturers; some also work on typewriters and adding machines. Duplicating and copying machines require about 6,500 servicemen in the United States alone. Duplicators are small offset printers that use special plates for reproduction. Copiers are electromechanical devices which produce single or multiple copies directly from an original. These machines may be simple and hand operated or highly complex. The copy-machine servicemen may also work on microfilm equipment, but such a job requires photographic knowledge in addition to an understanding of electronics and mechanics. Postage meters, addressing and imprinting machines and folding and inserting machines require roughly another 2,000 servicemen who have a full knowledge of electromechanical machines.

Business machine servicemen are employed in virtually every community in the country, but they are found most frequently in large urban centers where offices are concentrated.

What You Need Personally

A serviceman needs mechanical aptitude and manual dexterity. Good vision, including color vision, is important, as is hearing in order to detect small problems in the machines. These workers meet customers all day, and it is important that they get along pleasantly with them. A serviceman must also be honest and trustworthy. He works independently and is often working around large sums of money in banks or other offices. In some cases, employers require business-machine servicemen to be bonded.

What Education and Training You Need

Most employers require a high school education to enter this field, with background in shop courses, mathematics, physics, and English. Any studies in electricity and electronics would also be helpful. Employers are even more pleased to have applicants who have completed some training beyond high school, particularly in electricity or electronics. The more complex the equipment to be serviced, the more important extra training is.

Applicants have to pass tests for mechanical aptitude and often on basic electricity, manual dexterity, general intelligence, and abstract reasoning. After hiring, trainees are given extensive on-the-job instruction. Most companies provide schooling in the company's products, which takes from several weeks to several months, depending on the machine. Companies usually pay trainees during this period. They will also frequently pay part or full tuition for the employee who wants to take related courses in vocational or technical schools or through home-study courses.

Following introductory instruction the trainee usually has one to three years of on-the-job training and experience before becoming a fully qualified serviceman. Cash-register repairmen usually take two-and-a-half to three-and-a-half years to learn their jobs; calculating-machine servicemen about two years, accounting-bookkeeping-machine repairmen train for three to four years, including a year or two servicing adding machines, calculators, or cash registers. Typewriter repairmen may need two or three years to become skilled; adding-machine repairmen six months to a year.

Repairmen for data-processing equipment need knowledge of electricity or electronics and may attend college or technical school courses in engineering or may have had electronics training in the armed forces. They may also study computer programming. Applicants for data-processing work usually spend two months in on-the-job training, then three to six months in school, then another twelve to eighteen months getting specific on-the-job experience.

What the Occupation Has to Offer

This occupation should see rapid growth in the next decade. More and more businesses are using office machines, and new types of machines are continually being developed. Data-processing equipment repair will be a particularly big field for the future, but all types of servicemen should be in demand. The serviceman who knows electricity or electronics will be in the best position.

Wages within this field vary significantly, depending on geographical area, type of equipment serviced and experience of the employee. The highest salaries usually go to those who service electronic data-processing equipment, accounting-bookkeeping machines, postage and mailing machines, and the more complex duplicating and copying equipment. Those who work only on typewriters, adding machines, calculators, cash registers, or dictating machines receive lower salaries.

Trainees usually earn between $80 and $105 a week; those with previous electronics training start a little higher. Periodic merit raises are given by most companies, and experienced servicemen earn from $110 to $300 a week. In addition, some servicemen receive commissions for selling supplies or service contracts. Most companies provide insurance and benefit plans.

Promotions in this field are usually based on technical competence, leadership qualities and skill in self-expression. Some servicemen move into sales positions, which offer greater earnings. Others are promoted to foreman, service manager or another supervisory position. Still others train new servicemen or go into product engineering. Experienced servicemen sometimes open their own repair shops or may become independent dealers for manufacturers.

Points to Consider Before Going into This Field

This occupation offers excellent opportunities for a person with an interest in electronics and mechanics. Most schooling is provided by the employer, and the employee can learn useful skills that will be increasingly desirable in a modern world. These skills can also be built upon so that the worker can go on to more complex machines and greater earnings. There is very rarely any heavy work involved. Employment is steady and available throughout the country. Servicemen visit many different offices, meeting new people and working independently. Hours are regular; the work isn't usually too dirty.

There are very vew disadvantages to this occupation. Sometimes the serviceman must work in uncomfortable positions and they do get greasy when repairing some machines. Customers are often in a hurry to get their machines fixed and may put pressure on the serviceman, which he should be able to handle.

For more information, write:

Business Equipment Manufacturers Association
1828 L Street, N.W.
Washington, D.C. 20036

Department of Human Resources Development
800 Capitol Mall
Sacramento, California 95814
Ask for: *Office Machine Serviceman* pamphlet No. 405.

Also contact:

Dealers who sell and service business machines; brand-name sales and service offices; trade and technical schools which offer courses in electronics or office-machine repairs; state employment offices for information about training under the Manpower Development and Training Act.

Diesel Mechanic

The Job

Much of our heavy transportation and construction equipment is diesel-powered, with a fuel-injection system in which the heat of compression causes fuel to burn. To keep all these engines working requires a specialist known as a diesel mechanic. He works on heavy trucks, buses, ships, power boats, locomotives, bulldozers, cranes, tractors, generators, compressors, and pumps.

When a diesel engine isn't working properly, the mechanic finds out as much as he can about the particular engine, then looks at it, listens to it and inspects and tests the engine parts to find the problem. Once he decides what to do, he disassembles the engine and repairs or replaces the faulty part. Then the engine is reassembled, cleaned, lubricated, and tested. Diesel mechanics also perform preventive maintenance on engines, inspecting, testing, and adjusting engine components at regular intervals.

The diesel mechanic works with a variety of equipment, including hand tools such as pliers, wrenches and screwdrivers, measuring and testing equipment, welding tools, drills and special tools such as valve refacers and piston pin-fitting machines.

Diesel mechanics may have job titles referring to their specialities, for instance truck mechanic or heavy-equipment mechanic (bulldozers and earthmovers). Some diesel mechanics specialize in rebuilding engines or in repairing a particular part, such as a fuel-injection system or starter system. Others work on all types of diesel repair or install equipment for diesel-engine manufacturers.

More than 85,000 diesel mechanics are found throughout the country, but they are most heavily concentrated in California, New York, Illinois, and Texas—states with a lot of construction, industry, farming and commercial activity. The mechanics are employed by ship companies, railroads, construction firms, logging companies, bus lines, electric power plants, and state highway departments. Others work in the service departments of the distributors and dealers who sell diesel engines, trucks, farm and construction equipment. Still others are employed by the engine manufacturers and by the garages that service diesel equipment.

What You Need Personally

A diesel mechanic works with many different tools so needs a better than average aptitude for mechanics. He should be manually dexterous, quick-thinking and have a good sense of the relationships between parts. Because these engines and their parts are heavy and often hard to get at, the mechanic should be fairly strong and agile.

What Education and Training You Need

There are many different ways to learn this trade, but most employers prefer to hire trainees who combine a high school education with mechanical ability. Public high schools and vocational schools offer courses in automobile repair, machine shop, science and mathematics that are useful background for this trade.

Further training can be obtained from junior and community colleges, public and private vocation and technical schools, and colleges and universities. There are also correspondence courses, and the armed forces train many mechanics in all fields. A formal training program can take from several months to two years and combines classroom instruction with practical experience. After that, on-the-job experience and training is still needed to become a skilled mechanic.

Some diesel mechanics start by working on gasoline-powered engines for three or four years. It then takes another six to eighteen months of training to learn to maintain and repair diesel equipment, and some supplementary courses in a vocational or trade school are helpful.

Diesel-engine manufacturers and some other employers offer four-year apprenticeship programs which combine classroom training with practical experience. The classroom studies include blueprint reading, hydraulics, welding, and other subjects. On-the-job trainees learn about valves, bearings, injection systems, starting systems, cooling systems, and other parts of the engine. (See pages 52-63.)

Diesel manufacturers often offer additional training programs for experienced mechanics to learn to maintain and repair the newer engines, using the most modern equipment.

What the Occupation Has to Offer

There should be a large increase in jobs in this field in the next decade. The industries which use these engines are expected to grow, and the diesel engine is relatively economical to use. In many instances, diesel engines will replace gasoline-powered engines. It is expected that many job openings will be filled by mechanics who have worked on gasoline engines and who will be trained for diesel repair.

The range of earnings for diesel mechanics varies depending on geography and type of business. Unionized workers usually earn more than nonunion workers, but in general wages range from $3.70 to $5.50 an hour. Mechanics often have to work on weekends or at night on emergency repairs, for which they receive overtime rates. Paid vacations and holidays, insurance programs and other benefits are common.

Opportunities for promotion are particularly good for mechanics who work for organizations operating or repairing large fleets of diesels. Some possible positions are lead man, shop foreman, or service manager.

Points to Consider Before Going into This Field

One advantage to this field is that job opportunities can be expected to expand in the coming

years. The work is steady with no off-seasons, and pay and benefits are usually good. The mechanic learns to apply many different skills and to make independent judgments and decisions.

This work does have some disadvantages. The work is often dirty, noisy, smelly, and strenuous. Heavy lifting and reaching, bending, standing and crouching are common. To get at an engine part, the mechanic may have to stand or lie in an awkward position for a long period of time. If safety precautions are taken, there should be little danger of injury, however.

For more information, write:

Diesel Engine Manufacturers Association
122 East 42nd Street
New York, New York 10017

International Association of Machinists and Aerospace Workers
1300 Connecticut Avenue, N.W.
Washington, D.C. 20036

Departmentof Human Resources Development
Mail Control Unit
800 Capitol Mall
Sacramento, California 95814
Ask for: *Diesel Mechanic* No. 251, Free.

International Union, United Automobile, Aerospace and Agricultural Implement Workers of America
8000 East Jefferson Avenue
Detroit, Michigan 48214

Sheet Metal Workers International Association
1750 New York Avenue, N.W.
Washington, D.C. 20036

Also contact:

State employment offices for information on training programs and apprenticeships; firms that use or service diesel-powered equipment, such as truck and bus lines, truck, construction and farm-equipment dealers; local offices of the unions listed above.

Farm-Equipment Mechanic

The Job

Have you ever seen a farmer working his fields with a horse-drawn plow? Probably not! The modern farmer, using a dazzling variety of machinery to plant and harvest crops, is able to produce a greater yield with many fewer man-hours than even in his father's time. The electrical, mechanical, and hydraulic equipment used by today's farmer includes tractors, combines, pick-up balers, corn pickers, crop dryers, field-forage harvesters, elevators, and conveyors. To assemble, maintain, and repair all this equipment, more than 53,000 farm-equipment mechanics are hard at work.

Some mechanics assemble new farm implements and machinery that have been shipped in sections to farm equipment dealers or wholesalers, or they repair dented or torn sheet metal on the equipment. Other mechanics work on tractors, either diesel or gas-powered, which may be driven or hauled to a shop for repair. Emergency repairs are common, however, when the farmer is in the midst of harvesting his crops. In this case, the mechanic may have to go to the farm to fix the tractor.

Testing equipment is used by the machanic to determine the cause of malfunction. A dynamometer measures engine performance; a compression tester can determine whether piston rings are worn or if cylinder valves leak. Once the cause of trouble is determined, the mechanic sets about repairing or replacing broken parts, fixing the transmission or tuning or overhauling the engine. For this work, he uses hand tools and welding and power metalworking tools. Mechanics also perform preventive maintenance on farm machinery.

In large shops, mechanics may specialize in certain types of repair or in certain types of farm equipment. Mechanics who work for an equipment manufacturer may perform assembly and adjustment jobs to determine the most efficient future designs for farm work. Some farm-equipment mechanics repair equipment used for irrigation or plumbing.

Farm-equipment mechanics work in the service departments of the farm-equipment dealers, in independent repair shops, in repair shops on large farms and in service departments of farm-equipment wholesalers and manufacturers. About half the mechanics work in Illinois, Texas, Iowa, California, Minnesota, Ohio, Indiana, Missouri, Wisconsin, Nebraska, North Carolina, Pennsylvania, and Kansas.

What You Need Personally

The farm-equipment mechanic needs not only a knowledge of mechanics but also an understanding of agriculture. He should be in good physical condition, have good eyesight and be dependable. He must be able to get along with farm people; he must be honest, hard working, and have personal habits that are acceptable to a farm community.

What Education and Training You Need

Most employers prefer high school graduates with a farming background. Some experience in hydraulics, welding and diesel and gasoline engines is helpful and can often be obtained in a public or vocational high school. An additional year or two of training in a vocational or technical school is an asset, with emphasis on studies in mechanics, basic electricity, welding, blueprint reading and auto or shop mechanics.

On-the-job training is necessary for these jobs. This can be obtained in various ways. In most cases, mechanics are hired as helpers, and as such they assist experienced mechanics in assembling new farm equipment and performing repair work. Training time varies, but it usually takes at least three years to become a qualified mechanic.

Some mechanics complete an apprenticeship training program which lasts three or four years. Apprentices are usually chosen from among shop helpers, and they receive on-the-job training in all phases of maintaining and repairing farm equipment, plus classroom instruction. (See pages 52-63.)

Some manufacturers have service schools for trainees who have shown aptitude and ability in their work. Manufacturers also offer refresher training programs periodically to teach design, maintenance and repair of new farm equipment models.

What the Occupation Has to Offer

The field isn't overcrowded today. Farms will become more and more mechanized in the coming years, and there will be a steady demand for trained specialists who can maintain and repair equipment. There will be a decrease in the number of farms, however, which will somewhat offset this growth in openings. Farm equipment is also becoming more reliable and tends to need fewer repairs.

Earnings vary for farm-equipment mechanics, usually ranging from the minimum wage for beginners to $4.00 an hour for experienced workers. The hours are irregular, perhaps forty hours a week in the winter and as many as sixty hours a week during planting and harvesting seasons. Mechanics often receive paid vacations and holidays, plus insurance benefits.

The farm mechanic can advance from helper to mechanic to machinery repairman to maintenance repairmen to foreman. Some mechanics open their own repair shops. Keeping up with developments in the field is an important key to promotion.

Points to Consider Before Going into This Field

The farm equipment mechanic has the advantage of having a needed skill in a geographical location where there is often not a heavy concentration of industry. He is able to make an important contribution to the overall economic health of his region and can gain a feeling of satisfaction from working with and helping his neighbors. The work is independent, and the results are visible.

There are some disadvantages to this work. The hours during the heavy season can be exhausting, with hardly a day off to recuperate until winter. Mechanics often have to travel miles to fix a piece of equipment and may have to work on it in the middle of a field—in the rain! The work can be dirty and tiring.

The requirements for farm-equipment mechanics are that applicants be strong, mechanical, and knowledgeable about farming.

For more information, write:

Publications Manager
California State Polytechnic College
San Luis Obispo, California 93401
Ask for: *Mechanical Agriculture*.

Department of Human Resources Development
Mail Control Unit
800 Capitol Mall
Sacramento, California 95814
Ask for: *Farm Equipment Mechanic* No. 302, Free.

Farm and Industrial Equipment Institute
410 North Michigan Avenue
Chicago, Illinois 60611

National Farm and Power Equipment Dealers Association
2340 Hampton Avenue
St. Louis, Missouri 63139

Also contact:

Local state employment offices for information on training programs and apprenticeships; local farm equipment dealers and independent service shops.

Industrial Machinery Repairman

The Job

Modern factories are filled with huge, efficient machines which, although expensive to install, save the manufacturer a lot of money in production costs. But when these machines break down, all those savings are quickly wiped away. A long-term breakdown of an industrial machine can disrupt production and cost a company hundreds of thousands of dollars. To keep these machines in good condition and to do quick repairs when they are needed, industry

counts on the industrial-machinery repairman, also called a maintenance mechanic.

Preventive maintenance is an important part of this man's work. The mechanic regularly inspects machinery to see that it is working properly. He oils and greases the machines and cleans and repairs its parts. He may also keep maintenance records of the machinery he services.

Some repairmen specialize in certain kinds of equipment—boilers, furnaces, electrical or electronic components. Some specialize in a certain industry. Others work on any kind of machine they are assigned.

When a machine breaks down, the industrial machinery repairman confers with the machine operator and goes over the machine carefully to determine what is wrong with it. He listens for strange noises or any unusual movement that might reveal trouble. The machine is usually disassembled at least partially and the necessary repair made. After the repairman puts everything back together, he adjusts and tests the machine to make sure it's operating properly.

These mechanics need a wide range of knowledge to do their work. They often follow blueprints, lubrication charts, and engineering specifications to repair or maintain equipment. If a replacement part isn't readily available, they may sketch it so that it can be produced by the plant's metal fabricating shop in order to get the machine working again as quickly as possible.

The mechanic uses shop measuring tools to help him judge needed repairs and uses hand tools and portable power tools in repairing machinery. A machine may take from an hour to three days to repair.

Industrial machinery repairmen are employed in many kinds of industries and are most often found in manufacturing plants. A small plant may have one mechanic; a large aircraft plant may have dozens. The industries that most often hire the country's 180,000 repairmen are food and related products, primary metals, machinery, chemicals, fabricated metal products, and transportation equipment. Repairmen are also employed by the paper, electrical machinery, and rubber industries. Others work for companies who do maintenance for firms too small to hire their own full-time mechanics, and still other repairmen are employed by the manufacturers of the industrial machinery. Although these workers are found all over the country, their greatest concentration is in industrial states of New York, Pennsylvania, California, Ohio, Illinois, Michigan, New Jersey, and Massachusetts.

What You Need Personally

Mechanical aptitude is most important for this work, as the repairman will be working on a variety of different machines. Because the work is so diverse and the problems so unpredictable, the repairman must be adaptable and able to apply original thinking to each situation.

Manual dexterity is important for the industrial-machinery repairman, and he should be agile and in good physical condition. He will have to be prepared for reaching and climbing, and should have enough strength to lift heavy tools or boxes.

Patience and attention to detail are also necesary qualities for this job. Because the work often means doing fine measurements and fitting to close tolerances, the repairman cannot afford to work too fast or carelessly.

What Education and Training You Need

The skills of this trade are usually acquired by several years of related working experience. But there are ways to increase chances of success. High school studies should include courses in mathematics, mechanical drawing, blueprint reading, physics, metal shop, and wood shop. Model-building hobbies are also helpful. For additional formal training, the worker can take courses in two-year junior and community-college programs, at private or public vocational or technical schools, or through adult-education programs.

On-the-job training is most important in this field, and it is sometimes acquired through a four-year formal apprenticeship program. These programs include classroom instruction in shop, mathematics, blueprint reading, safety, hydraulics, welding and other relevant subjects. Practical experience includes the use and care of tools and the operation, lubrication, and adjustment of the machinery involved. An apprentice will usually start as an "oiler," lubricating machines, and will work himself up to journeyman status. Having reached that point, it is important that he keep up on new developments in the field. (See pages 52-63.)

What the Occupation Has to Offer

There should be a rapid increase in jobs for the industrial-machinery repairman in the 1970s. As machinery becomes more complex and more of it is used to fabricate, process, assemble, inspect, and handle materials in every industry, the need for trained mechanics will become ever greater. Companies stand to take heavy financial losses when this machinery breaks down, so the role of the industrial-machinery repairman is vital to the efficient and profitable running of factories.

Wages for these workers vary by geographical locale, but most earn more than $3.75 an hour. Most of these mechanics are union members, and their contracts provide paid holidays and vacations, insurance, pensions, and other benefits.

There are some opportunities for advancement open to the journeyman mechanic with ambition. He may become a supervisor, who not only is in charge of maintenance and repair but also supervises the installation of new equipment. Or, with long and proven experience or an engineering degree or both, he may become a master mechanic, the person in charge of choosing machinery and determining production capacity for new products and model changes.

Points to Consider Before Going into This Field

The industrial machinery repairman is a skilled worker, and the demand for his skills can be expected to increase in the years to come. His work is usually steady, the hours regular, and he is rewarded by good pay and benefits. This worker is challenged on the job as he makes independent decisions and evaluations. The success of his efforts is very important to his company.

There are some disadvantages to this work, however. It can be hard to get at machine parts, and repairmen may have to work in uncomfortable positions for long periods of time. The work is usually dirty and greasy; repairmen sometimes suffer minor injuries on the job. Adherence to safety regulations should make injury less likely, however. The repairman will occasionally have to work odd hours on an emergency repair, and the surroundings can be hot, smelly, and noisy. There will be pressure to get a machine fixed when it is holding up a vital operation.

The requirements for these workers are that the mechanic must be in good mental and physical shape, ready to meet the challenges offered by his work—problems to be solved that aren't always in the book!

For more information, write:

International Association of Machinists and Aerospace Workers
1300 Connecticut Avenue
Washington, D.C. 20036

International Union, United Automobile, Aerospace and Agricultural Implement Workers of America
8000 East Jefferson Avenue
Detroit, Michigan 48214

Also contact:
Local offices of these unions.

Instrument Repairman

The Job

One crucial part of today's sophisticated technology is the variety of complex industrial and scientific instruments that measure, control, and record pressure, heat, electricity, flow of liquids, and chemical composition. Each instrument is designed specially for its particular task, and it is always crucial to the operation in which it is involved. Therefore, we need trained specialists who can get malfunctioning instruments repaired and working properly before too much valuable time and money are lost. The instrument repairmen do just that.

Some instrument repairmen may specialize in a certain type of work. Some install and test new instruments and explain their workings and maintenance to operators. Instrument repairmen are important to industries involved with oil refining, nuclear energy, electricity, laboratory experiments, consumer product manufacture, aerospace operations, oceanography, sewage and water treatment, medicine, optics, dentistry, and photography.

When there is a malfunction in an instrument-controlled system, the repairman first checks to see whether it is the instrument or the related machinery that is causing the trouble. Using a variety of testing equipment like voltmeters, ammeters, pressure and vacuum gauges, the instrument repairman will go over the mechanisms and electrical circuits looking for defects. The repairman will often have to disassemble the instrument to make tests, and needs a thorough understanding of electrical components to do so. Using the instrument manufacturers' instructions as a guide, the repairman compares test readings with the readings he would get from a properly working instrument. The defective part is repaired or replaced, the instrument reassembled and then tested to be sure it is operating properly.

Instrument repairmen also perform preventive maintenance duties, inspecting instruments and cleaning, lubricating and adjusting them. They try to correct any problems that might result in later breakdowns.

The instrument repairman may work in a specially equipped shop or in the plant where the trouble is. He may perform anything from a minor repair to a major overhaul. A wide variety of tools and work materials are needed in this job: hand tools like screwdrivers, pliers and soldering irons, bench tools like jewelers' lathes, small buffer grinders and ultrasonic cleaners; micrometers and measuring devices; testing equipment; sometimes machine tools like drill presses or grinders. Instrument repairmen also work with instruction books for instruments and schematic diagrams, assembly drawings, and blueprints.

There are 95,000 instrument repairmen. Many of whom work for utility companies, petroleum and chemical plants, manufacturers of instruments and industrial controls. Others work for airlines, and manufacturers of pulp and paper, metals, rubber, aircraft, missiles, and automobiles. Most work in or around large metropolitan areas.

What You Need Personally

Mechanical aptitude, manual dexterity, and good eye-hand coordination are all important to this job. The repairman must have confidence in his own observations and be able to apply what he knows to all kinds of situations. He must be detail-conscious and able to do precise work. The work is usually done independently, so the worker must be able to work without supervision.

Because of the many situations he comes up against, the instrument repairman must be adaptable, reliable, tactful, and able to get along with others. There is sometimes pressure in this job, and the repairman must have the confidence, patience, and emotional stability to cope with it. He must think quickly and be flexible.

What Education and Training You Need

The first requirement for this job is graduation from high school. There are many studies that would be useful, including algebra, geometry, trigonometry, physics, chemistry, electricity, electronics, machine shop, mechanical drawing, English and social studies. Hobbies that include building electronic equipment are good practice.

Technical school training is becoming increasingly important for success in this field. Public and private vocational and technical schools and junior and community colleges offer two-year programs dealing with mechanical technology, electrical technology, basic engineering, or instrumentation. As instruments get more complex, these studies will become even more important. Armed forces technical schools also give training in instrument servicing that will often equip a person for a civilian job.

On-the-job training is also important to this trade, and four years of experience are usually necessary to become skilled. Some repairmen learn the trade just by assisting more experienced workers, but usually a more formal structure is used. A four-year formal apprenticeship program can provide the beginner with on-the-job training plus classroom studies. The courses can be taken during working hours, at night, or by correspondence study. They usually cover the more detailed procedures and theory the job involves and include physics, electronics, chemistry, blueprint reading, mathematics, process theory and instrument theory. (See pages 52-63.)

Some instrument manufacturing companies give special training to repairmen employed by their customers. The training, which lasts anywhere from one week to nine months, covers theory, maintenance, and operation of the manufacturer's instruments; students learn how to check instruments and where to learn more about their repair. (See pp. 247-248 and pages 297-298.)

What the Occupation Has to Offer

The use of sophisticated instruments is expected to increase in the 1970s as they become more generally accepted in current industries and find new uses in various technical, scientific, and industrial areas. They will be common in air and water pollution monitoring, in research laboratories, in laser technology, in temperature control of buildings and many other fields. The demand for instrument repairmen will thus increase, and those who can work with the more sophisticated instruments will be in excellent positions for jobs.

Most repairmen earn between $3.00 and $5.00 an hour. Some electronic instrument specialists may make more. Instrument repairmen are often union members and usually receive paid holidays and vacations, insurance, and retirement benefits.

Advancement possibilities exist for the instrument repairman, particularly if he has a knowledge of electronics. Those with supervisory ability may become group leaders or foremen in maintenance and repair departments. Some become service representatives in instrument manufacturing branch offices. A few become engineering assistants.

Points to Consider Before Going into This Field

The instrument repairman is a skilled specialist who works in an area destined for growth along with an increasing technology. The demand for his services can be expected to grow, and he receives good pay and benefits for what he does. The work is challenging, independent, and important to the proper function of industry.

There are some disadvantages to this work. The repairman may have to work under heavy pressure to fix an instrument quickly. Sometimes he will be blamed for the malfunction of the instrument, and he may be given a very hard time. The working conditions can be dirty or noisy, and some work may have to be done outdoors. In some places, instrument repairmen work on shifts and may be called in at odd times for emergency work; this work gets higher pay, however.

For more information, write:

Instrument Society of America
400 Stanwix Street
Pittsburgh, Pennsylvania 15222
Ask for: *Rewarding Technical Career in Instrumentation Awaits You*, $.50.

Scientific Apparatus Makers Association
Process Measurement and Control Section
370 Lexington Avenue
New York, New York 10017

Also contact:

State employment offices for lists of training programs.

Maintenance Electrician

The Job

Most industry and many of the comforts of everyday life are made possible through the use of electrical equipment. To keep all these systems operating properly, maintenance electricians, also known as electrical repairmen, are kept busy in many factories and large buildings. They maintain and repair—and occasionally install or modify—motors, transformers, generators, controls, instruments, compressors, and lighting systems.

The most important part of this worker's job is preventive maintenance. He gives periodic checks to all the equipment for which he is responsible and tries to find and fix any defects before breakdowns occur. When there is trouble,

More than half of the country's 250,000 maintenance electricians work in the manufacturing plants of industries that produce transportation equipment, primary metal products, fabricated metal products, machinery and chemicals. Others work for public utilities, transportation industries and government agencies. The largest numbers of these workers are in the heavily industrial states of New York, Pennsylvania, California, Illinois, and Ohio, but maintenance electricians are employed all over the country.

What You Need Personally

Maintenance electricians should have manual dexterity and agility and should be in good physical condition. Good vision is also important, particularly the ability to distinguish colors.

You'll find an interest in electrical equipment and a general curiosity helpful qualities for this job. You must be patient, responsible, and thorough in your approach to your work. In many situations, you must be able to work alone without supervision.

What Education and Training You Need

A number of high school courses will be useful to the maintenance electrician. Algebra, trigonometry, science, and electricity courses are recommended. More specific training is also available from the armed forces and from technical schools. These studies provide good theoretical background but must be combined with on-the-job training.

Sometimes the trade is learned by gradual, informal on-the-job training. A young worker may assist a skilled electrician and learn from him or work in the maintenance department of a plant, moving from job to job and picking up different skills. If you do it this way, it'll take more than four years to become skilled.

Usually recommended is a four-year apprenticeship program which combines on-the-job training with classroom instruction. In class, the apprentice studies mathematics, electrical and electronic theory, drafting, blueprint reading, and other subjects. Practical training includes wire splicing, motor repair, commercial and industrial wiring, installation of light and power equipment, installation and repair of electronic controls and circuits, and welding and brazing. Apprentices are usually chosen from among the work force in a particular plant. (See also pages 52-63.)

In an increasing number of cases, maintenance electricians are required to become licensed by passing a comprehensive test on electrical theory and its application. All maintenance electricians should know the National Electric Code, and some must be familiar with local building codes.

he has to find and repair the malfunction quickly to prevent production loss. If there is a major breakdown, he must let management know whether it is necessary to shut down the equipment.

A maintenance electrician's skills and duties are diverse. He may do splicing or use mechanical connectors to connect wires or may find himself replacing wiring, fuses, circuit breakers, coils or switches. He may have to adjust equipment controls or instruments or oil and clean the moving parts of electrical machinery.

To do his work, the maintenance electrician must be able to use a wide variety of tools and equipment. He sometimes works from blueprints, diagrams, or other specifications and may test equipment with test lamps, ammeters, or oscilloscopes. Sometimes he makes mathematical computations to figure the current carrying capacities of electrical wiring and equipment. Among the tools he regularly uses are pliers, screwdrivers, wire cutters, drills, conduit bending and threading tools, soldering irons, and other hand and power tools.

The specific duties of maintenance electricians vary depending on their places of employment. In a large plant, they are usually responsible for some or all of the electrical equipment used in manufacture. In a small plant, they will do all types of electrical repair work. In a large office building or hospital, they will work on compressors, elevators, lighting systems, and air-conditioning systems.

Maintenance electricians often continue their studies in order to keep up with the new equipment and skills needed to do their work.

What the Occupation Has to Offer

There should be some increase in job opportunities for these workers during the next decade as electrical energy is used in more industries and buildings.

Earnings for maintenance electricians vary according to industry, size of company and location, but in general they earn between $3.60 and $4.75 an hour. Some earn more than $5.00 an hour. Many maintenance electricians are union members, and most receive paid vacations and holidays, insurance, and other benefits.

Skilled maintenance electricians who work for large firms can advance to foremen, or even plant electrical superintendents or plant maintenance superintendents. Chances for promotion are limited if you work for a small company.

Points to Consider Before Going into This Field

There are jobs in almost every town and every industry for the maintenance electrician. He has adaptable skills and can go easily from one industry to another. Automation won't affect his skills as long as he keeps up with developments in his field. In his work, he gets a chance to use various skills and processes and usually works independently. His job is generally secure, his hours fairly regular.

There are some disadvantages to this work, however. Climbing ladders or scaffolds and working in cramped or awkward positions is common. Some work must be done in a noisy, dirty area. There is some danger involved in working near high-voltage equipment, and the electrician must be careful to remain alert and to observe all safety precautions pertaining to his work. Another drawback to this work is that there is often limited chance for advancement. (See also pages 192-193, 216-227, 243-244.)

For more information, write:

Edison Electrical Institute
90 Park Avenue
New York, New York 10016

International Brotherhood of Electrical Workers
1125 Fifteenth Street, N.W.
Washington, D.C. 20005

Also contact:

Local employers of maintenance electricians for information on training schools and apprenticeships; unions for lists of union-management apprenticeships; state employment offices for training information, aptitude tests and applicant screening.

Millwright

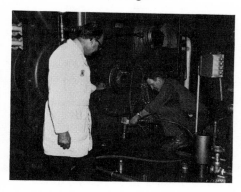

The Job

The monstrous machinery used in industry today cannot simply be purchased, set down, plugged in, and put to use. It requires special techniques of moving and installation, done by skilled workers known as millwrights. Automatic assembly equipment, milling machines, lathes, and other heavy equipment are handled by these workers.

The millwright prepares platforms and concrete foundations or makes metal frameworks or wooden platforms on which to mount the machinery. For these jobs, he must know how to read blueprints, work with wood, steel, concrete, and metal.

When new equipment arrives at a plant, the millwright unloads it from trucks and takes it to the specially prepared mount. For this work, he uses hoists, cranes, rollers, dollies, jacks, and crowbars. He is responsible for guiding the equipment into its proper spot. He then makes sure it is properly aligned and bolts it to the foundation. The next step is to assemble the rest of the machine parts and check the accuracy of the fitting with precision measuring instruments.

In order to assemble the equipment, the millwright must understand machinery, electricity, pneumatics, and hydraulics. He must also be able to use hand tools, power tools, and measuring and leveling devices. Some millwrights install a wide variety of machinery, while others specialize in what is used by a particular plant. The millwright has various other duties. He may replace worn or broken machine parts and perform other maintenance and repair work. He will be consulted in designing floor plans for new plants or for old plants which are being modernized.

The country's 80,000 millwrights work in virtually every industry, but most are employed in manufacturing—primary metals, paper, lumber and chemical products, metalworking plants, construction industries, furniture factories and others. Some work for companies that move, install, and maintain machinery on a contract basis, and others work for machinery manufacturers and government agencies. Most jobs are in industrial states such as New York, Michigan, Ohio, Pennsylvania, Illinois, and Indiana, although millwrights work all over the country.

What You Need Personally

Millwrights need good mechanical aptitude and must be able to visualize how things will work out. They must be able to plan and should have a good memory for details. Physical strength is necessary for this job, because of the enormity of the machinery involved. Agility, hand, arm and finger dexterity, and good eye-hand coordination are also important. The millwright also needs good vision for doing precision measurements and reading blueprints.

The millwright works with others and must be able to get along with them. He should be able to give and accept directions and must be extremely responsible because of the high value of the equipment he is working with.

What Education and Training You Need

On-the-job training is vital for a millwright, but a solid educational background will be very helpful. High school courses in science, mathematics, mechanical drawing, and machine shop are all good training for the job. Some vocational or technical schools or correspondence courses might also be useful.

On-the-job training can be acquired informally by working as a helper to a skilled worker for a number of years and gaining the necessary knowledge and experience. Where available, however, a formal apprenticeship is recommended. These programs usually last for four years and are open to applicants between 18 and 26, preferably high school graduates. (See pages 52-63.)

The apprentice gets classroom instruction and practical experience. In class he studies mathematics, science, electricity, safety, blueprint reading, hydraulics, and the use of precision measuring instruments. Practical training includes learning how to dismantle, move, erect, and repair machinery and training in floor layout, carpentry, welding, rigging and the use of structural steel, wood, and concrete.

What the Occupation Has to Offer

There should be some increase in jobs for millwrights in the next decade as economic growth promotes new plants, new machinery and modernization. Automation will increase, rather than decrease, the number of jobs, because automated equipment will require skilled installation.

Earnings for millwrights vary by area and industry, but most average about $4.00 an hour.

Some make more, particularly those employed by contract installation companies and construction companies. Those in the construction industry can earn more than $7.00 an hour.

Millwrights are frequently union members and receive various benefits, including overtime pay, paid vacations and holidays, and insurance.

Points to Consider Before Going into This Field

The millwright has a specialized skill which he can employ in any industrial area in the country. His work is usually steady and well-paid, and he gets a chance to make decisions and apply a variety of skills to each day's projects.

There are some disadvantages to the work, however. Oil, dirt and grease are unavoidable, and the noise from machines is a constant companion. The work can be dangerous; millwrights often work in high places or can be struck by moving or falling objects. Although millwrights employed by factories have steady work, many of the better paid jobs may involve layoffs and time spent away from home.

If you are considering this job, be sure you are in top physical and mental condition and can think and plan even under pressure. This is considered a man's job because of the physical labor involved.

For more information, write:

Department of Human Resourcs Development
Mail Control Unit
800 Capitol Mall
Sacramento, California 95814
Ask for: *Millwright (Any Industry)* No. 316, Free.
Millwright (Lumber and Wood Processing Industry) No. 312, Free.

National Machine Tool Builders Association
7901 Westpark Drive
McLean, Virginia 22101

United Brotherhood of Carpenters and Joiners
of America
101 Constitution Avenue, N.W.
Washington, D.C. 20001

Television and Radio Service Technician

The Job

There's hardly a home in America without a radio and television set; and some homes have them in every room! To keep all this equipment in working order requires the services of skilled technicians. Television sets are the items most often repaired, but technicians may also service radios, phonographs, tape recorders, and public address systems.

The service technician has a thorough knowl-

edge of electrical and electronic parts and understands the workings of the television or other electronic product he services. Technicians often make service calls in order to give customers estimates of repair costs.

To determine what is wrong with a TV, the technician gives it a routine check, looking for the most common causes of malfunction—tubes, loose or broken connections, charred or burned parts. If this check doesn't reveal the trouble, the technician uses test equipment, such as vacuum tubes, voltammeters, multimeters, oscilloscopes, and signal generators. The simplest tests are made with voltammeters. They may also check color TV circuits for excessive X-ray radiation.

When the problem is found, the service technician will change tubes or other easily replaceable parts or install or repair antennas. He also makes necessary set adjustments, including picture focusing or correcting color balance. The television and radio service technician uses many different tools, including soldering irons, wire cutters, wrenches, pliers, and measuring and testing instruments. He usually refers to wiring diagrams and service manuals to help with his work.

Radios and portable TVs are usually brought to the service shop for repair. Larger sets are brought to the shop by the technician if the problems are too complex for home repair.

More than 130,000 people are employed in this profession. They work in service shops or in stores that sell and service televisions, radios, and other electronic products. They are also employed by product manufacturers themselves. These workers are found in almost every community but are most concentrated in heavily populated areas. About one-third of the people in this field own their own businesses.

What You Need Personally

Television and radio service technicians must have an interest in electronics and understand

their function. They need good hand-eye coordination, manual dexterity, eyesight, color vision, and the ability to do detailed work. Because these technicians are frequently their employer's contact with the public, they should have a pleasant manner and appearance and be able to get along with people.

What Education and Training You Need

A good background for someone who wants to get into this field is high school or vocational school studies in mathematics, electronics, and physics. Hobbies like ham radio operating are good starts.

It usually takes two to four years to become a qualified television and radio service technician, and a formal training program can be very useful. Programs of public and private vocational and technical schools, the armed forces, home study courses, private electronics schools, and the Manpower Development and Training Act all give good instruction for this job. Study usually lasts six months to a year with training in general electronics and in specific methods of repair for television and radios. Many manufacturers, employers, and trade associations also conduct training programs when new models or new products are introduced to keep both new and experienced technicians up on the latest techniques and developments.

After some training, the technician will usually become an assistant, going on repair calls with a more experienced worker until sufficient skill and knowledge are acquired to make him qualified as a technician. Some states and cities require that service technicians be licensed; they must then pass tests in which they demonstrate their skill with testing equipment and their knowledge of electronic circuits and components.

What the Occupation Has to Offer

There should be a rapid increase in jobs for television and radio service technicians in the next decade as people continue to buy more televisions, radios, and stereo and tape equipment. More homes will have two or more televisions and there will also be more use of video tape recorders, closed circuit television, and two-way radios.

The growth of jobs will be somewhat offset by the fact that products are being made better and should need less repair. Tubes are being replaced by transistors and hand-wired chassis by printed circuit boards, making repairs less frequent and easier to accomplish. The field is still an expanding one, however.

There is a wide range of earnings for these technicians. Beginners will usually start at $125 a week, and experienced technicians may earn as much as $300 a week. Since many of these workers go into business for themselves, earnings can go even higher. Paid vacations and holidays and insurance benefits are offered in many cases.

Various opportunities for advancement are open to the skilled television and radio service technician. Those who work in large repair shops or service centers may become assistant foremen, foremen, or service managers. With increased electronics and engineering studies, they can become electronic mechanics or technicians for manufacturers or government agencies. Other service technicians employed by manufacturers can move on to such positions as technical writer, sales engineer, design engineer and service-training instructor. Men with some management ability and funding can go into business for themselves. (See pages 216-227 and 243-244.)

Points to Consider Before Going into This Field

This job offers work in a field that can be expected to continue to grow in the years to come. The technician has a skill that is in demand anywhere in the country and which can also be used as a base for building skills leading to better paying jobs. The initial training is relatively short and is easily available. The technician often gets to work independently and works normal hours in relatively comfortable surroundings.

There are a few disadvantages to the job. Repairmen may have to spend a lot of time driving between the shop and the customer's home lifting and carrying receivers. There is also some danger in installing or repairing antennas on rooftops.

Although most of the workers in this field are men, there is no reason why women can't perform the duties, and in fact, some women have begun to enroll in appropriate courses and are finding the way is smooth for repairwomen.

For more information, write:

Consumer Electronics Group
Electronic Industries Association
2001 Eye Street
Washington, D.C. 20006
Ask for: *The Electronics Service Technician*; list of approved schools and courses.

National Alliance of Television Associations
5908 South Troy Street
Chicago, Illinois 60629

Also contact:

Local service technicians; dealers who sell and service television receivers and other electric equipment; local television service associations; manufacturers who operate their own service centers; technical and vocational schools; state employment offices for information about training programs.

Watch Repairman

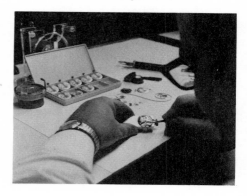

The Job

More than 90 percent of adults in this country own watches, and about half of these own more than one. Many children wear watches also. All these timepieces require skilled workmen to keep them operating properly. Watch repairmen clean, repair, and adjust watches, clocks, and chronometers.

When a watch isn't working properly, the repairman uses tweezers, a screwdriver, and other tools to remove it from its case and disassemble the movement. He uses a magnifying glass to go over all the parts of the mechanism to find out what's wrong and what must be done to fix it. He then replaces or repairs the malfunctioning part and cleans and oils all parts before putting the watch back together and testing it for accuracy. Most watch parts are interchangeable, but the repairman may have to adjust them to fit perfectly in the individual watch.

Watch repairmen use timing machines, cleaning machines, and hand tools in their work. When they work on electric and electromechanical watches and clocks, they also use electrical meters.

Of the country's 15,000 watch repairmen, about half are self-employed, usually owning small jewelry stores. Other repairmen work for retail jewelers, repair shops, wholesale establishments or manufacturing plants. Some trained watchmakers find jobs as instrument makers, repairmen or assemblers, laboratory technicians or microminiaturization specialists. They work throughout the country but are most often found in large commercial centers such as New York, Chicago, Los Angeles, Philadelphia, and San Francisco.

What You Need Personally

The watch repairmen must have finger dexterity, good eyesight, depth perception, and an attentiveness to detail. He must like to analyze and solve problems and be able to apply patience and concentration to his delicate work. The nature of the work requires sitting for long periods of time.

What Education and Training You Need

There are various approaches to this field, but high school education is considered desirable. Courses in mathematics, physics, chemistry, electricity, mechanical drawing, and machine shop will all be good background.

All training for watch repairing may be taken on the job, or the beginner may attend school for specific studies. Some public vocational high schools offer courses in this field, and there are also technical institutes and private watchmaking schools. The average formal course of study runs from one to two years, depending on what you are studying, your ability, and your attendance. The schools offer some academic courses but emphasize specific technical training. Students disassemble and assemble watch movements, remove and replace balance staffs, fit friction jewels, and learn how to use the instruments of the trade. They also learn to overhaul watches and may take courses in repairing unusual timepieces. Most schools ask students to furnish their own hand tools.

The American Watchmakers Institute offers two certification examinations for watchmaking-school graduates and for experienced watchmakers who want to prove their ability. The voluntary examinations are designed to test skill and can result in the awarding of titles of either Certified Watchmaker or Certified Master Watchmaker. The Institute also offers plaques of recognition for those who take annual voluntary upgrading examinations on developments in the field. Some states require that watch repairmen pass state licensing examinations which test skill with tools and knowledge of watch construction and repair.

The beginning watch repairman will usually take a job working with a more experienced worker in order to develop his skills. On-the-job training or apprenticeship programs are also used to develop skills in this field, rather than the formal school approach.

What the Occupation Has to Offer

There should be a relatively constant demand for skilled watch repairmen during the 1970s. Many workers in this field are near retirement age, and there are not as many young workers being trained to take their places. People will always be wearing watches, and some of the more complex—calendar watches, selfwinding watches, chronographs and electric watches—will need competent repairmen. Others will be inexpensive costume jewelry watches, however, and will not be worth repairing. There will also be jobs for skilled watch repairmen in industries making scientific instruments and electronic equipment.

Beginning watch repairmen usually earn between $90 and $125 a week, and more experienced workers make $125 to $200. In some cases, a watch repairman may also be a salesman in his jewelry store and might receive commissions on what he sells. Most watch repairmen who are in business for themselves have higher earnings. The best way to get ahead in this trade, in fact, is to go into business for yourself, either with a repair shop or a jewelry store.

Points to Consider Before Going into This Field

Watch repairing is a skill that can be practiced in any size community in any part of the country. It is also easily adaptable to skilled jobs in industry. The watch repairman works in a pleasant environment with regular hours, doing independent problem-solving work. Although this is not a growth field, there should continue to be a steady demand for a skilled watchmaker's services.

There are some disadvantages to the work, however. The watch repairman must sit for long periods of time doing very close work. For those who do not want to go into business for themselves, the opportunities for promotion are limited.

There are very few restrictions for this work. It is often recommended to handicapped persons whose hand and eye capacities are not impaired. There is no unusual physical effort involved.

For more information, write:

American Watchmakers Institute
P.O. Box 11011
Cincinnati, Ohio 45211
Ask for: *Careers in Watch Repairing*; list of watchmaking schools.

Department of Human Resources Development
Mail Control Unit
800 Capitol Mall
Sacramento, California 95814
Ask for: *Watchmaker*. No. 233, Free.

Retail Jewelers of America, Inc.
1025 Vermont Avenue, N.W.
Washington, D.C. 20005
Ask for: Job opportunities in retail stores.

The Performing Arts

Of all professions that attract young people today, the quotation "many are called, but few are chosen" applies particularly well to the performing arts. Music, acting, singing, and the dance attract thousands of young men and women annually, but since the supply far outweighs the demand, only a relatively small number of musicians, singers, dancers, models, actors and actresses find the employment they seek. Although competition is keen and the chances for employment limited, the appeal remains. Many people in the performing arts supplement their incomes by teaching, particularly in areas such as instrumental music, singing, and the dance.

"Show biz" remains a good example of a career where the college degree is sometimes helpful, but not necessary. Performing artists normally spend years in intensive practice and training before they are prepared to perform in public. Natural talent is a must, but determination along with understanding the need for long hard hours of practice and rehearsal is just as vital if you are a person with a dedicated interest in your chosen field. Preparation for an income-producing, *regular* occupation is strongly recommended, whether in related or nonrelated fields of employment!

Actors and actresses work in legitimate theaters, motion pictures, night clubs, radio and television. This category also includes radio and TV announcers, circus performers, disc jockeys, etc. The ability to memorize, physical stamina, and an ability to concentrate despite distraction are musts. Experience counts heavily in all fields here, and employment is often erratic. Knowing someone helps, too, as far as interviews go. Formal training in acting has become increasingly necessary over the years, whether in college courses or at special schools of the dramatic arts.

The dance attracts increasing numbers of young people, both men and women, since dance has become an important part of theater, musicals, night-club entertainment, and television programs. A few dancers become choreographers or dance directors. As television and motion pictures compete with live theater, opportunities for dancers in stage productions continue to decline over the years.

Models are classified as fashion models, photographic models, and television models. Fashion models are employed by clothing manufacturers, designers, department stores. Photographic models work through model agencies as a rule and are paid on an hourly or daily basis. Television models are employed by advertisers to do commercials. Competition is toughest in New York City, but other large cities provide opportunities for those interested in a modeling career.

Musicians may include instrumentalists from the rock guitarist to the French horn player. Some perform as soloists, some with bands, orchestras, folk, rock or jazz groups. Most specialize in either popular or classical music, very few excel in both categories professionally. A high percentage of musicians are engaged in teaching—in schools, colleges, and on a private-lesson basis.

Singers or vocalists may work in solo performance or with a band, chorus, orchestra, or other musical group. Most specialize in either classical or popular music. Classical singers may find work with religious institutions, professional choral groups such as the opera, or as teachers and music directors in schools or religious institutions. Popular music singers have a wider field of possibilities, including the recording field or even radio and TV commercials. The best opportunities for employment are in schools and colleges, as well as in private teaching.

Natural talent, determination, stamina and a willingness to train and practice for long hours are the demands for any career in the performing arts. Supplementary income and/or job training for regular income-producing work are realistic needs to consider as well.

Actor And Actress

The Job

Actors and actresses perform in the legitimate theater, in motion pictures and on radio and television. Their job is to make a character come to life before an audience. To do that most memorize lines and all must attend rehearsals and work under a director to create good char-

and a pleasing voice quality. A voice that records well is necessary in radio, TV, and motion picture work. The more skill and versatility you have, the longer your acting career will last.

What Education and Training You Need

Wide experience in acting is the most important requirement for an acting career, but the trend in the seventies calls for experience plus formal training in acting. Most special private training schools of the dramatic arts are located in New York City, but degree programs are offered in more than 500 colleges and universities throughout the country. Experience can be gained in local productions put on by community-theaters and in summer stock, high schools, and colleges.

The best training is found when you work under a teacher, coach, or director. There are many studios, schools, and amateur organizations in every large city where this kind of training can be acquired. Some schools also give the aspiring actor or actress a chance to be seen. This is called showcasing. Three of the best schools that offer this advantage are the American Academy of Dramatic Art in New York City, the Goodman Memorial Theater in Chicago and the Pasadena Playhouse in California.

If you want to teach in this field, a degree in drama and/or related courses are a prerequisite, and for college teaching a graduate degree in the fine arts or drama is expected.

What the Occupation Has to Offer

Most actors and actresses work only a portion of the year. The number of persons looking for work exceeds the demand to such a degree that it is vital to have savings or supplementary income for the long periods when there is no work available. Even Central Casting, an agency in Hollywood which lists names of extras for Hollywood film producers, has cut down its list to 4,000 names, a dropping of 13,000! The demand for extras is simply not there.

TV's popularity has affected the movie industry adversely; not as many films are being made. Off-Broadway opportunities have increased somewhat, but not enough to make a difference to the vast numbers of persons aspiring to an acting career. Competition is extreme for legitimate theater, but since new talent and fresh faces are always exciting, there will be work for those who are really determined to get it.

Members of the acting profession belong to various unions which set minimum wages, salaries, and other working conditions. In 1970, the minimum weekly salary for actors and actresses in Broadway productions was above $165. Off-Broadway shows paid a minimum of $75 a week. Road shows paid about $220 a week minimum. Motion picture performers had a minimum daily

acterizations. Roles portrayed may be serious or comic, parts may be walk-ons, bit parts, supporting roles, or leading roles. Because the actor or actress is a member of a team, in addition to acting ability he or she may be required to have dancing and singing talent. "Extras" are used in crowd scenes. They rarely have speaking parts, except in chorus or crowd response.

Rehearsal time varies according to the type of performance. Live theater requires long rehearsals of the entire production. TV and motion picture rehearsal time is usually in segments, particularly in TV where video tape is used often. The performer works amid technicians, stage hands and other theater personnel, and this can be distracting. So can cameras, lights or interruptions from technicians.

Actors and actresses find jobs not only in Broadway theater and film but also in TV commercials, summer stock (commonly called "little theaters"), repertory theaters, and dinner theaters.

What You Need Personally

Young persons planning a career in acting must have poise, stage presence and the ability to project themselves to the audience. Talent and creative ability and the stamina to endure long and often uncomfortable rehearsals are absolutely vital.

Self-discipline is needed in order to meet repeated disappointments. A good memory and the capacity to understand and work with people are as important as good physical appearance

rate of $120. Extras averaged about $33 a day. Performers on network TV shows averaged a $180 minimum for a half-hour program (including ten hours of rehearsal time).

Most actors and actresses are covered by a pension fund and receive hospitalization through their union memberships. Unemployment compensation is sometimes hard to collect because regular employment is erratic and performers have trouble meeting their states' eligibility requirements.

A possibility for future employment is seen in the establishment of professional acting companies in more and more cities. The number of summer stock and repertory theaters seems to be increasing also. The expansion of public broadcasting systems and expanded use of cable TV offer further opportunities for employment.

Points to Consider Before Going into This Field

Uncertain job opportunities, the need for supplementary income, and the erratic nature of the work are all points to be considered seriously by the person who wishes to act. While irregular and long hours would seem to be disadvantages to some, most young actors and actresses take this as a normal and even enjoyable part of "show biz." Acting is one of the few occupations where you work as an integral part of a team, where everyone strives toward the same goal of a fine performance. While very few ever make the top, the progress of the aspiring performer is always an exciting one, despite setbacks, periods of unemployment, and disappointment. A tremendous amount of determination and courage is vital not only for the beginner but also for the veteran performer. TV and filmed commercial opportunities can help to fill unemployed periods as can part-time work in other fields. Actors and actresses enjoy a sense of fellowship with their co-workers that is unique among the performing arts. An acting career is difficult to get into, harder to make money in, but most rewarding.

For more information, write:

Actors' Equity Association
165 West 46th Street
New York, New York 10036

American Federation of Television and Radio Artists
1350 Avenue of the Americas
New York, New York 10019

Vocational Guidance Manuals
235 East 45th Street
New York, New York 10017
Ask for: *Opportunities in Acting*, $1.65.

Additional Reading:

Moore, Dick. *Opportunities in Acting*. American National Theater and Academy, 245 West 52nd Street, New York, New York 10019; or from the Drama Bookshop, Inc., 150 West 52nd Street, New York, New York 10019

Dancer

The Job

Dancers usually specialize in one of five major categories: ballet, modern, musical comedy, exhibition, or ethnic. In most productions, dancers work together as a chorus, sometimes in small groups for special numbers, or in a few instances as soloists. A dancer may perform on the stage as a member of a large dance troupe, in clubs, circuses, hotels and resorts, at private parties, in recitals, at pageants and music festivals, even aboard ship or at industrial shows. Some dancers become teachers or choreographers. Others go into therapy work at clinics and hospitals, and some branch out into writing, reviewing, or promoting.

In 1970 there were about 23,000 dancers and dancing teachers in the United States. More than half of this number were teachers; most of the rest were performers on the stage, in motion pictures, or on television. Dancing teachers work mainly in large cities, but schools of the dance are located in smaller cities and towns as well. Some teach in private studios; others are associated with colleges and universities.

What You Need Personally

The dancer must keep in good physical condition. Rehearsal sessions and rugged travel schedules make good health a must. Besides a natural aptitude for dancing, the dancer should have good feet, an average body build and height, and the ability to function as part of a team since most dance work is in chorus. The aspiring dancer must be prepared to face the uncertainty of working conditions, show closings, audition failures, and other setbacks. A dancer who chooses to specialize in musical comedy should have acting and singing talents. Many years of dance training are required before one becomes a professional dancer, so dedication to the art and determination are vital.

What Education and Training You Need

The dancer graduating from high school is faced with an important decision: whether to continue training at a college or university where he or she can major in dance or to give up the formal college experience in favor of professional study in a major city. To spend four years at college is to fall four years behind in the performing competition. The dance major with a college degree, however, is usually one who seeks a less competitive performing level. Certainly, teachers of dance with college degrees in the dance have better opportunities for employment whether privately or with schools. A teaching position in a professional school usually requires performing experience. In colleges, degrees are generally required for the dance teacher; in some instances, experience as a performer may be substituted. There are about 200 colleges and universities which confer a degree on students who have majored in dance (or in physical education with concentration on the dance).

Some ballet schools offer scholarships to talented students: the school of American Ballet and the Harkness School, both in New York City; the San Francisco Ballet School in San Francisco; the Pennsylvania Ballet School in Philadelphia; the National Ballet School in Washington, D. C. In the field of modern dance, the Martha Graham School in New York City has a scholarship program.

What the Occupation Has to Offer

As in most of the performing arts professions, the number of performers is greater than the number of jobs. Opportunities in dance are limited by the small number of full-time openings and the relatively large number of persons seeking jobs. Irregular employment is expected to continue through the 1970s, although recent union-management contracts attempt to guarantee some dancers nearly full-time employment annually. It's the rare stage show that runs more than twenty-six weeks, however, and stage productions continue to decline because of the competition from television and the movies.

Female dancers find ballet work very difficult to obtain after the age of 30. Because fewer men than women choose a dancing career, male dancers face less competition. About 90 percent of all dancers are women, but about half of the dancers in ballet and modern dance are men. Broadway shows rarely hire women past the age of 25.

Some employment opportunities are increasing with the use of dancers at industrial exhibitions such as auto, boat, and housewares shows. A few new professional dance companies have been started around the country, and TV continues to offer some opportunities. Most job openings result from the need to replace those who leave the field.

The outlook for teachers of dance is much better, particularly for those who have education as well as experience as performers. Increasing college enrollments contribute to this as well as growing interest in the dance.

Dancers who perform professionally are members of one of several unions affiliated with the Associated Actors and Artists of America, part of the AFL-CIO. Minimum salary rates, working hours, and other employment conditions are specified in agreements worked out between the unions and the producers. A dancer signs a separate contract with the producer and may make more favorable arrangements (but never less than the minimum required by the union). A normal working week is 30 hours (rehearsals and performances). Extra compensation is paid for extra hours. Rehearsals usually require very long hours, frequently on weekends and holidays. Weekend travel is required when shows go on the road.

Unions provide for some sick leave and health benefits to the dancer. Earnings in 1970 averaged about $155 a week for dancers in ballet and stage productions. The minimum rate for rehearsal time was about $135 a week. Salaries for teachers vary with the school.

Dancers who belong to unions earn from $125 a week (nightclub work, for example) to $185 for an hour TV performance (with many hours of extra rehearsal beforehand, of course). Soloists are paid more. Principals in a stage or TV show make whatever their agent can negotiate for them. Industrial shows pay very well. Some dancers overlap careers, modeling or teaching some of the time, acting or even ice-skating at other times. There are summer dance camps where employment may be found, too.

Points to Consider Before Going into This Field

A close association with the other arts resulting in an integration of the arts through the dance is perhaps one of the most satisfying things about this profession. The dancer who performs enjoys all the satisfactions of translating human emotion through his or her bodily movements in a way that no one else can.

Rigorous training never ends, however, and the dancer must keep up his or her physical health at all times. Unsteady employment, unless supplemented by other sources of income, can make even the most dedicated of artists lose heart. The emphasis is always on youth in the dance, so with few exceptions a career in dance performance is a relatively short career. A career in the teaching of dance offers far better prospects, and the broader the dancer's education, the better the opportunities will be.

For more information, write:

American Guild of Musical Artists
1841 Broadway
New York, New York 10023
Ask for: information on working conditions and wages.

Dance Directory
National Education Association
1201 16th Street, N. W.
Washington, D. C. 20036
Ask for: list of institutions offering dance courses or a degree.

Additional reading:

Dance News magazine
119 West 57th Street
New York, New York 10019

Model

The Job

The person who models clothes, shoes, or other products is partly a member of the advertising world and partly a performer. For it is the model who attempts in a dramatic way to convey the idea that life can be better, more glamorous, even easier or more secure if we buy the products or services he or she advertises. It is the model who stimulates public interest in a new look or a new product.

Fashion models exhibit clothing. This is sometimes called mannequin work. The way a fashion model walks, moves, gestures or pivots is intended to induce the prospective buyer to purchase the apparel being worn. Showroom models are employed by apparel designers, manufacturers, and wholesalers. During peak seasons they may work constantly; during slack periods they might have to perform clerical duties. Fashion models working for department stores, custom salons, retail and specialty shops are called informal models. Informal models work at a more leisurely pace. Their audience is usually store customers, and often the fashion show is given in order to promote, through advertising and news coverage, a new line of apparel.

Photographic models are usually employed by advertising agencies or free-lance photographers who specialize in supplying pictures for catalogs, pamphlets, magazine and newspaper ads or features. It is more important that the photographic model be photogenic than that he or she, like the fashion model, conform to current standards of beauty. Photographic models need acting ability since they must convey moods of pleasure, surprise, even dissatisfaction (for long hours under bright lights and in a hard-to-hold pose).

Besides fashion or photographic work, some models demonstrate products or services in commercial or fashion films, on TV or at manufacturers' exhibits and industry trade shows. Some models pose for artists or sculptors; others are hired by designers for fittings.

About 55,000 models were employed in the United States in 1970, but many worked only part-time. Most models are employed in major cities, with the greatest number at work in New York City. Models also work in Chicago, Detroit, Dallas, Los Angeles, Miami, San Francisco, and Washington, D. C.

The largest number of full-time models work for manufacturers, designers, and wholesalers. Thousands of firms and designers in New York City, for example, employ from one to four models on a permanent basis. Other models work for advertising agencies, retail stores, mail-order houses, magazines as well as for commercial artists and sculptors, illustrators, fashion artists, and art schools.

What You Need Personally

Modeling demands more than perfect grooming, poise, and a pleasant personality. You must have physical stamina and plenty of determination. Long hours may be spent under hot lights; furs may be modeled in the summer, bathing suits in the winter. Schedules can be close, with quick changes one after another. Patience is a must, and the ability to wear clothes to great advantage is vital.

A fashion model is hired to fit the clothing, so young fashion models should be slim, wear small sizes and be well-proportioned. Shoe models should wear a size 5 (or less), and a hosiery model must have long and graceful legs. Male models should be able to wear trim clothing, usually size 40–41 long in a suit.

Usually women must be long-waisted and at least 5'6" tall. Good teeth and a face that is pretty, expressive, or reflects the style of the times are helpful too. The photographic model must be responsive to direction and able to move with spirit and grace. You must be able to adapt to erratic scheduling.

What Education and Training You Need

Many modeling jobs require no formal training, though some employers do require a high school diploma, and a few prefer some college work in addition. Courses in art, speech, drama, dancing, fashion design and salesmanship are useful, and the wise person who seeks a modeling career will have shorthand and/or typing skills in order to supplement income between modeling assignments. Training and knowledge of grooming methods, how to stand, walk and pose are essential. Knowing how to speak well is vital to the fashion commentator.

Many models learn through experience. A model can learn by watching other models, and of course a good photographer will help his model in every way he can. Attending an accredited modeling school is most helpful. There are modeling schools and charm schools which can give full training programs or mini-courses in such specialities as eye makeup. The job placement service at the modeling school you choose is most important. Be sure to investigate it thoroughly and read the section of this book devoted to choosing a school. (See pages 77-79.)

What the Occupation Has to Offer

Full-time modeling is expected to remain highly competitive through the seventies. Part-time modeling opportunities should be good. More jobs should be available in industries, such as apparel manufacturing, the wholesale and retail trade, and in advertising.

Female models average about eight years of work. For this reason, most openings occur as a result of replacement needs. In high fashion the accent is on youth. Some models are eased out of the field because they have become too closely identified with certain fashion lines or because the work with which they are associated becomes outdated. The working life of a male model is much longer—about twenty years!

Earnings in the field of modeling depend on the type of employment, the nature, frequency, and especially the duration of the assignment. Some top models earn more than $40,000 a year, but most models earn far less. Beginning fashion models working for manufacturers on a full-time basis usually earn about $100 a week, those with experience, $135 a week. Beginning models in retail stores make between $65 and $100 a week, but the experienced retail model earns between $100 and $125 a week.

A retail model can supplement earnings by modeling in fashion shows. Pay includes pre-show fittings at about $15 an hour in some cities, to $60 an hour for experienced models in New York City.

Beginning photographic models earned between $25 and $50 an hour in 1970. Beginners, however, work only a few hours a week, so don't let this figure fool you. Photographic modeling may seem to pay well, but many models in this specialty have to supply their own clothing and usually have to provide accessories and pay other expenses.

A TV model earns at least $35 per appearance as an extra, at least $135 as a principal character, plus an additional amount for each rerun. TV models must be members of the Screen Actors Guild, Inc. or the American Federation of Television and Radio Artists.

Models who work for manufacturers, retailers, and wholesalers on a permanent basis work five days a week, receive a two-week vacation and other benefits. Models working through an agency or on a free-lance basis do not receive these benefits. Most models are paid time-and-a-half for overtime (work after 5:30 p.m.) and for weekend work. The client pays travel expenses outside the model's city.

Points to Consider Before Going into This Field

Four out of five models are women. Because of the glamour attached to the job, the numbers of persons searching for full-time modeling work is expected to be greater than the number of openings throughout the seventies. Part-time opportunities remain favorable, however.

Modeling can be a safisfying part-time career for the ex-model who is raising a family, or if you are trying to combine careers. One of the disadvantages is that a model may have to limit her dating: the camera can highlight the effects of a late night out! Remaining slender is a must, too. Dieting for some models may be considered a disadvantage.

As a beginner, you'll discover that most employers want experienced models. You can find jobs through the employment office of your modeling school. You can register at a model agency, which requests a number of photographs to show prospective clients. The model must pay for these photos. Some models find that their work acts as a stepping-stone to further jobs in the fashion field: work on a fashion magazine, as a fashion consultant or fashion coordinator. The aura of former model is a strong one in fashion-related fields such as retailing, magazine work, newspaper feature writing (social pages). Models who serve as stand-ins in motion pictures or television occasionally become actors and actresses. If you have artistic talent you may go on to fashion illustrating. Modeling, then, while it may be a relatively short career for a woman, does provide the basis for development of other related talents. The male model may find that part-time work in the field can supplement his regular income.

For more information, write:

American Federation of Television and Radio
    Artists
1350 Avenue of the Americas
New York, New York 10019

Department of Human Resources Development
Mail Control Unit
800 Capitol Mall
Sacramento, California 95814
Ask for: *Model* No. 144, Free.

Screen Actors Guild, Inc.
551 5th Avenue
New York, New York
Ask for: information on TV modeling.

Also contact:
    State departments of education (for lists of modeling schools.)

Additional reading:

The Madison Avenue Handbook, New York: Peter Glenn Publications (19 East 48th Street), 1974. ($7.40; lists photographers, TV producers, ad agencies, illustrators, fashion houses in New York City.)

Musician, Music Teacher

The Job

The professional musician, whether a folk guitarist or cellist with a symphony orchestra, generally has spent many years in intensive study and practice. The musician who specializes in popular music may play the guitar, organ, drums, one of the brass instruments, piano, or string bass. Classical musicians play in opera and theater orchestras, symphony orchestras, or in small chamber groups. Pianists may be accompanists or soloists for vocal or instrumental performers, and most organists play in churches or synagogues, often directing the choir as well. Both classical and popular musicians make recordings, as soloists or as members of groups.

A high percentage of musicians teach in schools or colleges, or give private and/or group instruction in their studios or homes. Some mu-

sicians work in the area of music therapy in hospitals, clinics for the handicapped or corrective institutions. Other musicians enter the field of piano tuning or instrument repair, and some are music librarians with schools, colleges, radio and TV stations, or orchestras, and bands.

Working conditions vary. The rock musician may rehearse in a loft or in posh surroundings; the classical instrumentalist may rehearse in a concert hall or a church building. Dance bands perform in night clubs, in restaurants, or at parties. Rock groups may give concerts in TV studios or in public parks. Music teachers associated with schools or colleges work in the school or college atmosphere, living on campus or nearby. More than 200,000 musicians and music teachers are employed annually. Most professional musicians who perform are working in cities such as New York, Chicago, Los Angeles, Miami Beach, New Orleans. Teachers are associated with schools throughout the country, and part-time musicians may find work with community bands, orchestras, and choral groups.

What You Need Personally

Musical talent, creative ability, poise and stage presence are required of those entering the music profession. Self-discipline is vital, for the field requires constant study and practice. Physical and mental stamina are just as necessary since there may be a great deal of travel and often long hours of rehearsal. The ability to work with people and the ambition to study and improve oneself is important also. Teachers and therapists must be persons who inspire confidence, have patience, and possess a real desire to help other people.

What Education and Training You Need

You'll need intensive training, either in private study or at a college or music conservatory in order to achieve a career as a performer or music teacher. Technical skill, a thorough knowledge of music, and the ability to interpret music must be acquired before you can become a professional musician.

In general, a college degree is required for the musician who wishes to enter the teaching field, as well as for the music therapist or music librarian. Other occupations, such as instrumentalist, church organist, tuner and technician, do not require a college degree, although specialized training and/or experience is certainly a necessity. Private teaching would not require a college degree, but it would certainly help.

There are more than 550 music conservatories and college or university schools of music which offer a four year program leading to a B.A. in music education. Completion of one of these programs is necessary before you can qualify for a state certificate, which is often required for elementary and secondary school teaching positions. If you major in instrumental or vocal music, you may also receive a bachelor of music degree. Advanced degrees are usually required for college teaching positions; exceptions are sometimes made for well-known artists in individual fields of music.

Jazz, rock and other popular musicians usually learn under private teachers and through wide experience with small dance or rock groups. The more experience and exposure you get, the better your chances for a successful audition with a larger group or with a more widely known band or orchestra.

Instrumentalists, whether popular or classical, should have completed high school, should know how to read music, should have performing skill on one or more instruments and should have had experience with groups and as soloists.

What the Occupation Has to Offer

The employment outlook for instrumentalists is limited. Chances for concerts and recitals are not numerous enough to provide for all those desiring them. Jobs with major orchestras and teaching positions with colleges and conservatories afford some stability of income, but competition for these positions is keen. While it is easy to enter the field of private teaching, there are often more teachers than students in many areas. Chances for work as a private teacher are sometimes better in smaller communities than in larger towns and cities.

The music performer may find a number of short-term engagements, but again, there are more instrumentalists available than jobs. The exception to this is in the field of top-flight, well-trained accompanists and players of stringed instruments, where musicians are in demand. Fully qualified music teachers and music supervisors in the public school systems are in demand also.

For performers, employment opportunities are expected to increase slightly through the seventies, particularly in part-time employment, due to the increase in small community orchestras. A decline in opportunities in theater, radio, and motion pictures has resulted partly from the increased use of recorded music. The expanded use of cable television (paid TV) as well as future development and wider use of video cassettes should result in some increased employment opportunities.

Generally speaking, the employment outlook is better for teaching members of the music profession than it is for performers. Best opportunities for teaching are found in elementary and secondary schools and in part-time private teaching. Piano instruction leads the field of individual teaching jobs, while opportunities for teachers of various instruments depend largely upon community interests and needs. The community with a school system which provides instruction will not need as many private teachers as the one in which instrumental instruction is absent from the public school system.

Music teachers earn between $5,800 and $17,400 in the elementary grades through high school. Colleges and conservatories may pay from $6,000 to $27,000 annually. A private teacher makes between $3 and $25 an hour on the average. Music therapists earn from $6,000 to $12,500. An instrumentalist with a symphony orchestra may make as much as $270 per week, small ensemble players between $20 and $750 per concert. A fine concert soloist may make as much as $6,000 per concert, a church organist between $5,000 and $18,000 annually. A self-employed piano tuner makes between $10,000 and $20,000 a year, and a music librarian may earn as much as $16,000 a year.

Points to Consider Before Going into This Field

While the need for public school music teachers and supervisors is expected to remain relatively constant through the seventies, salaries depend upon school budgets. Earnings from private lessons are uncertain and depend upon the instructor's reputation and the needs of the community. Performers outnumber the available positions, so employment is uncertain. Night work and weekend work are customary as are daily practice and rehearsal.

Musicians employed by symphony orchestras have the advantage of working under master wage agreements which guarantee them a season's work up to fifty-two weeks. Musicians in other areas may find long periods of unemployment between jobs, and they normally do not work steadily for a single employer. Some performers cannot qualify for unemployment compensation due to the erratic nature of their jobs.

The satisfactions of music, whether performed or taught, are known well to those engaged in their respective fields. For other than regularly employed musicians and music teachers, however, a secondary and regular source of employment or income is usually imperative.

For more information, write:

American Federation of Musicians (AFL-CIO)
641 Lexington Avenue
New York, New York 10022
Ask for: information about wages, hours of work, and working conditions for professional musicians.

American Guild of Organists
630 Fifth Avenue
New York, New York 10020
Ask for: requirements for certification of organists and choir masters.

Music Educators National Conference
The National Education Association
1201 16th Street NW
Washington, D. C. 20036
Ask for: *Careers in Music*, Free.

National Association of Schools of Music
One Dupont Circle, NW
Washington, D. C. 20036 (Suite 650)
Ask for: list of accredited schools of music.

Additional reading:

Biegeleisen, Jacob I., *Careers and Opportunities in Music*, New York: E. P. Dutton & Company, Inc., 1969. $4.95.

Careers in Education, Washington, D. C.: National Commission on Teacher Education and Professional Standards, National Education Association, 1968. No. 681–18372, $.35.

Curtis, Robert E., *Your Future in Music*. New York: Richard Rosen Press, Inc. 1962. $2.79.

Egbert, Marion S., *Career Opportunities in Music*. Kalamazoo, Michigan. American Music Conference, 3505 East Kilgore Road, Kalamazoo, Michigan, 49002, 1966. $1.00.

Singer and Singing Teacher

The Job

The vocalist, whether a specialist in classical or popular singing, is usually required to have a fine voice, a highly developed technique, and a broad knowledge of music. Most professional singers of classical music are employed by churches and synagogues. These occupations can sometimes lead to teaching or perhaps concerts for the experienced soloist. Some classical singers become members of opera companies, oratorio, or concert groups. Some find jobs as directors of music in religious institutions, where they conduct the choirs and administer the music program for special and regular services.

Talented classical singers may find employment in the choruses of large opera companies. Auditions are required, and the vocalist must have some professional experience prior to auditioning or run the risk of auditioning too early in his career. Second auditions are difficult to obtain, so young singers should have the advice of a professional voice teacher before attempting to audition.

Popular singers perform in musical shows of all kinds—on radio and TV, on the stage, in motion pictures, at night clubs and other entertainment spots. Well-known singers make and sell recordings. Bands and orchestras employ singers for work in hotels, ballrooms, and at dances. The better known the vocalist is, the better the chances are for making independent engagements without being connected with any particular band or instrumental group.

Small vocal groups who perform folk or popular music may work in night clubs, on radio or TV, or may make recordings. Some singers and vocal groups find jobs making commercials for TV and radio stations. The ability to sight read music is vital, and since work for both soloists and groups is usually part-time, a supplementary source of income is recommended.

What You Need Personally

Before you decide to become a professional singer, you should audition before a competent voice teacher to decide whether the career ought to be pursued. If you do begin a singing career, you'll need great determination, musical ability, perseverance and an outstanding personality. An attractive appearance is more than helpful, and good contacts plus a fair amount of luck are often required as well. A singer needs the stamina to travel to concert and club engagements and the ability to adapt to demanding time schedules, which often include late-night hours of performance and/or rehearsal.

What Education and Training You Need

High school training for this field should include music and languages and as broad a background as possible in drama and the arts. Dancing ability is helpful also, since singers are sometimes required to dance. Participation in high school plays and musicals, choirs, talent shows, and even community musical productions is valuable not only for the experience gained, but also to help determine the singer's abilities and his effect upon an audience.

Those preparing for a career in classical music may enroll in a conservatory, or in the music school of a college or university, or take voice lessons privately. The classical singer needs training not only in voice, but also in understanding and interpreting music and in music-related subjects such as foreign languages (Italian, German, etc.). Sometimes dramatic training is needed also.

The singer wishing to enter the teaching field must have at least a bachelor's degree with a major in music and must complete requirements for state certification as well. More than 550 colleges and universities in this country provide such training. For college teaching, a master's degree is required and sometimes a doctorate degree. Occasionally exceptions are made for well-qualified artists.

Singers of popular music don't always require formal training; in fact, some very succesful popular singers have had no formal instruction. Talent is a must. Voice training is an asset for the popular singer, but popular songs seldom require the vocal range of classical music. Lack of voice projection can be overcome with microphone adjustments. Experience and exposure are vital in popular music. Participation in both amateur and paid performances in the community is good experience, as is singing with local bands. These engagements may lead to other contacts with larger bands or music groups or to radio and TV opportunities. A booking agent usually handles arrangements for professional vocalists.

What the Occupation Has to Offer

In 1971, about 75,000 persons were employed as professional singers. The country's chief entertainment centers, such as New York City, Los Angeles, and Chicago, provide the most opportunities for singing engagements. Nashville, Tennessee, is a major center for live performances of country-and-western music. The employment outlook is not as good in smaller towns and cities for the performer. A classical singer has the best chance to find openings in cities where there are major symphony orchestras and opera companies, such as Rochester, Boston, Cleveland, Cincinnati, Baltimore, and Philadelphia.

The employment outlook for singers who are music teachers is far better no matter where you live. Part-time positions are available in churches and synagogues. Opportunities for private teaching depend on the needs of the community and the economic status of the community as well. Professional singers often hold full-time teaching positions in schools and colleges, reserving evenings and weekends and holidays for performances. Some openings can be found in radio and TV and in cable TV (paid television) for singers who wish to record popular music and/or commercials. These openings appear to be on the increase in larger cities.

Earnings for teachers depend upon the salary scales of the schools where they teach, with public school salaries ranging from $4,000 to $11,000 annually. Yearly salaries at colleges and conservatories range from $5,500 to $20,000. Salary scales differ with the type of school and its location.

Soloists in church choirs receive a maximum of $25 per performance, vocalists in radio and TV shows from $58 to $100 per broadcast. Dance band singers may earn from $50 to $200 a week, members of concert choral groups from $10 to $50 per concert. Singers in an opera chorus receive from $50 to $100 per week, and opera stars earn as much as $3,000 for each performance. Concert soloists of high calibre may earn $4,000 per concert. Directors of church music may earn $10,000 a year. Private music teachers receive as much as $25 a lesson, earning as little as $1,200 or as much as $20,000 annually, depending upon whether it is full-time or part-time work and upon location.

Points to Consider Before Going into This Field

A career in singing provides the advantage of allowing you to budget your own time, to work at singing part-time for extra income if you like—as a private teacher with a few students, for example. While job opportunities may be limited, the singer does have many locations across the country to look for work. Travel opportunities can be interesting, and the satisfactions of providing entertainment to large numbers of people most rewarding.

The greatest disadvantage the performer must face is that job opportunities are limited—the supply is always greater than the demand. Competition is keen for both popular and classical singers, and only a relatively few singers reach the top. A great number of short-term jobs are expected in the entertainment field through the seventies, but not enough to provide many singers with steady employment. Also, the use of recorded music diminishes the demand for live performances.

Singing careers are sometimes relatively short since age can affect both the voice and public acceptance of the singer. Thus, unstable employment conditions and unreliable financial circumstances are serious disadvantages for the performer to consider. The teaching field has more advantages to offer: stability of income; opportunity for private teaching to supplement income; vacation periods concurrent with school calendars; and in colleges and conservatories, the opportunity for study or research. Opportunities in the teaching field on all levels are expected to increase somewhat through the next decade. In both the teaching and performing areas, men and women are equally welcome.

For more information, write:

American Guild of Musical Artists
1841 Broadway
New York, New York 10023
Ask for: information on opera and concert work.

See also: Music and Music Teachers, pages 330-332.

Sales Occupations

The Job

One of the most underrated job areas today is sales work. Without salesmen, business would simply fold. Almost five million people work in sales occupations of varying types and their work is indispensable. It is the sales worker who is the bridge between manufacturer and customer, wholesaler and retailer, retailer and consumer. The salesperson is like an ambassador representing his employer. He puts across both himself and his product, and it takes skill and knowledge to do that well. He is the one who persuades another person to part with his money to purchase a product or service.

The largest group of sales workers are employed in retail selling, working everywhere from the corner drugstore to Macy's to exclusive shops. As a salesman your duties vary according to the size and type of the operation. You give customers assistance, explaining the qualities of merchandise, its care, and how it works. Customer payments, receipts and charges are handled by the sales worker, as are returns and exchanges. You may also assemble and wrap customer purchases, help stock shelves and mark prices, set up advertising displays, or help purchase inventory.

Another group of salespeople are those who work for wholesalers. In these companies, large quantities of particular kinds of merchandise from different manufacturers are stocked, and retail firms, schools or other institutions buy directly from the wholesaler instead of having to go from one manufacturer to another. If you are a wholesale salesman, you may go to your customers, taking catalogs, pictures and other materials to show the customer what you have available. You must be very familiar with your company's stock, and with the customer's type of operation, and your most important function is to provide specialized service to the customer.

Other salesmen work for manufacturers, selling in most cases to other kinds of industries, to wholesalers and institutions. These salesmen, too, go to their customers with catalogs or samples of merchandise. They work closely with customers, trying to fill their needs and operating with a thorough understanding of their own industry and that of the customer.

Some salesmen are specialists. They sell such things as insurance, real estate, securities or other nonmanufactured products.

Selling has become a service field. Computers and electronic data processing are removing some of the routine work from all areas of selling, and service to the customer is growing more important all the time. Industry and retailing in this country are highly competitive, and good salespeople are a must for a successful business.

Salesmen are employed everywhere by businesses of all sizes. Large chain stores and various types of industry are actively soliciting and training people to work in sales.

What You Need Personally

Personal qualities are vitally important to a salesperson. You spend most of your time dealing with people, and the way you appear and the impression you give are very relevant to the sale of your product, no matter how good it might be.

You must like people, be able to communicate well with them, and be able to listen to their problems and ideas. Poise, tact, courtesy, sincerity and honesty are also important. A neat, well-groomed appearance and a certain amount of physical stamina are also necessary qualities for a career in sales.

Independence is also an important quality, especially for a sales person who has to go outside to get and keep customers. You have to be a self-starter, persevering but not obnoxious. You must know your product and your industry and communicate your own enthusiasm for it. You can't let yourself be discouraged by a "no sale." Optimism and belief in your ability to do the job are the salesman's best tools.

Salesmen who work on the road must be analytical, able to tackle customers' problems, and offer valid solutions. A good memory, some imagination and adaptability are also good qualifications.

What Education and Training You Need

The amount of training required varies, depending on the job and the company. In retail sales, for instance, post-high school training is rarely required. Most stores have some kind of on-the-job training, however.

For any career in sales, a high school education is an asset, and often a necessity. Courses in mathematics, English, social studies, and public speaking are all helpful. If you are looking toward a career in some specific field, particularly a technical one, you should also take as many courses as possible related to that field. Some high schools offer work-study programs for their students which combine formal schooling with work in a local business. The student can earn some money and get valuable experience while still in school.

More and more companies are looking for sales workers with at least some college training. In jobs that involve the sale of technical equipment, such as electronics, a college degree is preferred. College studies helpful to any salesman include marketing, advertising, business administration, sales management, economics, psychology, mathematics, geography, statistics, and sociology.

Educational requirements for sales in real estate, insurance or securities also vary. The more education the better. People in these fields take specialized courses, usually provided by their company, in order to pass qualifying examinations.

On-the-job training is offered in almost any kind of sales job. Retail workers receive training that ranges from a few days with an experienced worker in a small shop, to a formal training program of a few weeks in a large department store. In other kinds of sales, companies may have formal training schools or may have more informal training in which the salesman works at different jobs in the company for short periods of time in order to become familiar with the products and methods of his company.

What the Occupation Has to Offer

The increase in the population and the expected economic growth in the country in the next decade should result in some increase in jobs for sales workers on all levels. In retail sales, automatic equipment will take away some of the routine duties of the sales worker, but the ever increasing number of stores and longer business hours will create a need for more salespeople. The emphasis in retail sales will be increasingly on direct customer service.

Education will be more important in the hiring of sales workers, but there will be openings for those who are bright, ambitious, and hard working.

Earnings for sales workers vary considerably. Retail workers, for instance, may start at the minimum wage and average less than $3 an hour. Selling jobs which require special skills or knowledge in dealing with people pay more.

Other jobs start at salaries ranging from $7,000 to $9,000 a year and potential earnings are virtually unlimited. It is not unusual for a conscientious salesman to earn over $25,000 a year.

Methods of paying sales people vary. Most retail workers are paid a straight salary. Others receive salary plus commission on total sales, or straight commission. In other kinds of selling, commissions are used most frequently as part or all of salary, and bonuses may also be given.

Retail salesworkers usually receive a discount on the store's goods, ranging from ten to twenty-five percent.

Anyone with ambition and skill has great opportunity for advancement in sales. Promotions are made according to performance, not education, and there are many places to go. In all fields, many top executives started their careers in sales.

In retail selling, you can become a buyer, department manager, store manager or work up to an office position. A wholesale salesworker may advance to supervisor, sales manager or other executive position. A manufacturers' salesman can become a branch manager, supervisor, district manager, sales manager or may go into business for himself as a manufacturers' agent.

Promotion is usually wide open to the aggressive, successful salesman who keeps up with developments in his field. Some, however, stick with sales simply because they can be independent and still earn a good salary.

Points to Consider Before Going into This Field

Sales work has many advantages. In all but the most technical areas, you can get into it without much formal education, and advancement is entirely dependent on the individual. The work is for you if you like other people, can get along well and communicate with them. You are performing an important service to others, and your work is not too routine. In many cases, you work independently, setting your own schedule.

There are some disadvantages, though. In all kinds of selling, you may have to work long irregular hours that will probably include some nights and weekends. Retail sales people usually have to work Saturdays and at least one night a week. Insurance salesmen often have to make their calls at night. Wholesale or manufacturers' salesmen may find themselves traveling at night or on weekends to get to appointments, or working into the night on reports. In any sales job, there are also the frustrations of dealing with people, who may not always be as agreeable as you would wish. Income usually fluctuates and there is a certain amount of insecurity since you are often not on a fixed salary.

There are few restrictions on a career in sales

except that the individual be alert, healthy, outgoing, enthusiastic and knowledgeable about his field. Self-confidence is an absolute necessity for a successful salesperson.

Women are found in all areas of sales, but their proportion varies. In retail sales, for instance, over half the workers are women, but they are mostly in the lower paying jobs. Only about ten percent of manufacturers' salespeople are women, and most of them work for the food products industry. A small percentage of insurance and securities salespeople are also women. In general, there are no real restrictions against women in sales, but they have to work a little harder to succeed.

For more information, write:

Career Education Department
Sales & Marketing Executives International
630 Third Avenue
New York, New York 10017
Ask for: *The Salesman: Ambassadors of Progress*; and other information on careers in selling and training opportunities.

Insurance Agent and Broker

The Job

After an accident, a fire or a serious illness or injury, the first thing most of us check is our insurance. Are we covered? Will the policy pay all the bills? Insurance agents and brokers sell insurance policies which protect us or our businesses against possible future losses or financial pressures.

There are three basic types of insurance—life, property and liability, and health. Some agents sell only one kind of insurance while others may sell two or more. Some agents may also sell equity products, such as mutual fund shares.

Generally speaking, life insurance makes sure that survivors receive some payment in the event of the policyholder's death. Depending on the policy, other benefits may also be included, such as college funds for children or annuities.

Property and liability insurance policies protect policyholders from the financial losses that can be caused by car accidents, fire, theft or other such hazards.

Health insurance takes care of all or part of the hospital or other medical expenses, or for loss of income due to illness or injury.

In addition to selling policies, the insurance agent may offer customers other related services. Sometimes they help the customer plan the best insurance protection for his particular needs and family. Or he may suggest the best kind of insurance to protect the car, home, or business. He may also help a policyholder settle a claim.

Some agents work for insurance companies; others are independents who are under contract as an authorized representative of one or more insurance companies. The broker isn't under contract to anyone, but places his clients' policies with the companies he thinks will best fill their needs.

Agents and brokers spend most of their time with prospective customers, discussing policies. However, some office work is also necessary such as designing insurance programs for a particular prospect, preparing reports, keeping records, and drawing up lists of prospective customers. Some salesmen specialize in group policies and may spend time incorporating a program into a company's bookkeeping system.

There are about 350,000 full-time insurance agents and brokers, and many more who work on a part-time basis. About half specialize in life insurance and half in property and liability insurance. Both sell health insurance. Agents and brokers work all over the country, with the greatest number in the nation's population centers.

What You Need Personally

Because you are constantly dealing with people in this job, and trying to persuade them to buy something, a pleasant, outgoing manner is necessary to inspire confidence. You need enthusiasm for your work, and enough initiative to go out and get customers. A good memory and an ability to express things clearly are also important.

What Education and Training You Need

Although most insurance companies don't specify a particular amount of educational background for their employees, about half have some college training, and high school is almost a necessity. Most college courses are assets to an insurance agent or broker in that they help him to express himself better and communicate with others. Courses in insurance are available at many schools, and studies in liberal arts, accounting, economics, finance, and business law are also good background for this job.

All states require that agents and most brokers be licensed, and often have written tests covering insurance fundamentals and state regulatory laws that must be passed for certification.

On-the-job training is offered by all insurance companies, either at the company home office or at the firm where the employee will be working. In some cases, trainees work under the close supervision of an experienced employee. In others, the company holds classes in insurance principles and sales problems, which may last anywhere from a few weeks to a few months.

Established insurance agents and brokers often take further study programs to increase their knowledge of the business and expand their chances for success. Many junior and community colleges and universities give courses in insurance, and insurance organizations often sponsor institutes, conferences, and seminars.

The Life Underwriter Training Council, for instance, offers courses in life and health insurance for experienced agents; at the completion of a two-year program, you are awarded a diploma in life insurance marketing. The American Society of Chartered Life Underwriters gives experienced agents and brokers a series of examinations which, if passed, qualify them as Chartered Life Underwriters. Property and liability agents can take similar examinations given by the American Institute for Property and Liability Underwriters to qualify as Chartered Property Casualty Underwriters.

Training and education in this field never stops. If you want to be successful, you'll be expected to continue your education while you work in order to keep up with new developments and government regulations affecting your business.

What the Occupation Has to Offer

This should be a growing field in the 1970s, as more people turn to insurance for retirement income, medical care, college funds, and life insurance protection. Industrial expansion and the increased number of people buying homes and cars will contribute to a growth in property and liability sales. The growth in jobs will be only moderate, however, since many policies are sold on a group basis or by mail. Some jobs become available because there is a high turnover among beginners in this competitive field.

Earnings vary considerably for insurance agents and brokers. Beginners usually get guaranteed salaries or advances on commissions while they learn the business and build a clientele. This is usually a modest sum. After that, most agents are paid on a commission basis, with commissions varying, depending on the size of the policy, the type, and whether the policy is new or a renewal. Earnings can be anywhere from $8,000 to $20,000 yearly. There are successful agents and brokers who earn $30,000 a year or more.

Agents and brokers who run their own businesses must pay office expenses out of their earnings, and most agents and brokers pay their own car and travel expenses.

There are a variety of advancement opportunities in this field. By showing sales talent and leadership qualities, you can be promoted to district sales manager or to a managerial position in the home office. Some agents become agency superintendents or company vice-presidents or presidents. In many cases, agents or brokers establish their own firms.

Points to Consider Before Going into This Field

As a broker or an agent, you are able to work independently, with your rewards totally dependent on your own efforts. If you like to get out and meet people, this job gives you a chance to do that while providing a worthwhile service. The educational requirements for entry level jobs are not always strict, and success is more a matter of personality and initiative than previous training.

Some disadvantages do exist, however. If you have a poor month, when few policies are sold or renewed, your income will suffer, and hours can be long, and often irregular.

There are no restrictions against women in this field, but about 90 percent of the full-time agents and brokers are men.

For more information, write:

Educational Division
Institute of Life Insurance
277 Park Avenue
New York, New York 10017

Insurance Information Institute
110 William Street
New York, New York 10038
Ask for: information about opportunities as
property and liability agents and brokers.

The Life Underwriter Training Council
1922 F Street NW
Washington, D. C. 20006
Ask for: information about sales training in life and health insurance.

National Association of Insurance Agents, Inc.
96 Fulton Street
New York, New York 10038
Ask for: information about opportunities as property and liability agents and brokers.

The National Association of Life Underwriters
1922 F Street N.W.
Washington, D. C. 20006
Ask for: information about sales training in life and health insurance.

Also contact:

For more information contact the home office of many life insurance and property and liability insurance companies. The state department of insurance at your state capital will give you information on state licensing requirements.

See also: pp. 138-141 for more jobs in the insurance field.

Manufacturers' Salesman

The Job

No product automatically sells itself—and so most manufacturers employ salesmen to present their goods to potential customers. Manufactur-

ers' salesmen may handle anything from pens to computers, with most of their selling directed at other businesses or to institutions: schools, hospitals, factories, wholesalers, retailers, banks, etc.

A salesman usually has a particular territory to which he is assigned. He calls on firms in his area to try to sell his product. He must be well-informed about what he is selling and about the needs and requirements of his customer. To persuade the customer to buy, he has to present his product in a way that is meaningful to his customer's business, stressing those things that are most relevant about the product. Sometimes he puts together displays to promote his products and exhibits at conventions or conferences attended by large groups of potential customers.

If he sells technical products, like electronic equipment, he is sometimes called a sales engineer or industrial salesman. This kind of salesman needs all the product knowledge of the others, and must also be able to help customers with technical problems. For instance, he may have to spend days studying a particular firm and figuring out which piece of his equipment would be best for its operation. He then goes to the firm with his solution and tries to make a sale.

A sales engineer may also work closely with his own company's research and development department to come up with ways to adapt existing products to a customer's particular need. In many cases, he trains the customers' employees in the operation and maintenance of the new equipment and returns at regular intervals to be sure that everything is working properly.

A salesman spends most of his time visiting customers or prospective customers, but some time must be devoted to paperwork in the office. He prepares reports on sales prospects in his territory, reports on customers' credit ratings, plans work schedules, makes appointments and lists of prospects, has some correspondence, and keeps up on literature relating to the products he sells.

Although some salesmen work out of their company's home office, most work out of branch offices in large cities nearer their customers. Of the 500,000 people employed in this profession, the industry hiring the most salesmen is food products. Other salesmen work for printing and publishing companies, chemicals, fabricated metal products, and electrical and other machinery firms. About 45,000 sales engineers are currently at work, mainly employed by heavy machinery manufacturers, transportation equipment companies, fabricated metal products firms and companies that make professional and scientific instruments.

What You Need Personally

You should be able to get along well with all kinds of people, be outgoing, pleasant, and tactful. A neat and well-groomed appearance is also vital, since you are representing your company to its customers. Because you will have to walk and stand a lot, and sometimes carry heavy product samples, physical stamina is often necessary.

To be successful, a salesman must take his job seriously, learning all he can about his products, about his industry, and about the companies and industries to which he sells. He must be able to apply his knowledge well, work independently, and know when to be persistent and when to hold back.

What Education and Training You Need

Educational requirements vary for this job, but employers look more and more for college graduates. You should get as much background in business subjects—mathematics, economics, etc.—as you can, in addition to taking courses related to the type of industry in which you are interested in working. Liberal arts or business administration studies are considered equally acceptable. Some manufacturers' salesmen, however, don't have college training at all. For sales engineers' jobs, technical training is usually required, and drug salesmen, for instance, frequently have some training at a college of pharmacy.

Before they go out to sell, sales trainees are also given training by their companies. These programs vary in length, depending on the complexity of the product, but a formal program for a technical product may be as long as two years. In this type of program, the trainee may be rotated among jobs in the plant and office to learn as much as possible about production, installation and distribution of the product. Other companies give formal class instruction at the plant, followed by on-the-job training in a branch office.

What the Occupation Has to Offer

The outlook is good for manufacturers' salesmen in the 1970s, but competition for jobs will be high. The growth of the economy and the development of new products and improved marketing techniques will increase manufacturer competition, creating a need for extremely effective sales organizations. Because of the competition and the growing number of technical products, employers are expected to select salesmen carefully.

It is difficult to estimate earnings for these jobs. The average starting salary for a new salesman is about $8,500 a year; the highest starting salaries are usually paid by manufacturers of electrical equipment, construction materials, hardware and tools, and scientific and precision instruments.

The method of pay varies according to company. In some cases, the salesman is paid a straight commission, based on a percentage of the dollar amount of his sales. Other companies pay a salary. In most cases, some kind of combination plan is used: either salary and commission, salary and bonus, or salary-commission and bonus. Commissions vary, depending on salesman's efforts and ability, commission rate, sales territory, and product sold. Bonuses may be based on individual performance, the performance of all salesmen in a group or district, or on the company's sales performance. An experienced salesman can make between $16,000 and $32,000 a year, and some make much more.

Salesmen have various opportunities for advancement. Many transfer to better jobs with other companies or go into business for themselves as manufacturers' agents selling similar products of several manufacturers. Within a company, a salesman may be promoted to sales supervisor, branch manager, or district manager. From there, he can go to sales manager or other top executive positions. It is not unusual to find a top executive who started as a salesman.

Points to Consider Before Going into This Field

This is an ideal job for a person who likes other people and can communicate with them, who likes to work independently and on a flexible schedule, and who has a good store of knowledge about his product. If you want a job that is not confining, one in which ingenuity, aggressiveness, and a knowledge of your industry and product will make you a success, this is for you. Pay is often good, and personality is frequently more important than education in determining who gets ahead.

It has a few disadvantages, however. Some salesmen have to travel a great deal to cover large territories and may be away from home for days or weeks at a time. In these cases, the companies usually pay for car and hotel expenses. It is also not unusual for salesmen to work at night or on weekends, either calling on customers or writing reports. Many salesmen learn to budget their time in order to get time off to compensate for this, however.

About 10 percent of all manufacturers' salesmen are women, with most of them employed in food products industries.

For more information, write:

Manufacturers' Agents National Association
Suite 503
3130 Wilshire Boulevard
Los Angeles, California 90010
Ask for: information on job opportunity and
    training information.

See also: page 337.

Real Estate Salesman and Broker

sales staff sell residential property, although in larger cities, firms may specialize in industrial and commercial properties.

A real-estate office, whether it is in a large city or a small suburban town, is a busy, lively, and sometimes hectic place! Offices specializing in residential properties (a good place for beginners) are usually staffed by energetic people. A beginner is wise to select a firm located in his own hometown or college town, or at least a suburban area where residential development is on the upswing. Here the sales person will work in a small office, or where a new development is being built, in a model home office where business transactions are made.

There are close to a million persons in this country licensed to sell real estate. Over 200,000 are actively engaged in the business full-time, with large numbers of people also selling real estate on a part-time basis.

In big cities, firms are apt to have large sales staffs. Here a beginner may start with telephone answering, filing, acting as a rent collector or rental agent. In suburban areas, the beginner is likely to receive more on-the-job training from the broker or experienced salesperson. The important thing is to seek employment in the area with which you are most familiar—urban or suburban. Areas near growing cities offer the best opportunities for employment.

The Job

The real-estate business is concerned with a basic human requirement—the need for shelter. We need shelter for the family, for commerce, and for industry. The real-estate salesperson or broker is at the heart of most property transactions. He represents the property owner who wishes to sell and he looks for potential buyers for the residential or commercial property. (Salesmen and brokers may also be called real-estate agents, or if they are members of the National Association of Real Estate Boards, they can be legally called realtors.) Sometimes the real-estate person may be employed by the buyer. But whether working for buyer or seller, his principal goal is to negotiate an agreement between the two parties.

One of the most important duties of the real-estate salesperson is to obtain "listings," which entails getting sellers to place their properties for sale with the firm. Seeking listings and answering questions about properties involves a good deal of telephone work, and tracking down leads for listings through advertising and personal contacts.

Beginners in the real-estate business usually start by working for a broker, an independent business person who not only sells real estate, but sometimes handles rental properties, makes appraisals, and arranges for loans to finance purchases. Most brokers and their real-estate

What You Need Personally

A pleasing personality, honesty, and a neat appearance are important characteristics. Getting along with people is a must and a substantial measure of tact and enthusiasm are important too. You should have a good memory for names and faces as well as for business details, such as prices and zoning regulations.

You should have more than a passing acquaintance with the community, and a positive approach to the advantages of properties is necessary. Emphasis on the good features of a property combined with a determination to be honest are marks of the trustworthy real-estate salesperson. Your role as negotiator (when lower offers are made beneath the asking price) must be tactful, and objective, especially when it comes to fair compromise.

In this challenging field, a salesperson must be prepared to accept disappointments. A positive outlook, an optimistic approach, and a willingness to "keep trying anyway" are just as important as the ambition to obtain new listings. A sense of responsibility toward the client is a must, as is a detailed knowledge of the property involved. If you like people, like to help them, and believe that you have a certain amount of intuition about their needs and preferences, you're going to inspire trust, which is a basic requirement in the real estate field. Satisfied customers will refer their friends to you. In this way you can build your future sales.

What Education and Training You Need

In order to work as a real-estate salesperson or broker, a license is necessary. All states require prospective agents to pass written examinations which usually include questions dealing with the basics of real estate transactions as well as laws affecting real-estate sales. The exam for brokers is more comprehensive than that for salespeople. In most states, a candidate for a broker's license must also have a certain amount of experience as a real-estate salesperson (or related education/experience). State licenses can be renewed every year without further examination.

A high school education is preferred by employers (college is even better) and an academic program should include high school math, salesmanship, architectural drawing, business law, economics, and even public speaking. Many real estate agents are college graduates, and most have had some post-high school training.

Sometimes a beginner can get a job in his neighborhood where knowledge of the area is an advantage. Beginners and experienced salespeople alike may find training opportunities provided by local real-estate boards. There are more than 360 colleges and universities (including junior colleges and community colleges) offering courses in real estate and some offer real estate as a major subject leading to a degree. You can also study real estate through home study courses. Local boards of real estate, who are members of NAREB (National Association of Real Estate Boards) may offer courses, which are sometimes conducted at neighboring schools and colleges. Some of these courses are for beginners; and some are specialty courses such as appraising, mortgage financing, property development and management.

What the Occupation Has to Offer

During the 1970s, several thousand openings for real estate salespeople are expected. The anticipated increase in residential and commercial construction accounts for much of this projected opportunity, with turnover in personnel also helping.

Commissions on sales are the normal source of income for salespeople and brokers. A few are paid on straight salary but this is the exception. Sometimes commissions on sales are shared by members of the firm, with the salesperson originally listing the property receiving some of the commission, and the rest divided between the broker-owner of the firm and other agents.

A full-time real estate agent earns between $7,000 and $12,000 a year, though beginners earn less. As one gains more experience, earnings

increase. Since the commission-only system of payment is most common, the beginner should have some funds to rely on until commissions increase.

Advancement in the real-estate field comes in two ways: through experience and a mastery of the trade, and through specialization. After you gain broad experience in the field, specialization such as appraising, property management, mortgage lending, even land development may interest you. There are technical courses available to those who wish to specialize.

Points to Consider Before Going into This Field

When it comes to real estate, the sky's the limit. The rewards are great for the hard worker, and the job is satisfying and rewarding once your interest is stimulated. One disadvantage is that many openings are filled first by mature persons because experience counts for a great deal. Your age, therefore, may be a handicap in the beginning. A car is almost always a necessity, for prospective clients must be taken to properties. Also earnings are frequently subject to the ups and downs of the market, despite your capabilities. Commission arrangements vary greatly from area to area, and even from firm to firm. Weekend work is almost a necessity to the really enthusiastic salesperson, for often, especially in residential properties, this may be the only time when prospective buyers are able to shop.

Men and women are equally welcomed in this field. Real estate lends itself to part-time as well as full-time employment.

For more information, write:

Department of Education
National Association of Real Estate Boards
155 East Superior Street
Chicago, Illinois 60611
Ask for: information on jobs and places to get training in real estate.

Also contact:

Information on licensing requirements for salespeople and brokers may be obtained from a local real-estate office, or the state real-estate commission located in your capital. Many states can provide manuals that help applicants prepare for the required written examinations.

Retail Sales Worker

The Job

Every day we come face to face with salespeople in every possible kind of retail establishment. How they act and how good they are at selling often decides what we think of the store. Courteous and efficient service is the most important responsibility of any salesperson, but the

specific duties vary according to the kind of merchandise sold.

If you're selling books, clothes, furniture, or appliances, you must interest the customer in the store's merchandise and be able to answer questions about articles for sale. In some cases, you have to know how something is made, how it works, or how it can be cared for.

Some kinds of stores, like pet stores, require more specialized knowledge—in this instance knowledge about the care and feeding of animals.

Other responsibilities of salespeople include assembling and wrapping items the customer purchases, receiving payment, making out sales and charge slips, and giving change and receipts. They usually handle customer returns or exchanges, also.

Salespeople are responsible for keeping their work areas neat and, in small stores, may also be involved in stocking shelves, marking price tags, ordering merchandise, taking inventory, and preparing displays.

Salespeople work in every community in the country, although more of them are found in large cities. The 2.5 million people employed in this work may be found in corner drugstores, huge department stores, door-to-door sales companies, or mail order houses. The largest employers are department and general merchandise stores, food stores, and apparel and accessories stores.

What You Need Personally

Personal qualities are very important in this job. You must like people and be able to deal with them. Tact, courtesy, and an ability to communicate clearly are all necessary. You should have a neat, well-groomed appearance, be healthy, and able to stand for long periods of time. You should also have an interest in sales work, and preferably an interest in, and knowledge of the particular product you are selling.

What Education and Training You Need

A high school education is preferred for sales jobs, although it isn't always necessary. Home economics and arithmetic are helpful, and some schools give courses in merchandising and principles of retailing and retail selling. In some places, work-study programs in retail trade are offered by the schools in cooperation with local merchants.

On-the-job training is always included in this line of work. In a small store, the proprietor or an experienced employee will explain the procedures and products of the store. In a larger store, there will be a somewhat more formal program and perhaps even specialized training for selling certain items.

Some groups also offer training for their experienced workers. Booksellers, for instance, can take a five-day course on information techniques and problems related to this business.

What the Occupation Has to Offer

As the population and economy grow, more stores will open, selling a wider variety of items to the public. Overall, there should be many job openings for salesworkers, some resulting from persons retiring or changing occupations.

Some kinds of stores will need fewer salespeople because of the increasing use of self-service. But in areas where a salesperson must spend time with the customer there will be more positions open.

Earnings for salespeople vary according to the locale, the size of the store, the complexity of the work and the experience of the worker. Beginners are often paid at the minimum wage, particularly where duties are routine. Experienced workers, some of whom are covered by union contracts, may earn $3 an hour or more. Salespeople may be paid on a straight salary basis, salary plus commission, or straight commission. Among the highest paid are those who sell automobiles, major appliances and furniture, or anything that requires special skill or technical knowledge in dealing with customers.

Some salespeople, particularly those who work for large stores, get fringe benefits like health insurance, and they frequently get from 10 to 25 percent discount on the store's merchandise.

Opportunities for advancement are excellent for a person with ambition and ability. Education is often not a factor in promotion in this field, and you can become a buyer, department or store manager. In large stores, salespeople may advance to office positions. Although working for a small store has limited possibilities, any retail sales job can be good background for sales jobs for manufacturers or wholesalers.

Points to Consider Before Going into This Field

This kind of work requires no specialized training for entry positions, and chances for advancement are good for the person who works hard. You can work anywhere in the country, and you get to meet a variety of people every day.

Selling does have some disadvantages, though. The hours can be long and irregular and often include Saturdays, evenings, and heavy holiday season work. The pay is generally not too high.

About three-fifths of the nation's retail salespeople are women. Men often work in the higher paying jobs, though, and predominate in stores that sell furniture, household appliances, hardwood, farm equipment, shoes, lumber, and automobiles. Women are predominant in department and general merchandise stores, variety stores, apparel and accessory shops, and drugstores.

For more information, write:

American Booksellers Association
175 Fifth Avenue
New York, New York 10010
Ask for: information on bookshop work and booksellers schools.

Also contact:

For more information contact: the personnel offices of local stores; state merchants' associations; local unions of the Retail Clerks International Association; or ask about retailing courses given in high school at your local superintendent of schools office.

See also: page 337.

Securities Salesman

The Job

One of the more fascinating fields today is the stock market. Most large companies sell stock in their firm, both to individuals and to other companies, to help finance their operations. A securities salesman—also known as a customers' broker, registered representative, or account executive—services investors who want to buy or sell stocks, bonds, or shares in mutual funds.

A salesman has many duties to perform for his customers, whether they are individuals with a few hundred dollars to invest or large corporations investing millions. He first relays the buy-or-sell order through his firm's order room to the securities exchange floor. In the over-the-counter market, he sends the order to his firm's trading department. Later he notifies the customer when the transaction is completed.

The salesman also provides his customers with all kinds of related services. He must be thoroughly familiar with different kinds of investments so that he can give advice according to the customer's investment objectives. He may make suggestions about purchase or sale, or explain the details of stock market trading to a novice. He also gives the latest stock and bond quotations and information about what is happening financially and otherwise with various corporations.

Salesmen may be generalists, servicing all kinds of customers, or may specialize in, for instance, institutions. They may handle all kinds of securities, or only one type. The salesman spends much of his time with customers. In the beginning, he seeks customers; later, he spends most of his time servicing the accounts.

About two-thirds of the 200,000 securities salesmen work full time for brokerage firms, investment bankers, and mutual fund firms. Others work part time, usually selling shares in mutual funds or variable annuities. Securities salesmen work in offices all over the country.

What You Need Personally

If you go into this field, you have to be able to communicate with people, get them to trust you and your judgment. A neat, attractive appearance, a pleasant manner, and an air of conservative dependability are important. You should be able to express yourself well to any kind of person. Responsibility, maturity, and ambition are also important for this work, since you must work independently.

What Education and Training You Need

Specialized educational training is not usually required for this field. Employers sometimes prefer applicants with any kind of experience in either sales or financial work, and some college training is often considered important when hiring, because the job requires a thorough knowledge of economics and other related subjects. Studies in liberal arts, economics, or business administration are helpful, and any courses in finance will provide specific knowledge.

Most states require that securities salesmen be licensed, although requirements vary. Written examinations are sometimes given, and the applicant may have to furnish a personal bond.

Most salesmen must also be registered as representatives of their employer's firm, according to exchange regulations or to regulations of the National Association of Securities Dealers. Before being qualified, the salesman must pass the Securities and Exchange Commission's General Securities Examination or a similar test, which covers knowledge of the business. Character investigations are also required.

Most companies give salesmen training in meeting the registration requirements. All firms who are members of the New York Stock Exchange, and some others, too, give six-month training periods. In large companies this may include classroom instruction in security analysis, effective speaking, business school subjects, and on-the-job training. In smaller firms, the training is less formal and shorter, and the trainee may read assigned materials and observe experienced salesmen.

What the Occupation Has to Offer

This should be a growth business in the 1970s because more individuals will have more money to invest. People are joining investment clubs and associations, and are purchasing securities to put toward their children's education and their retirement. Institutions are also involved in buying securities, and the many new corporations and government projects needing backing will be bringing new securities to the market. New jobs will also be created by the high turnover of beginners in the field who are discouraged by the difficulty of establishing a clientele.

Earnings vary enormously in this field. Trainees usually get a salary of about $400 or $500 a month until they are licensed. In some instances the salary can be more, and it may continue after registration until the salesman is able to get established.

After training, salesmen get their earnings mainly from commissions. These vary in size depending on the type of security, policies of the employer, where it is traded, and fluctuations in the market. Most companies pay salesmen a "draw against commission," which is a minimum salary based on expected commissions plus commissions from any additional sales.

In general, securities salesmen earn between $8,000 and $17,000 a year, although it is not unusual for them to make over $25,000 a year when the market is good. Some earn much more. In addition, some companies pay bonuses when business is good.

Usually salesmen advance by increasing the number and size of the accounts they handle, thus increasing their commissions. In some cases, a salesman may become a branch office manager, supervising other salesmen and still handling transactions for his own customers. In a few cases, salesmen may become partners in their firms.

Points to Consider Before Going into This Field

There are many advantages to this work. It is always changing, always exciting, and is involved in the essential workings of our economic system. The salesman works independently, and can be very highly rewarded. Working conditions are usually pleasant, even if sometimes hectic, and working hours are fairly regular.

There are a few disadvantages, however. A securities salesman's earnings are dependent to a large extent on the state of the economy, and earnings can go way down in a period of recession or market inactivity. Because conditions change constantly, the job is often very pressured.

Most securities salesmen are men, but there are no restrictions against women (except the personal ones of some investors and employers), and women are starting to take more interest in the field.

For more information, write:

New York Stock Exchange
11 Wall Street
New York, New York 10005
Ask for: information about the work of securities salesmen.

Wholesale Trade Salesworker

The Job

While we usually do our personal buying from *retail* stores, these stores—as well as our schools, hospitals, business, etc.—do their buying from *wholesale* outlets. The wholesale trade salesworker is one of the important links between the factory and the consumer. He works for a company that distributes hundreds of similar products from different manufacturers. A wholesale warehouse may have a wide selection of drug and cosmetic products made by dozens of manufacturers, for example, or may stock hardware and construction materials. By going to a wholesale warehouse, the buyer is saved the trouble of having to deal with many different manufacturers.

The salesman pays regular visits to the people who do the purchasing for retail, industrial, and commercial firms or for schools or hospitals. His purpose is to convince these people to become regular customers, and he brings samples, catalogs, and pictures to give them an idea of what his company stocks. By giving prompt and dependable service, he gains and keeps customers.

There are many other responsibilities involved in this job, most of them centered around personalized service to the customer. The salesman may be responsible for checking the retailer's stock and ordering needed items. He may help store personnel utilize electronic data processing systems to facilitate their orders and inventory.

In some cases, a wholesale salesman advises retailers about advertising, pricing, and window and counter displays. If he handles technical products, he may even give technical assistance.

Salesmen also have paperwork to handle. They forward orders to the wholesale house, prepare reports and expense accounts, plan work schedules, make lists of prospects, make appointments, study literature that relates to their products, and sometimes collect money.

Although most wholesale houses are located in larger cities, a salesman's territory may vary. He may have just a small section of a large city, or may cover half a state in a less populated area. The largest employers of the nation's 540,000 wholesale salespeople are companies that sell foods and food products. Other major employers are drug wholesalers, dry goods and apparel companies, motor vehicle equipment wholesalers and electrical appliance outlets. Some are also employed by companies that sell machinery and building materials to industrial and business firms.

What You Need Personally

For a career in sales, personality is very important. You should like people, be outgoing and communicate well with others. A neat appearance and an enthusiastic, confident, knowledgeable approach to your work are also prerequisites.

What Education and Training You Need

High school education is a must for these jobs, including courses that build your arithmetic skills and your memory. The more technical the product being sold, the more likely employers are to want salespeople with some post-high school technical training.

Training programs vary from company to company. A college graduate will usually be given a formal training program that includes classroom instruction and short experiences in various nonselling jobs, such as work in the warehouse in order to familiarize him with the company's products and methods. In some instances, college students can participate in a work-study program while in school.

A high school graduate may start out in a nonselling job or be hired as a sales trainee. Either way, he will probably work at various nonselling jobs before he begins selling. He may start out in the stockroom or shipping department, or may study the prices and discount rate of articles. Next, he will probably become an "inside salesman," writing telephone orders. He'll also accompany experienced salesmen on calls to learn the firm's methods and meet the customers. It usually takes about two years for a trainee to become familiar enough with the company's products and techniques to be assigned a selling territory.

What the Occupation Has to Offer

There should be good job opportunities for wholesale salesmen in the 1970s. As business in general expands, and as large firms and chain stores centralize their purchasing, the demand for good salespeople in the wholesale area will grow. Computers will relieve these workers of some of their more routine duties, and more time will be spent giving customers personalized service.

The estimates of earnings are limited, but most beginning salesmen average about $9,000 a year. An experienced salesman averages about $15,000, but some make much more.

In most cases, salesmen get a salary plus a percentage commission on sales, although some companies pay a straight commission. Car and travel expenses are usually paid for by the company.

Opportunities for promotion are good for an ambitious, hard-working salesman, who may advance to supervisor, sales manager or other executive positions.

Points to Consider Before Going into This Field

A person who likes people and is outgoing and alert can find success in this field even without much education. The pay is quite good, and benefits are usually included. The work is steady and year-round, although there may be some seasons that are more popular than others for certain products. There is also diversity and a chance to advance.

However, a salesman often has to travel at night and on weekends and may have to be away from home for days at a time. Hours can be long, and evenings are often spent writing reports and orders.

For more information:

You can get information on jobs in wholesale selling from local wholesale houses or from associations of wholesalers in large cities.

See also: page 337.

Services Industries

Over 20 million people are employed in service industries. About three-fifths of them are white-collar workers and the industry employs the highest proportion of professional and technical workers of any major industry.

What do we mean by service industries? Education (teaching) services including public and private schools and institutions of higher education, account for nearly one-third of the service work force. Health services (doctors, dentists, nurses) are also a major area of employment.

Other professional service workers include lawyers, accountants, engineers, and architects. Hotels, laundries, repair services, and the entertainment industry also employ service workers.

Another group of service workers is involved in food preparation and service. Employed by hotels, restaurants, and school, hospital, and plant cafeterias, almost 3 million people work as cooks, chefs, kitchen workers, waiters and waitresses, counter and fountain workers, and bartenders.

Another 2 million people clean and maintain buildings as janitors, charwomen, chambermaids, and elevator operators.

Private household workers—including maids, handymen, cooks, and governesses—prepare and serve meals, clean and launder, take care of children and perform other household duties.

Almost one million people are employed as protective service workers, responsible for safeguarding lives and property. These workers are mainly policemen, guards, and firemen. Most are government employees, but some guards and watchmen are privately employed to protect plants, hotels, and stores. Other protective service workers include sheriffs, bailiffs, crossing watchmen and bridge tenders, marshals, constables, and FBI special agents.

Some are employed in jobs related to grooming, such as barbers and cosmetologists. Others are involved in recreational activities, such as ski instructors, ushers, and check room attendants. Airline stewardesses and travel guides also fall into this category.

Some service workers are employed in repair jobs such as auto repair, or employed by places like golf courses and bowling alleys.

Personal qualifications for service jobs vary a great deal because of the variety of jobs involved. All of them, however, require dealing with people and any service worker should be able to get along with people and be interested in helping them.

With our desire for more personal services resulting from larger incomes, employment in this industry can be expected to increase quite a bit during the 1970s. Greatest growth will be in educational services, medical health services, laboratory research facilities, policemen, beauty operators, food service workers, and people involved in providing recreation and entertainment. Most service fields will not be affected very seriously by the increased use of technology.

Earnings in the service industry range from minimum wage on up. Most of these occupations provide an opportunity for advancement. Many have a series of ranks for promotion, depending on seniority, education, and job performance. Other services are well-suited for individuals who want to go into business for themselves—caterers, or barbers, for example.

The opportunities in most service fields should be good in the years to come. People with specialized training in any of the areas mentioned should have no trouble finding steady employment. Many service occupations offer a chance for people to work independently and participate in a variety of duties.

One disadvantage is that some service occupations involve long or odd hours.

Women account for about three-fifths of the industry overall, but are mainly found in lower ranked jobs in hospitals, educational institutions, hotels, beauty shops, laundries, and serving as private household help.

Barber

The Job

Barbers provide men with many personal services, although their main job is to cut and style hair. In addition, they may give hair and

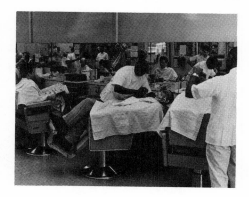

scalp treatments, shaves, shampoos, and facial massages.

In recent years as men have become more style-conscious, barbers have become hairstylists. Some men now request coloring, straightening, styling and setting, and some purchase hairpieces.

Barbers have traditionally worked with razors only for trimming but used scissors for the haircut. Today, however, razor cuts have become more common and stylish. Some barber shops have dryers or drying lamps for their longer-haired customers.

In addition to working on hair, barbers must keep their instruments sterilized and well maintained and their work areas clean. Barbers who own or manage a shop also are responsible for keeping records, ordering supplies, paying bills, and hiring and firing employees.

Barber shops are found in every city and town in the country, and more than half the 180,000 barbers in the country own and operate their own shops. Most shops are small, with only one or two barbers, and may be located in shopping centers, hotels, or office buildings.

A new trend in barber shops is the "unisex" shop, which offers services to both men and women. More and more women are being hired, both for the combination shops and for male only establishments.

What You Need Personally

You should like people and enjoy working and talking with them. Because you work with the public, you should have a neat and clean appearance. Patience is another good quality. Fairly good eye-hand coordination is needed, and some creative or artistic leanings are an asset in styling hair.

This is a good career for a person who likes to work in a clean place and enjoys working with his hands. If you have an artistic temperament, barbering may be for you because of its creativeness.

There are no physical qualifications for bar-

bers except stamina, as barbers often work long hours, many of them with their arms at a tiring shoulder level. Amputees and others with disability of the legs have gone into this profession with success.

What Education and Training You Need

Educational requirements for barbers vary from state to state. In most states, an eighth grade education is required, but high school graduates are preferred.

All states require barbers to obtain licenses. To get one, an applicant must be sixteen or eighteen years old, depending on the state, and must have graduated from a state-approved barber school.

Barber school courses usually last from six to eleven months and include 1,000 to 2,000 hours of instruction. The school provides chairs, instructors and supplies, and the student usually purchases his own tools at a cost of about $100. Studies include hair cutting, shaving, massaging, facial and scalp treatments, and skin care. There are also courses in anatomy, sanitation and hygiene, and the barber is taught how to recognize certain skin conditions. Because so many barbers run their own shops, courses are also given in salesmanship and general business practices. There are also instructions on how to use and care for instruments.

In addition to taking courses, the barber trainee practices his skills, under supervision, on fellow students and customers in school clinics.

Upon completion of schooling, most states require a beginner to take an examination for an apprentice license. After working one to two years, he takes a second examination to become a registered barber. Both examinations include a written test and a demonstration of haircutting ability. Examination fees range from $5 to $25.

A beginning barber may locate his first job through the school or through the local barber's union.

What the Occupation Has to Offer

The growth in employment opportunities for barbers will be limited in the next few years. Most job openings will be to replace older barbers who retire, die, or leave the occupation. Barbers are, on the average, older than many other professionals.

The trend to longer hair has resulted in men getting fewer haircuts. However, the growing popularity of the men's hairstyling salons should provide some new jobs for barbers trained in working with long hair.

Barbers who are not shop owners receive income from either commissions or wages, and from tips. Most employed barbers receive 65 to 75 percent of the money they take in at their stations. A few receive salaries. Information on earnings is limited, but the average barber probably makes between $150 and $175 a week including tips. Apprentices usually make $85 to $125 per week, while experts and shop owners can make over $250.

Earnings depend on the size and location of the shop, the number of regular customers the barber attracts and keeps, the prices charged, skill of the barber, and the amount of competition. Larger styling shops charge much more for a haircut, which increases the barber's income.

A barber can advance by becoming a manager of a large shop, teaching at a barber school, or opening his own shop. To open a shop requires some investment capital, but the amount varies depending on whether the equipment is new or used. Equipping a one-chair shop with new equipment costs from $1,500 to $2,800.

Points to Consider Before Going into This Field

Barbering offers a chance to provide a personal service and is a good occupation for someone who likes to meet and talk with many people. The surroundings are clean and pleasant, the career can be practiced anywhere, and the work is creative and independent. Good barbers are in demand twelve months of the year. You have the chance to operate your own business with a smaller amount of capital to start than in many other businesses.

One disadvantage is that most barbers work more than a forty-hour-week. The work is not constant, however; while Saturdays and peak hours may be very full, other periods give the barber time to himself. Some work by appointments to overcome this problem.

Some barbers belong to unions, which means they get paid vacations and insurance benefits. Those who don't belong rarely get paid holidays, insurance, or other benefits.

Although almost all barbers have been men in the past, the field is open to women. Many men are asking for women barbers, and increasing numbers of women are attending barber schools.

For more information, write:

Associated Master Barbers and Beauticians of America
219 Greenwich Road, P. O. Box 17782
Charlotte, North Carolina 28211
Ask for: information on this field. Enclose $.15.

Barbers, Beauticians and Allied Industries International Association
7050 West Washington Street
Indianapolis, Indiana 46240
Ask for: list of accredited schools and job information.

Department of Human Resources Development
Mail Control Unit

800 Capitol Mall
Sacramento, California 95814
Ask for: *Barber* No. 78, Free.

National Association of Barber Schools, Inc.
338 Washington Avenue
Huntington, West Virginia 25701
Ask for: information on schools and licensing.

Also contact:

Information on approved barber schools and state licensing requirements can be obtained from the State Board of Barber Examiners in your state capital.

Building Custodian

The Job

Every office, hotel, hospital, apartment house, and large building must be maintained and cleaned. This work is performed by a building custodian, also known as a janitor or cleaner. Building custodians are responsible for seeing that heating and ventilating equipment is functioning properly and that the building is neat and orderly. They perform many different jobs that keep a building functioning and in good condition. Included among their duties are cleaning floors, furniture, and other equipment, vacuuming carpets, getting rid of insects and rodents, and making minor repairs.

Many materials and tools are used by building custodians. Some are as simple as mops; others may include such things as electric polishing machines. In recent years, more mechanical equipment has been developed to help with these jobs and cut down on physical labor. Custodians must know all about the different materials used in their work because using a machine or chemical cleaner incorrectly could cause great damage.

Women in custodial work usually do lighter tasks like mopping, dusting, and furniture waxing. Men usually do the repairs and heavier work such as operating heavy floor polishers and buffers or moving furniture or other articles.

In large buildings, some workers act as supervisors and are responsible for an entire section or building. They have to make sure that jobs are being done properly throughout their area.

Building custodians are employed all over the country. Some work for contract firms that provide building maintenance on a fee basis. Although most building custodians work indoors, some have outdoor tasks such as sweeping walkways, shoveling snow, or mowing lawns.

What You Need Personally

You should be able to adjust to diverse duties and be able to follow instructions. You should be dependable, responsible, and able to work independently.

What Education and Training You Need

Most building custodians receive no formal training for their jobs. An inexperienced custodian starts with simple tasks and advances to more complex duties.

He should know simple arithmetic and it would be beneficial for him to take high school shop courses to learn handyman tasks like plumbing repair and carpentry.

Some unions and government agencies offer training programs for building custodians. Students learn the properties of different surfaces and the correct way to clean them. They are taught how to operate and maintain cleaning machines and learn how to make minor repairs on electrical and plumbing fixtures. Students are also taught to plan their work and are given suggestions on dealing with the public. Some training programs also include remedial courses in reading, writing, and arithmetic.

What the Occupation Has to Offer

There should be quite a few openings in this field in the 1970s. New buildings are going up all over the country as the economy grows, and they all have to be maintained. New apartment houses and office buildings, in particular, are expected to show growth. Some of this growth will be offset, however, by improved technology that makes cleaning easier. Buildings are being designed with surfaces that are easier to maintain and new cleaners and solvents do a better cleaning job today. New machines will also reduce maintenance work.

Earnings for building custodians depend on where you live and the type of building in which you work. Salaries tend to be higher in the large cities on the west coast and in the north central

part of the country. A male building custodian usually earns between $2.15 and $2.80 an hour, a female between $1.89 and $2.57 an hour.

Building custodians who work in places with large maintenance staffs can advance to supervisory positions. A high school diploma is an asset in such promotions. A custodian who has built up skills and reputation can go into business for himself and contract his services to buildings on a fee basis.

Points to Consider Before Going into This Field

There are always jobs for building custodians and many of them receive fringe benefits from their employers. They normally work in pleasant, heated, well-lighted buildings, and can usually set their own pace and work independently.

One disadvantage of the job is that custodial workers spend much of their time on their feet and are required to bend, stoop, and stretch for many jobs. Because many buildings are cleaned after the regular staff has left for the day, building custodians often work at night. Because they work with machines and chemicals they often suffer from minor cuts, burns, and bruises and may get dirty and greasy on the job.

About three-quarters of the 1.1 million custodial employees are men. Women tend to earn less than men in this profession.

For more information:

For information on openings in custodial work and on training programs set up by the Manpower Development and Training Act for this kind of work, contact your local state employment office. See also the custodial jobs advertised in the classified section of your newspaper.

Cosmetologist

The Job

Although hairdressing and professional beauty care go back to before the days of Cleopatra, cosmetology is really a modern art and science. The world of beauty and cosmetics offers many career opportunities for both men and women on a full or part-time basis. Cosmetologists, also known as beauty operators, beauticians, or hairdressers, may perform many services or specialize in a single area. They cut, set, shampoo, style, straighten, bleach and tint hair, and give permanent waves. Other services include giving manicures, scalp and facial treatments, makeup analysis, eyebrow shaping, wig cleaning and styling.

A salon manager or owner also performs managerial functions, such as record-keeping,

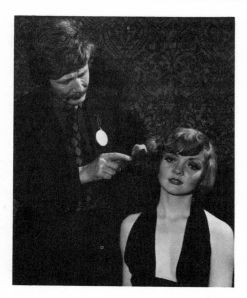

property maintenance, control of supplies and supervision of employees.

Most cosmetologists work in salons that are either independent shops or operated in conjunction with hotels or stores. Some shops are also found in hospitals, on ocean liners, or in motion picture and television studios.

There are beauty salons in towns and cities all over the country. Most are small and have under four employees. Over half are operated by their owners.

Almost half a million people work as cosmetologists and hairdressers, quite a few of them part time.

What You Need Personally

You should be able to get along well with people, be patient, tactful and courteous in dealing with them. Customers can sometimes be trying and demanding. You are rendering a highly personal service and you must be willing to deal with your customers' whims.

Good grooming and a pleasant appearance are important in dealing with the public. Manual dexterity, good eye-hand coordination and a good eye are also important for a cosmetologist. A sense of form and artistry is helpful, and you'll find it necessary to keep up with changing trends and techniques in order to give your customers the best service. The more artistic and creative you are, the better your chances of success.

Physical stamina is also important, as long hours, man of them standing, are required on the job.

What Education and Training You Need

All states require that beauty operators be licensed. Qualifications vary from state to state, but usually the applicant must be at least sixteen years old, in good health and have completed at least tenth grade. Some states require a high school diploma. Most states expect you to complete an approved cosmetology course, although some will substitute an apprenticeship period. License examinations include oral and written sections and a practical demonstration.

Cosmetology training is offered by over 3,500 public and private vocational schools that are state approved. The Cosmetology Accrediting Commission has almost 500 special cosmetology schools registered.

Many schools offer part-time night courses as well as full-time day school. The number of hours of required study runs from 1,000 to 2,000 and daytime courses usually take six months to a year to complete. Courses that include academic subjects last from two to three years. Apprentice training usually takes one or two years. Many states issue manicurists licenses which require much less training.

Be very careful in picking a school of beauty culture. While many schools have high standards, some give their students poor training while charging high tuition fees. Some exploit students as a source of free labor in shops run by the school. It is important to attend an accredited school of cosmetology where instructions, both theoretical and practical, are conducted with modern equipment and with textbooks that are recognized and endorsed by leading educators and state boards.

The study of cosmetology includes lectures, demonstrations and practical work. As a student you study the theory and practice of hairdressing, haircutting, shampooing, facial and arm manipulations, makeup, manicuring, and hair-coloring. You also learn to apply principles of physiology, bacteriology, circulation, chemistry, hygiene, and electricity. By practicing on other students or on manikins, you learn to work with hair and with makeup. After some preliminary training, you may practice on patrons in school clinics.

If you intend to manage a shop or open your own, you'll find a business course which includes bookkeeping, banking practice, and other commercial subjects very helpful.

What the Occupation Has to Offer

Job opportunities in the cosmetology field should grow somewhat during the next few years. The increasing population, larger incomes and the number of women working outside the home are expected to continue to create a demand for cosmetologists.

Earnings of cosmetologists vary a great deal,

particularly since part of their income comes from tips. Other variables include experience, skill, speed of performance, ability to build up a clientele and location of salon. Some cosmetologists are paid on a straight commission basis, some by salary and some receive a salary plus commission, in addition to tips.

Beginning operators, who are usually manicurists or shampooers, earn from $65–$90 per week. Top stylists or specialists may make as much as $300. Part-time workers, of course, make less. Many large salons and salons affiliated with stores or hotels offer insurance and other benefits to employees.

Employees are expected to furnish their own uniforms in most places, but are usually provided with combs, brushes, and other materials.

There are various ways to advance in the cosmetology profession. You can become a specialist in a large salon; can manage a shop or can own your own shop. Some operators advance to teaching positions in cosmetology schools. Others get jobs as demonstrators for cosmetic manufacturers, as beauty editors, or specialists who teach makeup techniques.

Points to Consider Before Going into This Field

Cosmetology offers a steady career that may be practiced anywhere, in a field that is expanding and developing. It offers security if you are capable. It can be practiced on a part-time basis and can be reactivated after a period of time away from work. Because each customer is different and styles and tastes change, the work is diverse and constantly changing. The educational requirements are not too demanding, and there is plenty of opportunity for advancement for the ambitious and intelligent operator.

However the hours are often long and irregular and the work is strenuous because you must spend so much time on your feet. Most full-time operators work forty hours or longer a week, including late afternoons and Saturdays.

While only about 10 percent of the country's licensed cosmetologists are men, the number will probably increase in the future.

For more information, write:

International Department of Education
Barbers, Beauticians and Allied Industries International Association
7050 West Washington Street
Indianapolis, Indiana 46240

Cosmetology Accrediting Commission
25755 Southfield Road
Southfield, Michigan 48075
Ask for: information on cosmetology schools.

National Hairdressers and Cosmetologists Association, Inc.
3510 Olive

St. Louis, Missouri 63103
Ask for: *Cosmetology As A Career*, Free.

Also contact:

For a copy of your state's law concerning this field, write to the Cosmetology Board at your state capital.

Firefighter

The Job

Firefighters are responsible for protecting us from fires that claim lives and cause untold damage each year. When an alarm sounds, a fireman, whether full- or part-time, must be prepared to put on protective clothing and drive the fire equipment to the scene of the fire.

Because of the dangers involved in firefighting, teamwork is of vital importance and firemen are well aware of their own and others' duties. A supervisor makes sure each fireman does his job. Some, using tools like axes and crowbars, force their way into burning buildings. Others lay out and attach firehoses to water hydrants and then turn the sprays of water on the fire. Rescue teams carry people to safety and give them first aid. Often a fireman will go into a burning building again and again to be sure that all residents have gotten out safely. The commanding officer watches over the progress of the firefighting and assigns and reassigns his men where they are needed.

After a fire is put out, the firemen make sure there's no further danger before they return to the firehouse.

When they aren't fighting fires, firemen are expected to continuously improve their knowledge of their work by practicing skills and maintaining equipment. Firemen who live at the station may spend some time keeping the living quarters in shape and checking alarms.

Fire prevention is another important responsibility of fire departments. In larger departments, a chief fire marshal and a team of inspectors are charged with inspection duties; in a smaller community, inspectors are appointed from the squad. They inspect buildings for fire doors, faulty wiring, stored flammable materials, fire escapes, and check conditions that may cause fires. They also check public buildings for compliance with safety regulations and report any dangerous conditions and violations.

Firefighters are also involved in educating the public about fire prevention and are often asked to speak before civic groups and school assemblies on this subject.

What You Need Personally

You must be at least twenty-one years old, meet certain height and weight requirements for your community, be in excellent physical condition and pass a medical examination. You must also pass a written intelligence test and tests of strength, stamina, and agility as specified by civil service regulations. You must be a citizen of the United States and, in most cases, a resident of the community for at least a year.

Because of the dangers involved in firefighting and its importance to the community, qualifications for firefighters are quite high. Courage, mental alertness, endurance and a sense of public service are all important. You must have initiative and confidence in your own judgment, because you will often have to make quick decisions that can mean life or death. You must be able to work as part of a team and follow directions when necessary. You must be responsible and aware of the dangers in your occupation.

What Education and Training You Need

Most fire departments require applicants to be high school graduates or the equivalent. Studies in physics, chemistry, and mathematics will be helpful, as will drafting, blueprints, and some knowledge of building construction and the law. Appointees to the fire department are chosen from men who receive the highest grades on the civil service examinations. Experience gained as a volunteer fireman or through firefighting training in the Armed Forces may improve an applicant's chances. Notice of qualifying examinations is posted in newspapers and public buildings. There are more applicants than jobs and so competition, especially in big cities, is keen.

Firemen do most of their training on the job, but large cities usually have a fire school where they give several weeks' training to beginners. Training includes classroom instruction and practice drills, and beginners study firefighting techniques, local building codes, fire prevention, and first aid. They learn to use axes, chemical extinguishers, ladders, hoses, and other equipment. Techniques of salvage and rescue are also studied.

There are other places to study firefighting. State and city fire departments give courses on fire prevention and fire fighting, and some state and community colleges offer fire prevention courses. Some universities offer courses in fire engineering to experienced firemen. A new area of study for firemen involves eighty-two hours of training to become emergency medical technicians. These are firemen trained by doctors to perform simple lifesaving operations on fire victims in the time before they can get to a hospital.

What the Occupation Has to Offer

There should be a moderate increase in firefighting jobs in the 1970s. Firemen usually retire at a younger age than other workers. Some new jobs will also occur as growing communities enlarge their staffs and switch from volunteer to paid fire departments.

Firefighters are employed by every town, city, federal and state agency, industrial plant, etc. Most full-time paid positions are in cities, while small towns usually have volunteers who are employed on an annual pay or pay-by-call basis. Special Forest Service firemen are trained to fight forest fires.

Firefighters in large cities usually have higher starting salaries. In cities with populations of over 500,000, the average starting salary is about $7,800; in smaller cities it is $6,100. Experienced firefighters earn between $7,000 and $10,000 per year. Chiefs average between $10,000 and $21,600.

Some allowance is usually given for uniforms and protective clothing such as helmets, boots, and rubber coats. An injured fireman usually receives full-pay compensation for the time he is out. If his injury is permanent, he is retired usually at half pay.

Most of the country's 180,000 full-time firemen are unionized and are municipal employees. As such they receive excellent benefits. Their health insurance plans are good, and they get liberal paid holidays and vacations. They can usually retire at age fifty or fifty-five at half pay after twenty-five years of service.

Chances for promotion are good. There are various grades of firemen. In most departments, a fireman is advanced automatically for the first few years until he becomes fireman first grade. When a vacancy occurs in any rank higher than that, all interested members of the department must take the appropriate examination and the highest ranking man in the examination gets the promotion. Usually, a fireman is eligible for promotion to lieutenant after five to ten years or more of service. After that, the line of promotion goes to captain, batalion chief, assistant chief, and finally to chief. A firefighter who continues his education in firefighting and fire prevention stands a better chance to be promoted.

Points to Consider Before Going into This Field

Fire fighting is one of the most valuable community services a man can perform. A fireman is called upon to save lives and property and has the satisfaction of knowing that by his successful performance, many people's families and homes are protected.

For men who like to work on a team and enjoy male companionship, firefighting is an excellent profession. Benefits are good and the work is steady and stable.

Because of the danger involved, there are disadvantages, of course. The hours can be rugged. In some cities firemen are on duty for twenty-four hours, then off for twenty-four with an extra day off periodically. Some work either a ten-hour day shift or a fourteen-hour night shift. The average workweek for firemen is about fifty-six hours, although some duty hours afford firemen time to read or study.

Firemen must also work many extra hours overtime bringing fires under control, but they either get extra time off, or extra pay to compensate for this.

Firefighting involves serious dangers. Every year more firemen are injured on duty than policemen. Even when they are not fighting fires, firemen are waiting with some tension for an alarm to come in. Alarms come in during any kind of weather, and firemen work in the cold, rain, even hurricanes. The pressures and strains are serious and the chance of injury or even death very real. There is always the possibility that a floor may cave in or a wall will fall down. In addition, there are the hazards of flames, smoke, poisonous and explosive gases and chemicals.

It is for these reasons that firemen must pass strict tests for physical stamina and mental alertness and men who do not stand up to stress would not do well in this work.

Firefighters are always men, although some small rural departments are considering using women as volunteers.

For more information, write:

Department of Human Resources Development
Mail Control Unit
800 Capitol Mall
Sacramento, California 95814
Ask for: *Fire Fighter (City and Suburban)* No. 241, Free.

International Association of Fire Fighters
905 16th Street, N. W.
Washington, D. C. 20006

Also contact:

Information on becoming a firefighter in your community can be obtained from your local fire department or civil service commission.

Household Worker

The Job

When you think of a household worker, do you think of Hazel, that wonderful gal on TV? Actually, private household workers have many different titles and perform a variety of services, but maid service is the most common. A general maid does all kinds of things, including cleaning household furnishings, floors and bathrooms; changing beds; watching children; buying, cooking and serving food, and washing dishes; and washing and ironing clothes. Similar duties are performed by a "mother's helper," who is basically a trainee.

There are quite a few specialties open to household workers. A personal maid assists her employer by keeping her clothes in proper condition and order, keeping her private quarters neat and helping her dress.

Some maids are involved primarily with children. A nursemaid cares for, bathes, and supervises children. She also prepares their meals, and washes and irons clothes. An infant's nurse is similar, but her duties include sterilizing bottles, making formulas, and feeding the baby at proper times during day and night.

Full responsibility for running a household may be given to a housekeeper, who usually operates with less supervision than a maid. She usually manages a house with a large staff of employees. She directs the others, orders food and cleaning supplies, keeps track of money spent, and may hire and fire employees.

Some private household workers specialize. The laundress, for example, is usually limited to washing and ironing household laundry. The cook prepares the meals, either planning her own menu or following her employer's instructions. The cook, who is sometimes assisted by a cook's helper, may also serve meals and perform special duties like making fancy pastries.

A companion lives with a convalescent or a person who is alone, and acts as aide and friend, attending to the employer's personal needs and looking after social or business affairs. She is often of the same social background as her employer and may spend time talking with or reading to the convalescent.

A governess is employed to look after children in a home. She often supervises their education, play, health and eating, and may ...so be charged with teaching and disciplining them.

There are some household jobs that are generally performed by men. The jack-of-all-trades, otherwise known as the handyman or odd-jobman, helps keep the home in order, waxing and polishing floors, washing windows, painting fences, repairing screens, tending the furnace, and caring for the yard. If he only tends the house, he is sometimes known as a houseman; if employed year-round, he may be called a caretaker.

A valet performs personal services for a male employer, such as caring for and laying out clothing, mixing and serving drinks, and running errands.

A butler receives and announces guests, answers the telephone, serves food and drinks, and sometimes acts as a valet. He may supervise and coordinate the duties of other household workers and may also act as chauffeur.

What You Need Personally

If you want to be a household worker, you should have a pleasant and agreeable nature and be trustworthy, neat, clean, and healthy. Some employers may require cooks or infant's nurses to have a health certificate.

Ability to get along with people—including children—is important, and a household worker should be prepared to do steady work, often without supervision.

What Education and Training You Need

No formal educational requirements are needed for most household workers. The duties of a general maid, cook, or nurse are often learned by girls at home as they grow up. You could also learn these skills by working for a year as an assistant to an experienced household worker.

Home economics courses in school and training courses sponsored by federal agencies, state employment services, and local welfare offices help to develop better than ordinary domestic skills. Most household workers are expected to be able to operate household equipment like vacuum cleaners and to floor waxers.

For a governess or companion, educational cultural background are more important than work experience. A companion should be of similar age, background and interests to her

employer, and, if the employer is ill, should have some practical nursing experience. A governess will find that a broad educational background, particularly in music, foreign language, and experience with children will be helpful.

What the Occupation Has to Offer

Openings are abundant and the demand should continue to increase with the rise in family income and the increasing number of women working outside the home.

Household workers' earnings vary according to the type of work performed, employer's income, and geographical location. Wages are higher in large cities, especially in the north. Workers who live at the employer's home are usually paid the same as day workers, but receive free room and board. Day workers usually receive a free meal and transportation costs.

Although wage information is limited, in most parts of the country household workers earn between $.90 and $2 an hour.

There are places for advancement within household work categories, but usually the worker will have to change jobs in order to obtain a higher position. A nursemaid or general maid could, for instance, increase her skills and get a new job as personal maid, infant's nurse, cook, or housekeeper.

Points to Consider Before Going into This Field

There are some advantages to household work, particularly for part-time workers. They are free to negotiate duties with their employer and frequently work unsupervised when the employer is not at home. Part-time workers also have time to themselves.

Disadvantages outweigh the advantages for many people. The result is usually more jobs than applicants. The hours, especially for live-in workers, are often long, and the work can be quite strenuous. Pay is not very high and fringe benefits are usually lacking. Live-in help in homes with no other workers are often lonely, since the length and irregularity of their working time isolates them from family and friends.

Most household jobs are distinctly divided into categories for men or women, as outlined previously.

For more information, write:

National Committee on Household Employment
1625 I Street, N. W.
Washington, D. C.

Also contact:

Information about employment opportunities or training programs for private household workers is also available from your local state employment offices.

Law Enforcement

The Job

If you have a sense of responsibility, like excitement, and feel a need to contribute to society, the growing field of law enforcement may be the right one for you.

Most policemen and detectives work for municipal, county, state, and federal government agencies. However, thousands more work for department stores, schools, hotels, business and industry. And some are self-employed private detectives.

What do different kinds of policemen and policewomen actually do? If you're a local policeman you begin on patrol duty in congested business districts or outlying residential areas. You cover "beats" alone or with another patrolman, either on foot or in police cars. You learn to recognize suspicious situations, safety hazards, and stolen cars. You direct traffic, investigate housebreakings, and give first aid to accident victims. You report to headquarters through call boxes, by radio or walkie-talkie. Finally, you learn to prepare reports and testify in court.

In large cities you may be assigned to specific duty, usually patrol or traffic. Some policemen receive special assignments in accident prevention, communications, or criminal investigation. Plainclothesmen are assigned to homicide, narcotics, and general detective squads. Still others become experts in firearms identification, handwriting and fingerprint identification, and lab work. Some cities maintain special units— mounted or motorcycle police, harbor patrols, helicopter patrols, canine corps, mobile rescue teams, and youth aid services.

As a state policeman you enforce laws governing highways. You spend most of your time patroling thruways, enforcing traffic laws, and giving out tickets. When necessary, you testify in court. You also help at the scene of an accident, conduct investigations, and write reports. In addition, you aid motorists in trouble and direct traffic during repairs, fires, other emergencies, and parades. Side duties include weighing commercial vehicles, giving exams, and serving as a public safety information officer. Some state police officers specialize in laboratory analysis, instructing trainees or flying police aircraft. In areas that do not maintain their own police force, state officers investigate crime. They also help the local police in criminal matters and riot control.

If you're interested in the FBI, you'll find a variety of jobs open to you. Although only law school and college graduates with specific training may be special agents, the bureau does have openings for typists, clerks, messengers, telephone and teletype operators, receptionists, radio technicians, and photographers. Two specialized FBI jobs involve working as a fingerprint clerk, where you learn to identify individuals on the basis of the unique characteristics of their fingerprints, and working in the lab (laboratory aid), where you help scientists examine documents, firearms, toolmarks, explosives, blood, poisons, hair, fibers, chemicals, soils, minerals, and metals.

A policeman's job is tough. He works a forty-hour week and in all but the smallest communities he may be on duty weekends, holidays, and at night. He's on call any time and in emergencies he may work overtime. The FBI has a forty-hour week and in many sections there are regular night and midnight shifts. Employees must be available for such assignments, and may also have to work weekends.

What You Need Personally

Honesty, good judgment, and a sense of responsibility are especially important in police work. An applicant's character and background are thoroughly investigated before he's hired as a policeman. The FBI subjects all candidates to a careful investigation for loyalty, reputation, and character.

Physical stamina, agility, and an interest in people are all qualities that help the policeman succeed in his work. And, as he advances in his career, an aptitude for psychology, sociology, and minority relations is useful. Since policemen of the future will need more specialized training, and since police departments encourage officers to continue their education, a desire for further study will prove helpful. A policeman must also be prepared to take competitive exams as he advances in his field. Naturally, he must expect to put in long, hard hours and, on occasion, face dangerous situations which require him to be courageous, resourceful and, above all, cool.

What Education and Training You Need

If you're twenty-one, a U. S. citizen, and can pass the strict physical and mental civil service exams, you'll probably qualify as a local or state policeman. Most departments require a high school diploma, but some cities demand college training while others hire law enforcement students as police interns. These paid civilian employees attend classes part time to learn police science and also do clerical work. At age twenty-one they may be appointed to the force.

In the future more officers will be recruited from post-high school training. To meet this need over 400 colleges and universities offer major programs in law enforcement. Michigan State University has one of the nation's oldest and largest programs in its School of Criminal Justice. Because you have to be twenty-one to enter police service, many applicants have the chance to go to college for two to four years before going into police work. College training may be required for women because of specialized assignments. In any case, experience in social work, teaching or nursing is helpful for women wishing to do police work.

Before a policeman gets his first assignment, he goes through a training period. In small communites instruction is informal as recruits work for about a week with experienced officers. In large city departments, training may extend over several weeks or a few months. Preparation includes classroom instruction in constitutional law, civil rights, state laws, local ordinances, procedures in accident investigation, patrol, traffic, and other work. Recruits learn how to use guns, defend themselves, administer first aid and deal with various emergencies. This training is usually given only after a person has been accepted as a member of the force.

Further training at police department academies and colleges keeps officers up to date on crowd control techniques, civil defense, legal developments and new law enforcement equipment. Many departments encourage officers to get college degrees, and some pay part or all of the tuition.

State police training lasts several months, with the minimum usually twelve weeks. Recruits receive classroom instruction in state laws and jurisdictions and, in addition to regular police training, they learn how to handle a car at high speeds. Later, some officers take specialized training in police science, administration, law enforcement and criminology. Classes are held at junior colleges, colleges, universities or special police institutions such as the National Academy of the FBI.

While special agents for the FBI must be law school or college graduates, you may join the FBI as a nonagent if you are a high school graduate, a U. S. citizen, at least sixteen, and in good physical condition. You must be able to pass a rigid spelling test, but no previous experience is necessary for many jobs because you receive on-the-job training. Fingerprint clerks, for example, take a training course that lasts ninety days. Lab assistants must have two years of college training in science or the equivalent in industrial experience. All lab appointments are probationary for the first year and applicants with experience in photography, use of scientific instruments or other technical work are given preference. FBI positions do not come under civil service appointment regulations.

What the Occupation Has to Offer

The employment outlook through the 1970s is very favorable. New positions will open up as the population grows, crime rates increase, and other officers retire. Since policemen usually retire at a younger age than most people, replacement rates are high. The number of police-women will increase, especially in work involving female offenders. The need for policemen and detectives in areas other than municipal police departments is also expected to rise.

Future jobs are likely to be affected by changes in methods and equipment. Specialists are becoming more essential, particularly in electronic data processing—to compile administrative, criminal, and identification records and to operate emergency communications systems. Specialists in engineering related to traffic control and social work techniques for crime prevention will be needed.

The need for state troopers will also increase with the demand mostly for officers on highway patrol. Our growing mobile population requires more state policemen to control high speeds, prevent accidents, and help stranded motorists. Specialists will be needed in crime labs and data processing centers.

In 1970 a policeman's earnings averaged $8,500 while more experienced officers received $10,000. Most men get regular increases during the first few years until a specified maximum is reached. Sergeants, lieutenants, and captains get higher wages. Top salaries are paid to chiefs or commissioners. In 1970 they averaged $11,000 in small cities and $23,000 in the largest. Special allowances are given for uniforms, revolvers, nightsticks, handcuffs, and other equipment. Some departments pay overtime at straight wages, others at time and a half and still others give officers an equal amount of time off. Liberal pension plans allow many officers to retire at half pay by age fifty-five, and other benefits include paid vacations, sick leave, medical, surgical, and life insurance plans.

In 1970 state policemen's beginning salaries ranged from $480 to $860 a month, with starting rates highest in the west and lowest in the south. Officers get regular increases based on experience and performance. In 1970 maximums ranged from $640 to $1,100 a month, with earnings increasing as a man was promoted to a higher rank.

FBI entrance salaries begin at $5,828 for fingerprint clerks and $6,544 for laboratory aides. Employees receive regular promotions. Fingerprint clerks, for example, earn $6,544 after six months, $7,319 after twelve months and $8,153 after twenty-four months. People with supervisory ability may eventually earn as much as $20,627 a year.

FBI employees can also earn cash awards by demonstrating superior work performance or by making valuable suggestions to improve efficiency and economy. The Bureau also offers tax-free medical, disability, health and life insurance benefits, with the government paying part of the premiums. There are also retirement benefits, depending on the length and type of service. The FBI specifies that a new employee should plan to have sufficient funds to enable him to live for at least one month before receiving his first salary check.

On most police forces men and women become eligible for promotion after specific periods. An officer may choose to specialize in one kind of police science, such as lab work, traffic control, communications, or work with juveniles. Promotions to sergeant, lieutenant and captain are made according to the man's position on the promotion list, determined by how well he's done on written exams and in his daily work. Advancement opportunities are greatest in large departments, where separate bureaus work under the direction of administrative officers and assistants. A detective's position is an advanced one to which a policeman may be promoted after several years if he has an outstanding record and special aptitude.

Further training is useful to a policeman in advancing his career. College or home study courses are available, dealing with criminal investigation, drug addiction, homicide, traffic control, criminology, crime prevention, arson, explosives, bombs, interrogation, first aid, jail administration and laws of arrest, search, and seizure. Courses such as those given by community and junior colleges and private vocational schools are open to police officers wishing to take special training. Some police departments give financial aid to employees who want to get college degrees or additional training.

State police recruits serve a probationary period of six months to two or three years. After that the men become eligible for promotion. Most states have merit promotion systems requiring officers to pass an exam in order to go on to the next rank: from private to corporal, to sergeant, to first sergeant, to lieutenant, and then captain. Especially able officers are considered for higher positions as commissioners or directors.

Advancement in the FBI depends on an employee's ambition, qualifications, and work performance. Promotions are based on merit rather than seniority, although no deserving longtime employee is overlooked. While the FBI doesn't give financial aid to people who want to attend college, it does urge its employees to attend business schools, colleges, universities, and professional schools in their spare time to prepare for positions of greater responsibility.

Points to Consider Before Going into This Field

The advantages of becoming a policeman are these: you provide a service for your community and you learn new skills both on the job and at police academies and colleges. You also have a chance to retire at an early age and pursue other interests, related or unrelated to your field.

The disadvantages are obvious: a policeman's job is more hazardous than most. You may be assigned to work outdoors for long periods of time in all kinds of weather. The injury rate is higher than in many occupations because of risks you face when you pursue speeders, capture lawbreakers, and deal with public disorders such as riots.

For a woman, police work offers increasing opportunities. More departments are hiring women to work with juvenile delinquents, locate lost children and runaways, and to search, question, book and fingerprint women prisoners. More women are also being hired to serve on detective squads, working mainly on crimes involving women. Women interested in law enforcement jobs must be aggressive and determined. It's often an uphill battle just to get the chance to take the examination.

A policeman or policewoman must be highly motivated to join a police force and highly dedicated to stay on it over a number of years. Those who choose police work will find an opportunity to serve both themselves and their communities.

For further information, write:

The International Association of Chiefs of Police
11 Firstfield Road
Gaithersburg, Maryland 20760
Ask for: *Directory of Law Enforcement and Criminal Justice Education; Requirements for a Police Career.*

School of Criminal Justice
Michigan State University
East Lansing, Michigan 48823
Ask for: information on obtaining a bachelor's or master's degree in law enforcement.

Also contact:

Information about local entrance requirements may be obtained from your local civil service commission or police department. Information on state police work may be obtained from your state civil service commission or the state police headquarters in your state capital.

For information on positions available in the FBI, go in person to any of their 49 field offices listed in the front of your phone book, or write to: Director, Federal Bureau of Investigation, Washington, D. C. 20535.

Library Technician

The Job

Libraries exist for everyone to use. Library technicians assist librarians in providing help to patrons. They perform a variety of tasks in almost every area of a library's operation. The technician helps people use and understand the library's resources and aids them in finding information through the card catalogs, almanacs, encyclopedias, and atlases. He or she also maintains files of newspaper clippings and pictures.

In a large library, technicians may maintain controls on checkouts, reserves, renewals, and overdue materials. They may operate and maintain audiovisual and data processing equipment including photographs, slide projectors, and tape recorders, as well as "readers" that magnify, project on a screen, and sometimes print information on microfilm and microfiche cards.

The library technician works under direct supervision of the librarian, but has specialized skills enabling him to assume responsibility for jobs requiring knowledge of library techniques and procedures. As a member of the library crew, the technician works with pages, clerks, librarians, and administrators toward a common goal: effective, efficient, and relevant service to the public.

The technician directly assists the professional librarian and is often called upon to train and supervise the clerical staff. One of his most important duties, which takes place behind the scenes, is the cataloging of books. This includes identifying the title, author, and other publication data.

Most library technicians are employed in public and school libraries although some work in business and industry. Their buildings or rooms are quiet, pleasant places in which to work without the pressures of more energetic but less contemplative occupations.

What You Need Personally

Although today's library technicians are apt to be of all ages, styles, and shapes, the important thing is that he or she is neat and clean, and congenial with the people who use the library's services. A respect for books is also a necessity. The library technician must be willing not only to help those people in need but must possess the verbal ability to explain the workings of the library.

The cataloging of books is repetitious and sometimes tedious but is one of the most necessary parts of the job. A neat handwriting is important for cataloging: others will have to be able to read and understand your numbers and letters. Typing ability is a definite plus but not essential in all libraries. You will need the ability to do a great deal of standing, stooping, bending, and reaching.

What Education and Training You Need

While an increasing number of library technicians have been receiving training in formal post-high school programs, most present library technicians were trained on-the-job in programs that required from one to three years to complete. The trend is toward education in a formal two-year program. About 130 community colleges now offer such training which leads to an associate of arts degree in library technology. A high school diploma or its equivalent is the standard entrance requirement for both academic and on-the-job training programs. Many programs require that a student be proficient in typing. A few schools require on-the-job experience under the supervision of a librarian. Curriculums generally include one year of liberal arts and one year of library related work, such as introductory courses in bibliographic science and cataloging. Some schools offer training to familiarize the student with data processing and audiovisual materials.

Professional librarianship requires a bachelor's degree in liberal arts or science plus a master's degree in library science. Credits earned in a two-year college program in library technology cannot always be applied toward a professional degree in library science.

What the Occupation Has to Offer

This job category is relatively new and the employment outlook is excellent for technicians, particularly for graduates of academic programs. A growing, more educated population and recent federal funding to construct, expand, and improve libraries will influence demand in the future. By 1980 we will need 124,000 library technicians, almost twice as many as we had in the 1960s.

Salaries generally range from $5,000 to $6,300 and experienced library technicians sometimes make over $9,000.

Technicians employed in public and private school systems usually work only during school hours, sometimes sharing the schools' vacations and holidays. Public and college libraries may include some weekend and evening hours. Most libraries provide fringe benefits such as group insurance and retirement pay. Some business and industry libraries provide special educational assistant programs.

The federal government itself employs 3,300 library technicians who work a forty-hour week and also receive the same benefits as other federal employees.

Points to Consider Before Going into This Field

Once learned, the skills of the library technician can be used in a variety of places, e.g., special libraries such as those of business and industry, public libraries, school libraries, and academic libraries. The main drawback is that while the work offers variety it can also be tedious and detailed.

The American Library Association stresses the fact that library jobs are open to all. It is not solely a woman's field. Most libraries are actively recruiting minorities as technicians.

For more information, write:

American Library Association
Office for Recruitment
50 E. Huron Street
Chicago, Illinois 60611

Secretariat Federal Library Committee
Room 310
Library of Congress
Washington, D. C. 20540
Ask for: information on careers in federal libraries.

Also contact:

If you're looking for more specifics on opportunities, visit libraries in the area where you wish to work. There you can obtain firsthand information on employment levels, training requirements, and job openings. Salaries and entrance requirements vary considerably and it is important to have a clear picture of local hiring patterns.

To locate college programs in library technology, check your local public library for the *Council of Library Technology, Directory of Institutions Offering,* or *Developing Programs for the Training of Library Technical Assistants.*

Information on scholarships can be obtained from your state library agency. State boards of education can also furnish information on job opportunities for school library technicians.

Recreation Worker

The Job

Americans live in a leisure-oriented society. As we have more free time, we look for new places to go, new things to do. A recreational worker helps others of all ages and all circumstances to make good and enjoyable use of their spare time. Recreation has become not only a business but a concern to many. Creative recreation can be pleasurable, constructive and, in some cases, therapeutic. The new interest in ecology combined with recreational interests has created a demand for trained people who can help to provide and maintain recreation for children and adults. Recreation workers not only help people to use their leisure time constructively, but they also run physical, social, and cultural programs. They operate recreational facilities as well as study and plan for the needs of individuals and communities.

There are all kinds of careers in recreation. Because recreation programs for the inner cities are badly needed, workers are hired by government and voluntary agencies to direct activities at playgrounds and indoor centers. They may give instruction in arts and crafts, or sports. They also work with social workers in creating programs at community centers and in correctional facilities.

Other recreational workers are employed by industry to plan activities for company employees such as bowling leagues. Some work for hospitals setting up recreational programs for the ill and handicapped. Others organize leisure-time activities for schools and for senior citizens.

More recreational workers are supervising national, state, country, district and municipal parks. Still others are being trained in zoological, wildlife and game management, and in conservation. They are also meeting public interest in zoos and aquariums and are putting new designs for such places into effect.

Private recreation clubs, planned communities, commercial recreation areas, and leisure-oriented housing complexes are all being built at a great pace. These offer many job opportunities for the recreation worker.

What You Need Personally

If you are a recreation worker, you should enjoy working with people in all capacities. You must be enthusiastic, able to teach, help, and supervise, and often must organize and initiate activities. Being responsible, organized, creative, and independent are all important traits. You'll work at a fast pace so good health and stamina are important. Many recreation jobs involve the out-of-doors.

A good recreation worker is very sensitive to people and able to understand and motivate them. Often you will be working with people who are handicapped, retarded, or ill—or simply hostile or ignorant. You must be able to deal effectively with all of them. This is a good field if you want to see the results of your work directly and want to feel you are doing something concrete for people.

What Education and Training You Need

Training required for recreation work varies according to the job. Most employers prefer applicants with a bachelor's degree in recreation,

social science, physical education, or health; but less than half of the workers now employed actually have such training.

To prepare for a career in recreation, students are urged to do volunteer, part-time or summer work in recreation departments, camps, or community centers.

There are opportunities at all levels dependent upon the amount and type of educational preparation you have. A two-year course in a junior or community college will prepare you for a job as a technician or specialist, the first rung on the recreation worker's ladder. On-the-job experience counts heavily in this field.

If possible, you should consider taking a four-year college program, and advanced courses leading to a master's degree are suggested for teaching and administrative positions.

A college program for a recreation worker should include courses in communication, natural sciences, humanities, philosophy, sociology, drama, and music. Specific recreation courses include group leadership, program planning and organization, health and safety procedures, outdoor and indoor sports, dance, arts and crafts and field work in actual recreational programs. Students interested in industrial recreation should consider courses in business administration, and anyone interested in working with the aged or handicapped should take courses in psychology, health education, and sociology. Recreational workers interested in parks or animals will need courses suited to these specialties.

Over 200 colleges and universities offer degrees in parks recreation and conservation. Scholarships are available from the federal government and some private institutions. Most college graduates enter the recreation field as leaders or specialists; those with graduate training may become recreational directors, supervising an entire facility.

The National Recreation and Park Association offers a national internship program that provides advanced training for high potential recreation graduates around the country. Stipends of $6,000–$8,000 a year are included in this program.

What the Occupation Has to Offer

Prospects for recreation workers during the 1970s are good. At present there are too few recreation graduates to fill the openings, which means persons with less than full professional training will continue to find jobs in the field. There is also a demand for part-time and volunteer workers.

The growth in this field can be expected to continue as people have more leisure time, higher incomes, earlier retirements and more travel opportunities. Concern for physical fitness and for the lack of recreational opportunities for urban youth all point to the need for more recreation workers. The importance of rehabilitative recreation is also being recognized.

Earnings vary according to amount of experience and education you have, and on the size of the community where you work. The average starting salary for an inexperienced college graduate is from $7,200 to $7,800. More experienced workers in supervisory positions earn from $8,500 to $14,200. Recreation directors and administrators can earn anywhere from $12,000 in a small community to $40,000 in a big city.

Opportunities for advancement are good. Most administrative positions go to people with graduate training, but workers with a combination of education and experience are often given good chances for promotion as well.

Points to Consider Before Going into This Field

The recreation field has many advantages if you want to make a contribution to society and if you enjoy working with people. Regardless of the special interest you follow, your fellow man benefits. There are jobs almost anywhere, city or country, and the field is expanding so rapidly that there will be even more opportunities in the future. There is a place in recreation work for virtually any kind of talent and plenty of chance to see results from your work.

Recreation workers often have to work long and irregular hours. They are usually working when others are enjoying leisure time, which may keep them from their families. And the work is physically and mentally demanding. To advance very far, a college education is necessary.

About half the recreation workers today are women but there are no restrictions in this field.

For more information, write:

National Industrial Recreation Association
20 North Wacker Drive
Chicago, Illinois 60606

National Recreation and Park Association
1601 North Kent Street
Arlington, Virginia 22209
Ask for: *Where the Action Is*, $.30; and information about training program in colleges.

Department of Medicine and Surgery
Veterans Administration
Washington, D. C. 20421
Ask for: information on opportunities in Veterans Administration Hospitals.

Social Service Aide

The Job

Social service aides are in great demand because of the number of social services offered and the shortage of professional social workers.

Social service aides, or social welfare aides, free the professional social worker to give time to more creative and supervisory responsibilities. This allows the agency to offer more and better service to the community. Most aides work under the direct supervision of a social worker or counselor.

Welfare aides often greet new applicants, help them fill out forms, and explain the purpose of the information needed. They give information about the agency's services, facilities, and procedures and gather information needed to determine the applicant's eligibility for public assistance. This can include making home visits, interviewing friends and relatives of the applicant and keeping files on clients. They keep files of reports and case reviews and do other routine paperwork. They help applicants with school enrollment, obtaining medical help or employment, or solving landlord-tenant problems. They may escort the elderly to medical clinics or take unemployed clients to job interviews. And they are also available for friendly counseling.

Homemaker aides may be assigned to a home for one or more days or may instruct a group of housewives at a community center. Their job is to help women improve skills in shopping, cleaning, sewing, budgeting, family health and hygiene, child care, and meal planning and preparation. The homemaker aide demonstrates homemaking skills, setting up a schedule of weekly activities. She may teach women how to clean a stove or refrigerator; how to prepare meals from leftovers; or how to make an attractive dress out of inexpensive materials. She encourages her clients to take advantage of surplus foods, thrift shops, free recreation, and other cost-saving opportunities.

Homemaker aides may also help housewives communicate effectively with schools, the welfare department of other institutions that can help them.

Outreach workers act as bridges between community agencies and the people they serve, keeping up communications between them. Neighborhood workers are in this category. They let people know about their agency's services, identify people's needs, and refer people to the appropriate agency. They may give community residents information about training, housing, or job opportunities. They may also assist in organizing neighborhood groups to benefit the residents, encourage people to participate in antipoverty programs, and try to foster a sense of community feeling.

Employment aides seek out the unemployed, even in poolrooms and on street corners, and inform them about services of state employment services and special training programs. They help them fill out application forms and counsel them on how to succeed in job programs. They may also contact employers to line up jobs. After workers are employed, the aide keeps in touch to help clients adjust to jobs and help straighten out their personal problems.

Teacher aides relieve teachers of routine jobs. They may supervise the lunchroom, playground and study hall, help load and unload school buses, arrange materials on bulletin boards and help in record keeping, filing, and other clerical jobs. Some aides help with lessons and correct tests.

There are over 50,000 social service aides and about 200,000 teacher aides in the country. Most are employed in the poverty areas of urban centers. Employment aides work in state employment service offices.

What You Need Personally

You need to be able to get along well with people, especially the disadvantaged. You should want to help society and enjoy aiding others. You must have patience, because disappointment is frequent and most projects take a long time to complete. You must also like problem solving and feel able to counsel people.

Because not all people will seek out help, it is especially important that social service aides be tactful and courteous and have leadership qualities.

What Education and Training You Need

There is usually no formal educational requirement for this field, although any skills and knowledge help. In some neighborhoods, it is important to be able to speak and understand Spanish, and some jobs require typing.

On-the-job training is provided for all these positions, but some junior colleges are establishing special training programs for aides.

When hiring aides, agencies are more interested in desire and need for work than in education. They look for potential for the particular job. For example, homemaker aides should show competence in running homes and rearing children.

Most training programs involve from one to several months of training, with the aide taking on greater responsibility as his or her familiarity with the program and skills increases.

What the Occupation Has to Offer

Most social service aide positions are funded by the federal government. The New Careers program, which is part of the Economic Opportunity Act, is designed to create entry level positions in public service. It encourages people to move up to higher level positions within the agency.

As long as funds are available, these positions should increase because there is a serious need for more competent workers in the overworked social service agencies and schools in urban areas.

Starting salary for social welfare aides in the New Careers program is about $2.25 per hour. Social work aides working for the federal government start at $4,125 to $5,212 per year. Employment aides start at about $4,200 per year. Experienced workers earn from $5,853 to $7,294. Many aides work less than a forty-hour week.

Advancement is possible in all these areas as skills increase through experience and education. Entry level jobs as employment aides, for instance, can lead to jobs as employment agents and coaches, then to employment interviewers and, after special training, to employment counselors.

Prospects for teaching aides are good as more school systems recognize their helpfulness as part of the teaching team.

Points to Consider Before Going into This Field

There is a great need for workers and the field offers an opportunity for you to help others and upgrade your community. It is also a way for a person with limited education and money to learn marketable skills to enter other professions.

Because most of these jobs are dependent on government funding, there is a certain lack of stability over a long period of time. The work can also be frustrating because it involves intricacies of bureaucracy and the whims of human nature.

Most of the workers in this field are women, but there is no reason why men cannot also seek jobs.

For more information, write:

Office of Education
Department of Health, Education and Welfare
Washington, D. C. 20202
Ask for: information on teacher aide positions

National Education Association
1201 16th Street, N. W.
Washington, D. C. 20036

Ask for: information on teacher aide positions

Also contact:

For more information on social service aide jobs, contact: your local city, county or State Department of Welfare; Department of Recreation; or a local Community Action Agency.

For information on employment aide positions contact: the local state employment office or the state civil service or Merit System office in your state capital.

Food-Service Industry

The Job

Whatever else may go in or out of style, the need for food will always be with us. There are many occupations involved in bringing food to people. Employees of restaurants and food stores make up the biggest group in this field.

One group of food-service workers is involved in the preparation and serving of food to people outside of their homes. They work in every kind of restaurant from luxury gourmet dining rooms to drive-in hamburger palaces. Some work in drug and department stores and in hospital, school, and factory cafeterias. Still others work for commercial airlines, railroads, and shiplines.

Restaurants employ cooks and chefs, pantrymen and women who prepare certain dishes, waiters and waitresses, counter attendants, bartenders, busboys and busgirls, and janitors and porters. In small places, many of these jobs are combined. The owner or operator may also perform one or more of these duties. Large restaurants may also employ cashiers, dieticians, accountants, and bookkeepers.

The other large group of food-service workers are employed by supermarkets. The retail food industry is the biggest business in America. Food stores vary in size from the small corner store to the large chain market. Employees include store managers, department managers, clerks, checkers, and delivery boys.

What You Need Personally

There are no specific traits for all food-service employees because there are so many different types of work. However, neatness and a pleasant manner are important for most employees who have to deal with the public. Good health and physical stamina are also recommended, since most of these jobs require the worker to be on his feet for long periods of time. Restaurant employees should be able to work under the pressure which builds when busy hours produce a great deal of tension.

What Education and Training You Need

Training and education vary according to the type of job. Small establishments require less training than larger ones. People with less than a high school education can be employed as kitchen workers, dishwashers, or busboys in many places, or as delivery boys in supermarkets.

Not much formal training is required for waiters and waitresses or for supermarket checkers. Most of their skills are learned on the job. Waiters and waitresses, for instance, are taught how to set tables, take orders and serve food in a courteous and efficient manner.

Training programs lasting twelve to fifteen weeks are available under the Manpower Development and Training Act for cooks and cook apprentices, waiters and waitresses, food-service supervisors and cook's helpers.

Public and private vocational schools provide training in food preparation and cooking, catering, restaurant management and other subjects. Various training programs exist for restaurant training through restaurant associations and trade unions, technical schools, junior and community colleges, and four-year colleges. These programs can range from a few months to two years of study. Supervisory training can be obtained by taking a two-year program at a junior or community college in food service management, for example. The Culinary Institute of America (a private vocational school) offers a two-year course leading to an associate degree in occupational studies. The program, which costs $1,175 per trimester, includes courses in culinary theory and demonstration, pantry, production kitchen, bakeshop, table service, storeroom procedures, buffet catering, classical pastry, principles of food service management, and many courses in different kinds of food preparation.

Supermarkets also have training programs for employees. A store manager, for example, should have a high school diploma and will be promoted much faster if he takes college level courses in food distribution. A number of colleges now offer degree programs in food distribution that include studies in merchandising, buying, marketing, and management. Scholarships are available in many cases for these studies with preference given to those who have had some experience in the food business. Schools that have these programs are Cornell University, Ithaca, New York; University of Southern California, Los Angeles; University of Delaware, Newark; Michigan State University, East Lansing; University of Massachusetts, Amherst; St. Joseph's College, Philadelphia, Pa.; Western Michigan University, Kalamazoo.

Cornell also has a noncredit home study program for people already working in this field, which includes courses in economics for business, food distribution, checkout management, business law, bookkeeping and accounting, and food marketing. These courses cost $25 each.

What the Occupation Has to Offer

The outlook is promising for people in these professions. The number of restaurants and supermarkets is expected to increase in the years to come, and mechanization will have little effect on these jobs.

Earnings vary according to the job, the size of the establishment, and the geographical area. In restaurants, many employees receive salaries and tips. Although figures are limited, it is estimated that waiters and waitresses average $.82–$2.15 an hour excluding tips; busboys and busgirls $1.01–$2.26; dishwashers $1.32–$2.26; pantry workers $1.46–$3.33; assistant cooks, $1.47–$3.86; porters $1.48–$2.60; kitchen helpers $1.53–$3.20; cashiers $1.57–$2.47; checkers $1.57–$2.73; cooks, $2.02–$4.12; bartenders $2.09–$3.87; and chefs $2.22–$4.65. Starting managers with college training may make from $7,000–$10,000 in large restaurants. Experienced restaurant managers can make from $10,000–$25,000.

Restaurant employees are usually provided with uniforms and get at least one free meal a day.

There is plenty of opportunity for advancement in the food-service industry. In a restaurant, a busboy or dishwasher can be promoted to waiter or cook's helper. With more training, he can become cook or chef, baker, or bartender. A restaurant hostess may become an assistant manager. The better managerial positions are more likely to go to people with special training.

In a supermarket, a packer can progress to clerk, assistant department head, department head, assistant manager, and then manager of the store.

In both restaurants and supermarkets, often it is necessary to change jobs in order to attain a promotion; any extra training you have will be helpful. Many people go into business for themselves, and franchises are available in both restaurant and food store operations.

Points to Consider Before Going into This Field

The food service industry offers a wide open area for employment for the future. There are a variety of jobs, many of them lacking trained people, and the field is unlikely to be seriously affected by technological developments. As people have more money, they spend more on food and more on eating out. There are good chances for advancement for a person with ambition, willingness to avail himself of special courses and training programs.

One drawback is the hours. Restaurant workers often work split shifts—on duty for a few hours at each meal time, with time off in between. Night hours are also common. Nights, weekends, and holidays are popular times in restaurants, and many employees have to work during those periods.

While many restaurants are clean, modern and well-equipped, some smaller ones are less desirable. All restaurants require workers to spend a long time on their feet, work near hot ovens, and lift heavy trays and other objects. There are work hazards such as injury from knives, broken china, or spills on wet floors.

Supermarket employees also have irregular hours, often working evenings, Saturdays and Sundays. They also tend to be on their feet all day and often have to do a lot of lifting.

Women are employed heavily in the food-service industry, but mainly in lower-paying and lower-status positions, almost none as store managers.

For more information, write:

Home Study Program
250 Warren Hall
Cornell University
Ithaca, New York 14850
Ask for: information on home study courses.

The Culinary Institute of America, Inc.
Hyde Park, New York 12538
Ask for: a list of schools and colleges offering courses in restaurant jobs.

Council on Hotel, Restaurant and Institutional Education
1522 K Street N. W.
Washington, D. C. 20005
Ask for: a list of school and colleges offering courses in restaurant jobs.

National Association of Food Chains
1725 Eye Street N. W.
Washington, D. C. 20006
Ask for: information on careers in food retailing.

National Association of Retail Grocers of the U.S., Inc.
Suite 620

2000 Spring Road
Oak Brook, Illinois 60521
Ask for: information on careers in food retailing.

Educational Director
National Restaurant Association
1530 North Lake Shore Drive
Chicago, Illinois 60610

Information Service Manager
Super Market Institute
200 East Ontario Street
Chicago, Illinois 60611
Ask for: *Sources for Career Opportunities in Food Retailing.*

Also contact:

For information on courses in nearby schools relating to restaurant work, write to your local Director of Vocational Education, your superintendant of schools, or your State Director of Vocational Education at the Department of Education at your state capital.

Baking Industry

The Job

The baking industry is one of the largest of the food services. Over 350,000 people work in a wide variety of occupations. Some workers make, wrap and pack bakery products. Others deliver them to stores, homes, and restaurants. Mechanics maintain and repair the machinery and service delivery trucks. Managers, chemists, sales specialists, and clerical workers also are needed in this industry.

Many employees in this field are employed in large bakery plants. The primary product is bread, but the same general principles apply to other baked goods. Production workers all load and unload machines, keep track of their operations and inspect the product, but there are many different phases of production. Mixers weigh ingredients and mix them in blending machines. They control timing and temperature which causes the dough to rise. When it has

risen, it is poured into other blending machines and mixed with additional flour, liquids, sugar, salt, and shortening. It then goes through another fermenting process and rises again before being shaped.

Dividermen operate the machines which divide the dough according to the weight of the loaf to be produced. The pieces of dough are rolled into balls and dusted with flour in a rounding machine.

Dough molders have machines that press air bubbles out of the dough and form it. Bench hands knead and form dough by hand for fancy shaped rolls or bread, and place it in pans. All dough goes to a final proofing room for an hour and then the ovenmen place it in the oven. Other workers may assist any of these specialties by greasing pans, removing bread, etc. In small bakeries, all-round bakers perform all these steps. In large bakeries they supervise the operations.

After the baked foods leave the oven and cool, the slicing and wrapping machine operators feed the bread into the machines and oversee the slicing and wrapping operations.

Others may work in the icing department as icing mixers, hand icers who work on decorated cakes, or run icing machines. Bakeries also employ receiving and stock clerks, packers and checkers, and machinists to keep machinery and delivery equipment in good shape.

Once baked goods are wrapped, they have to be delivered to consumers and stores. Driver-salesmen or routemen work for either wholesale bakeries or home-service bakeries. They have particular routes and deliver the baked goods to grocery stores and homes and collect payment for them. An important part of their job is to increase customers' orders and acquire new customers. At the end of the day, the driver-salesman returns unsold goods to the bakers, reports the days's business and turns in the money he's collected. He also suggests items he thinks people will buy the next day. Large bakeries also employ route supervisors who are in charge of six to ten driver-salesmen. Chain grocery store bakers employ truckdrivers who deliver large vans of baked goods to the company's stores. Administrators are included among other bakery employees. In a small bakery, the proprietor coordinates everything from purchase of raw materials to delivery of product.

Many large baking companies have laboratories and test kitchens where chemists, home economists and other technicians test ingredients and formulas for baked items. In small establishments, many baking operations are done by hand and five or six employees do all the work. These shops afford the beginner an opportunity to learn all aspects of the trade.

Bakeries are located almost everywhere, but more than half of all industrial bakeries are in

New York, Pennsylvania, California, Ohio, Illinois, New Jersey, Texas, and Massachusetts.

What You Need Personally

A baker must be in good health. Most states require a health certificate stating that the worker is free from communicable diseases. The irregular working hours and exposure to extreme temperatures also require good physical condition.

What Education and Training You Need

Training in baking varies according to the job. Some workers, such as slicing machine operators, can be trained in a few days, while baking specialists require at least three or four years training. Professional and administrative workers often need a college degree.

In many large bakeries, untrained workers are put to work as helpers, training with experienced bakers to learn the trade. Some places have formal apprenticeship programs and select people from among the helpers to participate in these programs.

Apprenticeship applicants should be between eighteen and twenty-six years of age and have a high school or vocational school education. The programs last three or four years and include on-the-job training in all baking operations and related classroom instruction.

Some training programs for bakers are being operated under the Manpower Development and Training Act. There are also available courses in vocational schools and the Armed Forces which may shorten apprenticeship periods.

To acquire baking expertise, experienced bakers can attend special schools. The American Institute of Baking offers many courses for people in this field and even has a post-bachelor's degree program for those who want managerial positions in the industry. The school also has a scholarship program for young people who want to enter the field.

The Baking Science and Technology course at the American Institute of Baking lasts twenty weeks and instruction includes lectures, laboratory, and shop courses. Classes cover the science of bakery ingredients, standard laboratory and experimental baking procedure, formula construction, product scoring, sweet goods production, bakery equipment and bakeshop mechanics, nutrition, sanitation and safety, personnel supervision, and modern management practice.

Other schools with baking programs include the William Hood Dunwoody Industrial Institute, which offers a sixteen-week course in the production of bread and rolls and a sixteen-week course in the production of cakes and pastries. You don't need a high school diploma, but you do need at least six months experience in baking. Kansas State university offers the only four-year program in Baking Science and Management in the country. Oklahoma State Technical College offers a full semester or a forty-eight-week course and two sixteen-week courses in cake and pastry and variety bread and roll production.

Some bakeries have apprentice programs for maintenance jobs; others hire only skilled maintenance men. Driver-salesmen or truckdrivers should have a high school education and usually start as stock clerks, packers, or checkers. Applicants for promotion are sometimes tested for driving ability and must be able to get a chauffeur's license. They may receive some classroom instruction in sales, display and delivery procedures, but get most training on the job.

What the Occupation Has to Offer

There may be fewer job openings in this field in the 1970s. The demand for bakery products is expected to rise, but more efficient production will offset this. There will, however, be a need for more truck drivers to service expanding sales territories and more maintenance workers to keep machinery and equipment in working order.

Earnings for bakery workers vary according to job and geographical location. Wage rates are usually higher in the west and north. On the average, an all-round baker makes between $3.55 and $5.03 an hour. Other production bakers make from $2.83 to $4.72 an hour.

Some bakeries run night shifts, which pay more, but this practice is being eliminated as freezing processes make it possible to prepare baked goods in advance.

Driver-salesmen usually get a guaranteed minimum salary plus a percentage of sales. Salaries average anywhere from $87 to $175 per week, plus the sales percentage. Truckdrivers are paid by the hour and make from $3.15 to $4.18 an hour.

There are opportunities for advancement in most areas of the baking industry. Production bakers can become all-round bakers or department supervisors. Those who have special skills in fancy cake or pie making may find jobs in hotel or restaurant bakeries. Some all-round bakers open their own shops. Driver-salesmen may be promoted to route supervisors or sales managers.

Points to Consider Before Going into This Field

Although working conditions in bakeries are good, there is still some strenuous physical work involved and oven areas can be hot and uncomfortable.

About twenty percent of industrial bakery workers are women, most of whom are clerical workers or operators of simple machines. Very few women are bakers.

For more information, write:

American Bakers Association
Industrial Relations Department
1700 Pennsylvania Avenue N. W.
Washington, D. C. 20006
Ask for: *Careers Unlimited in the Modern Baking Industry*, Free. Also ask for information on job opportunities and accredited schools giving courses in baking.

American Institute of Baking
400 East Ontario Street
Chicago, Illinois 60611

Department of Human Resources Development
Mail Control Unit
800 Capitol Mall
Sacramento, California 95814
Ask for: *Bakery Occupations*, No. 330, Free.

The Baking Department
William Hood Dunwoody Industrial Institute
818 Wayzata Boulevard
Minneapolis, Minnesota 55403

Kansas State University
Department of Grain Science and Industry
Manhattan, Kansas 66502

Oklahoma State Technical College
Okmulgee, Oklahoma 74447

Associated Retail Bakers of America
731–735 West Sheridan Road
Chicago, Illinois 60613
Ask for: *A Baker is . . .* , Free. (Includes job information, training and scholarship information).

Cook and Chef

The Job

About one out of four meals is eaten outside the home. The food-service business is booming and begging for trained people. The cook has the most essential job of all. His responsibilities vary according to the place where he works. In a small restaurant, a cook—perhaps assisted by a short-order cook or a kitchen helper—prepares all the food, which is usually relatively simple. Desserts may be purchased from a bakery.

Larger restaurants have more varied menus and their staffs usually prepare all food served right in their kitchens. The staff usually includes several cooks and kitchen helpers and a head cook, sometimes called a chef, who coordinates the work. The head cook or chef usually prepares certain foods himself and decides on the sizes of food portions served. He sometimes plans menus and purchases food supplies. He has the important responsibility of seeing that the food served looks attractive and tastes good. Some chefs have such skill at creating new dishes that they acquire international reputations.

The other cooks in large restaurants usually have a special assignment and often a title, such as pastry cook, fry cook, roast cook, or vegetable cook.

Most of the 740,000 cooks and chefs in this country work in restaurants, but some work in public and private schools, colleges, hotels, nursing homes, hospitals, industrial plants, day care centers, jails, private clubs, or prepare food for airliners.

What You Need Personally

If you want to be a cook, you'll need a keen sense of taste and smell. You should be clean, have physical stamina, and be able to work under pressure. A head cook must be organized and able to give instructions. Some states require that cooks and chefs have health certificates.

What Education and Training You Need

Most cooks, especially those who work in small eating places, learn their skills on the job as kitchen helpers. Occasionally they are trained as apprentices by large hotels or restaurants, or by unions.

To work in a large restaurant or hotel, a cook usually has to have some training. Many public and private vocational schools offer such courses. Other courses—often open only to high school graduates—are given in technical schools and junior community colleges or sponsored by restaurant associations, hotel management groups, or trade unions. The courses range from a few months to over two years in length. The federal Manpower Development and Training Act also has some programs to train people to be cooks.

Experts estimate there are about 17,000 openings for chefs—not cooks—in large restaurants, clubs, and hotels. Schools, like the Culinary Institute of America, offer a two-year training program leading to an associate degree to prepare you for such jobs. Most cooking courses involve a lot of time in actual practice in well-equipped kitchens. The student learns the art of baking, broiling, and frying, and other methods of food preparation. Instruction is also given in the use and care of kitchen equipment. Other areas of study include selecting and storing food, determining the size of portions, planning menus, and buying food supplies in quantity. Hotel and restaurant sanitation and public health aspects of food handling are also taught.

What the Occupation Has to Offer

There should be moderate increases in jobs for cooks and chefs in the 1970s due to the opening of more restaurants and hotels. As people have more money and leisure, they tend to do more traveling and eating in restaurants. More students attending schools and colleges, and more women working outside the home are expected to have a positive effect on the profession. Also more people can be expected to eat regularly in hospitals and other institutions with food facilities.

The greatest number of starting jobs for cooks will be in small restaurants and other places where simple food is served. There is a shortage of highly skilled chefs and cooks, so anyone with traning should have no trouble finding jobs in hotels and large restaurants.

Earnings vary considerably for cooks and chefs depending on the type of establishment and geographical location. Most are not covered by union contracts, so figures are limited. But for those who are covered, wages for assistant cooks range from $1.47 to $4.86 an hour; cooks earn $2.02 to $4.12, and chefs from $2.22 to $4.65. Large restaurants and hotels may pay considerably more and a chef with a major reputation can earn over $25,000 a year.

Most restaurant cooks also receive at least one free meal a day and are provided with uniforms. They usually receive paid vacations and holidays and various types of health insurance. Cooks who work in schools usually work school hours and only for nine months of the year.

Chances for advancement are quite good for cooks, particularly if they have training. Many institutions give on-the-job training for cafeteria workers who wish to become cooks and may select cooks from the workshops they conduct.

Inexperienced workers can usually qualify as assistant cooks or fry cooks after a few months of on-the-job training, but developing sufficient skills to become head cook or chef may take several years. Some acquire new skills by changing jobs frequently.

Some cooks go into business for themselves as caterers or restaurant owners or become instructors at vocational schools.

Points to Consider Before Going into This Field

Steady employment can be found in this field. A cook can be employed virtually anywhere, and many positions are available in attractive resort areas.

Disadvantages to the job are that cooks must spend long periods of time on their feet and work near hot ovens. They often have to lift heavy pots and other objects and, particularly in small eating places, the kitchens may not be especially pleasant, though most large kitchens are air-conditioned.

Almost three out of every five cooks are women, including about half the cooks in restaurants and many of those employed in schools and hospitals. Men are usually cooks in hotels and private clubs and most head cooks and almost all chefs are men.

For more information, write:

The Educational Institute
American Hotel and Motel Association
888 7th Avenue
New York, New York 10019
Ask for: information on job opportunities for cooks and chefs.

Council on Hotel, Restaurant and Institutional Education
1522 K Street N. W.
Washington, D. C. 20005
Ask for: a list of public and private schools offering courses in cooking.

Culinary Institute of America, Inc.
Hyde Park, New York 12538
Ask for: information on job opportunities for cooks and chefs.

Department of Human Resources Development
Mail Control Unit
800 Capitol Mall
Sacramento, California 95814
Ask for: *Chefs and Cooks (Fine Restaurants)* No. 93, Free.

Educational Director
National Restaurant Association
153 North Lake Shore Drive
Chicago, Illinois 60610
Ask for: information on job opportunities for cooks and chefs.

Also contact:

For more information on training in this field, contact your state employment service about the Manpower Development and Training Act courses.

Also, see descriptions of food-service industry and baking industry, pages 365-369.

Transportation

Traffic Management

The Job

Industrial traffic managers and their assistants arrange transportation of raw materials and finished products for industrial firms. After analyzing transportation options, traffic managers choose the most efficient methods of transportation—rail, air, road, water, pipeline, or a combination of these—the routes, and the particular carriers to be used for each job.

Traffic managers must have thorough knowledge of the complex pricing structures of carriers, knowledge of numerous routes, and services available as well as an understanding of the regulatory laws involved. A well-staffed traffic department is a necessity in almost every large manufacturing or commercial operation today. The how, why, when, and where of transporting goods can often make the difference between profit and loss, between holding or losing customers.

The traffic manager and his staff specify the methods of transportation, sizes and types of vehicles used, routes to be employed, when to seek a more favorable rate or classification, what services-in-transit are to be used, and how to do all this most efficiently and economically in the light of existing tariffs, classifications, and regulations. In many companies the industrial traffic manager supervises the shipping and receiving departments, helps decide the location of new plants and consults on the packaging and handling of products and the design of shipping and storage containers. To protect favorable rates for his company, he may participate in Interstate Commerce Commission or State Commission hearings, industry conference, and rate-committee hearings.

The carrier traffic manager works for one of our country's varied freight-handling lines—railroads, steamship companies, airlines, motor carriers, or freight forwarders. One of the most important functions of the traffic manager is to attract new business for his particular company through the establishment of competitive rates and the maintenance of company records of safety and efficiency.

Since many aspects of transportation are subject to federal, state, and local government regulations, traffic managers must be familiar with these and other legal matters that apply to their companies' shipping operations. Senior traffic managers represent their companies in front of rate-making and regulatory bodies, such as the Interstate Commerce Commission, state commissions and local traffic bureaus.

Traffic managers are employed throughout the world. Import-export traffic management is an open field, and the opportunity to travel while working in a lucrative job makes this appealing to many people. Here, knowledge of a foreign language, although not a requirement, can be a distinct advantage. The federal government and the military employ traffic managers as well.

What You Need Personally

Anyone interested in the field of traffic management should be reliable, competitive, and personable. Competitiveness is a must, since a large part of the job is the establishment of competitive rates. This is a field of rapid advancement, and ambition is an important quality in any applicant. Because of the nature of the work, traffic managers are often under pressure; anyone interested in this field should work well under strain. The ability to deal easily with people is also important. Traffic managers are doers, people who can give orders and make decisions with confidence.

What Education and Training You Need

In the field of traffic management a high school diploma or its equivalent is a must. For some kinds of work, college training may be required—or at least two years of college work in the specialized field of transportation and traffic management. More than 100 junior colleges, colleges, and universities offer courses in traffic management. Correspondence schools are also good places to start your education, or perhaps enrollment at one of the private vocational schools which specialize in traffic management would fill your training needs. You can take courses lasting from twenty weeks to two years, which will cost from $200 to $1,400. A few scholarships are offered by companies employing traffic managers.

What the Occupation Has to Offer

The field of traffic management is new, and job possibilities are almost unlimited. All large corporations and many smaller companies employ traffic managers. Starting salaries in this field are about $8,000 for the college graduate, lower for beginners with less schooling. Advancement is swift; anyone with ability can soon reach executive status. There is an emphasis on continued education in traffic management. Taking company-sponsored courses or others is often necessary to keep up with this changing field. Many traffic managers become vice-presidents, a tribute to their importance in the world of business.

Points to Consider Before Going into This Field

The advantages of working in traffic management are many, rapid advancement, high salaries, and open job markets being just a few. The person with the desire to continue learning and keep abreast of transportation developments will do best. Pressure is a part of this exciting, competitive work; it is not a field for the sedate under-ambitious person. Most traffic managers are men, but both men and women are sought, and traffic-management schools accept both if they meet enrollment standards.

For more information, write:

Academy of Advanced Traffic
50 Broadway
New York, New York 10004

Public Relations Department
Association of American Railroads
1920 L Street, N.W.
Washington, D.C. 20036

College of Advanced Traffic
22 West Madison Street
Chicago, Illinois 60602

International Correspondence Schools
Scranton, Pennsylvania 18515

Additional Reading:

Heine, Robert E., *Your Future in Traffic Management*, New York: Richards Rosen Press, Inc., 1967.

Liston, Robert A., *Your Career in Transportation*, New York: Julian Messner, 1966.

McGill, John P. and Robinson, W. L., *Aim for a Job in the Trucking Industry*, New York: Richards Rosen Press, Inc., 1972.

Truck Driving

The Job

More than 2.5 million truck, bus, and taxicab drivers moved passengers and goods over highways and city streets in 1970. They transported thousands of products and millions of people every day.

Some men who work in trucking spend practically all their working time behind the wheel. Others are occupied with loading and unloading goods, making pickups and deliveries and collecting money. Still others, like the routeman, spend a good deal of their time selling. The main job in the trucking industry is that of the truckdriver, whose responsibility it is to transport products throughout the country. Truckdrivers can be separated into three catagories: the over-the-road driver, the local driver and the routeman. The over-the-road driver spends most of his time driving large tractor-trailers or single-unit trucks long distances over major highways. He transports goods of great value which must be delivered safely and on time. Little if any of his time is spent in the loading or unloading of his truck, except for long-distance moving-van driving. Local drivers stay close to home and in many cases are deliverymen. They may also have to operate machinery, such as that found in oil trucks or the hoist equipment used in the transportation of machinery. Collecting receipts, filling out charts and collecting C.O.D. payments may also be part of the local driver's duties. The routeman is not only a truckdriver but also a salesman. Although a postman is sometimes referred to as a routeman, the term usually is applied to supervisors of deliverymen. The supervisor maps new routes, maintains office records, and handles customer relations.

Jobs for truckdrivers can be found everywhere, but the greatest concentration is in and around large cities. Over-the-road drivers work for private or for-hire carriers. Private carriers are businesses such as chain food stores that are large enough to support their own truck fleets. For-hire carriers deal with the general public and contract to ship goods for companies without private truck fleets. Local truckdrivers work mostly for businesses that deliver their own goods. Meat packers, department stores, and dry cleaners are a few types of businesses that utilize local truckdrivers. The federal government also employs local drivers, the best example being the post office's use of mailmen. Routemen are employed by both wholesale and retail businesses. Most routemen work for companies that provide personal services or distribute food.

What You Need Personally

Personal qualifications for drivers vary depending upon the type of driving involved and sometimes upon the standards of the employing firm. Standards for over-the-road drivers are the highest. The USDT (United States Department of Transportation) minimum requirements for interstate and foreign commerce states that the driver must be 21 years old and in good health. Vision, with or without glasses, should be at least 20/40. Hearing must also be good. Prospective over-the-road drivers must be able to speak and read English. The driver needs at least one year of driving experience and a good driving record. A chauffeur's license is also required. Road and written tests are given in order to demonstrate the applicant's driving skills and knowledge of regulations. Many firms will not hire over-the-road drivers less than 25 years old; they also may specify height and weight requirements.

Standards for local drivers are basically the same as for over-the-road drivers but usually are less stringent. Routemen must have sales ability and knowledge of their product in addition to driving skills. Simple arithmetic is needed, and most employers require routemen to have high school educations.

What Education and Training You Need

Driver-training courses are offered in many vocational and high schools and are given by private companies. Training methods vary between companies. Many include formal tests, indoctrination courses, physical examinations, and a break-in period. A course in automotive mechanics is recommended, and routemen are encouraged to take courses in arithmetic and salesmanship.

Most over-the-road drivers have local driving experience and progress from small trucks to larger ones. The high standards for over-the-road drivers are more strictly adhered to than those for local drivers, whose standards may be lowered when there are not enough applicants for jobs.

Tractor-trailers used in over-the-road hauling usually cost between $25,000 and $40,000, and the load may be worth more than $100,000. The owners of such valuable equipment only employ experienced drivers who also can accept responsibility.

Applicants for jobs as over-the-road drivers are required to pass a physical examination, which is usually paid for by the employer. In addition to the written traffic and driving tests, some employers give tests to measure factors such as sharpness and field of vision, reaction time, ability to judge speed, and emotional stability. The last step in the selection of drivers is the road test. The applicant is expected to demonstrate his ability to handle, under a variety of driving conditions, a vehicle of the type and size he will operate in regular service. A few states require such a test before licensing a driver to operate a tractor-trailer.

A man may begin as a helper to a local driver and gradually work into a regular driving shift. Routemen can begin as helpers but may also get industry or plant jobs in order to learn the business and then proceed into driving jobs when there are openings.

A small number of private vocational schools offer truck-driving courses. Students receive instructions in driving large vehicles in close quarters and on the highway, with emphasis on safe driving practices. Instructions also are given on the care of equipment and freight, and compliance with federal, state, and local regulations. Completion of such a course does not insure immediate employment as a driver. Graduates frequently must start as material handlers or drivers' helpers and advance to driving jobs. Prospective students should enroll only in truck-driving courses offered by schools which have been certified by their states. Accredited schools are approved for financial assistance to veterans under the G. I. Bill. Financial aid programs are offered to nonveterans by most large trucking companies.

What the Occupation Has to Offer

The trucking industry is a growing field of employment. Earnings are relatively high and many over-the-road drivers earn more than $200 a week, with the average about $12,600 a year. Experienced drivers can earn considerably more. Local drivers and routemen don't usually earn as much, but they too make a comfortable living, about $9,000 to $14,000 a year. Advancement in the trucking industry is limited and usually comes with seniority. Older drivers get the easier and more profitable driving runs. There are opportunities for a few drivers to advance to safety supervisor, driver supervisor, or dispatcher.

Points to Consider Before Going into This Field

Truck driving offers employment to the young man who doesn't want to go to college or learn a craft or technical skill. This is an opportunity to make a good living with fairly good working conditions. You may also enjoy the freedom from close supervision and the frequent contacts with people.

Truckdrivers are well paid and have many advantages afforded them by union membership. Most drivers receive six or more holidays per year. Paid vacations run from one to four weeks, depending on length of service. Health insurance and pension plans are also widespread in the trucking industry.

One of the main disadvantages is that opportunities for promotion are limited. Seniority is the only common means of advancement. Working conditions vary greatly in the industry. Truck driving is both physically and mentally demanding, but conditions have improved as a result of better highways, more comfortable seating, power steering and air-conditioned cabs. Over-the-road drivers frequently work at night and spend time away from home. Some truckers, such as over-the-road drivers, can expect to be away from their families two or three days a week. This isn't the most ideal job for family men. Local drivers usually work only during the day. A large number of trucking industry employees are members of the Industrial Brotherhood of Teamsters, Chauffeurs, Warehousemen and Helpers of America.

Truck driving jobs are held almost entirely by men. Nearly all women employees in the trucking industry are clerical workers.

For more information, write:

Educational Services
Public Relations Department
American Trucking Associations, Inc.
1616 P. Street, N. W.
Washington, D. C. 20036
Ask for: *Opportunities in the Trucking Industry.*

Department of Human Resources Development
Mail Control Unit
800 Capitol Mall
Sacramento, California 95814
Ask for: *Long Haul Truck Driver* No. 255, Free.

Other Manual Occupations

Boilermaker

The Job

In many industries and aboard many ships enormous receptacles are used to hold gasses and liquids under pressure. Skilled craftsmen, such as boilermakers, layout men, and fitup men assemble, repair, and disassemble these boilers, tanks, vats, pressure vessels, heat exchangers, and other metal containers. Boilermakers have all-round skills and are usually involved in construction and repair. Layout men and fitup men most often are employed in the manufacturing of new boilers and heavy tanks.

Boilermakers assemble prefabricated parts and fittings at construction sites where pressure vessels are used, or assemble complete units at fabricating plants. After the boilers are assembled, they are checked for defects. Boilermakers also maintain and repair pressure vessels in industrial power plants. Installation and repair of boilers and similar vessels must comply with state and local laws.

Boilermakers who do repair work diagnose the problem, dismantle the unit and make minor repairs, such as patching weak spots with metal or strengthening a joint, or more comprehensive repairs that may require replacing an entire section. The boilermaker must be familiar with welding and riveting tools, power shears, power rolls, and oxyacetylene torches. He may also use rigging equipment (hoists, jacks, and rollers, for example) when assembling units.

Layout men prepare metals that are used to manufacture boilers, tanks, etc. They mark curves, lines, points, and dimensions on metal plates and tubes to instruct other workers who will cut or shape the parts. They work with compasses, dividers, scales, surface gauges, hammers and scribers; and following blueprints or sketches lay out parts to scale.

Before final assembly of boilers at construction sites, fitup men fit and temporarily assemble parts in the shop. They bolt or tack-weld parts and correct any irregularities on parts, such as pipes and nozzles, that would prevent a tight fit. To make sure parts meet specifications, the fitup man follows blueprints and drawings. The equipment for his job includes hammers, sledges, wrenches and punches, welding machines, drills, and grinding tools.

Of the 25,000 craftsmen employed in this field most are found in manufacturing plants that produce boilers and other pressure vessels; nearly all layout and fitup men work in these plants. Boilermakers also work in the construction industries, in maintenance and repair departments of oil refineries, electric and gas utilities, iron and steel manufacturers, and railroads or for the federal government.

Most boilermaking craftsmen work in the Middle Atlantic and East North Central regions where the metalworking industries are concentrated.

What You Need Personally

Good health, physical stamina, and agility are important in this job because of the heavy equipment involved. You should have coordination, manual dexterity, a mechanical aptitude and should enjoy working with your hands without minding filth. Because much of this work is done cooperatively, every boilermaker should be able to get along with fellow workers.

What Education and Training You Need

Graduation from high school or vocational school is recommended. High school courses in mathematics, blueprint reading, and metal shop are good background.

Most layout and fitup men get their training

on the job. It usually takes two years to qualify as an experienced layout or fitup man in a mass-production shop; workers move from helper status to craftsman.

A boilermaker may also learn his craft on the job, but a formal apprenticeship lasting four years is recommended. Such programs include approximately 600 hours of technical instruction in subjects such as mathematics, blueprint reading, welding techniques, and shop metalurgical science covering stress capacities of metals. On-the-job training includes about 8,000 hours of work experience. The apprentice works under a journeyman boilermaker, learning the techniques, tools and machines needed in the trade. (See pages 52-63.)

What the Occupation Has to Offer

There should be an increase in jobs in this field during the next decade, although most openings will fill vacated positions. Public and private utilities, as well as chemical, petroleum, steel, and shipbuilding industries will be using boiler products as will construction firms and atomic-energy facilities. Some growth will be offset, however, by more efficient production techniques and equipment.

Earnings are relatively high for these workers, although rates vary by industry, location, and the experience and skill of each employee. Boilermakers employed by the construction industry for field assembly and installation usually earn more than those who work in industrial plants, although their work is less regular. The average wage for these workers is almost $7 an hour. In industrial plants, minimum hourly wage rates for these job categories exceed $3 an hour; most workers earn more. In general, layout men have the highest incomes, followed by boilermakers, then by fitup men. Most of these workers are union members and generally receive all the usual fringe benefits. They can become foremen for contractors specializing in boiler installation and repair or may go into business for themselves, but opportunities for promotion are otherwise limited.

Points to Consider Before Going into This Field

There are a number of advantages to this work. Jobs exist in most geographical areas, and the work requires a variety of skills. Craftsmen in plants are assured steady work; their hours are usually regular. Pay is good, and no financial investment in training is necessary.

This work does have some disadvantages, however. It is dirty, and work sites are often damp, wet, or badly ventilated. The boilermaker must work in cramped positions for long periods of time, and noise levels around him can be deafening. A lot of heavy lifting is involved. There can be injuries if safety precautions are not carefully observed. This is considered a

man's occupation; and physical examinations are given to prospective employees.

For more information, write:

American Boiler Manufacturers' Association
Suite 317
1500 Wilson Boulevard
Arlington, Virginia 22209

International Brotherhood of Boilermakers, Iron Shipbuilders, Blacksmiths, Forgers and Helpers
Eighth Street at State Avenue
Kansas City, Kansas 66101

Electroplater

The Job

Many items are electroplated to give them a protective surface or more attractive appearance. Such products as automobile bumpers, silverware, costume jewelry, electrical appliances, and jet-engine parts are coated with chromium, nickel, silver, gold, or other metals. The process involves the use of a plating solution and electric current or electrolysis. A process called electroforming is used in the manufacturing of spray-paint masks, search-light reflectors, and molds used to manufacture plastic.

While platers in production shops usually perform relatively simple and specialized assignments, a plater with general skills is often responsible for many different tasks. He may analyze solutions, calculate time and current needed for various types of plating, order supplies, or do many kinds of small-lot plating.

When an item is to be electroplated, the parts not requiring plating are covered with lacquer, rubber, or tape. The item is scoured in a cleansing bath, then placed in the plating solution. It must be checked periodically since mistakes are expensive. Platers must use micrometers, calipers, and electronic devices to check their work for defects that are often invisible.

About half of the 17,000 electroplaters in the United States work for independent shops that specialize in metal plating and polishing for manufacturing firms and individuals. The rest work for plants that manufacture plumbing fixtures, cooking utensils, wire products, electric appliances, electronic components, motor vehicles, mechanical measuring instruments, and other metal products.

Although electroplaters work throughout the country, most jobs surround the metal-working centers in the Northeast and Midwest. New York, Cleveland, Chicago, Providence, Newark, Detroit, Los Angeles, and San Francisco all have large numbers of electroplaters.

What You Need Personally

It is important to be careful in this work, because some solutions used are poisonous and because mistakes in plating can cost the company quite a bit of money. Sometimes lifting is required, and an electroplater should be able to lift and carry objects weighing as much as 100 pounds.

What Education and Training You Need

High school or vocational school training is advisable for an electroplater. Courses in chemistry, electronics, physics, mathematics, and blueprint reading are valuable background. Many branches of the American Electroplaters Society offer basic courses in electroplating, and one- or two-year courses are available in some vocational schools, technical institutes and colleges.

Most electroplaters learn their trade on the job. Training for platers who perform specialized tasks in production shops can be completed in relatively short time. All-round platers usually need about three years to learn the trade. A small percentage of platers work for three to four years as apprentices in programs that combine on-the-job training with classroom instruction in chemistry, the properties of metals and electricity as applied to plating. By the end of the training period, these electroplaters are able to do plating without supervision, determine cleaning methods, make solutions, examine plating results, and supervise less skilled helpers.

What the Occupation Has to Offer

During the 1970s, employment opportunities for electroplaters are expected to show a modest increase, with most openings the result of experienced workers retiring, dying, or changing occupations. Electroplating is expected to be used with a larger group of metals and plastics in the future.

Although there are no national figures on electroplaters' earnings, a survey in late 1970

showed that most experienced platers earned $2 to $4 an hour. Trainees made 60 to 70 percent of that. Many platers belong to unions, and most receive benefits and paid holidays from their employers.

A skilled and qualified electroplater can advance to foreman in his shop or department.

Points to Consider Before Going into This Field

Electroplating is a useful skill with a steady future. There are some occupational hazards, however. Humidity and odor are problems in most electroplating plants, and many of the solutions used are highly acid, alkaline, or poisonous. Ventilation systems and safety devices help to reduce these hazards, as do protective clothing.

For more information, write:

American Electroplaters' Society, Inc.
56 Melmore Gardens
East Orange, New Jersey 07017

Department of Human Resources Development
Mail Control Unit
800 Capitol Mall
Sacramento, California 95814
Ask for: *Electroplater* No. 116, Free.

National Association of Metal Finishers
248 Lorraine Avenue
Upper Montclair, New Jersey 07043

Foreman

The Job

In order to see that work is performed correctly and activities are coordinated, all industries employ foremen. Millions of dollars worth of equipment, material, and labor are under their control. They supervise the work of skilled and unskilled laborers alike in all kinds of operations: assembly, service, loading, or almost any similar activity you can name. Some foremen are given titles that are used only in a particular industry; in construction, they are known as overseers, pushers, straw bosses or gang leaders, for instance. A number of foremen work at a specific craft in addition to supervising other workers. This is common in construction.

A foreman's primary responsibility is to provide discipline and guidance to workers under him. He passes on company policy and gives instructions for various work assignments. Foremen schedule work loads, keep records on employees and production, sometimes prepare reports on production, cost, personnel, and safety and participate in meetings to discuss these topics.

Almost 1.5 million foremen are employed in this country. They are found in every state and in every business and government agency that

employs blue-collar workers. More than half the foremen work in manufacturing firms that produce machinery, metals, transportation equipment, food, chemicals, and paper products. Construction, trade, and service industries also employ many foremen.

What You Need Personally

A foreman must be able to communicate well, command respect, and motivate employees to perform without causing resentment. He should also be industrious and dependable.

What Education and Training You Need

Foremen are almost always promoted through the ranks and are expected to be thoroughly familiar with the work to be done, company policy, and their fellow workers. Performance on the job and acquired skills are more important than education, although most foremen are high school graduates. In some of the technical industries, persons with college training in business administration, industrial relations, mathematics, engineering, or science are hired as foremen. The more jobs a worker has mastered, the more likely he is to be made a foreman.

What the Occupation Has to Offer

There should be some increase in foremen's jobs during the 1970s as business operations grow larger and more foremen are needed to supervise individual processes. Although most

foremen will continue to be in manufacturing, there will be many new positions in construction, trade, service, and public utilities.

Earnings for foremen vary widely depending on the industry, geographical area and each employee's experience. Foremen usually make from 10 to 40 percent more than the workers they supervise. They are usually salaried and not paid for overtime. The average salary for foremen is almost $10,000 a year.

Foremen who show good ability, particularly those with higher education, can advance to positions such as department head, general foreman, or plant manager. In some businesses, foremen who acquire enough skills go into business for themselves.

Points to Consider Before Going into This Field

Most foremen are well paid for handling responsible, prestigious positions. Their work is not usually as physically strenuous as that done by the workers they supervise. A foreman is in a good position for promotion within the company.

There are some disadvantages to the job. The foreman may sometimes feel as if he's in a no-man's land—neither labor nor management. Because of the responsibility of his position, he may find himself working longer hours than other workers and in some instances he will be getting as dirty and tired as they do.

Although nearly 90 percent of foremen are male, women are occasionally promoted to this position, particularly in the apparel, electrical-machinery, leather-products, and laundry-and-drycleaning industries.

For more information, write:

American Management Association
135 West 50th Street
New York, New York 10020

Foundry Workers

Thousands of the products we use from engines to pots and pans are made from metal castings produced by foundry workers. A casting is used to form molten metal into a particular shape. First a mold is prepared with a cavity in it that has been shaped by a pattern or model of the object to be cast. The foundry worker then pours heated metal into the mold cavity, where it cools and solidifies, emerging as a railroad-car wheel or missile component, or cast-iron frying pan.

Foundries employ many types of help, mostly skilled, and are generally located near plants that use castings. Many of the jobs available in foundries will be described in this section. (See also pages 248-249.)

Employment opportunities in foundries will remain about the same through the 1970s because of newly automated equipment; job opportunities for unskilled workers will continue to decrease.

Most foundry workers are male because the work, other than for coremakers (see below), is strenuous.

For more information, write:

American Foundrymen's Society
Golf and Wolf Roads
Des Plaines, Illinois 60016

Foundry Educational Foundation
1138 Terminal Tower
Cleveland, Ohio 44113
Ask for: list of job opportunities and scholarship grants.

Gray and Ductile Iron Founders' Society, Inc.
Cast Metals Federation Building
20611 Center Ridge Road
Rocky River, Ohio 44116

International Molders' and Allied Workers' Union
1225 East McMillan Street
Cincinnati, Ohio 45206

National Foundry Association
9838 Roosevelt Road
P. O. Box 76
Westchester, Illinois 60156

Non-Ferrous Founders' Society, Inc.
21010 Center Ridge Road
Cleveland, Ohio 44116

Also contact:
Local foundries, state employment services, state apprenticeship agencies.

Coremaker

The Job

A coremaker prepares the "cores" which are placed in molds to form the hollow cavities required in metal castings. Poured metal solidifies around the core so that when the core is removed, the desired shape remains.

A core may be made by hand or by machine. In both cases, prepared sand is packed into a core box (a block of wood or metal into which a hollow space the size and shape of the desired core has been cut). After the core has been removed from the box, it is hardened by baking or other methods. When hand methods are used, the coremaker works with mallets and other handtools to pack and ram sand into the core box.

In hand coremaking, you may work as a bench coremaker, making small cores on a workbench, or as a floor coremaker, producing bulky

cores on the foundry floor. There is a wide range of skill required here. As an all-round hand coreman (journeyman), you prepare large and intricate cores; you may also be employed as a supervisor. Some kinds of coremaking require a high degree of manual dexterity. Coremaking is repetitive work because you produce large numbers of identical cores.

As a machine coremaker, you operate machines that make sand cores by forcing sand into specially shaped hollow forms, usually through the use of compressed air. You could be required to set up and adjust your machine and do finishing operations on the cores, but coremakers are primarily machine tenders who have their machines adjusted for them and are closely supervised.

What Education and Training You Need

An eighth-grade education is usually the minimum required for coremaking apprentice training; however, some employers require graduation from high school. A skilled hand coremaker will have completed a four-year apprenticeship training program or will have the equivalent in job experience. Only a brief period of on-the-job training is needed for less skilled hand coremaking and for most machine jobs. Other foundry workers may be upgraded to apprentice coremakers. Training in both coremaking and molding is often combined in a single apprenticeship. Apprenticeships are sometimes required for the more difficult machine-coremaking jobs. (See pages 52-63.)

As an apprentice, you work with journeymen coremakers in routine duties and gradually move on to more advanced work, such as making simple cores and operating ovens. During this time you acquire experience in benchwork and floorwork and in the operation of coremaking machines. This training is usually supplemented by classroom instruction covering subjects such as arithmetic and the properties of metals.

What the Occupation Has to Offer

There were about 25,000 coremakers in 1970, and this employment figure is expected to show little or no change through the seventies. Though foundry production is expected to increase, the demand for coremakers will not keep pace because of the growing use of machine-made rather than handmade cores. There will be several hundred job openings each year in order to replace experienced coremakers whose jobs are vacated. Hand coremakers with all-round training may be promoted to supervisor.

Earnings depend on several factors including the specific requirements of the job, the type of metal poured and geographic location. In a 1970 survey of fifty-two labor areas, straight-time average hourly earnings were as follows: floor coremakers, $3.55; bench coremakers, $3.35; machine coremakers, $3.25.

Points to Consider Before Going into This Field

Light coremaking is not very strenuous work, and women are frequently employed.

For more information, write:

Department of Human Resources Development
Mail Control Unit
800 Capitol Mall
Sacramento, California 95814
Ask for: *Molder and Coremaker (Foundry) No. 37, Free.*

See also: page 379.

Molder

The Job

Molders prepare the hollow forms into which molten material is poured. The mold is made by packing and ramming a specially prepared sand around a pattern (a model of the object to be duplicated) in a box called a flask. This flask is usually made in two parts so it can be separated to allow removal of the pattern without damaging the mold cavity. Molten metal is poured into the cavity, and when it solidifies, it forms the casting. As a molder, you use pneumatic-powered rammers and such hand tools as trowels, shovels, and mallets for handling, compacting, and smoothing the sand in molds made by hand.

Most of the 55,000 molders in 1970 were machine-molders; the rest were bench- and

floor- (hand) molders. As a machine-molder, you assemble the flask and pattern on the machine table, fill the flask with prepared sand and operate the machine by levers and pedals. Many molders set up and adjust their own machines, but semiskilled workers operate machines set up by experienced molders or maintenance men.

As a bench-molder, you use hand methods to make molds for smaller castings usually made on the workbench. A floor-molder uses hand methods also, but for larger and bulkier castings which are made on the foundry floor. An all-round hand-molder makes many kinds of molds, while a less skilled man does more repetitive work and specializes in a few simple types of molds.

What You Need Personally

Molding jobs require fairly good physical conditioning. Hand- and floor-molders stand at their work, move a great deal and are frequently required to lift heavy objects. As a hand-molder, you need manual dexterity and good vision.

What Education and Training You Need

An eighth-grade education is usually the minimum requirement for apprenticeship, but many employers prefer applicants with additional education for skilled hand-molding or machine-molding jobs.

Completion of a four-year apprentice training program or the equivalent in job experience is needed to become a journeyman molder and thus qualify both for all-round hand-molding and for specialized or supervisory jobs. This kind of training is preferred for some machine-molding jobs also.

As an apprentice, you work under the supervision of journeymen, and about half your training is devoted directly to molding. You begin with simple jobs such as shoveling sand and go on to ramming molds, withdrawing patterns and setting cores. You also learn to operate various types of molding machines. As training progresses, you make complete molds, beginning with simple ones and advancing to the complex. Training includes both floor and benchwork, and you may be asked to work in other foundry departments in order to develop an all-round knowledge of foundry methods and practices.

Apprentices usually receive at least 144 hours of classroom instruction every year in subjects such as shop, arithmetic, metallurgy, and shop drawing. (See p. 52-63.) Molders' helpers and less skilled hand-molders often learn molding skills informally on the job, but this method takes longer and is not as reliable as apprenticeship.

Hand-molders who do very repetitive work learn in a brief training period. "Learners" (men without previous experience or upgraded foundry helpers) work with a molder on a particular kind of mold. After two to six months, the learner can usually make this mold or a similar one without close supervision. The more difficult and responsible machine-molding jobs require formal or equivalent on-the-job training, but most machine-molding jobs can be learned in sixty to ninety days of on-the-job training.

What the Occupation Has to Offer

Employment in this field is expected to show little or no change through the 1970s. Demand for molders will not keep pace with increased production, because the trend is toward more machine-molding and use of permanent and shell molds. The need to replace experienced molders who die, retire, or transfer out of the occupation will provide more than 1,000 job openings each year. Several hundred will be for molding apprentices.

Earnings depend on several factors, including type of molding work (hand or machine), skill requirements, type of metal poured, and geographic location. In a 1970 survey of fifty-two laborareas, straight-time average hourly earnings were as follows: floor-molders, $3.55; bench-molders, $3.45; squeezer-machine-molders, $3.35; and heavy-machine-molders, $3.35.

Since molding work is strenuous, few women are employed.

For more information:

See also: page 379.

Patternmaker

The Job

A foundry patternmaker is a highly skilled craftsman who builds patterns used in making the molds in which metal castings are formed.

Most workers in the occupation are metal patternmakers, although some are wood patternmakers. A growing number work with both materials. Plastics and plaster have been introduced into this craft in the past decade. Some patternmakers work only with these two materials, but plastics and plaster can also be used by metal and wood patternmakers.

As a patternmaker, you work from blueprints supplied by the company engineering department or by a customer's design engineer. From this blueprint you make a precise pattern for the product, allowing for shrinkage of molten metal used in the casting process and for other factors. Patterns are prepared from metal stock or from rough castings made from an original wood pattern. In order to shape and finish the work, you use a variety of metal-working machines, such as the engine lathe, drill press, shaper, milling machine, power hacksaw and grinder as well as small hand tools.

In wood patternmaking, you select the proper woodstock, lay out the pattern, mark the design for each section on the proper piece of wood and saw each piece roughly to size. Next, you shape the rough pieces into final form, using woodcutting machines, such as circular saws, lathes, planers, band saws, and sanders as well as hand tools. Finally, you assemble the pattern pieces by hand, fastening them with glue, screws, and nails. You finish the pattern with standard colors.

Great accuracy is required in making patterns, because any imperfection in the original pattern will be reproduced in castings made from it. Throughout the patternmaking operation you carefully check each dimension of the pattern, using measuring instruments such as shrink rules, calipers, micrometers, and gauges. You also make core boxes (much the way you make patterns) and repairs patterns.

More than half of the U. S. patternmakers work in foundry pattern shops of plants making products such as machinery, transportation equipment, and fabricated metal products. Others work in plants that make patterns to order or in pattern shops in independent foundries.

What You Need Personally

Although patternmaking is not strenuous, it calls for considerable standing and moving about. You need manual dexterity for this job because of its precise nature. You also need the ability to visualize objects in three dimensions.

What Education and Training You Need

Apprenticeship is the principal means of qualifying as a journeyman patternmaker. Employers generally require apprentices to have at least a high school education. Trade school courses in patternmaking provide useful preparation for you as a prospective apprentice. These courses may be credited toward completion of your apprenticeship period, but keep in mind that they do not substitute for your apprenticeship or on-the-job training.

Because of the high degree of skill and the wide range of knowledge needed for this job, it is difficult to learn informally on the job. The usual apprenticeship period is five years. At least 144 hours of classroom instruction in related technical subjects are normally provided each year with separate programs for wood and metal patternmakers.

As an apprentice, you begin by helping journeymen with routine duties. You make simple patterns under close supervision, and as you progress the work becomes more complex and the supervision is more general. (See pages 52-63.)

What the Occupation Has to Offer

There were about 20,000 foundry patternmakers in 1970. This employment figure is expected to show little or no change through the rest of the seventies. Most openings will be for metal patternmakers. Though there will be an increase in the number of castings made, the need for patternmakers will not keep pace, because patterns can be used many times to make identical molds.

Patternmakers usually have higher earnings than other skilled foundry workers. Their earnings, however, depend on the skills which each job requires, the type of metal poured, geographic location, etc. In January, 1970, the average straight-time hourly earnings of wood patternmakers ranged from $3.95 in steel foundries to $4.50 in gray-iron and malleable-iron foundries, according to a survey of fifty-two labor areas. In general, metal patternmakers have higher earnings than wood patternmakers.

Points to Consider Before Going into This Field

Because patternmakers learn either basic metalworking or woodworking, they are prepared for employment in related fields. For instance, as a wood patternmaker, you could qualify for woodworking jobs, such as cabinetmaker, and as a metal patternmaker could transfer to machining operations such as machinist or layout man.

For more information, write:

Department of Human Resources Development
Mail Control Unit
800 Capitol Mall
Sacramento, California 95814
Ask for: *Patternmaker (Foundry)* No. 349, Free.

See also: page 379.

Jeweler and Jewelry Repairman

The Job

Creating, appraising, and repairing jewelry is both an art and a skill. Work in these areas gives you exposure to natural and man-made objects of great beauty and a chance to develop and use precision crafting.

Jewelers are skilled craftsmen who make and repair jewelry, working with precious or semiprecious stones set in metals such as gold, silver, or platinum. They also repair watches and are often retailers in the bargain. Among the procedures used by jewelers are metal working, casting, stone setting, and engraving. Many workers specialize in one of these operations, while others become expert in repairs and resettings or perhaps in watch repair. Watch repair has become, for economic reasons, an essential part of most jewelry repair businesses. (See p. 322.) About half of the 15,000 jewelers in the United States are self-employed, and about half of the others work in jewelry manufacturing establishments.

Gemologists, experts on gems, are able to grade and evaluate stones, determine real from fake, and judge how a particular stone can best be used in a piece of jewelry. Gemologists serve as jewelry buyers and appraisers or may run their own jewelry businesses.

Today, some jewelry is mass-produced by factory workers, but skilled jewelers are still needed to design and make the models and tools required for mass production. They also perform finishing operations such as stone setting and engraving.

What You Need Personally

Jewelry work is precise and delicate and involves the mastery of a number of small tools. A jeweler needs concentration, patience, good eye-hand coordination, and finger and hand dexterity. Patience is very important, as jewelers must often sit for long periods of time. To work with precious stones and metals, a person must be bonded and investigated for honesty, trustworthiness, and respect for the law. Jewelry design requires a natural creative flair, and an appreciation of beauty and fine work will aid anyone working with stones.

What Education and Training You Need

For a career in this field, specialized training is necessary. A high school education is desirable, and courses in chemistry, mechanical drawing, and art will provide useful background. One place to get this special training is through a school such as the Gemological Institute of America which offers courses for jewelers both on a residential basis at the school in Los Angeles and through a home-study program. A gemologist diploma is awarded for completion of the home-study courses, and a graduate gemologist degree is presented to those who either take a full-time course at the school or take a two-week program at the school combined with the completion of the home-study course. Courses offered include Diamonds, Colored Stones, Gem Identification, Pearls, Jewelry Designing, Creative Display, and Jewelry Retailing. These are often taken by experienced jewelers to expand their knowledge and business opportunities. Courses in jewelry repair are also offered by some trade schools.

The Gemological Institute of America resident training program, which requires a high school diploma or the equivalent for admission, offers a twenty-week course for $1,315. The cost for the correspondence courses required for a degree is $620, which includes necessary study materials and loans of gems. The home-study courses usually take two to three years to complete, although they can be done in less time. The American School of Diamond Cutting in Gardnerville, Nevada, takes about a dozen students, and its very specialized course of study can be expected to take three years. There are other private vocational schools that also offer training for jewelers and repairmen.

Jewelry work also requires either formal or informal on-the-job training. Another way to get your training is through formal apprenticeship, which lasts three or four years depending on the specific job area. Such an apprenticeship offers trade school instruction combined with training on the job. The apprentice will progress from simple soldering or rough polishing to more difficult and complex work. Jewelry manufacturers are usually fairly small firms, so the number of trainees accepted for apprenticeship is limited. This is even more true of jewelry repair shops, which are often one- or two-man operations. (See pages 52-63.)

What the Occupation Has to Offer

The jewelry field, although small, always has openings in all areas. Many workers are older, and their retirements or deaths create vacancies, which are often filled by people with specialized skills in both production and repair. All-round jewelers have been in short supply in recent years, and there is a continuing demand for them.

As the American standard of living continues to rise, it can be expected to create a larger market for jewelry. Costume jewelry, costly jewels, and engagement and wedding rings are all in increasing demand. More efficient means of production are also being developed, however, so it can be expected that the demand for jewelers will remain stable.

Information on earnings in the field is limited, but beginning pay for jewelers and jewelry repairmen is usually $80 to $125 per week. Experienced workers earn as much as $240 weekly, with highest earnings predictably reported in major metropolitan areas. Highly skilled specialists can earn more. A diamond cutter, for example, can make at least $400 per week.

Retail jewelry stores and repair shops are located throughout the country, with heaviest concentrations in major commercial centers like New York, Chicago, Los Angeles, and San Francisco. New York City is the manufacturing center for precious jewels; 75 percent of all precious jewelry manufacturers are in New York, New Jersey, Rhode Island, and California.

There are various ways to advance in the jewelry industry. In manufacturing, workers can become shop foremen. In retail stores, they can become department heads or store managers. Some jewelry workers open their own retail or repair shops. This is a highly competitive area, requiring substantial financial investment, and anyone planning to go into business for himself is advised to get experience in selling and repair work first and to build up a reputation.

Points to Consider Before Going into This Field

The jewelry business offers an opportunity for creative, productive work, a chance to learn and practice a skill that will never go out of style. A jeweler works with materials of great beauty and value and can create and repair things that will probably outlive him and give years of pleasure to the people who own them. Because of the precision necessary for the work, however, a very active person would probably find it tedious. A person with coordination difficulties would have trouble with the fine work involved.

Unless you go into business for yourself, jewelry does not offer an exceptionally high income, although it does provide a comfortable one. A high-income jeweler, almost always self-employed, will probably have acquired a combination of skills and experience, including salesmanship. The field is open to women as well as men.

For more information, write:

Gemological Institute of America
11940 San Vincente Boulevard
Los Angeles, California 90049; or

580 Fifth Avenue
New York, New York 10020
Ask for: information on job opportunities and training program.

International Jewelry Workers' Union
Local No. 1
133 West 44th Street
New York, New York 10036
Ask for: information on employment opportunities in manufacturing firms.

Manufacturing Jewelers and Silversmiths of America, Inc.
Biltmore Hotel & Motor Inn
Room S-75
Providence, Rhode Island 02902
Ask for: information on employment opportunities in manufacturing firms.

Retail Jewelers of America, Inc.
1025 Vermont Avenue N. W.
Washington, D. C. 20005
Ask for: information on watchmakers, jewelry repairmen, and schools offering training programs.

Motion Picture Projectionist

The Job

No motion picture theater can operate without a projectionist. As the person behind the scene, he or she works from an elevated room at the back of the theater, operating projection machines and audio equipment to provide the audience with high quality screen and sound presentation.

A projectionist showing a feature-length movie, uses two projectors, audio equipment, a film rewinding machine, and at least seven reels of film. Before the feature begins he or she checks the equipment to see that it is running properly and loads the projectors with the first and second reels. Most projectors burn a carbon rod to provide light for the screen. After igniting the rod, the projectionist starts the first projector, opens a shutter which throws the picture on the screen, then makes necessary adjustments.

A film reel lasts about twenty minutes. When the first reel is almost finished, cue marks (small circles) appear on the upper right hand corner of the screen, signaling the projectionist to start the second projector. When a second series of cue marks appear, he simultaneously closes the shutter on the first projector and opens the shutter on the second, without interruption to the viewer. Next, the used reel is rewound, and the process is repeated until all the reels have been shown. If the film should break, the projectionist must rapidly rethread it so the show may continue.

Besides operating the equipment, a projectionist cleans and lubricates it, checks for defective parts and damaged film and makes minor repairs and adjustments. Major repairs are made by servicemen who specialize in projection and audio equipment.

About 15,000 projectionists, almost all of them males, were employed in the U. S. in 1970. More than three-fourths worked in indoor theaters; most of the remaining were employed in drive-in theaters. Some large manufacturers, television studios, and federal, state, and local governments employ projectionists also. Most theaters employ one projectionist for each shift.

The projection room (called a booth) in most theaters has adequate lighting, ventilation, and work space, and many are air-conditioned. There are few hazards except for the danger of electrical shock and burns if proper safety precautions are not taken. The work is not strenuous. Although you frequently lift and handle film reels, most weigh no more than 35 pounds. You must be on your feet much of the time but can sit for short periods.

Projectionists work in cities and towns throughout the country. In a small theater, the owner or a member of his family often acts as projectionist.

Most projectionists work evenings, four to six hours, six days a week. They may work more than six hours on weekends when matinees are featured. Some work at several theaters, for example two evenings in each of three theaters. Those employed in drive-in theaters, particularly in the north, may be laid off for several months during the winter. Many projectionists receive two or three weeks of paid vacation and premium pay for weekends and holidays. Some are also covered by hospitalization and pension plans.

What You Need Personally

If you are thinking of becoming a projectionist, you should have good eyesight, including normal color perception, and good hearing. You should be temperamentally suited to working in close quarters. Manual dexterity and mechanical aptitude are also important to the job. You should also be able to work well without supervision, because most projectionists have little contact with other theater employees.

What Education and Training You Need

Most theaters in urban areas are unionized and require a projectionist to serve an apprenticeship. To apprentice, you must be at least 18 years of age and preferably have a high school diploma. The length of time you serve before taking the examination for union membership varies from one to two years, depending on local union policies. However, if you are capable of doing the work, you may be assigned a full or part-time job at journeyman's pay before you become a union member. (See pages 52-63.)

As a union apprentice, you learn the trade by working with an experienced projectionist. You begin by threading and rewinding film and progress to adjusting and repairing equipment. You might work in several theaters in order to become familiar with different types of equipment. Some apprentices receive no pay while being trained.

In a nonunion theater you may start as an usher or helper and learn the trade by working with the projectionist. Practical experience you gain from operating small projectors at home, at school or in the armed forces for instance, is also helpful. In a few cities and states projectionists must be licensed.

What the Occupation Has to Offer

Employment of motion picture projectionists is expected to increase slowly through the 1970s. Most openings will arise as projectionists retire, die, or transfer to other fields. Competition for these jobs may be keen, however, with many being filled by underemployed experienced projectionists. Employment of projectionists depends on the number of motion picture theaters in operation. This number declined rapidly in the 1950s, leveled off in recent years, but is expected to increase slightly in the seventies.

Earning averages are not available on a national basis. In large metropolitan areas, however, average straight-time hourly earnings ranged from $2.95 to $8.75 in 1970, according to information from several union-management contracts. Generally, downtown theaters pay higher rates than suburban or drive-in theaters.

For more information:

For more information about apprenticeship programs and employment opportunities, contact any local union of the International Alliance of Theatrical Stage Employees and Motion Picture Machine Operators of the United States and Canada.

Photographic Laboratory Workers

The Job

All photographs, whether snapshots, magazine illustrations, or home movies, must be developed in laboratories. Skilled workers are employed by these laboratories to develop film, make prints and slides, and do other things such as enlarging and retouching.

An all-round darkroom technician performs all the tasks needed to develop and print film. The developing process varies according to whether the film is black-and-white negative, color negative, or color positive. Black-and-white is the simplest. Some laboratories employ special color technicians to process color film, which is more complex.

The procedure for developing black-and-white film first requires that the technician unwind a roll of film and place it in a developer solution that brings out the image on exposed film. After it has been in the developer for a specified amount of time, the technician transfers it to a stop bath (another chemical solution) to prevent overdevelopment. Then it is placed in a fixing bath that makes the film insensitive to light and prevents further exposure. These steps are all performed in the dark. The film is then washed with water to remove the fixing solution and placed in a drying cabinet. The whole process can be performed manually or by automatic machines regulated by technicians.

To make a photograph, the darkroom technician transfers the image from a negative to photographic paper. This is often done on a projection printer, which has a fixture for holding negatives and photographic paper, plus an electric lamp and magnifying lens. The technician puts the negative between the lamp and the lens and the paper below the lens. When the lamp is turned on, light passes through the negative and lens and records a magnified image on the paper. The technician can vary the contrast of the image or remove unwanted background by using his hand or paper to shade part of the photographic paper from the lamp light.

When the photographic paper is removed from the printer, it is developed (the process is similar to that used on negatives) and may also be mounted in a frame or on paper or cardboard backing.

Darkroom technicians may also set up lights and cameras or otherwise assist photographers, a number take professional photographs themselves. In some laboratories technicians are assisted by helpers, who do general work or may specialize in a particular task, such as developing, printing, or photograph retouching.

In larger, more mechanized laboratories, semiskilled workers are employed for special duties and are supervised by the darkroom technicians. These workers are film numberers, who sort film for identification purposes according to the type of processing needed and number each roll; film strippers, who unwind rolls of film and place them in developing machines; printer operators, who operate machines that expose rolls of photographic paper to negatives; print developers, who operate machines that develop rolls of exposed photographic paper; chemical mixers, who measure and mix the chemicals used in developing solutions; slide mounters, who operate the machines that cut, insert, and seal film in cardboard mounts; or photo checkers and assemblers, who inspect finished slides and prints and package them.

About half of the 37,000 photographic laboratory workers are darkroom technicians, the other half semiskilled workers. Most darkroom technicians work for laboratories operated by portrait and commercial studios or for those run by manufacturers, newspaper and magazine publishers, advertising agencies and federal, state, and local governments. Some are employed in small commercial laboratories that process the work of free-lance photographers, advertising agencies, etc. Most semiskilled workers are found in the large commercial laboratories that specialize in processing film for amateur photographers.

What You Need Personally

For skilled and semiskilled jobs, manual dexterity, good eye-hand coordination, and good vision and color perception are important. Darkroom technicians must be careful, diligent, and neat in their work.

What Education and Training You Need

Darkroom technicians usually learn their work through on-the-job training, both in skilled and semiskilled positions. The length of training varies.

For semiskilled workers, a high school education is not necessary, but it is usually needed for advancement. Most semiskilled positions can be learned within a few months. Film numberers and slide mounters usually only need a few weeks to learn their work, but printer operators and chemical mixers may need several months or more.

Darkroom technicians are usually expected to have a high school education, with courses in chemistry, physics, and mathematics considered helpful. Further background can be gained by film-processing hobbies, armed-forces training and photography courses in high school or trade school.

Some junior community colleges offer two-year programs leading to an associate degree in photographic technology, especially useful for those interested in moving into managerial positions. Training is also available through private vocational schools.

Darkroom technicians are first hired as helpers and learn to print and develop film through experience. Some become specialists in a particular activity, while others go on to become all-round technicians. It usually takes three to four years to become fully qualified.

What the Occupation Has to Offer

There should be a sizable increase in job opportunities for workers in this field during the 1970s. More and more amateurs are taking up photography as a result of increased income, simpler cameras, and increased leisure and travel. Improved mechanized film processing will partially check the growth in jobs, however.

All-round technicians will be especially in demand as business and government use more photographs in brochures and advertisements. Photography is also being used more in research and development. In general, photographic laboratory jobs should be plentiful.

There is a great variation in earnings for photographic workers depending on skill, experience and geographical area. Semiskilled workers earn between $2 and $3.50 an hour in most cases, with printer operators and chemical mixers earning most. Beginning darkroom technicians earn $2 to $3.10 an hour and more experienced technicians from $2.50 to $5 an hour. Some technicians make more. These workers also receive benefits, such as paid holidays, vacations, and health insurance.

Opportunities for promotion are fairly good in this field. Semiskilled workers can improve their skills and become supervisors or darkroom technicians. Darkroom technicians often become professional photographers. Others become supervisors in laboratories. (See pages 122-124.)

Points to Consider Before Going into This Field

There are a number of advantages to photographic work. The demand for photographic services should continue to grow in the years to come, and while mechanization may slowly increase in jobs, it will not eliminate the need for workers. Photographic laboratories are found throughout the world. The work is steady, the hours fairly regular and the job not physically strenuous in the least. Most laboratories are clean, well lighted and air-conditioned.

There are a few disadvantages to this work. In laboratories that process amateur film, there is often a big rush at Christmas or during the summer, creating pressure and overtime demands. The overtime is well paid, however. The semiskilled jobs can be repetitious and tiring on the eyes.

Many women are employed in photographic laboratories, but mainly in semiskilled jobs. Nearly all darkroom technicians are men.

For more information, write:

Master Photo Dealers and Finishers Association
603 Lansing Avenue
Jackson, Michigan 49292
Ask for: information on job opportunities and schools offering degrees in photographic technology.

Professional, Commercial and Industrial Markets Division
Eastman Kodak Company
Rochester, New York 14650
Ask for: information on job opportunities and schools offering training.

Professional Photographers of America, Inc.
1090 Executive Way
Des Plaines, Illinois 60018
Ask for: information on job opportunities and schools offering degrees in photographic technology.

Stationary Engineer

The Job

Stationary engineers are responsible for the operation of the heating and air-conditioning equipment in structures like large apartment and office buildings, commercial and industrial establishments, factories, hospitals, hotels, mines, power stations, and schools. These skilled people operate and maintain the equipment in accordance with state and local laws, since the safety of so many people depends upon proper functioning.

Stationary engineers must detect and identify any trouble that develops. To do so they watch machinery carefully, listen to it and analyze readings of meters, gauges and other instruments. The engineer knows how to operate levers, throttles, switches and valves and also repair equipment using hand tools of all kinds, including precision tools. Common repairs include such things as reseating valves, replacing bearings and gaskets, and adjusting piston clearance. The stationary engineer also supervises the activities of semiskilled stationary firemen and air-conditioning mechanics. His duties depend on the size of the establishment in which he works, but his primary responsibility—safe and efficient operation of the equipment—is much the same in all plants.

Because stationary engineers work in so many industries, they are employed throughout the country. Most, however, work in heavily populated areas where large industrial and commercial establishments are located, rather than in rural areas.

As a stationary engineer, you might find work in a power station, factory, brewery, food-processing plant, steel mill, office or apartment building, hotel, or hospital. Federal, state, and local governments also hire large numbers of engineers.

Most engine rooms, power plants or boiler rooms are clean and well-lighted. Nevertheless, some stationary engineers are exposed to high temperatures, dust, dirt, contact with oil and grease, and fumes from oil, gas, coal, or smoke. Some have to crawl inside boilers and work in crouching or kneeling positions to clean or repair interiors. They have to be alert to avoid burns or electric shock.

What You Need Personally

In order to be well suited to stationary engineering you should have mechanical aptitude, manual dexterity, and be in good physical condition.

What Education and Training You Need

Training authorities in this field recommend formal apprenticeship as the best way to learn this trade because of the complexity of the machines and systems involved. Most joint labor-management apprenticeship committees prefer as applicants high school or trade school graduates between 18 and 25 who have had courses in mathematics, mechanical drawing, machine-shop practice, physics, and chemistry. (See pages 52-63.)

An apprenticeship usually lasts three to four years. As an apprentice, you learn to operate, maintain and repair boilers, pumps, air-conditioning and refrigeration machinery, and to use such things as electric grinders, lathes, precision instruments, and equipment used to move machines. On-the-job training is supplemented by classroom and home study. Those who become stationary engineers without this formal apprenticeship do so only after years of experience as assistants to licensed engineers.

Eight states, the District of Columbia, and more than fifty cities require licenses for stationary engineers. Requirements differ somewhat, but usually you must be over 21, have resided in the state for a specific period of time and must show that you meet the experience requirements for the class of license you desire.

Generally there are three classes of licenses, first-class, second-class, and third-class. The different classes specify the steam pressure or horsepower of the equipment you may operate. As a first-class engineer you can operate all types and capacities of equipment. As a lower-class engineer you are limited in what you may operate without supervision from a higher rated engineer.

What the Occupation Has to Offer

In 1970 about 200,000 stationary engineers were employed in the U. S. in a wide variety of establishments. Employment through the rest of the 1970s is expected to show little or no change. While industrial growth will increase the use of boilers and other equipment in factories and power plants, the need for more engineers will be limited by trends to more centralized equipment and automatic controls.

According to a 1969-70 survey covering seventy-five metropolitan areas, stationary engineers averaged straight-time hourly earnings of $4.14. This covered a range of from $2.84 in Oklahoma City, Oklahoma, to $4.98 in Chicago,

Illinois. Work is usually year-round and steady, with a straight eight-hour day, and forty-hour week.

As a stationary engineer, you advance to more responsible jobs by being placed in charge of larger, more powerful or varied equipment as you obtain higher grade licenses. However, advancement is not automatic. Although you get a first-class license, you may still have to work some time as an assistant to another first-class engineer before a vacancy occurs. Usually the broader your knowledge, the better your chances of advancement. Stationary engineers also advance to jobs as plant engineers and building and plant superintendents.

Points to Consider Before Going into This Field

Many stationary engineers are employed in plants which have union-management contracts. Most of these contracts provide fringe benefits which include hospitalization, medical and surgical insurance, life insurance, sickness and accident insurance, and retirement pensions. Similar benefits may be provided by plants which do not have union-management contracts.

For more information, write:

Department of Human Resources Development
Mail Control Unit
800 Capitol Mall
Sacramento, California 95814
Ask for: *Stationary Engineer* No. 234, Free.
Stationary Engineer, Stationary Engineer Apprentice No. 361, Free.

International Union of Operating Engineers
1125 17th Street, N. W.
Washington, D. C. 20036

National Association of Power Engineers, Inc.
176 West Adam Street
Chicago, Illinois 60603

Also contact:
State employment services, state and local licensing agencies, locals of the International Union of Operating Engineers.

Stationary Fireman (Boiler)

The Job

Stationary firemen operate and maintain the steam boilers that are used to power industrial machinery and to heat factories, offices, department stores, and other buildings. They are considered semiskilled workers. Some highly experienced firemen can be responsible for inspecting boiler equipment, lighting boilers, and building up steam pressure. Others are limited to keeping equipment in good working order by cleaning, oiling, and greasing parts.

As a stationary fireman, you would operate mechanical devices that control the flow of air, gas, oil, or powdered coal into fireboxes to keep proper steam pressure in the boilers. You would read meters to be sure boilers are operating efficiently and according to safety regulations. In some plants you would make minor repairs. You might be supervised by a stationary engineer. (See page 387.)

Most stationary firemen work in manufacturing industries. Leading employers are plants which manufacture lumber, iron and steel, paper, chemicals, and transportation equipment. Public utilities also employ many firemen. Although firemen are employed in all parts of the country, most jobs are located in heavily populated areas where large manufacturing plants are located.

Modern equipment and safety procedures have reduced accidents considerably in this field in recent years. However, most firemen are at times exposed to noise, heat, grease, and fumes from oil, gas, coal, or smoke. They may have to crawl inside a boiler and work in crouching positions. Stationary firemen also are subject to burns, falls and injury from moving machinery.

What You Need Personally

If you wish to be a stationary fireman, you should have normal vision and hearing and understand the operation of machinery. Because of the mechanization of equipment, strength is no longer a major requirement for this job.

What Education and Training You Need

Some large cities and a few states require a stationary fireman to be licensed. There are two types of licenses: one for low-pressure and one for high-pressure boilers. As a low-pressure fireman, you operate boilers generally used for heating buildings. As a high-pressure fireman, you operate more powerful boilers and the auxiliary boiler equipment used to power machinery and heat large buildings. With either license, however, you may operate equipment of any pressure class as long as there is a stationary engineer on duty.

You can obtain the knowledge and experience to pass a license examination by first working as a helper in a boiler room or by working as a stationary fireman under a conditional license. License requirements vary from city to city and state to state. In general, you must prove that you meet experience requirements, and you must pass an examination which tests your knowledge of the job. For specific information on licensing requirements, consult your state or local licensing authorities.

What the Occupation Has to Offer

In large plants where turbines and engines are housed under a separate roof and where there is need for constant surveillance of boilers, firemen will be needed through the 1970s. In general, however, there will be a decline in employment because of a trend to automatic and more centralized equipment. About 70,000 stationary firemen were employed in 1970.

A survey of sixty metropolitan areas made from 1969 to 1970 shows that stationary firemen had average straight-time hourly earnings of $3.47. Averages in specific areas ranged from $2.18 in Greenville, South Carolina, to $4.53 in Detroit, Michigan.

Stationary firemen can advance to the jobs of stationary engineer and maintenance mechanic. To help qualify for advancement you might supplement on-the-job training by taking courses in practical chemistry, elementary physics, blueprint reading, applied electricity, and the principles of refrigeration, air conditioning, ventilation, and heating.

Points to Consider Before Going into This Field

Many stationary firemen are employed in plants that have labor-management contracts, most of which provide benefits that include paid holidays and vacations, hospitalization, medical and surgical insurance, and retirement pensions.

For more information, write:

International Brotherhood of Firemen and Oilers
200 Maryland Avenue, N. E.
Washington, D. C. 20002

Also contact:
State employment services, state and local licensing agencies, locals of the International Brotherhood of Firemen and Oilers.

Welder and Oxygen and Arc Cutter

The Job

Everywhere we turn, we are using products that have been welded together; cars, planes,

the edges to be welded. The resultant heat melts the edges and the electrode tip; the molten metal from the electrode is deposited in the joint, where it bonds with the molten metal edges for a solid connection.

With materials like aluminum and stainless steel that are hard to weld, a process that uses inert gas to shield the weld area may be used. In gas welding, the intensely hot flame comes from a gas torch which is applied to the metal edges.

Oxygen cutters and arc cutters can be skilled or semiskilled. The semiskilled worker uses hand-guided torches to cut or trim metals. The oxygen cutter directs a fuel gas flame burning with oxygen to the cutting area until the metal starts to melt. Then an additional stream of oxygen is released to cut the metal. The torch cuts along previously marked lines or follows a blueprint pattern.

Arc cutters, or flame cutters, use an electric arc. There are special versions designed to be used for such things as underwater cutting. Arc or oxygen cutters sometimes work with torches mounted on electrically controlled machines which automatically follow patterns.

The nation's 535,000 welders, oxygen and arc cutters are employed throughout the country, although about half of them work in Pennsylvania, California, Ohio, Michigan, Illinois, Texas, and New York. More than half the welders and cutters are employed by manufacturing industries, which produce transportation equipment and fabricated metal products. Others work for construction firms, repair services, and miscellaneous industries.

water faucets, and refrigerators work because they have been properly welded. Welding is basically a process which applies intense heat and pressure to metal edges in order to bond them together permanently and can be used on metal parts as large as building structures.

There are more than forty different welding processes, but most fall into three categories; gas, arc, and resistance. Arc and gas welding can be done either by hand or by machine. Resistance welding is usually done by machine.

Oxygen and arc cutting are very similar to welding. In these processes, metal objects are cut or trimmed to the desired shape and size. It is also possible to cut excess metal from castings or cut scrap metal into pieces of manageable size using oxygen or arc cutting.

Semiskilled workers in this field often operate welding machines and do repetitive jobs that only require the welding of surfaces in one position. In resistance welding, machine operators feed and align the work into the machine and remove it after the welding has been completed. They sometimes have to adjust the machine controls for current or pressure.

The skilled welder has more diverse duties and broader knowledge of the business. He must know the welding properties of steel, stainless steel, cast iron, bronze, aluminum, nickel, and other metals and alloys. He may, when his skill is developed, specialize in welding one or more of these metals. He also must be able to make plans from drawings or blueprints, determine the proper sequence of work operations for a job, and weld all types of joints in varying positions. Welding is also used by plumbers and pipe fitters, sheet-metal workers, structural steel workers, and other skilled workmen.

The welding process varies depending on the type of metal being welded and the type of connection desired. In a common arc-welding process, the welder adjusts electric current on a suitable electrode, creates an electric circuit by touching the metal with the electrode and then guides the electrode at a suitable distance from

What You Need Personally

Manual dexterity, mechanical aptitude, and physical stamina are important qualities for these jobs. You also need good vision and good eye-hand coordination. Because the work is quite precise, concentration is necessary. You will frequently have to work independently, so you should be dependable.

What Education and Training You Need

No particular educational background is needed for semiskilled welding jobs, but a high school education is always an asset. Courses in high school or public or private vocational schools that include welding methods are helpful, as are studies in mathematics, mechanical drawing, and blueprint reading.

There are other places beside vocational schools where you can acquire welding training. Manpower Development and Training Act programs teach welding and may include classroom work or just on-the-job training. The U. S. Navy has four-year welding apprenticeship programs for some civilian employees. A few large companies, such as automobile manufacturers, have formal apprenticeship programs for welders. (See pages 52-63.)

The amount of necessary on-the-job training varies. Most resistance-welding machine operators and oxygen and arc cutters learn their jobs in a few weeks. Skilled jobs, which may require a knowledge of blueprint reading, welding symbols, metal properties and electricity, may take longer. In general, it takes a few years to become a skilled manual arc or gas welder and a little longer to become a skilled combination welder able to use both techniques. Most beginners start in simple production jobs, using the same metals and positions repeatedly. Occasionally, beginners start as oxygen or arc cutters, then move into manual welding.

In some instances, welders have to pass qualification tests. This usually applies in jobs where the strength of the weld is critical, such as missile manufacture. Tests may be given by an employer, municipal agency, naval facility, or private agency. In some places, welders are required to have a license for certain types of outdoor construction.

What the Occupation Has to Offer

Metalworking industries are expected to expand in the next decade, and since more welding will be used, there'll be many new jobs. Manual welders will also be needed for maintenance and repair work, in the manufacturing of structural metal products and in the construction industry. Oxygen and arc cutters will also be in demand, but the increased use of machines in their work will restrict the growth in job opportunities.

Earnings for welders vary according to skill, industry, and experience. Machine operators usually earn between $2 and $4 an hour. Skilled manual welders earn between $2.50 and $5 an hour. Many welders and cutters belong to labor unions and are provided with fringe benefits, such as insurance, paid vacations, and holiday and retirement pensions.

There are many opportunities for advancement in this field. Machine operators can become manual welders, and a skilled welder can become a specialist or a supervisor. With two years of technical training, he can also become a welding technician, a growing area which involves interpreting engineers' plans and instructions. Other welders become inspectors, who check to see that welds meet specifications. In addition, welders open their own welding or repair shops.

Points to Consider Before Going into This Field

There are many advantages to going into this field. Welding is a skill and one that is increasingly in demand. Because it is used in so many different industries, the welder can get a job anywhere in the country or in the world. Hours are usually regular and the pay good. Educational requirements are not too stiff, and the chances for advancement are very good for the worker who takes additional courses on his own.

The main disadvantage to this job is the many hazards the worker encounters. Safety clothing and devices are used, but there are still dangers from burns, eye injuries, and fumes from toxic gases. You need to be in good physical shape, coordinated, and alert.

Although there are few women in this field, there is no reason why a woman cannot perform the job. During World War II, labor shortages forced industry to train and use many women as welders. Their work was often better than that done by men. It's still not always easy to get an employer to give you a chance to prove how good you are!

For more information, write:

The American Welding Society
2501 N. W. Seventh Street
Miami, Florida 33125

Ask for: *Opportunities in the Welding Industry* and a list of two-year welding technology institutions.

International Association of Machinists and Aerospace Workers
1300 Connecticut Avenue N. W.
Washington, D. C. 20036

International Brotherhood of Boilermakers, Iron Shipbuilders, Blacksmiths, Forgers and Helpers
Eighth at State Avenue
Kansas City, Kansas 66101

International Union, United Automobile, Aerospace and Agricultural Implement Workers of America
8000 East Jefferson Avenue
Detroit, Michigan 48214

United Association of Journeymen and Apprentices of the Plumbing and Pipe Fitting Industry of the United States and Canada
901 Massachusetts Avenue, N. W.
Washington, D. C. 20001

Also contact:

State employment services for information on apprenticeships, the Manpower Development and Training Act and other training programs.

Where You Can Find Out More About Career Education

These are sources of general information about career education other than those sources listed at the end of each chapter throughout the book.

Arnold, Arnold. *Career Choices for the 70s.* New York: Crowell-Collier Press, 1971. $4.95.

Barron's Educational Service, Inc.
113 Crossways Park Drive
Woodbury, New York 11797
Ask for: *Barron's Guide to 2-Year Colleges and Occupational* Program Selector (revised), 1972. $2.50.

Belitsky, Harvey. *Private Vocational Schools and Their Students. Limited Objectives, Unlimited Opportunities.* New York: Schenkman, 1969. $7.95.

Biegeleisen, J.I. *Getting a Job with a Future.* New York: Grosset & Dunlap, 1967. $1.95.

Brown, Newell. *After College ... Junior College ... Military Service ... What?* New York: Grosset & Dunlap, 1971. $3.95.

Brunetti, Cledo and Higgerson, Clifford H. *Your Future in a Changing World.* New York: Richards Rosen Press, Inc., 1970. $3.99.

National Business Education Association
1201 16th Street, N.W.
Washington, D.C. 20036
Ask for: *Careers in Business,* free.

Cass, James and Birnbaum, Max. *Comparative Guide to Junior and 2-Year Community Colleges.* New York: Harper & Row, 1972. $3.95.

Chronicle Guidance Publications. *Trade and Technical School Directory.* Moravia, New York, 13118.

Counselor's Information Service
B'nai B'rith Career and Counseling Services
1640 Rhode Island Avenue, N.W.
Washington, D.C. 20036
Ask for: Quarterly Annotated Bibliography of current literature on educational and vocational guidance, $7.00 per year.

Department of Human Resources Development
Mail Control Unit
800 Capitol Mall
Sacramento, California 95814
Ask for: Occupational Guide Index and Mini-Guide Index (includes list of hundreds of occupations for which descriptive material is available without charge).

Detjen, Mary Ford and Detjen, Ervin Winfred. *Your Plans for the Future.* New York: Whittlesey House, 1947.

Encyclopedia of Education (10 volumes), New York: The Macmillan Co., 1971.

Evers, Dora R. and Feingold, Norman. *Careers in Exotic Occupations.* New York: Richards Rosen Press, 1972. $3.99.

Ferguson, J. G. (editor). *Concise Handbook of Occupations.* New York: Doubleday & Co., 1972. $11.95. (Also a series of books on career opportunities in various fields by same publisher.)

Forrester, Gertrude. *Occupational Literature—An Annotated Bibliography.* New York: H. W. Wilson, 1971. $15.00.

Friedman, Sande and Schwartz, Lois C. *No Experience Necessary.* New York: Dell Publishing Company, 1971. $1.25.

Haight, Tim. *Careers After High School.* New York: Collier Books, 1970. $1.25.

Hopke, William E. (editor). *The Encyclopedia of Careers and Vocational Guidance.* Chicago: J. G. Ferguson Publishing Co., 1972.

Lembeck, Ruth. *380 Part-Time Jobs for Women.* New York: Dell Publishing Company, 1968. $.95.

Louisiana Power and Light
R.L. Polk and Co.
2001 Elm Hill Pike
Nashville, Tenn. 37217
Ask for: *After High School What?* 1972-73 edition, $.25 (careers not requiring four years of college).

Lovejoy, Clarence E. *Lovejoy's Career and Vocational School Guide.* New York: Simon and Schuster, 1973. $3.95.

Lukowski, Susan and Piton, Margaret. *Strategy and Tactics for Getting a Government Job.* Washington, D.C.: Potomac Books, Inc. (P.O. Box 40604, Palisades Station, Washington, D.C. 20016), 1972. $2.75 (describes areas of civilian employment in federal government).

Miller, A. E. and Brown, Betty I. *National Directory of Schools and Vocations.* North Springfield, Pennsylvania: State School Publication, 1967.

National Council of the Young Men's Christian Association of America
291 Broadway
New York, New York 10007
Ask for: *You and the YMCA* (YMCA career opportunities), 1971, free.

National Vocational Guidance Association
Career Information Review Service Committee
1607 New Hampshire Avenue, N.W.
Washington, D.C. 20009

Ask for: NVGA bibliography of current occupational literature.

Navy Recruiting Command (code 34)
Washington, D.C. 20370
Ask for: *Navy-Marine Scholarship Program: 1973 NROTC Bulletin,* free.

Russell, Max M. (editor). *The Bluebook of Occupational Education.* New York: CCM Information Corporation, 1971. $29.95.

Science Research Associates, *Directory of Vocational Training Sources.*

Scobey, Joan and McGrath, Lee Parr. *Creative Careers for Women.* New York: Essandess Special Edition, 1968. $1.00.

Splaver, Sarah. *Paraprofessionals.* New York: Julian Messner, 1972. $4.95.

Splaver, Sarah. *Your Career If You're Not Going to College.* New York: Julian Messner, 1963.

Superintendent of Documents
U.S. Government Printing Office
Washington, D. C. 20402
Ask for: *Job Training Suggestions for Women and Girls,* Leaflet 40 (rev) $.15. *Working for the USA, How to Apply for a Civil Service Job, What*

the Government Can Offer You as a Federal Worker. 1972. CS 1.48: BRE 37/2 S/N 0600–0647. $.20. *Occupational Outlook Handbook.* U.S. Department of Labor, Bureau of Labor Statistics. Bulletin 1700. $6.25. *Accredited Postsecondary Institutions and Programs,* U.S. Department of Health, Education, and Welfare, Office of Education, 1973. $1.25.

Thomson, Frances Coombs (editor). *The New York Times Guide to Continuing Education in America,* New York: Quadrangle/The New York Times Book Company, 1972. $12.50.

Vocational Foundation, Inc.
353 Park Avenue South
New York, New York 10010
(212-889-1550)
Ask for: information about the free community center and referral service.

Whitfield, Edwin A. and Hoover, Richard. *Guide to Careers Thru Vocational Training.* San Diego, California: Robert A. Knapp, 1968. $5.95.

Index

Date Due